1981
Yearbook of Science and the Future

1981 Yearbook of Science and the Future

Encyclopædia Britannica, Inc.

Chicago Toronto London
Geneva Sydney Tokyo
Manila Seoul

1981 Yearbook of Science and the Future

Editorial Advisory Board

Contents

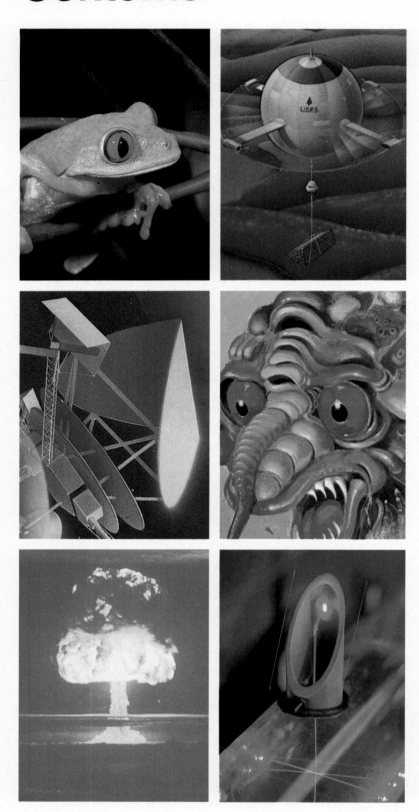

243

425

Frontiers for the 1980s
by Kendrick Frazier

Scientists face the new decade challenged by unsolved problems in many fields. Among their hoped-for achievements are unification of the four forces of nature and full understanding of the way in which genetic information is transcribed.

The decade of the 1980s promises exciting advances across the whole range of the sciences. Trying to anticipate what the discoveries may be is a risky but enjoyable activity. The process is made more uncertain by the serendipity factor—the wonderful way inquiry has of achieving totally unexpected revelations about the nature of the world. The objects of hoped-for discoveries range through the intricacies of life (where we still have examples from only one planet) to the nature of the physical universe, small and large.

In the 1980s scientists will strive to achieve a further unification of the four forces of nature. They may find evidence for a final, sixth quark, completing the set of particles thought to make up the proton, neutron, and other particles in the nucleus of the atom. They may gain more insights into the nature of evolution from studies of newly discovered regions on genes. They will map human chromosomes with techniques never before available. They will discover more natural chemicals in the brain and learn more about how they affect body processes. They will use recombinant DNA techniques for commercial manufacture of insulin and other hormones and to peel back layers of ignorance about fundamental workings of genetic mechanisms. (Recombinant DNA techniques involve excising specific pieces of DNA from an organism and then enzymatically splicing them into a carrier molecule.)

Scientists will continue to probe—remotely and in person—the dynamic processes of the ocean bottom at sites where new crust and minerals are formed. They will set up experimental observation networks to monitor and warn of severe forces such as thunderstorms and tornadoes with a rapidity and accuracy never before possible. They will make intense efforts to better understand one of the crucial problems of our time—the future course of climate change, its myriad causes, and the possible ways human activity may be affecting climate.

Scientists will look to the Sun and try both to resolve some perplexing mysteries that have come to light in the past few years and to understand how changes on the Sun are linked to changes in weather and climate on Earth. In the latter part of the decade they will for the first time observe the Sun via spacecraft from "above" and "below," thus suddenly widening human perception of that neighboring star.

They will put a large telescope into space for the first time. And, if experience is any guide, the introduction of such a new observing tool above the Earth's atmospheric screen will lead to many new discoveries about the universe. Astronomers will chart high-energy emanations from distant cosmic events, and seek to understand quasars and confirm the existence of black holes.

The space shuttle will introduce the world to a new era of routine orbital flights. Relatively inexpensive insertions of space experiments and private satellites into orbit will become common. Many astronauts who have never

"Scientists will continue to probe—remotely and in person—the dynamic processes of the ocean bottom...."

KENDRICK FRAZIER *was formerly editor of* Science News. *He is now a free-lance science writer and editor of* The Skeptical Inquirer.

(Overleaf) © Erich Hartmann—Magnum

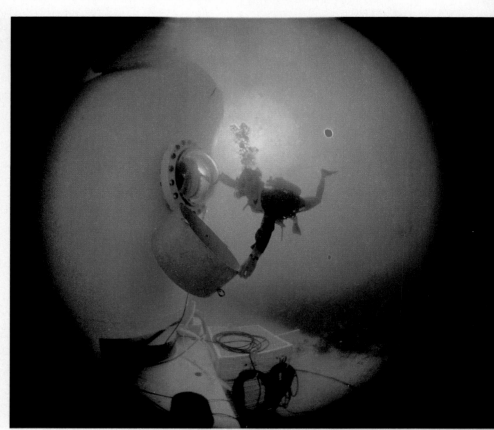

Flip Schulke—Black Star

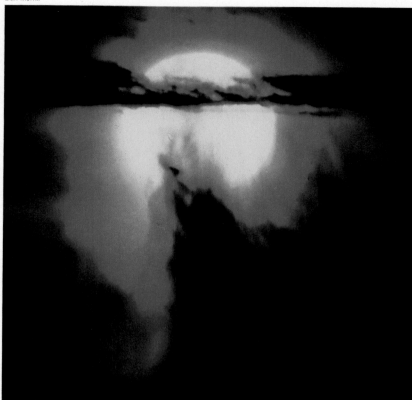

"Scientists will look to the Sun and try to resolve some perplexing mysteries....The space shuttle will introduce the world to a new era of routine orbital flights."

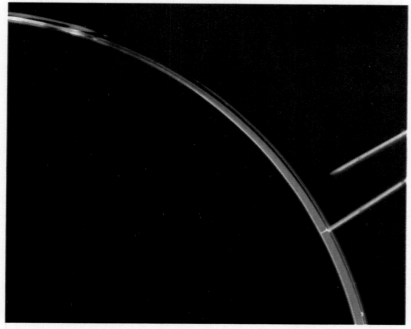

been trained as pilots but are primarily scientists will go into space, and perhaps a ship will even carry the first private passengers. (It is interesting to speculate about who that first private passenger will be: one of the several noted writers who popularized space flight, some current science journalist, a politician-supporter of the space program, or just a pay-to-be-first millionaire?)

The first-ever rendezvous mission to a comet is planned for mid-decade. If funding is forthcoming, the U.S. National Aeronautics and Space Administration (NASA) and the European Space Agency will send a spacecraft to Halley's Comet in 1985, where it will fire a sampling probe into the comet. The spacecraft will then continue on to rendezvous in 1988 with another comet, Tempel 2, and perhaps even fly side-by-side with it for a year or more. The mission should greatly increase knowledge of comets.

The Galileo space mission, the only new planetary spacecraft project of the decade, will place a craft into orbit around the giant planet Jupiter and send the first-ever probe down through its dense and turbulent atmosphere. Launchings are now planned for 1984, with arrival at Jupiter in 1986.

We may, if all goes well, get our first close look at the outer planets Uranus (in 1986) and Neptune (in 1989). The views would be courtesy of the Voyager 2 spacecraft, which is in the middle of a mission of planetary exploration. It would also be courtesy of Saturn, which, if conditions are correct, will hurl Voyager off toward Uranus after the spacecraft flies by in August 1981. (Voyager 1 will have already passed by Saturn eight and a half months earlier, in November 1980.)

There will also be much discussion during the 1980s about the possibility of future new missions to Mars (especially a landing craft that could move about the surface) and to four "new planets" in the solar system, the Jovian moons Io, Europa, Ganymede, and Callisto. The eye-opening observations of

The only new planetary space probe of the 1980s, the Galileo project, will place a craft into orbit around Jupiter and send a probe down through its dense atmosphere. On the opposite page is a composite picture of Jupiter (upper right) and its four largest moons. On this page Jupiter's faint ring system is revealed by the two orange lines protruding toward the planet's limb. The photographs were taken by Voyager 2.

13

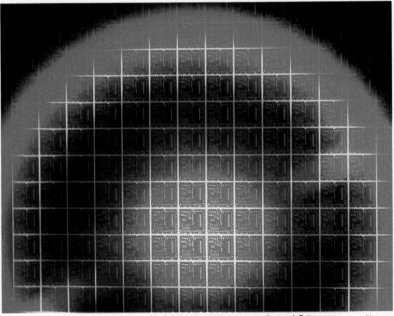

"In the home the electronics revolution will enter with a rush. The home microcomputer will become commonplace." Top, electric computer wire; bottom, abstract rendition of a computer board.

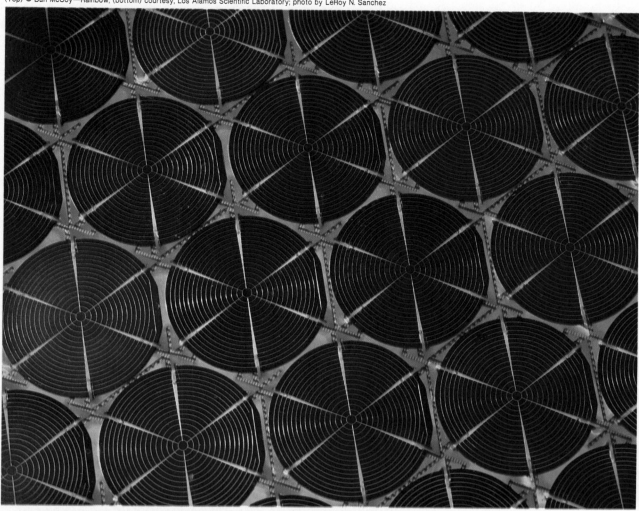

"The forced retooling... of homes, automobiles, and buildings so that they will better conserve energy will profoundly change lifestyles and the physical environment." Above, photovoltaic cells; left, oil in shale burning.

these large moons by the two Voyager spacecraft in 1979 revealed four fascinating and incredibly diverse worlds. They pose a number of intriguing questions about the evolution of planetary bodies. Planetary scientists will in the future undoubtedly want further close-up observations and perhaps even a landing mission.

In the home the electronics revolution will enter with a rush. The home microcomputer will become commonplace. It will do everything from paying monthly bills (by electronic banking, naturally) to instructing and entertaining the family. Even a fully electronic telephone to replace today's electromechanical devices will be readied for introduction. More phone calls will be transmitted optically or digitally. The old idea of electronic facsimile newspapers may never have got off the ground (except for the transmission of made-up page forms to printing plants), but electronic mail relayed by satellite will be introduced for certain users. The multiplicity of home video channels through the use of cable television and the introduction of participatory viewing, in which viewers can give immediate feedback of opinions on public affairs issues, will pave the way toward a more diverse, interactive communications system.

The forced retooling, already under way, of homes, automobiles, and buildings so that they will better conserve energy will profoundly change lifestyles and the physical environment. All the many alternate energy sources will be explored, and advances meriting the term "breakthrough"— such as low-cost photovoltaic conversion—will be earnestly sought. But many of the obstacles are social, political, and economic rather than technological. Which of the many possible paths to new energy sources will prove most promising may be more clear to everyone by the end of the 1980s. Right now the nation is in too early a stage of petroleum-withdrawal shock to exercise clear and decisive judgment. The following paragraphs will discuss a few of the possible scientific advances of the 1980s in more detail.

Life and medical sciences

There is extraordinary new ferment in molecular genetics that will result in changing ideas about the way genetic information is transcribed. This rebirth of activity is a result of recent discoveries indicating that in higher organisms only a portion of the DNA in the nucleus serves as a source of genetic information for the coding of proteins. A strand of DNA contains numerous extra, or "silent," segments scattered along its length, and somehow these inactive segments are snipped out and the gaps closed up in the process of transferring coded information onto RNA (from which protein manufacture is guided). The molecular machinery, in other words, carries out a vast editing operation, one totally unsuspected only a few years ago.

The many questions raised by this realization will produce intense inquiry. Molecular biologists will seek to learn exactly how the intervening sequences are removed and will try to identify the enzymes involved. They will search for the way instructions for this complex process are given and will strive to understand the purpose behind segmented genes and what seems at first glance to be an inefficient production of large portions of unproductive DNA. There may be evolutionary purpose in the spreading out of genes

16

over longer-than-necessary lengths of DNA. Some scientists believe that this distribution helps drive evolution by promoting increased genetic recombination between companion chromosomes; others think it may be a way to preserve stability by holding genes in place. Whatever the implications for evolution, one of the basic sets of ideas about molecular genetics has been shattered and many new insights are likely to result from the inquiries into this perplexing area.

One humane and dramatic goal of neuroscientists is to reverse nerve paralysis in human beings. Such an achievement would enable paraplegics to walk again. Only a few years ago such a possibility seemed hopelessly beyond reach, and there are still formidable obstacles to overcome. But many neuroscientists see encouraging signs from work in laboratories, indicating that restoration of severed nerve pathways may be an achievable goal. The mammalian nervous system does seem to show evidence of attempts to regenerate itself. At least one area of the brain in mammals has demonstrated an ability to sprout new nerve connections. Proteins called nerve growth factors have been discovered that help nerve cells regenerate.

Research into nerve regeneration has blossomed in recent years, and some prominent scientists believe that now is the time for a concentrated effort to gain the needed basic information to learn how to make severed nerves grow. The goal of nerve regeneration so that a paralyzed person can walk

"There is extraordinary new ferment in molecular genetics that will result in changing ideas about the way genetic information is transcribed." Below is a model of the DNA molecule.

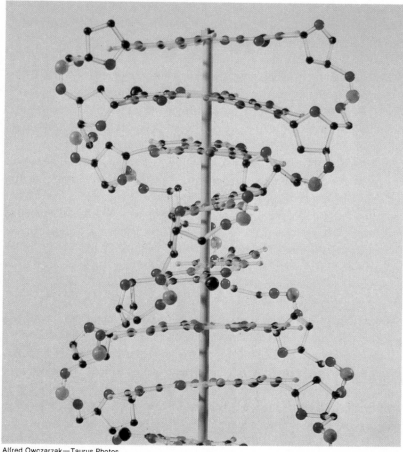

Alfred Owczarzak—Taurus Photos

again is anywhere from 5 to 50 years off, depending on whom one listens to. But most authorities agree that important new advances will be made in the 1980s.

Further revelations about a series of remarkable natural chemicals in the brain seem certain to be made during the next ten years. By the end of the decade a whole new class of drugs based on these chemicals may reach the market. The brain chemicals identified by the end of the 1970s are called endorphin (of which there are three types, alpha, beta, and gamma) and enkephalin. They are all segments of different lengths of a long protein molecule known as beta-lipotropin, which is produced in the pituitary gland, just beneath the brain.

When extracted from the pituitary and reinjected into animals or humans, enkephalin and the endorphins produce a variety of fascinating psychopharmacological effects. Most are beneficial. They have been shown to relieve pain, produce pleasure, improve concentration, enhance memory, and relieve some symptoms of mental retardation or schizophrenia. They have rightly been called one of the exciting potential drug finds of the century.

New properties of these brain chemicals are still being found and tested. And there is general agreement that still more natural brain chemicals will be identified. Not all segments of beta-lipotropin have yet been fully analyzed, and there is evidence that beta-lipotropin is itself only a portion of a still larger pituitary protein molecule that is about three times as large. Its uncharted segments may well prove to produce still more psychopharmacological effects. Nobody yet knows how many more such useful chemicals will eventually be identified. One scientist has said he believes there will be "a whole zoo of them."

Recombinant DNA techniques, the subject of much debate in the 1970s, will be put to use in many ways in both basic and applied research in the 1980s. For instance, human growth hormone is much in demand to treat pituitary dwarfism in children. It may have other clinical uses as well. Its only commercial source now is human cadavers, and 50 cadaver pituitaries are necessary to produce enough hormone to treat one child for a year. Scientists may soon be able to produce enough of the hormone in the laboratory by inserting the gene for its production into bacteria, which then manufacture it in quantity. Similar techniques will be used in the 1980s to produce on a large scale insulin needed by diabetic persons. Still further in the future is the use of recombinant DNA techniques to produce other hormone products, vaccines, and antiviral drugs. They might even be used to produce catalytic enzymes necessary in some industrial processes. It is clear that recombinant DNA technology has a bright future.

Recombinant DNA research will also be used to learn more about the human body. Identifying the action and location of genes on human chromosomes is now a slow and difficult task. The linkage in the 1980s of recombinant DNA techniques with other cell procedures is expected to speed the task significantly. The new gene mapping techniques will eventually allow a detailed portrait of the human gene and also are expected to lead to insights into the control mechanisms that govern which genes are active throughout an organism's lifetime.

"A human clone is still only a writer's fantasy, but the 1980s will see progress in the cloning of laboratory mammals." Natural chemicals newly discovered in the brain will be extracted and used for many purposes, among them relieving the pain of an arthritic hand.

18

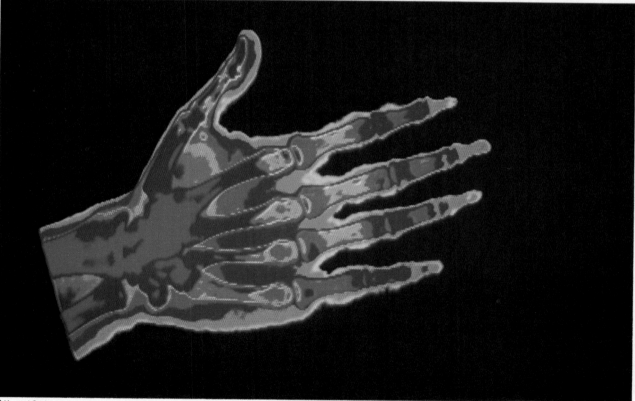

A human clone is still only a writer's fantasy, but the 1980s will see progress in the cloning of laboratory mammals. The first successful transfer of the nucleus of one mouse embryo cell into an egg cell of another mouse, leading to the birth of a normal mouse by a foster mother, was announced in 1979. It was the first such success with laboratory mammals. Further research should make full cloning of laboratory mice possible.

The goal of this research is not the eventual development of a human clone. (Scientists and scientific ethicists have been almost unanimous in their disapproval of the desirability of that.) Instead, the hope is to gain insights into some basic biological mechanisms, such as aging, the initiation of cancer, and the way gene action is regulated during development. Another goal is to produce genetically identical laboratory animals for use in immunological research.

Couples who wish to do so may in the coming years be able to select the sex of their infant. That is already possible in a limited sense. A method that is a by-product of techniques to surmount the inability of some males to produce sperm vigorous enough for fertilization of the female egg led to a way to isolate Y sperm preferentially from the general mass of sperm. The fertilization of an egg by Y sperm results in a male baby. No equivalent way to isolate X sperm preferentially (with fertilization resulting in female babies) has been possible because the procedure is based on the ability of Y sperm to swim faster than X sperm. But work on that problem is now under way, and the 1980s may well see progress toward full sex-selection ability for would-be parents.

A new procedure to diagnose genetic defects in fetuses—one that is far safer than the present amniocentesis technique of withdrawing fetal cells from the womb with a needle—may be developed. It is based on the somewhat surprising discovery that some cells from the fetus find their way into the mother's bloodstream. Simple extraction of a blood sample from a pregnant woman's arm may thus yield fetal cells for genetic analysis. Several obstacles must be overcome before the technique can be feasible for routine use. But the new technique opens the possibility that all pregnant women could safely have fetal cells tested.

Physics and chemistry

In the physical sciences the search for a sixth quark will animate discussion among those physicists probing the fundamental constituents of matter. Quarks are hypothesized particles of which most of the known subatomic particles such as protons and neutrons are thought to be composed. Evidence of five different kinds of quarks has been found. But theory demands six, or perhaps eight. So far the sixth quark (sometimes called the top quark) has not been found despite some expensive and high-powered accelerator experiments designed to reveal it, and its absence is puzzling. If repeats of the previous experiments still fail to unveil this quark, the searches will have to be carried out at still higher energies.

The long-sought dream of physical scientists to unify the four classes of force in a single framework will be pursued intently in the 1980s. Scientists were greatly encouraged by work in the late 1970s that dramatically fulfilled

The search for new subatomic particles will continue in the 1980s as physicists seek to unify the four classes of force in a single framework. Neutrinos are tracked at the left; above is a pion accelerator.

an important part of the goal, a unification of two of the four forces, electro-magnetism and the weak interaction. That achievement brought the 1979 Nobel Prize for Physics to the theorists of that union. If those two forces can now be considered one—dubbed perhaps the "electroweak" interaction—then it, gravity, and the strong interaction (the force that binds the nuclei of atoms together) remain to be joined in a unified field theory. In the 1980s physicists will be exploring the possibilities of a newly developed concept known as supersymmetry (and its subcategory supergravity). To many prominent physicists it seems the route to further unification of the forces. Supersymmetry has the possibility of unifying both the long-range interac-

21

tions (gravity and electromagnetism) and the short-range ones (the weak and strong). The hoped-for order sought in the scientific-philosophical quest for unification may or may not actually exist in nature. But a number of not-yet-discovered particles would be a consequence of the existence of supersymmetry, and physicists in the 1980s will be searching for them with great diligence.

Such particles are sought in high-energy accelerators. In this regard West Germany might well be the scene of some of the most significant discoveries in experimental particle physics in the 1980s. The Deutsches Elektronen-Synchrotron (DESY) laboratory in Hamburg, West Germany, has the PETRA facility, the world's most advanced machine for colliding electrons and positrons at high energies. Because these two particles are matter and antimatter, their collision results in annihilation. The enormous energy released is immediately transmuted into the mass of new particles. Observing what happens to them can lead to new insights into the nature of matter.

The PETRA colliding-beam facility is already responsible for demonstrating the existence of gluons, the particles that bind quarks together. It is undoubtedly also going to be valuable in experiments probing more precisely the now-unified domains of electromagnetism and the weak interaction. Past experience shows that when such a powerful new tool for exploring matter is put to work all sorts of surprises can result.

The Europeans are looking beyond even PETRA's capabilities. Scientists and governments of many European countries are actively planning an electron-positron collision facility called LEP that would be two to three times as energetic as the PETRA unit. The design of LEP has been under way for several years, and sometime in the 1980s it will become available for what will probably be even more revealing particle studies.

Physicists will also continue to search for further evidence of fractional electric charge. Using niobium spheres, several laboratories have found evidence that electric charge having a fraction (one-third) of the charge of a single electron does exist.

Gravitational waves will also continue to be sought, although hopes of finding them in the near future are not especially high. Such waves are predicted by Einstein's theory of general relativity, but direct evidence of their existence has been elusive. Gravitational-wave detectors consisting of large masses of metal and associated instrumentation are in place at a number of laboratories, but experience shows that unambiguous direct detection will be difficult. Tentative indirect evidence for their existence has been reported by one radio-astronomy experiment observing and calculating the rate of change of the orbital period of a pulsar in binary orbit with another object. (Theory predicts that the radiation of gravitational waves should cause the orbital period to change at a certain rate.) Such astrophysical searches may have to suffice until such time as a gravitational wave's vibration can be detected on Earth. (*See* Feature Article: THE SEARCH FOR GRAVITATIONAL WAVES.)

Solid-metallic hydrogen may be produced in the laboratory in the next few years. Room-temperature metallic hydrogen is expected to be a superconductor, a material in which electrical current flows with no resistance. A

Superconducting cable, in which electrical current flows with negligible resistance, requires elaborate windings of insulation and coils of liquid helium to maintain it near a temperature of absolute zero. Physicists hope to develop a room-temperature superconductor, which could have exciting applications in the production and transmission of electrical energy.

room-temperature superconductor could have exciting applications in electrical energy production and transmission as well as in many other technological fields. Already laboratory experiments have produced solid hydrogen at room temperature. All that is required to make it metallic is to increase the pressure used in the process to about one million times atmospheric pressure, and that seems achievable fairly soon.

During the 1980s there will also be increased activity in the search for superheavy elements. Theory predicts the possible existence of stable atoms having atomic numbers clustered around certain "islands of stability," such as 114 and 164. (The heaviest element now known conclusively is element 106.) So far the search for such superheavies has turned up some tantalizing possibilities but nothing that has been able to stand up in the court of science. Some nuclear chemists and physicists are discouraged about their inability to find conclusive evidence for such elements, either in nature or in accelerator experiments. But their discovery would be a major breakthrough, and the quest will continue in the 1980s.

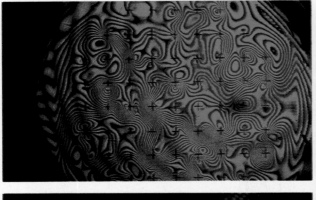

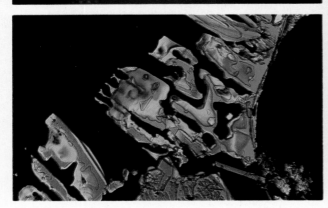

Applications of lasers (top left, center left, and right) and of electron microscopes (bottom left and opposite page) to scientific research will increase in the 1980s.

Lasers will be applied more and more to chemistry in the 1980s. Traditionally, chemists search for the right combination of temperature, pressure, and concentrations of catalysts necessary to weaken or break chemical bonds and bring about chemical reactions. A better way would be to deliver only the precise amount of energy necessary to break the desired bond. Lasers can supply that capability. They provide an intense source of energy, and they can be tuned to any desired frequency from the ultraviolet to the microwave. The principal drawback is cost of operation. Therefore, the first commercial applications of laser chemistry will probably be in the production of specialty products such as fine chemicals, drugs, catalysts, and rare isotopes. But as laser technology advances and the devices become more efficient, unit costs of output will decline. Laser chemistry, many think, will eventually have a near-revolutionary effect on many segments of the chemical industry.

24

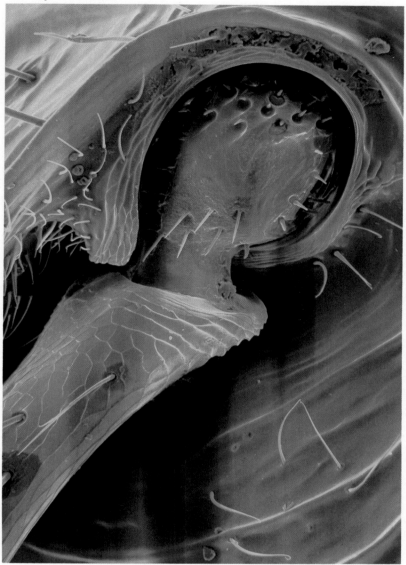

Earth sciences and astronomy

Earth scientists in the 1980s will work to develop ways of forecasting the likelihood of certain earthquakes. Full prediction, with anything like the precision and accuracy one thinks of with weather forecasting, will probably not be achievable in the decade. Nevertheless, lives can be saved and property protected if present research on the identification of earthquake precursors and earthquake-overdue "seismic gaps" progresses as expected.

Weather modification is an area in which hopes have exceeded achievements for several decades. But a research program that successfully caused Florida cumulus clouds to grow in size and produce more rain will be transferred to the U.S. Middle West in the early 1980s. The hope is that a careful program of research will discover ways to increase rainfall over major crop-producing areas.

The Sun and its possible connections to weather and climatic change on

25

"...as with carbon-14 the record of beryllium-10 contained in such natural long-term repositories as the ice caps of Greenland ... also contains the record of solar activity."

the Earth will be a target of considerable research in the 1980s. A number of basic solar processes, some of which have posed substantial intellectual puzzles, will be studied in detail. What, for example, is responsible for the Sun's magnetic cycle? What role do the recently discovered oscillations of the Sun play? Is the "solar constant" constant or variable to a small extent? How do the outputs of the Sun change over periods from years to thousands of years? And how do solar changes and events affect terrestrial weather and climate? (There is strong circumstantial evidence that they do.)

Another question is the mystery of the missing solar neutrinos. Only about one-third of the expected flux of particularly energetic neutrinos from a certain reaction expected to be taking place in the center of the Sun has been detected on Earth. Solar physicists would like to know why. The neutrino detector that has produced these disturbing results is a large tank of perchlorethylene located deep underground in a gold mine in South Dakota (where neutrinos but not cosmic rays can penetrate and cause the reaction that is considered a detection). Two other materials that could capture a wider range of solar neutrinos (including those from the main proton-proton reaction in the Sun) are being considered for neutrino "telescopes" in the 1980s. One is gallium-71, and the other is indium-115. Both are expensive, and large quantities of either would be required. However, a detector consisting of one of these materials may be set up in the 1980s. Then scientists may be able to learn what is awry with the Sun (or with neutrinos or with their theories).

26

Another chemical isotope scientists now think can tell them something important about the Sun in the coming decade is beryllium-10. In this case the concern is not what is going on in the Sun right now but how its activity may have varied over the past several tens of millions of years. And that could be important in gaining a better understanding about the Sun's role, if any, in past episodes of climatic change on Earth.

Carbon-14 has been used in recent years to determine the effect of solar activity on climate, but beryllium-10 has added advantages that promise to unlock far more of the past history of the Sun. Cosmic rays from outside the solar system produce carbon-14 when they impinge on nitrogen in the Earth's upper atmosphere. That carbon-14 eventually (over 40 or 50 years) finds its way to the surface and into living organisms. At times of high solar activity the Sun's greater emanations block some of the cosmic rays, and so less carbon-14 is produced and smaller amounts of it are found in tree rings formed shortly after that time. Thus, tree rings contain a record (when suitably unraveled) of solar activity extending back some 5,000 years.

Beryllium-10 also is produced in cosmic-ray collisions in the atmosphere. It has a much longer half-life than carbon-14, and it precipitates out of the air very quickly, in about a year. In the same manner as with carbon-14 the record of beryllium-10 contained in such natural long-term repositories as the ice caps of Greenland and Antarctica also contains the record of solar activity. The problem in the past has been that beryllium-10 is not nearly as radioactive as carbon-14, and so its presence in samples cannot easily be detected. But that problem recently has been resolved by the development of a new technique using particle accelerators to measure directly in a sample of material the concentration of radionuclides, such as beryllium-10. Thus, once full experimental techniques are set up and suitable ice cores are released for analysis, this isotope is expected to reveal much-sought secrets about the Sun.

These are, of course, only a few of the many possible scientific advances of the 1980s. The wondrous thing about the process of discovery called science is the surprises it may bring. Many dead ends and many suddenly opened pathways await investigators into the mysteries of nature. Nobody really can predict where all the routes of inquiry may lead. But of one thing we can be sure: by the end of the 1980s some of the questions now being posed by scientists will be answered. And because research seems always to reveal a new enigma for every one it solves, science will have a whole new list of questions and mysteries to confront in the 1990s.

Bards of the Sciences
by Jerry Pournelle

"Gather round," said the storyteller, "and I'll sing to you of humans who wrote fiction about science and themselves. And how what they wrote changed what they wrote about."

Much of mankind—certainly anyone of a culture that takes an interest in the events in this yearbook—lives in a science fiction world. That statement is true on several levels. As the mass entertainment field enters the 1980s, *Star Wars* ranks as one of the all-time moneymaking motion pictures. Hundreds of science fiction titles are published each month. Science fiction magazines proliferate like desert flowers after rain. A whole generation is growing up watching "Star Trek" reruns on television. Not only is science fiction popular, but it also has become respectable, a development that some of its proponents find pleasant but quite surprising. Not very long ago science fiction was "Buck Rogers stuff"; now there are university courses in the genre. Yet there is a deeper sense in which people live in a science fiction world, for the world around them, the real world of everyday life, was science fiction not many years ago—and science fiction can claim to have had a major influence in creating it.

The elusive definition

There are currently 500 members of the Science Fiction Writers of America and many more practitioners in other countries. There are also several hundred academic teachers of SF. (Most science fiction authors prefer the abbreviation SF for science fiction, rather than the popular term sci-fi.) Although most have tried at one time or another to define science fiction, probably no two have ever agreed. Is there a difference, for instance, between "science fiction" and "speculative fiction"? Does science fiction include disaster stories set in the near future? Two examples of this type are J. G. Ballard's *The Crystal World*, in which all life on the Earth begins to crystallize, and *Lucifer's Hammer*, by Larry Niven and Jerry Pournelle, which describes the Earth's encounter with a large meteor. And what about fantasy, sword and sorcery, the ghost story, the fairy tale, or such social satire as Jonathan Swift's *Gulliver's Travels*? John W. Campbell, Jr., whose influence on modern science fiction was greater than that of any other editor, once defined science fiction as the real mainstream of literature, with everything else—including that which most people call mainstream—as a subcategory.

Defining science fiction is an impossible task, but certainly some agreement is needed in order to consider the impact of science fiction on science and society. Philosopher José Ortega y Gasset wrote that "to define is to exclude"; accordingly, this article will ignore fairy tales and fantasy and will be concerned primarily with what is usually called hard-science SF; *i.e.*, stories that attempt, within limits, to be faithful to known laws of science. Nevertheless, other kinds of stories will inevitably enter into the discussion.

A poor prophet

Although often popularly supposed to predict the future, science fiction has seldom done that, nor do most science fiction writers claim any such ability. True, many SF editors of the so-called classic era from the mid-1920s to the early 1940s, particularly *Amazing Stories* magazine editor Hugo Gernsback, insisted on up-to-the-minute scientific accuracy and encouraged writers to project technological advances into the future. True, there have been numerous instances of correct "predictions," the most dramatic resulting in the 1944 visit by Manhattan Project security officers to *Astounding Science Fiction* magazine editor Campbell to discuss an alarmingly accurate fictional description of atomic energy. And true, the tradition of projecting technology into the future remains an important technique of modern science fiction. Yet, for all that, few SF authors would claim either the ability or the intent to predict the future.

Consider why any such claims would be untenable. The predictions of science fiction resemble those of the fortune-teller. A great many prophecies are made. Most are ambiguous, so that a large range of events can be counted "successful predictions"; these "successes" are loudly trumpeted while the many more numerous failures are conveniently forgotten. If science fiction is trying to predict, then the literature has a dismal record, not much better than the average soothsayer. There would be little point to examining its impact.

JERRY POURNELLE has written or co-authored several works of science fiction, including A Spaceship for the King, The Mote in God's Eye, *and* The Inferno. *He is a former president of the Science Fiction Writers of America.*

Illustrations by Ron Villani; illustration text by Charles Cegielski

It can likewise be argued, on a case-by-case basis, that the best SF is not deliberately trying to predict. One example is Frank Herbert's *Dune*, a work remarkable for its realistic, detailed evocation of a desert planet, including its physiography, ecology, and human society. Nevertheless, it is this very complexity—this dependence on the interplay of so many coincident events—that makes it highly unlikely that the combination of environment and society in *Dune* will ever come to pass. It is difficult to suppose that Herbert could have crafted such a world without this understanding. Moreover, in some cases the book taxes known science; for instance, in its assumption that a breathable atmosphere could be created and maintained on a planet lacking water or some other source of oxygen. *The Mote in God's Eye*, by Niven and Pournelle, postulates an intelligent alien race that has altered its own evolution in a highly unexpected way, but its authors would be much surprised if future astronauts found any such creatures. Yet these are examples of two hard-science SF novels. A great deal of SF is not hard science; many authors have never attempted to make their works consistent with known science and technology.

Even hard-science SF authors have written nonscientific SF stories. As an example, Poul Anderson, justly known for stories incorporating the very latest in scientific developments, also wrote *Three Hearts and Three Lions*, in which a 20th-century engineer is transported to the faerie world found in the chansons de geste, where modern physics interacts with magic in delightfully strange ways. One might dismiss that novel by saying that it is not science fiction at all but fantasy. How then should one classify his dozens of "puzzle" stories, in which a known scientific law is used as the solution to an obviously contrived problem? Readers of Anderson's "The Three-Cornered Wheel" do not really expect future astronautical entrepreneurs to be stranded on a world where they must transport a large object over bad roads, but find that there is a religious taboo against constructing or even drawing circles and round wheels.

Science fiction does not predict the future. It does, however, often succeed at technological forecasting. Although the success record of SF authors as a group is not startling, the best of them are most likely on a par with such professional forecasting institutions as the Hudson Institute or the U.S. government's Office of Technology Assessment. This should not be surprising because many science fiction writers have training in technological assessment that equals or surpasses that of the professional forecasters and draw on the same source materials. The famous "secret" letter to U.S. Pres. Franklin Roosevelt in which Albert Einstein pointed out the possibilities of an atomic bomb did no more than reflect what was known to anyone familiar with the open technical literature of the time. Einstein's equation ($E = mc^2$) demonstrating the possibility of converting matter to energy had been discussed in physics journals for more than 20 years, and when the United States began the Manhattan Project other major powers (Germany, Japan, and Great Britain) had already begun research on practical devices for accomplishing what had long been known to be possible in theory.

Sometimes the relationship has been more direct. Given that during World War II such SF writers as Robert Heinlein and L. Sprague de Camp, who were both engineers, had been assigned work on pressure suits that would withstand total vacuum, it is no great surprise that the space suits worn by early astronauts were quite similar to those described in science fiction stories of the late 1940s and early 1950s.

Finally, many science fiction writers routinely maintain close relationships with the technological community. Thus what is often seen as a startlingly successful forecast is in fact no more (and no less!) than the first popularization of an already accomplished laboratory breakthrough.

Discussion of science fiction as a literature of prediction can easily founder in a quagmire of definitions—not only of SF but of prediction itself. As an example, most writers active between 1940 and 1960 were interested in the then-infant computer sciences. Many important stories included very large and very complex computers. The science fiction machines—even those of the rather distant future—generally resembled real computers of the time: enormous things, occupying many square feet of floor space and filled with thousands of vacuum tubes and hundreds of thousands of discrete electrical parts. What was not foreseen, either by science fiction writers or professional forecasters, was that within two decades computers would become not only vastly more complex and capable but also small and cheap. Does one claim a successful prediction of powerful computers, or failure because science fiction has not to this day dealt with the consequences of widespread distribution of computers and information systems?

To quibble over this question is to show the futility of such a discussion. At best, science fiction has no more utility in either predicting the future or accurate technological forecasting than does popular nonfiction science literature. Its claim to significance must rest on something more substantial, as in fact it does. Rather than merely predicting the future, SF can make a good claim to shaping it. In fact, it can claim, with justice, to be among the most influential literature of the century.

A better proselytizer

One important influence of science fiction becomes obvious at any major scientific convention or event: the career choices of many, perhaps a majority, of the scientists and engineers present were profoundly influenced by early exposure to science fiction. They may no longer read science fiction—modern science is a harsh mistress and leaves little time for amusement—but thousands of scientists first became fascinated with science and technology through science fiction. Indeed, it would not be hard to make the case that without the stories of Heinlein alone, the already difficult task of aerospace company recruiters would be impossible.

It is generally agreed that the world needs a steady supply of good engineers and scientists. Unlike the liberal arts, hard-science courses are unforgiving. Failing science majors soon find it of no use invoking cultural relativism or explaining that they "have an open mind" and thus do not accept the current theory of the differential calculus. A physicist may advance to a point at which his refutation of Einstein's theory of gravitation will be taken seriously, but not without first having demonstrated to some instructor in his academic past that he understands general relativity. In

June
25 CENTS
Canada 30¢

1929

Science SEER Stories

NEW

The Myth of the Crystal Ball
Special Eye-Witness Report
20 Noted Authors
Ascend the Mountain

A:

Q: WHAT WILL
YOU LOOK
LIKE IN 1980

PLUS   The Wheel • Fire • Marriage • Income Tax   And   Other Incredible Tales of the Future

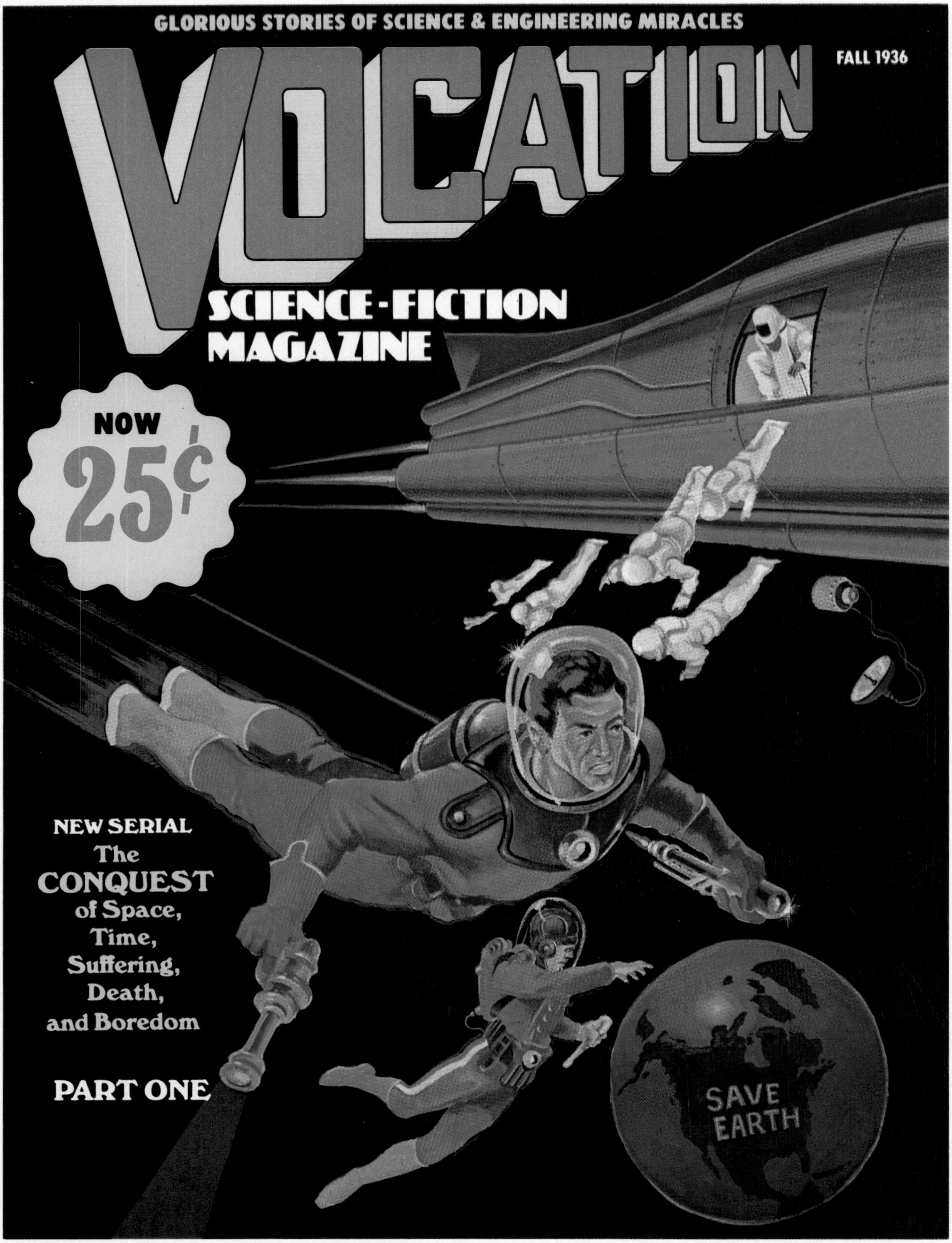

GLORIOUS STORIES OF SCIENCE & ENGINEERING MIRACLES

FALL 1936

VOCATION

SCIENCE-FICTION
MAGAZINE

NOW
25¢

NEW SERIAL
The
CONQUEST
of Space,
Time,
Suffering,
Death,
and Boredom

PART ONE

SAVE
EARTH

contrast, the social sciences and liberal arts have significantly less intractable content, and in those fields the ability to argue one's case can be as important as scholarship. The hard sciences need bards to sing their praises if they are to attract new converts, and science fiction serves that need.

It is more difficult to measure the influence of science fiction on the lives of individuals in fields apart from the sciences, although that influence cannot be negligible and may be important. However, the spell that SF casts over a small but significant population segment is both direct and nearly total. The phenomenon of science fiction fandom is unique. No other literary genre has developed such a large and well-organized cult; nor is there another genre in which such routine, massive, and direct contact exists between authors and readers. Moreover, for many SF readers there is a period—sometimes a few years, sometimes decades—during which science fiction is the only literature read.

The few studies attempting to characterize readers of science fiction unanimously show that the majority are considerably above average in both intelligence and potential social influence. While those who long remain total addicts to SF seldom have great influence outside SF fan organizations, the same is not true of those merely temporarily addicted. Many of today's scientific, academic, political, business, and social leaders literally lived in science fiction story worlds during their adolescence, and although the stories of that era seem today almost hopelessly conservative, they were thought radical in their time. To many of those young readers the worlds of SF were more real and more natural than the actual world in which they grew up. It is small wonder that they have been willing to act as midwives in creating those worlds.

A voice in the wilderness

A second, more profound influence is easily seen but difficult to pin down: the preparatory impact of SF on both the general public and the scientific community. Science fiction, wrote *Future Shock* author Alvin Toffler, "widens our repertoire of possible responses to change." It does this by "dealing with possibilities not ordinarily considered." Marshall McLuhan stated in *The Medium is the Massage* that the problem of modern man is "to adjust, not to invent," and that science fiction will "enable us to perceive the potential of new technologies." Science fiction is needed to "find the environments in which it will be possible to live with our new inventions."

One excellent example is the U.S. space program. As late as 1955 few people believed they would live to see humans reach the Moon. Most had grown up in times before widespread use of electricity, and many were convinced that they had "seen the future" with the initiation of scheduled airliner service. But during the 1950s a major boom occurred in science fiction. A dozen magazines sprang up, although most of these flourished only briefly. Hollywood made dozens of SF movies, most banal and some dreadful but all fairly popular. For the first time it was possible to buy whole books of science fiction, for SF outside magazines was almost nonexistent prior to 1950. Television made its contribution with "Captain Video," "Space Patrol," and other such series. Eventually the demand for science fiction was

Many of today's scientific, academic, political, business, and social leaders literally lived in science fiction story worlds during their adolescence. It is small wonder that they have been willing to act as midwives in creating those worlds.

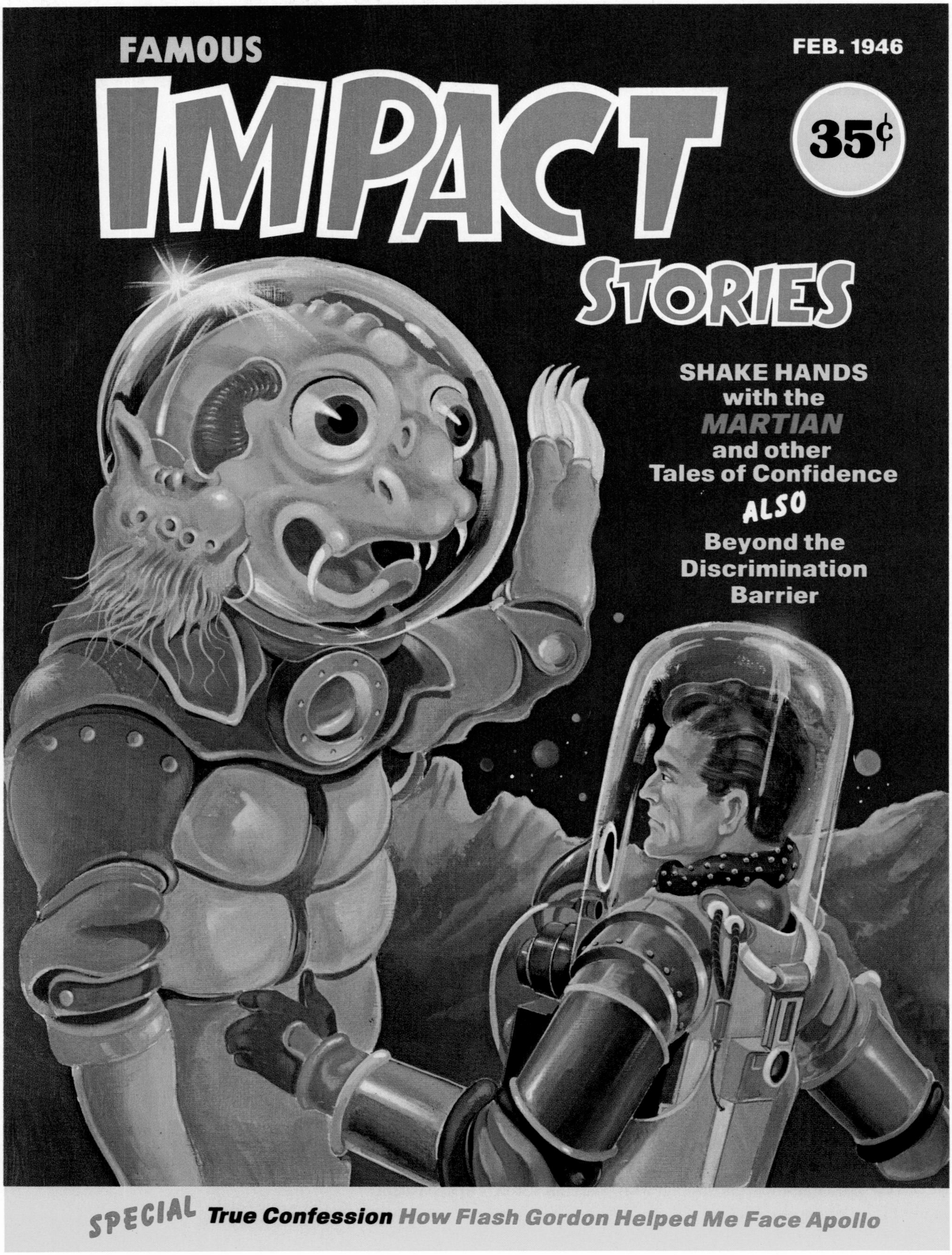
FAMOUS
FEB. 1946
IMPACT
35¢
STORIES
SHAKE HANDS
with the
MARTIAN
and other
Tales of Confidence
ALSO
Beyond the
Discrimination
Barrier
SPECIAL True Confession How Flash Gordon Helped Me Face Apollo

so great that a great deal of very low-grade material was published and filmed. Nevertheless, the impact had been made. The idea of manned space flight was no longer "far out," "weird," and "not for our lifetimes." It was in the air, something thought of every week, and not farfetched at all compared with what movies were offering. After all, if scientists could unerringly save mankind from Godzilla, giant ants, and other Hollywood creatures, what could stump them?

Although probably impossible to prove, it can be argued that without the preparatory influence of SF, the U.S. Apollo program would not have been possible. Certainly Pres. John F. Kennedy's announcement of a manned Moon landing before 1970 would not have been well received. He would have been thought a frivolous dreamer, not an imaginative leader. Moreover, much of the popular acceptance of the Apollo program must be laid to science fiction and definitely not to the technological community. When Kennedy made his announcement in 1961, most aerospace engineers were agreed that his goal was mere moonshine. In fact, the more closely they were attached to the space program, the more likely they were to insist vehemently that getting to the Moon in nine years was impossible.

The same kind of preparatory role can be seen operating today. Throughout the history of science fiction, writers have offered hundreds, perhaps thousands, of stories of the first contact between mankind and intelligent life of extraterrestrial origin. In some of these works the setting is the past, present, or future Earth; in others it is in space or on another planet. A few authors have even finished in fiction the real-life drama of scientists who presently listen to radio noise from space for broadcasts from other civilizations among the stars. If on some future day Earth's inhabitants discover they are not alone in the universe, they will be better equipped to deal with the biological, social, philosophical, and religious implications for having experienced them in the literature of science fiction.

Although science fiction's preparatory role is most dramatically illustrated in the field of technology, there has been a more subtle, but perhaps deeper, effect on social relations. It is impossible to measure the actual contribution of such stories as Anthony Boucher's 1943 novelette "Q.U.R." Ostensibly about robots and robot psychology, the story presents a black man as president of a World Federation of nations. Heinlein's novels written for a juvenile audience regularly employed women as scientists and engineers. Although science fiction legitimately can be faulted for retaining accepted stereotypes and for lacking sufficient boldness in asserting sexual and racial equality, as early as 1955 Heinlein presented Captain Helen Walker, a soldier of the Imperial Army, in *Tunnel in the Sky*. The influence of such stories in shattering cultural stereotypes can certainly be exaggerated, but it should not be underestimated.

Everyday miracles

Closely tied with the preparatory function of science fiction is its tendency to change people's expectations, sometimes directly, sometimes in rather subtle ways. Moreover, this type of change interacts with science and the real world.

Science fiction, wrote Future Shock *author Alvin Toffler, "widens our repertoire of possible responses to change." If on some future day Earth's inhabitants discover they are not alone in the universe, they will be better equipped to deal with the biological, social, philosophical, and religious implications for having experienced them in the literature of science fiction.*

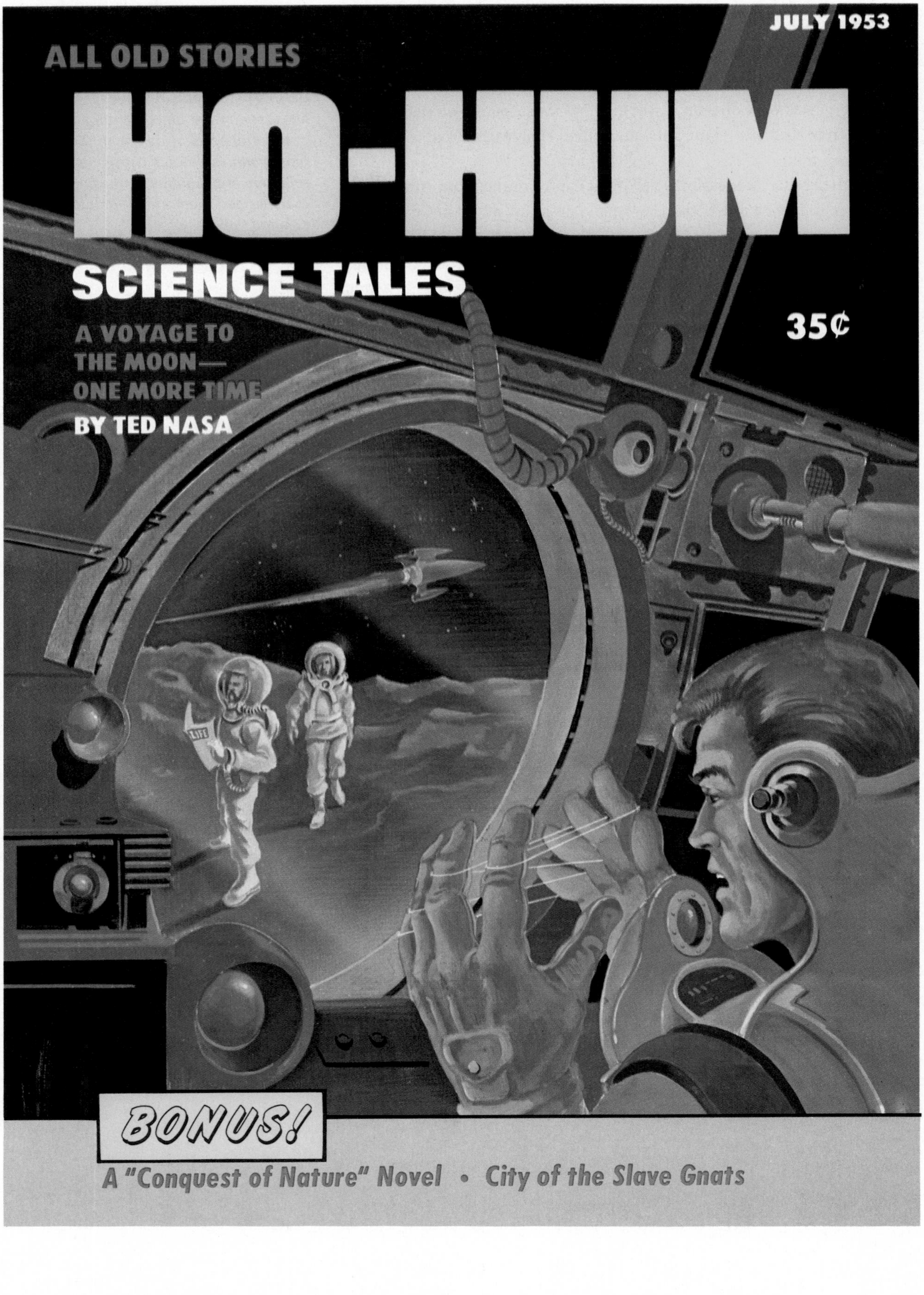

JULY 1953
ALL OLD STORIES
HO-HUM
SCIENCE TALES
35¢
A VOYAGE TO
THE MOON—
ONE MORE TIME
BY TED NASA
BONUS!
A "Conquest of Nature" Novel • City of the Slave Gnats

As an example, one of the least studied but most important results of the Apollo program was that those involved learned how to manage incomprehensibly complex tasks. Hundreds of thousands of people worked on thousands of separate projects—some of which involved discovering how to do things previously not possible—and the products of all this activity were brought together at a single time and place to produce a result. This degree of coordinated activity was unprecedented in human history. The only activity remotely as complex has been war, and wars have hardly been famous for good management. The invasion of Normandy on D-Day, 1944, may have approached Apollo in numbers involved but hardly compares in technological complexity. Apollo was unique; moreover, it was on time and very nearly within a budget set years before anyone knew how the mission would be accomplished.

Yet, although the Apollo program was a milestone in history, the difficulty of the task has not been appreciated by the general public—nor, indeed, by science fiction, which had usually shown the first flight to the Moon as a fairly simple accomplishment, sometimes as a backyard project. Although science fiction may have made the flight possible, by underplaying the difficulties it also diminished public sensitivity to what had been done.

The result of this interaction between public expectation, often shaped by science fiction, and scientific accomplishment has been fairly consistent. The public expects miracles and cannot understand why they are not routinely forthcoming. Science fiction encourages people to dream, while the knowledge explosion leads them to demand that the dreams come true.

Of course not all such demands can be ascribed to the influence of science fiction. It has long been an insistence of Western civilization that nature adapt to mankind, not mankind to nature. The biblical book of Genesis tells man to subdue the Earth and have dominion over every living creature. Although there is a school of SF that explicitly exhorts human beings to live in amity with nature, the vast majority of the literature disagrees.

It is noteworthy that the optimistic hard science story of the individual triumphant is popular chiefly in the U.S., with its long tradition of "American know-how" and inventive heroes like Benjamin Franklin and Thomas Edison. It is probably also significant that SF's dramatic rise in popularity during the 1930s and 1940s came during a period when mainstream literature concentrated largely on stories of men and women destroyed by an impersonal society. (Interestingly, a lot of science fiction stays in print for a very long time; even an average SF novel is likely to be available years after many Pulitzer prizewinning works have become unobtainable. Again, one is tempted to ask which is mainstream.)

Turn back, o man

Another indirect influence of science fiction is as warning. It is an old and honorable tradition: some of the best-known SF is pure jeremiad; for example, George Orwell's *1984* and Aldous Huxley's *Brave New World*. The generic type is what Heinlein once called the "If This Goes On" story: take a current trend, carry it to extremes, and show a society—usually a dystopia, *i.e.*, a perverted and malevolent utopia—built from the results. There are

39

thousands of examples of stories warning against hundreds of trends, some significant, some utterly trivial.

It is impossible to know just how influential such stories have been. For instance, if Western society is not in fact moving toward a world dominated by advertising agencies, how much of its safety has been due to the warning delivered by C. M. Kornbluth and Frederik Pohl in their 1952 classic, *Gravy Planet*? Nor is such a question absurd; at least some of the present skepticism toward the media appears strongly influenced by science fiction. Even more specifically, one may wonder just how much influence Poul Anderson's popular and prophetic 1954 novelette "Sam Hall" had on passage in the U.S. of the Privacy Act of 1974. This legislation regulates the dissemination of information about individuals that has been collected in government dossiers and permits persons to see their own files.

It might be argued that society would be the same today if the above two stories and many other SF jeremiads had never been written. Certainly it is difficult to show the influence of any single story or book, or even of an important author. Yet it is also probable that attitudes have been changed by their cumulative influence. For example, an almost uncountable number of stories showing the grim consequences of war in the nuclear age were published at a time when military and civilian policymakers still believed wholeheartedly in nuclear war as an instrument of national policy.

Although the majority of science fiction has presented science and technology as beneficial, there is a very strong countertrend denouncing science as Faust's bargain. Often those who cry warning have outshouted the larger number of bards who act as technology's harbingers, at least in the opinion of literary critics. Whether the dystopian theme produces better works than the more traditional stories of triumph is debatable, but certainly the gloomier works are more likely to win academic critical acclaim. Indeed, some critics go so far as to say that nothing can be literature that does not recognize man's fallen state.

Although fewer in number, there are also jeremiads warning against the rejection of technology and depicting societies that have sunk hopelessly into misery as a result of foolish attempts to "return to nature." This type of work has not often succeeded in gathering popularity or literary acclaim, probably because protechnology authors do not find such societies interesting, while antitechnology factions do not find them believable.

Who sings to the bards?

If science fiction or, more accurately, science fiction writers have a significant influence in shaping the future, what influences them? Perhaps the most consequential factor is fandom. SF fans are important far beyond their numbers or economic impact. It has been estimated that all of fandom— everyone who regularly reads one of the SF amateur publications called fan magazines or "fanzines," plus everyone who attends science fiction conventions—does not number more than 25,000. Whereas this figure would represent a very respectable sale for a hardbound book, it is well known that no large number of fans buys hardbound books; most wait for the paperbacks. Thus, even if an author sells a copy of every paperback he writes to

41

FAN & WRITER

50 cents

WEIRD SF ROMANCES   March 1974

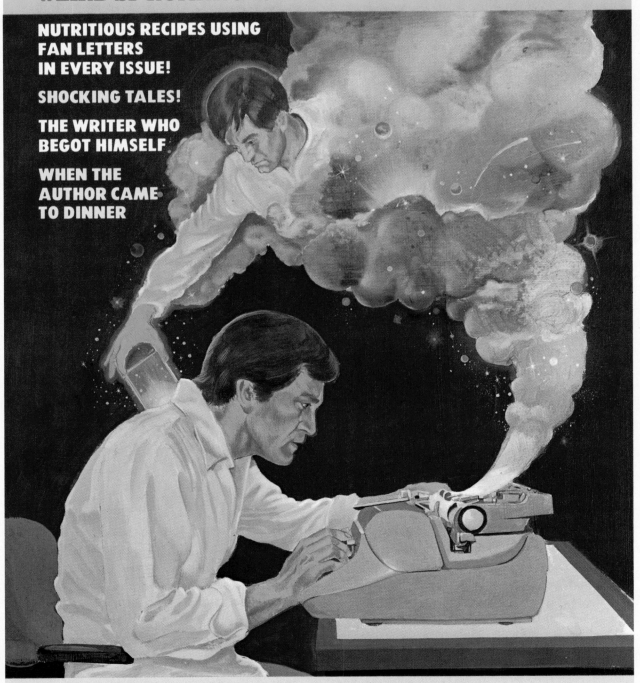

NUTRITIOUS RECIPES USING
FAN LETTERS
IN EVERY ISSUE!

SHOCKING TALES!

THE WRITER WHO
BEGOT HIMSELF

WHEN THE
AUTHOR CAME
TO DINNER

AN ASTONISHING NOVELET OF THE UNNATURAL SF CONVENTION

every fan in existence, but to no one else, the author will starve. Simple economics dictates that SF writers must appeal to a larger audience and that, if fans' tastes conflict with those of the general public, on economic grounds the fans ought to be ignored.

Yet few authors do this, for the very good reason that SF fans are usually the only readers an author meets, and it would be an unemotional writer indeed who could ignore the preferences and sentiments of hundreds to thousands of readers. The life of the average professional writer is an unnatural one. He spends many waking hours in a room alone save for beings of his own creation. It is no wonder that many writers seem unfit for social intercourse. And while this situation may apply to any professional novelist, it is even more descriptive of the science fiction writer, who is not often invited to academic parties and in general is not accepted in mainstream literary circles, but who will always be welcomed by fans. The temptation to please organized fandom is extreme.

If fans are important to science fiction writers, so are other science fiction writers. The late author Richard McKenna once described a gathering of SF writers as "a trapper's convention." Only those who have served the lonely hours on the trap lines are full companions in the order. Certainly SF writers form a close-knit community unique among laborers in the literary vineyards; no other genre has anything faintly resembling their fellowship. Most science fiction writers have received substantial assistance from some of the most famous names in the field, and there is a long-standing tradition that such aid should be "paid forward" to newcomers. New developments in science, even new story ideas, are regularly exchanged. While some SF writers delight in outraging their colleagues, few can entirely ignore them. Most will admit to their influence.

Thus a strange phenomenon has occurred: the creators of the future have in large part created themselves. Although a substantial minority of SF writers have not been fans, they are often drawn into the SF community after they become writers. Fandom and other writers are the major influences on science fiction. Science fiction created fandom. The serpent eats its tail.

The land of dreams

There have always been bards. They have often held high status. They have sometimes been more important than kings. In ancient days they roamed the land, seeking listeners who would feed them, searching for the campfires of some wandering band, approaching to say, "If you will carve me a slice from that roast and fill my cup with wine, I'll tell you a truly marvelous adventure in a land where men fly, light burns cold like the firefly, and wagons move without beasts to draw them."

Then as now they hoped to sing for more than supper; they imagined that their songs might sway kingdoms and powers and armies. Sometimes they did. Yet, was that their true work? Or is the true work of the bard to dream and, having dreamt, to tell his dreams? Then as now they could not know their influence. They could only tell stories. But nothing happens unless first a dream.

A strange phenomenon has occurred: the creators of the future have in large part created themselves.

The Airship Returns
by Norman J. Mayer

Aviation experts believe that the venerable technology
of lighter-than-air craft can be modernized and reapplied
to current transport problems.

Smithsonian Institution

German "Graf Zeppelin" (above), a hydrogen-filled airship of rigid design, was decommissioned in 1937 after nine years of successful continuous service carrying passengers, mail, and freight. That same year its successor, the "Hindenburg," exploded in flames while landing at Lakehurst, New Jersey, killing 35 passengers and crew and leaving behind a burnt, twisted mass of wreckage (facing page).

NORMAN J. MAYER is Program Manager and Consultant for Lighter-than-Air Systems at the U.S. National Aeronautics and Space Administration.

Illustrations by John Youssi

On May 6, 1937, the German dirigible "Hindenburg," carrying 36 passengers and 61 crew members and inflated with 200,000 cubic meters (seven million cubic feet) of hydrogen gas, burst into flames above the landing mat at the Naval Air Station in Lakehurst, New Jersey. Thirteen passengers and 22 crew personnel died in the crash and fire. Compared with modern aviation casualty figures these losses were small, yet the event remains today as one of the most spectacular air accidents. Not since that time have large dirigibles ever operated again in any kind of passenger service. A few years later the entire German dirigible industry was abolished, and most of the facilities were destroyed by Allied bombing in World War II.

Nevertheless, in the past decade many people have asked about and have even advocated a return of the dirigible. Their arguments emphasize the major advantage of lighter-than-air flight; namely, the ability to remain aloft without consuming energy. This feature, combined with such other characteristics as zero take-off distance and low noise levels, would seem to provide many practical benefits. Despite such justification and enthusiasm there are at present no serious ventures aimed at reestablishing dirigible transport service similar to the German operations. Today's economics and the complexity of aircraft development dictate that new vehicles can only be created in response to large markets. Recent analyses indicate that, when all costs are considered, Hindenburg-type operations would be at best marginally competitive and probably more expensive than jet plane transport. However, assessments made by the U.S. National Aeronautics and Space Administration (NASA) and others give a positive indication that important missions do exist for certain types of airships. A key to this future role may be provided by a review of the past.

Past applications

Beginning in 1783 and for about a century thereafter, the unguided, unpropelled balloon provided mankind's only means of flight. The dirigible came upon the scene sporadically, and it was not until the year 1900 that Count Ferdinand von Zeppelin began a really new era with the first successful test of his concept for large rigid airships. His Zeppelin dirigibles became the world's first long-range bombers during World War I, after having demonstrated their possibilities in civil passenger transport by carrying some 34,000 passengers inside German borders prior to the war.

The basic concept of the Zeppelin was adopted by the British and the French and later by the United States, but use of rigid airships as military aircraft vanished soon after the war. Their vulnerability, due to the use of hydrogen gas, eliminated further consideration. Only the U.S., with its abundant supply of nonflammable helium, continued with the construction of large flying rigid scouts and aircraft carriers during the early 1930s.

In postwar Germany the Luftshiffbau-Zeppelin organization turned its attention once again to the commercial world. In 1929 the dirigible "Graf Zeppelin," with a hull volume of 105,000 cubic meters (3.7 million cubic feet) demonstrated its potential by flying around the world, carrying 20 passengers and making only four stops. The "Hindenburg" began operations in 1936 and was of a more modern design. Until these airships discontinued

Drawn in 1910, an artist's vision of warfare in the year 2000 (right) includes use of gun-laden airships. Two important craft in airship history are the first successful dirigible balloon, built by French inventor Henri Giffard and flown in 1852 (below left), and one of Count Ferdinand von Zeppelin's earliest dirigibles (bottom), the first of which flew in 1900. An early French nonrigid airship (below right) dates from 1907.

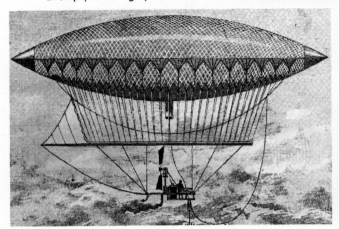

operations in 1937, they offered the only means of nonstop scheduled air transport between continents, having carried some 16,000 passengers a total distance of two million kilometers (1,250,000 miles), which included more than 181 ocean crossings.

In contrast to the well-publicized demise of the German operations, it is generally not known that the U.S. found the smaller, nonrigid dirigible, or blimp, to be of unique service during World War II as an antisubmarine patrol vehicle. By the end of the war, the U.S. Navy had operated 138 patrol blimps from 62 sites and bases along both the east and west coasts of the U.S. and from Newfoundland to southern Brazil. Six U.S. airships were stationed in the Mediterranean region in 1944, some having been flown across the Atlantic.

This record was so impressive that the Navy continued the use of nonrigid airships until 1962. Several new and larger types were developed, one of which carried a 13.7-meter (45-foot) rotating radar antenna within its helium-filled envelope. A combination of economy measures and the improved capability of airplanes and helicopters to perform antisubmarine patrol missions brought the service to an end.

The reasons, then, for the periods of success are clear. The balloon and simple dirigible gave man easy access to flight despite unreliable power plants and crude materials. There was comparatively little risk involved or technical skill required, and until the key to winged flight was provided by the Wright brothers in 1903, competition did not exist. The slow progress of the airplane toward reliable long-endurance flight gave the rigid airship an unquestionable advantage as a long-range bomber and scout during World War I and, later, prior to World War II, there was essentially no competition against the airship as an intercontinental transport. Finally, no aircraft but the blimp could provide the long-endurance, low-altitude patrol missions the Navy needed during and after World War II. In each instance the dirigible in some form performed a unique function and fulfilled an important need.

Moored to the ground, the gas-filled envelope of the early French airship "Patrie" (above) floats above a cable-suspended open framework for carrying crew and engine. French newspaper illustration (below) depicts the sinking of the German Zeppelin L-19 in the North Sea after a bombing raid over England in World War I.

Towering like a giant cocoon, the metal framework of a large rigid dirigible of the past takes shape in an airship assembly shed (right). German workers construct the control gondola of the "Hindenburg" (above).

Although conditions that once favored dirigibles for scheduled passenger transport no longer pertain, other developments have created new requirements. These include heavy-lift cargo transport, increased need for accessibility to remote areas, and patrol and surveillance of coasts and borders.

The changing world of transportation

The first development, heavy-lift transport, was partly dictated by the need for more efficient methods of maritime transport. In 1951 containers were initiated as a better means of handling the vast assortment of items transported by merchant ships. Containers are aluminum boxes measuring 2.4 meters (8 feet) square in cross section and as much as 12.2 meters (40 feet) in length. They can weigh as much as 27 metric tons (60,000 pounds) when filled but average around 22 metric tons (48,000 pounds). Containers allow and require the use of highly mechanized loading and unloading systems, and currently about 65% of all U.S. dry cargoes are shipped this way. They are most visible as the trailer part of many truck shipments since they can be moved easily from ship to road. Although most container trade is conducted between countries which have proper port facilities, the U.S. Department of Defense has been at work on the problem of port facilities in wartime, when rapid unloading of containerized cargo may be denied by port location or condition.

The container is a light load compared with those units of cargo classified as heavy lift. This category is defined by shippers as any single cargo weighing 100 metric tons (220,000 pounds), measuring 4.6 meters wide by 24 meters long (15 feet by 80 feet), or both. World trade in heavy-lift cargo, both intercontinental as well as within national borders, has been increasing. One reason for this increase is that efficiency and quality can be improved by manufacturing large components. Another is that items which fall in the heavy-lift category are typically associated with industries that are experiencing rapid growth. These include energy source exploration and development and mining, agriculture, and forestry development.

Heavy equipment does not easily lend itself to breakdown into smaller units for reassembly on site. Nuclear power generating equipment is a good example, in which the hazards of poor manufacturing or assembly would present unacceptable risks. Also, although the shipment of heavy-lift cargoes is no particular problem on water, it is much more difficult over land—even impossible in some cases. Such factors tend to force new facilities to be limited to navigable waterways where transport by ship or barge is comparatively easy.

The problem of heavy-lift transport is a subject of continuing study by a number of organizations, including agencies of the U.S. government and several foreign groups. A few examples, taken from such studies, illustrate the complexities and economics involved in heavy-lift transport.

1. In western and northwestern Canada, many natural resources have been discovered, particularly oil and gas. Establishing extraction facilities and pipelines for transport would require construction in some of the most difficult and climatically hostile terrain of the Canadian Northwest. Movement of hundreds of workers and many hundreds of tons of equipment into and out of construction sites must be completed between yearly winter freezes. It has been calculated that the combination of an extension of the working period and the time saved in transportation of equipment could reduce costs by more than $3 million (U.S., 1978) per year for three sites if a more direct transport method could be found. Another savings, of more than $180,000 per day of lost time, would result from bypassing such natural obstructions as rivers and gorges when transporting equipment. Larger subassemblies, requiring fewer trips and less assembly time on site, would save $400,000 per site. Lastly, once a pipeline is built, the benefits of having repair crews and equipment readily available could continue.

2. Another example can be found in a fossil-fuel steam electric generating plant to be constructed in the southwestern U.S. Three major cost savings are possible in this case: $8 million if fully assembled turbine and shaft and pressure components could be transported from the manufacturing plant to the lay-down area (a place where supplies are arranged in an orderly manner near the construction site); $1.2 million if all heavy components could be transported from the lay-down area to the plant site; and $1.1 million by elimination of a rented heavy-lift crane.

3. In the U.S. two million acres of forest stand on steep slopes or fragile soils where conventional logging is either not economical or not environmentally acceptable. Ground machinery can penetrate forested areas less than a half mile from the logging roads when such roads can be built. On steep slopes or environmentally sensitive areas, aerial methods must be employed to lift logs above the ground or tree line; cable yarders or "skylines," for example, which are cables supported above treetop level by towers, have been used up to distances of one mile. In many areas in the West and Alaska, however, even gaining access within a mile by road is not feasible. A long-
continued on page 53

51

Nonrigid airships, or blimps, served the U.S. Navy well as antisubmarine patrol craft during World War II. They also functioned in minesweeping operations, shipping control, and search and rescue missions.

UPI

Kinds of lighter-than-air craft

The term dirigible literally means "steerable." As a shortened form of "dirigible balloon" it strictly applies to all lighter-than-air craft that can be propelled and controlled in flight. Both ordinary balloons, which are unpropelled and unsteerable, and dirigibles belong to the class of aircraft called aerostats, a term indicating that their lift is derived from buoyancy, or displacement of air by a lighter gas. Dirigibles are also called airships. The "Hindenburg" was classed as a rigid airship because its hull was formed by a fabric-covered rigid metal framework that enclosed the lifting gas in a number of separate cells. This framework also provided support for engines and tail surfaces and space for passengers, crew, cargo, fuel, and ballast.

Another type of airship is the nonrigid. Its streamlined hull is literally a fabric envelope, and the internal gas pressure maintains the shape. Nonrigids, which are also called blimps, can be deflated for shipment or storage. A third type, the semirigid airship, utilizes a rigid keel in combination with a pressurized envelope.

These three types constitute the major classes of airships. A fourth, rare type can be called a pressurized rigid. This version consists of a rigid, nondeflatable hull that requires internal pressure for structural integrity when in flight. An example is a small metal-skinned airship built in 1929 for the U.S. Navy, the ZMC-2.

Examples of four basic types of airship appear below. (Clockwise, from top left) The rigid dirigible "Akron," completed in 1931 for the U.S. Navy, featured swiveling propellers to provide vertical and reverse thrust and was capable of launching and recovering planes in flight. The "Norge," an Italian-built semirigid, carried a team of explorers over the North Pole in 1926. The U.S. Navy nonrigid type ZPG-2, basically an antisubmarine patrol craft, played a part in the Navy's program to improve blimp performance after World War II. Another Navy craft, the ZMC-2, is a rare example of a pressurized rigid; constructed in 1929 with an all-metal, aluminum-alloy skin, it depended upon internal pressure to maintain hull strength in flight.

(Top) Brown Brothers; (bottom) Smithsonian Institution

(Top) The Lighter than Air Society Collection, Bierce Library, The University of Akron; (bottom) Pictorial Parade

continued from page 51

distance, high-capacity vertical-lift system could remove this barrier.

These examples illustrate conditions that exist in many areas, not just those cited. Less developed countries in particular often have resources in remote places and few if any established transportation facilities.

Heavy-lift airships

Vertical airlift is the obvious answer to heavy-lift transport. Currently the only type of heavier-than-air craft providing vertical lift is the helicopter. In the mid-1970s the largest helicopter in the world, of Soviet design, was capable of handling about 33 tons over short distances, and for U.S. helicopters the maximum cargo load is 18 tons. Developments have been under way to increase capacity by building larger helicopters, but the high cost of design and development has thus far stymied further support of such programs in the U.S.

Several people in various countries have suggested that some form of aerostat could be a simpler, less expensive, and more certain development than larger helicopters. One concept, originated in the mid-1970s by Frank Piasecki of Piasecki Aircraft Corporation in the U.S., proposed an aircraft using aerostat components and existing helicopters to achieve a heavy-lift capability of 25–160 tons. Buoyancy of the helium gas in this "Heli-stat" would lift the empty weight of the vehicle, while the helicopters could support the payload. Thus, this craft would be a hybrid of the helicopter and the airship operating in a predominantly heavier-than-air or "heavy" condition. In early 1980 the U.S. government contracted with Piasecki to build a vehicle with a 25-ton lift capability for aerial logging, with delivery in two years. In France a vehicle similar to the Piasecki concept was proposed in 1975 to carry a million pounds more than a thousand miles.

A more advanced version of this idea has been proposed by the Goodyear Aerospace Corporation in the U.S. It would utilize a 70,800-cubic-meter (2.5 million-cubic-foot) nonrigid envelope together with helicopter rotors and gearboxes mounted on streamlined power pods. Separate shafts from turbine engine gearboxes would drive propellers for forward and reverse thrust. The craft would carry a nominal 75-ton payload.

These new hybrid vehicles would not only raise the current limits on vertical-lift payload, but by virtue of the static lift from buoyancy would also demonstrate high cost savings over helicopters. Analyses show that even early-generation hybrid heavy-lift airships with helicopter components would have about 30% lower total operating costs than helicopters alone on a payload ton-mile basis. The helicopter-airship hybrid is considered to be the closest to reality in terms of time for development, since comparatively little new technology is required, and would be a first step across the threshold to true heavy lift.

Other concepts have been suggested for moving heavy payloads. One solution studied by the Grumman Aerospace Corporation in the U.S. is the modular unit. Each module would be a complete airship with a volume of 708,000 cubic meters (25 million cubic feet) and a payload capability of 330 tons. Three could be combined laterally to achieve close

53

to 1,000 tons. Each would be powered by four turbine-driven ducted fans that could be vectored (swiveled) for control as well as propulsion.

An interesting departure from the above approaches can be found in the "Aerocrane," a concept initially proposed by the All-American Engineering Corporation of Wilmington, Delaware. This vehicle would consist of a large spherical balloon and four blades or wings mounted at the balloon equator. The entire vehicle would rotate like a giant fan, power being provided by engines and propellers mounted on the wings. A stationary pilot's car would be attached at the bottom. Rotor lift combined with buoyant lift would allow carrying loads up to 50 tons. Other rotating concepts are also being studied by the originators of the Aerocrane idea.

Incorporation of helicopter-type features or vectored thrust also solves one of the major problems of aerostats: hovering with adequate control. An airship can hover because it literally floats in the atmosphere. It is difficult for it to do so, however, for more than a short period of time. Solar radiation can warm the lifting gas to create a condition called "super heat," resulting in a temporary increase in lift and causing the vehicle to rise. Likewise, if the surrounding air becomes warmer than the gas, a negative condition can exist, causing a loss of lift. Propeller thrust can be used to hold the vehicle against a prevailing wind, but horizontal or vertical gusts cause considerable deviations from an original position. Normally the control surfaces at the airship's stern correct its pitch and yaw motion, but these lose their effectiveness below certain airspeeds. The need for some design compromises

Examples of three designs for heavy-lift airships are shown at work at a construction site. Goodyear Aerospace Corporation's hybrid (facing page) uses a nonrigid envelope with pod-mounted helicopter rotors for vertical lift and propellers for forward and reverse thrust. The Aerocrane (below left), developed by the All-American Engineering Corporation, consists of a round balloon with wings jutting horizontally from the balloon's equator. Powered by engines and propellers mounted on the wings, the vehicle rotates about its vertical axis like a giant fan. The stationary pilot's car and cargo hang below from a swivel. Another hybrid, Piasecki Aircraft Corporation's Heli-stat (below right), combines a buoyant envelope and existing helicopters.

Photos, Musée de l'Air

French "Helicostat," a small nonrigid airship built by Étienne Oehmichen in 1931, could hover, rise and descend vertically, and fly backward. Its open-framework car carried a single pilot, four swiveling propellers, and a 40-horsepower engine.

among weight, drag, and control force usually sets this limit at about 15 knots. (One knot is about 1.85 kilometers per hour or 1.15 miles per hour.) Below this speed conventional dirigibles are largely controlled by static forces, such as shifting weight or air.

Although propulsion on conventional airships has been used primarily for forward flight, early dirigible designers recognized the advantages of low-speed control and auxiliary lift that could be provided by thrust devices. A notable example was a development by Étienne Oehmichen in France in 1931 called the "Helicostat." It contained four tilting propellers driven by one 40-horsepower engine. Flown by a single pilot, it could hover, rise and descend vertically, and fly backward. The U.S. Navy dirigibles "Akron" and "Macon," built in the early 1930s, incorporated tilting and reverse thrust on all eight engines so that as much as 4,500 kilograms (10,000 pounds) of vertical thrust could be generated.

A modern version of the Oehmichen design has been offered by the French firm Aerospatiale, co-developer of the supersonic Concorde. This experimental vehicle would incorporate helicopter rotors instead of propellers and use separate small rotors for forward and reverse thrust. It would demonstrate principles to be incorporated in larger machines.

56

Patrol and surveillance

In 1976 the U.S. passed the Fishery Conservation and Management Act, which established U.S. control over a coastal area extending out to 322 kilometers (200 miles). In this zone American fishing activities would be limited and those of foreign nations excluded unless specifically licensed. The total area covers 5.7 million square kilometers (2.2 million square miles) of ocean, equal to about three-quarters of the U.S. mainland.

The enforcement of this act is the responsibility of the U.S. Coast Guard, which employs a variety of ships, planes, and helicopters in the task. The ships are limited by speed, the aircraft by endurance. Wind and waves often combine to slow surface vessels to crawl speeds. Although aircraft are not affected by waves and are fast enough to negate normal wind effects, they consume expensive fuel at a high rate, and in those capable of long patrols, crew fatigue is a factor.

Recent studies have shown that airships could overcome these problems. The fuel consumed per mission would be a fraction of that used by an airplane, and the vibrationless environment of the airship would allow greater concentration on the mission and less fatigue. Because large quarters or crew facilities are easy to incorporate in airships, longer patrols and relief crews could be accommodated. Designed as a blimp, the modern coastal patrol airship could have substantial hover capability. Whereas most of its lift would be derived from buoyancy of its helium, propellers would furnish both propulsion and control by means of vectored thrust.

In application, the airship would cruise over areas in which fishing or other coastal activities are in progress, monitoring them by means of modern electronic gear and visual observations. When suspicious actions are noted, the airship would descend near the vessel, hover above it, and dispatch a boarding party either directly or via a small boat carried aboard.

Law enforcement

Tethered balloons and remotely controlled airships may offer solutions to problems of crime detection and law enforcement. City police currently use helicopters for low-altitude patrol of streets and traffic. As outstanding as these vehicles are, several problems still exist in their use. The first is cost: only large cities can afford the purchase and operating expense. The second is emitted noise, especially above residential neighborhoods. And the third is the relatively short endurance of both vehicle and crew.

Studies have been made of the potential of small blimps that could cruise at low altitudes and at low speeds, piloted remotely via television and infrared sensors by an officer seated in a building miles away. Without pilots and space for them these airships could be quite small in size yet carry all necessary equipment for viewing the scene below, even in low-visibility conditions. Cost of operation could be a fraction of helicopter expense, and the low power requirement would generate less noise and allow almost continuous aerial surveillance. In addition to municipal police work, balloons and airships offer potential for border patrol smuggling surveillance needed by immigration authorities, narcotics control groups, and the U.S. Customs Service.

57

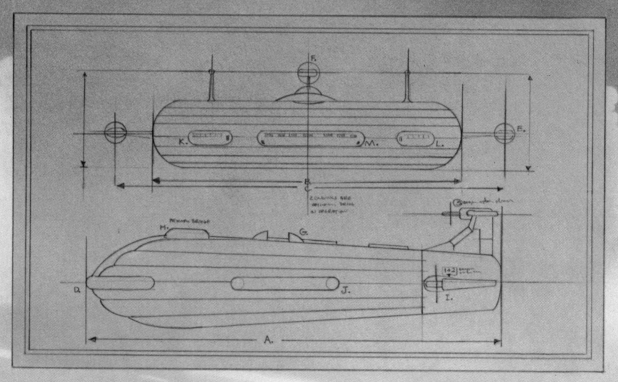

Other applications and designs

Jobs may exist for large rigid airships in Navy and antisubmarine patrol missions over the world's oceans, either close to or away from the surface fleet. Because much of the mission time would be spent in very slow speed flight, average power and fuel consumption requirements would be very low. Although no decisions have been made to develop such airships, a program of this kind also could yield modified designs for special civil passenger transport: cruise ships, hospital ships, disaster relief assistance vehicles, or long-range heavy-lift transport to remote areas.

Certain newer concepts in hybrids could replace the more conventional streamline-shaped airship for missions where full buoyancy is not required. For a number of years, a small U.S. group known as the Aereon Corporation of Princeton, New Jersey, has studied a design that combines aerodynamic lift with buoyant lift. This delta-shaped vehicle allows somewhat higher speeds and improved efficiency over the conventional airship for certain ranges of travel when operated as a semibuoyant aircraft. Aereon has flown a nonbuoyant small-scale version to check out aerodynamics and control. Variations combining conventional and deltoid shapes have also been investigated by others with favorable conclusions.

Shape variations seem to be a favorite subject for experimentation. French and British groups have proposed use of saucer shapes as offering certain advantages, such as reduced resistance to crosswinds, especially at or near the ground. One concept would combine helium and hot-air lift to achieve varying degrees of buoyancy.

Two airships designed for specialized service assist at the scene of a sea disaster. The deltoid-shaped vehicle, outfitted as a hospital ship, derives from an Aereon Corp. concept that combines aerodynamic lift and buoyant lift. Its flat top deck permits helicopter launching and retrieval. The U.S. Coast Guard patrol ship follows the basic blimp design and is equipped with swiveling propellers for vectored thrust.

The small blimp also continues to intrigue a number of entrepreneurs wanting to enter the world of dirigible manufacture and flight in the U.S. and abroad. One noteworthy example is an airship developed in England that incorporates extensive use of composite materials in its car, nose stiffening, and tail structure. Such composites are usually combinations of high-strength, high-stiffness fibers and polymeric resin plastics with properties superior to those of metals. The airship also uses vectored thrust by means of tilting fans mounted on each side of the car and driven by two automotive Porsche engines. The combination of lightweight structure and envelope gives this airship a payload of almost twice the weight that could be lifted by past airships of similar size.

Studies at NASA also identified a limited market for a so-called "airport feeder." This craft would resemble a small blimp but would actually be a hybrid since it would combine buoyant and rotor lift.

The future

There is no doubt that a flyable hybrid vehicle could be built, but the element of risk is high unless certain research is accomplished first. Little information exists concerning the interaction between large rotors and aerostat hulls, and control and flight characteristics are not yet precisely predictable. A program to investigate these unknown factors is under way at NASA. It will provide design criteria and determine flight characteristics in computerized flight control simulators. The program will also involve wind tunnel tests and possibly a piloted scale-size research aircraft.

Patrol and surveillance airships would not require such extensive development. Their design could be a more straightforward application of current aerospace technology. Consequently their costs would be much lower than those of hybrids.

It is interesting to note that current space-age materials and design procedures can contribute to lighter and stronger airship structures. Advanced composite materials, for example, can be used in such hard structures as cars and tail surfaces and in rigid-airship hulls. New plastics like Mylar offer much improvement over older materials for gas cells or in combination with synthetic cloths for the entire envelope. Weight savings of as much as 50% are possible for particular components, and overall weight reductions of 20–30% could be achieved.

The future of dirigibles and other lighter-than-air craft depends on new applications in transportation and other fields, particularly where there is great need, good economic justification, and little or no competition. The most promising use is in the transport of heavy-lift cargoes to and from otherwise inaccessible or remote areas, and airships that perform these operations will probably be hybrids of aerostats and helicopters. More conventional airships and drones will be useful for offshore coastal patrol and other surveillance missions. The large rigid dirigible of the 1930s is not likely to return as a commercial carrier, but it could appear in the form of a long-range naval patrol vehicle. If this occurs, variations of the basic design could be applied to special civil uses, perhaps including specialized passenger transport.

Small, remotely piloted police craft, a "miniblimp" concept of Developmental Sciences, Inc., of California, cruises at low speed among the high rises of a large city. Its television camera, infrared sensors, and directional microphone function as the eyes and ears of an officer seated at its controls in a building perhaps miles away. Parked on a rooftop landing pad and detailed at the top of the illustration is an airport shuttle, a blimplike hybrid airship designed by Goodyear to carry 80 passengers. A helium-filled envelope and four tilting rotors powered by turboprop engines provide lift.

61

Primate Intelligence

by Sue Savage-Rumbaugh and Duane M. Rumbaugh

Research with monkeys and apes has led to the conclusion that intelligence is not a fixed quantity in any species but is instead a set of abilities that can be altered by experience.

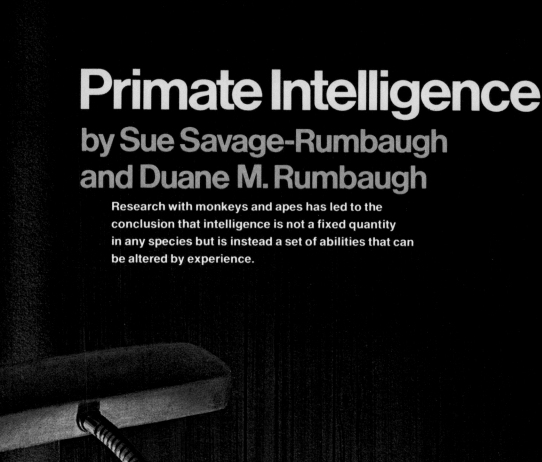
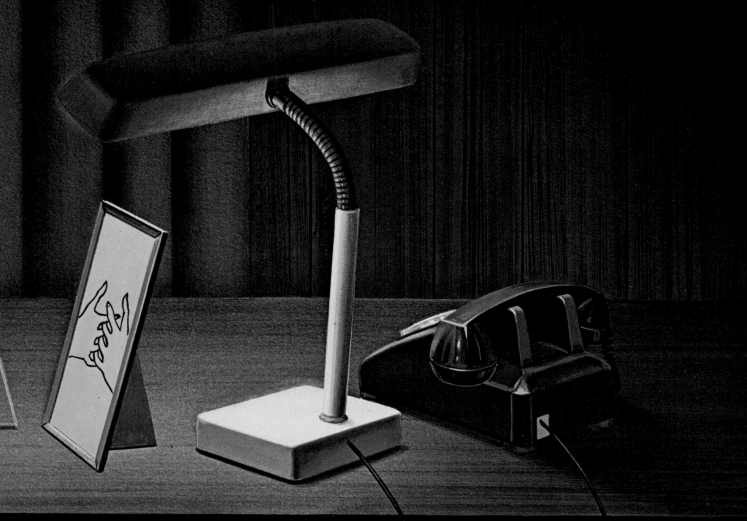

People have long been interested in and speculated about primate intelligence. How smart are monkeys and apes? This question is intriguing, for in the nonhuman primates strange caricatures of mankind not found in other animals may be seen. Only primates share with human beings (who are themselves primates) similar body proportions, true hands and feet, true binocular vision, and prolonged infant dependency leading to a strong parent-infant bond and a complex, hierarchically organized social unit of existence. People have occasionally even been tempted to attribute superhuman capacity to nonhuman primates. The orangutan of Southeast Asia, for example, is said by legend to avoid learning to speak because he knows that when he does so he will also have to work. Men, so the legend continues, were not so smart. They came out from the forest, learned to speak, and now they must work every day. Although scientists now know that the orangutan is not as intelligent as the human being, they are still searching for precise and equitable means of comparing intelligence across primate species.

The order Primates is comprised of a remarkable array of diverse forms, including prosimians (including, among others, lemurs and tarsiers), New and Old World Monkeys, the lesser and great apes, and the human species. It is generally accepted that the great apes (orangutan, gorilla, and chimpanzee) approximate human beings more closely than do the lesser apes (gibbon and siamang). Additionally, all of the apes approximate mankind more closely than do the monkeys, tarsiers, and lemurs. The order Primates is believed to have had its roots in a now extinct form of tree shrew; a close approximation thereof still lives in present times.

The concept of intelligence is admittedly a difficult one. There is great controversy regarding its definition and how to measure it properly. In the past, attempts to measure intelligence in humans have emphasized knowledge accrued through the experience of living in the United States. More recent efforts are exploring the feasibility of assessing intelligence through methods that presume that the human brain is a system that collects and processes information. It is beyond the scope of this article to review the diverse perspective of human intelligence; however, reference to David Wechsler, a leader in the field of intelligence testing, might be helpful in the interpretation of data emanating from primate research. For Wechsler intelligence is defined as "the capacity of an individual to understand the world about and his resourcefulness to cope with its challenges." The components of intelligence are viewed as many and diverse. Its systems include: (1) awareness of what is being done and the reason for it; (2) meaningfulness, in that behavior directed by intelligence is goal-directed and not random; (3) rationality, in that behavior directed by intelligence is consistent and logical; and (4) usefulness, in that intelligent behavior is adjudged worthwhile by others. Value judgments are inevitably entailed in assessments of intelligence if for no other reason than that intelligence is a construct and as such can be measured and inferred only indirectly through behavior.

It is clearly a difficult task to apply Wechsler's concept of intelligence to species other than man. How do we determine whether or not animals are aware of what they are doing and their reasons for doing it? From what value system do we determine that their behavior is logical and rational?

SUE SAVAGE-RUMBAUGH is Assistant Research Professor at the Yerkes Regional Primate Research Center of Emory University, Atlanta, Ga. DUANE M. RUMBAUGH is Professor of Psychology at Georgia State University, Atlanta.

(Overleaf) Illustration by Eraldo Carugati

64

Irven DeVore—Anthro-Photo

When an ant or a bee uses the elements at hand to construct a nest, are we to conclude that its behavior is resourceful and worthwhile and, thus, intelligent? When we attempt to study the behavior of other animals, we realize that the human concepts of intelligence have been narrowly defined and that we cannot easily apply these concepts to other species. For this reason there have arisen various approaches to the study of primate intelligence. These approaches differ significantly, but they share the common goal of assessing the relative intelligence levels and processes of primates.

A baboon pushes a rock aside in search of worms and grubs that may be under it. One method of assessing the intelligence of primates is to observe their behavior in natural settings.

Field studies

One such approach can be identified as the ecological orientation. It postulates that the intelligence of animal behavior can best be assessed by means of observations in natural settings. The creative adaptation of behaviors as generated in response to novel problems (which the animal finds occurring naturally in its environment) thus serves as the basis for inferring the "intelligence" of the animal. These flexible and novel behaviors are contrasted with those that are basically unlearned and structured by heredity (genes) as they interact with environmental factors. The use of various methods to extract nuts from shells can serve as an example. Nuts are extracted by use of the teeth to crack the shell (an unlearned technique) or by the use of clubs and rocks as instruments to crack the shell by impact (learned techniques that are often transmitted across generations).

Chimpanzee bends close to a termite mound in search of an opening (left). After finding one, it inserts a blade of grass (center). Termites in the mound grasp the blade and, when it is removed, provide a treat for the chimpanzee (right). Primates that manipulate objects in nature solve laboratory problems more readily than those that do not.

The variety and effective functioning of such learned or acquired behavioral tactics are used to infer the intelligence of the various primate forms. Considerable evidence has been collected that reveals that the degree, form, and function of object manipulation serve as excellent indicators of intelligence. Primates who manipulate a wide variety of objects in many different ways and contexts also solve formal (laboratory) problems more readily than those that do not and possess larger, more convoluted brains. The great apes are far more creative and versatile in this respect than are gibbons and monkeys, both in the field and in captivity. For example, all of the great apes use tree or bush branches to construct nests every evening. Orangutans even break off large leafy branches to use as umbrellas during heavy rains. No monkeys have ever been observed to construct nests or to modify their environment in any way to facilitate sleeping or to avoid the elements. Chimpanzees strip twigs, lick them, and then insert them into termite and ant mounds to catch insects. (Termites react as though the stick is an animal invader and try to repel it by grasping onto the stick with pincers. Ants race up the stick to attack the invader.) Baboons living in the same area also eat termites but make no attempt to use twigs, or any other object, to catch them. Also, chimpanzees throw sticks and rocks at animals that they perceive as potentially dangerous. Although they throw with an underhand, imprecise, arm-slinging motion, their aim is accurate enough to land the object in the general vicinity of the other animal. Monkeys have never been observed to actually grasp and throw objects, though there are scattered reports of baboons pushing rocks off of cliffs onto intruders below. Figure 1 illustrates the relationship between the complexity of brain development and the tendency to manipulate objects.

Evolution of the primate brain can be assessed from various perspectives. One is the absolute size of the brain. A cranial capacity (in cubic centimeters) for a human being is approximately 1,400; for a gorilla, 480; for a

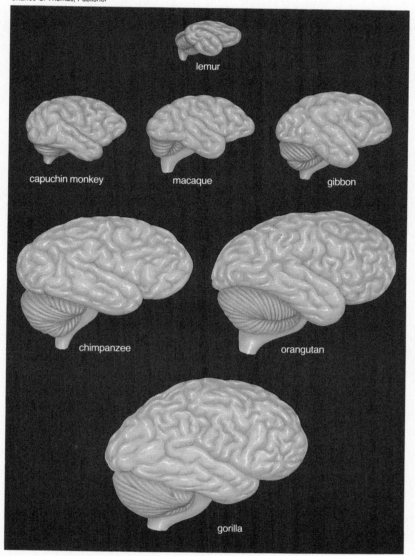

chimpanzee, 365; for an orangutan, 375; and for a gibbon, 100. In terms of brain development the human brain is several times larger than what would be predicted given that the human being is a primate and given the average human body size.

Laboratory research

A second approach to the assessment of primate intelligence is represented by laboratory studies in which the abilities of various primate species to learn with high levels of efficiency are assessed quantitatively under carefully controlled conditions. These efforts might be traced to the early speculations by Wolfgang Köhler (1925) and by Robert and Ada Yerkes (1920) which asserted that qualitative differences exist in the learning processes of apes and monkeys. These researchers regarded apes as being capable of abstract or ideational learning, in contrast to monkeys, which learned primarily by the association of specific responses to specific stimuli.

Figure 1. Complexity and size of primate brains correlate generally with the tendency to manipulate objects. During a study over an extended time the orangutan spent 36% of its time manipulating objects with respect to other objects or to itself. It was followed, in order, by the chimpanzee (29%); gorilla (13%); capuchin monkey (6%); macaque (5%); gibbon (4%); and lemur (3%). Considerable evidence reveals that the degree, form, and function of object manipulation are excellent indicators of intelligence.

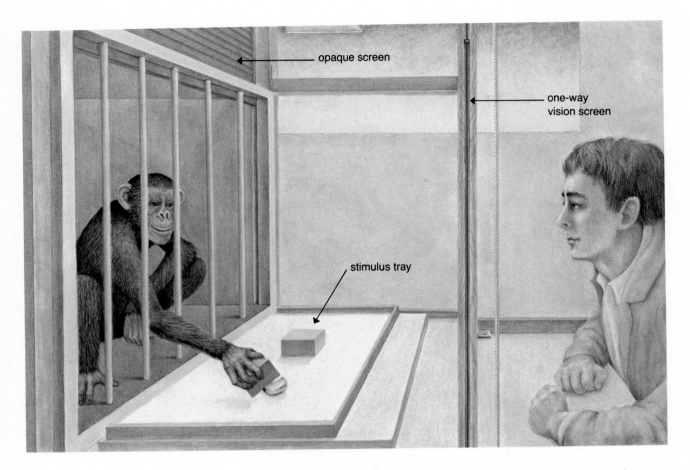

opaque screen

one-way vision screen

stimulus tray

Figure 2. A primate is presented with two objects that differ in color or other ways from one another. One object has food under it, and the other does not; the primate must determine which one covers the food. Such two-choice visual discrimination tasks have been used for many years to measure primate intelligence.

Work by Harry Harlow (1949) revealed a systematic relationship between the amount of experience in attempting to learn how to solve two-choice visual discrimination problems and the rate at which new problems of the same type were learned. Two-choice visual discrimination tasks represent the classic measure of primate intelligence. In such problems the animal is presented with two objects or "stimuli." These stimuli may differ either in many ways (color, form, shape, size, etc.) or only in one way. One of these objects is arbitrarily designated "correct," the other "incorrect." The correct object has food hidden under it, and the incorrect object does not. The primate's task is to determine which object is correct. An example of the classical two-choice discrimination training apparatus is shown in figure 2.

As the animals in Harlow's studies repeated the tasks, they became more facile learners and were said to have formed "learning sets." This meant that they became better and better learners in terms of accuracy of choice when presented with new problems, even though they were not given enough trials to learn any single problem well.

This improvement in accuracy was believed to reflect a generalized form of cumulative transfer of knowledge. Improvement in performance was charted as a function of successive blocks of problems, a block being an arbitrary number of problems. By the end of their training the primates chose the correct object on all trials following the first trial on each and every new problem they encountered; thus, they had formed a learning set.

This stood in dramatic contrast to their very poor performance on the first several trials of problems that were encountered early in their training.

Research from various laboratories indicated that there was reason to believe that the more highly evolved the brain of a given primate species, the more likely it was to excel in learning-set tasks like those employed by Harlow. Also, within a species, there was an orderly relationship suggested between its ontogenetic development and its ability to form learning sets. The problems encountered in making comparisons of the learning-set skills of various species and genera were recognized by Harlow and his students, and caution was advised by Harlow, who stated, "Diversity in receptor-effector mechanisms frequently renders exact comparisons of learning between species and genera questionable and poses major problems when we attempt comparison among orders, classes and phyla."

Duane Rumbaugh in a study published in 1969 reported the development of the Transfer Index, designed to circumvent or at least minimize the risks involved in learning-set studies of various primate species. Differences in species' morphologies, sensory-motor systems, learning and attentional processes, and strengths of appetites for foods (used as rewards for correct responses) are representative of the many sources of difficulties encountered when one tries to compare the performance levels of diverse species in an absolute sense in order to draw conclusions as to levels of intelligence.

The Transfer Index attempted to circumvent these problems by requiring that the subjects learn each two-choice discrimination problem to a well-defined level of competence prior to any attempt to make performance measurements that would be used to infer species' differences in cognitive skills. Subjects were allowed certain numbers of trials (not to exceed 60) within which to achieve a preselected "criterion"—a level of performance, such as, for example, that 67% or 84% of the responses given were correct. Upon achievement of the criterion by the subject, the object that had been correct and that, if chosen, had led to a food reward became incorrect and not rewarded if selected; choice of the formerly incorrect second object was rewarded with food. Ten trials under these conditions were then given, and the performance of the subjects on them relative to the levels required prior to cue reversal was used as the basis for calculation of the Transfer Index.

Achieving performance that meets a criterion level prior to testing ensures that the subjects are attending and learning and that they have learned to approximately the same levels of efficiency. The ten test trials in which the cue values are reversed provide for a quantitative assessment of the subject's ability to cope with that new situation. The Transfer Index testing procedure, then, allows for some latitude in terms of rate at which the criterion is achieved, but provides only a limited and equal opportunity for the demonstration of ability to transfer learning from training during the criterion-achievement period to the reversal-test situation.

Interestingly, though diverse species might learn the original discriminations to the identical criterion with equal facility, they do not perform with equal proficiency on the reversal test trials. For example, great apes and rhesus monkeys frequently continue to improve when the correct and incorrect objects are reversed. They may, in fact, do better after such a reversal.

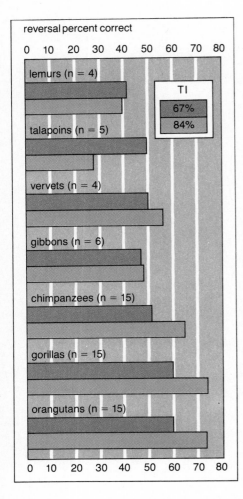

reversal percent correct

	TI
	67%
	84%

lemurs (n = 4)

talapoins (n = 5)

vervets (n = 4)

gibbons (n = 6)

chimpanzees (n = 15)

gorillas (n = 15)

orangutans (n = 15)

Figure 3. Performance of primates varies on tests requiring transfer of previous learning to a new situation in which the cue is reversed. (TI = Transfer Index; see accompanying text.) On the opposite page chimpanzees demonstrate how they have learned to scale a wall by using a pole.

This is not the case for the smaller Old and New World monkeys or the prosimians. Invariably these forms do less well on reversal test trials than they did prior to reversal. In other words, if they have met a criterion of 84% correct prior to reversal tests, they perform at a level appreciably less than 84% correct on reversal tests, while certain apes and rhesus monkeys do reliably better than 84% correct on their reversal tests.

The reversal tests are essentially transfer-of-training trials. If an animal is capable of transferring its previous learning set (for example, choosing the "funny-shaped green one" and not the "fat round red one") to a new situation in which the problem is the same but the opposite response is required, then it is said to be able to transfer knowledge. It is generally true that the more highly evolved the primate brain, the more adroit the primate in its ability to transfer knowledge—a basic dimension of intelligence.

Transfer Index data for selected primate forms are portrayed in figure 3. That these data are significant with regard to the assessment of primate intelligence is evidenced by the fact that there is a high correlation between the Transfer Index performance levels of four-and-a-half-year-old children and their intelligence as otherwise measured. The high statistical correlation found here indicates that individuals with a high Transfer Index score will most likely have high scores on other independent tests of intelligence, while individuals with a low score on one test are likely to have low scores on other intelligence tests. The correlation is +.76, about as high as can be expected between any subtests of intelligence and scores obtained from an entire intelligence test.

The inferred intelligence levels of primate genera are in close correspondence not only with the development of their brains, but also with the development of their perceptual capabilities and their abilities to integrate and to equate information that they derive either concurrently or sequentially from different senses. Cross-modal perception is well established as a phenomenon among nonhuman primates, though not too many years ago it was thought to be a uniquely human capability. Richard K. Davenport and Charles M. Rogers demonstrated that apes are able to select the one of two stimuli sensed by touch that matches a visual sample in tests where materials are used that are unfamiliar to the subjects. They also demonstrated that without special training apes are able to use high-quality photographic representations as visual stimuli to be matched with objects sensed by touch and that they are able to retain such information for a minimum of 20 seconds prior to their choice. This information was used to argue that apes are able to store information representationally beyond the commonly accepted limits of short-term memory even though they have no formal linguistic competency to mediate that storage.

Concepts of Piaget

A third approach to the study of primate intelligence has been the application of the concepts of renowned Swiss psychologist Jean Piaget. These concepts were designed as measures of intellectual development in the human species, but are now being fruitfully employed as indices of comparative intellectual development across species. Piaget views intelligence as

the purposeful invention of new procedures or applications of old procedures in a new context to solve a problem. This concept has intuitive appeal, but its real applicability lies not in the concept itself but in a set of precise behavioral descriptions that Piaget has provided for clarifying the development of intelligence in the human child. These descriptions lend themselves to cross-species comparisons, providing for the first time a common behavioral framework for the study of intelligence in monkeys, apes, and mankind. They also lend themselves to determination of neurological correlates, thereby making it possible to draw conclusions regarding not only comparative intellectual capacities but also comparative brain structures and maturational processes.

The intellectual capacities of human beings, monkeys, and apes differ in many ways. However, all of the differences can be thought of as falling into one of two groups: those intellectual capabilities that are present in all three of the primate groups but are far more highly differentiated in one than in others, and those abilities that are completely absent in one group but are present in another. In reality this situation is made slightly more complicated by the fact that some cognitive abilities may exist in one modality (for example, complex bodily actions) but be absent in another (for example, complex vocal actions).

Beyond the ages of 18 months for the human infant, 4 years for the ape infant, and 6 months for the macaque monkey infant there is little further significant intellectual development in either the ape or the monkey. Yet there remain considerable cognitive skills to be acquired by the human infant; this additional development in the human species is heavily dependent upon language acquisition. Nonhuman primates do not spontaneously acquire language, and the most meaningful comparisons between human and nonhuman primate intelligence are to be made prior to the emergence of complex sentences in the human child. It is clear that human infants display significant capabilities not seen in monkeys even as early as one month of age. These differences continue to be pervasive throughout development and reflect in a general way significant differences in autonomy, intentionality, and cause-effect reasoning between man and monkey. Human and ape infants choose to repeat interesting behaviors and also attempt to gain control over them and to explore cause-effect relationships. Monkey infants do not.

The most significant distinctions between human and ape infants lie in the purposeful vocal capabilities that appear very early in humans but are completely lacking in apes. It is this vocal ability that becomes the medium of arbitrary symbolic representation and, later, of language, and thus assumes the key role in the distinction between ape and human.

Apes and sign language

A fourth approach to the study of primate intelligence has only recently appeared, yet at the present time it proposes to be one of the most exciting and productive means of investigating the entire phenomenon. It entails attempts to teach primates to communicate by means of arbitrary language-like symbols.

71

Chimpanzees Sherman and Austin use symbolic communication to identify hidden foods to one another and to request from one another the tools needed to extract food from embedded sources. Clockwise from top left, Austin licks food obtained through use of a stick-tool; Sherman presses symbol on keyboard to obtain desired food; Austin holds a straw while Sherman sucks liquid through it; Austin removes stick-tool used to obtain food.

Would apes make greater cognitive advancement if they could engage in voluntary vocalization? Recent work with apes has attempted to answer this question by providing them with arbitrary symbol systems that facilitate the emergence of languagelike capacities. Apes provided with these arbitrary symbol systems have displayed abilities that have not previously been found in their species; however, these symbol systems have not permitted them to make the cognitive advances that all normal human children have achieved by four to five years of age. Furthermore, the abilities of apes have been observed to increase very slowly and only with extensive training. This indicates that language alone is only partially responsible for the development of human intelligence.

The advances made by chimpanzees who have been taught symbol systems are important because in many ways they reflect stages that our hominoid ancestors probably passed through as cognition and language developed. Of particular interest in this regard are the studies of symbolic communication between animals.

Two chimpanzees, Sherman and Austin, have employed symbols to identify hidden foods to one another and to request tools from one another. These tools were requested because they were needed to open an embedded food source. Food sharing between these two animals emerged as environmental situations were designed that forced them to share tools to extract food from embedded sources. The linguistic, cooperative-social, and motor skills that

72

emerged in Sherman and Austin are not typical for apes, and appeared as the laboratory environment was structured in a manner that stressed cooperative tool use for extraction of embedded food sources. This was done in an effort to find ways to induce the animals to cooperate with one another and teach them object reference.

While many approaches failed, the use of tools to extract embedded foods emerged as a successful way of initially inculcating these skills and was therefore intentionally elaborated upon. This suggests that the need to coordinate joint action toward objects gave rise to early language. When Sherman and Austin employ symbols during food division, they regulate their turn-taking by gestures, and they use symbols to regulate object exchange. These behaviors emerged without specific environmental structuring or training. As they have appeared, the complete gestural repertoire has also become increasingly elaborate. Both symbols and gestures function in this context to permit a degree of object-related behavioral coordination and cooperation between the two that was not previously present.

Although other apes have not been reported to use symbols to communicate with each other, they have reportedly used symbols to communicate with their human experimenters. Washoe, a chimpanzee and the first ape to receive training in a human symbol system, was said to have acquired a vocabulary of 132 items. She was taught a modified version of ASL (American Sign Language for the Deaf) signs in which hand movements represent objects (for example, the "look" sign is made by placing both palms together and then opening and closing the hands as one would open and close the covers of a book). Washoe repeatedly combined signs without specific training into strings such as "Roger you tickle" and "Please sorry good." She also appeared to use signs in new contexts without being taught. For example she signed "more" when she wanted more food, even though she had only been taught to use this sign for more tickling. (However, she had often been asked by her human companions if she wanted more to eat.)

Penny Patterson attempted a similar study with a gorilla named Koko. By age seven Koko was said to have learned 375 signs, and she also used them in novel contexts and formed spontaneous combinations. According to Patterson, Koko also uses signs to comment on past and future events, to lie, to rhyme, and to insult.

The longest and most grammatically complex symbol sequences produced by apes have been those of Lana, a chimpanzee at the Yerkes Regional Primate Research Center. Lana produces these symbol sequences by touching keys embossed with geometric figures said to represent a variety of English words. Like Washoe and Koko, Lana used symbols for other than the originally intended purpose and formed novel sequences to request items for which she had no name (such as "?You give apple which is orange"), to lie, to request objects that were not present, and to ask for the names of things.

A number of problems arise concerning the remarkable skills reported for Lana, Washoe, and Koko. All these achievements have been demonstrated only in interactions with human beings, who might possibly overinterpret them and also inadvertently cue the apes. Furthermore, none of the three

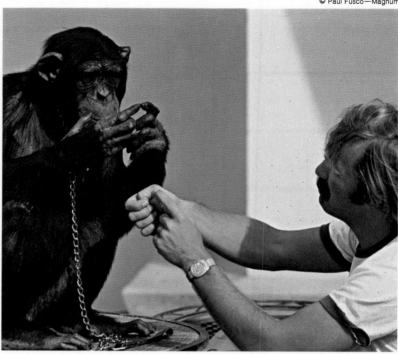

Chimpanzee Lana makes the sign for "hurt" for trainer Roger Fouts. Lana has also produced symbol sequences by touching keys embossed with geometric figures that represent words.

have been tested with regard to their ability to comprehend signs, only to produce them. A more recent ape-signing project undertaken by Herbert Terrace revealed that while apes readily learn to make a number of signs and to combine those signs, their combinations tend to be imitations of their teachers' recent signs. (*See* Year in Review: PSYCHOLOGY.)

The only ape-language study that has emphasized comprehension and conceptual development is the inter-animal communication project involving Sherman and Austin. These chimpanzees are able to use symbols to answer questions presented through symbols, and they are capable of using symbols communicatively without the presence of human experimenters.

With the study of language acquisition skills the field of primate intelligence is beginning to develop an approach that encompasses and goes beyond the previous endeavors. Object manipulation has been placed within the context of cognitive development. It is recognized as an important sensorimotor adaptation that logically precedes the onset of symbolization. As the developing primate learns to use objects intentionally, to act upon and produce changes in other objects and other individuals, it is acquiring skills that are important precursors to the ability to operate upon or effect changes in the world about him by means of symbols.

When a primate learns that symbols can replace objects, it begins to use those symbols as "tools" themselves to effect change in the behavior of others (by requesting specific foods, tools, outings). At this point such a primate has moved into a domain that was formerly reserved for human beings. In so doing, it raises in a striking way the question of the effect of experiences upon intelligence. Surely if the intelligence of apes can be so altered through experience as to permit the appearance of important cognitive advancements formerly alien to the species, the brain must be a highly

74

flexible organ. The conclusion seems inescapable that intelligence is not a fixed quantity in any species, but is rather a set of abilities alterable by experience.

Gorilla Koko operates a computer terminal. When each key is pressed, it produces a spoken word. Koko is also said to have learned approximately 375 signs and used them to comment on past and future events, to rhyme, and to insult.

FOR ADDITIONAL READING

S. Chevalier-Skolnikoff, "A Piagetian model for describing and comparing socialization in monkey, ape and human infants," in S. Chevalier-Skolnikoff & F. Poirier (eds.), *Primate Bio-Social Development: Biological, Social and Ecological Determinants* (Garland, 1977).

R. K. Davenport and C. M. Rogers, "Intermodal equivalence of stimuli in apes," *Science* (April 10, 1970, pp. 279–280).

G. Ettlinger, "Interactions between sensory modalities in nonhuman primates," in A. Schrier (ed.), *Behavioral Primatology: Advances in Research and Theory,* vol. 1 (Lawrence Erlbaum Assoc., 1977).

K. R. Gibson, "Brain structure and intelligence in macaques and human infants from a Piagetian perspective," in S. Chevalier-Skolnikoff & F. Poirier (eds.), *Primate Bio-Social Development: Biological, Social and Ecological Determinants* (Garland, 1977).

H. Harlow, "The evolution of learning," in A. Roe and G. G. Simpson, (eds.) *Behavior and Evolution* (Yale University Press, 1958).

W. C. McGrew, "Socialization and object manipulation of wild chimpanzees," in S. Chevalier-Skolnikoff & F. Poirier (eds.) *Primate Bio-Social Development: Biological, Social and Ecological Determinants* (Garland, 1977).

D. M. Rumbaugh, "Learning skills of anthropoids," in L. A. Rosenblum (ed.), *Primate Behavior: Developments in Field and Laboratory Research* vol. 1 (Academic Press, 1970).

D. M. Rumbaugh and T. V. Gill, "The learning skills of the rhesus monkey," in G. Bourne (ed.), *The Rhesus Monkey:* vol. 1 *Anatomy and Physiology* (Academic Press, 1975).

S. Taylor-Parker, "Piaget's sensorimotor series in an infant macaque: A model for comparing unstereotyped behavior and intelligence in human and nonhuman primates," in S. Chevalier-Skolnikoff & F. Poirier (eds.) *Primate Bio-Social Development: Biological, Social and Ecological Determinants* (Garland, 1977).

Life in the Jungle Canopy

by Donald R. Perry
and
Sylvia E. Merschel

The canopy of the tropical rain forest, an overlapping mat of leaves 15–40 meters above the ground, is home to unique associations of plants and animals.

A taut white rope hangs motionless in front of me. I am above the least-studied habitat on earth, balanced on the limb of an "emergent" tree, the tallest class of trees in the tropical rain forest. In a moment I must make the unsettling transition to the rope, but first I recheck my gear to be certain every connection is secure.

When I jump from the limb, the rope sags under my weight. I glide, hanging from a pulley, into open space above the treetops to a place no person has been before.

Below, the forest forms a continuous undulating carpet, an unexplored zone of life known as the canopy. An observer on the ground who is gazing up will, most likely, not see me. The canopy is an opaque, overlapping mat of leaves. More than 80% of the jungle's food is produced there. It is a mixture of familiar and unfamiliar organisms that maintain the whole jungle environment, yet little or nothing is known about their life histories. To reach them, I tie a rope to the web and descend, spiderlike, into the thick layer of vegetation below.

Early studies

This was not the first, but it is the most recent and ambitious attempt at unlocking the door to the canopy. Before the 20th century little canopy work had been done. What was known about it came primarily from the notes and stories of such 19th-century naturalists as Alfred Wallace and Henry Bates. Only during the present century has direct canopy work begun and then only by a few scientists.

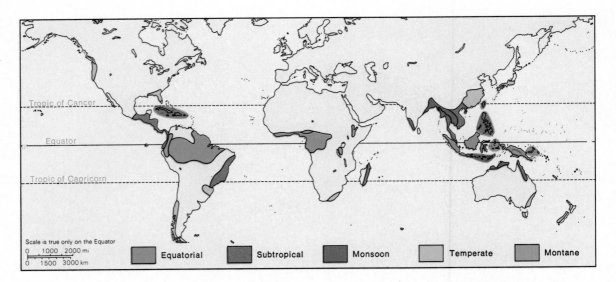

Scale is true only on the Equator
0   1000   2000 mi
0   1500   3000 km

Equatorial Subtropical Monsoon Temperate Montane

Jungles and rain forests are distributed throughout the world, mainly in tropical regions. The tropical rain forest described in this article lies in the lowlands of Costa Rica. On the preceding page Donald Perry moves along the web he has constructed over the jungle canopy, about 30 meters above the ground.

Epidemiologists started studying the treetops because they were found to be a reservoir for disease vectors, especially malaria-carrying mosquitoes. Botanists were drawn to the numerous plant species that resided in the trees, some of which offered breeding places for mosquitoes. Ornithologists began observing the bird life because many birds restricted their activities to the canopy. Most of this work was done from the ground. Trees were cut down to collect plants. Animals and birds were shot for museum specimens, and observations were made with field glasses. Some scientists built permanent facilities such as towers, platforms, and catwalks. These were the first observation posts with direct access to the canopy.

The arrival of the 1950s brought with it a new interest in the tropics, perhaps the result in part of the intimate contact with jungles experienced by many troops during World War II. Scientific research grew through the 1960s and early 1970s. During that time a new concern developed over the future of tropical forests. Predictions still considered accurate today stated that most jungles would disappear by the year 2000 because of worldwide deforestation. With the hopes of saving as many organisms as possible from extinction more scientists then became committed to tropical research. The canopy, however, with its unique community that contributes much to the tropical ecosystem, remained unexplored and, therefore, unstudied. It was not until 1975, and as recently as 1979, that methods were developed that would truly open the door to canopy research.

Ecology of tropical rain forests

What were the problems and difficulties that slowed the development of canopy research? This question is best answered by looking at the structure and environment of tropical rain forests.

Tropical rain forests can be found in a belt around the earth between 10° North and South latitudes. Within certain areas of this region annual rainfall, temperature, and humidity combine to produce the Earth's most complex ecosystems. The forests that have the highest development of arboreal life are inundated by three to seven meters of rain each year. (One meter

DONALD R. PERRY *is a Research Scientist associated with the Department of Biology at the University of California at Los Angeles and the builder of the canopy web.* **SYLVIA E. MERSCHEL** *is a writer and educator.*

(Overleaf) Photo by Nalini Nadkarni

78

is approximately 3.3 feet.) The relative humidity remains above 90%, while the temperature stays near 80° F (27° C). The climate is much like that inside a greenhouse.

Traditionally, students of this jungle community divided it into a well-defined layer system. The forest was considered to have several strata, each with its own tree species. Trees that did not grow up into the sunlight and, in fact, were adapted to a shaded, humid environment, were residents of the subcanopy. They were found between 3 to 15 meters above the ground. Trees that formed the elements of the sunlit upper surface were said to be in the canopy. They were between 15 and 40 meters high. The very tallest trees, the ones that stuck up above the others so that their crowns looked like puffballs on the horizon, formed the emergent layer. They reached above 40 meters in height.

Today the forest is not considered to be so easily divided into layers. In fact, it is widely accepted that layering does not occur. Nevertheless, strong differences do exist between the ground and canopy environments.

Until recently the jungle has been accessible to scientists up to a height of ten meters. This corresponds to the height beyond which a long or multi-segmented ladder becomes unwieldy and dangerous. The height of the canopy, however, can extend above 35 meters. That leaves about 25 meters of unexplored, biology-filled space, two and a half times the volume of the historically accessible area of forest.

A further complication is the variety of species of plants in the tropical rain forest. The number of different species in any area is staggering, and in some cases individuals belonging to the same tree species are separated by large distances. In any given area of forest it is likely that all the trees

The interior of a tropical jungle reveals typical dense growth and abundance of vines.

E. A. MacAndrew—Natural History Photographic Agency

The canopy web of author Donald Perry incorporates a network of ropes and pulleys. Above is the sleeping platform. At right Perry takes photographs next to a tree, and below he swings from the web as he collects samples of tree pollinators.

are of different species. Distances of separation vary from between a few to several thousand meters.

A tower or platform placed in a forest like this is hopelessly isolated. As far as the eye can see the forest is composed of different plants, a concept known as spatial heterogeneity. From the tower at Finca La Selva, a tropical rain forest research station in Central America, only about 2% of the estimated 300 tree species are actually accessible for investigation.

Towers are even less useful in the face of seasonality in the flowering, fruiting, and leafing of trees. Animals are very sensitive to the state and condition of the trees. They are, in a way, the canopy's migrant fruit pickers, and it is impossible to track them on their daily rounds when confined to a stationary position.

But perhaps the primary obstacle thwarting tropical treetop research is the height of the trees. Some attain heights of 70 meters, although most are between 20 to 40 meters tall. Their crowns are not usually visible from the ground. Low-level vegetation is so dense that it effectively blocks the view. The large tree trunks, between one and two meters in diameter, stand as limbless pillars that jut skyward. Branches are found only at the top, where they may spread out horizontally for 25 meters, adding to the canopy's inaccessibility.

The "canopy web"

These were the problems I faced in 1974 when I first decided to study the canopy. It was clear that any new method had to be mobile. Some scientists were, in fact, climbing trees. I studied their methods and found each had major limitations. All required contact with the trunk; some injured the tree. All methods failed to provide good access to all canopy plants.

By the summer of 1975 I had developed a mobile, easy-to-use method of canopy access. It incorporated diverse techniques used by parachutists, mountain climbers, and archery fishermen. Basically, I used a crossbow to shoot an arrow that was connected to a lightweight fishing line over the top of a tree. The fishing line was too weak to pull up a climbing rope, and so I used it to pull a stronger braided nylon line into place. This line in turn lifted the climbing rope.

Once the rope was over the top of a tree and the free ends were at the ground, I tied one of them to a strong tree trunk. The free end of the rope was then climbed by using rope ascenders, a foot sling, and a parachute harness. While climbing, I could stop at any point along the rope to rest and make observations through the canopy's vertical space. With this equipment the rope became a movable lightweight tower that could be placed in any large tree in the forest. Unlimited numbers of trees became accessible, and much research was done.

In 1978, in order to increase my contact with the canopy, I built a small sleeping platform in a tree. From that vantage point I reflected on the forest structure and came to realize that my methods, too, were limited. This was mainly because the forest was largely composed of weak-limbed trees that stood like a sea around the large sturdy climbable ones. These unclimbable trees were tall, reaching 30 to 33 meters in height.

It is within the unclimbable trees that the common canopy animals such as monkeys, sloths, snakes, insects, toucans, parrots, and other birds spend much of their time. No less important is the air space above the trees. It is probably the most active region in the whole rain forest. Birds as well as butterflies of all kinds fly there along invisible flyways. Clouds of insects surround the tops of blooming trees. Somehow, the unclimbable trees and the air above their crowns had to be made accessible. But how could that be done?

The answer lay in the forest's uneven upper surface. In the distance, to my right and left, loomed two large climbable trees. These were forest giants, each exceeding 50 meters in height. I wondered if I could use them and my platform tree to support an aerial web of access ropes. Above the forest and mobile, I could hang down, explore the rest of the canopy, and overcome the problem of weak trees.

At first, I was reluctant to proceed because the safety problems appeared formidable. This method was unparalleled in the field of tropical biology, and its development would have to cover new and untested ground. During the fall of 1978 I discussed the problems with John Williams, an engineer. Our plans worked on paper as did the scale model. If they were successful in practice, more than an acre of forest could be studied from ground level to above the treetops.

Two varieties of parrot, the red-cheeked (below) and the blue-headed (below right), are among the many colorful birds inhabiting the jungle canopy.

In March 1979 we traveled to the lowland rain forest of Costa Rica, and in three weeks the "canopy web" was in partial operation. Subsequently, it has proved to be useful and safe and may well mark the start of a new era of research in the canopy. All the plants and animals under the web are accessible, and research can now be experimental as well as observational.

The world of the canopy

A new world opens with the ascent to the canopy. It is a world apart from the ground. This can be seen on a climb up one of the ropes.

The forest floor is dark, and the air is dank and stagnant. It remains like this until the lowest dense layer of leaves is reached at eight meters up. The air then becomes fresh and bright, and there are new smells. The flowers of vines and small trees become visible. This is a new zone of wide-open spaces dotted by the tops of medium-sized trees. Only gentle breezes wash the leaves here. As the climb continues, the tops of the medium-sized trees fuse into a carpet. At about 25 meters one hangs in virtual empty space between the lower vegetation and the tops of the highest trees. At least five meters higher is the first huge limb. On arriving at the crown another characteristic of the tropical rain forest becomes apparent. The upper surfaces of the limb are covered with plants not found on the ground.

These plants form the canopy. There the tall and medium trees actively compete for light by expanding growth of their crowns until they have fused into an uneven carpet. Canopy plants are so efficient at filtering light that only about 1% makes it to the forest floor and only 3% to the subcanopy. Because light energy powers growth and development, it is not surprising that a large number of plants have "learned" to exploit the limbs of canopy trees, where light intensities reach 25% or higher. These are the epiphytes, plants that lack communication with the ground and only use the host for support. They include bromeliads (pineapple family), aroids (philodendrons, etc.), orchids, melastomes, cacti, gesneriads, ferns, lycopods, mosses, liverworts, algae, and fungi.

Exploiting limbs has not been accomplished without overcoming a major problem. Even in the wettest areas rain does not fall continuously, and

Epiphytes, plants that use the limbs of trees rather than the ground for support, are abundant in the canopy. Two flowering examples include bromeliads (below) and gesneriads (bottom).

(Top) M. P. L. Fogden—Bruce Coleman, Inc.; (bottom) W. H. Hodge—Peter Arnold, Inc.

The monkey pot tree exemplifies the interdependence between plants and animals that is characteristic of life in the canopy. Each pod on the tree protects from 20 to 40 seeds from animals that would distribute them before they mature. When the seeds are ready, the pods open after dark to allow bats to eat the fruit and drop the seeds where they have a good chance of survival.

sometimes drought conditions will last several weeks. This is a serious matter in the canopy because bare limbs have little or no water-absorbing capacity. The air is at about 80% relative humidity, and constant breezes provide a drying influence.

The simplest adaptation of epiphytes to these desiccating conditions is the development of dense root masses that tend to collect detritus and hold water. Another line of protection, nearly universal, is the presence of large fleshy leaves that store water. The most successful modifications seem to be among plants that have a form of subdivided storage tanks formed by tightly overlapping leaves. For example, a large bromeliad can span a diameter of two meters and have tanklike storage that holds several gallons of water. It is easy to see how a limb choked with bromeliads would bear a tremendous amount of weight.

Adding to the burden tropical trees carry on their limbs are vines that start at the ground and grow up the trunks. Lianas, which also start life at the ground, may grow into huge plants in their own right. Since vines and lianas connect with the ground, they are independent of canopy "droughts." They are at times so vigorous that they overtake a whole tree crown. Some vines are so extensive that portions of a plant have been found dispersed over an acre of forest, with roots communicating between them. *Clusia,* a hemi-epiphyte, begins life as an epiphyte but then sends to the ground long hanging roots that wrap around the host's trunk and choke it. Then it continues growing where the host was.

It has been theorized that the abundance of epiphytes, vines, and lianas contribute to another tropical phenomenon. Tree falls are very frequent, so frequent that the half-life of a tropical rain forest has been calculated at about 120 years. The huge plant loads may unbalance the trees and predispose them to toppling, especially when the weight of water is added. Far from being a detriment, this keeps the tropical rain forest dynamic by allowing for the growth of new trees, frequently of different species.

Vines and lianas have other beneficial side effects. They weave and hang between trees in great numbers. The connections thus made between trees are sometimes so strong that large trees have not fallen even after their bases have been cut.

Plant reproduction

Reproduction is a major "preoccupation" of canopy plants. Seed dispersal and pollination are the two major problems, and in this regard there are big differences between epiphytes and canopy trees.

Epiphytic plants seldom or never produce large numbers of flowers, and their total resources must be considered low. Their flowers are inconspicuous. The few pollinators that are seen around them, such as bees and hummingbirds, are thought to memorize an extended foraging path. This path, in the case of euglossine bees, is potentially several kilometers long, and numerous plants are visited. The seeds of epiphytes are wind-dispersed since they would not survive on the forest floor, or they are carried to other sites in the guts of birds. Usually the fruit of these plants is brightly colored to help the birds find it.

Canopy trees, on the other hand, face the problems of reproduction in a different manner. They are also dependent on animals. An early theory suggested that due to the isolation of most species from others of their kind, there may be little movement of pollen between trees. This would result in the evolution of autogamy and self-compatibility. A tree could produce fruit without needing to be crossed with another tree. But later studies showed that a canopy tree does need pollen from another tree in order to bear fruit. Thus, a large population of each tree species is essential to its continued existence.

Canopy trees produce a large number of flowers daily, which are visited by groups of pollinators. These pollinators are opportunistic and visit trees that have high quantities of resources. Some trees even resort to "deceit" in their manner of attracting these opportunists. *Dipteryx panamensis* is a towering emergent tree that produces fragrant pink blossoms that bloom for one day. But after each blossom has opened and its petals fall off, petal-colored calyx lobes remain and the flower continues to appear as if it were blossoming. Thus the whole tree seems to be massively blooming during its flower-producing period, even though only a small percentage of flowers may actually be doing so at any one time. This maintains the tree's long-distance attractiveness, enticing pollinators from surrounding areas to come close and thereby giving the tree a greater chance of cross-pollination.

The monkey pot tree, *Lecythis costaricensis,* on the other hand, attracts few pollinators. Perhaps because of its specialized flowers only a few species of bees will visit it. However, the *Lecythis* reproduces in a different way. It produces fewer than 200 fruit, which are heavy and as large as a man's head. Built like a vault, these fruits protect 20 to 40 delicious seeds with fleshy attachments. The "vaults" must shield these seeds from animals that would eat them before they mature. In keeping with the close associations that are facets of canopy life, the monkey pot tree is perfectly suited to a specific type of seed disperser. Bats fly in during the evening after the pods open. They fly off, eating the fleshy attachment, and drop the seeds where they have a better chance of survival.

Trees usually have large fruit and seeds that are dispersed by large mammals in the trees or on the ground. The seeds carry stored nutrients to help the seedling survive in the dark forest floor. During fruiting time the trees become noisy marketplaces, where the search for nutritious fruit is intense.

Animals in the canopy

Animals may compete for food sources in the canopy, but they are just as likely to cooperate. Feeding flocks consisting of many species are standard, and it is possible to predict what animals will be found together. There are indications that mixed-flock foraging is good for all concerned. A mixture of species, with their differing sensory specializations, may aid the group in locating the forest's widely scattered food sites while providing increased protection against surprise attacks by predators.

Within the treetops movement may be facilitated by trails or paths denoting preferred routes between feeding sites and nests. Highways of this type are common on the ground, and it is interesting to note that no one had

(Top) Peter Ward—Bruce Coleman, Inc.; (bottom left) Medford Taylor—Black Star; (bottom right) James H. Carmichael, Jr.—Bruce Coleman, Inc.

Animals of the tropical canopy include, on the opposite page, howler monkey (top), sloth (bottom left), and kinkajou (bottom right). Insects, many of them found in hollow trees (left), include the weevil (top), damsel fly (below), and fulgorid (below left).

anticipated their presence in the canopy. In one tree (*Lecythis costaricensis*) there were paths more than 20 meters long. They formed corridors through the miniature jungles on a limb's upper surface and were apparently maintained by numerous types of canopy animals. These include white-face monkeys, squirrels, howler monkeys, kinkajous, spider monkeys, and various marsupials. Tiny animals, such as some ants, also maintain their own minuscule paths.

Although animals can be destructive to the epiphytes on tree limbs, they can also encourage their growth. Nutrients are so rare that the collection of any that are available is an essential part of survival. Thus, bromeliads may benefit from the nitrogenous wastes of mosquitoes, aquatic insects, and frogs that spend considerable portions of their life cycles in the moisture-rich bases of these plants.

Maybe the best example of fertilization of epiphytes is found on hollow trees. *Anacardium excelsum,* a giant emergent tree, is often hollow, with openings high above the ground; it provides roost sites for bats. The spacious interior of one housed hundreds of animals: huge cockroaches, crickets, scorpions, centipedes, whip scorpions, pseudoscorpions, a marsupial, a climbing tree viper, and hundreds of bats. This dense accumulation of animal life was probably due to the bat feces, upon which numerous insects feed. Guano was also dropped on the outside, and its fertilizing effects were obvious. The tree trunk had a thick carpet of epiphytes, vines, and lianas unmatched by any other tree in the forest.

The canopy is very good at hiding its inhabitants. Even so brightly colored a bird as a parrot can hide among the vegetation. Not long after I built my sleeping platform, I discovered a large, odd-looking bird sitting in a distant tree. Its coloration and patterning almost identically matched the lichen-covered bark. It was an enigma, fitting no description of birds known to be in the area. Further investigation revealed it to be a great potoo, a nocturnal bird that is rarely seen. After becoming familiar with its call, I heard several other great potoos in the same area. But this bird disappeared, and I have yet to see the others.

Such observations are not limited to birds. I once saw a *Basiliscus plumifrons* lizard two-thirds of a meter long sitting on a bromeliad near the top of an emergent tree in an area without rivers. This was surprising because such lizards were believed to live on the ground and in trees near waterways.

These examples suggest what can be taken as a rule. The habits of jungle animals, even ones found near the ground, will not be fully known until the canopy is explored. Who would guess that earthworms dig in humus on limbs more than 30 meters high or that a diurnal cockroach might be a pollinator?

Misconceptions abound and will continue to occur until the canopy is further studied. For example, the lack of gliding lizards in the tropics of the Western Hemisphere has long puzzled scientists. Much of what is known about arboreal animals is inferred from visible characteristics, such as the "winged" gliding *Draco* lizard of Asia, which resembles a midget dragon. Because there are no *Anolis* lizards in Central America that have easily recognizable flaps such as are found on *Draco*, none were believed to

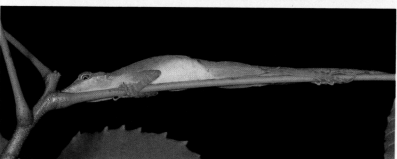

Among the reptiles and amphibians native to the jungle canopy are the red-eyed tree frog (top), green snake (above), tree viper (above left), and Anolis lizard (left). Brightly colored animals are often well disguised by the luxuriant vegetation.

The flying fox, a large bat, is among the many gliding animals found in the canopy of a tropical rain forest.

be capable of gliding. However, I observed an *Anolis* gliding between limbs at the very top of the canopy. Other observed tropical gliders in the canopy include frogs, snakes, marsupials, and rodents.

Since gliding is a precursor to flight, the large number of tropical gliders establish the forest habitat as the most prolific producer of experiments in flight and, likely, the center of its origin. In the canopy there is a strong selection for unerring locomotion and small body size. The primates have paid dearly for being large and not having some means of "parachuting" to the ground. X-rays of monkey legs sometimes reveal bones that have had multiple fractures, which must be attributed to long falls from trees. Injuries and even death are the price that must be paid by large canopy animals when they fall.

Higher primates tend toward a larger body size and refinements in body structure that ensure safe locomotion. Binocular vision and most probably an enlarged brain were necessary for accurately judging long jumps between trees and for finding one's way through the canopy's twisted maze of plants. Long arms and legs have several uses. Outstretched during a jump, they help to distribute the force of landing over a large area, while ensuring contact with many small branches. They are used in brachiation, a means of travel by swinging from arm to arm, most highly developed in the gibbons of Asia. Long arms help when reaching for food at the tips of weak branches. "Hands" on both the arms and legs give secure footing and a solid grip on objects. And in New World monkeys a prehensile tail becomes an extra limb for hanging on to branches.

Among primates there is a strong correlation between increased time spent on the ground and greater body weight. Large primates like human beings, gorillas, and chimpanzees are primarily terrestrial. This is probably related less to unerring locomotion than it is to the strength of tree limbs. The canopy's pathways, vines, lianas, and small branches will not hold large weights reliably. Chimpanzees, quite reasonably, are only seen climbing up trees and staying on large limbs and then climbing down if they want to go to another tree.

For most primates today and for the ancestors of ground dwellers, including humans, a life spent in the trees is the rule. But for those primates that became too large to adapt effectively to such conditions a new body plan gradually evolved. This plan adapted our ancestors to a new way of life on the ground.

The future of the rain forest

For more than sixty million years the canopy of tropical rain forests has been the breeding place for new evolutionary developments. Its plants and animals constitute a vast gene pool with unstudied potentials in agriculture and medicine. No other terrestrial habitat has existed as long. Yet now its future is entering a critical new phase.

In some ways the future is here now. Sizable chunks of the forest have been cut down for farming. The threads uniting the canopy are strained or broken. Epiphytes in trees left standing may show fresh vigor. They now have unlimited amounts of light for growth. New animals may appear. But

these signs of health are only temporary. Seedlings cannot grow in pastures maintained by plow or grazing.

Can the jungle survive the present wave of deforestation? Certainly tropical forests will not remain intact, and so the question becomes "How much will be left?" Research on canopy trees and organisms shows that large reserves are essential for the survival of most species.

What species could survive in the face of deforestation? I've followed parrots to their roost sites in pasture trees, but their feeding routes often include the jungle canopy. Most types of pollinators will probably die. What then will be the fate of isolated pasture trees? Would threatened forest animals migrate? Where would they go, and would they present a burden to their new environments? Or would they, like ancient man, be forced to evolve, adapting themselves to new conditions?

What is the threat of agriculture? Would an alternative be to farm the canopy as do the animals that live there? Would mankind be able to map food sources and harvest them? Would human beings then also disturb the equilibrium? Perhaps the jungle can be made profitable in a way that is beneficial to mankind and nature.

Fortunately, reserves have been or are being established worldwide, but many more should be set aside. Tropical rain forests are often located in small countries that lack funds. International cooperation is needed. Established reserves will ensure that enough forest is preserved so that essential scientific investigations can continue. This is of no minor importance to the human species, which evolved in the canopy environment, and though it has left, mankind still might have connections to some of its plants. For example, new foods or pharmacological products beneficial to mankind are likely to be discovered in the forest canopy.

My methods have, in a practical way, opened up the long-dormant field of canopy biology. I am optimistic that this unexplored community will prove useful while at the same time stimulating our imaginations and prompting new insights concerning our origins and ourselves.

Trees covered with vines are a common sight in the tropical rain forest. In areas where some trees have been cut down, the vines on the trees left standing have grown vigorously because they are receiving more light.

91

Biological Pest Control
by Richard L. Ridgway

Mankind's increasing ability to manipulate the natural enemies of plant and animal pests is creating exciting new opportunities for dealing with many pest-control problems.

Great fleas have little fleas upon their backs to bite 'em,
And little fleas have lesser fleas, and so *ad infinitum*.
And the great fleas themselves, in turn, have greater fleas to go on;
While these again have greater still, and greater still, and so on.

—Augustus De Morgan

Literally tens of thousands of insects, plants, fungi, viruses, bacteria, nematode worms, and other living organisms are potential pests of agricultural crops and forests and of human beings, their domestic animals, and other belongings. The number of pests includes at least 10,000 species of insects and mites, 2,000 species of weeds, 8,000 species of fungi, and 2,000 species of nematodes. In North America about 700 species of insects and other arthropods are considered serious pests; of these, more than one-third have been accidentally introduced from other parts of the world.

Modern pest-control technology, including the use of more than a billion pounds of chemical pesticides in the United States annually, has firmly established itself in agriculture. During the past three decades, however, growing use of these synthetic substances has produced undesirable consequences, including development of resistance by the intended target and threats to human health and the environment; at the same time, costs of developing and producing pesticides have increased greatly.

"Great fleas have little fleas...." Scanning electron micrograph reveals a mite wedged into the joint between head and thorax of a termite. Magnification is about 1,000 times, from which the width of the mite is calculated to be about a tenth of a millimeter, or four-thousandths of an inch.

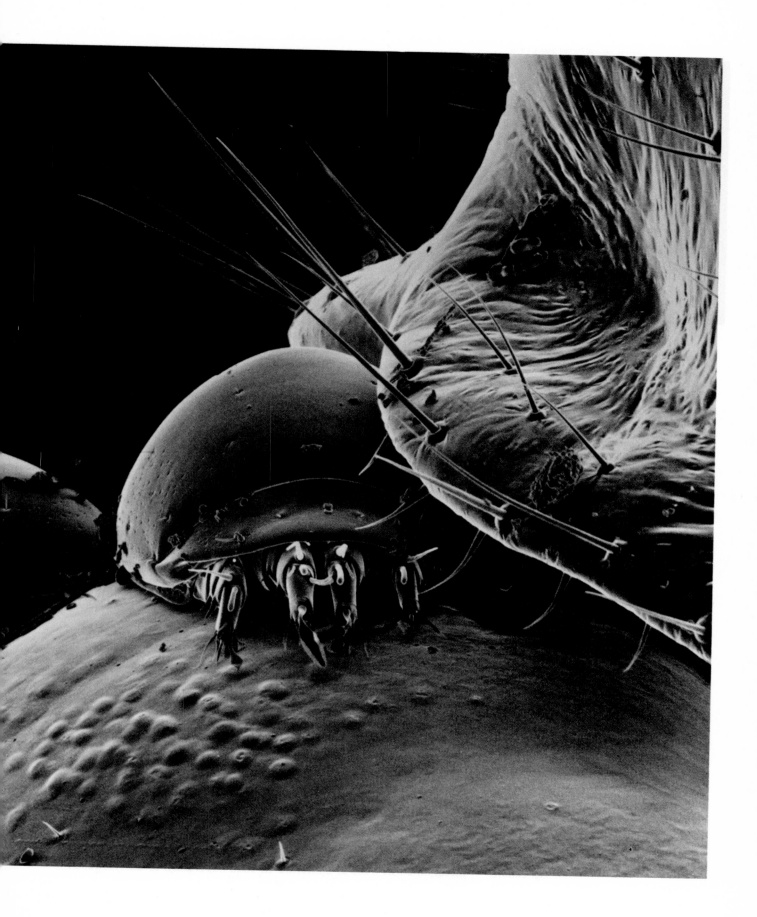

but it does not survive well through the winter months in the U.S. Therefore, deliberate releases of this exotic parasite each spring to swell its ranks, followed by conservation practices to encourage further multiplication, result in effective control of the Mexican bean beetle on soybeans.

Future prospects

The many examples of current and potential uses of biocontrol agents make it clear that there is opportunity for considerable expansion. Also, recent successes using genetic engineering to constitute new microorganisms provide a means of developing a potentially unlimited number of new biological agents that can be tailored for specific uses. Successful modern agriculture, however, has evolved together with pesticide use, and substantial quantities of pesticides thus are likely to be required for the foreseeable future. More attention, however, should be devoted to identifying those situations in which biological control is economically acceptable and socially preferable. Specifically, comprehensive cost-benefit analyses are needed from the perspective of both the individual user and society.

To the individual user—*i.e.,* the producer of an agricultural product—the short-term benefit is the added profit that results from using pest control minus the cost of the control. The individual user, therefore, is primarily concerned with reducing losses to pests or pest-related risks. It is possible that some long-term benefits, such as avoiding pest resistance, may influence the user's selection of a control method. Nevertheless, the user will normally choose the method that has the lowest short-term cost. To society, the short-term benefit of pest control relates to the effect of its cost on the cost of food, fiber, timber, aesthetics, and human health. The long-term benefits in using biological control in preference to other methods include reductions in environmental and health hazards. Measurement of such costs and benefits is difficult. Analyses of benefits are further complicated because biological control is basically preventive rather than corrective. Thus, the problem becomes one of determining the economic benefits resulting from a pest situation that does not develop, rather than determining the benefits of controlling an existing situation.

Expanded use of biological agents may also require some institutional changes. For instance, natural enemies on one farm may be harmed by pesticide drift from another farm. Or some mass-produced agents may be so mobile that they will not be effective if released simply on a farm-by-farm basis. Therefore, it may be necessary to form pest control districts or other similar arrangements. Again, because many biological agents are highly selective and therefore effective against a limited number of pests, market potential is limited. In addition, opportunities for patent protection appear to be rather limited for living organisms until legal controversy regarding their patentability is resolved. Thus, the incentives for the private sector to invest in biocontrol agents may be considerably less than for certain other methods of pest control.

The rate at which biological pest control will expand will most likely be limited primarily by the rate at which new knowledge is obtained—and thus by the nature of the research and development programs in both the public

104

specific *Colletotrichum* species reduced infestations of northern jointvetch in rice by more than 95%.

Viruses, bacteria, and fungi all have potential for use in the control of plant diseases. Agricultural scientists know that at least three different mechanisms—induced resistance, hyperparasitism, and antagonism—may become involved in this control. Induced resistance results when the interaction between one disease agent and a host makes the host more resistant to another disease agent. For instance, tomato transplants may be protected from severe infection with tobacco mosaic virus by prior inoculation with a noninfectious form of the virus. Hyperparasitism, in which one parasite attacks another parasite, is common among microorganisms that infect plants and may occur between two fungi, two bacteria, bacterium and fungus, virus and bacterium, or virus and fungus. Although many cases of

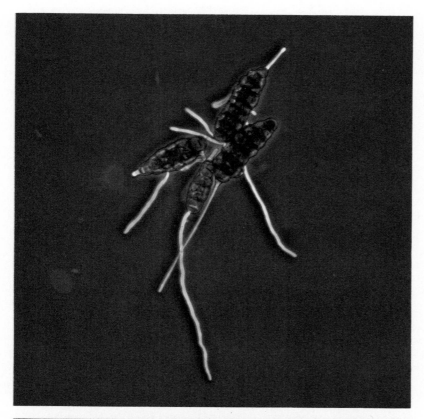

Photos, H. L. Walker, USDA, Southern Weed Science Laboratory

naturally occurring hyperparasitism have been documented, manipulations of the phenomenon so far have been limited.

Control by antagonism occurs when a relatively harmless species competes with a disease-causing species for a limited resource like food or space and thereby interferes with the pathogenic process. Microorganisms can also interfere antagonistically with each other by secreting such detrimental metabolic products as antibiotics. Many natural examples are known, and some experimental attempts to exploit antagonism have been successful. Damping-off, a diseased condition of plants caused by fungi, has been prevented or reduced in pine, corn seedlings, and tomato seedlings by coating seeds with competitively antagonistic bacteria. Beet seeds have been protected from seedling blight by coating them with common saprophytic fungi, which live on decaying matter. Coating oat and corn seeds with species of *Penicillium*, which produce antibiotics, has also succeeded in affording protection to the emerging seedlings.

On a commercial scale antagonists have been developed in the U.S. for use in at least two different instances. The fungus *Peniophora gigantia* currently is being used to control a forest-tree disease, pine stump rot, which is caused by another fungus, *Fomes annosus.* And crown gall disease, caused by the bacterium *Agrobacterium tumefaciens,* is being controlled by inoculating transplants or cuttings of plants with a harmless strain of a related bacterium, *A. radiobacter.*

Nematodes and snails under harness

Although nematodes and snails are invertebrate animals, in evolutionary terms they are far removed from insects and other arthropods. Nevertheless, these groups do contain some useful biological control agents. Nematodes, commonly called roundworms, are particularly useful in the control of insects. One of the first nematodes so used, *Neoaplectana glaseri,* de-

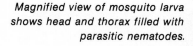

Magnified view of mosquito larva shows head and thorax filled with parasitic nematodes.

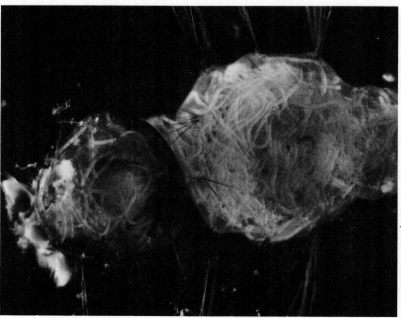

Research Institute, Belleville, Ontario

stroyed large numbers of Japanese beetles in New Jersey. More recently another strain of this nematode has been used experimentally to combat against a wide range of hosts including the codling moth, the Colorado potato beetle, and the white-fringed beetle. And yet another nematode, *Reesimermis nielseni,* has been tried against mosquitoes. Several species of nematodes have been found to attack aquatic weeds and fungal infections of forest tree roots, and at least one species shows promise for control of a weed, silverleaf nightshade.

Snails probably provide limited opportunity for use as biocontrol agents. Investigators, however, are studying the virtues of two species of South American snails for control of submerged aquatic weeds.

Arthropod approaches

Species of arthropods—particularly insects, mites, and spiders—are perhaps the best known among biological control agents. Functionally they can be divided into insect-feeding (entomophagous) and plant-feeding (phytophagous) varieties.

Probably in excess of a million species of insect-feeding arthropods prowl the Earth, of which perhaps only 15% have been discovered and named. They are often further subdivided into parasites and predators. Parasites develop on or in a single host from eggs laid on, in, or near the host; by contrast, predators feed on many different individuals.

Insect-feeding parasites fall into two major taxonomic groups: wasps and flies. The wasps, which may include 100,000 parasitic species, attack caterpillars, sawfly larvae, adults and larvae of beetles, scales, aphids, true bugs, and ticks. A number of very small, highly specialized wasps attack the eggs of a wide range of insects. In addition, some wasps have developed into hyperparasites, attacking other parasites.

Wasps that parasitize larvae or adult forms of pests account for many successes in biological control projects. In a recent dramatic example, importation into Florida of two wasp parasites of the citrus blackfly—*Amitus hesperidum* and *Prospaltella opulenta*—resulted in complete control of a pest that had been threatening the state's citrus industry. Similarly, importation of two wasp parasites—*Microctonus colesi* and *Bathyplectes curculionis*—of the alfalfa weevil into the Middle Atlantic states has reduced annual losses by several million dollars. Other imported wasps have effectively controlled the olive scale and the walnut aphid in California. A less mobile parasite, *Neodusmetia,* successfully suppressed Rhodes-grass scale in Texas after being widely distributed by airplane, and *Spalangia endius,* a pupal parasite of the housefly, has been shown to suppress housefly and stable fly populations when released on a sustained basis. In many countries of the world another wasp, the egg parasite *Trichogramma,* is used to control a wide range of caterpillar pests.

Parasitic flies are important natural enemies of such insect pests as caterpillars, beetles, and true bugs. One species is important in suppressing armyworm populations in North America, and other species parasitize caterpillars that bore in stalks. Mass rearing and release of the fly *Lixophaga diatraeae* have been promising for control of the sugarcane borer.

Trichogramma *wasps, less than one millimeter in length, deposit their eggs within the eggs of a wide range of caterpillar pests. Wasp larvae consume the parasitized eggs and then emerge as adults.*

99

Predator arthropods occur in a wide variety of taxonomic groups and have diverse habits and host preferences. Important predators in nature are found among the beetles, lacewings, ants and wasps, flies, true bugs, and other groups. Among the beetles, which all have chewing mouth parts, ladybird beetles are perhaps the most important. The vedalia beetle, which was used to control cottony-cushion scale on citrus, is the most famous of the group. Others feed on such soft-bodied pests as aphids, mealybugs, white flies, and mites. Among the more unique beetle predators are the dung beetles (*Onthophagus*), which control such insects as horn flies, a serious cattle pest, by destroying cattle dung in which the flies breed.

The green lacewings are the most common of their group. The larvae, when seen under magnification, appear particularly ferocious because of their large curved mandibles, which are used like forceps to pierce soft-bodied prey and search out the body fluids. One species of green lacewing, *Chrysopa carnea,* has been mass-reared and used successfully to control mealybugs on pears, aphids on greenhouse crops, and bollworms on cotton.

Ants are important in the natural control of populations even though many are classed as pests themselves. They are fostered particularly in Europe in the biological control of certain citrus pests. Vespoid and sphecoid wasps are important predators of a wide range of insects. They usually paralyze their prey and carry it back to their nests to feed their young.

Of the several groups of predaceous flies, syrphid fly larvae, which are valuable predators of aphids, are perhaps the best known. However, the tiny larvae of a substantial number of species of midges also prey upon aphids, scale insects, whiteflies, thrips, and mites. The true bugs, with their sucking mouthparts, are predominantly plant feeders, but a number of species are predaceous. Such groups as the damsel birds, big-eyed bugs, flower bugs, and soldier bugs attack economically important crop insects and are considered to be of great importance in natural control of pest populations.

Some important predaceous arthropods other than insects also contribute, including many spiders and mites. Spiders feed on a wide range of insects, whereas mites are particularly important as predators of other mites that attack crops.

Plant-feeding arthropods, often called herbivores, that are useful for weed control are generally not as selective of their diet as are their insect-eating relatives. This is understandable because of the wide range of pest arthropods that feed on beneficial plants and of the sometimes narrow differences that exist between beneficial plants and undesirable plants. A weed is often defined as a "plant out of place," and the same species of plant can be either unwanted or desirable depending on the beholder. Therefore, choosing plant-eating arthropods for use as biological agents often means choosing insects with preferences for the specialized habitats that are unique to the habitat of the weed. There are species of arthropods, however, with very strong predilections for specific weeds.

Arthropods useful for weed control are known among the beetles, moths, thrips, mealybugs and scales, true bugs, and flies. Among the beetles, perhaps the leaf-feeding chrysomelids have been the most useful for weed control in the U.S. The poisonous Klamath weed (*Hypericum perforatum*) is being controlled by two species of these beetles on 2.3 million acres of rangeland in California alone. Another chrysomelid has proved very useful as an aid to control the aquatic alligator weed. Other plant-feeding beetles, particularly the weevils, have also proved their worth for control of thistles and puncture vine.

The moths are perhaps unique in that they have been useful predators of weeds but not of insects or other arthropods. The larva of one moth, *Cactoblastis cactorum*, somehow prepares the way for a species of bacterium to invade plant tissue and is largely credited with the spectacular control of cactus in Australia. The larva of the cinnabar moth (*Tyria jacobaeae*) is the most important biological agent yet evaluated for combating a poisonous weed, the tansy ragwort, in pastures and rangelands in the Northwest. Moth larvae are also the most important insects that feed on dwarf mistletoes, a damaging parasite of ornamental and timber trees.

Help from vertebrates and higher plants

Although relatively few vertebrates appear to be exploitable as control agents, through their natural behavior many species play significant roles as predators. Birds, especially flocks of gulls that feed on white grubs, crickets, and grasshoppers, are definitely useful. On the other hand, starlings, which naturally control insect pests in some parts of the world, are generally considered pests themselves in the U.S. and Great Britain. Lizards, toads, bats, mice, and shrews also consume large quantities of insects.

Of all the vertebrates, fish seem to be proving the most manageable for the control of pests. The mosquito fish (*Gambusia affinis*) has been used to suppress mosquitoes, and certain herbivorous fish show promise for aquatic weed control in rice paddies and artificial fish ponds.

Like antibiotic-producing bacteria, certain higher plants may function as biological control agents by releasing chemical substances that kill or inhibit the growth of competitors or natural enemies. This phenomenon, often

Three species of insect that have proved their worth in biological pest control efforts are pictured at their jobs on the facing page: (top to bottom) the seven-spotted ladybird beetle (Coccinella septempunctata) preying on aphids; the green lacewing (Chrysopa species) among aphids; and the South American flea beetle (Agasicles hydrophila) at work on a leaf of alligator weed, its natural host.

The mosquito fish (Gambusia affinis), a topminnow with a large appetite for mosquito larvae, has been introduced in many parts of the world for mosquito control.

Jeff Foott—Bruce Coleman Inc.

called allelopathy, is believed to contribute to the ability of the low-growing plant spikerush to prevent growth of much larger and more troublesome species of aquatic weeds in irrigation canals. Such plants as crotalaria and marigold control several major parasitic nematodes that cause extensive losses in crop plants, and planting marigold among vegetables has become a popular strategy with home gardeners as a pesticide alternative. Another plant, pangolagrass, although more limited in its scope, is effective against at least one group of nematodes.

Mustering the troops

Effective use of biological agents in pest control requires considerable knowledge of the biology of the pest, the agents to be used, and their interactions with the environment. Due to the complexity of biological systems, any classification of strategies is somewhat artificial, but such terms as importation, conservation, and augmentation help in describing the various approaches currently being employed.

Importation entails the search for natural enemies in foreign countries and their introduction into infested regions. The underlying principle of this approach is that many pests were accidentally introduced into new habitats without their normal complement of natural enemies. To date, importation has received the greatest emphasis in biological control. In the U.S. this approach is currently being implemented primarily by state and federal agencies. Exotic agents are processed through approved quarantine facilities to ensure that undesirable organisms are not inadvertently imported as well. Organisms from foreign countries are usually quarantined for at least one generation to permit detection and removal of such contaminants as secondary parasites, plant disease organisms, and hazardous or unwanted host materials. In some cases, as with plant-feeding arthropods being considered for weed control, extensive testing is done before importation or during quarantine to ensure that desirable plants will not be harmed.

Thus far, the importation approach has concentrated on the introduction of insects to control other insects and weeds. It has achieved the permanent control (complete, substantial, or partial) of some 200 species of pest insects in various countries of the world, including substantial control of 19 insect pests in the U.S. during the past decade. About one of every two tries has succeeded. Similarly, a 75% success ratio has been reported in attempts to control about 50 species of weeds. The value of these efforts is reflected in estimates that indicate a $30 return from every dollar invested.

Conservation emphasizes the maximum use of natural enemies in a particular habitat, regardless of whether they are imported or native. This method works at enhancing the environment of biological agents, for instance, by providing favorable habitats or reducing mortalities. A number of such beneficial modifications have been demonstrated experimentally. Researchers have planted alternate, less troublesome host plants to provide nectar and pollen for parasites and predators of plants in order to increase their numbers. Insect food supplements such as sprays containing sugars and fermented milk whey have also been successful. Other conservation techniques include harvesting such crops as alfalfa in alternate strips

U.S. quarantine officer examines foreign shipment of insects in isolation box. Exotic organisms are usually held in quarantine for at least one generation to permit removal of living and nonliving contaminants. About ten facilities in the U.S. are authorized to receive imported biological agents.

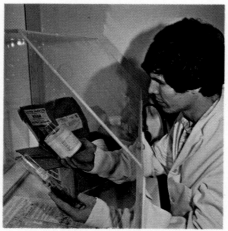

USDA, Beneficial Insects Research Laboratory; photo, William H. Day

to preserve a favorable environment for parasites and predators and the use of cultural practices to create a soil environment favorable to beneficial microorganisms.

Although environmental manipulation is useful in conserving natural enemies, actions to limit their direct killing—primarily through more judicious selection and use of pesticides—probably has had the greatest practical effect. The advantages of selective synthetic organic insecticides were demonstrated in Europe in the 1950s when low dosages of a systemic insecticide succeeded in controlling cabbage aphids without killing beneficial insects. Since then, numerous selective insecticides that help conserve biological agents have been discovered, but the technique of fostering pesticide resistance in natural enemies has been one of the more unique advances. For example, a particularly effective pest management system for apple trees has been developed that employs predaceous mites bred for insecticide resistance. These mites, which attack plant-feeding mites, are spared from the insecticides used to control such other pests as the codling moth.

New ways of encouraging the judicious use of broad-spectrum pesticides can also result in more benefit from natural enemies through conservation. The development of statistical concepts, improved monitoring devices, and computer models for predicting the behavior of pest populations has resulted in considerable improvement in pesticide use in recent years. For example, a computer-based prediction system for the bollworm and tobacco budworm on cotton in Texas has significantly reduced insect control costs by allowing more efficient use of naturally occurring parasites and predators and of insecticides.

The third approach, augmentation, usually involves mass production and periodic distribution of biological organisms. It is particularly appropriate when the number of naturally occurring enemies is inadequate to provide the degree of control desired. Augmentations with a wide range of organisms for control of most classes of pests have been successfully demonstrated throughout the world.

Augmentation efforts to date have stressed microorganisms for the control of insects. In the U.S. bacteria are manipulated to produce toxins or spores for the control of insects on as many as ten million acres annually. Limited use is also being made of viruses and fungi to control insects. Additionally, several microorganisms are exploited to control plant diseases.

Augmentation with insects for insect control is difficult to document precisely because the greatest use is probably in the Soviet Union and China. Large-scale practical use of egg parasites to control caterpillars reportedly is practiced on more than 20 million acres in the Soviet Union. Augmentation with mites and insects is also used for control of greenhouse pests in Western Europe and the Soviet Union. About ten species of insect are being sold commercially through about 30 retail outlets in the U.S., but the volume of sales is small compared with other methods of pest control.

The three approaches described above are not exclusive; in fact, a combination of at least two of them is usually desirable. In some cases, a combination of all three approaches is needed. The imported wasp *Pediobius foveolatus,* for example, is an effective parasite of the Mexican bean beetle, but it does not survive well through the winter months in the U.S. Therefore, deliberate releases of this exotic parasite each spring to swell its ranks, followed by conservation practices to encourage further multiplication, result in effective control of the Mexican bean beetle on soybeans.

Future prospects

The many examples of current and potential uses of biocontrol agents make it clear that there is opportunity for considerable expansion. Also, recent successes using genetic engineering to constitute new microorganisms provide a means of developing a potentially unlimited number of new biological agents that can be tailored for specific uses. Successful modern agriculture, however, has evolved together with pesticide use, and substantial quantities of pesticides thus are likely to be required for the foreseeable future. More attention, however, should be devoted to identifying those situations in which biological control is economically acceptable and socially preferable. Specifically, comprehensive cost-benefit analyses are needed from the perspective of both the individual user and society.

To the individual user—*i.e.,* the producer of an agricultural product—the short-term benefit is the added profit that results from using pest control minus the cost of the control. The individual user, therefore, is primarily concerned with reducing losses to pests or pest-related risks. It is possible that some long-term benefits, such as avoiding pest resistance, may influence the user's selection of a control method. Nevertheless, the user will normally choose the method that has the lowest short-term cost. To society, the short-term benefit of pest control relates to the effect of its cost on the cost of food, fiber, timber, aesthetics, and human health. The long-term benefits in using biological control in preference to other methods include reductions in environmental and health hazards. Measurement of such costs and benefits is difficult. Analyses of benefits are further complicated because biological control is basically preventive rather than corrective. Thus, the problem becomes one of determining the economic benefits resulting from a pest situation that does not develop, rather than determining the benefits of controlling an existing situation.

Expanded use of biological agents may also require some institutional changes. For instance, natural enemies on one farm may be harmed by pesticide drift from another farm. Or some mass-produced agents may be so mobile that they will not be effective if released simply on a farm-by-farm basis. Therefore, it may be necessary to form pest control districts or other similar arrangements. Again, because many biological agents are highly selective and therefore effective against a limited number of pests, market potential is limited. In addition, opportunities for patent protection appear to be rather limited for living organisms until legal controversy regarding their patentability is resolved. Thus, the incentives for the private sector to invest in biocontrol agents may be considerably less than for certain other methods of pest control.

The rate at which biological pest control will expand will most likely be limited primarily by the rate at which new knowledge is obtained—and thus by the nature of the research and development programs in both the public

104

and private sectors. Rapid advances will require increased research in fundamental biology, mass production, and population biology, as well as expansion of foreign exploration, field evaluation, information systems, technical assistance to users, and cost-benefit studies. Thus, future prospects for biological pest control are excellent, but the extent to which it will be used will depend on society's willingness to make the necessary financial and institutional adjustments.

FOR ADDITIONAL READING

P. DeBach, *Biological Control by Natural Enemies* (Cambridge University Press, 1974).

R. L. Ridgway *et al.,* "Pesticide Use in Agriculture," *Environmental Health Perspectives,* vol. 27 (1978, pp. 103–112).

U.S. Department of Agriculture, *Biological Agents for Pest Control* (U.S. Government Printing Office, 1978).

Spraying chemical pesticides on one farm risks the possibility of drift to nearby farms and consequent harm to biological control agents that may be present. An expanded future role for biological agents may warrant the establishment of multifarm pest control districts, in which control practices can be integrated and coordinated for best results.

The Chemistry of Good Cooking by Gary A. Reineccius

Coaxing the best in attractiveness and taste from food traditionally has been an art founded on hard-won practical experience. From the viewpoint of modern chemistry many rituals of cooking make sense, but the scientific cook knows better than to follow them blindly.

Down through time, from the first person who charred his game over an open fire, there stretches a tradition of learned lessons that make up the fine art of cooking. Along the way, everyday cooks and great chefs alike have used certain ingredients in specific rituals, with little idea of what was actually taking place in their mixing bowls and ovens. It was enough that their trial-and-error methods produced good food; knowing exactly what was happening to the food was of no value.

Yet, as has proved true in medicine, smelting, leather tanning, and many other former arts, the modern, rapidly changing world has depended on fundamental scientific understanding when tradition was no longer satisfactory. Likewise in cooking, a modern chef may discover that blind faith in recipes and established procedures can lead to problems that could have been avoided with a little knowledge of basic food chemistry. For example, a chemist once attended a class in modern French cooking in which the instructor was making an egg custard dessert. The instructor added vanilla extract to milk and then boiled the mixture, obviously losing much of the bouquet of the pure vanilla. As the chemist wondered about this contradiction, he realized that many traditional recipes involving vanilla called for a vanilla bean to be heated with milk to extract the vanilla flavor. Employing that technique with modern vanilla extract, however, detracted from the flavor. The instructor knew tradition, but not when to break with it.

GARY A. REINECCIUS is an Associate Professor in the Department of Food Science and Nutrition at the University of Minnesota, Minneapolis.

(Overleaf) Painting by Kinuyo Y. Craft; illustrations by John Craig

108

While there are still many unanswered questions, research has provided considerable insight into the art of good cooking. To demonstrate, this article will consider the chemistry involved in cooking an attractive green vegetable, creating hollandaise and white sauces, preparing a tender and flavorful beef entrée, mastering the egg, and stirring a smooth fudge. By appreciating what is happening to such foods as they are prepared and heated, anyone who cooks should be able to make better decisions on how to serve appetizing and tasty meals.

Kitchen colors

What happens to the color of vegetables during cooking—processes that are dependent on chemical reactions—can have an important psychological effect on enjoyment. Cooked peas, for instance, may be an appetizing shade of green or simply a rather drab olive, depending on preparation. Peas get their basic color from chlorophyll, the complex pigment involved in photosynthesis. The chlorophyll molecule is a head-and-tail arrangement in which the head consists of a magnesium atom held centered in a large flat ring-shaped structure. Presence of the metal atom in the ring gives the native state of chlorophyll a rather bright green color. But peas also contain a substantial amount of natural acids, and when the vegetable is heated, these acids attack the chlorophyll, replacing magnesium with hydrogen atoms and causing the pigment to fade to olive.

This knowledge of the chemistry of peas can readily be applied in the kitchen. If one wants to cook peas or other green vegetables in water, use a minimum amount of liquid and start cooking in an uncovered pan. A great deal of the natural acids boil off with the water and are not available to change the color of the vegetable. After one to two minutes of boiling, cover the pan, reduce the heat, and cook until tender. (To preserve color, heat exposure during cooking should also be minimized. Vegetables may lose 50–75% of their chlorophyll simply to destruction by heat during normal cooking.) The reader is invited to try an experiment at home. Divide a package of frozen peas into two pans. Add water to both pans until the vegetables are covered. Then add three tablespoons of vinegar (an acid) to one pan and one teaspoon of baking soda (an acid neutralizer) to the other pan. Cover both pans and simmer for ten minutes. A considerable difference in color will be seen between the two pans of peas, a result of the difference in acidity.

Canned peas earn part of their reputation for dullness from the fact that during the canning process their natural acids are trapped inside the container, where they set to work altering chlorophyll. Until relatively recently food processors were permitted to precook their vegetables for canning in copper kettles. Copper atoms from the kettles would replace magnesium in chlorophyll and give the vegetables a bright green color that withstood canning. Copper is relatively toxic, however, and consequently this practice has been banned in the U.S.

Another vegetable that changes color during cooking is carrots. Carrots do not have a significant amount of chlorophyll but get their color from long hydrocarbon chains called carotenes. Carotenes are responsible for the yel-

Comparison of peas cooked with vinegar (left) and baking soda (right) reveals the color-altering effect of acid on chlorophyll.

109

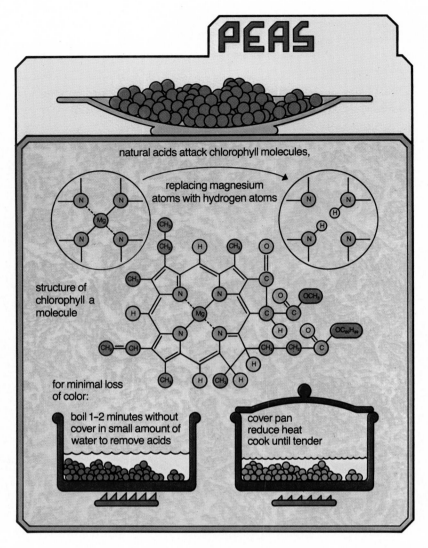

natural acids attack chlorophyll molecules,

replacing magnesium atoms with hydrogen atoms

structure of chlorophyll a molecule

for minimal loss of color:

boil 1–2 minutes without cover in small amount of water to remove acids

cover pan reduce heat cook until tender

Presence of a central magnesium atom (Mg) in chlorophyll's ring structure gives this natural pigment a bright green color. Cooking green vegetables often provides an opportunity for natural acids to attack this structure, causing the color to fade. A simple cooking procedure can help minimize color loss.

lows, oranges, and a few reds in nature and are the compounds in the human diet that are converted in the liver to vitamin A. On cooking, carrots change from a yellow-orange to a lighter yellow. The cause of this color change has not been satisfactorily resolved. The majority of researchers support the theory that structural changes, *i.e.*, changes in shape, in the carotenes themselves are responsible for a lightening in color. Others suggest that destruction of carrot cellular order causes the color change. Again, as with peas, in order to preserve color (and vitamin content) carrots should be cooked as little as is practical.

Smoothing the savage sauce

Although the cook who has failed at the chemistry of cooking vegetables may wish to obscure the results under a classy hollandaise sauce or a simple white sauce, the primary purpose of these creamy dressings is good eating. The respective chemistries of hollandaise and white sauce are fascinating and quite different. Hollandaise is based on egg yolks and butter, the butter

110

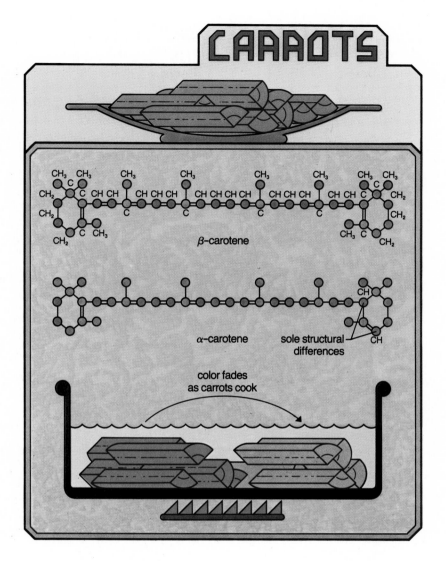

β-carotene

α-carotene

sole structural differences

color fades as carrots cook

existing as an emulsion of droplets dispersed in water. Although oil and water normally separate very quickly, hollandaise is nevertheless rather stable and not as delicate as the beginning cook is led to believe. In addition to egg yolks, water, and butter, the sauce contains salt, lemon juice, and cayenne pepper.

The egg yolks in hollandaise serve several purposes: they contribute to richness, smoothness, and sauce stability. Eggs contain compounds called phospholipids, which resemble detergent molecules in that their structure allows them to bridge the worlds of oil and water. Each phospholipid has a fatty end that avoids water and a phosphorus-containing segment that has an affinity for water and carries an electric charge. When water, egg yolk, and butter are mixed, phospholipids accumulate at the surface of the oil droplets, directing one end into the oil and the other end into the water to form a kind of membrane. The water-binding property of phospholipids helps to put a shell of water around the butter droplet, and their charged ends add to each droplet a small electric charge that acts to repel nearby

Alpha- and beta-carotene belong to a family of molecules responsible for the color of carrots, squash, sweet potatoes, oranges, and many other similarly colored vegetables and fruits. As in the case of chlorophyll, cooking causes the color of carotenes to fade, although scientists do not agree on the reason for the color change.

111

droplets. The net effect of this chemistry is to keep the droplets from joining to each other and rising to the top of the sauce. As long as they do not coalesce, the sauce will be stable. Egg also helps stabilize the sauce by making it thick. The thicker the sauce, the more difficult it is for butter droplets to come together.

Water in hollandaise sauce serves primarily to dilute the sauce to proper thickness, and cayenne pepper adds flavor. Butter gives richness, smoothness, body, and flavor to the sauce. Although many recipes call for unsalted butter that has been clarified (freed of water and suspended matter), one can generally make very good hollandaise sauce using unclarified salted butter just by eliminating salt from the recipe. Salted butter resists spoilage; if one chooses unsalted butter, it should be purchased frozen and kept frozen until use.

Lemon juice adds flavor to the sauce, and its acidity retards spoilage due to bacterial growth. Fresh or fresh frozen juice is best for hollandaise; bottled and canned lemon juices suffer in flavor due to damage from the heat treatment necessary to make them shelf-stable. Bacterial stability is not particularly important to the home cook since the sauce is generally eaten shortly after it is made. Restaurants, however, must be concerned about spoilage because they may keep the sauce for several hours at temperatures ideal for the growth of disease-causing microorganisms.

Either of two perennial problems can vex the person making hollandaise: the egg may curdle on heating or the sauce may become unstable and separate into butter and egg mixture. Curdling of the egg (the chemistry of which is discussed below) can be avoided only by keeping the sauce from overheating. Once curdled, egg cannot be redissolved. Sauce separation (called "breaking" of the emulsion) can be corrected in several ways. One common method is to put another egg yolk in a second pan, beat it gently with a whisk, and then slowly add the broken hollandaise emulsion with continued beating. The emulsion will reform and the sauce will become smooth again.

The white sauces are quite different from classic hollandaise. The most common generally consist of butter, flour, salt, milk, and pepper. Simple gravy is a variant, using meat drippings in place of butter. Problems with white sauces are generally limited to lumpiness, but an understanding of food chemistry will make it possible to make an excellent white sauce consistently.

White sauce gets its thickness—and its lumps—from gelatinization of the starch present in the flour. Native starch is a rather large long chainlike molecule assembled into crystals and covered with a protein coat. The coated starch crystal, called a granule, is rather small but can be seen under a microscope. When placed in cold water, this granule absorbs only a little liquid. Hot water, however, has enough energy to break apart the starch crystal in the granule into individual chains. The water then bonds directly to the starch chains, allowing a large amount of absorption to occur. Eventually the starch granule absorbs so much hot water that the protein coat bursts, and the starch chains spill out into the water. If this mixture is cooled, the starch chains bond to each other to make a rigid paste called a

Each ingredient in hollandaise sauce serves a purpose, although richness, smoothness, and stability of the sauce depend on the proper interaction of butter, water, and egg yolk. Egg yolk contains lecithin and other phospholipids; these molecules are each made up of a segment that has an affinity for water and a double "tail" that avoids water. When water and butter are beaten with egg yolk, the phospholipids in the yolk arrange themselves naturally to form a membrane on the surface of each oil droplet, thereby keeping the droplets tiny and dispersed throughout the sauce.

112

SAUCE-HOLLANDAISE

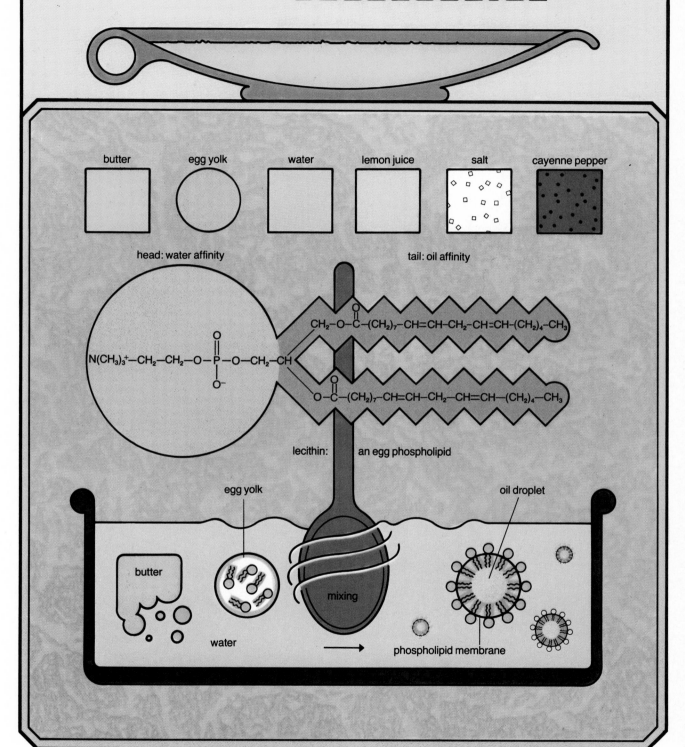

butter   egg yolk   water   lemon juice   salt   cayenne pepper

head: water affinity   tail: oil affinity

$N(CH_3)_3^+$—CH_2—CH_2—O—$\overset{\overset{\displaystyle O}{\|}}{P}$—O—$CH_2$—CH

CH_2—O—$\overset{\overset{\displaystyle O}{\|}}{C}$—$(CH_2)_7$—CH=CH—$CH_2$—CH=CH—$(CH_2)_4$—$CH_3$

O—$\overset{\overset{\displaystyle O}{\|}}{C}$—$(CH_2)_7$—CH=CH—$CH_2$—CH=CH—$(CH_2)_4$—$CH_3$

lecithin: an egg phospholipid

egg yolk   oil droplet

butter

mixing

water   phospholipid membrane

SAUCE-WHITE

butter   milk   flour   salt   pepper

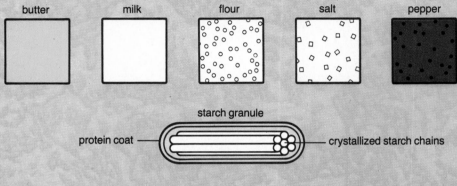

starch granule

protein coat — crystallized starch chains

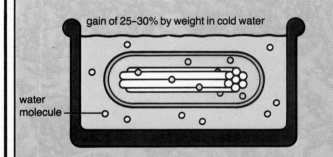

gain of 25–30% by weight in cold water

water molecule

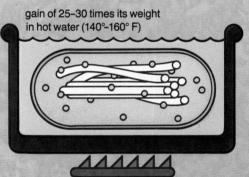

gain of 25–30 times its weight in hot water (140°–160° F)

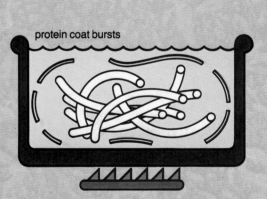

protein coat bursts

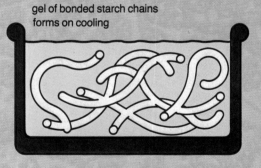

gel of bonded starch chains forms on cooling

gel. White sauce becomes lumpy when starch granules are put directly into hot water. The granules swell quickly, and some burst early. The free chains then serve as excellent glue to stick the remaining starch granules together.

The secret of smooth white sauce is to keep the starch granules apart while they are swelling and bursting. One common method is by making a roux. A roux is prepared by melting butter in a pan (or using meat drippings if for gravy), adding flour, and heating while stirring. Milk or other watery liquid can then be added with stirring and heated to thicken without lumps forming. The butter coats each starch granule in the roux and keeps free starch molecules from sticking the granules together. Another method of keeping lumps out of white sauces, employed in commercial food processing, involves premixing the starch with sugar before adding the hot liquid. A third procedure calls for mixing the starch with cold water and then adding a hot stock or milk with constant stirring. These last two methods are not as foolproof as the use of a roux.

Some chemistry to chew on

Once the basis has been laid for preparing a nice vegetable dish, what about the meat entrée? Knowing what happens to meat during cooking and how those phenomena influence flavor and tenderness can prevent the occasional inedible steak. Typical meat flavor is the result of heating during the cooking process; raw meats lack the characteristic roasted, browned flavors and tend only to be "fleshy" and metallic. In the parlance of food-tasting professionals, cooked meat flavor is generally considered to consist of two parts: meaty, brothy "base notes" and lighter "species notes." Base notes in effect announce "you are eating meat" and are similar in character irrespective of the species of meat being tasted. They come from the reaction of muscle sugars and amino acids (the chemical building blocks of proteins in muscle) due to heating. Species notes are, for example, what make beef taste like beef and not like lamb or chicken. These notes are primarily due to compounds in the fat as they react or vaporize during heating.

The system of chemical reactions that produce meat flavor is extremely complex and poorly understood. It involves probably more than 30 different starting compounds and is dependent upon acidity, types of chemicals and their concentrations, cooking temperature, cooking time, the degree of moisture present during cooking, and many other factors. Despite this complicated situation, it is possible to understand why different cuts of meat or meat cooked by different methods (*e.g.*, braising, broiling, and stewing) do not taste the same. Generally, the greater the heat treatment—higher temperatures or longer times—the more flavor develops in the product. Depending on the cut or grade of meat, however, cooking conditions that produce the most flavor can result in a very tough product. Therefore, it is necessary to consider the chemistry of meat tenderness. In broad terms animal muscle tissue, which is the common interpretation of "red meat," consists of two types of proteins. The proteins in muscle fiber make up most of the mechanism responsible for muscle contraction; the proteins in connective tissue help organize and hold the muscle fibers in place. Muscle fibers are most concentrated in the red portions of meat. The connective tissues appear as

Thickness in white sauce derives from the gel-forming properties of the starch granules present in flour. In cold water these protein-coated crystals absorb comparatively little liquid. In hot water, however, they swell tremendously as the crystallized starch within the granules comes apart into individual water-bonding chains, and eventually their protein coats burst. When the starch-water mixture is allowed to cool, the freed starch chains bond to each other into a rather rigid network to form a gel.

115

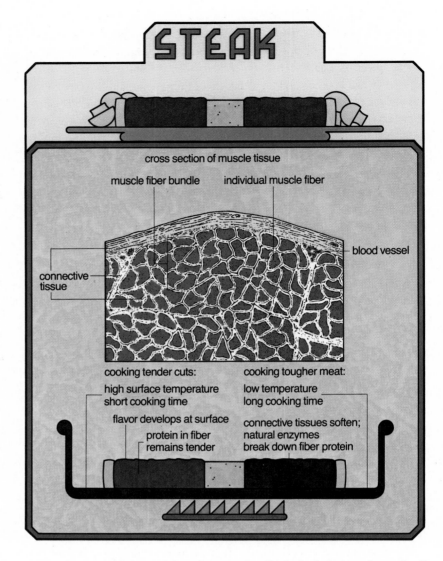

STEAK

cross section of muscle tissue

muscle fiber bundle   individual muscle fiber

connective
tissue

blood vessel

cooking tender cuts:

high surface temperature
short cooking time

flavor develops at surface

protein in fiber
remains tender

cooking tougher meat:

low temperature
long cooking time

connective tissues soften;
natural enzymes
break down fiber protein

Red meat derived from muscle tissue consists primarily of two kinds of protein: from muscle fiber and from connective tissue. Each kind of protein exhibits different characteristics in the raw and cooked states, and the relative proportion of each in a cut of meat largely determines whether the cut is inherently tender or tough and, consequently, what form of cooking should be used to elicit the best combination of flavor and tenderness.

white areas in and surrounding the muscle, all of which fuse at the ends of the muscle to form the tendons that connect the muscle to skeleton.

Muscle fiber is generally quite tender when raw, the degree of tenderness being determined by how much it is contracted in rigor mortis. Muscle that goes into rigor mortis in a relaxed state is tender; the extreme example of this is beef tenderloin. When muscle fiber is subjected to any degree of cooking, its proteins tend to change in a way that causes the muscle fiber to dehydrate and toughen. By contrast, connective tissue is extremely tough in the raw state. Cooking—especially with moist heat or extended, low temperatures—tends to soften and tenderize its proteins. In fact, the end product of cooking one of these proteins, collagen, is gelatin. Hence, contrasting effects occur during cooking: muscle fiber becomes tougher and connective tissue becomes more tender. A piece of meat such as tenderloin steak, which is very low in connective tissue, is actually toughened by cooking. Such meat should be cooked only as much as is necessary to develop the desired flavor and aesthetic appearance. On the other hand, a cut such

116

as round steak, which is higher in connective tissue, may be cooked substantially more. In this case, the softening of connective tissue during cooking is much more important to tenderness than is the toughening of muscle fiber.

This kind of chemical know-how should be of use to anyone preparing a steak for best flavor and tenderness. If the cut is high in muscle fiber, it should be broiled over an open flame (or fried in a very hot pan) for a very short time. High heat produces drying of the meat surface and very high surface temperatures. This elicits a lot of flavor from the outer portion of the steak but does not toughen the remaining interior fiber proteins. For cooking a tougher cut of meat, two options are available. The first is to cook it only very slightly; that is, prepare the meat rare. Such cooking results in minimum toughening of muscle fiber proteins although it has little effect on connective tissue. If one does not care for rare meat, then it should be prepared well done. On prolonged heating the muscle proteins become dehydrated and toughen to their maximum, but the softening of connective tissue more than compensates for this effect. Current research indicates that long-time, low-temperature cooking is best, because it apparently prolongs the lifetimes of natural meat enzymes that break down protein and thus assist in the tenderizing process. Oven temperatures as low as 200°–250° F (90°–120° C) are becoming very common in restaurants and in the future will be more common in the home. The current risk is that without proper instruction and adequate temperature control (which typical home ovens do not provide) people will use temperatures that are low enough to produce food-borne bacterial illnesses.

The ubiquitous egg

It would be unreasonable to discuss the chemistry of cooking without including eggs. They are cooked and eaten as is and are added to cakes, brownies, muffins, pancakes, and other flour-based creations. In addition, they form the basis of custards, meringues, cheesecakes, sauces, soufflés, and a number of other foods. It is doubtful whether any other ingredient is used in as wide a variety of applications.

In composition the egg is about 65% white and 35% yolk. The white is mostly water (87.6%) with some protein (10.6%), sugar (1.1%), and small amounts of other ingredients. The yolk contains less water (49%) but is higher protein (16%) and contains significant fat (34%). The difference in composition between yolk and white gives these portions quite different properties and functions in foods. Earlier in the article the emulsification properties of egg yolks were considered in making hollandaise sauce. Egg yolk is an excellent emulsifier due to the phospholipids and cholesterol contained in its fat portion and is used as such in mayonnaise, salad dressings, cream puffs, and other products.

The protein portion of the egg contributes some unusual properties. One of these, the binding property of coagulation, is of importance in such tasks as making meat balls that hold together or brewing a cup of egg coffee. Mixing coffee grounds with egg is a rather old technique; as the egg coagulates during heating, it binds the coffee grounds and sediment together and

Photomicrographs, Mary Lou Percy; courtesy, Thayne R. Dutson, Texas A&M University

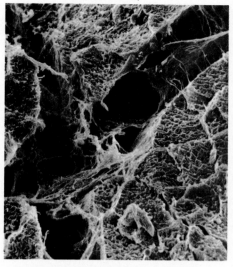

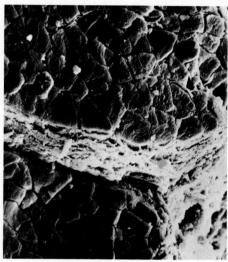

Scanning electron micrographs of raw (top) and cooked (above) muscle tissue samples that have been fragmented in liquid nitrogen depict changes produced as a result of the cooking process. Connective tissue lying between bundles of muscle fiber is transformed in appearance from an open, fibrous mass to a coagulated, more compact one. In addition, the individual fibers making up each bundle appear much smoother and stand out more clearly in the cooked state.

117

EGGS

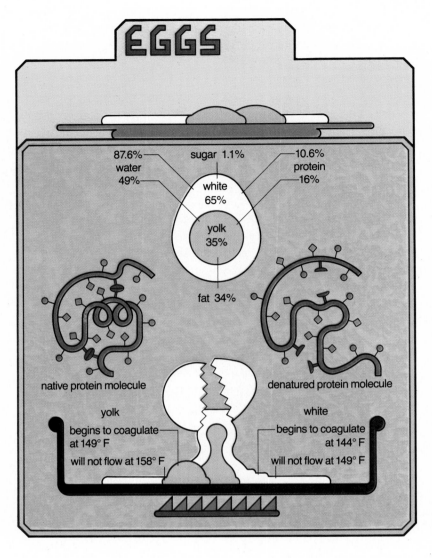

87.6% water — sugar 1.1% — 10.6% protein

49% — 16%

white 65%

yolk 35%

fat 34%

native protein molecule

denatured protein molecule

yolk

begins to coagulate at 149° F

will not flow at 158° F

white

begins to coagulate at 144° F

will not flow at 149° F

The white and yolk of an egg differ in basic composition and in the nature of their proteins. When heated, both yolk and white proteins coagulate, but within different temperature ranges. Protein coagulation, an irreversible process, begins when the normally coiled protein structure unfolds, or denatures, to expose previously hidden reactive side chains (yellow squares in the figure). Individual protein molecules then bond to each other to form a rigid interlocking structure.

keeps the beverage clear. Coagulation of eggs also lies at the heart of a successful custard or meringue. Heat-induced coagulation is caused by changes in the egg proteins. In raw egg these large, long-chain molecules exist as coiled, roughly spherical structures that are held in this compact form by a large number of weak bonds. Heating the protein puts energy into the system; the bonds holding the protein in a coil break, and the molecule unfolds and stretches out. As it unfolds, reactive groups of atoms that were previously hidden are bared, and these can then interact with other protein molecules to form a continuous series of bonds that give a rigid structure, or gel. The process just described is called denaturation.

Egg white proteins differ considerably from yolk proteins. White proteins begin to coagulate at a temperature of about 144° F (62° C) and will not flow at 149° F (65° C). Yolk proteins begin to coagulate at about 149° F and will not flow at 158° F (70° C). This is one factor that permits making a cooked egg that has a hard white and a soft yolk.

Coagulation of egg proteins cannot be reversed. Only nature can put them together such that they are stable and the egg is liquid. Unfortunately, as is indicated by the temperatures cited above, a rather small temperature range exists within which the egg will become thick but not actually coagulated. When one makes hollandaise sauce the egg should be so heated that it starts to thicken but does not coagulate. In making custards the egg should be only slightly coagulated. If the custard is overheated, the egg proteins bind together rather strongly and squeeze water out of the gel structure. Then the custard curdles and assumes a mottled appearance and some water separates out. If the custard is heated in a pan of water it will warm slowly, lessening the chance of overheating. Slow heating also gives the egg proteins better stability against coagulation.

Although whipping of egg white for such specialties as meringues, soufflés, and chiffon cakes does not involve heat, it is also related to changes in proteins. Egg white proteins normally exist in the presence of water (egg liquid). When one whips air into the system, the proteins begin to lose contact with water and instead become stretched across air bubbles. Contact with the air causes changes in the proteins; again they unfold, stretch out, and interact with each other to form a somewhat rigid foam structure. Overbeating the whites allows the proteins to interact too much. They lose their elastic properties and appear dry and mottled. Instead of holding water in a smooth foam, the proteins hold on to each other, and the water around them tends to separate.

Freshness of the egg can influence some of the properties mentioned. The white of a newly laid egg is thick and has a pH of about 7.6. (The pH of a food is a measure of its acidity: the lower the pH, the more acidic.) As the egg ages, its white thins due to protein breakdown, and water moves from the white to the yolk, thinning it as well. Therefore, a fresh egg will not spread out in a pan as much as an older egg. This factor is important in preparing poached or fried egg, when a thick, compact egg is desirable. An aging egg also loses carbon dioxide, a process that causes an increase in pH. This change in acidity influences the ease of peeling a boiled egg and the whipability of the white. When boiled, an older egg peels substantially more easily than a fresh one. Whipping a fresh egg takes more time but results in a larger volume. When an egg is used for its gel-forming or emulsifying properties, however, its age does not appear to be important.

Fudge factors

Just as dessert is usually the finale to a meal, so it is to this article. This article features fudge, and making a smooth fudge can often be a very difficult task. Fudge has a tendency toward graininess, which results from the formation of large crystals of sugar that can be felt by the tongue. To discuss the chemistry of successful fudge making, one needs to consider both the ingredients and the process. The recipe calls for placing cocoa, salt, sugar, milk, and corn syrup in a pan and then heating until the syrup reaches a boiling point of 234° F (112° C). Butter and vanilla are then added without mixing, and the fudge is cooled until it reaches 122° F (50° C). The concoction is then beaten vigorously and poured into a pan.

From a chemist's point of view this process makes excellent sense. Boiling

Both the yolk and white of a fresh egg stand firm and high when the egg is broken into a bowl (below). As an egg ages, its white thins due to protein breakdown and water moves into the yolk. Consequently the white of an older egg (bottom) tends to be runny and its yolk broad and flat.

Photos, Linda Moore—Rainbow

119

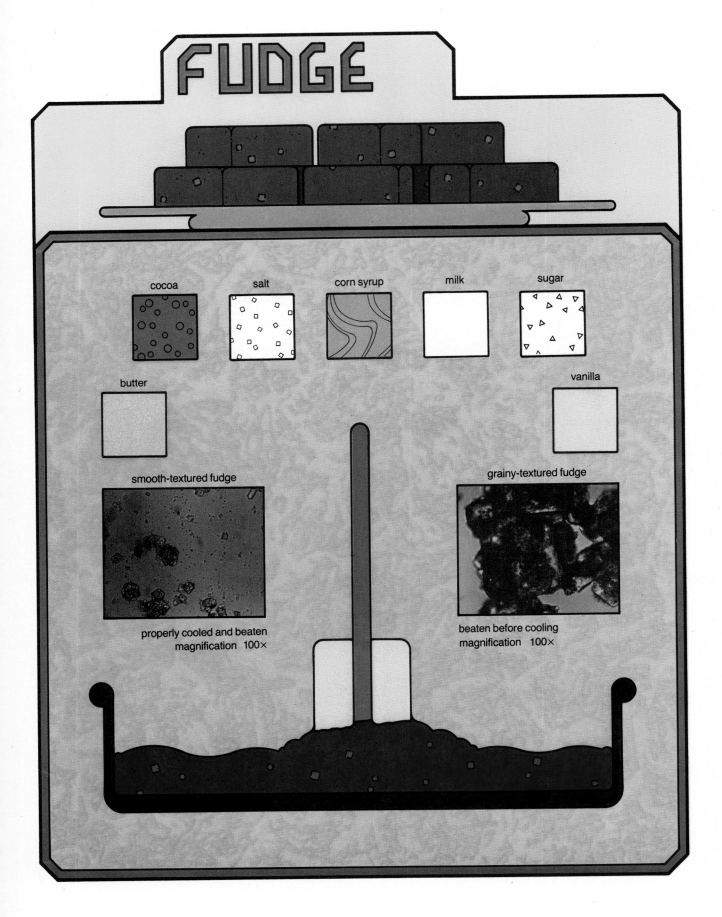

FUDGE

cocoa salt corn syrup milk sugar

butter vanilla

smooth-textured fudge

properly cooled and beaten
magnification 100×

grainy-textured fudge

beaten before cooling
magnification 100×

point in this case is a measure of water content: as the boiling point increases, water content decreases. When the boiling point reaches 234° F the fudge contains about 20% water and consequently will have about the proper consistency when cooled. At this boiling point the other ingredients are added and the fudge allowed to cool without stirring. If the fudge were stirred at all during cooling, the sugar would start to crystallize too early. At 234° F the sugar is completely dissolved, and there is enough energy in the system to prevent sugar crystallization. As the temperature drops, the sugar becomes less soluble and there is an increasing tendency to crystallize. If the fudge is not disturbed, by the time it reaches 122° F it has become greatly supersaturated and has a strong driving force for crystallization. Stirring at this point initiates crystallization. Because the sugar solution in the fudge is highly concentrated, a lot of small crystals are suddenly formed, and complete crystallization takes place rapidly. On the other hand, if the fudge were stirred at a higher temperature, for instance, 212° F (100° C), there would only be a weak tendency to crystallize and few crystals would form. As the fudge cooled further, these few crystals would grow large and become quite objectionable.

Whereas temperature control in making fudge is very critical to smoothness, the ingredients also contribute. The presence of fat (as butter), corn syrup, and cocoa help slow crystal growth. Fat tends to coat the sugar crystals, keeping new sugar molecules from attaching and thus adding to crystal size. Instead, the molecules form small new crystals. Corn syrup also contains sugar, but of different types—primarily glucose and maltose—than ordinary table sugar, which is sucrose. The sugars in corn syrup become incorporated in the growing structure of sucrose crystals but do not fit properly. They change the shape of the growing crystal such that additional sucrose molecules can no longer add to the structure. Cocoa helps to keep the fudge from forming large crystals by adding thickness. A thick fudge mixture makes it difficult for sucrose to move any distance through the medium to form large crystals. The ingredients other than sucrose are generally called interfering substances because of their action inhibiting the crystallization of the sucrose.

Bon appétit—par la chimie

Although an exhaustive excursion through the chemistry of food could fill many volumes, the "menu" discussed above should give the kitchen dweller a new and different approach to preparing good meals. It should also indicate that not all recipes are correct or as satisfactory as they could be if offered a little help from chemistry and common sense. Moreover, a fundamental knowledge of foods can free one from recipes to serve one's own tastes—and not the tastes of others.

In addition to adding flavor and richness, most of the ingredients in fudge serve as interfering substances that inhibit growth of large, grainy sugar crystals. The most important factors in producing smooth fudge, however, are temperature control and proper mixing procedure. The photomicrographs on the facing page compare the extent of crystal growth in fudge beaten after sufficient cooling and fudge that was stirred too soon.

Photomicrographs, courtesy, Hershey Foods Corporation

The Remarkable Cell Membrane

by Stephen L. Wolfe

Traffic control station, lookout post, mint—these words figuratively describe some remarkable new findings about the living cell's outer "skin." An even deeper understanding of its nature may spur important medical advances.

Photo sequence surrounding magnified view of living cells shows the progress of a settling soap membrane. Essentially an ordinary soap bubble, the membrane is formed from a solution of detergent in water and is supported by a steel ring. Like the lipids found in cell membranes, detergent molecules immersed in water organize into bilayers. Regions of soap membrane that are hundreds of bilayers thick scatter light in a rainbow effect, whereas regions consisting of only one bilayer transmit light and thus appear black. Extension of the techniques used to form such soap membranes has allowed scientists to produce artificial lipid bilayers under water and to compare their properties with those of natural membranes.

One of the great biological principles developed during the 19th century was the concept that all living beings are organized into cells. Every integrated function and activity, even of an organism as large and complex as the human body, is subdivided among these individual, microscopic compartments. Each cell is a functional unit of the whole that carries out a specialized task with the greatest possible efficiency.

Cells are kept as separate compartments by an exceedingly thin surface layer of molecules. This boundary, the cell membrane, was first thought to be little more than a passive "bag" that simply held the contents of the cell together and kept them separate from the external environment. Today this picture has changed greatly. From decades of research the cell membrane is now known to be a region of purposeful, dynamic activity that maintains the cell interior as a distinct biochemical environment by controlling what molecules enter and leave. It selectively transports raw materials inward and secretory and waste products outward. In addition it carries specialized receptor molecules that function as the eyes and ears of the cell and provide it with the means to react to outside stimuli—hormones and other natural regulatory substances, many types of drugs, and even other cells. Moreover, Nobel-prizewinning work has demonstrated that cell membranes provide the basis for synthesizing most of the molecular "energy currency" required for cellular life.

122

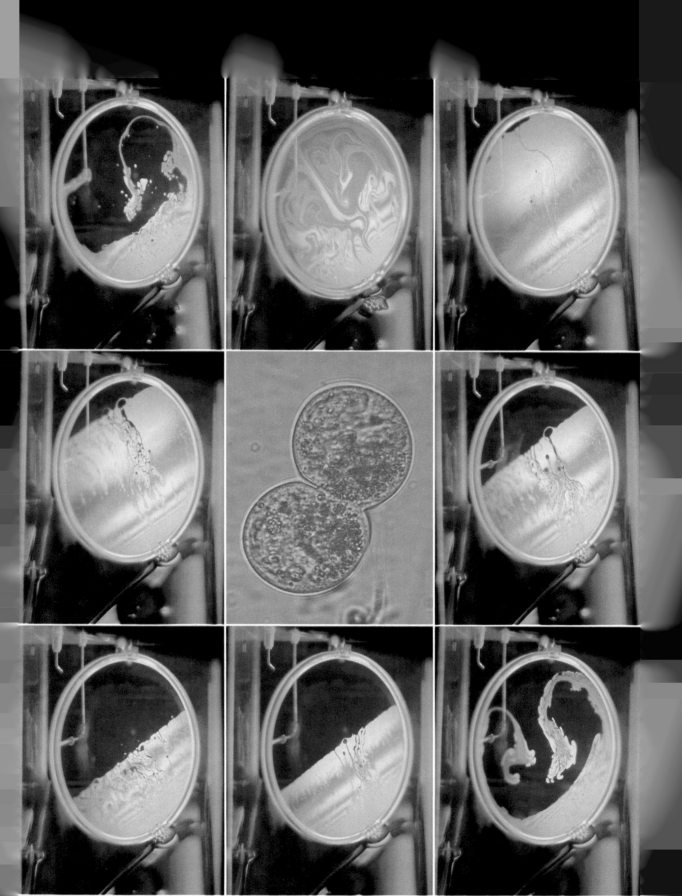

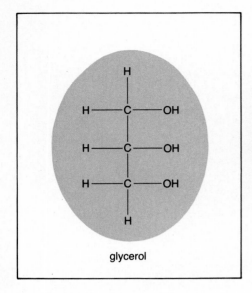

glycerol

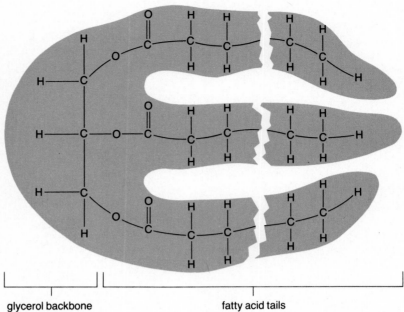

| glycerol backbone | fatty acid tails |

generalized lipid structure

Figure 1. Lipid molecules found in natural oils and in the cell membrane share a common structure based on glycerol (above). In natural oils lipids consist of a glycerol backbone linked to three "tails" of long carbon-chain molecules called fatty acids (right).

STEPHEN L. WOLFE *is Associate Professor in the Department of Zoology at the University of California at Davis.*

Illustrations by Leon Bishop

Part of the control of molecular traffic between a cell and its surroundings is passive and depends simply on the fact that oil and water do not mix. The cell interior and the exterior fluids bathing the cell are watery solutions. The cell membrane, by contrast, is oily in character. Because of this arrangement neither the molecules of the cell interior nor those of the fluids surrounding the cell mix readily with the molecules of the cell membrane. Superimposed on this control is another system based on the existence of minute, watery channels in the oily film of the cell membrane. These watery channels are selective: they have the capacity to recognize and admit only certain kinds of water-soluble substances. Both control systems depend upon the two kinds of cellular molecules that are known to serve as structural elements of cell membranes: lipids and proteins.

Membrane lipids

Lipids, which give the cell membrane its oily characteristic, are defined as biological molecules that dissolve more easily in organic solvents, such as benzene, than they do in water. Although they form a highly varied group, most of the membrane lipids share a common structure based on glycerol, a relatively small chain of three linked carbon atoms. Each carbon in glycerol carries an —OH (hydroxyl), an active chemical group that can bind to other molecules. In a pure natural fat or oil, such as olive oil, each of these active sites is linked to a long carbon-chain molecule called a fatty acid. The resulting structure is a glycerol backbone linked to three long fatty acid "tails." (See figure 1.)

Molecules so structured are typically electrically uncharged substances that "prefer" oily environments—so exclusively, in fact, that they can be suspended in water only by a considerable expenditure of energy. Such

124

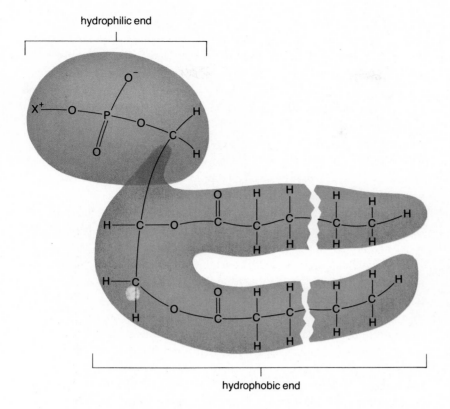

hydrophilic end

hydrophobic end

generalized phospholipid structure

substances are called hydrophobic, meaning literally "water-fearing." The oil and water in a bottle of salad dressing, for example, can be mixed by shaking the bottle vigorously. The suspension of oil droplets in water is temporary, however, and lasts only as long as energy is put into the system by shaking it. Once at rest again, the mixture will separate spontaneously because all molecular systems, whether part of living or nonliving matter, tend automatically toward a state that requires a minimum energy input for their maintenance. For oil in water, the minimum energy state is one in which the two are as separate as possible. If left at rest, the oil will layer on top, with minimum surface area exposed to the water. If forced beneath the water, oil will round up in spherical droplets to satisfy the minimum energy requirement, because a sphere has the smallest surface area for a given volume of liquid. This tendency of hydrophobic molecules to remain associated together in their own nonwatery environment provides the major force holding cell membranes together.

The lipids of membranes are like pure natural oils with one vital substitution in their structure (figure 2). In place of one of the three bound fatty acid chains, the glycerol backbone carries a fundamentally different structure. Part of this structure is a carbon-based group (generalized as X in the figure) with the properties of an alcohol. The significance of the alcohols found in membrane lipids is that they are water-soluble substances. The alcohol is linked to the glycerol by a phosphorus-containing group that also has an affinity for water solutions rather than oils. The result, called a

Figure 2. The lipids found in cell membranes are called phospholipids. They differ from those in natural oils in that one fatty acid chain is replaced by a phosphorus-containing group and a group with the properties of an alcohol (represented as X).

125

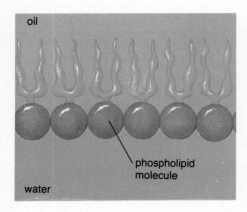

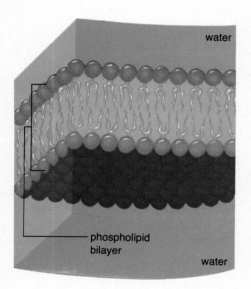

Figure 3. Phospholipid molecules orient preferentially if introduced into an oil-water boundary; added in the right amount, they will form a film between the oil and water just one molecule thick (top). When immersed under water, phospholipids form extended layers exactly two molecules thick (above).

Figure 4 (facing page). The folding pattern of proteins reflects their compatibility with the medium in which they are normally immersed. A protein that normally functions in a watery medium folds so as to collect its hydrophobic regions within the protein, while its hydrophilic regions face outward. Membrane proteins fold so as to create separate hydrophobic and hydrophilic surface regions.

phospholipid, is a molecule with a split personality. The two fatty acid chains and the end of the glycerol backbone containing them retain their hydrophobic character and find their minimum energy level when associated with a hydrophobic environment. The opposite end of the molecule, containing the alcohol and phosphate group, finds its minimum energy level when suspended in a watery solution. This end thus has a hydrophilic, or "water-loving," character.

Phospholipids satisfy their dual solubility preferences in patterns that have fundamental significance for cell membrane structure. If introduced into the boundary formed by an oil resting on water, phospholipid molecules will orient so that their fatty acid chains extend into the oil, and their phosphate-alcohol groups face the water (figure 3). If introduced in the right amount, the layer of phospholipids will form a stable film between the water and oil just one molecule in thickness.

If phospholipids are introduced beneath the surface of water, they satisfy their dual preferences by forming extended layers exactly two molecules in thickness. In the double layers, individual phospholipid molecules orient so that the fatty acid chains of each layer line up end-to-end in an interior, water-excluding environment, while the phosphate-alcohol groups face the surrounding water molecules. These double films, called bilayers, are highly stable because any change in the orientation of the molecules would force the hydrophobic fatty acid chains into the watery medium, an effort that would require a large energy input. These automatically formed, stable phospholipid bilayers have been shown to make up the basic structural framework of cell membranes.

Membrane proteins

The proteins of cell membranes also contain distinct hydrophobic and hydrophilic regions. Proteins are complex molecules built up from long, folded chains of amino acids; some of these individual amino acids have hydrophobic tendencies, and some are hydrophilic. The chains fold automatically into a three-dimensional structure that satisfies the solubility properties of the individual amino acids. Proteins that are normally suspended entirely in a watery medium fold in such a way that the hydrophobic amino acids are collected together within the protein, while the hydrophilic amino acids cover its surface (figure 4). Membrane proteins take up a folding pattern in which hydrophobic amino acids face the surface in some parts of the molecule, giving these regions a hydrophobic character. In other regions, hydrophilic amino acids are exposed at the surface, making these parts hydrophilic.

Other facets of protein structure also have great significance for cell membranes. Although cells use only 20 different amino acids in assembling proteins, essentially any one of the 20 can appear at any position in an amino acid chain. Since the chain may contain a minimum of 50 or so to more than 50,000 amino acids, a virtually endless variety of different proteins is possible. The significance of this vast potentiality for membrane structure and function is that proteins can be made in myriad forms to suit the special activities of every cell type.

126

Another significant characteristic of proteins is that the final, three-dimensional folding pattern taken by an amino acid chain is flexible. Since the folding pattern results from chemical interactions between individual amino acids, the pattern is sensitive to conditions that affect chemical interactions; *e.g.,* temperature, pressure, acidity, and exposure to other reactive molecules. The variations in folding pattern that result from changes in such conditions are central to protein function in membranes and in other locations in cells.

protein folded to
function in watery medium

Accessory carbohydrates

Carbohydrate accessory groups occur as complex chains attached to some of the phospholipid and protein molecules of membranes. These chains are built up from individual units of six-carbon sugars such as glucose, and they take the form of straight and branched structures that are totally hydrophilic. Because of this property, they attach only to the parts of membrane lipids and proteins that face the membrane surfaces and do not function as internal structural elements of the membrane. In animal cell membranes, branched carbohydrate chains extend outward from the membrane surface like rooftop antennas. The presence of these carbohydrate groups on the outer cell surface gives the cell what is often described as a "sugar coating."

The evolving concept of membrane structure

Current understanding of the way in which lipid and protein molecules combine together in membranes is based directly on a series of scientific investigations that extends back to the turn of the century. In the 1890s a Swiss investigator, E. Overton, discovered that the ability of many substances to penetrate through membranes is directly related to their solubility in lipids. From these findings Overton was the first to propose that the cell surface is covered by a layer of lipids. The first clues about the physical arrangement of the lipid molecules in the surface layer were developed in Holland in the 1920s by E. Gorter and F. Grendel. These investigators broke open the red blood cells of animals to release their contents, leaving behind empty cell membranes called red cell "ghosts." By measuring the ghosts under a light microscope, Gorter and Grendel were able to come up with an average figure for the total area occupied by a single red cell membrane. They then extracted the lipids from their sample and estimated the lipid quantity per red blood cell ghost. Comparing this result with the surface area per cell revealed that just enough lipid is present to make a layer exactly two molecules in thickness around the cell. On this basis Gorter and Grendel proposed for the first time that the lipid molecules in cell membranes occur in bilayers.

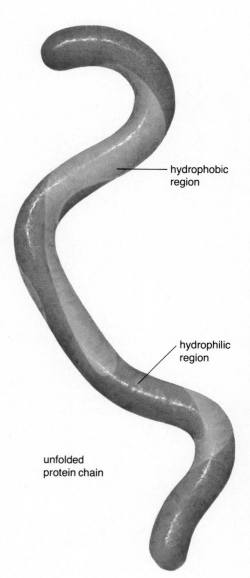

hydrophobic
region

hydrophilic
region

unfolded
protein chain

Proteins were first implicated as membrane components through cooperative research carried out from the 1930s to the 1950s by two Englishmen, James Danielli and Hugh Davson. These workers made measurements of the surface tension of oil droplets in water and compared them with values obtained for living cells. If cells were covered with a layer of lipids, as the earlier work suggested, then the surface tension of oil droplets and cells ought to be similar. Their actual results turned out to be quite

127

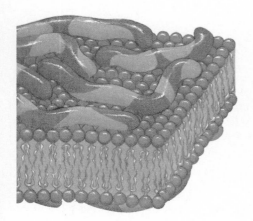

Danielli-Davson model

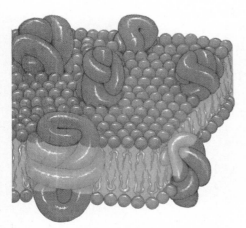

fluid mosaic model

Figures 5 and 6 (top and above). According to the Danielli-Davson model of cell membrane structure, lipid molecules in the form of an oriented bilayer make up the basic membrane framework, while membrane proteins lie completely unfolded on both surfaces of the bilayer. Experimental findings eventually revealed inadequacies in this model and led to a new idea for membrane structure. The fluid mosaic model retains the notion of the lipid bilayer but proposes that membrane proteins exist as folded, compact units suspended on or within the bilayer.

different—the surface tension of cells was consistently much lower than that of oil droplets. They found, however, that they could mimic the surface properties of cells by adding proteins to the oil droplets. The proteins formed a hydrophilic film over the surface of the droplets and reduced their surface tension to levels much like those of living cells.

From this information Danielli and Davson developed a model for membrane structure that was to shape biological thinking for many years to come. They proposed that lipid bilayers form the basic structure of membranes and that the lipid bilayer is coated on both sides with a layer of protein that reduces its surface tension. To accommodate a complete layer of protein on both surfaces within the very thin dimensions actually observed for biological membranes, the proteins were considered to extend over the lipid bilayer as completely unfolded chains only one amino acid in thickness. (See figure 5.)

The Danielli-Davson model attracted wide attention and provided the conceptual framework for essentially all of the thought and experimentation concerning membrane structure until the 1960s. During these years a variety of experiments confirmed that proteins are important constituents of membranes. Some clues as to their possible functions came from a series of interesting studies in which the properties of artificial bilayers and cell membranes were compared.

Investigators working with bilayers of pure phospholipids noted that highly lipid-soluble molecules pass through them about as fast as they do through natural membranes, confirming Overton's original results and conclusions. Certain other molecules, however, such as glucose and some amino acids, were found to penetrate through natural membranes very rapidly, even though they are highly water-soluble. In keeping with expectations from their hydrophilic character, the same molecules passed through artificial lipid bilayers only very slowly or not at all. Ions, which are atoms or small chemical groups carrying a positive or negative charge, were also found to pass through natural membranes much faster than through pure phospholipid films, some of them millions or even billions of times faster. Since the primary difference between the artificial films and natural membranes is the presence of proteins in the latter, these observations suggested that the unexpectedly rapid transport of some hydrophilic molecules depends in some way on protein.

The fluid mosaic model

While this information implicating proteins in cell membrane structure and function was accumulating, inadequacies in the Danielli-Davson model were becoming increasingly apparent. In 1966, S. J. Singer, working at the University of California at San Diego, found that membrane proteins transmit light in a pattern indicating that as much as 30% of their amino acid chains is folded into an extensively coiled formation. This made it seem unlikely that membrane proteins could be completely unfolded, as Davson and Danielli had proposed. Singer also noted that the total content of the coiled formation is characteristic of proteins with a spherical rather than flattened shape. Further, Singer observed that unfolding membrane proteins into essentially

128

two-dimensional layers is also extremely unlikely from an energetics standpoint. Proteins achieve a minimum energy level when they fold into spherical or elliptical shapes. Unfolding them requires considerable energy input, much greater than the amounts required to maintain structures as stable as cell membranes. Singer also noted that spreading proteins in thin layers on membrane surfaces would expose hydrophobic amino acids to either the surrounding aqueous medium or to the hydrophilic ends of the phospholipids at the bilayer surfaces. A consideration of energetics also makes this condition extremely unlikely.

Observations of the actual behavior of phospholipids in water made it clear that it is unnecessary to assume that phospholipids must be coated with proteins to reduce their surface tension when they are placed in water. The substances used by Danielli and Davson in their experiments were pure, totally hydrophobic oils. Substances of this type, as noted, round up into spheres when placed in water and resist deformation to more flattened shapes. This resistance to deformation is reflected in the relatively high surface tension of the droplets. Phospholipid droplets, in contrast, can take up the bilayer arrangement, in which all exposed surfaces are hydrophilic. This allows them to assume essentially any shape in water and reduces their surface tension with no requirement for surface coats of protein. Thus, as sometimes happens in science, Danielli and Davson arrived at a correct conclusion—that proteins are important in membrane structure—for the wrong reasons.

In 1972 Singer and a colleague, Garth Nicolson, combined this information into a new idea for membrane structure, the fluid mosaic model (figure 6). In simplest terms their model retains the oriented lipid bilayer framework and proposes that proteins, rather than being spread in layers, are suspended as individual compact units in or on the bilayer. The model proposes in addition that the membrane lipids are in a mobile, fluid state, and that individual lipid molecules are free to exchange places and move through the bilayer. This is the "fluid" part of the fluid mosaic model. Proteins in the membrane are considered to float in the fluid bilayer like icebergs in the sea. Some penetrate entirely through the membrane and are exposed on both sides, and some penetrate only partway through. The distribution of proteins in membranes, in dispersed units rather than as continuous sheets, is the "mosaic" part of the model.

According to the model, membrane proteins are held in suspension in the fluid lipid bilayer by their dual solubility properties. Proteins that pass entirely through the membrane have two hydrophilic ends and a hydrophobic middle region. The hydrophobic middle region remains in association with the membrane interior, and the hydrophilic ends extend into the watery medium at the membrane surfaces. Proteins that extend only partially through the membrane have a hydrophobic end suspended in the membrane interior, and a hydrophilic end facing the watery medium. Within these limitations, the proteins are free to displace phospholipid molecules and move laterally.

Singer and Nicolson included a provision in their model for the selective transport of water-soluble substances by membrane proteins. This transport

129

might take place in either of two ways, both of them involving proteins that are long enough to completely span the cell membrane. An individual protein floating in the lipid bilayer, held in place by hydrophobic associations with the membrane, might fold so that a hydrophilic channel extends through its interior, from one membrane surface to the other. Alternatively, several proteins might link together in such a way that they enclose a hydrophilic channel through the membrane.

The tenets of the fluid mosaic model also provide a molecular basis for other activities of cell membranes. In addition to transport functions, some of the protein molecules floating in the lipid bilayer are specialized for reception and recognition functions. In these proteins, the segments extending outward from the cell surface are shaped so that they fit, and can bind, molecules from the fluids surrounding the cell. Some are also specialized to recognize and bind molecules that form part of the surfaces of other cells. Most of the membrane proteins active in this function carry a carbohydrate "antenna" that forms a part of their recognition and binding sites.

The fluid mosaic model developed by Singer and Nicolson opened new avenues in membrane research and allowed an extensive reevaluation of earlier findings. The results of this investigative effort clearly support the major ideas of the model.

Types of membrane transport

Two kinds of transport are moderated by the proteins forming hydrophilic channels in membranes. One requires no energy input and depends for its driving force on naturally occurring concentration differences in the substances being transported. The second pushes molecules across membranes whether or not favorable concentration differences exist. This second process, called active transport, requires an energy input and in many cell types accounts for much of the total cellular energy expended.

The existence of a concentration difference means simply that there are more molecules per unit volume on one side of a membrane than on the other. This concentration difference represents a source of energy that can be used for transport because of the universal tendency of molecular systems to run toward a minimum energy level, which in this case is a uniform distribution of molecules on both sides of the membrane.

The energy available from a concentration difference can be more easily understood by considering an example. Suppose that a person is assigned the improbable task of stacking bricks in a pile during an earthquake. Stacking the bricks and keeping them stacked requires considerable and continuous human effort. At any time the person stops returning bricks to the pile, they cascade downward until they assume a layer of more or less even thickness on the available surface. In falling from the pile to the surface, the bricks release the energy expended in piling them. If harnessed in some way, the energy released as the bricks fall could be used to do useful work.

This situation is paralleled by molecules distributed unevenly on two sides of a cell membrane. The constant motion of molecules at all temperatures above absolute zero ($-273°$ C) corresponds to the earthquake in the example. For each degree the temperature increases above absolute zero, molecu-

130

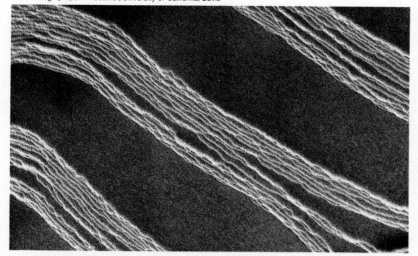

Some of the best experimental support for the fluid mosaic model comes from studies involving freeze-fracturing, a technique used to prepare specimens for electron microscopy. In this technique a specimen quick-frozen in liquid nitrogen is fractured in two by striking it with a knife edge. When cells are split in this way, the line of fracture follows the interior of cell membranes, splitting the membranes into inner and outer halves of equal thickness. The measured thickness of each half is equivalent to the length of single phospholipid molecules. In addition, under high magnification, globular structures the size of protein molecules can be seen embedded in the membrane interior, giving the exposed surface a pebbled appearance. Freeze-fracture studies of artificial phospholipid bilayers provide further support. Microscopic examination of pure phospholipid membranes containing no proteins shows smooth fractured surfaces (top). By contrast, artificial membranes containing added proteins possess surfaces strewn with globular units (bottom) that resemble the units visible in fractured natural membranes.

lar motion becomes more violent. At the temperature of the human body, which amounts to 310° on the absolute scale, this motion is violent indeed. The region of greater concentration represents a pile of molecular bricks on one side of the membrane. The pile tends constantly to fall until the molecules are evenly distributed throughout the available space on both sides of the membrane. The amount of energy available for this movement depends on the height of the pile of bricks or, in other words, on the magnitude of the concentration difference on the two sides of the membrane. Whether the molecules can become evenly distributed on both sides depends simply on whether they can get through the membrane. The membrane transport proteins act by providing the channels of entry for these molecules. Moreover, through their capacity to recognize different molecular types, they select from the available piles of cascading molecular bricks only the types needed by the cell. The transport mechanism involving these proteins is believed to work as illustrated in figure 7 on p. 132.

Selective transport of this type enables cells to absorb many of the hydrophilic molecules, including glycerol and several kinds of sugars, that are required for the activities of life. Such waste products as urea and other

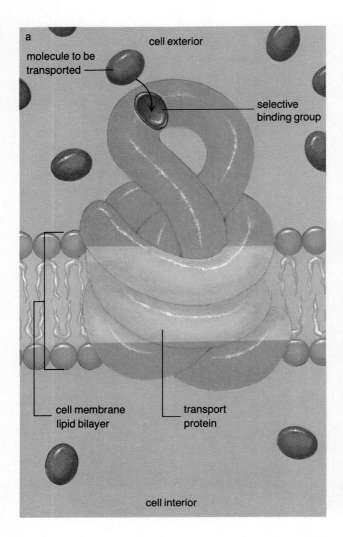

a

cell exterior

molecule to be transported

selective binding group

cell membrane lipid bilayer

transport protein

cell interior

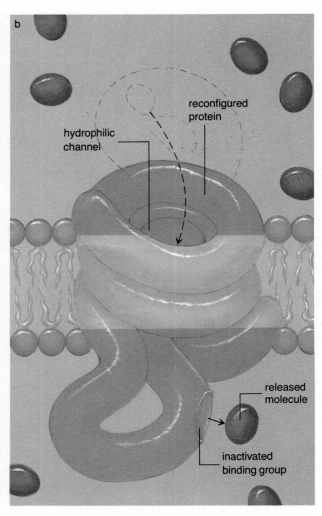

b

reconfigured protein

hydrophilic channel

released molecule

inactivated binding group

molecules in greater concentration on the inside are also moved to the outside by the same selective mechanism.

In contrast to the system described above, membrane proteins engaged in active transport move molecules inside or outside the cell against concentration differences. In effect, they continuously add molecular bricks to piles inside or outside the cell in opposition to the constant tendency to run to equal concentrations inside and outside. The effort proceeds only at the expense of cellular energy.

The required energy is supplied by a molecule that serves as the "dollar" of energy currency in all organisms from bacteria to humans. This is the ATP molecule, known technically as adenosine triphosphate. The part of ATP that makes it so useful as an energy source is its triphosphate segment, which consists of three phosphate groups attached in a row to one end of the molecule. Each of these phosphates contains a phosphorus atom surrounded by four oxygen atoms. One of the oxygens of each phosphate carries a strongly negative charge. In the ATP molecule, the three phosphate groups line up side by side in a position that brings the negative charges close together in space. Since like charges repel, the nearness of the negative charges imposes an internal strain on the molecule. This strain is relieved, with release of energy, if the phosphates are removed. (See figure 8.)

The ATP molecule functions as an energy carrier in all living cells. At sites where energy is captured for cellular use, as in the reactions of photosynthesis, phosphates are added. At sites where energy is required, as in cell membranes transporting molecules against a concentration difference, phosphate groups are removed from ATP to supply the needed energy. Usually in this energy cycle only the last of the three phosphates is added or removed, converting the molecule between ATP, with three phosphates, and ADP (adenosine diphosphate), with two.

The active transport mechanisms that use ATP as an energy source, like the concentration-dependent mechanism, depend on the ability of proteins to take up a variety of folding patterns. This transport process is depicted in figure 9 on pp. 134–135.

A variety of substances is transported actively by cell membrane proteins. Glucose and amino acids are two kinds that have already been mentioned. In addition, cell membranes transport ions of various kinds by active mechanisms. This ionic transport is of special significance, because movement of charged particles amounts to generation of an electric current. Currents generated by active transport of sodium ions (Na^+) and potassium ions (K^+) across nerve cell membranes set up the conditions required for generation of electrical impulses by nerve cells. These impulses provide the basis for the complex activities of the brain and nervous systems and the sensory functions coordinating the rapid and complex behavior of animals, including human beings.

Active transport and cellular energy

Active transport of substances across membranes is also directly related to the fundamental cellular mechanisms that capture chemical energy and store it in ATP. The active transport process uses ATP energy to pile up molecular or ionic bricks inside or outside the cell. It is obvious that, if the same mechanism could be made to run in reverse, the transporter proteins would make ATP from ADP, rather than break it down. In this case the bricks would be piled so high that their tendency to fall would force the active transport mechanism to run backward. This situation has actually been shown to occur in active transport systems that have been forced to run in reverse. For example, one of the known systems in cell membranes normally pumps sodium ions outward, greatly reducing the concentration of sodium ions inside the cell and increasing it outside. If the outside concentration of sodium ions is raised to levels high enough to swamp the pumping system, the system runs in reverse and synthesizes measurable quantities of ATP inside the cell.

The idea that ATP synthesis might proceed in this way in living cells was first proposed by Peter Mitchell of the Glynn Research Laboratories in England. In Mitchell's hypothesis, the energy of sunlight in photosynthesis, or the energy released from oxidation of fuel molecules such as sugars, is used to build up a difference in the concentration of hydrogen ions (H^+) on two sides of a membrane. The concentration difference is then used by

Figure 7. One type of protein-moderated transport across cell membranes is powered by concentration differences in the molecules to be transported. The kind of transport protein involved in this mechanism has a hydrophilic channel running through its interior and is fixed in the lipid bilayer with hydrophilic ends exposed at both inside and outside membrane surfaces. On the outside surface, where molecules to be transported are in greater concentration, the protein is so folded that a small segment of it can bind chemically to the transported molecule. When a molecule of the proper type collides with the protein, it attaches to this selective binding group (a). The binding induces a change in the folding pattern of the protein such that the segment holding the molecule moves through the channel to the cell interior. This inward movement also disturbs the folding arrangement of the binding group so that it no longer fits the transported molecule. As a result the molecule is released on the inside (b). Release causes the protein to return to its original folding pattern, ready to combine with another molecule.

133

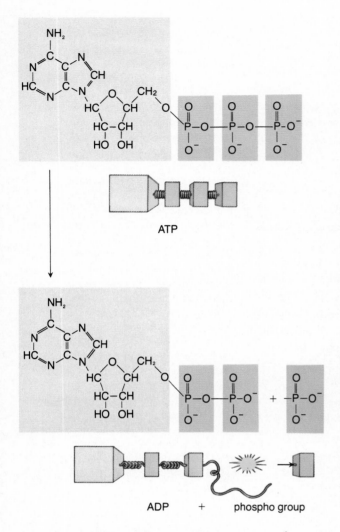

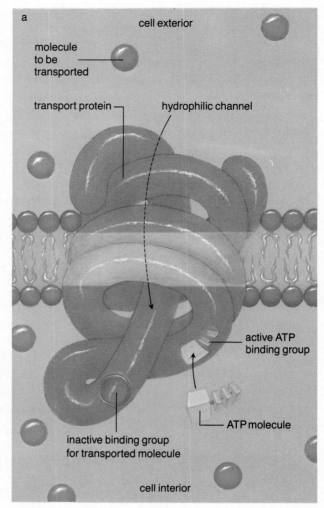

Figure 8 (above left). The usefulness of ATP as an energy source derives from its chain of three phosphate groups. Negatively charged oxygen atoms in each group are aligned in such a way that their mutual electrostatic repulsion places a strain on the molecule. This strain is relieved in increments, with the release of energy, as phosphate groups are removed one at a time. The effect is much like compressing or releasing a spring. Adding phosphates to the molecule compresses the spring and stores energy in the molecule. Removing them releases the spring and makes energy available for work.

membrane proteins as the energy source for adding the third phosphate to the ATP molecule, in a mechanism much like the active transport pumps running in reverse. Mitchell's idea that hydrogen ion concentration differences power ATP synthesis in this way has been amply demonstrated by experimentation and is now accepted as the primary basis for ATP synthesis in all living organisms. Mitchell received the Nobel Prize for Chemistry in 1978 for his hypothesis and his experimental contribution to one of the most significant findings of biology.

In bacteria, ATP synthesis via the mechanism described by Mitchell is now known to be concentrated in the surface membrane that forms the cell boundary. In higher organisms, synthesis is concentrated in closed, saclike membranous structures located in the cell interior. There are two kinds of these interior structures associated with energy metabolism in plants and animals. One type, the chloroplast, synthesizes ATP in response to energy absorbed from sunlight in plants. The second type, the mitochondrion, uses energy derived from oxidation of sugars and other fuel molecules to power ATP synthesis. This second, oxidative system occurs inside both plant and animal cells.

134

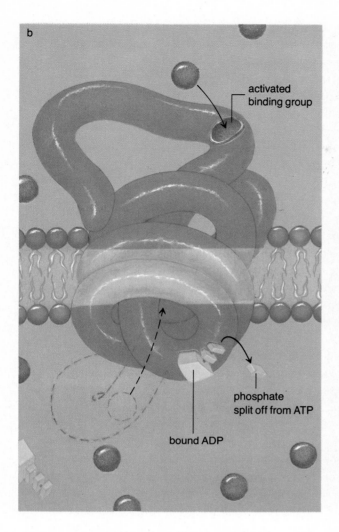

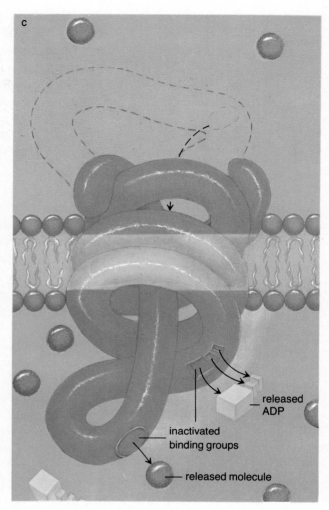

Figure 9 (facing page, right, and above). The type of protein involved in active transport processes uses ATP as an energy source. On the inside surface of the membrane, the exposed, hydrophilic end of this protein has a folded region that binds to ATP molecules, which are circulating in the cell interior and are constantly colliding with the inside membrane surface (a). When this selective binding group binds an ATP molecule, it splits off a phosphate group, converting ATP to ADP, and releases energy. This binding and energy release changes the folding pattern of the protein in such a way that (1) a selective binding group for the molecule to be transported is activated and shifted to the outside membrane surface and (2) a strain is imposed on the protein chain (b). The effect in this situation is much like using the energy liberated by release of the ATP spring to cock a second spring within the protein molecule. The activated external site then binds a molecule of the substance to be transported. This binding releases the transporter spring, pushing the molecule through the protein's hydrophilic channel to the cell interior. This movement changes the protein folding pattern once again so that the binding groups no longer fit either the ADP or the transported molecule. As a result both molecules are released from the transporter protein into the cell interior (c). This release triggers a final change in the protein folding pattern, returning it to its original state in which it is ready to bind a fresh ATP and begin the transport cycle again.

Membrane proteins and surface reception

In addition to transport and energy metabolism, membrane proteins also function in recognition and binding of molecules at the cell surface. Binding of a recognized molecule by a receptor frequently results in transfer of a "signal" across the cell membrane to the cell interior. The signal, in turn, triggers a specific internal biochemical response, such as an increase in synthesis of specific proteins or cell division. Transfer of the signal across the membrane is also believed to depend on the ability of proteins to take up alternate folding conformations.

The process of recognition, binding, and response of cells to the insulin molecule provides an excellent example. Insulin is a hormone secreted by the pancreas in mammals. Body cells have receptor proteins, embedded in the cell membrane, that are shaped so that they fit a portion of the insulin molecule. Collision between insulin and a receptor protein results in immediate binding of the hormone to the cell surface. In response, the cell increases its rate of glucose intake and use. Only a relative few of the surface receptors need to bind insulin, and none of the insulin molecules actually has to penetrate the surface membrane to elicit a full cellular response.

Protein molecules that act as receptors, like transporter proteins, are considered to extend entirely across the cell membrane. Binding a "signal" such as a hormone molecule on the outer surface of the membrane causes a rearrangement in the folding pattern of the receptor protein. Through this rearrangement, the opposite end of the protein is activated to release an internal trigger. The internal trigger may take different forms in different receptor systems. In the insulin system, it is believed to involve an increase in the activity of another membrane protein that transports calcium ions (Ca^{2+}). The resulting increase in calcium ions then triggers the internal cellular response. In other systems, change in the folding pattern of the receptor protein activates an enzyme on the inner membrane surface. Activation of the enzyme results in increased synthesis or release of the triggering substance. (For an account of the significance of recent research into the opiate drug receptors of nerve cell membranes, see *1979 Yearbook of Science and the Future* Feature Article: THE BODY'S NATURAL OPIATES.)

Most of the membrane molecules active in the reception and recognition function have an accessory carbohydrate "antenna" that forms a part of their structure. Carbohydrate groups are also important as parts of the molecules that are recognized by the cell surface. For example, the surfaces of most human body cells are marked by a group of molecules called the HL-A antigens. Each person carries a unique combination of the antigens and, by means of the particular combination present, body cells can distinguish between their own kind and those of another individual. Cells transplanted from another individual are recognized as foreign and destroyed by the recipient's defense mechanisms against disease. These HL-A antigens, which form the main barrier to successful tissue and organ transplants, have been identified as carbohydrate-containing membrane proteins. The "antigen" part—that is, the part that is recognized as foreign and stimulates the defense response—is the carbohydrate portion of the molecule.

136

Current efforts and future prospects

The insights brought about through the research of Singer, Nicolson, Mitchell, and others, while providing solutions to some of the most fundamental problems of cell membrane structure, open new vistas for future research and pose a host of new questions. Now that the general structure of membranes is known, what is the detailed arrangement of lipid and protein molecules in membrane bilayers? What differences appear in these molecules and in their arrangement within membranes that carry out specialized functions in cells, such as the membranes of mitochondria and chloroplasts? What is the precise relationship between the lipid layers forming the inner and outer halves of cell membrane bilayers, and how are differences between them maintained? Because the fluid nature of membrane structure allows the constituent molecules to move freely, how are membrane regions with specialized functions maintained as separate locales with distinct populations of lipids and proteins? How are new membranes assembled during cell growth and division? Exactly how do the carbohydrate "antennas" at the cell boundary function in cell-to-cell recognition and surface reception? Is it possible to modify the recognition mechanism to allow organs to be transplanted successfully between individuals?

One of the most exciting future prospects from membrane research comes from work with artificially made, closed membranous sacs called liposomes. Under the proper conditions, these small spherical vessels can fuse with the membranes of living cells. In so doing, they become continuous with the boundary membranes of the recipient cells and dump their contents inside. By enclosing drugs inside liposomes, it may be possible to deliver corrective medicines directly to the cells of the body without the risks inherent in placing them in general solution in the bloodstream. By including the correct recognition groups in the membranes used to make liposomes, it may even be possible to restrict delivery of the enclosed drugs to specific cell types within the body. Malignant cells come immediately to mind as targets for drugs applied in this way. Finally, because liposome membranes become continuous with cell membranes on fusion, it may be possible to use the artificial sacs to add desired recognition groups to cell surfaces. In this way, the cell surfaces of a transplanted organ might be disguised to "trick" the cells of a recipient individual into accepting the organ as part of "self." Alternatively, cells of a malignant tumor could be marked as foreign and allowed to be destroyed by the natural immune reactions of the body. By exploring and exploiting these avenues, contemporary research may eventually provide remedies for some of mankind's most ancient and destructive diseases.

See also Feature Article: THE CHEMISTRY OF GOOD COOKING, which relates the membrane-forming properties of phospholipids to food preparation in the kitchen.

The Two Brains of Man
by Monte S. Buchsbaum

The halves of the human brain differ in their size and shape, abilities, and responsibilities. Understanding these differences and the way in which the two halves cooperate is a major pursuit of medical science.

Two hands, two feet, two ears, two kidneys—most of the parts of the human body come in pairs, or in two mirror-image halves as do the nose and mouth. Mankind shares this bilateral symmetry not only with familiar family pets but also with grasshoppers, crabs, and even worms. Having two legs for running seems a clear and understandable advantage over having one or three. But having two brains, a right and a left one, for reading this article, making love, or reaching decisions seems superfluous at best and a prescription for insanity at worst. How the two brains work separately and together to think, feel, and act, as well as to produce the introspective impression of a single personality and consciousness in their owner is a neuroscientific problem that challenges researchers from zoologists to psychiatrists. Clues to understanding differences between men and women, human intelligence, and the roots of serious psychiatric illness may lie in the patterns of this cooperation and of its disturbance.

Evolution, laterality, and function

To an amoeba there is no left or right side. These single-celled organisms at the bottom of the phylogenetic tree move by flowing movements of their bodies. Although they respond to chemical and mechanical stimulation, they have no nervous system to coordinate movement or maintain a specific orientation or locomotion. A nervous system first appears in the jellyfish and other members of the phylum Cnidaria, the most primitive group of animals that can move very far. Jellyfish coordinate their swimming motions through a network of nerves devoid of a tissue mass that functions as a central controller. They have a top and bottom but are arranged on a circular, or radial, plan with their organs arranged in a ring. While one edge may lead in swimming for a time, this pacemaker shifts, and no one neural center is a permanent leader.

Development of a single center to control behavior was the next evolutionary step. An animal with such a control center would be able to coordinate its activity toward a specific goal, a clear advantage in the struggle for survival. Ancestors common to the jellyfish and some other marine invertebrates went part way to have two generalized regions of neural control, but the flatworms, of the phylum Platyhelminthes, are first with a clearly recognizable head. The flatworm's single central control center—the most primi-

138

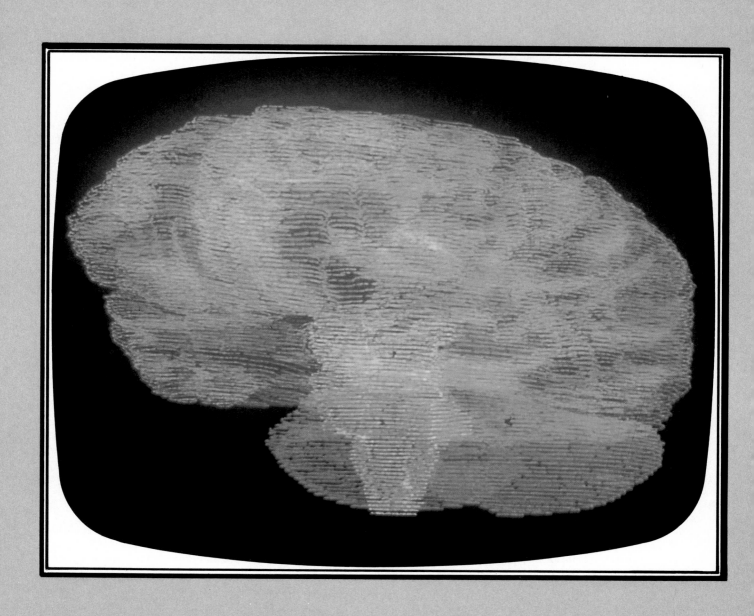

Dual nature of the primitive brain and its development in progressively higher forms of life are shown in a representative series of animals from the flatworm through a primate. In the flatworm and insect the brain comprises paired concentrations of nervous tissue, or ganglia. In the vertebrates shown, drawings to scale of the cerebrum make evident the progressive increase in its size and complexity.

MONTE S. BUCHSBAUM *is Chief of the Section on Clinical Psychophysiology, Biological Psychiatry Branch, National Institute of Mental Health, Bethesda, Maryland.*

(Overleaf) Photo by Robert B. Livingston, University of California, San Diego; Illustrations by Leonard Morgan

tive brain—and the concentration of sense organs near it yield a recognizable animal that can select a course of action and carry it out, unlike the radially organized jellyfish. In the flatworm's centralized control lies the evolutionary potential of individual personality and consciousness. Yet it retains from its forebears a pairing of neuronal control regions—right and left cephalic ganglia—that define right and left sides for the first time. The adaptive advantage of this pairing is clear as phylum after phylum of animals through successive evolution maintained this plan, and human beings carry the ancestral flatworm design, although greatly modified, within their own skulls today.

In humans some paired organs function merely as a backup system. For example, if the right kidney is injured or surgically removed, the left one is available to maintain vital function. Other organs like the heart are really made up of a pair of simpler organs. The right heart pumps blood to the lungs for oxygenation and carbon dioxide release, and the left heart pumps blood to supply the body. This specialization leaves no reserve. If the muscle of the left heart has its own blood supply reduced by a heart attack, the right side cannot take over its function. Fish and amphibian hearts lack such full specialization; their left and right ventricular pumps are only partially divided, allowing some capacity for backup at the expense of mixing oxygenated and spent blood and less precise and efficient control over blood pressure. Thus a biological tradeoff occurs, one that can be extended as well to the concept of two brains: increasing specialization of left and right, or lateralization, allows more adaptive and complex control but perhaps less capacity to sustain function after injury or under the handicap of a birth defect.

Full lateralization of the mammalian heart with its completely separated left and right halves prevents mixing of blood from the body and lungs. Such isolation of function might also be another potential advantage of two brains: incompatible or independent modes of thought can separately go forward without interference.

For very simple kinds of behavior a lateralized brain makes sense. If one touches a hot coal with the right hand, sensory messages go to the right brain and the right hand is withdrawn. If there is food to the left, one extends the nearest hand in that direction. Some communication to the opposite side may be necessary—for example, for two-legged balance—but for fighting, avoiding danger, feeding, and sex there is usually a clear orientation between spatial position in the external world and behavior.

As the central nervous system takes on more complex tasks and memory, planning, and abstraction are called for, this spatial relationship becomes attenuated. "Yesterday a snake bit me over by the white rock" is not clearly spatially lateralized. And the logical response to avoid that situation henceforth may have to be weighed against other information perceived in another part of the brain, such as "A lot of ripe strawberries are growing just on the other side of the white rock." This potential of the left and right brain for conflict represents a problem that has somehow been resolved during evolution, but in a manner that is complex and not fully understood. Moreover, the nature of this solution is especially difficult to explore in humans, whose abstract reasoning and language abilities provided the first clues to

140

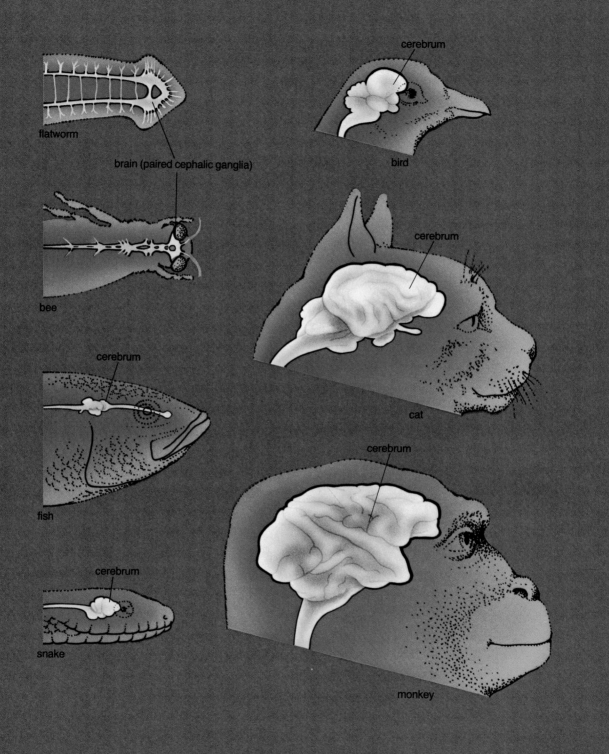

flatworm

brain (paired cephalic ganglia)

bee

cerebrum

fish

cerebrum

snake

cerebrum

bird

cerebrum

cat

cerebrum

monkey

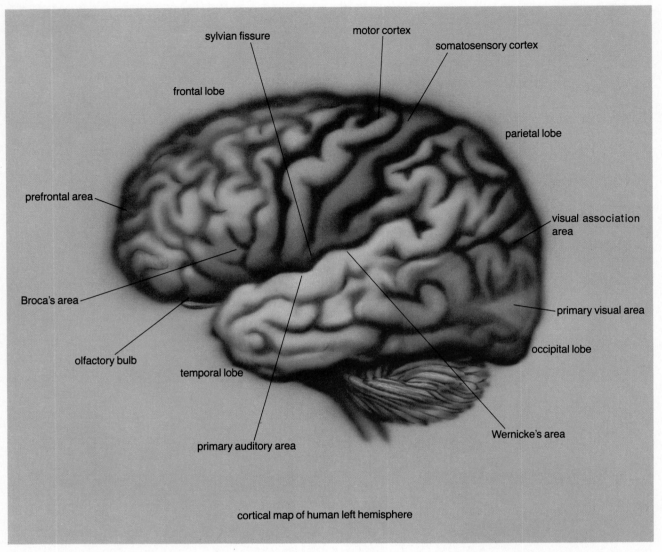

cortical map of human left hemisphere

the brain's double identity but whose fragile cerebral integrity is protected by law, cultural ethics, and thick skulls.

In the past few years knowledge about lateralization has advanced dramatically for two main reasons. Surprisingly, brain lateralization has been found in songbirds, monkeys, and even rats, allowing neurophysiological experiments not possible in human beings. And new techniques that allow scientists to study human brain activity without invading the skull have brought new images of the two brains at work.

First suspicions

Earliest hints of the brain's lateralization came from the wounds of war. Observant physicians noted that left-side head wounds sometimes affected speech and right-hand movement. As autopsy procedures developed in the 19th century, victims of strokes (interruptions of blood flow to particular regions of the brain) and brain tumors became other sources of information. A series of intellectual deficits could be noted in a patient, and when the

142

patient died, a correlation could be made between the specific difficulty—such as the inability to name things—and damage to a specific region of the cerebral cortex, the so-called gray matter that forms the outer layer of each hemisphere of the cerebrum.

From these clinical techniques the concept of a verbal, logical left hemisphere and a visual-spatial, emotional right hemisphere has emerged—a picture that holds for virtually all right-handed persons and most left-handed ones. Difficulties with naming objects, mixing syllables within words, and being able to repeat words but not speak them spontaneously are typical symptoms of left-hemisphere damage, especially in regions of the brain around a feature called the sylvian fissure. Pretended or pantomime movements, such as driving a screw or brushing teeth, may be impossible to carry out but may be successfully performed with an actual screwdriver or toothbrush. Damage to the left parietal region of the brain may leave the victim unable to do mental arithmetic, to name his or her own fingers when asked (thumb, index, etc.), or to identify his or her own left and right sides correctly (*e.g.*, "touch your right elbow with your left thumb").

In contrast, a person with right-side damage may have difficulty reproducing a geometric drawing, identifying pieces of music, reading maps, or building with blocks. A wristwatch may be drawn with only the numbers on the right side of the dial. A shirt may be turned and shaken randomly in a disordered effort to orient it for dressing. Parts of the body may be neglected and left unwashed and undressed. Screams may erupt as persons with such damage find a "strange arm" (actually their own left arm) in bed with them.

All of these effects occur among injured adults. In young children injuries to either side of the brain may cause verbal difficulties, but recovery may be fairly complete, suggesting a potentiality of either side for verbal skills—a backup capacity of adaptive advantage available for the more vulnerable child. Women seem to have greater resistance to cerebral damage from strokes than do men. Not only do they appear to recover speech function more fully, but they also appear less likely to lose verbal skills acutely.

Crossed systems

If one catches a ball thrown from the right, several kinds of sensory signals —visual, tactile, and kinesthetic (a sense of body position and movement)— must be brought together. For a fish, a horse, or any other animal with eyes on the side of its head, sight on the right side of the body is a job for the right eye; the visual fields of its eyes overlap little. But for a human being to perceive the distance from ball to hand, two visual signals from the left and right eyes are needed for comparison. Without such binocular stereoscopic vision the hand is far less useful. In fact, hand and eye evolved together in the primates, who generally have two large forward-facing eyes with greatly overlapping fields of vision.

Along with the benefits of depth perception, however, come complications. If the ball is on one's right, the light from it passes through the lens of each eye to fall on the left half of each retina. Hence, the left halves of the two retinas are jointly responsible for sensing light from the right half of the full visual field. The images projected on the two retinas are reunited in the

Map of left hemispheric surface in a human locates regions of cortex whose specialized functions have been identified in the course of more than a century of medical observation and experiment. Running parallel to each other across the roof of the brain are the somatosensory cortex, which is responsible for receiving sensory signals from the skin, bones, joints, and muscles of the right side of the body, and the motor cortex, which handles voluntary muscular control of that side. Nearby is the primary auditory area, which is the center of sound reception for the right ear. On the occipital lobe and surrounded by the visual association area is the primary visual area, which integrates sensory information from the left half of each eye. Whereas the functional regions listed above have counterparts on the right hemisphere, other regions are unique to the left hemisphere. These include Broca's and Wernicke's areas, which are positioned close to the auditory and facial motor centers and function together in the production and understanding of language.

143

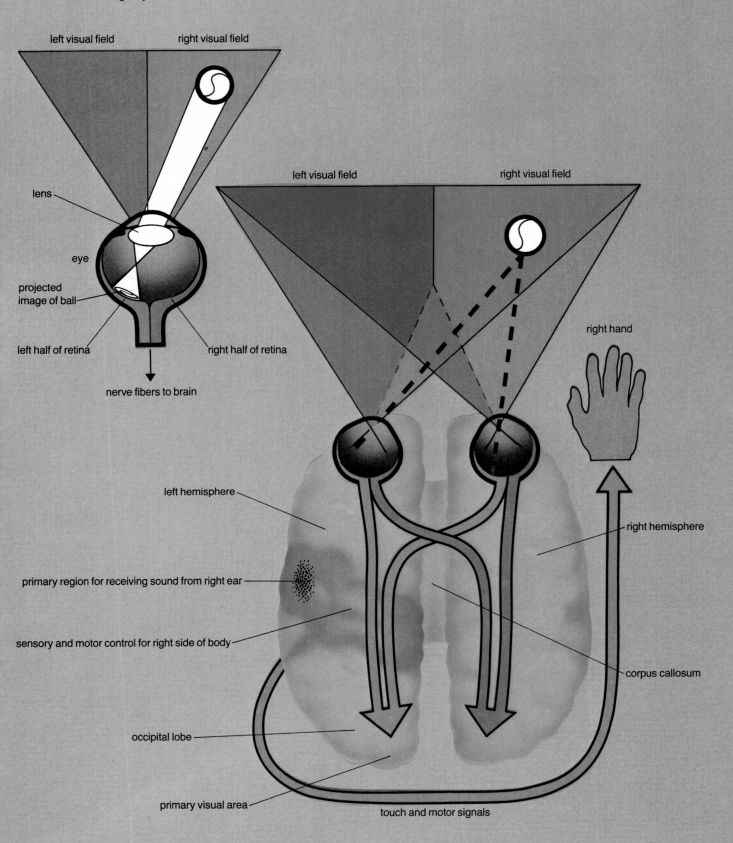

single-eye vision

left visual field

right visual field

lens

eye

projected
image of ball

left half of retina

right half of retina

nerve fibers to brain

left visual field

right visual field

right hand

left hemisphere

right hemisphere

primary region for receiving sound from right ear

sensory and motor control for right side of body

corpus callosum

occipital lobe

primary visual area

touch and motor signals

binocular vision

left brain's visual region of the occipital cortex. Nearby, also on the left, are the brain's centers for fine sensory and motor control for the right hand as well as receipt of sound information from the right ear. Thus, the primate brain apparently evolved in a way that unites the visual signals from those halves of the two retinas that together report on everything of interest to one side of the body with the fine motor and tactile systems of that side.

This situation requires much crossing of signals: visual nerve fibers from the left half of the retina of the right eye cross to the left cortex; fine touch signals from the right fingertips cross from right to left to reach the left cortex; motor signals descend from the left cortex and cross to the right to terminate in the right hand. This crossed system is a recent addition on the evolutionary time scale, and more primitive uncrossed systems remain in place supplementing and backing up sensory and motor function, but with less precision. Individuals differ widely in the proportion of crossed and uncrossed systems, complicating studies of laterality and making each human unique in the relationships between left and right brains.

Researchers have taken advantage of the predominant crossed system to study the responsibilities of the right and left brains. In a typical experiment the subject is given a simple cognitive task with two possible responses (*e.g.*, yes/no) to be made, one with each hand. Each problem in the task is then presented to the right or left visual field (or right or left ear). If the left brain handles the task, the fastest response should occur when the problems are presented to the right visual field or ear and the correct answers require a right-handed response because perception, processing, and muscle response can all be performed by the left hemisphere. Other combinations would require transmitting information between hemispheres to request help from the right brain.

Consider the visual problem explored by John Bradshaw and co-workers in Australia of distinguishing the letter A from the letter B. One letter is pointy, one is round; hence, there is no need to read (to use the verbal left hemisphere) to tell them apart. But what about distinguishing the letter a from A or B? One might argue that the A/a/B task requires either the verbal left hemisphere or the shape-sensitive right hemisphere. To settle this question Bradshaw and co-workers gave subjects two keys to press (to signal "same" or "different") and a string of pairs—Aa, Ba, AA, aa, bb, and so on—to identify by name as the same letter. Of the four possible combinations of visual fields and hands that were tried, the combination of right visual field and right hand gave the fastest response time, which is consistent with a primary left-hemisphere role in letter-naming. Such a strategy has been used with a wide variety of tasks including identifying symbols, pictures, spoken words, and musical notes. Pictures of faces, for example, have been better identified by the right brain.

The emotional right brain

Is the right brain the emotional, affective, feeling counterpart of the left brain, separated by nature to perform independent assessments of plans and goals? Some suggestions of emotional differences between hemispheres have come again from clinical cases in which right-brain defects were

Studies of the way brain and body interact have shown that such a commonplace activity as catching a ball coming from the right with the right hand involves a complex system of crossing nerve signals. Each eye in a human being independently receives light from within a certain cone-shaped volume of space called the visual field. Because of the way light behaves when it is projected through a lens like that of the eye, light from one half of the visual field falls on the opposite half of the light-sensitive retina at the back of the eye. Thus, the image of a ball coming from the right will be projected on the left half of the retina. In binocular vision, in which the visual fields of the eyes greatly overlap, the left halves of the two retinas are jointly responsible for sensing light from the right half of the full visual field. For the two retinal images of the ball to be perceived as a single object, signals from each eye must be brought together. The human nervous system does this by routing the visual nerve fibers from the left half of each retina to the visual region of the brain's left occipital lobe. Nearby, also on the left side of the brain, are the somatosensory and motor regions of the cortex, which receive signals from and control the right side of the body, including the right hand. Also nearby is the primary auditory area (not directly visible in this perspective), which receives sound information from the right ear. Hence, the crack of a baseball bat or the hiss of the ball through the air may also be assimilated by the brain as it coordinates a successful catch.

correlated with unusual emotional behavior. Other indications have come from diagnostic procedures that transiently sedate one half of the brain by injecting a drug into the blood supply of the right or the left hemisphere, the right or left carotid artery in the neck. Striking also are the pioneering observations by U.S. psychobiologists Roger Sperry and Michael Gazzaniga of subjects who had had the major neural line of communication between hemispheres, the corpus callosum, severed as a treatment to ameliorate and contain severe epilepsy. For example, when a picture of a nude was suddenly presented to the right hemisphere of such a subject in a series of standard psychological stimuli, the person "broke into a hearty grin and chuckle." When questioned as to what was funny, the subject could not say, except that "the machine was funny or something." When the same picture was presented to the verbal left hemisphere, it was quickly reported as a nude figure. Thus, although the right brain was inarticulate, it understood the incongruity of the nude among the standard shapes and patterns of the laboratory tasks.

This right-hemisphere emotionality has been ingeniously pursued by S. J. Dimond in the U.K. in subjects with normal hemispheric interconnections who were fitted with contact lenses blacked out to occlude either their right or left visual fields. They viewed films ranging from cartoons to medical operations and rated their own emotional responses. Subjects who viewed medical films with their right hemisphere (left visual field) rated them more horrific than did those who saw them with their left hemisphere.

Emotions also seem to be expressed more intensely with the left half of the face, the muscles of which are controlled by the right hemisphere. To demonstrate this idea, composite photographs of faces showing emotions were assembled by Harold Sackeim and co-workers in the U.S. Photographs consisting of a left side of a face and its mirror image were rated as more intensely expressive than the normal face or a composite of two right sides. This experiment, in conjunction with the contact lens experiment, raises the possibility that in a face-to-face encounter one views the other person's more emotionally expressive half face with one's less emotionally responsive visual half field. This situation may have advantages or disadvantages for emotional communication or for diminishing emotional distraction. Or, greater expressiveness of the left side of the face may represent a compensation made by nature in order to overcome the diminished emotional sensitivity of the left field.

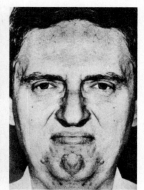

From "Emotions are Expressed More Intensely on the Left Side of the Face," H. A. Sackeim, R. C. Gur, M. C. Saucy, SCIENCE, vol. 202, pp. 434–5, fig. 1, October 27, 1978, © AAAS

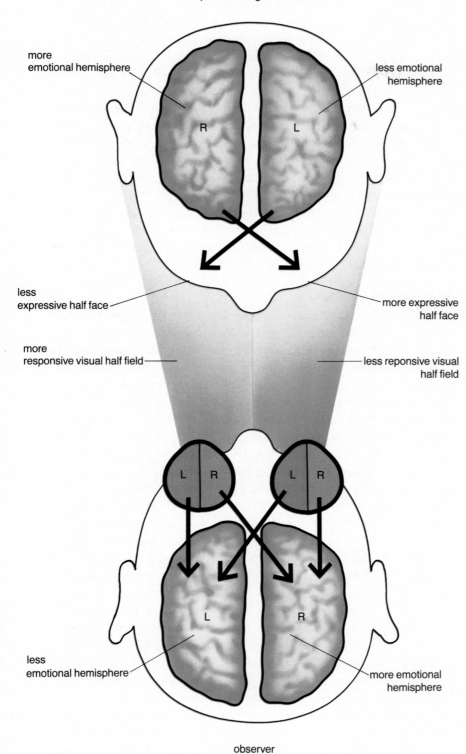

person being observed

more
emotional hemisphere

less emotional
hemisphere

R   L

less
expressive half face

more expressive
half face

more
responsive visual half field

less reponsive visual
half field

L | R   L | R

less
emotional hemisphere

more emotional
hemisphere

L   R

observer

Unaltered photograph of a face registering disgust (facing page) is flanked on the left by a composite of two left sides — the original and its mirror image — and on the right by a composite of two right sides. Human subjects who viewed this sequence and other sequences featuring different emotional expressions judged the left-side composites to be the most intensely expressive of the three choices. These results support the concept that the right brain hemisphere, which controls the muscles of the left side of the face, is the more emotional hemisphere. They also imply that, in situations involving face-to-face encounters (left), the more expressive half face of the person being observed falls within the observer's less emotionally responsive visual half field, which projects to the less emotional hemisphere. This situation could be interpreted as advantageous or disadvantageous, depending on the desirability of emotional communication. It also raises the possibility that the more expressive left side of the face may have evolved to compensate for the reduced emotional sensitivity of the left hemisphere.

If the right hemisphere is concerned with emotional response, could such an affective mental disorder as depression be primarily dysfunction of the right brain? Electroconvulsive therapy, a common treatment for depression, can be given to the whole head or just to one hemisphere. Usually the patient is anesthetized and an electric current is passed briefly across the head; a series of such treatments frequently ameliorates severe depression. Some confusion and loss of memory, especially for recent events, frequently occur after both hemispheres are shocked. Physicians who experimented with administering shock separately to the left and right hemispheres found that such questions as "What is the color of grass?" were answered more poorly after left-side shock. Indeed, this result is consistent with the other indications that the left hemisphere is the speech center. In addition, some patients make better recoveries after right-side shock, suggesting to some that depression may be a right-hemisphere illness. Yet, this observation may merely reflect the fact that the diminished memory loss following right-side shock is less upsetting, rather than offering evidence of an actual effect on lateralized emotional centers.

New ways to study the brain

Although examination of patients with gunshot damage to the brain has yielded valuable hints about differences between right and left brain function, the unpredictable and uncontrollable effects of such injuries limit their usefulness in studies of the brain. Strokes, tumors, and electroshock therapy are clinical tools available by accident rather than by design in brains not fully normal. But new computer techniques are making it possible to study the function of undamaged brains. Without breaking the skin, medical scientists can record the electrical activity of groups of neurons in the brain as they process incoming information. Flashing a picture to the left visual field, for instance, evokes activity that can be recorded as an electroencephalogram by amplifying about 10,000 times the activity picked up by small metal electrodes pasted on the scalp. Such a stimulus tends to break up the normal resting pattern of brain-wave activity, the regular undulating alpha rhythm, and to produce a more irregular, faster, lower amplitude pattern. This loss of the alpha pattern has been used as an indicator of activation of the visual-spatial right hemisphere in such tasks as making designs with blocks. But, hidden in this general low irregular electrical activity is the specific brain response evoked by the stimulus, often only a millionth of a volt in amplitude. This "evoked potential" can be distinguished from continuous brain-wave activity by a computer technique called averaging.

In the first experiments exploring verbal laterality with evoked potentials, Monte Buchsbaum and colleagues in the U.S. showed subjects three-letter words and dot designs that looked like words but were unreadable. They presented the material so that it appeared only in the subjects' left or right field of vision. Only the left hemisphere was found to produce clearly different evoked potentials for words and dots; the right half, because it lacked the other hemisphere's verbal ability, apparently failed to recognize the difference between them. These experiments have been extended by others to examine lateralization with spoken words and linguistic distinctions and

From "Right-Left Asymmetrics in the Brain," Albert M. Galaburda, SCIENCE, vol. 199, pp. 852–6, fig. 4, February 24, 1978, © AAAS

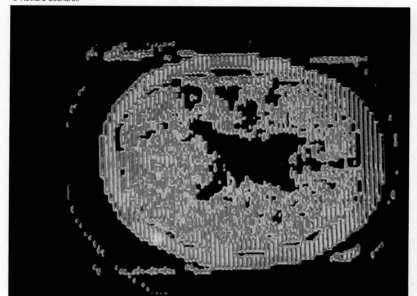

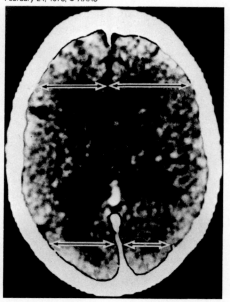

to time the transfer of information across the corpus callosum. By the early 1980s cortical maps of cognitive function using many scalp electrodes were being produced.

The differences between the right and left brain so far discussed have been differences in function, not structure. Measurements of sliced brain tissue by U.S. neurologist Norman Geschwind and others, however, suggest that the verbal left brain has a larger region of cortex for processing language-related sounds. A larger occipital pole (the tip of the occipital lobe) also appears frequently on the left, and other asymmetries may be revealed. Not everyone shows these asymmetries, and variation in the amount and location of cortex in the left hemisphere could help to explain individual differences in cognitive skills or left-hemisphere advantages.

With the development in the past decade of computerized axial tomography (CAT; also called computed tomography, or CT), such asymmetries may now be assessed in living persons. (Physicist Allan Cormack and electronics engineer Godfrey Hounsfield shared the 1979 Nobel Prize for Physiology or Medicine for their contributions to CAT; *see* SCIENTISTS OF THE YEAR.) The CAT scan uses X-ray views taken at many different angles; these are mathematically reconstructed into a two-dimensional image of a slice through the body. In a CAT scan of the head, structures within the brain can be seen because such computerized reconstruction is sensitive to very small differences in the amount that X-rays are absorbed by differing neural tissue. Differences between cerebral regions composed largely of nerve cells or nerve fibers (the gray matter of the cortex and the white regions below) have been resolved by scanners available in the late 1970s. The normally larger left occipital region of the brain is readily apparent in CAT scans, and it is expected that future advances will allow asymmetries in the sylvian fissure, in the ventricles (fluid-filled cavities), in the thickness of the cortex, and in the size of portions of the temporal lobe to be measured. Even the

Asymmetrical pattern of the ventricles of the brain stands out in black in CAT scan of the head of a living person (above, left). The reconstucted X-ray image is of a cross section of the brain as seen from above the top of the head; front is to the right. In the late 1970s this technique could depict in living brains many structural asymmetries that had been first noted in work with cadavers. CAT scan of the brain of a right-handed person (above) reveals typical pattern of hemispheric asymmetry: wider right frontal lobe (compare upper arrows), wider left occipital lobe (lower arrows), and protrusion of the left occipital pole past the midline of the brain into the right side. The view again is from the top of the head; front is up.

149

Michael E. Phelps and David E. Kuhl, University of California, Los Angeles

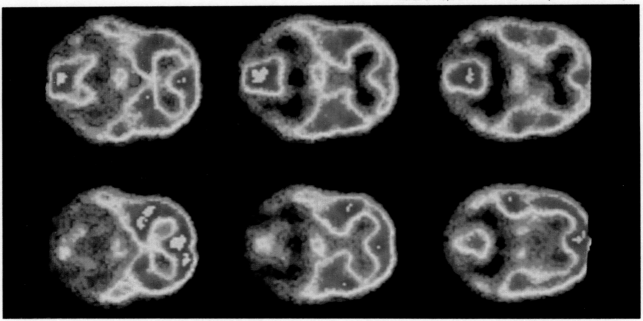

Brain activity in a living human subject given a radioactively labeled glucose analogue is followed in photographic images made with a PET scanner. Each sequence of three images maps local glucose metabolism at three successive horizontal levels of the brain, the colors red and white indicating comparatively high levels of glucose use. The top sequence was made with the subject's eyes open and the bottom one with the eyes closed. With the eyes open high levels of activity appear in the primary visual areas of the occipital lobes (extreme left portion of each slice). The scans also reveal changes in activity in the frontal areas (right portion of each slice) and differences in activity between left and right hemispheres.

length of the corpus callosum might be determined by reconstructing a series of vertical images.

The sites of damage from strokes can now also be accurately delineated in living persons with the aid of new radiological techniques. In one the patient is injected with a radioactive isotope, *e.g.,* of technetium, which leaks out through blood vessels that have been damaged by stroke and localizes in the region of brain tissue that has recently lost its blood supply. By scanning the head with a radiation detector, the site of isotope concentration can be pinpointed. A second technique makes use of the CAT scan, which, if taken after the brain is allowed to heal somewhat, can locate a region of tissue that is less dense than normal (an indication of blood-starved tissue). This procedure presents a defined defect to the investigator for neuropsychological studies and gives the patient's physician precise information on the extent of the damage and amount of healing.

Tomographic X-ray scans can supply information about the brain's structure, but they reveal nothing about its activities. Other recently developed techniques promise to revolutionize studies of brain function by producing images that correspond to localized activity within the working brain. Such radioactive isotopes as fluorine-18 decay by emitting subatomic particles called positrons and may be attached to metabolically active molecules, including the sugar glucose. Like muscle work, brain work uses glucose for energy involved in neural activity. But because glucose is rapidly broken apart, a radioactive label attached to its structure would be lost. A modified glucose, however—deoxyglucose—is abnormally metabolized by the cell, essentially becoming trapped in active brain cells. When labeled with fluorine-18, it becomes a tracer of local brain activity.

Development of this brain-activity tracer technique by Louis Sokoloff and others in the U.S. has focused primarily on animal studies and extremely high resolution images made from the sliced brains of animals injected with

Michel M. Ter-Pogossian, Washington University, School of Medicine

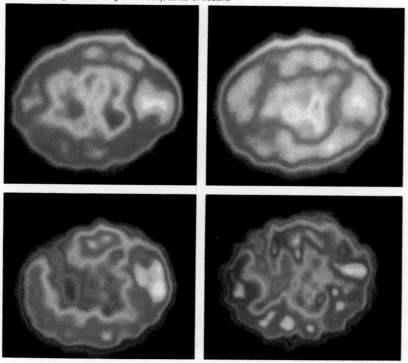

radioactive tracer. But, combined with a computerized tomographic process explored by U.S. workers Alfred Wolf and David Kuhl and others, the tracer technique permits neural activity of the brain to be mapped from outside the skull. This synthesis of techniques, called positron emission tomography (PET), can be safely applied to human volunteers, and such psychological tasks as reading or listening to a story may be identified with specific left-hemisphere centers to provide direct evidence and supplement the more indirect studies that have been done to date. This remarkable technique not only will extend knowledge about lateralization but also will produce un-dreamed-of maps of psychological functions.

Another method for assessing brain work, developed in Europe by Niels Lassen, David Ingvar, and colleagues, involves a two-dimensional mapping of cortical blood flow. Active regions of the brain receive more blood flow, and by using radioactive tracer injected into the brain's blood supply, precise outlines of active regions of thought can be visualized as a function of the rate at which the tracer is cleared from brain tissue.

Animals and humans: similarities and differences

The complex, musical trill of a canary is called song because of its resemblance to human vocalization, and the neural arrangements for canary song also resemble human lateralization. Fernando Nottebohm in the U.S. found that left-side brain operations largely reduced the number of musical syllables the birds could sing and disorganized their song patterns, whereas many birds sang as well after right-side surgical defects as before. Young birds in which the left brains were experimentally damaged before they had learned to sing were able to learn using their right brains, but birds given surgi-

Pairs of PET scans taken horizontally through the heads of two subjects are compared. The top pair is of a healthy subject, and the bottom pair is of a stroke victim. The images map the distribution in the blood of a radioactive oxygen isotope inhaled by the subjects. Scans making up each pair were taken several minutes apart; the differences between them reflect the redistribution of oxygen by blood circulation. In the bottom images the abnormal distribution of oxygen in the center and on one side of the brain is easily seen.

151

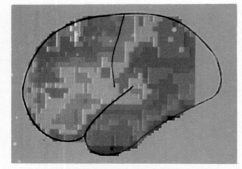
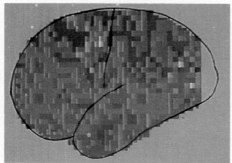
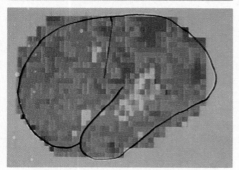
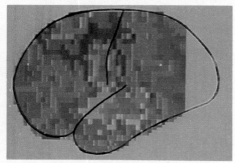
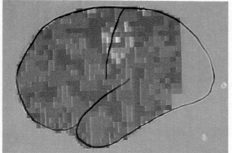

Niels A. Lassen, Bispebjerg Hospital, Denmark

cal defects as adults still had unstable, poorly controlled voices a year later. Thus, like human children, young birds have some backup capacity in their right brains for vocalization, a capacity largely lost in maturity.

Vocal communication in monkeys may also depend on their "verbal" left hemispheres. Michael R. Petersen and co-workers in the U.S. studied the cooing sounds female Japanese macaques use to call for male companions and similar sounds used by both sexes, young and old, for contact seeking. Japanese macaques discriminated their own tape-recorded calls better when played to their right ear (left hemisphere), whereas other monkey species, for whom vocalizations of the Japanese macaque meant little, showed no clear hemispheric advantage.

Animal models of man's right-hemispheric emotionality have also appeared. For example, Robert G. Robinson in the U.S. produced experimental strokes in rats by tying off the arteries that supply blood to the brain. It was found that rats who had had their right middle cerebral artery tied showed hyperactivity and changes in certain brain chemicals, the catecholamines, which have been implicated in regulation of emotions. Tying off the corresponding artery on the left did not produce the same results.

Despite these similarities in hemispheric specialization, handedness or "pawedness" in animals does not parallel the clear right-side preference in humans. Whereas mice show stable paw preferences, these seem dependent on environmental training, and even monkeys seem trainable to use either hand. Orangutans and chimpanzees in the wild show no clear hand preference. Greater cerebral specialization, enhanced speech abilities, and prevalence of manual tasks learned by verbal instruction may enhance human right-handedness. Although right- or left-handedness does tend to run in families, a clear dominant or recessive pattern of inheritance, as there is for brown and blue eyes, does not appear. In addition, unlike eyes, which are either one color or another, handedness may be incomplete with varying degrees of ambidexterity for different tasks. Nor does left-handedness imply right-brain speech control: most left-handers have left-brain verbal centers.

Recently Jerre Levy in the U.S. suggested that writing posture may reveal the hemisphere/hand link. She noted that right-handers with normal upright writing posture and left-handers with hooked, inverted writing posture show left-hemisphere verbal lateralization as inferred from task performance tests presented to the left or right visual fields. Left-handers with normal posture and right-handers with inverted posture (both relatively rare combinations) showed the reverse. This relationship seemed stronger when tests involving sight, rather than hearing, were used to determine brain lateralization. Thus, not only is lateralization incomplete, but it varies across skills and sensory modalities in its expressions. The very lateralization of human skills allows alternate specialized brain mechanisms to develop, often permitting options as to whether the right or left functions.

One, two, or three brains

Although the distribution of special cognitive tasks between brain hemispheres is dramatic, many functions, including memory, gross movements, and aspects of feeding, change little if one hemisphere is damaged or suc-

152

hemispheric specialization	
left hemisphere	**right hemisphere**
language and memory functions	
controls spontaneous speaking, writing	uses expletives
	draws geometric shapes
formulates reply to verbal commands	may act on simple commands
	recognizes faces
recognizes words	remembers shapes, music
remembers words and numbers	may repeat words
sensory and motor functions	
receives input largely from right visual field, right ear, right side of body	receives input largely from left visual field, left ear, left side of body
controls fine movement of right hand	controls fine movement of left hand
controls pretended and complex movements	
controls pantomiming responsible for finger naming	
perceptual and other cognitive functions	
orchestrates sequences of movements (e.g., lighting a cigarette)	responsible for orientation of clothes in dressing
	functions in map interpretation
	functions in mental rotation of images

Table (left) summarizes some of the known functional specializations of the two brain hemispheres. Five side-view images of nerve-cell activity in the left hemisphere of normal human subjects (facing page) were produced by a radioactive xenon tracer technique that maps blood flow in the brain. Shades of pink, red, and yellow indicate comparatively high levels of blood flow and, hence, of functional activity. Even in the awake, resting state (top), the frontal areas of the brain are seen to be active (compare with illustration on p. 142). With the subject looking at a moving object (second from top), changes in blood flow with respect to the resting state reveal local activity in the visual association area, as well as in that part of the motor cortex dealing with eye movement. With the subject listening to spoken words (center), both the primary auditory area and Wernicke's area are active. When the subject counts repeatedly to 20 (second from bottom), activity is seen in the mouth area of the somatosensory and motor cortices, the auditory area, and the supplementary motor area in the upper frontal lobe. Rhythmic clenching of the hand opposite the hemisphere being scanned activates the corresponding area of motor cortex (bottom).

cessfully continue with a single hemisphere. This spare or backup function is highly adaptive and may be crucial for survival since neurons in the brain have very limited capacities for repair or regrowth. Similar "brain" problems have been faced by designers of computer-controlled interplanetary spacecraft. Sent far from the local repair service, these computers must function correctly for as long as ten years.

Some U.S. planetary missions have used a two-computer system, one in a standby state ready to go into action if the first fails. This recalls the left-brain/right-brain system for vocalization in humans and canaries, in which recovery from early left-side failure can occur as the right side takes over. The guidance system of some U.S. space-launch vehicles used a three-computer system with action taken after majority vote. Most recently, self-repairing spacecraft computers have been developed with special self-checking circuits that bring new substitute elements on-line if malfunctions are detected in the primary components.

The human brain needs to last 70 years or more, and evolution seems to have chosen a two-unit model. Not all brain functions have a spare, especially in adults, but writing and remembering music may not head nature's list of survival skills. Neuroscientific advances will make it possible to better identify lateralized tasks and to follow repair and substitution processes as they occur after injury. Under normal circumstances the right and left hemispheres work not only separately and cooperatively but also redundantly to produce the surprisingly skilled, creative, and reliable human mind.

153

How Fast is Fast?
How High is High?

by Marvin I. Clein

In recent years athletes have run and swum faster, jumped higher and farther, and thrown weights greater distances than ever before. Their continued assault on sports records raises the question: Are there limits to human physical performance?

The physical achievements of humans have always been a topic of popular interest. Primitive tribes celebrated the physical conquest of the hunt. Aristotle, Epictetus, Spinoza, and other thinkers wrote of physical courage as a "cardinal virtue." Contests of physical ability have been an integral part of most societies. Their victors have been idealized by the public, sculptured by artists, and often generously rewarded.

Throughout their history humans have extended themselves beyond all predictions. Individuals have run faster, jumped higher, and thrown farther than anyone thought they would. They have descended into the Earth's deepest known chasm nearly seven miles to the ocean floor, climbed to the top of the world, and ventured some 240,000 miles across the dark recesses of outer space to stand on the Moon. Even before all this some humans withstood long journeys over frozen polar ice fields, carved trails through perilous and torrid tropical jungles, and survived free falls through the Earth's atmosphere of up to 16 mi.

At best it can only be a tentative conclusion that men and women have met every challenge in their quest for excellence in physical performance. The theoretical limits of physical achievement have been continually expanded. Unanimity of opinion as to the final limits has been difficult to find. In search of measurable evidence record performances in sports appear to provide the most dependable base of information.

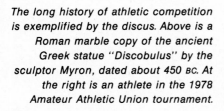

The long history of athletic competition is exemplified by the discus. Above is a Roman marble copy of the ancient Greek statue "Discobulus" by the sculptor Myron, dated about 450 BC. At the right is an athlete in the 1978 Amateur Athletic Union tournament.

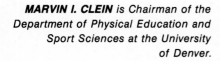

MARVIN I. CLEIN *is Chairman of the Department of Physical Education and Sport Sciences at the University of Denver.*

(Overleaf) Illustration by Marilyn Shimokochi

Athletic performances

In the Sport Sciences Laboratory at the University of Denver researchers have observed, measured, and studied human physical performance. This has been a complex undertaking because the variables implicated in the process of human physical attainment are numerous. Physical attainment depends not only upon natural endowment but also upon such factors as learning, opportunity, emotions, intellect, and the physical environment.

Few international records of athletic achievement were kept before 1850. Since that time performances in certain activities have displayed continuous improvement. Some, however, have remained intact over long periods and would appear to represent unique physical efforts. One of these is the 8.9-m (29 ft 2½ in) long jump Bob Beamon achieved in the 1968 Olympic Games at Mexico City. This mark exceeded the previous world record of Ralph Boston by 0.55 m and may stand for many decades in the future. Still another unique physical effort was that of Nadia Comaneci of Romania, who was awarded perfect scores of "10" seven times for her gymnastic performances during the 1976 Olympic Games at Montreal.

The shape of the performance curve for men can best be characterized by plotting record times in the mile run since 1860 (page 166). The curve is vertical during the early years (1860–1880), indicating a rapid improvement. From about 1880 to the present it flattens out, showing a steady but more gradual improvement. The rapid gains during the early years may be attributed to the expanding number of participants. During this time competition began in the schools, and many athletic clubs were organized. Not to be minimized was the psychological effect of maintaining international records, motivating among participants a willingness to break them.

Two landmark performances in track and field include Bob Beamon's 29-ft 2½-in long jump in 1968 (above) and the first mile ever run in less than four minutes, by Roger Bannister (above right) in 1954. The steady improvement in running times can be seen in the graph below.

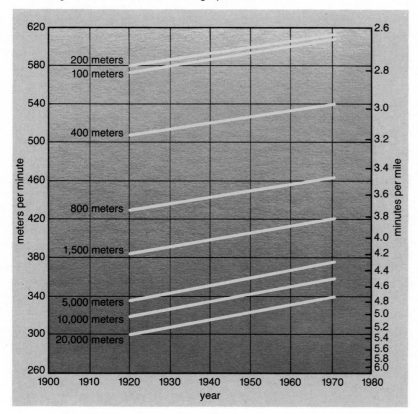

Shirley Babashoff swam the 400-meter freestyle in the 1976 Olympic Games almost two seconds faster than did Don Schollander when he won first place in the 1964 Olympics.

The performance curve among women at present describes the same accelerated improvement as the men's record prior to 1900. This may be attributed to the recent growth of women's sports programs, changing public attitudes about competition for women, the availability of facilities, and the ability to discard certain culturally prescribed values that may run counter to athletic achievement. The rapid rate of improvement may be illustrated by the fact that of the 15 world swimming records approved by the International Amateur Athletic Federation in August 1978, all but 3 were set during that same year. The opposite was true for the men.

Women have displayed outstanding levels of physical achievement. Research has supported the fact that women are different from men anatomically, physiologically, and behaviorally, although there is overlap that exists between the two sexes. Still, some women are swimming faster and running faster in some events than most men in history. For example, in the 1976 Olympic Games both Petra Thumer (East Germany) and Shirley Babashoff (U.S.), with times of 4 min 9.89 sec and 4 min 10.46 sec, respectively, swam faster in the 400-m freestyle than did Don Schollander of the U.S., who set a world record and won a gold medal in the 1964 Olympic Games at Tokyo with a time of 4 min 12.2 sec.

A number of factors appear to have been responsible for the continued record performances during the past 100 years. A few of these include increase in human size, improved training, new technology, medicine, nutrition, and increased leisure and time to train.

Increase in human size

Evidence supports the fact that the size of humans has increased during the past 100 years. For example, researchers have indicated that college-age females today are about one inch taller and males two inches taller than their parents at that same age. The main reason for increased size during the past century would appear to be better nutrition and less illness. These and other factors that have led to a higher standard of living seem to have been more important than genetic causes.

Increased size has influenced an improvement in physical performances from at least two standpoints, a greater mechanical advantage and an increased physiological capacity. In the first case increased size has provided a greater range of motion, and, if the necessary muscle mass exists, it should provide an advantage in the performance of a number of skills. Examples include projecting an implement, running stride range, and leverage in running and jumping. A higher center of gravity resulting from increased size provides advantages in the performance of such skills as high jumping, pole vaulting, and hurdling.

The effects of increased size on physiological capacity can best be explained by considering that measurements of volume (such as body mass and heart stroke volume) increase as the cube of any linear measurement (such as height). Also, measurements of cross-sectional area, such as muscle cross section, increase as the square of any linear measurement. Caution should be exercised in applying geometric scaling, however, because individuals are not geometrically similar.

158

Improved training

There has been a steady increase in scientific research during the past several decades related to preparing the human body for record performances. Accumulation of scientific information, its dissemination through professional journals and clinics, and the professional preparation of coaches in the foundational sciences of physical education have had a marked influence on improved training techniques.

Athletes have progressed from training regimens that reflected ill-founded beliefs to programs tailored to their unique physiological attributes. Competitive sport has passed through the days when weight training was believed to hinder flexibility, and long, low-intensity training sessions were the rule, to training that has been continuously monitored for effects of intensity and duration. Collaboration between coaches, physicians, and other specialists has contributed toward record performances. Training for optimal performance requires an understanding of such factors as training specificity, seasonal requirements, training devices, diet, and training intensity. The training regimens of many outstanding performers display an understanding of theoretical concepts developed from scientific study. These may include the following:

(1) Training involves not only conditioning for the event itself but also for the specific physiological base that supports the event.

(2) Transfer of training does not exist. Training must follow the specific components of the event in every dimension, or time is being wasted.

(3) Work effort is more important than work load.

(4) Training work load must be maintained and gradually increased or a deconditioning effect will occur.

(5) The more highly skilled one becomes during training the greater is the probability of deconditioning.

New technology

New equipment and facility designs have paved the way for improvement in physical performance. These improvements have been of varying importance. They have ranged from the development of the sliding seat in rowing shells to artificial playing surfaces and controlled environments.

Not until the middle of the 1800s did mass production methods help standardize sports equipment. Since that time the ingenuity of inventors and the growing public interest in sport performance have resulted in continued refinements in both equipment and facilities. The most dramatic example of new equipment design influencing record performance was the introduction of the fiberglass pole in pole vaulting. Up until that development in the early 1960s aluminum and bamboo were the principal materials used, and the world record vault was 4.79 m (15 ft 8^1/$_2$ in) by Cornelius Warmerdam (U.S.), in 1943. The adoption of the fiberglass pole allowed changes in the technique, which eventually led to vaults of more than 18 ft. The catapulting technique required less muscular power, and by 1980 high school-aged vaulters had achieved heights of almost 17 ft.

Other equipment has undergone similar changes. Athletes are running in shoes tailored to their specific sport. Lightweight shoes, as well as other

159

Equipment made of new materials has contributed to many record-breaking performances. Before the introduction of the fiberglass pole (top), only Cornelius Warmerdam (top right), using a bamboo pole, had vaulted higher than 15 feet. The flexibility of fiberglass allowed athletes to catapult over 18 feet. Metal cleats on shoes (above left) often caused injuries and so evolved into lighter weight shoes having rubber nubbins.

equipment, have afforded performers greater speed and conservation of energy. Cleated shoes, which contributed to injuries in football and other sports, have been continuously modified. They have evolved into shoes with rubber soles and rubber nubbins molded in tirelike treads. Titanium and graphite have been replacing wood and metals in tennis rackets, and metals are replacing wood in baseball bats; new designs reduce vibrations in both.

The use of synthetic surfacing similar to grass has spread throughout many parts of the world. These carpets have been manufactured in varying pile heights and thicknesses to accommodate specific uses in baseball, football, and other sports. This surface has provided a more predictable bounce to the ball and better footing under adverse weather conditions. It has provided year-round playable surfaces in many places where this was once not possible. Other manufacturers have made use of urethanes, polyvinyl chlorides, and rubber. Such surfaces, like the grasslike carpets, have provided participants with year-round facilities for training and competition.

Building technology has followed the synthetic surface breakthroughs. Inflatable and pre-engineered structures can be built quickly and often are portable. These structures, along with permanent buildings and indoor stadia that provide ideal climatic conditions, have allowed participants every advantage in which to extend themselves toward new levels of performance.

Medicine

Advances in health care practices have lightened the burden of illness from infectious diseases, contributing to a higher level of physical, mental, and social well-being in many parts of the world. Larger numbers of healthier people participating in athletic activity can only promote a higher degree of physical achievement.

But from a different perspective sports produce their own medical problems. Sprains and strains, contusions, fractures, dislocations, abrasions and lacerations, and concussions occur among a high percentage of participants.

160

More and more physicians are turning their efforts toward keeping athletes healthy. According to Allan J. Ryan, a physician and editor of *The Physician and Sportsmedicine,* the most significant advances in sports medicine have occurred during the last 25 years. These advances have been in the areas of diagnosis, therapeutics, and prevention.

In regard to diagnosis the use and practical application of computer systems have allowed prompt feedback of multiple test results. A speedy diagnosis often can be of paramount importance in competitive athletics. Advances in diagnostic techniques have allowed physicians to assess a person's total body strength symmetry and specific muscle group imbalances, both of which may be predictive of injury. By means of physical examinations predictions can be made regarding ideal participation weight as well as safe levels of weight loss.

New diagnostic techniques have resulted in improved assessments of joint and soft-tissue injuries. Arthrograms (X-rays of a joint that has been injected with an opaque substance) have provided a high degree of validity to diagnosis of tissue tears and joint injury in sport. Arthroscopy (examination of the interior of a joint by inserting an endoscope through an incision) allows for a direct visual examination of the knee joint without extensive surgery. Also not to be minimized has been the continuous development of techniques to control infectious disease, thereby reducing the loss of important practice time.

Astrodome in Houston, Texas, was designed to provide athletes with ideal climatic conditions, thereby helping them achieve new levels of performance.

Nutrition

The dependence of physical performance on the physiological mechanisms of the body has been well established. From this standpoint nutrition has played an important role in athletic achievement. Over the years the continuous improvement of the social and economic conditions throughout many parts of the world has contributed to better nutrition for many people. This in turn has had a positive influence on the level of physical attainment in at least three ways: by causing increased growth and reduction in illness, and by contributing an appropriate energy supply for an athlete. The first two have already been discussed. In the case of the third there are two important points to be made. First, the key to improved performance is training. Not only must the individual possess the physiological characteristics to train at a level that will allow him or her to achieve selected standards of performance but the nutritional demands of such training must also be met. In this regard proper nutrition must depend upon training intensity, duration, and the individual's body weight.

The second point concerns the specific characteristics of the event. The nutritional program should be suited to the type of event itself. In East Germany sports physicians and coaches have divided athletic activities into five groups for the purpose of providing sound nutritional programs: (1) cyclical activity such as marathon racing, crew racing, swimming, and cross-country skiing; (2) noncyclical activity such as ice hockey, basketball, and soccer; (3) activities that require quick responses for a very short period of time such as bowling and sailing; (4) jumping and running types of activities such as running races up to and including middle distances, diving, boxing, and pole vaulting; and (5) activities with high demands for an equal amount of reaction, strength, and endurance such as gymnastics, shot put, karate, and hammer throw.

Much has been learned about nutrition as it relates to performance in sports. Many athletic endeavors have been hampered unwittingly by improper diet. For example, hypoglycemia, an inadequate amount of glucose

(Top) Eric Schweikardt—Sports Illustrated; (bottom) Gale Constable—DUOMO

(Top) Tony Triolo—Sports Illustrated; (center) © Joseph F. Viesti; (bottom) Alain DeJean—Sygma

in the blood, affects performance adversely. Also, the feeling of "heavy legs" in a sprinter is caused by the metabolizing of increased amounts of glycogen, which results in the formation of metabolic water. In addition, too large a dosage of salt to compensate for water loss during practice sessions or competition may actually exacerbate the problem of dehydration. As these problems have been dealt with successfully, the result has been improved athletic achievement.

Increased time to train

The enormous increase in leisure time over the past 100 years along with changing attitudes about leisure has had a dramatic influence on physical achievement in sports. This influence has provided increased amounts of time to train and to develop the necessary skills and also afforded time for larger numbers of people to participate, thereby increasing the number of competitive athletes.

As leisure time increased, athletics became a major activity among youth. Sport sociologist John Loy indicated that over 80% of U.S. schools serving the grades from kindergarten through eight support at least one inter-scholastic competitive program. The figures on athletic competition for the young have been impressive, with more than 2,000,000 involved in age-group baseball programs each year. It is estimated that more than 500,000 boys and girls have been participating in age-group swimming.

Why individuals excel

During the past decade many individuals have been studied in the Sport Sciences Laboratory at the University of Denver. They ranged from the very young to Olympic and professional champions. Those who genuinely excelled in their sports appeared to possess a natural endowment that favored one or more of five factors.

The first is an individual's capacity to take up oxygen and to accumulate an oxygen debt during high work loads. Maximum oxygen intake per body weight has been the appropriate measure of an individual's ability to sustain work over a prolonged period of time. A near maximum work stimulus has been imposed in tests on the respiratory and circulatory systems of athletes. Some responded with exceptional results; they appear to have been born with an oxygen-carrying system that is more than adequate.

A second factor is an individual's ability to exert a force explosively. Leg power has been tested by measuring the speed at which an individual moves his or her body weight through a vertical rise or simply by the height of a vertical jump. Outstanding professional football running backs, whose success depends on their ability to get to the point of attack quickly or to accelerate their speed at any time, average about 33 in on the vertical jump test. One professional basketball player had a vertical jump of 46 in. The average college freshman male has a vertical jump of less than 20 in.

Those who excel also appear to have a body structure that favors a mechanical advantage for that activity. For example, the narrow hips of a sprinter provide the mechanical advantage for running a straight line efficiently. The bowed legs of a football running back favor greater than average

164

lateral mobility. There appears to be a process of natural selection. That is, the higher up the ladder of athletic achievement one advances, the greater the importance of this factor. Among outstanding performers in many activities researchers have found great similarities in body type occurring within each event.

A fourth factor is a mature sensory feedback system. The ability of an athlete to direct, adjust, and coordinate his or her movements appears to be a characteristic of those who are highly skilled, especially in fine motor performance. Tests have included measurements of accuracy, steadiness, sensitivity to specific tasks, position judgment, response times, and visual processing skills. Such measures have been viewed in terms of movements that are parts of specific sport skills.

Used as synonymous with the term "athletic intelligence," the fifth factor is fluid intelligence. It relates to an athlete's ability to see the relationships between the parts and the whole, and to interpret and solve problems. These factors represent important aspects of physical performances in which strategy and value judgments must be applied. In tests given to members of the men's and women's 1972 Olympic ski teams a very high positive relationship was found between those who scored highest in the area of fluid intelligence and those who were the most successful racers.

At least one other factor appears to be related to those best suited for physical achievement. That is the ability of the individual to function in a stress-related environment. The degree to which an individual is able to cope with the stress associated with a competitive event relates to many of his or her past and present experiences. In this way an individual's perceptions, attitudes, emotions, and motivations represent learned patterns of behavior that help shape the final physical achievement.

Large numbers of young people participate in sports, some beginning intensive training in a specialty at an early age. The great increase in leisure time during the last century has helped make this possible.

Have the limits been reached?

In some activities such as men's running events, new records have recently been set so gradually and by such small amounts of time that many believe that in this sport at least man has reached the outer limits of his physical capabilities. The improvement in the times of men's running events during the past 50 years is illustrated in the chart on page 157. This graph presents data plotting record performances from the 100-m dash to the 42,200-m run. The graph line indicates slow progress during this period.

Throughout many parts of the world the trend has been to help individuals achieve higher levels of physical performance by the application of sports sciences. Training centers have been established and financed by national governments, most notably in East Germany and the Soviet Union. Since the 1976 Olympic Games the U.S. and some Western European countries have also established such facilities.

For the future it seems likely that athletes working in a laboratory with scientists will be the new frontier of sports. Young, physiologically mature males and females may run on treadmills as physiologists determine how efficiently their bodies are using oxygen. Others may undergo muscle biopsies by physicians to determine their muscle-fiber composition. And specialists in the science of kinanthropometry may take precise measurements of

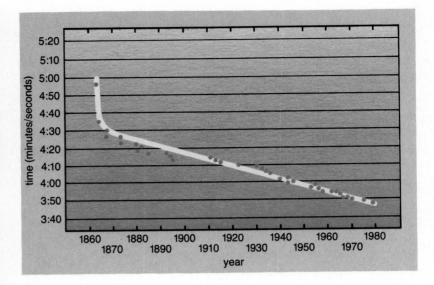

Starting technique of a luge racer (above) is tested in a laboratory. By using two cameras, as many as 30 light-emitting diodes taped to the athlete's body at various points, and a special computer program, the researcher is able to perform a three-dimensional motion analysis. The plywood ramp simulates the starting gate. The graph at the top right reveals the steady lowering of times for the one-mile run from 1860 to 1980.

body-segment proportionality. Combined with psychological data, these measures provide an individualized profile describing an athlete's suitability for a specific sport. An athlete's work in such a sport sciences laboratory will take on added importance with the growing realization that no ideal training exists for all sprinters or all marathon runners. The duration, intensity, and frequency of training must be based on each athlete's unique characteristics in order to guarantee best results.

In pursuit of record achievements athletes will have even greater incentives than in the past. The continued unbridled nationalism of the Olympic Games generates the major impetus for national interest in athletic achievement. More and more nations seem likely to follow the lead of the Eastern Europeans in providing government subsidization of sports.

Women should continue to improve at a faster rate than men, at least through the year 2000. The difference in athletic performance between the top men and women will decrease in some events, with the smallest difference—less than 10%—expected in swimming. Women's events in international competition are likely to take on added significance, which will lead to increased national support for outstanding female performers.

As with the men, when the international emphasis on the women's competitive programs increases, there will be a pressure to get a "competitive edge." This may lead to an increased use of amphetamines and androgenic steroids as well as newly discovered drugs. In this regard the verification of sex of women will be emphasized to a much greater extent than when first adopted for all females in the 1968 Summer Olympic Games. Studying the sexual chromatin on X-type chromosomes and the fluorescent tests of Y-type chromosomes will be supplemented with tests for use of drugs and blood doping.

International competition in sport is likely to reach such a level that drug monitoring will be given special attention by international governing bodies. Biochemical research will be stepped up to develop new and practical methods for detecting the use of drugs by athletes. An increased international

166

educational effort will be made to show the long-range harmful effects of certain drugs.

By the year 2000 it seems likely that a process of natural selection will become increasingly evident. Scientific, medical, and technological advances as well as such sociological trends as athletes marrying athletes will contribute to the continued physiological improvement of humans. The world standards in athletic achievement are likely to improve accordingly.

The applications of computer science in sports seem certain to reach an even more sophisticated level and play an important role in future athletic achievement. Computer terminals will generate daily updated training regimens for each athlete. These regimens will represent optimal training based on each athlete's physiological and psychological assessment by a sport sciences laboratory as well as on his or her response to the previously prescribed training. Energy expenditure data will also be processed and a daily dietary recommendation made that will facilitate the specific energy requirements of training. Computer simulation techniques that will predict performance as a result of an athlete's changes in technique and application of force will also be part of training.

The standard of living in most parts of the world should continue to rise. As a result, it would seem that humans will continue to grow larger. Physiologically, this would serve to increase human physical work capacity as well as to improve upon the oxygen delivery to the muscle tissue per unit of time. Other physiological functions would improve as well. This should result in a continued improvement in performances requiring strength, endurance, and power. And, under the right conditions, there will continue to be occasional exceptional performances. These will exceed existing records to the same degree as those exceptional feats of Jesse Owens and Bob Beamon. Then, as now, the question as to the limits of human physical performance will still be pondered.

In award ceremonies at the 1936 Olympic Games Jesse Owens of the United States (center on platform) receives the gold medal for his record-breaking long jump of 26 feet 5⁵/₁₆ inches. Second was Luz Long of Germany (right), and third was Naoto Tajima of Japan.

Fractals and the Geometry of Nature

by Benoit B. Mandelbrot

Guided by the mathematics underlying a recently revived family of "monstrous" geometric shapes, computer drawing machines are producing realistic representations of some familiar but grossly irregular patterns in nature.

Before beginning to understand what fractals are, one should know what they look like. The reader is therefore asked to begin this article with a careful examination of its illustrations and to read the captions only after the introduction below.

Now pay special attention to figure 1, at right. It does not represent what it may seem to. It is neither a photograph of a landscape on the Earth, the Moon, or any other planet, nor is it a painting by a science fiction artist. None of the illustrations in this article represents any actual facet of nature, and none is what is ordinarily called a work of art. All are guaranteed 100% geometric fakes. They are computer-generated and computer-plotted representations of selected members of the family of purely geometric shapes called fractals.

*Figure 1 (overleaf): a fractal
landscape that never was.*

Fractal geometry can imitate nature

The illustrated fractal shapes are really very simple in the sense that every one of their details has been deduced unambiguously from a few lines of instruction given to the computers that drew them. These shapes are extremely involved, however, and are strikingly unlike anything in the familiar discipline of classical geometry, or "Euclid." The new fractal geometry that they exemplify is very different from Euclid. Especially conspicuous is the fact that the number of dimensions, or dimensionality, of a fractal may be a fraction. This idea is by no means "geometry fiction" but part of a chapter of mathematics that is classical but was obscure until recently for lack of widely interesting applications.

The applicability of fractal geometry in describing some grossly irregular and fragmented facets of nature is so strikingly evident from the illustrations that it is reasonable to wonder why it had not been heard of before 1975, when this author's first comprehensive publication on fractals introduced the term and marked the founding of the discipline. For, had it been founded earlier, though doubtlessly under a different name, it would have filled an obvious need for describing some of many conspicuous natural patterns—including the shapes of mountains, coastlines, and clouds—at which the straight lines, circles, ellipses, squares, and other components of classical geometry are almost completely inept.

The answer is a hard-to-believe tale of extreme self-delusion on the part of many great minds over a full century. "Fractional dimension" and several other basic components later to be fitted into the system of fractal geometry had been known to mathematicians and to a few scientists and philosophers since the period 1875–1925 but were knowingly left to remain as unrelated odds and ends of specialized consequence. No one favored them with careful attention because they were believed to deserve none; hence no one even felt the need of a word to denote them.

Some unexpectedly simple shapes

Before touching again on history, it will be helpful to contrast some fractal shapes with those in Euclid. The circle, the square, the sphere, and the cube are the very simplest Euclidean shapes because, position aside, one needs only one parameter to describe any of them; say, a diameter or a diagonal length. Any alternative parameter is merely a fixed multiple of the one chosen as a base. A circle is simpler than a square because it involves fewer position parameters. A rectangle, an ellipse, or several circles strung shish-kebab style involve only two parameters. In addition, it is obvious that each of the parameters required by these examples is a scale of length.

This last feature leads to a strong temptation to identify the notions of scale and of parameter and to conclude that a geometric shape which is simple to describe must also involve few distinct scales of length. However, fractal illustrations suffice to demonstrate that this temptation has no merit at all. To take an example, the fake mountain view in figure 1 includes identifiable hills and hillocks of every conceivable scale, between barely perceptible ones and ones that nearly fill the picture. If the picture were more finely grained, an even wider range of hill sizes would be seen. On the

BENOIT B. MANDELBROT *is IBM
Fellow at the Thomas J. Watson
Research Center, Yorktown Heights,
New York, and a Visiting Professor of
Mathematics at Harvard University.*

*Illustrations implemented on computer
by Richard F. Voss (figures 1 and 5),
Mark R. Laff (figures 2, 3, 6, and 7),
and Sigmund W. Handelman (figures 3
and 4) of the IBM Thomas J. Watson
Research Center.*

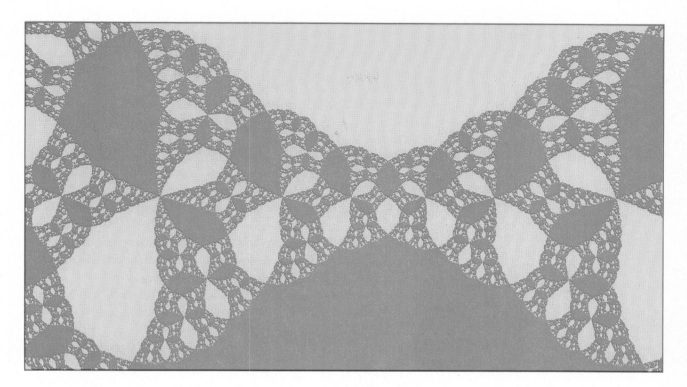

Figure 2: a fractal attractor.

other hand, only three parameters suffice to identify this mountain scene within a certain colossal "portfolio" of alternative scenes to which it belongs. (Not counted are the parameters that control the angles of lighting and of observation.) Furthermore, only one of the three parameters is related to length: it doubles when altitudes of the landscape double.

The second parameter, denoted D, is the most interesting and the most important one. In the case of surfaces it lies between two and three. Its most obvious role in the construction of these landscapes is to control the relative numbers of large and small hills: when D is close to two, the scene has a huge hill with tiny pimples, while when D is close to three, the scene contains many middling hills with barely a trace of a large one. The term denoted by D is "fractal dimension," which demands some explanation. D differs from the standard view of dimension as the number of distinct coordinates needed to specify a point in space. For instance, on a straight line one needs but a single coordinate to identify a point; on a plane or a landscape one needs two coordinates. The notion of dimension, however, has more than one meaning, and fractals are characterized by the fact that different definitions of dimension yield distinct numerical values. (This issue is discussed further in the box on pp. 176–177.)

The third and last parameter, called "random seed" or "chance," is best thought of as a scene's page number in the portfolio of alternatives mentioned above. The notion of chance in this sense is a subtle one. Ordinarily a game of, say, 1,000 coin tosses is viewed as a sequence of 1,000 independent chance events, each the outcome of one coin toss. But one can also imagine that there exists somewhere a big book of 2^{1000} pages (a number greater than 1 followed by 300 zeros), in which the progress of each possible outcome of 1,000 coin tosses is recorded on a separate page. Thus, any game of 1,000 tosses can be specified by selecting a page in this book. The parameter of chance is simply the page number so selected. Landscapes are a more complicated story, but again the computer program responsible for such fractals as figure 1 has a finite number of conceivable outcomes. The specific figure that one obtains depends on a number that one gives in advance, called "seed," which can be viewed as a page number in a virtual portfolio of different landscapes.

Some of the preceding assertions may be clarified by examining their counterparts in the case of other fractals—notably of the snowflake curve in figure 3 on p. 173. Whereas a computer that is programmed to draw a circle will perform that single task and then stop, a typical fractal-drawing computer is programmed to loop endlessly. In other words, after it has performed a simple task assigned to it and has finished drawing a curve with a limited amount of detail, it immediately starts again to perform the same task on a smaller scale of length, thus adding more detail—and so on to infinity. The ratio r between the scales involved in successive stages enters into the principal parameter, D, characteristic of such pattern-generation loops. For the snowflake curve this parameter is 1.26; for variants of the snowflake it lies between one and two and is again a fractal dimension. Endless looping is the trick that makes it possible for geometric shapes that involve many scales of lengths to be counted among the simplest in geometry. Thus, the product of an interrupted loop that stops after a finite number of steps is, paradoxically, less simple than that of an endless loop: to be able to know when to stop, the drawing program must include an additional signal; *i.e.,* one more parameter, such as a counter or a smallest scale.

It will be noticed that in loop-generated fractals, successive scales of length fall in a discrete, geometric sequence. This is an undesirable and unnatural feature in most cases in which one seeks a faithful model of nature, but it vanishes in such other fractals as fake mountains, whose scales are continuously governed by the chance parameter. When a loop is absent, a shape is typically extremely smooth. When a purely repetitive loop is present, a shape is typically extremely rough and irregular and in some cases also fragmented into separate islandlike pieces. These extremes happen to be much simpler than intermediate shapes of moderate irregularity.

Taming the mathematical monsters

This author's search for a word to denote the fake mountains, loop-generated curves, and their kin eventually led to coining the term fractal. The word is related to the Latin verb *frangere,* which means "to break." In the Roman mind, *frangere* may have evoked the action of breaking a stone, since the adjective derived from it combines the two most obvious properties of broken stones, irregularity and fragmentation. This adjective is *fractus,* which led to fractal. Eventually this author proposed a precise definition of the mathematical term fractal set (see box). The etymological kinship with "fraction" is also significant if one interprets "fraction" as a number that lies between integers. Indeed, a fractal set can be considered as lying between the shapes of Euclid.

3a: four stages in the construction of the Koch snowflake

3b: four stages in the construction of a snowflake sweep

3c: rounded approximations of 3a and 3b, superposed

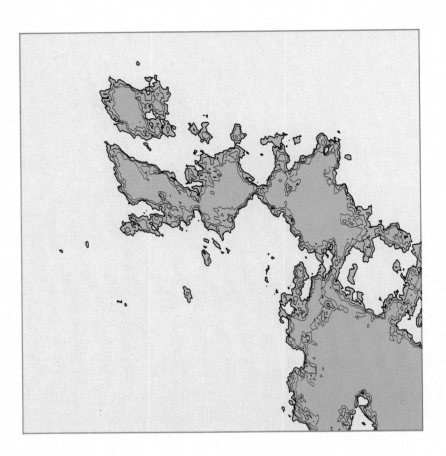

The reason for coining the term fractal and founding fractal geometry
was well stated by Freeman J. Dyson in the journal *Science*:

"Fractal" is a word invented by Mandelbrot to bring together under one heading a
large class of objects that have [played an] . . . historical role . . . in the development
of pure mathematics. A great revolution of ideas separates the classical mathematics
of the 19th century from the modern mathematics of the 20th. Classical mathematics
had its roots in the regular geometric structures of Euclid and the continuously
evolving dynamics of Newton. Modern mathematics began with Cantor's set theory
and Peano's space-filling curve. Historically, the revolution was forced by the discovery of mathematical structures that did not fit the patterns of Euclid and Newton.
These new structures were regarded by contemporary mathematicians as "pathological." They were described as a "gallery of monsters," kin to the cubist painting and
atonal music that were upsetting established standards of taste in the arts at about
the same time. The mathematicians who created the monsters regarded them as
important in showing that the world of pure mathematics contains a richness of
possibilities going far beyond the simple structures that they saw in nature. Twen-
tieth-century mathematics flowered in the belief that it had transcended completely
the limitations imposed by its natural origins.

Now, as Mandelbrot points out [in his book, *Fractals*] . . . nature has played a joke
on the mathematicians. The 19th-century mathematicians may have been lacking in
imagination, but nature was not. The same pathological structures that the mathematicians invented to break loose from 19th-century naturalism turn out to be
inherent in familiar objects all around us in nature.

Thus, the theory of fractals is not properly an application of 20th-century
mathematics, but the sudden revival and belated blooming of odds and ends

174

not intended to become a theory. In the 20th century more so than in preceding ones, mathematics is influenced and often dominated by the search for generality for its own sake. The results that this search achieves (for example, the properties true of all curves) are typically of little use in science. Science had exhausted the old curves of Euclid and was in dire need of new ones, but it needed curves that are sufficiently special to have interesting properties subject to comparison with natural phenomena. Mathematics of intermediate generality created around 1900 involved a cache of curves and other shapes that the "mainstream" had leapfrogged much too hastily, and fractal geometry is the new discipline that is being built around this cache.

The fact that mathematics, viewed by its own creators as "absolutely pure," should respond so well to the needs of science is striking and surprising but follows a well-worn pattern. That pattern was first set when Johannes Kepler concluded that, to model the path of Mars around the Sun, one must resort to an intellectual plaything of the Greeks—the ellipse. Soon after, Galileo concluded that, to model the fall of bodies toward the Earth, one needs a different curve—a parabola. And he proclaimed that "the great book [of nature] . . . is written in mathematical language and the characters are triangles, circles and other geometric figures . . . without which one wanders in vain through a dark labyrinth." In the pithy words of Scottish biologist D'Arcy Thompson: "God always geometrizes." With the advent of fractal geometry, the meanings of further geometric "characters" have been revealed, and a few more pages of the great book of nature have become understandable.

Selected facets of fractals are discussed below in descriptions of the illustrations and in a separate box.

Figure 1: a fractal landscape that never was

In order to determine the degree of validity of a scientific principle, scientists seek formulas that follow from this principle and compare them with empirical formulas derived from actual observations. The correspondence between the fractal model used to generate this mountainous relief and real mountains can be shown to be surprisingly excellent given the model's simplicity. By contrast, other mathematical models of landscape that compete with fractal landscapes lead to drawings remote from reality.

This figure is an example of an unsystematic, or random, fractal. Formally it is a "truncated fractional Brownian surface" of fractal dimension $D = 2.3$. The word truncated simply means that at all points where the mathematical model called for altitude below some threshold value labeled as zero, the altitude was arbitrarily reset to zero. In the illustration these points appear as depressions filled with water. The meaning of the word fractional is technical; it refers to a smoothing operation applied to a markedly rough surface, called a Brownian surface, to make it more in conformity with a natural Earth landscape. The word Brownian calls attention to the fact that each vertical cross section of a Brownian surface is a Brownian function: very nearly a random walk that steps up or down with equal probability independently of its past steps.

175

Self-similarity and fractal dimension

A straight line segment has a property that is self-evident but deserves to be set out as the basis of a later generalization. Given any integer N, a segment of length L is the sum (union) of N straight segments of length $r = L/N$, each of which can be obtained from the original segment by a similarity of ratio r, with an appropriate focal point. In the same vein a square of side L is the same as the sum of N^2 squares of side $r = L/N$, each of which can be obtained from the original by a similarity of ratio r. The line segment and the square are therefore described as being self-similar entities, and all line segments and squares are simply reduced or enlarged replicas of each other. In Euclid, all self-similar shapes are deducible to the above examples; hence self-similarity is not an especially useful notion. Fractals, however, can be self-similar in a truly overwhelming variety of ways. For example, each third of the snowflake curve in figure 3 is self-similar. It is made of four replicas of itself reduced in the ratio $r = 1/3$.

For the rare self-similar figures in Euclid it is easy to see that the ratio $D = \log N / \log (1/r)$—*i.e.*, the logarithm of N divided by the logarithm of $1/r$—is identical to the figure's dimension, which is one for curves like straight lines and circles and two for planar domains like the interior of a square. The same ratio also deserves to be considered for fractal self-similar shapes. But the values it yields are most surprising. For the snowflake curve, $D = \log 4 / \log 3 = 1.26\ldots$, which is a fraction! And for the snowflake sweep in figure 3, a more general formula (slightly more involved than a ratio of logarithms and applicable when the reduction ratios of the parts are not all the same) yields $D = 2$, which reflects the property of the planar domain that the curve fills rather than its curvelike nature.

More generally, the property of a geometric shape that is revealed by D is something that one may informally call "heft." Progressing from shapes

Figure 2: a fractal attractor

The boundary of the blue-colored region in this illustration, meant to contrast with the previous one, is an example of a very systematic (though very complex) fractal curve. The rationale behind it involves dynamic physical systems. A physical system may have a stable attractive point, meaning a point to which it converges in due time and to which it returns if disturbed. For example, a marble tossed into an upright funnel will tend toward a stable point at the funnel's neck. A physical system may also have a stable attractive cycle; say, a circle or an ellipse. The planets and satellites of the solar system, for instance, have established stable, nearly elliptical orbits around their parent bodies. However, dynamic systems whose attractors are points or near circular cycles or other Euclidean shapes are exceptions, and the behavior of most dynamic systems is incomparably more complicated. Viewed in terms of fractal geometry, a remarkable finding by the mathematicians Henri Poincaré (circa 1885) and Pierre Fatou and Gaston Julia (circa 1918) can be expressed by saying that, save for certain simple exceptions, attractors are fractals.

of lower dimension to those of higher dimension, a square is heftier than a line segment, and a cube heftier than a square. From the viewpoint of heft, fractals prove by simple construction that a shape can well lie between standard values of dimension.

But heft does not exhaust all the nuances of dimension. For example, the top third of the snowflake curve has the same kind of connectedness that a straight line segment has: if a few points are deleted from it, it breaks into disconnected pieces. Consequently, mathematicians say that for both the straight line and the snowflake curve the topological dimension is one. It is apparent that this value coincides with the number of coordinates needed to identify a point on either of these curves. The mathematician Georg Cantor, however, demonstrated that identifying dimension with numbers of coordinates is a treacherous notion, and modern mathematics prefers to stress the topological facet of dimension. In a similar manner, instead of noting that a plane or a landscape requires two coordinates in order to identify a point on it, mathematicians stress that both figures possess a topological dimension of two because either can be disconnected by deleting curves from it.

It should be clear that dimension is a notion more delicate than first appearances would indicate. Its dissection into distinct facets is of practical significance, and the author therefore was led to define a fractal set (the entire family of fractal shapes) as being a mathematical set such that D is greater than the topological dimension, D_T. In mathematical symbols, $D > D_T$. To describe fractals requires a number of different parameters, but the topological dimension, D_T, and the fractal dimension calculated as $\log N / \log (1/r)$, or by more general formulas when needed, are the crucial parameters.

Among the many reasons why this finding remained little known (and interest in this topic waned for half a century) is that the original papers are difficult and devoid of illustrations: fractal attractors are very difficult to draw. The few examples laboriously produced about 1885 keep being reproduced seemingly without recognition that they are incorrect and quite misleading. Drawing fractals is a task for computer graphics, as exemplified by the figure, which is excerpted from a varied and extensive collection developed in the course of the author's most recent research.

Figure 3: the Koch snowflake and a snowflake sweep

While the main display for these figures is shown in 3c, the more sober figures 3a and 3b give a clearer idea of the constructions. In order to construct the snowflake (3a), a shape derived by H. von Koch, one begins with an equilateral triangle with sides one unit long. Next, one attaches to the external middle of each side an equilateral triangle of side $r = 1/3$. Then one attaches to the middle of each side a triangle of side r^2, and so on. The "skin" of the snowflake is called a snowflake curve. A striking characteristic is that

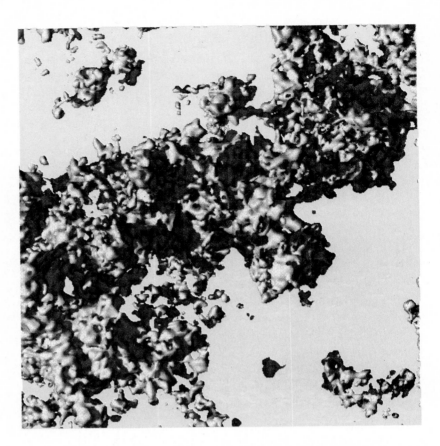

Figure 5: fractal clouds that never were.

its ultimate length is infinite: each time a new series of triangles is attached, the skin's length is multiplied by $^4/_3$. A related fact is that the curve has no tangent at any point. For example, try to draw a tangent at a corner point by drawing the chord which joins this point to another point on the curve that moves increasingly close to the first. It is apparent that this chord oscillates endlessly (within an angle of 30°) without even settling down to a limit one would call a tangent to the snowflake curve.

Is not a curve that has infinite length and is devoid of tangents too bizarre for words or for applications? The theory of fractals advances and defends the opposite view, as is discussed below in figure 4.

In order to construct the snowflake sweep (3b), a curve devised by the author, one starts with a string of length one. Then one stretches and pulls it into a 13-segment shape, called the generator, that fills a regular triangle reasonably uniformly and in any event passes at a distance that is less than $^1/(_2\sqrt{3}) = 0.2886\ldots$ from any point in the triangle. Then one stretches and pulls each segment of this generator into a reduced-size version of the whole, thus filling a star hexagon more uniformly than in the preceding stage, by a curve that passes at a distance less than $^1/_{12}$ from any point in this hexagon. And as one repeats the same stretching and pulling, the construction converges to a curve that comes infinitely close to any point within the snowflake (3a) described above.

The fact that a curve can be contrived to fill an area of a plane was first demonstrated by Giuseppe Peano using a different example. Yet, granted

178

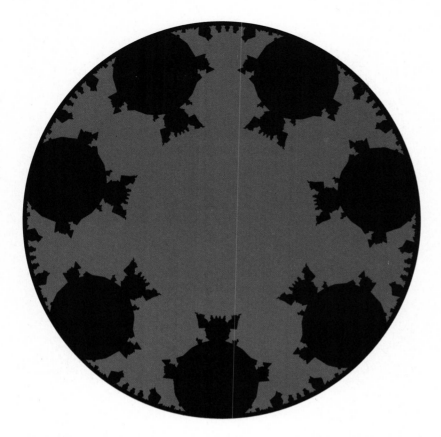

Figure 6: a seven-headed Poincaré
fractal curve.

that one can achieve such a monstrous goal in theory, is it not clear that the
outcome cannot be anything but extravagant and contrary to all intuition?
The theory of fractals shows otherwise. As evidence, figure 3c shows variations of stages of construction of the snowflake curve and snowflake sweep,
each being smoothed out by replacing every line segment by an arc, namely
$1/6$ of a circle. In the variant stages of the snowflake curve, these arcs all bow
inward, but in the snowflake sweep stages they bow toward the side along
which the next stage of construction will occur. In the resulting pattern one
may well find it possible to sense branching trees, licking tongues of fire, and
other familiar patterns of nature. In particular, if narrower lines are laid
along the middles of the red-colored "fingers," one obtains a branching
pattern bearing a strong resemblance to river networks. And this similarity
emphasizes the basic requirement of a river network that drains some area
effectively: that its cumulative shore should pass within a very small distance of every point of the area to be drained.

(The second stage of rounded approximation in figure 3c awaits a "fractal-
man" to adopt it as his symbol.)

Figure 4: map of a country that never was

This illustration is made up of selected contour lines of a fractional Brownian relief constructed along the same principle as figure 1.

How long is the coast of Britain? This is a deceptively simple question to
which the curves in figures 3 and 4 call attention. There is no need to seek

179

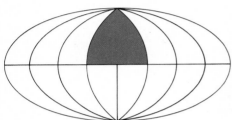

Figure 7: one-eighth of a sky that never was (above right). In the accompanying map (above) the celestial sphere centered on the Earth is projected on a plane. Shaded portion corresponds to the illustrated region of fractal sky.

the answer in an encyclopedia, because a little thought shows that the only sensible answer is "it depends." For example, when the length is measured by walking a compass or dividers along a coastline it is obvious that the result of the measurement depends on how far apart the legs are set: the less broadly they are opened, the better they take account of fine details of coastline and the longer the coastline length they yield.

If a coastline's shape extends to endlessly small detail by self-similarity (*i.e.*, if the irregularity of a coastline segment of any size is the same as that of a segment of any other size), then as the dividers' opening tends to zero, the total measured length will tend to infinity. This behavior exemplifies a surprisingly common phenomenon. When mathematicians concluded about a century ago that the seemingly simple and innocuous notion of "curve" hides profound difficulties, they thought that they were engaging in unreasonable and unrealistic hairsplitting. They had not determined to look out at the real world to analyze it, but to look in at an ideal in the mind. The theory of fractals shows that they had misled themselves.

Figure 5: fractal clouds that never were

The construction of this illustration bears many similarities to that of the fractal landscape in figure 1. The figure is again a fractional Brownian surface that can be thought to represent all points in a three-dimensional space, such as that filled by the Earth's atmosphere, at which the temperature equals 0° C (32° F), the freezing temperature of water. Following this interpretation, the surface bounds a region in the atmosphere that allows the formation and existence of clouds of ice crystals.

180

Figure 6: a seven-headed Poincaré fractal curve

Much of the caption describing figure 2 applies as well to this curve, which is also a fractal attractor, although of another kind. Its main characteristic is that it is not self-similar, as are the other illustrated figures. Instead it is self-inverse; that is, unchanged by geometric inversion with respect to any of 14 circles.

Figure 7: one-eighth of a sky that never was

Fractal "dusts" of totally disconnected points play a central role in fractal models of the distribution of stars in the Galaxy and of galaxies in the universe. Such dusts are variants of a celebrated mathematical monster called Cantor set. The creators of early models of the sky, not realizing that they were dealing with Cantor sets, largely operated by trial and error. The theory of fractals not only explains the early models but also allows present modeling to proceed systematically in full knowledge of what is actually being done.

In this figure, the distribution of stars is part of a planar projection of the sky, which is a sphere centered on the Earth. The map covers the portion of the Northern Hemisphere between the longitudes $-45°$ and $+45°$. In the illustration it takes the form of an ogive shape colored a dark blue. The "stars" distributed throughout it have been generated according to a model developed by the author; the principal mathematical input of the model consists of several parameters, of which the main one is the estimated fractal dimension of natural stellar distribution in the Galaxy.

FOR ADDITIONAL READING

Benoit B. Mandelbrot, "Getting Snowflakes into Shape," *New Scientist* (June 22, 1978, pp. 808–810).

Benoit B. Mandelbrot, *Fractals: Form, Chance, and Dimension* (W. H. Freeman, 1977).

Martin Gardner, "Mathematical Games," *Scientific American* (November 1976, pp. 132–136, and April 1978, pp. 16–32).

The Search for Gravitational Waves
by Barry Parker

Exploding stars and other cosmic objects undergoing violent change should exhibit detectable ripples in their gravitational fields. Reliable detection of this phenomenon may usher in a new branch of astronomy.

In 1969 Joseph Weber, a physicist working at the University of Maryland, reported experimental results that gave cause for jubilation among scientists around the world. If proved true this find would be the most important of the decade—perhaps of the past 50 years. But, as with all discoveries, confirmation was important before the results could be accepted, and soon several similar experiments were set up. Within a few years, however, it was evident that confirmation was not forthcoming: no one could duplicate Weber's results.

From a record of what he termed coincidence events, Weber believed that he had detected gravitational waves. Whether he actually succeeded, he must be given credit for igniting a spark that may soon flare into an entirely new branch of astronomy—gravitational wave astronomy. Most scientists in the field are confident that the waves will eventually be found and that they will become an important tool in astronomy. But as physicist Richard Price of the University of Utah commented, "It may take a lot of money and more time than we would like."

One major reason for optimism is the widespread faith in the existence of the waves. A simple argument is likely to persuade one of their abundance even on Earth. Consider an object falling to the surface of the Earth. The distribution of the Earth's mass will change as a result of the fall. The change may be exceedingly small; nevertheless it will cause a slight change in the Earth's gravitational field, as measured from any point in the universe. This change cannot be detected instantaneously at each measuring point; something has to carry information about the change. In essence, a disturbance of the field must propagate outward from the Earth to effect the change. This disturbance is a gravitational wave.

X-ray picture of the Crab supernova remnant (opposite page), taken by the Earth-orbiting satellite HEAO 2 (Einstein Observatory), displays a prominent bright spot corresponding to the Crab pulsar, a source of potentially detectable gravitational waves. The inset shows a test fixture used to develop a laser interferometer for detecting gravitational waves.

H. Tananbaum et al., Harvard-Smithsonian Center for Astrophysics; (inset) courtesy, Robert L. Forward; photo by Robert Reed, Hughes Aircraft

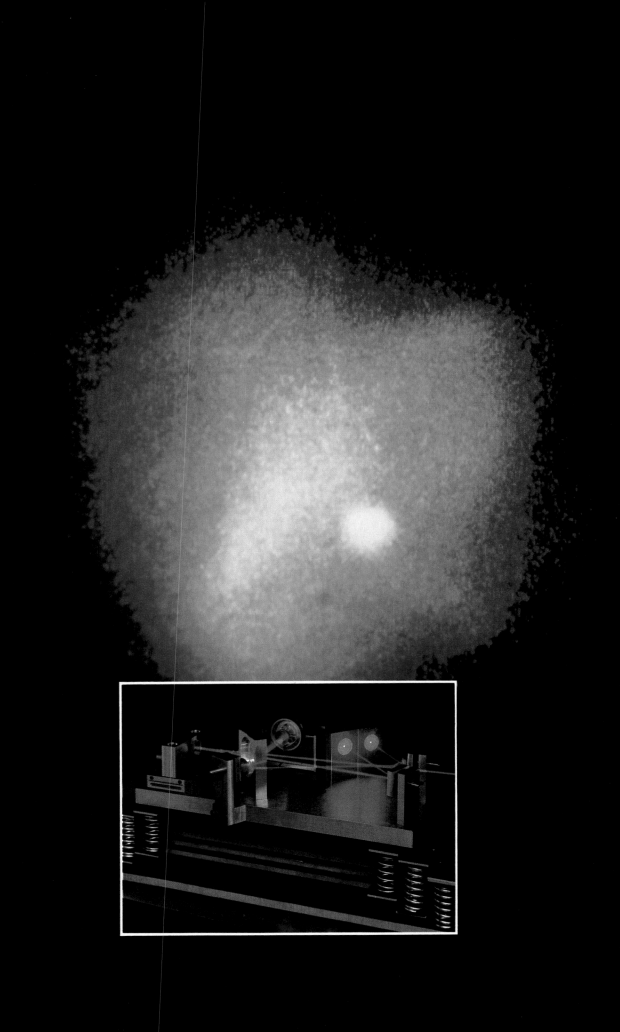

Courtesy, David K. Lynch, Hughes Research Laboratories

The first gravitational wave antenna, built by Joseph Weber and co-workers, stands on display near a photograph of Albert Einstein at the Smithsonian Institution in Washington, D.C. (above). A comparison of the natures of electromagnetic and gravitational waves (opposite page) is detailed in the text at right.

BARRY PARKER *is Professor of Physics and Astronomy at Idaho State University, Pocatello.*

Illustrations by John Youssi

Predictions and properties

Although the simple argument above may indicate that gravitational waves should exist, it reveals almost nothing about their nature. It is within the context of general relativity that their characteristics emerge. Gravitational waves were, in fact, predicted by Albert Einstein shortly after he published his work on general relativity in 1916. He found that they should be given off by matter whenever it was subject to acceleration. As a first example, Einstein calculated the expected intensity for a rotating rod. The numbers were disappointingly low—far too low to be measurable. He then turned to stellar binary systems, for two stars in orbit around one another would also be a source of the waves. But again his calculations, which were based on binaries then known, showed that the wave intensity would be too low to be measurable. The stars would have to be exceedingly dense and close to one another for significant emission. And, of course, in the early years of the 20th century the compact, but massive stars known as white dwarfs were just being discovered.

Within a few years scientists became skeptical of gravitational waves. Many believed that they were just an artifice of the mathematics and most likely had no physical reality. This point of view continued for several decades, but by the mid-1950s it was shown that the arguments against them were based on a defective analysis and consequently were incorrect.

To understand gravitational waves better, it will be helpful to consider electromagnetic waves. Electromagnetic waves are generated by accelerating electric charges. For example, when an electron moves back and forth along an antenna, an electromagnetic wave propagates into space. This wave possesses a number of properties: it has a wavelength (the distance between equivalent points of the wave), it carries energy, and it is polarized. A polarized wave possesses a preferred orientation in its direction of vibration. Moreover, the wave from the antenna belongs to a class of waves called dipole waves. Such waves vibrate in a single plane, called the plane of polarization, perpendicular to their line of travel.

Gravitational waves are, according to theory, similar to electromagnetic waves in many respects, but quite different in others. Like electromagnetic waves they are generated by accelerating objects, but the objects need not be charged. The only requirement is that the objects have mass. Gravitational waves are extremely weak compared with electromagnetic waves, and accelerations of exceedingly large masses are needed if the waves are to be detectable. Also, as in the case of electromagnetic waves, gravitational waves have a wavelength, carry energy, are polarized, and travel at the speed of light. Unlike electromagnetic waves, though, they are not dipole in nature. The simplest gravitational waves allowed by theory are quadrupole waves. Waves of this type have two planes of polarization, both of which are perpendicular to the direction of travel.

A simple example illustrates the difference between the two cases. Consider an electromagnetic wave striking a cloud of charged particles. As it passes through the cloud the particles move back and forth in the plane of polarization of the wave. At any given time, in a sufficiently small region, they are all moving in the same direction. On the other hand, when a

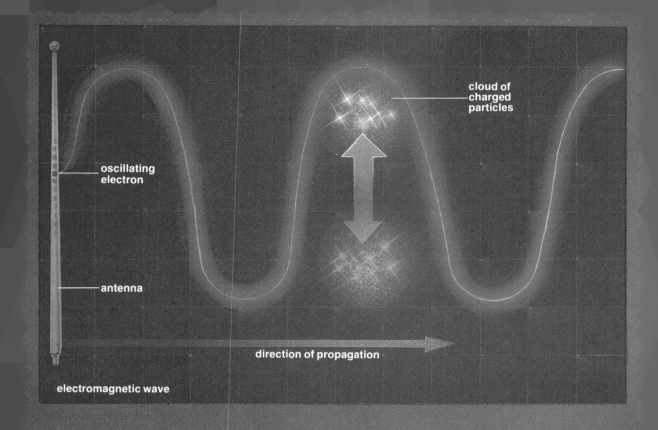

cloud of
charged
particles

oscillating
electron

antenna

direction of propagation

electromagnetic wave

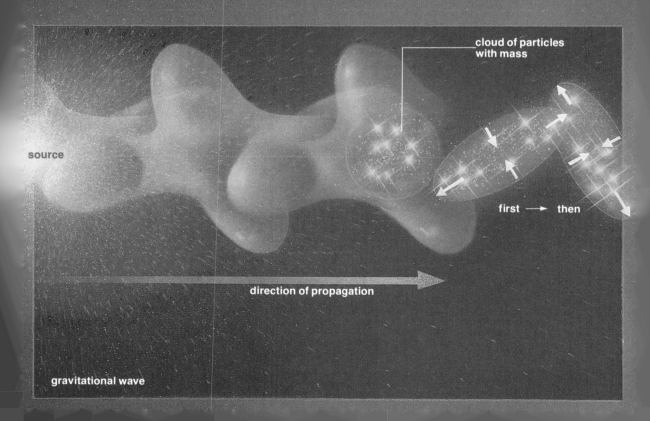

cloud of particles
with mass

source

first → then

direction of propagation

gravitational wave

Weber's refinements to his original room-temperature resonant antenna include a low-temperature variety, cooled in a special chamber to reduce unwanted motion of the metal cylinder due to heat.

gravitational wave encounters a cloud of particles, the motion is quite different. If an observer takes one of the particles as a reference, particles to the right and left may both be moving toward it, while particles above and below will be moving away from it. A moment later their roles will be interchanged. In other words, there will be motion in two planes, the two planes of polarization.

Weber's experiments

Joseph Weber began looking into the possibility of detecting gravitational waves in the late 1950s, when almost nothing was known about detector design. Most of his colleagues thought there was little chance of detecting them, but a number of them encouraged him. One of the first problems he had to overcome was related to the size of the waves. Gravitational waves are given off by all oscillating objects, and the waves in turn produce slight oscillations in objects they encounter. On this basis it might seem that detector design would be relatively simple; all that would be needed is an appropriate object — for instance, a bar — and the instrumentation necessary to monitor its vibrations. Unfortunately, all matter responds to gravitational waves in the same way and, depending on the properties of the particular wave that is incident on the apparatus, everything may vibrate in unison. To overcome this problem the detector must be sufficiently large compared with the wavelength of the incoming wave so that different parts of the detector respond to different sections of the wave.

The three design possibilities that presented themselves to Weber are now referred to as the free mass detector, the almost-free mass detector, and the resonant detector. A good example of a potential free mass detector is the Earth-Moon system. If a gravitational wave passes through them in a direction perpendicular to the line between them, they will both oscillate slightly. A sufficiently accurate measure of their separation at any time would then allow detection of the wave. How accurate would this measurement have to be? Current estimates indicate one of the order of one part in 10^{17}, or approximately one ten-millionth of a centimeter. There was, of course, no possibility of accuracy of this order when Weber was designing his detector. Even in the 1970s laser ranging could measure the Earth–Moon distance with an accuracy of only a few centimeters.

An example of the second type of detector, the almost-free case, consists of two large suspended masses that function as antennae, with a separation detector placed between them. When a wave passes through this system, the two masses undergo minute oscillations. These oscillations can then be monitored either by laser or by a piezoelectric crystal detector, which is sensitive to strain.

Weber decided to use the third type of detector, the resonant detector. In this case, a large cylindrical mass is suspended by a wire; when a wave passes through this antenna it resonates, or vibrates slightly in tune with the frequency of the wave. These vibrations cause a tiny strain in the antenna that can be measured by a series of ultrasensitive piezoelectric strain gauges attached around the antenna. A considerable amount of shielding is required to avoid vibrations from electromagnetic waves due to such phenomena as surges in power lines, television broadcast signals, and electrical storms, and also from various seismic events. One of the disadvantages of resonant detectors is that they are tuned to a single frequency and consequently can detect waves effectively only at this frequency. On the other hand, their resonant property gives them an advantage. When a very weak pulse passes them, they resonate, like struck bells, for a period considerably longer than the duration of the pulse.

Over the years Weber built several such resonant detectors. Representative of them was one with an aluminum cylinder 153 centimeters (5 feet) long and 66 centimeters (26 inches) across. It was capable of an accuracy of about one part in 10^{16} and had a resonant frequency of 1,661 hertz, which corresponds to a wavelength of about 180 kilometers (110 miles) and is near the frequency range within which gravitational wave energy was expected to be most concentrated. To his system at the University of Maryland Weber later added a detector at Argonne National Laboratory, near Chicago, at a distance of some 1,000 kilometers (600 miles) from the Maryland laboratory. The two cylinders were identical, and both were aligned in approximately the same direction. With two detectors he was able to record coincidence events or, more exactly, events that had a slight but specified time lag between them as a wave first struck one detector and then the other. This arrangement considerably increased the probability that coincidentally detected events indeed were caused by gravitational waves and not by some local disturbance.

Weber reported his success in 1969 after he had received about 260 coincident events over a period of four months. In 1970 he made plots of his events against both solar time and sidereal time (time measured by the apparent motion of the stars, rather than the Sun). His sidereal time plots were of considerable interest; they showed an apparent maximum when the antennae were aligned along the axis to the center of the Milky Way. Weber concluded on the basis of this correlation that the waves were being generated in this region. Later, however, several Soviet scientists looked carefully at his data and were not convinced that the evidence was conclusive.

Others join the search

Soon after Weber's announcement in 1969, other scientists began looking for gravitational waves; in most cases their instruments were similar to Weber's. Vladimir B. Braginsky of Moscow State University was one of the first, and like Weber he used two large cylindrical antennae. A unique feature of his system was his oscillation detector; it consisted of two capacitor plates mounted on the antennae. A small displacement produced a small but measurable change in electrical capacitance. Braginsky initially reported a few suspect events but later became certain that none of them were genuine coincidences.

J. A. Tyson of Bell Laboratories near Holmdel, New Jersey, used considerably larger antennae than Weber. They were tuned to a frequency of 710 hertz—about half that used by Weber. But, like Braginsky, he also failed to detect any events. Ronald Drever, who was then at the University of Glasgow in Scotland, and Richard L. Garwin and James L. Levine of IBM were among

Track of the output of a resonant detector over several hours presents a record resembling a tangled mass of thread. Sudden, distinctive changes in the position of the track, possibly indicative of gravitational waves, must be sorted out by computer from the general pattern of "thermal wandering" due to the effects of heat.

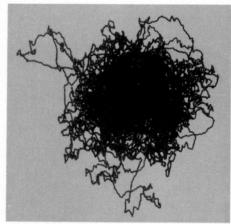

J. A. Tyson, Bell Laboratories

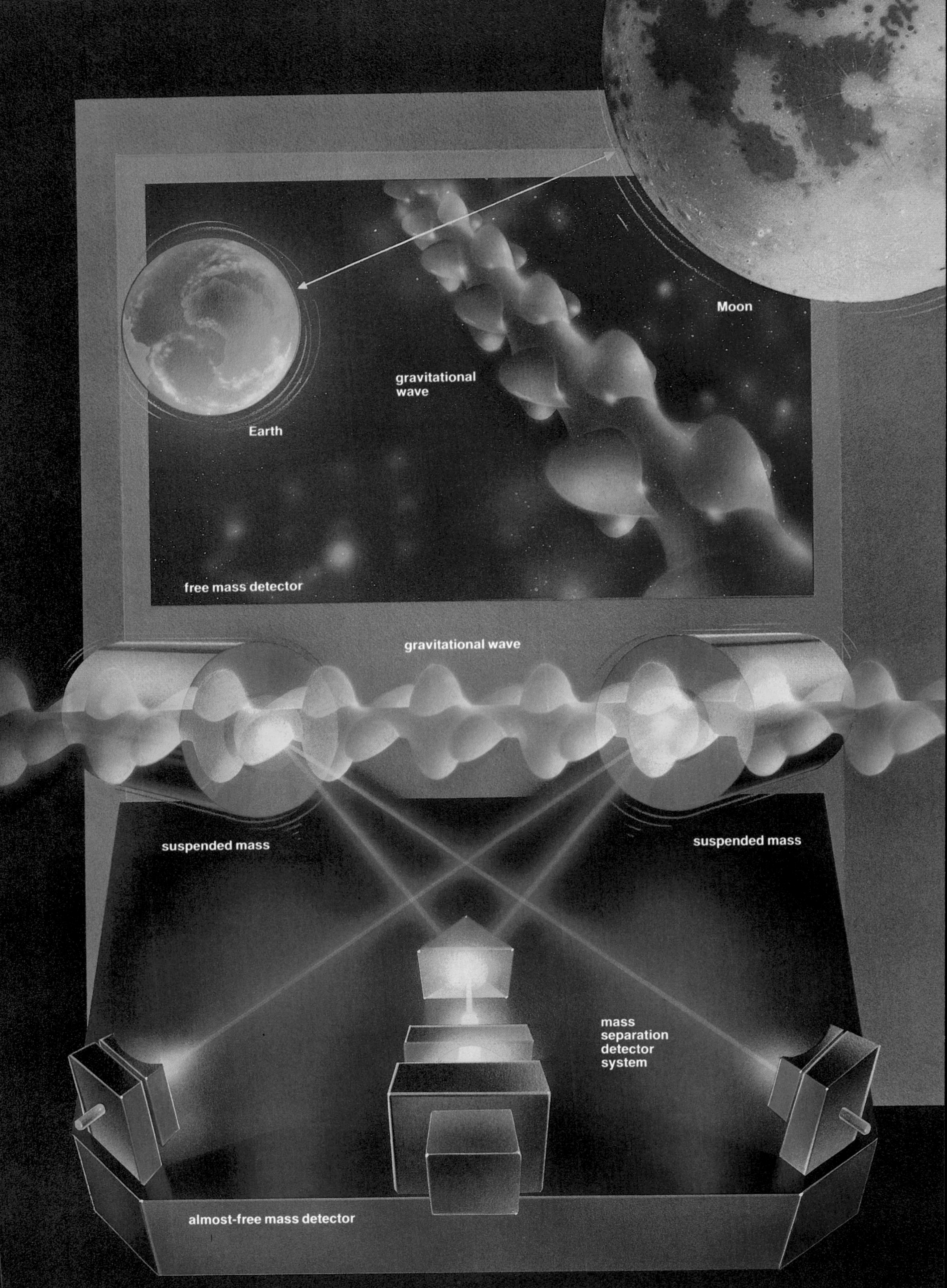

Earth

Moon

gravitational wave

free mass detector

gravitational wave

suspended mass

suspended mass

mass separation detector system

almost-free mass detector

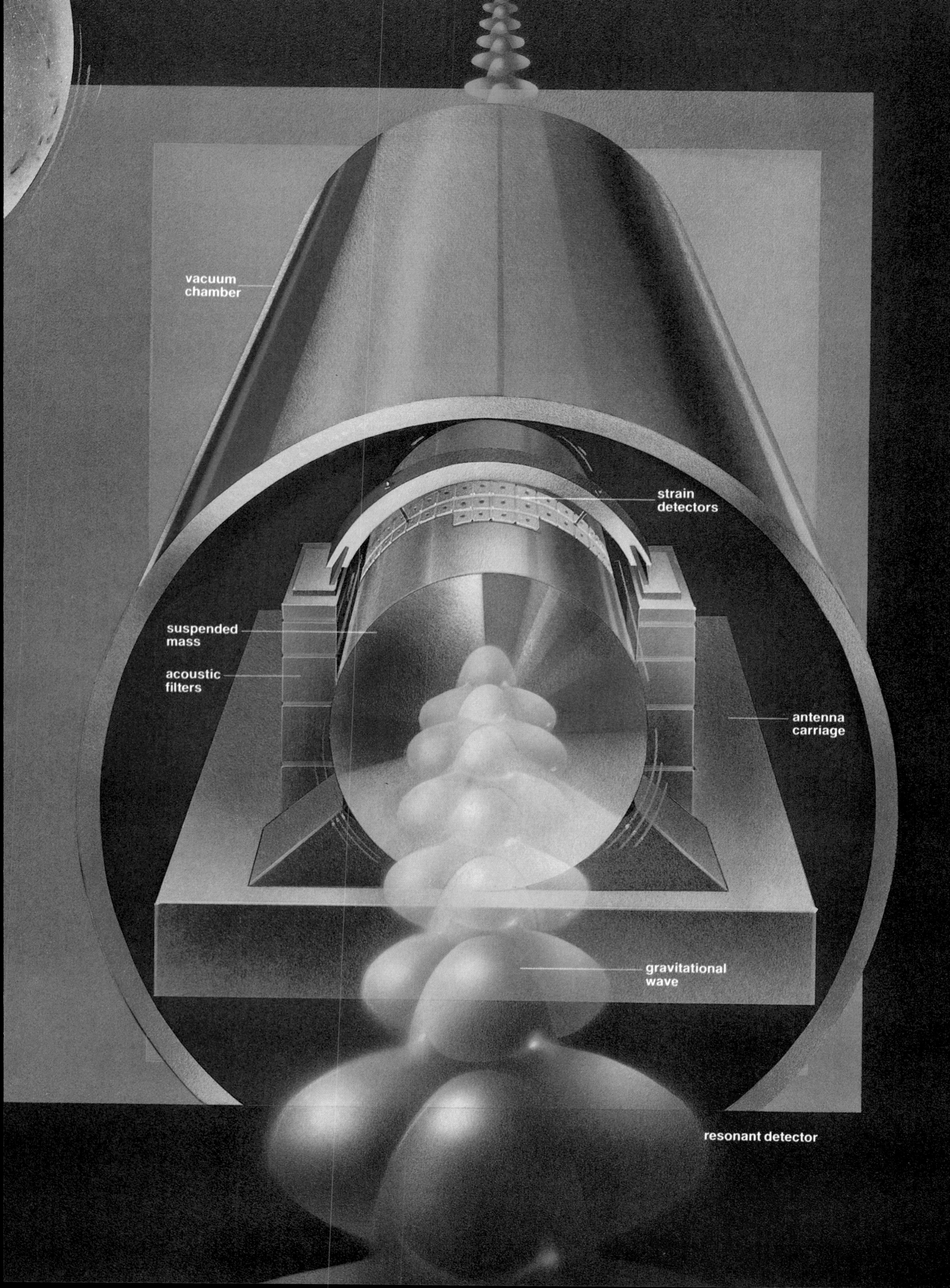

vacuum
chamber

strain
detectors

suspended
mass

acoustic
filters

antenna
carriage

gravitational
wave

resonant detector

Examples of three types of gravitational wave detectors appear on pp. 188–189. The Earth-Moon system would serve as a free mass detector if ways could be developed to measure wave-induced changes in their separation distance with sufficient accuracy. One version of the almost-free mass detector consists of two large suspended masses and a laser interferometer to measure their separation distance. Weber's original antenna system is of the third type, the resonant detector, which employs an array of piezoelectric strain detectors to sense vibrations from gravitational waves in a single suspended mass. An evacuated chamber for the antenna and acoustic filters on its suspension system serve to isolate it from other sources of disturbance.

several others who set up similar, though unsuccessful, experiments.

Some of the more recent attempts have used laser interferometry to sense gravitationally induced oscillations in large suspended masses. This technique depends on the ability to detect minute changes in the travel distances of laser beams as they reflect from mirrors attached to the masses. Among the first to experiment with this kind of system were Robert Forward and Gaylord Moss of Hughes Research Laboratories in the U.S. who used it to measure minute oscillations in two loosely suspended bodies of the almost-free mass variety of detector. This type of detector has an important advantage over the resonant type in that it is broadband; in other words, it is not restricted to a single frequency. But again no significant events were detected in the Forward-Moss experiment.

Interestingly, even while others were reporting negative findings, Weber continued to observe coincidences. But, as it turned out, nonconfirmation was not the only problem with Weber's results. The rate and intensity of his events were also much higher than could reasonably be expected. To understand why, it is necessary to consider what causes these waves.

Sources of gravity waves

In theory, all that is needed to produce gravitational waves is an accelerating mass. Two weights on the end of a spring will radiate gravitationally if they are set in motion, although the output will be much too small to be measurable. It is, in fact, quite unlikely that gravitational waves will be detected from any terrestrial source in the near future, even though such events as nuclear explosions are feasible sources. At the present time astronomical events or objects are the only known sources that are capable of producing detectable waves.

An important requirement of a source is asymmetry. For example, a sphere that oscillates uniformly in a radial direction, expanding and contracting like a balloon, will not produce gravitational waves; neither will a spinning sphere. A binary star system, however, has the required asymmetry, and if its component stars are sufficiently dense, the system will be a relatively strong source. Calculations show that it will radiate a wave with a frequency twice that of the orbital period of the stars.

Among the strongest potential sources are cataclysmic stellar explosions known as supernovas. Supernovas are believed to occupy a late stage in the evolution of stars that are at least about four times as massive as the Sun. As such a star nears the end of its lifetime, the nuclear reactions that supply the star with its energy suddenly change their character and use up energy instead of generating it. In a very brief time the core of the star collapses, its outer layers are blown off into space, and a pulse of broadband gravitational radiation is given off. A second pulse may also be produced by a cloud of elementary particles called neutrinos as they rush outward from the core. Finally, for stars with masses about four to eight times that of the Sun, the tiny neutron star that is left after the explosion may also become a source. In all probability it will be spinning at a high rate when first formed, and if any asymmetry is present from a deformity in its shape, gravitational waves will radiate from it. Estimates of the intensities of radiation have, in fact, been made for both the Crab and Vela pulsars, two rapidly rotating neutron stars that emit extremely regular pulses of radio emission. According to Mark Zimmermann of the Kellogg Radiation Laboratory at the California Institute of Technology, technology for detecting gravitational waves (if there are any) from neutron stars should be available during the 1980s.

Gravitational collapse or implosion of old stars even more massive than those that become neutron stars is expected to be another particularly important source. Gravitational waves will most likely be given off both during their collapse and later by the infinitely contracted, gravitationally powerful entities, called black holes, that remain. Black holes, which inexorably absorb all light and matter that approach within a certain critical distance, have taken the spotlight in the last few years as potential sources. Donald Lynden-Bell and Martin J. Rees of the University of Cambridge have suggested that certain galaxies with high radio wave emissions and perhaps even quasars—objects of enormous energy output that are believed to lie near the edges of the observable universe—may have gigantic black holes at their cores. A giant elliptical galaxy, called M87, with a jet of matter emanating from it has been of particular interest. According to some astronomers a black hole at its core may be absorbing nearby stars. As it devours star after star vast amounts of gravitational radiation would be produced. More recently interest has centered on an object discovered in the 1960s called SS433. It has two sets of rapidly and simultaneously shifting spectral lines: one set shows a huge shift toward the red end of its spectrum, indicating that it is receding from the Earth at high velocity; the other set shows a large blue shift, indicating an approach. Some astronomers have suggested that it is an unusual binary system or a single object with a massive black hole at its core. Whatever proves to be the nature of SS433, it may play an important role in the future of gravitational wave astronomy.

In light of the above information the major difficulty with Weber's results is the frequency of his events, which were detected at the rate of several per day. If they are being caused by supernovas or black holes at the center of the Milky Way, they indicate that an incredible amount of energy is being released, an energy equivalent to the annihilation per day of about 300 stars the size of the Sun. In a year this rate would give 100,000 annihilations. Although there is some evidence for violence at the galactic nucleus, the energy output seems to be too high by several orders of magnitude.

There are, however, a number of ways around this problem. If the source was not at the core, for example, but much closer, it would not have to be as violent to account for Weber's rate of detection. Also, Charles Misner of the University of Maryland pointed out that if waves from the center of the Galaxy somehow are not being radiated in all directions, but are being focused in the galactic plane—and thus toward the Earth—then, again, their source need not be as violent to account for Weber's results.

A recent breakthrough

Five years after Weber's announcement no one had yet detected any direct or even indirect evidence for the existence of gravitational waves. Though there was still optimism, it was fading. Perhaps the waves did not exist after

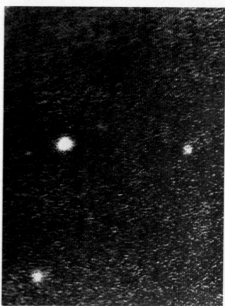

Photos taken through a stroboscope-equipped telescope record the ''on'' and ''off'' phases of the Crab pulsar, which blinks visibly about 30 times per second, or each time a directional beam of radiation that rotates with the star sweeps past the Earth. This pulsar is the core remnant of a supernova that occurred in AD 1054. Any asymmetry still present in its shape should make it a source of gravitational waves.

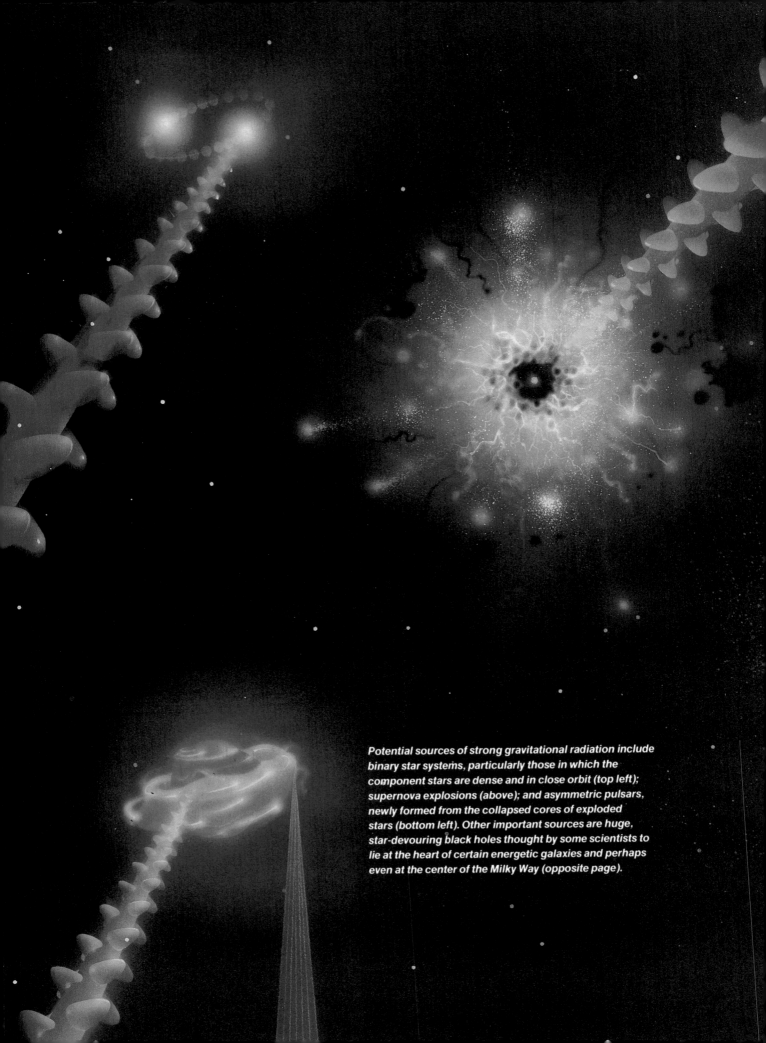

Potential sources of strong gravitational radiation include binary star systems, particularly those in which the component stars are dense and in close orbit (top left); supernova explosions (above); and asymmetric pulsars, newly formed from the collapsed cores of exploded stars (bottom left). Other important sources are huge, star-devouring black holes thought by some scientists to lie at the heart of certain energetic galaxies and perhaps even at the center of the Milky Way (opposite page).

all, or perhaps they were beyond the sensitivity of any detector that could be built. Then came the first inklings of a breakthrough. A binary pulsar system—one in which at least one component is a pulsar—was discovered in 1974 by Joseph H. Taylor and Russell Hulse of the University of Massachusetts using the gigantic 305-meter (1,000-foot) radio telescope at Arecibo, Puerto Rico. A binary pulsar system should be a strong source of gravitational waves, but until this discovery none could be studied since none had ever been found.

Taylor has explained why he believes such pulsar systems are relatively rare. Binary systems of ordinary stars are extremely common. If one of the two stars in such a system is sufficiently massive, when it explodes and collapses it will form a pulsar. The second star, however, would most likely be blown apart in the explosion of the first. The only presently conceivable way that a system of this type can arise is if, during the collapse of a single star, its core somehow splits into two separate objects. The system discovered by Taylor and Hulse is on the border between the constellations Sagitta and Aquila and is known as PSR 1913 + 16 (the numbers refer to its coordinates). One of the two objects is definitely a pulsar with a mass about 1.4 times that of the Sun. Like other pulsars detected thus far, it is believed to emit a directional beam of radio waves that sweeps past the Earth once each time that the star rotates, giving rise to its characteristic radio pulses. Its unseen companion emits no detectable pulses, but it may also be a pulsar with its radio beam pointed away from the Earth. A second possibility is that it may be a black hole.

The two stars orbit one another in about eight hours. At first the observed pulsar was believed to be relatively young because its pulse rate—and thus its rotation rate—was the second shortest known. (The Crab pulsar has the shortest known rate.) According to theory a pulsar spins fastest when it first forms; as it ages it gradually radiates away energy—both electromagnetic and gravitational energy—and slows down. After the system was studied for some time, however, it was determined that it was considerably older than first thought, probably about 100 million years old.

Taylor soon realized that the system could be used for an indirect, but good, test of the existence of gravitational waves. According to general relativity the pulsar and its companion should gradually move closer to one another as energy is released in the form of gravitational waves. As they approach, their orbital period will decrease. The expected decrease was calculated; it was small but measurable—about $1/10,000$ of a second per year.

For four years Taylor and two colleagues, Peter M. McCulloch of the University of Tasmania and graduate student Lee A. Fowler of the University of Massachusetts, carefully studied the pulsar. After more than a thousand observations they announced in late 1978 that its period had decreased in four years by 0.000414 seconds. This result was in reasonable agreement with theory: the binary system was indeed acting as if it was giving off gravitational waves.

The announcement was greeted with considerable excitement, but within a few months it was evident that not everyone was convinced. Taylor's estimate for the slowdown rate of the pulsar is based on a formula originally

In the photograph below, the peculiar stellar object known as SS433 appears as a reddish spot in the center of the supernova remnant W50. The picture was produced from radiotelescope observations at a wavelength of 11 centimeters; a computer translated variations in radio intensity into a spectrum of visible colors. Preliminary studies suggest that SS433 and W50 arose in the same supernova explosion about 40,000 years ago. Spectral readings of SS433 appear to show rapid cyclical acceleration of large amounts of matter, a characteristic that may make it an important object of study for gravitational wave astronomy.

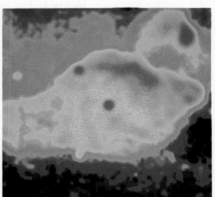

Bernard J. Geldzahler, Massachusetts Institute of Technology

194

Hiromasa Hirakawa, University of Tokyo

Recent searches at the University of Tokyo for gravitational radiation coming from the Crab pulsar have employed a square resonant antenna housed in a vacuum tank (left). The aluminum alloy plate is tuned to a frequency of 60.2 hertz, or twice the rotation rate of the pulsar. Another current effort, at Louisiana State University, involves use of a levitation cradle (below) lined with superconducting magnets to float a supercooled resonant antenna. Prior to operation the cylindrical antenna is slid on rails into an insulated tank (bottom), where both antenna and magnets are chilled to temperatures near absolute zero.

derived by Einstein, now frequently called the Einstein quadrupole formula. A number of scientists have suggested that this formula may be inaccurate, among them Arnold Rosenblum of the Max Planck Institute of Physics in West Germany and F. I. Cooperstock and P. H. Lim of the University of Victoria in British Columbia. Taylor and his colleagues, however, believe that their data suggest that any inaccuracies in the quadrupole formula are exceedingly small and therefore that the results are valid. Most others working in the field agree with them.

The future: a new window on the universe

The binary pulsar discovered by Taylor seems to have satisfied many scientists of the existence of gravitational waves, but direct evidence is still needed. It may well come with the next generation of detectors, which are expected to be millions of times more sensitive than the early ones. One of the first courses of action will be to cool the resonant antennae nearly to absolute zero (−273° C) to remove as much interference from heat as possible. William Fairbank of Stanford University and William Hamilton of Louisiana State University are two among several who are involved with this new generation of detectors. They are working with 5,400-kilogram (12,000-pound) cylinders that will be cooled and levitated magnetically to minimize outside disturbances. Laser interferometry has already played an important role in the search and will probably become increasingly important in the future. With the help of much larger and more powerful lasers, the sensitivity of detectors could be increased significantly.

Satellites will also play an important new role. Plans are now on the drawing board for a scientifically instrumented spacecraft called the solar probe, which will be built to pass within three million kilometers of the Sun's visible surface. It will first travel to Jupiter to achieve the proper velocity for a solar approach, and one of the projects envisioned for it during this

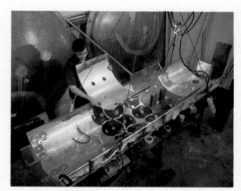

Photos, William O. Hamilton, Louisiana State University

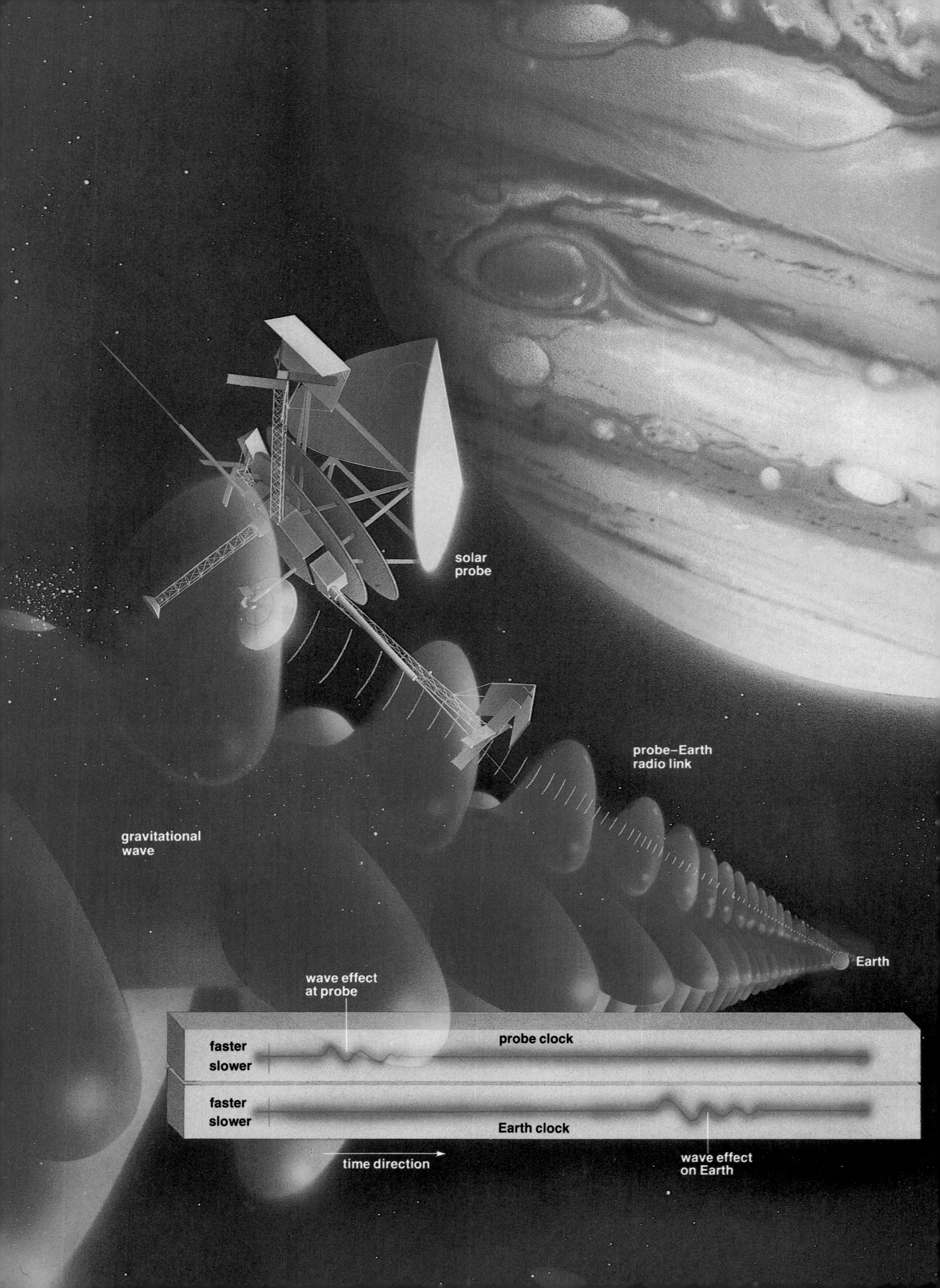

solar probe

probe–Earth
radio link

gravitational
wave

Earth

wave effect
at probe

faster	probe clock
slower	
faster	Earth clock
slower	

time direction

wave effect
on Earth

preliminary outbound trek is a test for gravitational waves from cosmic sources. One prediction of general relativity—and one that has been confirmed in a variety of experiments—is that gravity affects the measurement of time. A gravitational wave passing through a clock aboard the solar probe and through another clock on the Earth would cause separate infinitesimal changes in their timekeeping. A comparison of the two clocks via a communications system would then allow scientists to determine if a wave had been received.

Kip S. Thorne of the California Institute of Technology emphasized that there is still considerable work to be done on the theoretical side of the problem. So far, due to the mathematical complexity of solving Einstein's equations, most calculations have been based on what is called the weak field approximation. This simplified approach is satisfactory as long as the gravitational fields are indeed weak, but it is not when one deals with such compact objects as black holes. One of the few calculations involving no approximations (other than those used to get the problem on the computer) was one recently done by Larry Smarr of Harvard University, who found the expected gravitational wave intensity from a head-on collision of two black holes to be relatively small. S. L. Detweiller, however, showed that the expected intensity is quite large for particles spiraling into a black hole.

It is reasonable to ask why there is so much interest in detecting these waves. They do, of course, carry energy, but it is quite unlikely that man could harness it in sufficient quantity to be of use. On a theoretical level their detection would lend support to models of the physical universe which, like that based on general relativity, predict the existence and characteristics of the waves. More practically, however, they are quite important because in essence they would be a new window on the universe—a completely different way of seeing things. At the present time almost everything known about the universe has been gained by observing the light, X-rays, radio radiation, and other forms of electromagnetic waves that have been detected in it. But electromagnetic waves are a limited source; in general, they tell little about what is going on deep inside a star, at the heart of a supernova explosion, or at the core of the Milky Way. Events such as these are obscured by dense layers of matter.

Gravitational waves, on the other hand, easily penetrate all matter. Their detection, followed by analysis of their frequency, strength, direction, polarization, and other characteristics, would therefore greatly extend mankind's knowledge of their sources. They may even become a valuable tool in the study of black holes. The volume within a black hole is hidden from observation by a strange one-way "membrane" called the event horizon. Electromagnetic waves can pass inward through this horizon, but once inside, the gravitational field of the black hole prevents them from escaping. Gravitational waves, however, can propagate outward through the event horizon. Hence, once they are detected they will afford a technique for probing the secrets inside.

So, although the future looks bright, there appears to be a considerable amount of work to do before the age of gravitational wave astronomy dawns. The rewards, however, will no doubt be worth the effort.

General relativity predicts that gravitational radiation passing through a clock will affect its timekeeping. Consequently a gravitational wave that intercepts two clocks—one on Earth and the other on a spacecraft millions of kilometers distant—should be detectable by noting similar timekeeping discrepancies in the two clocks and the time delay between them, which would correspond to the travel time between the two clocks for a wave moving at the speed of light. A space probe on a proposed close-encounter mission to the Sun could carry one of the clocks, using the mission's outbound leg to Jupiter for the experiment.

197

Looking Deeper, Seeing Farther

by Jay M. Pasachoff and Naomi Pasachoff

A new generation of telescopes is extending the frontiers of optical astronomy to levels of faintness and resolution never before achieved.

Along with the spectacular advances resulting from observations in other parts of the electromagnetic spectrum, optical astronomy—investigations in the visible wavelengths and portions of the infrared and ultraviolet—in recent years has been transformed with new telescopes and new technology. Few large telescopes had been constructed in the 1950s and 1960s. The Palomar 5.08-meter (200-inch) reflector, completed in 1950, for many years stood almost alone at the pinnacle of optical astronomy. The 3-meter (120-inch) telescope at the Lick Observatory, opened in 1959, and the 2.7-meter (107-inch) instrument at the McDonald Observatory, completed in 1968, were the only U.S. telescopes constructed after Palomar that were larger than the old Mount Wilson 2.5-meter (100-inch) reflector, which dates back to 1917. The U.S.S.R. also built a telescope in this period, a 2.6-meter (102-inch) instrument completed in the Crimea in 1961.

This last group of telescopes has been recently joined by a current generation, most of them constructed since 1970. The new instruments have increased by a considerable factor the amount of surface that is available worldwide to collect starlight. Incorporating new developments in construction and located in the most advantageous sites possible, these telescopes are pushing optical astronomy to new frontiers of faintness and resolution. The new techniques and sites also allow the current generation of telescopes to be used in a somewhat wider range of the spectrum—extending into the infrared in particular—than had previously been accessible from the ground. In addition, fitting older telescopes with electronic detectors has brought them up-to-date, making them as useful as if their size had been increased. For the future, lasers and other new technologies are allowing astronomers to plan a next generation of telescopes on the ground with collecting areas as large as 25 times those now available.

AURA four-meter telescopes

Most of the current generation of telescopes are about 4 meters (158 inches) across or less. The most widely used is the four-meter Mayall reflector at the Kitt Peak National Observatory (KPNO) in Arizona, completed in 1974. A twin telescope, completed in 1975, was constructed in the Kitt Peak optical workshop in Tucson, Arizona, and installed at the Cerro Tololo Inter-American Observatory (CTIO) in Chile. Both KPNO and CTIO are operated by Associated Universities for Research in Astronomy (AURA), a consortium of more than a dozen U.S. universities that operates with support from the U.S. National Science Foundation.

Compared with the Palomar reflector both of these four-meter telescopes have much wider fields of view in which an image in good focus can be photographed. The Palomar telescope followed the traditional design in which a paraboloidal mirror reflects light to a focus. But paraboloids can perfectly focus only light that is incident along the axis of the paraboloid. This leads to a narrow field of view in good focus, only about two minutes of arc ($\frac{1}{30}$ a degree) across, though correcting optics near the film can provide a good focus over a somewhat larger region. The Kitt Peak and Cerro

Major optical observatories include that at Palomar Mountain in California (above), which houses a 5.08-meter (200-inch) reflector that was completed in 1950. Developed during the 1960s and 1970s were the Kitt Peak National Observatory in Arizona (right) and the Cerro Tololo Inter-American Observatory in Chile (right bottom).

JAY M. PASACHOFF *is Director of the Hopkins Observatory of Williams College, Williamstown, Mass., and author of the texts* Contemporary Astronomy *and* Astronomy: From the Earth to the Universe. ***NAOMI PASACHOFF*** *is a Research Associate in the English Department of Williams College.*

(Overleaf) © Gary Ladd; illustrations by John Draves

Tololo four-meter telescopes, like most of the current generation, are of the Ritchey-Chrétien design.

To make a Ritchey-Chrétien one changes the shape of the primary mirror from that of a parabola by deepening the center of the mirror about 10%. All large telescopes have several foci, including a Cassegrain focus, which falls just behind a hole in the center of the main mirror. The light is brought to a focus there by a secondary mirror suspended in the telescope tube closer to the main mirror than the prime focus; the Cassegrain focus is more readily accessible to observers and equipment than the prime focus. In the Ritchey-Chrétien design the Cassegrain secondary mirror is given a complex shape to correct for the optical aberrations introduced by the non-paraboloidal main mirror. These two mirrors together give a field of view about one degree across, twice the diameter of the full Moon. This wide field of view allows the structure of extended objects or groups of objects to be better understood. The image, however, appears in focus on a curved rather than a flat surface, which makes it difficult to put photographic plates there. To simplify the placement of such detectors a flattening lens is usually used.

Cutaway drawing reveals the 19-story building housing the 4-meter (158-inch) Mayall Telescope at the Kitt Peak National Observatory in Arizona. By the use of the Ritchey-Chrétien design, in which the primary mirror is not paraboloidal in shape, the telescope provides a wide field of view, twice the diameter of the full Moon.

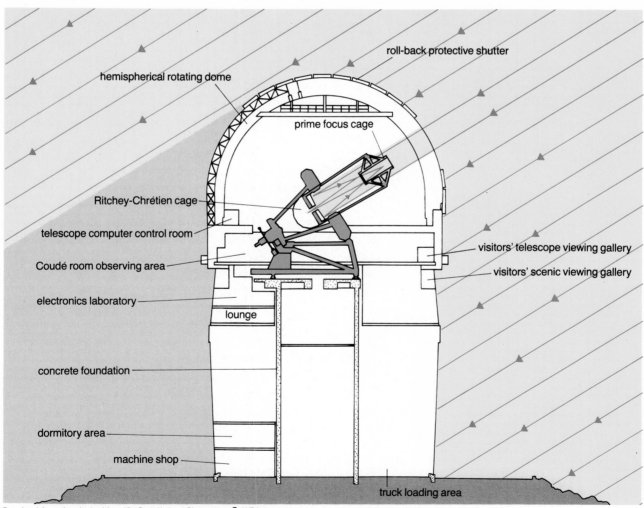

roll-back protective shutter

hemispherical rotating dome

prime focus cage

Ritchey-Chrétien cage

telescope computer control room

Coudé room observing area

electronics laboratory

lounge

visitors' telescope viewing gallery

visitors' scenic viewing gallery

concrete foundation

dormitory area

machine shop

truck loading area

Based on information obtained from Kitt Peak National Observatory. © AURA

The four-meter reflecting mirror of the Mayall telescope at the Kitt Peak National Observatory is washed (above). The telescope after installation is seen at the right.

Updating old telescopes

New developments in film emulsions and the addition of electronic devices to older telescopes, such as the five-meter reflector at Palomar, have made them as up-to-date as the new generation of instruments. Because of new video devices observers no longer need look through eyepieces to see where their telescopes are pointing. The vidicon systems are many times more sensitive than the human eye, and so much fainter features—even the spiral arms of galaxies—are now available for guiding and orientation.

Charge-coupled devices (CCD's) and an instrument that can count individual photons are routinely used on both old and new telescopes. CCD's are integrated-circuit devices that sense light on a surface and simultaneously scan the image on that surface with internal circuitry. The name CCD refers to the scanning method, which involves shifting the electrical signal from each point to its neighbor, one space at a time, in a manner analogous to the transfer of water in a firefighting bucket brigade, where buckets of water are passed from one individual to the next. CCD's and other self-scanned arrays create images by scanning elements line by line, as do television sets, using circuitry internal to the detectors themselves.

Yet another instrument in use is the image tube scanner. It consists of a standard spectrograph and an electronic device that amplifies the image of the spectrum in three stages. The final stage is scanned by an image dissector, which registers in a computer the intensity of incoming photons at each wavelength. The "Robinson-Wampler scanner" at the three-meter Lick telescope is such a device. A similar device, called the intensified image dissector scanner, is used at the 2.1-meter (84-inch) telescope at Kitt Peak and the 4-meter telescope at Cerro Tololo.

New observatories in the Southern Hemisphere

Though the region toward the center of the Milky Way, which contains many of the most interesting objects of the sky, can best be seen from southern latitudes, most of the telescopes of the last generation were in the

202

Northern Hemisphere. This imbalance has recently been remedied by the construction of many new telescopes in the Southern Hemisphere.

Many of the new sites are on coastal mountains west of the Andes range in Chile. At the Cerro Tololo Inter-American Observatory a host of other smaller telescopes, some of which were moved there from other sites, are alongside the four-meter reflector. On another mountain peak in Chile a consortium of European observatories and universities erected the European Southern Observatory. A 3.6-meter (142-inch) Ritchey-Chrétien telescope is the largest of the dozen instruments on the mountain. On Cerro las Campanas, another Chilean peak, stands the 2.6-meter (101-inch) Irénée du Pont telescope. It joins the Palomar, Mount Wilson, and Big Bear Solar observatories as a part of the Hale Observatories.

A joint British-Australian telescope has been erected on Siding Spring Mountain in eastern Australia. This 3.9-meter Anglo-Australian Telescope, whose usable aperture is intermediate between the usable 3.96 meters (156 inches) of the Kitt Peak telescope and the 3.81-meter (150-inch) usable diameter of the Cerro Tololo telescope, was completed in 1975.

Also at the Siding Spring Observatory is the British 1.2-meter (48-inch) Schmidt telescope, which began regular observations in 1973. Schmidt telescopes, also called Schmidt cameras, are designed to provide a wide field for direct photography, and they are therefore used to make sky surveys. A 1.2-meter Schmidt telescope on Palomar Mountain was used in the National Geographic Society-Palomar Observatory Sky Survey during the 1950s. While it mapped the entire sky that is visible from Palomar, fully one-quarter of the sky cannot be seen from that latitude. Together with another new large Schmidt, the one-meter telescope of the European Southern Observatory (ESO) in Chile, the Schmidt at Siding Spring is being used to produce a photographic atlas of the southern sky. The survey is taking advantage of recent advances in photographic and telescope technology not only to reach much fainter and more distant stars and galaxies than had any previous survey of the southern sky but also to go deeper into space than

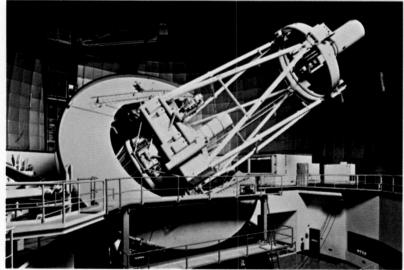

Anglo-Australian Observatory

The 3.9-meter Anglo-Australian Telescope at Siding Spring Observatory in Australia points low in the east. Capable of looking anywhere in the sky more than 20° above the horizon, the telescope can achieve this by swiveling on two axes. The large yellow horseshoe bearing rotates to determine the motion following the stars from east to west. A second motion around an axis between the arms of the horseshoe allows the white structure holding the large mirror to tip north and south.

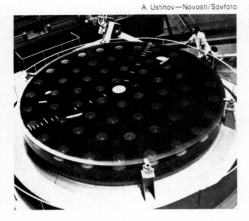

At an optics factory in Leningrad the Soviet Union's 42-ton, 6-meter reflecting mirror, the world's largest, awaits final control polishing (above). Later the reflector was placed in the Soviet Astrophysical Observatory in the Caucasus Mountains. On the opposite page at the top right a sign on a structure housing a multiple-mirror telescope (MMT) at the Smithsonian's Mt. Hopkins Observatory warns that the building rotates. Below is spiral galaxy NGC 4565 photographed using the 60-inch Mt. Hopkins telescope. At the bottom left is a secondary mirror of the MMT, and at the bottom right is the MMT in its building.

the earlier Palomar survey of the northern and equatorial sky. The U.K. Schmidt is observing in the blue region of the spectrum, and the ESO Schmidt works in the red. Both are using new types of photographic emulsions that are especially sensitive and have a very fine grain.

After the initial survey is complete, the U.K. Schmidt may be used to do a survey in the near-infrared region of Milky Way fields or to extend the current survey northward to the Equator or even farther. Meanwhile, the Palomar Schmidt is carrying out a survey in the infrared.

Other European plans involve setting telescopes at relatively low northern latitudes, compromising between convenient access, good weather, and coverage of the southern sky. The 2.5-meter (98-inch) Isaac Newton telescope, for example, is being relocated from the Royal Greenwich Observatory in England to a new site on the Canary Islands known for the excellent quality of the viewing it provides astronomers. A new mirror, 102 inches across, is being made for it.

Soviet six-meter telescope

The largest single optical telescope in the world has been erected by the Soviet Union atop Mt. Pastukhov in the Caucasus Mountains. This 6-meter (236-inch) reflector of the Soviet Astrophysical Observatory went into operation in 1976. The first six-meter mirror, made of the Soviet equivalent of Pyrex, is being replaced with a better one of the same material. Another new mirror is being prepared out of the Soviet equivalent of Cer-Vit, a ceramic that resembles glass but expands or contracts with heat even less than other materials in use; this property limits distortion of the shape of the reflecting surface. This mirror is expected to be installed about 1983.

The fact that ceramic mirrors are not as transparent as glass is not important, because the bulk of a telescope mirror is only present to provide a surface that is coated with a reflective layer of an aluminum compound and perhaps further coated with hardening and protective layers. Consequently, many of the new telescopes throughout the world are being made with ceramic mirrors.

Unlike all the telescopes mentioned previously the Soviet six-meter instrument has an altazimuth mounting, in which one axis rotates in the horizontal plane (azimuth) and the other axis allows the telescope to move up and down (altitude). The other telescopes are all on equatorial mounts, in which one axis points at the celestial north pole and the second axis of rotation is perpendicular to the first.

An advantage of equatorial mounts is that a uniform motion around the polar axis alone will keep up with the rotation of stars in the sky. Thus the equatorial mounting makes it relatively easy for astronomers to find and track celestial objects. In the altazimuth design motions around both axes simultaneously are necessary, and the rate at which each of these motions takes place varies continuously. Thus it is no longer possible for a single motor moving at a constant rate to allow the telescope to track the stars. A digital computer is required to drive the telescope, adjusting the rates as is necessary; such computers are now available and are relatively inexpensive. Altazimuth mounts make it simpler to balance the telescope and often allow

204

a more compact dome, thus providing considerable financial saving. The Soviet design also eliminates much of the stress in the mirror that accompanies equatorial mounting, which can lead to distortion of incoming light.

Multiple-mirror telescope

On a high mountain some 40 miles south of Tucson, Arizona, stands a boxy structure that contains six main mirrors and a small guide telescope, all linked together on a single support structure. Each of the mirrors is 1.8 meters (72 inches) in diameter, but together the collecting area they provide is equivalent to that of a single 4.5-meter (176-inch) traditional instrument. The MMT is thus the third largest optical telescope in the world, exceeded only by Palomar and the new Soviet instrument. Like the Soviet telescope the MMT has an altazimuth mounting with computer controls.

The individual mirrors of the MMT move together in their common structure, and fine corrections of the pointing of the mirrors with respect to one another are controlled by a delicate feedback system. Laser beams are reflected through each of the six independent sets of primary and secondary mirrors in such a way that a misalignment of the mirrors with respect to one another also shows up as a lack of common alignment of the laser beams. Sensors detect the laser beams and generate electrical signals that are used to align the six main mirrors so that the light from all of them is focused to within one second of arc, comparable to the finest resolution allowed by the distortion of the Earth's atmosphere.

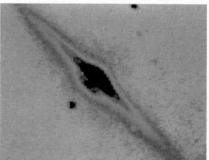

One common lack of efficiency in telescopes is the fact that the light from a star is focused as a round spot, while the slit through which light enters a spectrograph is rectangular. The MMT can direct its six beams so that they form a rectangular pattern instead of being exactly superimposed on one another, thus making spectrographic observations especially efficient.

One new feature that the MMT shares with many other large telescopes

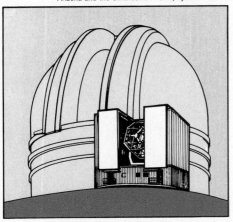

Multiple-mirror telescope (inset) is compared in size with the dome of the Palomar observatory. The dome measures 41.8 meters (137 feet) across the base and 41.2 meters (135 feet) from its highest point to the bottom.

Proposed next-generation telescopes (facing page) are of varying designs. A multiple-mirror model (top left) would require six ten-meter primary mirrors in a single support structure. The rotating shoe (top right) would comprise a 75-meter by 25-meter spherical mirror enclosed in a shoelike rotating frame. Another possibility is an optical-infrared array consisting of rings of identical telescopes (six ten-meter mirrors, center, or 108 with 2.4-meter diameters, bottom) that would transmit beams into a single image at a central focus.

is a television-type guiding system. It allows for careful orientation of the telescope on objects of interest. For example, at the MMT, galaxies with spiral arms swim into view as the telescope is moved across the sky.

Since each of the six main mirrors of the MMT is relatively small, the focal length of each is relatively short; the MMT is, therefore, relatively compact. Thus the building that surrounds the telescope need not be very large and, in fact, is less than half the diameter of the Palomar dome. The fact that the multiple-mirror telescope is mounted not in a dome but in a rectangular building, all of which rotates with the telescope, also allows for the efficient use of space.

In addition, the six mirrors used were left over from a space project and were thus available at relatively low cost. Prior to the inception of the MMT it had been believed that the cost of a new telescope was proportional to approximately the third power of the diameter of a single-mirror telescope's main mirror. That is, it was thought that a telescope of twice the size would be $2^3 = 8$ times more expensive. Through its many economies the MMT has broken this geometrical rule of thumb and has cost only one-half to one-third of the amount for a single-mirror telescope of equivalent aperture.

Mt. Hopkins is at an altitude of 2,600 meters (8,500 feet), considerably higher than Kitt Peak. At this height the MMT is above much of the water vapor in the Earth's atmosphere, which blocks infrared radiation. The MMT is thus especially well situated for infrared work. Plans for the multiple-mirror telescope accordingly include observations in both the visible and infrared wavelengths.

The MMT is a joint project of the Smithsonian Astrophysical Observatory of Cambridge, Massachusetts, and the University of Arizona at Tucson. Dedicated in 1979, it had by 1980 already proved itself a success. This led to the belief that such a multiple-mirror design may well be one of the best ways to construct a new generation of telescopes that would have collecting areas many times larger than those of the MMT, Palomar, or Soviet telescopes. The MMT may thus be a prototype of telescopes for the future.

Both the Kitt Peak National Observatory and the University of California, as well as Soviet groups, are investigating plans for giant telescopes in this next generation, with collecting areas of from 10 to 25 meters in diameter. In addition to the multiple-mirror model (which requires six 10-meter primary mirrors in a single support structure), the Kitt Peak study group outlines three other basic ways of constructing a 25-meter telescope. Each of the designs uses an altazimuth mounting, and each poses technical problems. One, the so-called rotating shoe design, consists of a 25-meter by 75-meter spherical mirror enclosed in a shoelike rotating frame. The primary mirror is made up of hundreds of hexagonal segments. A second possibility is a 25-meter steerable-dish telescope, resembling a traditional radio telescope. The paraboloidal primary mirror is made up of many "petals." The third approach is an optical-infrared array consisting of rings of identical telescopes (single rings of six 10-meter instruments or sixteen 6.25-meter ones, or a four-ring configuration of 108 telescopes, each with reflector diameter of 2.4 meters), transmitting beams into a single image at a central focus.

206

Based on information obtained from Kitt Peak National Observatory, © AURA

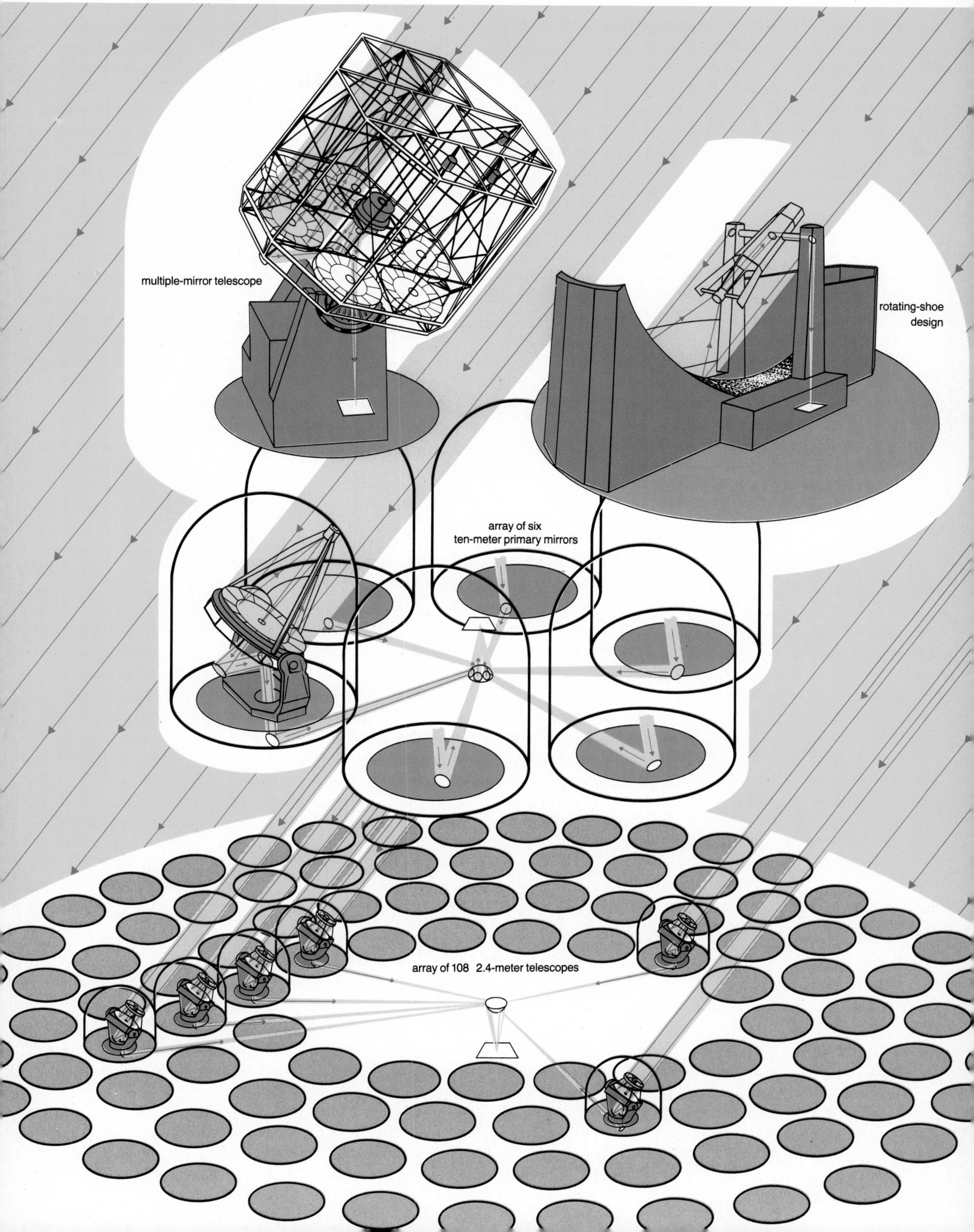
multiple-mirror telescope
rotating-shoe design
array of six ten-meter primary mirrors
array of 108 2.4-meter telescopes

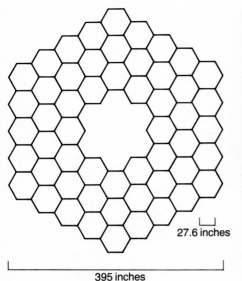

27.6 inches

395 inches

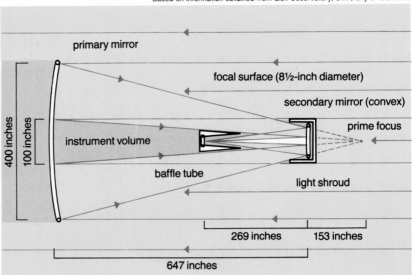

Based on information obtained from Lick Observatory, University of California

primary mirror

focal surface (8½-inch diameter)

secondary mirror (convex)

prime focus

400 inches

100 inches

instrument volume

baffle tube

light shroud

269 inches 153 inches

647 inches

Future telescope planned by the University of California would have a primary reflecting mirror 10 meters (400 inches) in diameter. The mirror would consist of a honeycomb pattern of segments in which an inner ring of seven hexagons (one enclosed by six others) would be surrounded by 54 hexagons in three outer rings. The movable support structure would be regulated by computer.

The University of California's prospective 10-meter (400-inch) "next generation telescope" will be more closely related to the single dish than to the multiple-mirror design. The primary reflector will be a honeycomb pattern of mirror segments. Seven hexagons (one enclosed by six others) will be surrounded by 54 hexagons arranged in three rings and independently controlled. A computer-regulated movable support structure will maintain the exact curvature. Though the University of California is funding the design stage, California astronomers hope for a single benefactor, who, like James Lick more than 100 years ago, will pay for the telescope.

A Soviet group is also considering a mosaic design for their version of a next-generation telescope. Their prime design is a 25-meter Cassegrain telescope made up of 500 hexagonal segments.

Infrared telescopes

Astronomers learn about the universe by studying not only visible light that comes from planets, stars, and galaxies, but also other types of radiation undetectable by the eye. It has always been difficult to detect infrared radiation because each infrared photon has a relatively low energy compared with an optical photon—too low, for example, to expose a photographic plate in most cases. Studies of infrared radiation have been boosted in recent years by the availability of new sensitive electronic infrared detectors and by the realization that many of the objects observed in the infrared may be stars in formation.

The use of the multiple-mirror telescope for infrared observations has been mentioned above. In addition, three large telescopes (two exclusively for infrared studies and one for optical and infrared work) became operational in 1979 at Mauna Kea Observatory, and a 2.3-meter (92-inch) infrared telescope located atop Jelm Mountain in Wyoming was completed in 1977.

Mauna Kea is a 4,200-meter (13,800-foot) extinct volcano on the island of Hawaii. Several factors were taken into account in selecting it as the

208

site of three large new telescopes (as well as the 2.2-meter optical-infrared telescope of the University of Hawaii, which has been located there since 1970). The atmosphere above Mauna Kea is especially dry (and therefore transparent to infrared radiation). The air is clear and steady, and because Mauna Kea is at a considerable distance from large urban concentrations its nighttime sky is extremely dark.

The weather atop Mauna Kea is a far cry from the beach climate that tourists normally associate with Hawaii. During the winter several feet of snow are the norm. In addition, the site is so high that astronomers have to spend a day acclimatizing themselves at an intermediate-altitude rest station on their way up to the telescopes. But the advantages of the site make its drawbacks seem relatively insignificant.

The largest of the new telescopes at Mauna Kea is the United Kingdom's infrared telescope (UKIRT). At 3.8 meters (150 inches) the UKIRT is the largest telescope in the world designed specifically for observing infrared radiation. It has several novel design features, of which the most notable is its very thin, and therefore lightweight, primary mirror. As compared with the 300 to 400 tons that a telescope of traditional design with comparable aperture would weigh, the 3.8-meter weighs only 80 tons. Indications are that the image quality that can be achieved with the thin mirror compares favorably with that obtainable with one of conventional optical design.

The next largest of the three new telescopes at Mauna Kea is the 3.6-

Mauna Kea Observatory in Hawaii as photographed in 1979. From left to right are the Canada-France-Hawaii 3.6-meter telescope dome, a 61-centimeter telescope dome (tiny), the 2.24-meter telescope dome of the University of Hawaii, the 3.8-meter telescope dome of the U.K., the 61-centimeter telescope dome of the University of Hawaii (tiny), and, in the foreground, the dome of the 3-meter telescope operated by the University of Hawaii for the U.S. National Aeronautics and Space Administration. Three of the large telescopes are used for observations in the infrared region of the spectrum.

University of Hawaii

Photos, Dale P. Cruikshank

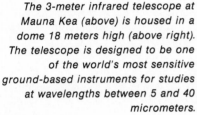

The 3-meter infrared telescope at Mauna Kea (above) is housed in a dome 18 meters high (above right). The telescope is designed to be one of the world's most sensitive ground-based instruments for studies at wavelengths between 5 and 40 micrometers.

meter (140-inch) instrument, built jointly by the National Research Council of Canada, the Centre National de la Recherche Scientifique of France, and the University of Hawaii. Although its main use will be at optical wavelengths, it was also designed to do infrared research.

Finally, the U.S. National Aeronautics and Space Administration (NASA) erected a 3-meter (120-inch) Infrared Telescope Facility atop Mauna Kea. Administered by the University of Hawaii, the facility was set up to support NASA space studies in addition to basic research in infrared astronomy. Its first task, for example, was to return data in support of the Voyager 2 encounter with Jupiter. For the study of Jupiter's "hot spots" (areas much hotter than the surrounding regions), ground-based telescopes are needed to locate the regions. The facility also provided support for the subsequent Voyager missions to Saturn.

The 2.3-meter (92-inch) Wyoming Infrared Telescope, funded jointly by the state of Wyoming and the U.S. National Science Foundation, was opened in 1977. It is located 35 miles southwest of Laramie, Wyoming, atop 2,943-meter (9,656-foot) Jelm Mountain. Infrared telescopes differ in several subtle ways from telescopes used for visible light observations. For example, the Cassegrain hole in the Wyoming Infrared Telescope's primary mirror is made as small as possible in order to limit the amount of radiation coming through the opening that might be reflected into the detector. Other parts of the structure are cooled to prevent them from emitting infrared radiation that might reach the detector.

A "chopping" technique is often used for infrared work at many telescopes. For example, the secondary mirror can be rocked back and forth by 3.5 arc minutes at frequencies up to 40 times per second. This allows alternate viewing of adjacent areas of sky, one with the source under study and the other presumably of uniform background. The difference between the two indicates the strength of the infrared source.

210

Space telescopes

Observational astronomers today are no longer limited to telescopes on remote mountains to make their observations. They can also use data sent back from satellites in space.

Space telescopes are studying radiation of different types. Since the Earth's ozone layer prevents all radiation at the short end of the spectrum from penetrating the Earth's atmosphere, astronomers have launched telescopes and other detectors in rockets and in orbiting satellites to study gamma rays, X-rays, and ultraviolet light.

Because X-rays would pass through ordinary mirrors they were approaching directly, one cannot merely use parabolic mirrors face-on to make images in X-ray studies. Instead, grazing incidence optics must be used. By carefully choosing a variety of curved surfaces that suitably allow X-radiation to "skip" along, as a stone can be skipped along a lake surface, astronomers can now fashion telescopes that actually form X-ray images. But the appearances of these telescopes are very different from those of optical instruments.

The study of X-rays and gamma rays is called high-energy astrophysics. The astronomical community recently has placed a high priority on work in this field. The first High-Energy Astronomy Observatory, HEAO 1, was launched by NASA in 1977. Its main instrument was able to survey the X-ray sky with about ten times the sensitivity of previous instruments, and it recorded about 1,500 X-ray sources. A second instrument was able to help ground-based optical telescopes locate objects more accurately. Other instruments aboard HEAO 1 studied an apparently steady background X-radiation and also observed X-rays in a higher energy range and gamma rays. HEAO 2, launched in 1978, was able to point at and study in detail the interesting objects mapped by HEAO 1. Called the Einstein Observatory, HEAO 2 uses grazing incidence optics to bounce X-rays off first a paraboloidal surface and then a hyperboloidal surface at an angle of less than 1° to make an image. A third HEAO was launched in 1979, to study cosmic rays and gamma rays, in particular.

Until 1980 the largest astronomical telescope that had been sent into space was the 0.9-meter (36-inch) instrument aboard the Copernicus satellite, the third Orbiting Astronomical Observatory, launched by NASA in 1973. The International Ultraviolet Explorer (IUE), launched under a joint effort of NASA and the British and European space organizations in 1978, carries a 0.45-meter (18-inch) telescope with two spectrographs for studies of the ultraviolet region. It carries a vidicon system that records data much more efficiently than Copernicus's detector and thus gives spectra more quickly. In synchronous orbit above the Atlantic Ocean, it is controlled for 16 hours each day by astronomers in a control room in the Goddard Space Flight Center in Greenbelt, Maryland, and for the other 8 by astronomers in a control room in Spain. An interactive system for examining the data quickly allows astronomers to modify their observing programs on the spot, thus making especially effective use of their telescope time. IUE has been used to study a wide range of astronomical objects, including planets, stars, galaxies, and quasars.

211

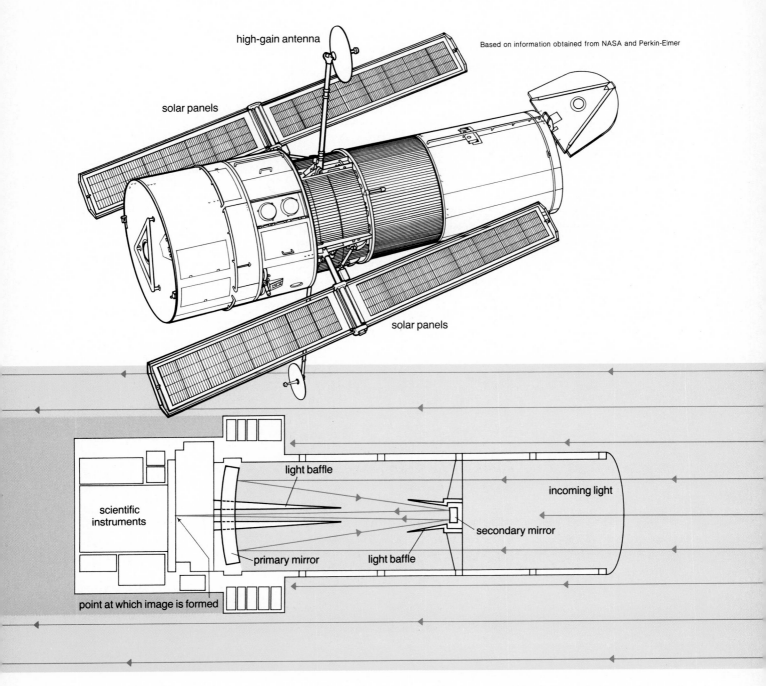

high-gain antenna

Based on information obtained from NASA and Perkin-Elmer

solar panels

solar panels

light baffle

incoming light

scientific
instruments

secondary mirror

primary mirror

light baffle

point at which image is formed

Space Telescope, scheduled to be placed in orbit by the U.S. National Aeronautics and Space Administration in 1983, will concentrate on studies in the visible and ultraviolet portions of the spectrum. At about 485 kilometers (300 miles) above the Earth, it will avoid the distorting effects of the Earth's atmosphere. Its 2.4-meter (95-inch) primary mirror will direct light to one of several analyzing instruments.

Space Telescope (ST), with a mirror 2.4 meters (95 inches) in diameter, is scheduled for launch in 1983 to concentrate on visible and ultraviolet studies. Free of the twinkling effects caused by turbulence in the Earth's atmosphere and located above the atmosphere in perennially black skies, ST will be able to observe details of objects in space about seven times finer than can be viewed with ground-based telescopes. Also, ST will be able to observe objects about 50 times fainter than can be observed with ground-based telescopes, partly because the sky is darker and partly because images will be concentrated better on the detectors. This will allow astronomers to see objects about seven times more distant than they can now, which will give them access to a volume of space about 350 times larger than is now possible. Thus, their understanding of many astronomical problems will be greatly improved by the capabilities of Space Telescope. For example, they should be able to improve their knowledge of distances to thousands of galaxies and thereby increase their understanding of the overall cosmic scale of distances. It should become possible to study quasars so far back in time that conditions in the universe must have been very different from the way they are now.

Space Telescope's primary mirror, of the Ritchey-Chrétien design, will direct light to one of several analyzing instruments. The major instruments are planned to be a wide-field planetary camera, a faint-object spectrograph, a faint-object camera, a high-resolution spectrograph, and a high-speed photometer/polarimeter. The use of charge-coupled devices will play a primary role in providing sensitivity.

Work on the faintest objects will be very slow, for at the limit of its observing ability ST will receive only one photon (that is, one particle of light energy) per minute. Thus there will continue to be much for ground-based telescopes to do, even though they are limited to working nights while ST can observe all the time.

Designed to operate for at least 15 years in orbit, Space Telescope will be launched by NASA aboard the space shuttle. It will then fly freely and be controlled from Earth. The European Space Agency is cooperating with NASA by providing the solar array, one of the instruments, and some of the staff. Astronauts in a space shuttle will be able to visit Space Telescope to make repairs, carry out maintenance, and even change one of the scientific instruments that receives the light from the primary mirror. Such visits are expected to be necessary every two and a half years. ST is designed to be brought down to Earth, refurbished, and launched again.

The space shuttle will also be used to carry other telescopes. NASA plans a cryogenically cooled Shuttle Infrared Telescope Facility, with an 0.85-m mirror. It will be operated aboard the European Spacelab in 1986 or 1987. A large solar optical telescope, for launch aboard Spacelab in the mid- and late 1980s, is also being planned. It will have a 1.25-meter (50-inch) aperture, which will allow resolution of features on the Sun ten times smaller than the smallest that can now be studied from the Earth. This telescope will be sensitive from the far ultraviolet through the visible and near infrared. It will be of a Gregorian type. Gregorians, like Cassegrains, have a secondary mirror that reflects the light back through a hole in the center of the primary mirror. Unlike Cassegrains, though, the secondary is located beyond rather than in front of the prime focus, which for solar telescopes serves the important purpose of putting the secondary mirror beyond the strongest concentrations of solar heat. Until this characteristic was realized, the Gregorian was thought of by some as an outmoded design.

And so astronomers will launch the 17th-century Gregorian design in a 20th-century space shuttle. Thus science draws on the wisdom of the ages to explore the past, present, and future of the universe.

Hazards of Low-Level Radiation

by Karl Z. Morgan

Exposure to low levels of ionizing radiation can be harmful to human health. The risk of developing cancer is greater than it was considered to be a decade ago.

Three Mile Island nuclear power plant near Harrisburg, Pennsylvania, experienced an accident in 1979 that caused radioactive gases to escape into the atmosphere. The incident focused concern on the hazards to human health of low levels of radiation.

KARL Z. MORGAN *is a Professor in the School of Nuclear Engineering at the Georgia Institute of Technology, Atlanta.*

(Overleaf) Photo by Dan Morrill

The accident in 1979 at the Three Mile Island nuclear power plant in Pennsylvania thrust into sharp relief an issue that has become one of the most controversial and sensitive in modern technology—the hazards to human health of low levels of radiation. Concern for these hazards had already led many people throughout the world to oppose the building of nuclear power plants, opposition that was intensified after the Three Mile Island episode. The related issue of the disposal of radioactive nuclear waste also came to the forefront and caused additional controversy.

Scientists have long known that large amounts of radiation can cause cancer in man and can be harmful in other ways, but most also believed that low doses produced few or negligible ill effects. Recent studies, however, have produced strong evidence indicating that low levels not only cause cancer and genetic damage but may indeed be even more harmful than higher doses per unit exposure.

Types of radiation

Radiation is often classified as either ionizing or nonionizing. Ionizing radiation is that which has sufficient energy to separate one or more electrons (each with a negative charge) from an atom, leaving it with a positive charge. As a matter of convention radiations with energy greater than about ten electron volts (eV) are classed as ionizing. Most substances have ionizing

216

potentials greater than 15 eV; for example, the ionizing potential of molecular nitrogen (N_2) is 15.5 eV. Above this potential about half the energy of the radiation is used in producing ionization and the rest in exciting the atoms and molecules.

Radiation can be further classified as mechanical, particulate, and electromagnetic. Mechanical radiations consist of sound, ultrasound, and infrasound, all of which are nonionizing. Particulate radiations are of many types, the most common of which are alpha, beta, neutrons, protons, and mesons. All of these are ionizing radiations except neutrons. Fast neutrons are not directly ionizing, but they can give up their energy to atoms so that the atom or part of it recoils as a heavy ion that produces ionization along its track. Slow neutrons (thermal) can be captured by the nucleus of an atom in such a way that the atom becomes radioactive, giving off electromagnetic radiation (X- and gamma rays) and particulate radiation (such as alpha or beta). Such an atom is then termed a radionuclide.

Electromagnetic radiations can be either ionizing or nonionizing. At the high-energy end of the scale cosmic radiation can have tremendous energies, as high as 10^{18} eV, and can be either particulate or electromagnetic. Common X-rays have energies from about 30 KeV to 50 MeV. Ultraviolet radiations have energies ranging from 3.18 eV to 100 eV so that at the high end they are slightly ionizing, but at the low end the energy is not sufficient to produce any ionization. As the energy decreases, there is next the narrow band of visible radiations, 1.57 eV to 3.18 eV; infrared or heat, 1.2×10^{-3} eV to 1.57 eV; microwave, 6×10^{-7} eV to 1.2×10^{-3} eV; radio frequency, 4×10^{-8} eV to 6×10^{-7} eV; and long wavelengths of energy less than 4×10^{-8} eV. None of these radiations can produce ionization, and so they release energy by current induction and excitation.

Even low levels of these nonionizing radiations can be damaging to man. For example, skin cancer can be caused by ultraviolet and cataracts by microwave radiation. There is considerable uncertainty regarding what should be the maximum permissible exposure (MPE) levels for these radiations. The occupational MPE in the U.S.S.R. for microwave radiation is set at ten microwatts per square centimeter, while in the U.S. the level is ten milliwatts per square centimeter.

The quantity expressing the energy density delivered by ionizing radiation is absorbed dose (D), the unit of which is the rad; one rad corresponds to 100 ergs delivered per gram of the medium. The quantity that is considered to relate most nearly to human damage from exposure to ionizing radiation is dose equivalent (H). The unit of dose equivalent is the rem. Dose equivalent is given by H(rem) = D(rad) × Q × N, in which Q and N are modifying factors. Values of Q are determined by the ion density along the track of ionizing radiation, but it is common practice to set Q = 1 for X-, gamma, and beta radiations, 20 for alpha, and 8 for chronic exposure to fast neutrons. N is a biological correction factor and is taken as equal to one for all external exposure and for all internal X- and gamma-ray exposure. N = 1 for all organs except bone and whenever radium is the parent element in the organ. N = 5 for alpha and beta radiations in the bone when radium is not the parent element.

217

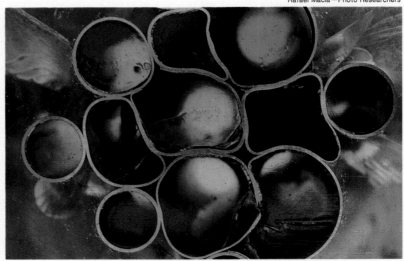

Fuel rods like those used in nuclear power plants would swell and contort from their normal round shapes by exposure to high temperatures as seen in a laboratory simulation. Such temperatures could be produced if an accident drains the reactor of coolant; the subsequent distortions of the rods might prevent the circulation of emergency coolant and allow the rods to melt through the containment, releasing radioactivity.

Sources of ionizing radiations

There are both natural background and man-made sources of ionizing radiation. Natural background radiation consists both of cosmic radiation from outer space and the Sun and the terrestrial alpha, beta, and gamma radiations from radionuclides (radioactive atoms) in the rocks, soil, air, food, and even from radionuclides such as potassium-40 and radium-226 in our bodies. Man-made radiations come from fallout from atmospheric testing of nuclear weapons, from medical X-rays and radioisotopes used in medicine, luminous watch dials containing hydrogen-3, smoke detectors containing americium-241, the nuclear power industry, and many other sources. In the U.S. the average natural background dose to the total body is about 105 millirem per year, that from medical applications about 90, that from weapons fallout about 4, and that from all other sources including nuclear power plants about 3.

When exposure results from a radiation source external to the body, it is referred to as external exposure. When a radionuclide is contained in a body organ, the body receives internal exposure. Exposure may result from a relatively insoluble form of a radionuclide as it passes through the gastrointestinal tract, from a soluble radionuclide such as hydrogen-3 or sodium-24 that is relatively uniformly distributed in the body, or from radionuclides such as iodine-131 that go selectively to the thyroid gland and plutonium-239 that localizes in bone. External radiation takes place when a person is near a source, but for internal exposure a person carries the source in his body where it continues to irradiate him until it is eliminated by biological excretion and radioactive decay. The term "low-level radiation" is not well defined, but in general it is considered to be at levels less than five rem per year, the occupational MPE for total body exposure.

Genetic hazards

Early studies of H. J. Muller on fruit flies indicated that ionizing radiation is a major mutagen (a substance that tends to increase the frequency or extent of mutations). This caused some people to suggest that perhaps

218

low-level exposure to ionizing radiation is beneficial because it accelerates the mutation rate and results in more rapid evolution and improvement of the human race. A few moments further reflection, however, should convince one that such radiation should be avoided as much as is practicable. Though this radiation increases the mutation rate, the improvement in living organisms comes about only by the survival of the fittest. Such radiation has been beneficial over the long centuries of time only in the same sense that certain diseases, blizzards, and man-eating tigers were beneficial in that they more frequently eliminated the weak that might otherwise have been our forebears.

Muller not only showed that dominant and recessive mutations increase in direct proportion with the accumulated dose of ionizing radiation but also emphasized that a more serious consequence of low-level radiation exposure was its production of what he called nonvisible mutations. These mutations were difficult to study in animals, and he held that they could produce insidious and comparatively subtle effects such as greater susceptibility to disease, lack of resilience, and failure to attain peak performance. He estimated that there are about 10,000 nonvisible mutations produced by radiation per visible mutation and that because of their nature they persist a very long time and spread widely in the gene pool of every living organism. As a consequence of these findings most of the maximum permissible exposure levels were originally set to reduce the risk of genetic damage.

Concern for radiation-induced genetic mutations was somewhat diminished in 1965 when W. R. Russell in his studies on mice found the mutation frequency (mutations per rem) at low doses and low dose rates was only about 10% of that at high doses and dose rates above about 5,000 roentgens per hour. This seemed to be a particularly important finding because most exposures except those used in medical therapy are of low doses and at low dose rates. More recently, however, Mary F. Lyon and coworkers collected

Courtesy, Brookhaven National Laboratory

Fruit flies have undergone a genetic change as a result of exposure to radioactive material. A normal male fruit fly was fed a tiny amount of radioactive phosphorus, and this affected its reproductive cells in such a way that offspring grew wings that were short and rudimentary. This characteristic also appeared in later generations, thus proving to be a true mutation.

and studied other data on low-level genetic effects and reported that there is strong evidence that at doses and dose rates lower than those studied by Russell and approaching natural background levels the mutation frequency actually seems to increase. Thus there may be no genetic safety factor at low doses and low dose rates, and the genetic hazards of low-level radiation may be as great or greater than predicted by Muller.

Somatic hazards

The only well-recognized somatic hazard of serious consequences from exposure to low levels of ionizing radiation is radiation-induced cancer. Low levels of radiation exposure do shorten the lives of mice by about 10^{-4} life spans per rem (equivalent to about $2^1/2$ days per rem for man), but it is not well established whether there is life-shortening in man that is independent of cancer induction. Although there are changes in the human system brought on by low-level exposure to ionizing radiation, such as an increase in the number of chromosomal aberrations, the relation to human damage is not well established.

The hazard of cancer production by ionizing radiation has been recognized since the early years of the century, but until the past two decades most radiobiologists and health physicists believed in the threshold hypothesis; that is, that there was a safe dose of radiation and so long as one did not exceed this threshold dose there was no risk of that radiation producing cancer or other forms of damage during a person's lifetime. They believed that at doses less than the threshold dose any radiation damage would be repaired, or, if a cancer were initiated, the incubation period until the cancer is recognized clinically would exceed the remaining life span of the exposed individual. During the past two decades, however, there has accumulated a vast amount of data on many kinds of animals, including man, which reject the threshold and support a so-called linear hypothesis for cancer induction.

During cell division in a Trillium erectum chromosomes normally separate into two sets and withdraw to opposite ends of the cell (below right). When a cell has been exposed to X-rays, the chromosomes do not all go to the ends of the cell and one pair fails to separate, forming a bridge (below).

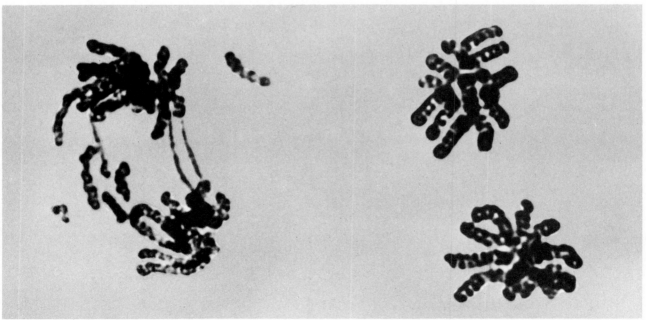

Photos, courtesy, Carmia Borek, Radiological Research Laboratory, Columbia University
College of Physicians and Surgeons; (bottom) NATURE, vol. 283, pp. 776–778

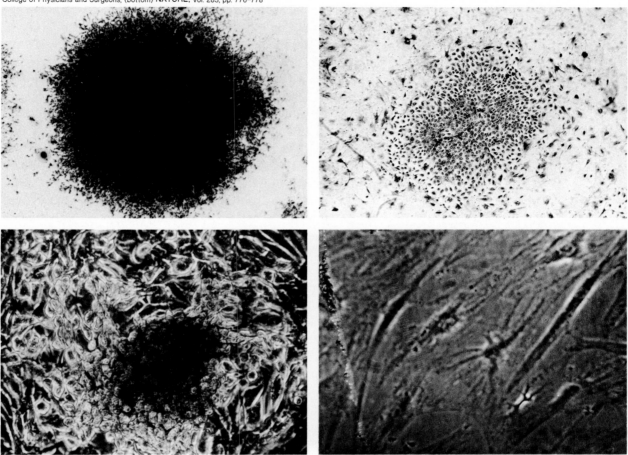

The International Commission on Radiological Protection (ICRP) in a 1971 working paper noted that the risk of radiation-induced cancer might be much greater than had been considered earlier, stating that further observation could lead to the conclusion that "the ratio of somatic to genetic effects after a given exposure is 60 times greater than was thought 15 years ago." It is interesting and instructive to observe that this ratio of the estimate of cancer risk to genetic risk has continued to rise since 1971 in spite of the fact that the estimates of genetic risk have risen in this period also.

There are many mechanisms of chronic radiation damage to body cells. They include damage to the blood vessels that supply the cells, damage to a cell's membrane, the formation of harmful chemicals such as hydrogen peroxide, damage to the body's repair and maintenance system (the reticuloendothelial system) such that these white blood cells fail to recognize and remove foreign protein and early-developing cancer cells, and direct damage to the nucleus of a cell. At low dose levels probably the last two forms of damage are most significant in causing cancer in man. In the nucleus of the normal somatic cell of man there are 46 chromosomes comprising the genes that were inherited from one's father and mother. Combinations of information among the genes along these chromosomes correspond to the amount of data in a huge library. In even a small dose of one-half of a rem of X-rays as is commonly delivered in a diagnostic X-ray procedure, more than

X-radiation at various levels can cause normal cells to become malignant. At the top right is a colony of normal cells of a hamster embryo that have been grown in a petri dish; at the top left are hamster embryo cells that have been made malignant by a dose of one rad of X-rays. At the bottom right is a culture of normal human skin cells, and at the bottom left are human skin cells in a culture made malignant by 400 rad of X-rays.

221

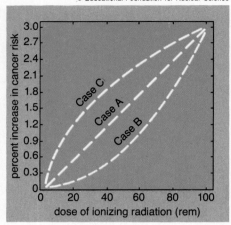

Adapted from "Cancer and low level
ionizing radiation," Karl Z. Morgan, THE BULLETIN
OF THE ATOMIC SCIENTISTS, p. 36, September 1978
© Educational Foundation for Nuclear Science

The relationship of cancer risk to doses of ionizing radiation describes different paths on a graph, depending upon the hypothesis used. Case A illustrates the linear hypothesis, in which the risk increases in direct proportion to the dose received. In Case B, the threshold hypothesis, the risk is low at a low average dose per person and increases rapidly with higher doses. Case C, in which the risk is greater at low than at high doses, may be applicable to leukemia among the young and old and to most other forms of cancer regardless of the victim's age.

a billion photons (bundles of electromagnetic energy) are absorbed per square centimeter of the body, and for the most part the cell nuclei are the most likely targets for radiation damage. When these photons stream through the cells of the body, there are four possible consequences: the photons pass through or near a particular cell without producing any damage; the cell is so damaged that it is killed or no longer able to reproduce itself by cell division; the cell is damaged, but the damage is repaired; and the cell nucleus is damaged, but the cell survives to reproduce itself in its disturbed form. It continues to divide and multiply, forming a clone of cells that eventually is diagnosed as a malignancy, perhaps 5, 10, or 50 years after this one photon damaged this single body cell.

Fortunately, this latter event is very unlikely because every day millions of photons from natural background radiation pass through the human body. Early in a person's life his immune system usually recognizes and removes these damaged cells before they can develop into a clone unless, as in the case of exposure in the uterus, the precursor cells to the immune system (the red bone marrow cells) are damaged. Unfortunately, as a person gets older, less of his bone marrow is active (an increasing fraction is inactive or yellow rather than red marrow). Therefore, his immune system is weakened, and at the same time he has received through the years more and more radiation so that the chances increase that he carries within his body one or more clones of cells that are incubating and developing into a clinically diagnosed malignancy.

Some types of cancer may require two or more damaging insults to a cell before they can be generated. These insults to the cell may come from a virus infection, a carcinogenic drug, ionizing radiation, or in some cases there may be a contributing inherited defect. This genetic factor may be the reason some families or races of people have a probability higher than the average of developing certain types of cancer.

On this simple theory of cancer development it is seen that the induction of cancer by ionizing radiation is simply one of chance. A person might develop cancer from the chest X-ray he received 20 years ago or from natural background radiation received 50 years ago. The more exposure a person gets the greater the chance he will die of a radiation-induced cancer, but there is no way of predicting except on a statistical basis who will die of a radiation-induced cancer or when it will occur following a given exposure. This is like most other risks in a person's life. For example, a fatal airplane accident may come during a person's first plane ride or on his 79th, but on a statistical basis the more rides one takes on a plane the greater the chance one will die in a plane accident. This analogy would be even better if one likens the radiation exposure that eventually leads to a malignancy to a rough landing of a plane that caused a small crack in the plane structure that led to the crash some years later.

Thus it can be concluded there is no "safe" level of radiation exposure, and no dose can be set so low that the risk is zero. This is why the standards-setting bodies are emphasizing that people should keep all exposures "as low as reasonably achievable" and should have no exposure unless the associated benefits exceed the risks of radiation damage.

Studies of low-level exposures

During the early period until about 1955 most of the information on the effects of ionizing radiation on mammals was on mice and rats, and for the most part such experiments were conducted at relatively high doses above 50 rem. Almost no data were available on chronic human exposure. What was available was information on such conditions as human exposure from body burdens of radium, and this was mostly data on high-level exposure of women who had worked in the radium-dial industry. Although R. D. Evans in his early analysis of this data presented it in support of the threshold hypothesis, many other researchers have shown that such data are best represented by a linear hypothesis. In fact, recent analysis of such data shows that the equation giving the best fit is: Effect $=$ (constant) $\times$ (dose)^n in which n is less than one. Thus, the cancer risk per rem is greater at low doses than at high doses. For practical purposes the threshold hypothesis can be represented by this equation when $n = 2$, and of course the linear hypothesis is given by this equation when $n = 1$. As discussed below there is strong evidence from other data to suggest that n should in many cases (and especially for alpha or neutron radiation) be less than one, and that not only is the threshold hypothesis ($n \simeq 2$) nonconservative but also the linear hypothesis ($n = 1$) tends in some cases to underestimate the radiation hazard from low-level exposure.

By far the most extensive studies of human exposure to low-level radiation are the many investigations of in utero exposure. The largest of these studies, which involved hundreds of thousands of children exposed to diagnostic X-rays, or pelvimetries, during the nine-month period before they were born, was conducted in the U.K. by Alice M. Stewart and George W. Kneale. They found that the human is most radiosensitive during the time of the fertilized ovum and the fetus, and that there is an increased risk of a radiation-induced malignancy in a child even from a single pelvimetry to its mother with an average dose of about 0.5 rad. The researchers found the risk of leukemia is about 3 per 10,000 children exposed to one rad in the uterus and that the total cancer risk is about twice this. This risk decreased linearly with decreasing number of pelvimetries down to a single pelvimetry, and presumably there is no dose to the unborn so low that the risk of inducing cancer is zero. Because of this high risk of cancer to the fetus the ICRP in 1964 recommended that diagnostic X-rays to the abdomen or pelvic region of women of child-bearing age be avoided except during the ten-day interval following the beginning of menstruation or for emergencies.

The largest study of a normal adult population exposed to low levels of ionizing radiation is that by Thomas F. Mancuso, Alice M. Stewart, and George W. Kneale concerning the radiation workers at the nuclear reactor facilities in Hanford, Washington. The average dose of the 442 radiation workers who died of cancer in the period 1944 to 1972 was about one rem, and 7 to 8% of these cancers were radiation-induced. The total deaths in the study group numbered 3,520, and so the risk of fatal cancer was about 8 per 1,000 persons exposed to one rem. This risk per rem is about 20 times higher than that found in other studies where the human populations were exposed to much higher doses.

Nuclear reactor at Hanford, Washington, was the site of the largest study of a normal adult population exposed to low levels of ionizing radiation (see accompanying text).

223

From a distance of eight miles and with their eyes shielded observers (top) watch a nuclear bomb explode (bottom) in 1955 near Yucca Flats, Nevada. Decades later those living in the fallout area from such tests were developing leukemia at rates significantly above normal.

The Hanford study has led to a great controversy because the reported hazard of low-level exposure is much greater than many persons had believed. About the time this study began to show evidence of a cancer hazard, the U.S. Department of Energy canceled its support of the program. This led to numerous claims and counterclaims in subsequent congressional hearings, but as of 1980 the program was being supported by another government agency, the National Institute for Occupational Safety and Health (NIOSH). New data from this extended study have tended to confirm and strengthen the earlier findings.

Several groups were engaged to find fault with and refute the Hanford study. However, the more thorough of these were forced to conclude that there is a statistically significant increase in cancer related to the recorded radiation dose received by the Hanford workers in at least two of the three malignancies earlier reported on the rise.

The studies revealed several other interesting observations about the Hanford population: workers who had received five or more rem had an increased longevity of ten years; there was a slight decrease in the total cancer risk in spite of a significant increase in cancers of bone and of the pancreas; and there was no significant increase in leukemia. It has been suggested that these developments may be the result of some unknown factor other than radiation or were due to the so-called "healthy worker syndrome." The Hanford radiation workers were carefully screened for good health before employment and kept under constant medical surveillance.

Thus one may take sides and draw his own conclusions, but the final answer will come only with further studies of this and other similar populations of radiation workers whose accumulated dose from external and internal exposure has been recorded. One such group is the population of radiation workers at Oak Ridge, Tennessee, which Mancuso, Stewart, and Kneale planned to examine in detail if their financial support continued. Other radiation workers under study by NIOSH are those at the Portsmouth (New Hampshire) Naval Shipyard. Preliminary studies by Thomas Najarian and Theodore Colton indicated a statistically significant increase in leukemia among these workers.

The studies of B. Modan and coworkers of the induction of head and neck tumors among immigrants into Israel who were treated with X-rays to combat ringworm are of particular interest because these researchers found a risk of thyroid carcinoma of 1.2 carcinomas per 10,000 persons whose thyroid glands were exposed to one rad. This supports the linear hypothesis down to the average dose of 6.5 rad used in those treatments. This dose may be compared with the present 30-rad maximum permissible annual dose to the thyroid tissues of radiation workers.

More recently there have been disquieting reports of other large human populations that were exposed to low doses of ionizing radiations decades ago and are now showing an increase of statistical significance in malignancy rates. Some of these population groups are those once in the military who developed leukemia years after taking part in atmospheric testing of nuclear weapons, U.S. Marines who helped clean up the Japanese cities of Hiroshima and Nagasaki after they were devastated by atomic bombs during

225

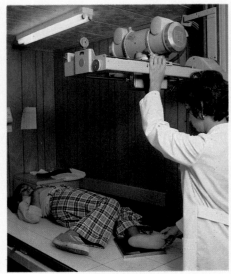

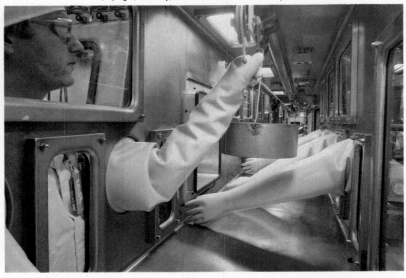

Modern technology has caused many people to be exposed to various levels of radiation, some on a daily basis. Above, a broken foot is X-rayed, and at the top right workers in the plutonium processing facility at the Los Alamos (New Mexico) Scientific Laboratory wear protective gloves. At the center right is the control room of a nuclear power plant, while at the bottom right radiation workers check gauges on a panel.

World War II, and residents of Utah who were in the high fallout area during atmospheric testing of nuclear weapons at a Nevada test site.

The two population exposure groups that have been studied extensively since the end of World War II are the survivors of the atomic bombings of Hiroshima and Nagasaki and patients who were treated with ionizing radiation as a palliative treatment of ankylosing spondylitis. Since 1960 these two groups have served as the principal sources of information on the effects of ionizing radiation on man. But unfortunately, as pointed out below, there is overwhelming evidence that both these studies tend to underestimate the hazards of low-level exposure.

Reasons for controversy

There are many reasons for the large difference in opinion regarding the hazards of low-level exposure. This difference exists among scientists and engineers as well as concerned members of the general public. One reason why many people tend to underestimate these hazards is that they still cling to the threshold hypothesis, and some groups seem to have the mistaken view that an admission of potential harm from exposure to low-level radiation would seriously weaken their profession. Good examples of such groups are radiologists and nuclear engineers. On the other hand some members of the public have developed a serious case of radiation phobia that is directed almost exclusively against the nuclear power industry. They fail to recognize two important facts: a 1% reduction in unnecessary exposures of the population of the United States to the diagnostic use of X-rays and medically applied radioisotopes would reduce the population dose more than the complete elimination of the nuclear power industry; and at least for many decades to come the principal sources of energy available in the U.S. for the generation of electricity are coal and nuclear energy, and both of these choices present serious attendant problems regarding environmental pollution and public health.

Today all the standards-setting organizations make use of the linear hypothesis in establishing radiation protection policies and the levels of MPE. Members of these bodies claim that the use of this hypothesis, assuming the risk of cancer per rem is the same at low doses as at high doses of radiation, provides a generous safety factor and a large measure of conservatism. Unfortunately, as mentioned above, the contrary seems to be true in most cases of human exposure. Some of the reasons that many scientists underestimate the risks of low-level radiation and why the linear hypothesis actually underestimates the cancer risk are as follows:

---

(1) Overkill: most studies on animal and human exposures have been at high doses, and the cancer risk at these levels has been extrapolated down to low doses. However, at these high doses many of the exposed population do not survive long enough to die of the malignancies under study.

(2) Cell Sterilization: Several scientists and standards-setting bodies have, for example, extrapolated the incidence of thyroid cancer from very high doses of ^{131}I down to the risk of low-level exposure to the thyroid. They fail to recognize that the high doses selectively destroy most of the tissue that

Researchers attempt to determine whether low doses of gamma radiation induce mutations in mice at the U.S. Department of Energy's Oak Ridge (Tennessee) National Laboratory. Caged mice are arrayed in a circle around an in-floor radiation source which is operated by remote control.

may be incubating a cancer, thereby preventing a malignancy from originating from the dead thyroid cells.

(3) Short Follow-Up Period and Fractional Life Span Studies: Most animal studies are of animals that live only 5 to 10 years, while man is a 70-year-animal; the risk of cancer in many cases relates to the time since the radiation exposure occurred and not (as often assumed) to the effects of radiation exposure over a certain fraction of the normal life span of the animal.

(4) Heterogeneity of Human Populations: As with all animals there is a wide variation in response to a radiation exposure among young and old, sick and well, fat and slim, smokers and nonsmokers, etc. Studies of Irwin D. J. Bross confirmed the work of Stewart and others and showed that a single pelvimetry gives the unborn child a 50% increased risk of dying of cancer before the age of ten, while if the child had received in utero X-ray exposure and in the first few years of life developed certain respiratory diseases he has a highly increased risk of dying of cancer.

(5) Differences in Response of Different Animals: Many of the conclusions regarding the effects of low-level radiation on humans are drawn from animal studies, yet it has been shown that there are extremely large differences in leukemia incidence and life shortening not only among different kinds of animals (rats, dogs, monkeys, etc.) but even among various strains of mice. One should not be surprised, therefore, at even greater differences between human and mouse.

Most of the controversy over effects of low-level exposure seems to arise from what many believe is a misuse of the data on effects of exposure of the survivors of Hiroshima and Nagasaki nuclear explosions and the effects of radiation treatments given to ankylosing spondylitis patients. Both of these sets of human exposure data conform with the linear hypothesis but suggest a cancer risk of only about 2 cancer deaths per 10,000 persons exposed to one rem. By contrast, human data from many other studies suggest a cancer risk ranging between 6 to 80 cancer deaths per 10,000 persons exposed to one rem.

The problem with the data on the survivors of the bombings of Hiroshima and Nagasaki is that the control group consists of those survivors that received low exposure, and if, as indicated above, the (effect) = $C \times (\text{Dose})^{1/2}$, then the cancers per rem are greater at low doses than at high doses. Furthermore, as indicated above, there are overkill and cell sterilization at high doses that tend to depreciate the cancer risk. Perhaps of even greater importance is the fact that these survivors were victims of blast, fire, trauma, disease, and deprivation; studies of other victims of fires, earthquakes, etc., show that such populations tend to have a reduced cancer risk because the incubation period for diseases such as pneumonia is much shorter than that of cancer and the weaker members of the population who are more likely to have cancers die of these diseases before the cancers have time to reach the recognizable stage. Joseph Rotblat compared the cancer incidence among early entrants into Hiroshima following the bomb explosion against the cancer incidence of late entrants after the residual activity from fallout

228

and neutron-induced activity had mostly died out and found a much higher cancer incidence among early entrants than among the survivors who had been exposed to other harmful effects of the bombing in addition to ionizing radiation exposure.

Normally man's immune surveillance mechanism holds in check all sources of foreign protein, including small colonies of mutant cells. However, this system seems to be relatively radiosensitive, and those Japanese who received numerous body insults at the time of the catastrophic atomic bombing died early of the radiation syndrome and common diseases, with which the weakened immune system was not able to cope. Kneale has shown that the terminal phase of preleukemia is associated with a high risk of dying of pneumonia, and the latter disease was a common cause of death in the early period following the bomb explosion. Only the stronger and more resilient of the population survived, a few of whom died later of cancer, but the weaker members of the population who were probably more likely to develop cancer died too soon of other causes to be so diagnosed.

The situation is much the same with the ankylosing spondylitic patients who were treated with radiation. In these studies the control group was the general population but should have been nonirradiated patients with ankylosing spondylitis. Kneale and Stewart have shown that persons with ankylosing spondylitis have less chance of dying of cancer because the disease shortens their life span.

Future outlook

In conclusion, it should be emphasized that there are great uncertainties concerning the kind and magnitude of risk not only from ionizing radiation but also from nonionizing radiations, from chemical pollutants in the environment, food supplements, drugs, pesticides, and many others. Unfortunately, in most cases the answers that are most trustworthy can come only from long-range studies of large human populations in which man serves as the guinea pig. There is no question but that there are both genetic and somatic risks (mostly cancer) from low-level exposure to ionizing radiations and that the cancer risk is far greater than scientists had considered it to be a decade ago.

Since there is no threshold or safe exposure level and because the risk of cancer per rem exposure appears in many cases to be greater at low doses than at high doses, it is important to keep all exposures as low as reasonably achievable. Population studies should be continued in order that people can make wise choices about the food they eat, the source of electrical energy that is safest, and the kind of environment in which they will live.

Surveyors of a Nation

by Harold L. Burstyn

From mapping the West to analyzing data from satellites the United States Geological Survey has provided invaluable aid to the nation in understanding its land and resources.

Earth offers both promises and threats to human society. It promises the resources with which to build industrial civilization. Water feeds crops, slakes thirst, and carries away wastes. From minerals are fashioned the artifacts of abundance. Fuels from the Earth transport us farther and faster than we can walk, turn darkness into daylight, cook and preserve food, and keep us in touch with one another across great distances. The structures that we build—the dams, bridges, buildings, tunnels, and power stations—rival the Earth's own features in size and complexity.

But the fragile Earth also threatens, holding mankind hostage to its mobility. Landslides, floods, earthquakes, volcanoes, and sea waves can destroy homes, factories, and cities unless close attention is paid to where and how they are built.

To cope with the demands that society and the Earth make on one another one needs foresight, which in turn requires understanding. Where will the energy, minerals, and water that industrial society uses in ever increasing amounts come from? What are the constraints that the Earth's mobility puts on the design and siting of our structures? What are the natural processes and habitats that our activities can harm? The people who understand the Earth, what it is made of, and how it works are the geologists, geophysicists, hydrologists, geographers, and engineers—Earth scientists, to use a single term. The largest organization of Earth scientists in the United States is the U.S. Geological Survey, founded a century ago.

Methods of mapping have changed during the 100 years of the U.S. Geological Survey. Above, a 19th-century topographer works with an alidade and plane table; on the opposite page is a color-enhanced photograph of the Colorado-Utah region taken from the Landsat satellite.

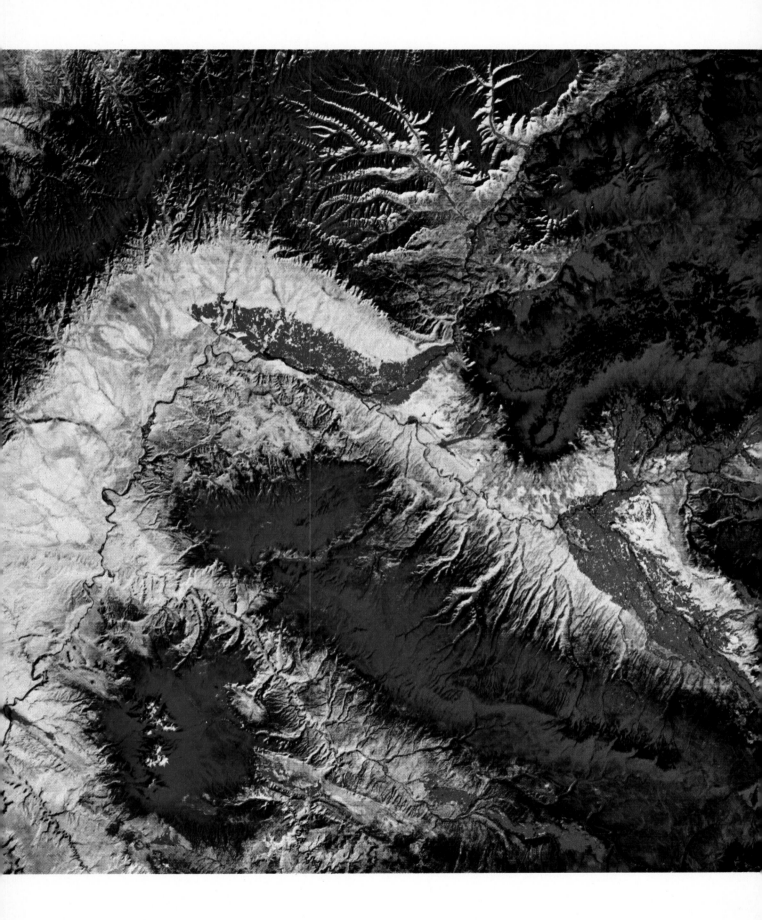

Harry Yount, first ranger of Yellowstone National Park, explores Berthoud Pass in Colorado for the Survey in 1874.

HAROLD L. BURSTYN *is the Historian of the United States Geological Survey.*

Industrialization and growth: mapping the West

Until the 19th century most of the world's people gained their living through farming, often raising by themselves everything they needed: food for nourishment, fiber for clothing, and wood for shelter and warmth. But beginning in Great Britain in the 1700s and spreading in the next century to the rest of Europe and to North America, industry replaced agriculture as the principal source of people's occupations. Farming for the market replaced farming for subsistence; food production grew even faster than population. Minerals dug from the earth replaced wood as the chief material for fuel and for building. During the 19th century Europe's population doubled, and North America's increased 12 times. Yet fewer and fewer farmers fed the growing numbers, more and more of whom, attracted by new industrial occupations, flocked to the cities.

The demands of this growing, industrializing population on the Earth's resources were unprecedented. In the colonial period in the U.S. a small amount of iron and other metals and of building stone sufficed, but by the 1830s coal for factories and steamships, coal gas for street lighting and cooking, iron for railroad rails and locomotives, and gold and silver for money were all needed in greater and greater amounts. At the same time the sciences of the Earth had developed to the point where their practitioners could help in the search for these ores and minerals. In Europe the national governments and in the U.S. the state governments began to set up geological surveys to inventory their resources.

In the United States the federal government promoted the settlement of the vast public domain beyond the original seaboard states. Though a geologist would occasionally be sent with a surveying party to investigate reports of minerals, the government's chief aim was to settle the land, and it paid little attention to the minerals. Before 1865 the federal government made only sporadic efforts to inventory the resources of the unsettled parts of the country. As a result most of the nation's mineral resources in the eastern half of the U.S. passed into private hands.

232

Astronomical observatory of the territorial surveys, photographed probably near Ft. Ruby, Nevada, in 1868. From 1867 to the end of the 1870s the territorial surveys mapped the West.

After the Civil War the pace of settlement increased. In one of history's great migrations the American people settled 430 million acres between 1870 and 1900. It took them only a single generation to occupy more land than their forebears had in ten. The headlong rush westward of people seeking new opportunity on the frontier made it hard for government explorers to keep pace with the settlers. Yet they tried. From 1867 to the end of the 1870s four separate groups, known collectively as the territorial surveys, mapped the West to determine its mineral resources and assess the possible uses for its land.

After a decade and a half of expansion, during which the territorial surveys were carried out, Pres. Rutherford B. Hayes and Secretary of the Interior Carl Schurz took office in 1877 as political reformers in the midst of a depression. They hoped to reduce the cost of government by merging the territorial surveys and placing in the hands of scientists the parceling of land for settlement. In 1878 the National Academy of Sciences prepared for Congress a plan for surveying and mapping the territories. Though Congress rejected any changes in the land system, it did consolidate federal geology into a single agency: the Geological Survey, established on March 3, 1879, was charged with "the classification of the public lands and examination of the geological structure, mineral resources, and products of the national domain."

Clarence King (far right) served as the first director of the U.S. Geological Survey. With him (left to right) are colleagues James Gardiner, Richard Cotter, and William Brewer.

To direct the new Geological Survey, President Hayes chose Clarence King, leader of the first territorial survey. From 1867 to 1878 King and his civilian colleagues had reconnoitered the natural resources along the route of the first transcontinental railway and had published a series of monographs that set high scientific standards for the geology of the American West. King, to U.S. Assistant Secretary of State John Hay "the best and brightest man of his generation," organized the new agency to demonstrate how useful science could be to the burgeoning mineral industry. His geologists and topographers went first to the major mining districts: Leadville in Colorado, Eureka and the Comstock Lode in Nevada, and the gold fields

233

of California. They hoped that their study of the principal ore bodies would show U.S. miners where to look for new ones and how to get more metal from the ores. The research could also help investors in U.S. mines choose their prospects. Success crowned the Survey's efforts when the report on the Leadville mining district, published in 1886, became the miners' bible. King and his colleagues also collected statistics, preparing for the Tenth Census of 1880 the first reliable inventory of U.S. mineral production and resources.

King wanted to extend the Survey over the entire country, but the Department of the Interior, uncertain about Congress's mandate, confined it to the public lands. Frustrated by the petty politics of the time and anxious to seek his fortune in mining, King resigned in 1881. To replace him U.S. Pres. James Garfield chose another territorial survey leader, John Wesley Powell. Powell and his colleagues had found in the stark landforms of the Rocky Mountain region the principles of a new approach to the Earth. By their emphasis on the role of erosion and deposition in forming the landscape, Powell, Grove K. Gilbert, and Clarence E. Dutton changed the direction of geomorphic thought.

On taking over the Survey Powell expanded it to cover the whole country, using the Congressional authorization (1882) "to continue the preparation of a geologic map of the United States." He countered the "states' rights" argument against his federal agency by beginning in 1884 a joint program of topographic mapping with Massachusetts, which as one of the original states had never contained any public lands. From Massachusetts, cooperation extended into other states and from topography into geology and hydrology until it covered the entire nation and all its resources. In 1886 Congress, after an investigation, renewed the Survey's mandate for Earth science in the public interest.

As an explorer Powell had paid as much attention to the human as to the

Above is the entrance to the headquarters of the Survey in Washington, D.C., as it appeared in about 1890. At right is a "cable car" on the Arkansas River near Canyon, Colorado, in 1890. The Survey used this device for measuring the velocity of rivers and streams.

natural environment, concluding that most of the interior United States lacked the rainfall to support the kind of family farm he knew from his youth in the East and Middle West. To raise crops on the plains would require irrigation, which would be limited by the shortage of water to 3% of the land. The rest was fit only for grazing. Because water rather than land limited settlement, the division of public lands into uniform rectangles would invite monopoly by those controlling the banks of the streams. These ideas lay behind the land reform of 1879 that Congress had rejected.

Powell's chance to change U.S. land policy came with the droughts that began in 1886, after seven years of heavy rainfall had encouraged the establishing of farms on the Great Plains. "Rain follows the plow" had been the farmers' cry, and their hopes gained the support of scientists such as Ferdinand V. Hayden, leader of the largest of the territorial surveys and King's chief rival in 1879 for the directorship of the Geological Survey. But in 1888, after drought and blizzards had destroyed the open-range cattle industry and three consecutive dry seasons had brought despair to farmers in the central Great Plains, Congress authorized Powell to conduct an irrigation survey.

Powell began an ambitious program of topographic mapping, measuring

Geologist Robert Bridges stands in an anticline consisting of shales and sandstones from the Upper Silurian Period in Washington County, Maryland. The photograph was taken in 1897 by Charles Walcott, director of the Geological Survey.

235

Replica of a Geological Survey plant for testing coal was built for the Louisiana Purchase Exposition at St. Louis in 1904.

the flow of streams and designating the sites for irrigation works and the lands they would irrigate. Because no one could set lands aside before they were surveyed, Congress closed the remaining public lands until Powell's men were finished. When the law authorizing the irrigation survey took effect in 1890, it generated such opposition that Congress reversed itself and abolished almost all of the irrigation survey. At the same time the Geological Survey suffered the first of a series of cuts in its budget that drove Powell to resign in 1894. His successor was paleontologist Charles Walcott.

The Survey and politics

Though the reductions owed more to both party politics and the depression that began in 1893 than they did to opposition to Powell, his colleagues and successors in the Geological Survey never forgot the lesson of the 1890s. Science might suggest the answer to a question of land use, but that answer might not be acceptable to the politicians in power or to their opponents who could become their successors at the next election. Thus to advocate specific policies or to have the duty to carry them out was potentially dangerous for scientists. What Congress had given, it might take away in the next budget. Furthermore, Congress until the 1940s supported research primarily in the service of regulation, and in times of fiscal constraint the regulatory function could usurp the resources devoted to research, however meager the latter might be.

From the failure of Powell's irrigation survey the Geological Survey's leaders learned that science could thrive only if administrative power was shunned. Every regulatory opportunity they had was transferred to another agency until the 1920s. Management of forestry, irrigation, and mining began in the Geological Survey but came to rest elsewhere: in the Forest Service, the Reclamation Service (now the Water and Power Resources Service), and the Bureau of Mines, respectively. Not until 1925, after Secretary of Commerce Herbert Hoover pulled the Bureau of Mines out of the Department of the Interior into his own department, did the Geological Survey regulate. With Interior unwilling to lose control over the public lands, the supervision of mining in the public domain became the responsibility of the Survey.

This transfer followed from the effort of George Otis Smith, Walcott's successor as director, to carry out the Survey's original mandate to classify the public lands, a task that had been neglected because of political opposition. By the 1920s the public lands that the Survey found to contain minerals or sites for water power could no longer become private property; they had to be leased instead.

In 1934 Congress ended the selling or giving away of public lands that had begun with the first settlements three centuries earlier, thus fulfilling Smith's dream to hold the continent's resources in trust for future generations. The Survey then hoped to achieve what it had long sought, the wisest and best use of the land as determined by impartial scientists. Shaped by the political climate of its first 50 years, the Geological Survey concluded that it would find the facts but not be an advocate, relying instead on its scientific reports to provide the basis for society's decisions.

236

Diversity of achievements

Besides the Survey's achievements in mapping and in managing resources, what have the people of the U.S. received for their 100-year investment in the Earth sciences? First, the Geological Survey has educated industrial society about its land and what it can be used for. Second, the Survey, in the words of historian Daniel J. Kevles, "shaped the intellectual thrust of the entire geological profession," becoming almost from its founding "the keystone in the institutional structure of American geology." Third, when the U.S. began to run short of essential mineral commodities during World War II, the Survey expanded overseas, bringing to less developed countries the expertise to organize their own inventories of their resources. Fourth, when the frontiers of science moved from the Earth to the rest of the solar system, the Survey began to investigate the planets in the hope of achieving a better understanding of the Earth and also began to adapt the techniques of space exploration to our own planet.

All these tasks were carried out by people chosen as much for their commitment to the research ideal of science as for their practical experience. Thus, there was generally available, somewhere in the Survey, the knowledge needed to address whatever resource or land use problem society presented to it.

Only a sample of the Survey's undertakings can be mentioned here. With the federal government's return in 1879 to a currency backed primarily by gold and secondarily by silver, the economy could expand only if the supply of gold and silver expanded as well. As the U.S. industrial machine grew, it needed iron ores that were low in phosphorus for steelmaking. After Edison developed electric lighting, the demand for copper soared. The Geological Survey responded to these needs with detailed studies of the major mining districts that showed how their ore bodies had developed, studies that were both practical examples to miners and contributions to fundamental knowledge. At the same time the Survey began to reconnoiter the rest of the country to suggest other areas where miners might look for ores.

The Survey tested the coal that fueled U.S. industry and classified the coal-bearing public lands to insure that they would not be taken into private ownership as farmland. When the development of the automobile after 1900 gave a push to the petroleum industry, the Geological Survey began, according to U.S. geologist Sidney Powers, "to map the structure of the rocks in and near oil fields in order to discover the various types of structural conditions under which oil and gas are trapped." This effort marked the beginning of modern petroleum geology in the U.S. As the U.S. increased its consumption of electricity, the Survey searched the rivers for sites for hydroelectric dams. Worries after World War I broke out in Europe that the world's petroleum would soon be gone led the Survey to investigate the oil shales of the western U.S. During and after World War II the Survey scoured the U.S. for leads to uranium and thorium for nuclear weapons and reactors. Discoveries of petroleum on the continental shelf launched research into the marine environment in the 1960s. More recently the demand to develop geothermal energy to replace fossil fuels has led to a major effort to map the country's hot spots in detail.

237

William Henry Jackson—U.S. Geological Survey   JoAnn Verburg—© The Rephotographic Survey Project

After a century the natural landscape near Colorado Springs, Colorado, has changed. Eroded sandstone conglomerate columns (above left) were photographed in 1873. At the right, after further erosion, is the same view in 1977. On the opposite page the landscape has been altered by man. At the top is Clear Creek in Colorado as it appeared in 1873. Below is the same area in 1977 after engineers had built a dam that created the Clear Creek Reservoir.

The scientific and technical public learned the results of the Geological Survey's investigations from its many publications, tens of thousands of monographs, professional papers, bulletins, circulars, open-file reports, and maps of every description. From its earliest years the Survey has answered inquiries from all over the country; more recently it has published pamphlets for the general reader.

Both the research and its dissemination have led to the development of new techniques. From such Survey innovations as a new plane table and telescopic alidade for field mapping in the 1880s, photogrammetry in the 1930s, and mapping from satellites in the 1970s, the Survey's mapmakers have pioneered improvements in the speed and accuracy with which they delineate the surface of the land. The Survey's chemists developed the methods of inorganic analysis in the late 19th century in their studies of rocks and minerals. The use of the airborne magnetometer for prospecting for ferrous metals and of the gravimeter to help find petroleum both began in the Geological Survey.

Hand in hand with technical innovation went the growth of theory and experiment. Survey hydrologists founded the science of groundwater; Survey geologists demonstrated that many metallic ores are deposited by hot waters that come from deep inside the Earth. During the 1960s Survey geophysicists developed the timetable of the reversals of the Earth's magnetic field, which convinced the Earth science community to embrace the theory of plate tectonics.

238

U.S. Secretary of the Interior John Payne (left) meets with American Indian leaders in 1920. The Conservation Division of the Geological Survey manages the extraction of minerals from Indian lands.

During World War I the Survey searched for strategic materials at home. In World War II the search expanded beyond the borders of the U.S. and its territories. South America was the principal destination of Survey geologists and hydrologists helping other countries search for strategic minerals. Yet no resource was more important than oil, and the Middle East had the greatest reserves of it. Saudi Arabia's huge reserves and lack of people trained to find and develop them made that country especially anxious to obtain U.S. assistance. Training Saudi scientists and helping them search for water and minerals became important tasks that continue. By 1980 more than 1,200 of the Survey's scientists and engineers had helped more than 73 countries. Among their achievements were modern geologic maps of Liberia, Libya, and Saudi Arabia.

When U.S. astronauts first began training to go to the Moon, someone had to teach them what the Moon would be like and to plan where on the Moon they should go and what they should do there. The Geological Survey's astrogeologists chose the landing sites, trained the astronauts, and analyzed the rocks they brought back. Then, as the adventures in space shifted from manned trips to the Moon to the sampling of the planets by automated probes, Survey scientists continued to study our nearest neighbors in space and to make maps of their surfaces. And the same devices that show us what the other planets are like can tell us more about our own. Satellites have orbited the Earth, sending back pictures that can be analyzed to reveal its undiscovered features and clues to its remaining resources.

Though it was founded almost a decade before the United States made its Civil Service competitive and nonpolitical, the Geological Survey from the beginning selected its employees for their professional merit. Thus it became an ally of the reformers of the Civil Service, and they in turn allowed the Survey to set the standards for Earth scientists employed by the federal government. Until written examinations for such posts were abolished in 1960, Survey scientists wrote the questions and graded the answers. This control of the qualifications for entering the federal government helped the Survey shape U.S. education in the Earth sciences, since virtually all colleges that taught geology encouraged their students to take the examination. Though the examination system may at times have reinforced the prevailing orthodoxy, it maintained in the Earth sciences the high standards begun by the territorial surveys.

As well as influencing geological education through the Civil Service examinations, the Survey financed the research of most of the leaders of U.S. Earth science in the colleges and universities. By offering funds for summer fieldwork or part-time work at the college itself, the Survey subsidized the scientific research of academic scholars.

All these activities keep busy the Geological Survey's more than 10,000 staff members—most of them in professional positions. Their work has one central direction: to inform the makers of policy. In its reports, publications, and maps, the Survey attempts to provide the deepest understanding that current science can offer of the Earth and its vagaries. The Survey's Conservation Division applies this knowledge to its management of the extraction of minerals from public and Indian lands, but its application to the rest of the national domain depends on federal, state, and local governments.

Not all of these governments can understand the information that the Survey provides them or how best to use it. As a scientific agency the Survey has tended to couch its communications in technical language, which is often beyond the ken of those who need the information. The Survey is now making strong efforts to translate its findings so that the public can readily understand them. In this way the Survey hopes to achieve in its second century the goal for which it was founded—to make science the basis for the use of the land and its products.

Future prospects

What will the next hundred years hold for the U.S. Geological Survey? Though it remains, a century after Congress established it, a single agency with the same name, the Survey, like any other federal bureau, is subject to the demands of government and the preferences of the party in power. Since its four principal tasks—studying the Earth and inventorying its resources, keeping track of the supply of water, compiling and publishing maps, and managing mineral exploration and production on public lands— can be independent of one another, reorganization of the bureau is always a possibility. (U.S. Pres. Jimmy Carter proposed such a reorganization in March 1979 as part of his plan to turn the Department of the Interior into a Department of Natural Resources. Though the administration withdrew its plan in May 1979 when Congress opposed it, the plan might come forward again at some future date.) Whether or not the Survey survives in its present form for another century, the duties it performs will remain and the federal government will continue to perform them. One cannot reasonably expect either the states or private business to provide the fundamental knowledge of the environment and its mineral resources that is needed to maintain society.

The nature of mining, whether for fuels or for minerals, is that mankind consumes what mining supplies, and so must constantly seek out new sources. They become harder to find as the more readily available materials are exhausted. The U.S. can expect to use up as much of the Earth's resources in the final 25 years of this century as it has used since the country was colonized by Europeans almost 400 years ago. To find this much material will require the most careful searching with all the newest tools of science, and only the most advanced geology can tell scientists where to look. The U.S. Southwest faces the same problem of depletion with its water supply and needs hydrologic science to help solve it.

The hazards that natural forces pose to human life must be understood so that people can be protected. Nowhere is this need greater than in California, where the combination of a large population and a substantial danger from earthquakes puts many lives at risk. Though earthquakes, floods, and seismic sea waves are more spectacular, the landslides and slumps caused by unstable ground do much more damage to property, estimated at several billion dollars a year in the U.S.

In all these areas the U.S. Geological Survey has substantial research programs, and the environmental movement of the 1960s and 1970s has made it more aware of the importance of communicating the results of its research. Though Survey scientists continue to make major contributions to the scholarly scientific literature, they have recently undertaken the task of making their studies more useful to policymakers. Planning for land development has always begun with Geological Survey topographic maps. Recently the Survey published *"Nature to be commanded must be obeyed":* *Earth-Science Maps Applied to Land and Water Management* (U.S. Government periodical 78-15538) to show planners how geologic and hydrologic information might help them serve the public, as it has helped California pass laws to keep public buildings out of areas where the danger of earthquakes is great. Rather than wait to be asked for advice about the consequences for the Earth of the development of synthetic liquid fuels, the Survey in 1979 published *Synthetic Fuels Development: Earth-Science Considerations* for the guidance of policymakers. In order to give policy advice when the scientific evidence is ambiguous, the Survey undertakes to find a consensus among the most knowledgeable of its scientists.

Foretelling the future is a hazardous game, for it never turns out quite as one expected. But industrial progress will continue to depend on water, fuels, and minerals from the Earth. The very processes by which these resources are obtained and used have the potential to degrade the environment beyond recovery, by pollution and perhaps by change of climate. To continue to live on Earth as humans have lived for thousands of years, to bring to everyone on the planet the decent standard of living that most people in highly industrialized countries now enjoy, demands a better understanding of the Earth and the willingness to act on that understanding with wisdom and with foresight. The U.S. Geological Survey enters its second century dedicated to increasing its knowledge of the Earth and the planets and to helping make that knowledge the basis for the important decisions that face civilization in the years to come.

Science
Year in Review

Science
Year in Review
Contents

Anthropology

The emphasis in anthropology during the year was on the development of theories capable of integrating various levels of analysis (*e.g.*, biological, psychological, social, cultural). Correspondingly, research was increasingly designed to ask questions within this specific framework. A considerable amount of the work was conducted by interdisciplinary teams, epitomizing the cross-fertilization of ideas that took place among the social sciences throughout the 1970s. Trends evident at the end of the decade indicated some of the promise of the anthropology of the future. The year in which the first microcomputer was successfully employed in a fieldwork assignment was also characterized by lively debate on philosophical issues and on biological constraints on culture.

The "Golden Fleece" award. Because much anthropological research is conducted among marginal and distant ethnic groups, the practical applications of such studies are often presumed to be minimal by persons outside the field. As the U.S. entered the 1980s under austere budgetary conditions, federal support for basic research in the social sciences was expected to be greatly reduced. Under these circumstances, U.S. anthropologists responded vigorously to the selection by Sen. William Proxmire (Dem., Wis.) of the National Science Foundation as a recipient of his "Golden Fleece of the Month" award for its support of an an-

thropological project. Proxmire established the monthly "award" in 1975 to bring public attention to what he considered the "biggest, most ironic, or most ridiculous example of excessive spending" in government. Undoubtedly, the esoteric-sounding title of anthropologist Sherry Ortner's NSF-funded project, "Himalayan Mountaineering, Social Change, and the Evolution of Religion Among the Sherpas of Nepal," had caught Proxmire's attention.

Ortner and several other anthropologists defended the project, while the American Anthropological Association passed a motion deploring Proxmire's attack as a "threat to basic research in all fields." Mountaineering, although it may have sounded to Proxmire like mere recreation, is the Sherpas' most direct connection with the world economy. That religion is a tremendously authoritative—but poorly understood—force in the contemporary world was supported by the explosive developments in Iran late in 1979. Thus work such as Ortner's can be important to both social science and the practical world. This is not to say that social scientists believed themselves to be above public questioning, but in such instances as the Golden Fleece affair, some of the best social scientists in the country were having to defend themselves from ridicule by engaging in dialogue with politicians concerning the very nature and survival of their disciplines.

The recent U.S. Supreme Court decision in *Hutchinson* v. *Proxmire*, which denied congressional immunity

A study of social change and religion among the Sherpas of Nepal (above) was criticized as a waste of the U.S. taxpayers' money. However, the importance of religion as a force for change in some parts of the world was dramatically illustrated by events in Iran (left).

against libel action for public statements made by legislators outside of Congress, promised some protection for specific researchers. The climate for basic research in 1979 was not healthy, however, and scientists expected to be "closely confined to narrow patterns of expenditure and performance" (*Science*, July 13, 1979). Anthropologists began to learn how to be creative under discouraging circumstances.

A departmental anniversary. The department of anthropology at the University of Chicago celebrated its 50th anniversary in the autumn of 1979. Festivities included an exhibition of documents illustrating aspects of the department's history and growth and the publication of a short history of the department by George Stocking (*Anthropology at Chicago*, 1979). The appearance of a history of this important department provided an opportunity for disciplinary self-appraisal. The effect of the Chicago exhibition and celebration was measured not only by the department's worldwide influence in its field but also by the fact that so many of the issues with which the Chicago faculty had struggled—and which it continued to confront—were consistent with circumstances elsewhere.

Initially the department had to deal with the problems of subjugation within a combined department of sociology and anthropology. It had to confront the inappropriateness of museum anthropology as a setting for the entire discipline. It looked to English social anthropology for ideas and for contrast with the emerging version of cultural anthropology. There were repeated debates over purpose. In the 1930s A. R. Radcliffe-Brown's ahistorical scientism was pitted against the humanistic concern with meaning associated with the work of Edward Sapir. The controversy in the 1950s involved the status of applied anthropology, this time with Robert Redfield and Sol Tax on different sides. An interest developed in symbolic anthropology, which, in its most prevalent form, studied culture independently of social systems.

The department was fractionated and reconstituted several times, most recently around neo-evolutionary theory. Yet there was a belief among several current observers, including Stocking, that the sense of theoretical malaise that began in the 1950s had continued to the present. The traditional balance in the department between the various subdisciplines was lost in the 1960s with the appointment of several cultural anthropologists who did not fit into particular slots in the departmental scheme and who had no particular theoretical concerns in common with the physical anthropologists or paleoanthropologists.

The latest of several revisions of the graduate program set up separate programs for students of the various subdisciplines, acknowledging lack of unity in the department and promising to perpetuate it. Several departments around the country, facing similar fragmentation, looked toward sociobiology as a possible synthesizing theory. Chicago, however, was not swayed by sociobiology, although some of its leading members were involved in the continuing debate over the merits of that theory.

Sociobiology and culture. Sociobiology utilizes the principles of evolutionary biology and emphasizes group and population-wide processes. One of the key concepts of sociobiology, "kin selection," refers to a selective advantage of certain genes over others based on the survival and reproductive fitness of relatives. Edward O. Wilson of Harvard University, whose *Sociobiology: the New Synthesis* (1975) launched sociobiology and brought it to the attention of social scientists, speculated on the "kin selection" advantages of homosexuality in his latest book, *On Human Nature* (1978). According to Wilson's "kin-selection hypothesis" homosexuals have genes that predispose them to assist close relatives, since they usually are freed from the duties of parenthood themselves. Thus, the work of homosexuals benefits the group in various ways, while genes for homosexuality are passed on by the collaterals of the nonreproducing individual.

In *Human Sociobiology* (1979) Daniel G. Freedman, a psychologist who had done extensive cross-cultural work on early infancy, reported his observations of newborn infants of Afro-American, Caucasian-American, Cantonese, Navajo, and Japanese parentage. Freedman was able to correlate certain behavioral dispositions of these newborns with their "ethnicity." For example, he found Chinese newborns to be amenable and accepting of intrusions and testing by their handlers, while Caucasian babies expressed frustration and annoyance. However, his extension of his findings to sweeping comparisons of art and philosophy in the East and West represented, for many anthropologists, the dangerous extravagances of sociobiology.

Anthropologists and biologists collaborated to produce *Evolutionary Biology and Human Social Behavior* (1979), edited by Napoleon Chagnon and William Irons. Though its title carefully avoided the word "sociobiology," the book aroused considerable interest as the first empirical study within the sociobiological framework to utilize intensive ethnographic or cross-cultural data. Among the subjects discussed, study of genetic considerations in societies where the relationship between mother's brother and sister's son is stressed was indicative of the line of inquiry being employed by sociobiologically minded anthropologists. It is well known that in certain societies mother's brother and sister's son engage in an important relationship. The sociobiological explanation of "fathering" by uncles, advanced by Jeffrey A. Kurland and supported by Wilson and Freedman, argued that uncles/nephews enjoy a guaranteed genetic association whereas, since paternity is never certain, men may have no genetic bond with their wives' children. Kurland speculated that mothers' brothers are in fact behaving in

Police in London guard a parade of the National Front, a right-wing organization in Great Britain that has cited sociobiological literature to justify racism.

accord with the theory of inclusive fitness when they favor nephews over reputed "sons."

Debate about specific sociobiological explanations, such as Kurland's, continued to grow in intensity and to draw on recent research. For example, Marshall Sahlins's argument that cultural and not biological factors are at work in the abovementioned case of Polynesian adoption was countered by Freedman, who pointed out the inbred nature of these island populations. Sahlins correctly noted that Polynesian kinship systems do not follow strict biological coefficients of relationship, while Freedman and others insisted that some measure of biological relationship must nevertheless be present.

The politics of sociobiology also received attention. Opponents worried about the adoption of sociobiological ideas by right-wing groups in the U.K., France, and the U.S. In the U.K. the right-wing National Front party cited sociobiological literature to justify racism as a legitimate strategy for ensuring genetic survival, and in Paris the right-wing Club de l'Horloge supported its stand about the inevitability of hierarchies in social organizations with sociobiological arguments. Sociobiologists, insisting that the scientific enterprise must be kept separate from its political uses and abuses by poorly informed people, maintained that sociobiological ideas were entirely the product of new advances in the study of animal behavior, primarily ethology. Other anthropologists agreed with geneticist Jonathan Beckwith, quoted in *Nature* (Nov. 22, 1979) as saying that the political uses of sociobiology were inherent in its construction.

Some pronouncements by sociobiologists themselves reinforced the belief among many social scientists that the theory was part of a larger ideological movement to the political right. Thus Wilson wrote, "We are not compelled to believe in biological uniformity in order to affirm human freedom and dignity" (*On Human Nature,* 1978). Marvin Bressler, cited by Wilson, was even more pointed: "An ideology that tacitly appeals to biological equality as a condition for human emancipation corrupts the idea of freedom."

Other anthropologists argued the scientific case against sociobiology without touching on the politics of the matter. Marvin Harris of Columbia University echoed a general sentiment among anthropologists that sociobiological premises cannot be applied to human social behavior. For Harris, complex learning circuits operate independently of genetic feedback. The range of variation in human cultural systems, therefore, defeats species-specific explanations of genetic programming. Harris's critique of sociobiology was important in the promotion of his own theory, *Cultural Materialism* (1979).

Clifford Geertz, Sahlins, and David Schneider wrote and spoke about culture as a domain of study which cannot be reduced to a biological substratum. Sahlins's discussion was specifically addressed to sociobiology and its tendency to assume isomorphic connections between biology and culture. Rather than seeing culture as an extension of biology, Sahlins portrays culture as an interruption in nature. In *The Use and Abuse of Biology* (1976), Sahlins wrote: "In the symbolic event, a radical discontinuity is introduced between

247

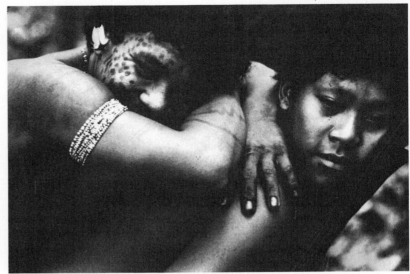
Claudia Andujar—Photo Researchers, Inc.

Yanomamo Indians of Brazil were the subject of a resolution by the American Anthropological Association in 1979. The AAA urged the Brazilian government not to place these Indians on widely separated and inadequate reserves but instead to set aside one tract of land large enough to guarantee the physical and cultural survival of these people.

culture and nature." Wilson countered this criticism in his 1978 publication: "It is a misconception among . . . a still surprising proportion of anthropologists and sociologists that social behavior can be shaped into virtually any form."

Some anthropologists who rejected sociobiology on theoretical principle, such as Alexander Alland, nevertheless defended Wilson's objection to anthropologists who grossly exaggerate the separation of human beings from biological control. Alland's new textbook (*To Be Human*, 1980) warned, however, of the serious need to separate the biological origins of human traits from their subsequent operation in the evolved species. For a majority of anthropologists, nonbiological, historical, and, for some, ecological factors were still considered necessary for the study of human culture.

—Lawrence E. Fisher

Archaeology

A restudy of certain classic Lower Paleolithic artifact collections from southern England could have revolutionary implications for the understanding of some of the earliest stone-tool industries of Europe. A lithic (stone) assemblage of large flakes and choppers discovered at Clacton-on-Sea and nearby localities near the end of the 19th century had long been of major interest to students of Paleolithic archaeology. This industry was very different in appearance from the Acheulian hand-ax industries previously discovered in France and England and now known to have existed over vast stretches of Eurasia and Africa during Lower Paleolithic times.

Whereas Acheulian industries prominently featured well-made core-biface hand axes of such consistent pattern that the type could be recognized throughout

Europe and Africa, Clactonian assemblages lacked this consistency. They gave the impression of ad hoc tools, crude and primitive in comparison with the Acheulian specimens, and many archaeologists concluded that the Clactonian was older, perhaps comprising the culture from which the Acheulian sprang. An interpretation still widely held is that the Clactonian was a derivative of a much more ancient pebble-tool tradition such as those, for example, at African sites like Olduvai Gorge in Tanzania and Koobi Fora in Kenya, dated about two million years ago. According to this view the Clactonian might have been the lithic industry of the first human beings to enter Europe and the stratum out of which subsequent cultures of the Lower Paleolithic period arose.

Reanalysis of the old lithic collections and consideration of new evidence led Milla Y. Ohel of the University of Haifa, Israel, to a quite different interpretation. He concluded that the Clactonian industry, despite its radically different appearance, is not a cultural entity separate from the Acheulian tradition but is actually contemporaneous with it and technologically related to it. A recent major surge of interest among prehistorians in the experimental replication and study of ancient tool types led to observations about the process of stone-tool manufacture that allow the Clactonian industry to be seen in a new perspective.

In reanalyzing old Clactonian collections Ohel found that those excavated under carefully controlled circumstances contained a significantly broader range of specimen types than those which had been selectively surface-collected from eroded and exposed situations. He further noted that some of these collections contained specimens that approached Acheulian hand axes in form, although they tended to be heavier, more crudely shaped, and sometimes broken. In addition, comparative study of flakes from both Acheulian and

Clactonian sites indicated that many of the Clactonian flakes could not be distinguished from their Acheulian counterparts.

From the comparative evidence Ohel's interpretation, informed by recent experimental advances in the understanding of lithic manufacture, was that Clactonian sites were simply localities where the initial working of rough stone nodules into preliminary Acheulian tool forms was carried out. Clactonian sites, according to this interpretation, were actually workshops near the source of the raw material where tools were roughed out, to be carried off and finished into Acheulian hand axes and other artifacts at the regular settlements.

This new interpretation is appealingly simple and straightforward and resolves certain troubling paradoxes in previous theories, which saw the Clactonian assemblages as representing a separate and distinctive culture. It seems to be gaining support among Paleolithic specialists, but the idea remains controversial. No doubt it will be some time before a broad consensus is achieved.

Butchering practices of early humans. An experimental study that involved butchering an elephant with chipped-stone tools comparable to those found at Clovis Paleo-Indian mammoth-hunters' sites in North America provided intriguing insights into the problems and methods of the early hunters. One of the most interesting observations reported by the experimenter, Bruce Huckell of the Arizona State Museum, was the rapid rate at which his stone tools became worn and dull. The effective use time between resharpenings of

New analysis of Paleolithic stone tools indicates that those described as Clactonian (right) are roughed-out versions of Acheulian forms (left) rather than being artifacts from a different culture.

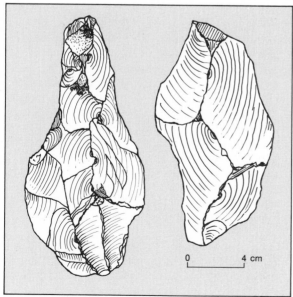

0   4 cm

Based on drawings from Milla Y. Ohel, University of Haifa

a hand-held bifacial tool employed in skinning the elephant varied between one and two and a half minutes. Resharpening, achieved by striking off tiny flakes along the cutting edge of the biface with a deer-antler hammer, took only a few seconds but was required so frequently that the shape and size of the tool were changed significantly over periods of only a few minutes. The fact that stone tools wear so rapidly and hence have a very short useful life helps to explain why such large quantities are often found associated with ancient sites.

The experience also made clear the importance of teamwork in butchering a large carcass with stone tools. In order for the butcher to make deep cuts with small hand-held stone flakes and bifaces, it proved almost indispensable to have someone else maintain tension on the parts being cut apart, thus facilitating cutting and preventing binding of the cutting tool.

Measurements of the thickness of the elephant's hide over various parts of the body also provided insights into the problems faced by Paleo-Indian hunters. Over most of the torso and upper limbs the elephant's hide ranged between 20 and 30 mm (0.8–1.2 in) in thickness. Over the throat, however, it was only about 8 mm (0.3 in) thick, and over the chest and belly, only about 2 mm (0.08 in) thick. It is difficult to imagine that a hunter could hurl a stone-tipped spear with sufficient force to penetrate an elephant's hide and go deep enough to do it serious injury, and the simple anatomical facts suggest that the early Paleo-Indians probably dispatched their quarry at extremely close range, using thrusting spears to penetrate the thin skin of the underbelly, where the heart or other vital organs might be reached most easily. Even today, the Mbuti Pygmies of Africa kill elephants in this way.

A further contribution to archaeological interpretation of the butchering practices of ancient hunters was reported by Andrew Hill of the International Louis Leakey Memorial Institute. Hill studied the way in which skeletons of the African topi, a large bovid, fall apart when a dead animal is left to decompose naturally. Using statistical methods on a sample of dead animals found near Lake Rudolf, it was possible to infer the relative order in which different body segments broke apart under natural conditions. This order was then compared with the order in which North American Paleo-Indian bison hunters of 7,000 years ago disarticulated their prey in a butchering process carefully documented by Joe Ben Wheat at the Olsen-Chubbuck site in eastern Colorado. The natural and cultural sequences of disarticulation were strikingly similar, showing that the human butchering procedure followed a path of least resistance and greatest efficiency dictated by the anatomy of the animal itself. These observations go far toward explaining why human butchering practices have changed so little over extremely long periods of time. They also suggest that

Fred Wendorf, Southern Methodist University

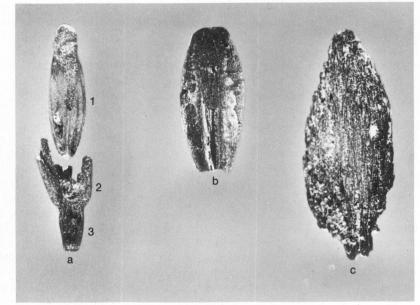

Carbonized grains and spikelets of einkorn wheat and barley found at Wadi Kubbaniya, a tributary of the Nile River in Egypt, suggest that this grass may have been tended and harvested as far back as 18,000 years ago. Wheat grain in a partially decayed hull similar in size to wild wheat is seen in a; a(1) is the grain, a(2) is the decayed hull, and a(3) is the rachis. These contrast with a barley grain without the hull, similar in size to domestic barley (b), and a barley spikelet, also similar in size to domestic barley (c).

primarily anatomical rather than cultural reasons lie behind the use of different butchering practices for different species of game animals.

Grain culture in Egypt. Several grains of carbonized barley recovered from a Late Paleolithic site at Wadi Kubbaniya, a tributary of the Nile River which enters the main valley near Aswan, Egypt, imply that this native grass may have been tended and harvested as much as 18,000 years ago. This is some thousands of years earlier than previous evidence had suggested for horticultural beginnings anywhere in the world. An international team headed by Fred Wendorf of Southern Methodist University, Dallas, Texas, reported that the barley grains were associated with grinding stones, mortars and pestles, and a typical Late Paleolithic stone-tool inventory. The site was firmly dated by a series of carbon-14 determinations to a period 18,300 to 17,000 years ago.

The seed grains exhibited some characteristics of both wild and domesticated forms of the barley which grows today throughout the eastern Mediterranean region. Indeed, the modern forms are so varied that some specialists consider both wild and domesticated types to belong to a single species, *Hordeum vulgare*. It is not possible, therefore, to say with any assurance whether the grains from Wadi Kubbaniya were wild or domesticated. The most important consideration, however, is that barley was exploited as a major food resource in a region where, there is reason to believe, it was not very common under natural conditions.

Only during years of very high Nile floods would there have been sufficient soil moisture at the Wadi Kubbaniya site to allow barley to grow. The investigators suggested that wild barley may have been deliberately sown in good years by the human occupants of the region, who subsisted by hunting and gathering a broad range of plant and animal foods. This interpretation implies that as early as Late Paleolithic times, 18,000 years ago, hunting-gathering societies in Upper Egypt were engaged in a mutual relationship with wild plant populations that led ultimately to domestication and the settled village-farming way of life.

Near Eastern village life. From sites on the Upper Euphrates River in northern Syria came additional important archaeological finds bearing on the transition from a hunting-gathering existence to a Neolithic village-farming way of life. A remarkably rich record came from the mound called Tell Abu Hureyra, near the previously studied and important sites of Buqras and Mureybat, which overlap it in time. The huge tumulus of Abu Hureyra, the largest of its period anywhere in the Levant, covered 11.5 ha (28 ac) and accumulated to a height of nearly 8 m (26 ft) between the time it was first occupied in the 10th millennium BC and its abandonment some time after 6000 BC.

Andrew M. T. Moore reported that excavations into the virgin soil beneath the mound disclosed a cluster of pit dwellings that had been occupied by sedentary hunting-gathering Mesolithic folk at some time prior to 8500 BC. In many important respects the Mesolithic remains prefigured the Neolithic way of life attested in the upper levels of the same mound. Milling stones, pestles, and small lithic flakes that may have served, among other uses, as blade insets for reaping knives or sickles were common in both the Mesolithic and Neolithic levels.

Careful screening of the excavated earth yielded more than two tons of animal bone, while flotation processing produced about 1,000 l (1,057 qt) of ancient plant remains from the various levels of the site. An agriculture based on domesticated einkorn wheat, emmer wheat, barley, and lentils was certainly (and not surprisingly) present at Abu Hureyra by Neolithic times, but the exciting result of the plant flotation analysis was that wild einkorn wheat, wild rye, wild barley, and a wild type of lentil were recovered from the preceding Mesolithic levels. It thus seems clear that a progression from the gathering of native seed-producing plants to their tending and eventual domestication took place at the site.

More and more clearly, the transition from a hunting-gathering to a farming way of life in the Near East was being seen as an increasingly successful human adaptation to the vegetal food resources of grassland environments, reaching optimum levels during the climatic amelioration of terminal Pleistocene and immediately post-Pleistocene times. An economy focused on gathering the seeds of abundant wild grasses allowed sedentary occupation and population growth. At the same time, the process of gathering led to tending and eventually to selective harvesting and replanting of the native grasses, culminating in the domesticated forms that emerged during Neolithic times.

Dating procedures. For three decades, since the carbon-14 dating method was first developed by University of Chicago chemist Willard Libby, many historians have believed that the dates provided by that method are not compatible with the historical chronologies of ancient Egypt and Mesopotamia. Since the Egyptologists first informed Libby that his dates were in error, a new, more accurate half-life for the radiocarbon isotope—a quantity that lies at the heart of the method—has been calculated. Futhermore, fluctuations over time in the amount of radiocarbon in the Earth's atmosphere, a critical parameter of the dating method not originally controlled by Libby, have now been measured and graphed. This was done by making carbon-14 assays on hundreds of wood samples of known calendric age, precisely dated by counting the annual growth rings of still-living trees that are as much as 7,000 to 8,000 years old.

In a recent synthesis James Mellaart of the University of London attempted to reconcile newly "corrected" carbon-14 dates with the historical chronologies of Egypt and Mesopotamia. Such a reconciliation is extremely important to an overall understanding of the early Near Eastern civilizations, because many aspects of the cultural record are known only through archaeology and dated only through the carbon-14 method. Mellaart's synthesis allows better correlation of purely archaeological information with what is known from historic sources, lengthening the generally accepted historical chronology by 200 to 400 years. This added time also makes it possible to resolve some conflicts in historians' interpretations of the original historical evidence itself, which is often somewhat ambiguous. One of the most striking implications of the revised

Wide World

Marble caryatid 2,500 years old is removed from the Acropolis in Athens for storage indoors in an effort to prevent further decay from air pollution. Cement replicas were made to replace this and other caryatids.

chronology is that early Mesopotamian writing, long believed to have been the oldest in the world, apparently does not actually predate that of Egypt. The new framework, certain to be controversial, may bring about a number of significant alterations in our understanding of early Near Eastern history.

The Hochdorf Tomb. Excavations at Hochdorf, in southwestern Germany, by Jörg Biel of the State Service of Antiquities of Baden-Württemberg produced an unusually rich series of Iron Age artifacts from the tomb of an early Celtic chieftain. The burial was made about 550 BC in a spacious log tomb over which an earth mound some eight meters high had been raised. On a high-backed couch wrought of sheet bronze lay the remains of a large man with a golden ring about his neck, a gold band on one arm, and a broad, gold-ornamented belt around his waist. A dagger with a gold-plated hilt had once hung from the belt. The man's shoes were embellished by thin strips of embossed gold

Exhibition of 5,000 years of Korean art featured a wide variety of works. At the left is a bronze rattle with eight jingle bells from the 3rd–2nd centuries BC. At the right is the gilt bronze Seated Maitreya (future Buddha) from the early 7th century AD.

Courtesy, Asian Art Museum of San Francisco

sheeting. Gold brooches had once fastened his clothing, which was made of a woven fabric embroidered with what appeared to be Chinese silk.

A great bronze caldron of more than 400-I (430-qt) capacity, placed at the foot of the chieftain's bier, still held the powdery, dried remains of a fermented honey-based drink called mead. An ornamental ring, on which lions crouched, encircled the rim of the caldron, which was identified as being of Greek manufacture. A golden drinking bowl, probably of local Celtic make, was found within the caldron. Across the room were the remains of a large four-wheeled wagon, on which had been placed plates and platters of bronze along with slaughtering and carving tools. Fragments of woven cloth found within the tomb suggested that its walls had been hung with rich fabrics.

Other such tombs have been found in Europe, but this one was unusual in having escaped plundering, and it gives a remarkably rich impression of the Celtic life of 2,500 years ago. It is clear from such finds that even in the early Celtic period Europe was the home

252

of socially stratified societies in which a dominant aristocratic class was able to garner great personal wealth. Objects of Greek manufacture demonstrate contacts with the Mediterranean, and the embroidery of the Hochdorf chieftain's garment hints that even then the ancient Europeans had established links with the Far East across Central Asia.

—C. Melvin Aikens

Architecture and civil engineering

The marriage of architecture and structural engineering has never been an easy one. Today, when much of architectural thought appears to be concerned with issues of modernism, historicism, and postmodernism, there seems to be no coherent and consistent development of working relationships between architecture and structural engineering in the design of buildings. But the design of bridges is providing new ways of demonstrating that architecture and engineering can be brought together in harmonious form. Two bridges, one designed for California and one for Switzerland, have been acclaimed and admired by both architects and engineers.

Model of the 390-meter-long Ruck-a-Chucky Bridge, which will be built between steep rock canyon walls northeast of Sacramento, California.

Hedrich Blessing

Photos, Christian Menn, Swiss Federal Institute of Technology, Zurich

The Ruck-a-Chucky Bridge will be built between steep rock canyon walls 55 km (35 mi) NE of Sacramento, Calif., at the middle fork of the American River. Approximately 390 m (1,300 ft) long, it will span the reservoir to be created by the construction of the Auburn dam and will connect two existing roads on the canyon walls. A straight bridge would have incurred the expensive and disruptive procedure of cutting large turning radii into the rock. A curved bridge was, therefore, designed.

The deck of the bridge will not be supported by piers because in a water depth of 135 m (450 ft) high piers would have been subject to strong seismic forces. Instead, it will cross the reservoir in a clear span and be supported by high-strength steel cables arranged in a hyperbolic paraboloid formation. These cables will be anchored into the rock canyon walls. The deck will have a width of 15 m (50 ft) and carry four lanes of traffic: two for automobiles, one for pedestrians, and one for horses. The radius to the center line of the bridge is 455 m (1,500 ft), producing a gentle and beautiful curve.

The U.S. Bureau of Reclamation sponsored extensive studies in which models of the bridge were subjected to testing on shaking tables to determine the bridge's potential dynamic behavior and possible response to earthquakes. The results of the tests and the analysis of the design of the bridge were extensively reported in the journal of the Structural Division of the American Society of Civil Engineers and attracted the attention of designers and engineers throughout the world. *Progressive Architecture* magazine, by awarding the bridge its First Award in architectural design, recognized that the bridge is not only an example of imaginative engineering but is also good architecture. The structural engineers were T. Y. Lin International and Hanson Engineers Inc. The architects were Skid-

The 678-meter Ganter Valley Bridge crosses Ganter Creek in Switzerland at a height of 150 meters. Model of the bridge (top) reveals the S-shape and long spans. Above, workers erect one of the reinforced-concrete supports and cantilevered girders. The bridge is scheduled for completion in 1980.

more, Owings and Merrill, with Myron Goldsmith partner in charge of design.

The Ganter Valley Bridge by Christian Menn is the latest example in the Swiss tradition of bridge design. The pioneering work of Robert Maillart, who played a

253

major role earlier in the 20th century in the development of both modern architecture and structural engineering, produced some remarkable bridges that drew on both disciplines. Menn, professor at the Federal Technical University in Zurich, continued that work. The Ganter Valley Bridge, his latest, is located near the southern border of Switzerland on the road through the Simplon Pass across the Alps. The bridge has the longest span in the country and passes high over the Ganter Creek between the steep slopes of the Ganter Valley. It was scheduled to be completed in 1980.

Two alternative solutions for the Ganter Valley crossing were considered. The first was a tunnel, approximately one kilometer (0.62 mi) long, to be bored in the immediate vicinity of an old bridge built over the creek by Napoleon. The tunnel would have avoided dangerous rockfall areas but, because of its alignment through heavily fissured rock, would have cost 30 million Swiss francs. The second alternative, which was adopted, was a 678-m (2,224-ft) bridge crossing the valley at a height of 150 m (492 ft) to avoid the dangerous rockfall slopes. The height of the bridge, coupled with the strong winds in the valley, required careful studies of the problems created by wind forces, especially their dynamic effects.

The bridge is an S-shape in plan. It leaves the northern side of the valley with a right-handed curve 200 m (660 ft) in radius. The curve is followed by a 230-m (755-ft) straight path, which is the transition to a left-handed curve 200 m in radius. The bridge is 10 m (33 ft) wide and slopes from south to north by approximately 5%.

The great height of the bridge, the steep slopes of the valley sides, and the delicate geological conditions all provided arguments for minimizing the number of difficult and expensive bridge supports. Long spans were therefore developed, including a main span of 174 m (571 ft). These conditions also argued for the cantilever as the most efficient and economic method of construction. Standard forms of reinforced concrete were employed for the prestressed cantilever girders and the supporting columns.

The most remarkable aspect of the design is the form of the prestressed cantilever girder: the main prestressing tendons rise well above the girder at the columns. These tendons are encased in concrete, giving the bridge the appearance, as Menn observed, of a Maillart bridge upside down.

The remarkable beauty of the Ruck-a-Chucky and Ganter Valley bridges is the result of brilliant design combining the best of modern architecture and engineering. In the words of David Billington, author of an analysis of Maillart's work, they achieve a "strong sense of the integration of the engineers' ideals—efficiency in materials, economy in construction and elegance in form."

—Robert L. Geddes

Astronomy

Major achievements in astronomy during 1979 included planetary explorations, successful operation of ultraviolet and X-ray observatories, and progress toward the interpretation of several unusual stars or systems of stars. New instruments were also added to help gather the data needed to understand the universe.

Instrumentation. The first instrument of its kind, and the possible predecessor of large optical telescopes of the future, was dedicated on May 9, 1979. The multiple mirror telescope (MMT) consists of six 1.8-m (72-in) mirrors mounted in a hexagonal array and arranged to bring their combined light to a common focus. The new instrument was constructed jointly by the Smithsonian Astrophysical Observatory and the University of Arizona. It is located at the summit of Mt. Hopkins, at 2,600 m (8,580 ft) elevation, roughly 60 km (37 mi) south of Tucson, Ariz.

The six large mirrors are mounted concentrically to a small (0.76-m) telescope that serves as the finding and guiding system for the array. The entire array is mounted in a cage which can be rotated in turn about a horizontal and a vertical axis, allowing the instrument to point anywhere in the sky. A computer is used to control the vertical and horizontal drive motors so as to follow an object in its daily motion across the heavens. An intricate feedback system continuously adjusts the secondary mirror of each primary mirror to correct for alignment and focus errors. It is this system, which senses and corrects the errors, that is the heart of the telescope.

The MMT is the largest telescope specifically designed for use at infrared wavelengths. It has the equivalent aperture of a 4.5-m single-mirror telescope. Design specifications were such that it can also be used for spectroscopic work in both the visible and ultraviolet regions. By the fall of 1980 the instrument was expected to be fully operational, but early in the year it was already contributing significant observational results. Many astronomers looked on it as the prototype for much larger telescopes, such as the ten-meter instrument being planned at the University of California. The cost of such a large telescope would be prohibitive if conventional designs were used.

An example of international astronomical cooperation was coming to fruition on the Mauna Kea Observatory site of the University of Hawaii. This site, the highest location in use in the world for large telescopes, has exceptionally favorable transparency, or clarity, in the infrared range and also remarkable astronomical seeing. In May the three-meter telescope sponsored by the U.S. National Aeronautics and Space Administration (NASA) was dedicated. First light for the Canadian-French-U.S. 3.6-m reflector was obtained in August, and the 3.8-m United Kingdom telescope was dedicated on October 10. These telescopes

Dale P. Cruikshank

Orchid leis and the appropriate flags decorate the 3.6-meter Canadian-French-U.S. telescope on Mauna Kea in Hawaii at its dedication in 1979.

will add nearly 29 sq m of new collecting surface for astronomical observations at Mauna Kea, a site with such excellent observing conditions that the instruments will be much more effective than if they were located elsewhere.

The first application of waveform analysis to the interpretation of radio radiation from an external galaxy was made during the past year. Joseph Erkes and Ivan Linscott of the Dudley Observatory developed an instrument that samples and digitizes a signal at a rate of 20 million points per second. The digitized data are then fed to a fast Fourier transform processor, which analyzes sets of 2,048 points that give the strength and timing of the signal at 1,024 different frequencies.

Using this device, the two investigators detected pulses in the radio signal from M87, a giant elliptical galaxy more than 70 million light-years distant. (One light-year = 5,878,000,000,000 mi.) The pulses are emitted about once each second and contain 10^4 times the amount of energy that the Sun emits each second. They are 10^9 times more energetic than the pulses emitted by pulsars detected in our Galaxy. Since the pulses themselves are very short in duration, about one millisecond, the source emitting them must be less than 300 km (185 mi) in diameter, the distance light travels in $1/1{,}000$ of a second. Astronomers have speculated that the source may be a massive black hole embedded in the central region of M87.

The solar system. The Voyager 1 space probe passed by Jupiter in March, while Voyager 2 reached Jupiter's vicinity in July. Both space vehicles had been launched nearly two years earlier. Later, in September, Pioneer 11, which had passed Jupiter in 1974, finally caught up with Saturn, giving astronomers their first close-up examination of that majestic planet. And ear-

lier, in December 1978, the Pioneer Venus and Soviet Venera spacecraft reached Venus. The exciting results of the Venus probes began to become known in early 1979, just in time to be overshadowed by the results from Jupiter.

The radar experiment aboard the orbiter of Pioneer Venus measured surface features on the planet that rival some of those detected on Mars. For example, Venus has a huge rift valley like the one on Mars. It is at least 1,400 km (870 mi) long in an east–west direction and is approximately 7 km (4.3 mi) deep. Such a rift is taken as evidence of tectonic plate activity on the planet. In addition, the orbiter radar confirmed earlier observations from the Earth of a towering feature called Maxwell, which stands eight kilometers (five miles) above the feature named the Great Northern Plateau. The plateau itself is anywhere from 3 to 5 km (1.9 to 3.1 mi) above the average surface of Venus. Thus, the top of Maxwell rises higher above the surface of Venus than does Mt. Everest above sea level on the Earth.

Close examination revealed the atmosphere of Venus to have a more complicated circulation pattern than expected. The atmosphere was found to be made up almost entirely of carbon dioxide. At the surface of the planet the atmospheric pressure is more than 90 times that on the Earth. The clouds, which keep the planet's surface hidden from view, appear to occur in four distinct layers. Below the bottom clouds the atmosphere is surprisingly clean and transparent. The particles that constitute the clouds are concentrated droplets of sulfuric acid and grains of pure sulfur.

Possibly the most surprising result was the large amount of argon-36 relative to argon-40 as compared with that found on the Earth. This is significant because argon-36 is the form of that element expected to be most abundant when the planet formed, while argon-40 is the decay product of radioactive potassium-40 accumulated over the lifetime of the planet. Thus, Venus must have retained a larger portion of the solar nebular gases from which the planets formed than did the Earth—just the opposite of the belief commonly held until these measurements became available. Another major surprise was the considerable amount of lightning and thunder on Venus.

The Voyagers showed Jupiter to be more colorful than anyone could have imagined. The circulation pattern of its atmosphere has a plethora of intriguing vortices and alternating bands of east- and west-flowing clouds. The Great Red Spot, known to Earthbound observers for centuries, is a huge high-pressure bubble with an anticyclonic circulation (counterclockwise in the southern hemisphere) trailed by a low-pressure confused wake. It is accompanied by three large white ovals that have been observed for the past 40 years, each of which is now known to have its own anticyclonic rotation.

Jupiter has a large, intense magnetic field that rotates in synchronism with the ten-hour period of the planet. Charged particles and electrons trapped within this field move around the planet at tremendous velocities. A "flux tube," within which there is an electrical current of several million amperes, connects Jupiter to its satellite Io. It would take more than 20 times the power-generating capacity available on the Earth to equal the power expended by this current.

The satellites of Jupiter observed by the Voyagers displayed a surprising diversity in characteristics. Io, the innermost of the major satellites, is the only body in the solar system besides the Earth on which active volcanoes have been seen. It is craterless but is marked with dark volcanic calderas on a strikingly colored surface that is mottled in yellow, red, and brownish black. The heat to drive the volcanism of Io arises from the tremendous tidal flexing it undergoes due to Jupiter. The density of the satellite implies that it is composed of silicates, but the silicate magma never reaches the surface. Instead, it heats the overlying sulfur and frozen sulfur dioxide crust, giving rise to the sulfurous mushroom-shaped plumes that spew forth from the surface.

Europa, on the other hand, has the smoothest known solid surface in the solar system. It is streaked with white and dark markings. The satellite appears to have a rocky interior covered by an ice crust no more than 100 km (60 mi) thick. The highest features on its surface are ridges and hummocks that are no more than about 50 m high.

Ganymede and Callisto, in contrast, have severely cratered surfaces. On Callisto there are impact craters side by side everywhere. The satellite has an ice and rock crust overlying a water or flowing ice mantle. Ganymede, besides its craters, reveals grooves cutting

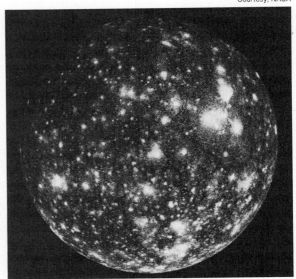

Courtesy, NASA

Callisto, a moon of Jupiter, was photographed by Voyager 2 from about 1.1 million kilometers. The bright areas are ejecta from impact craters.

across its surface with intricate fracture marks. The outer surface is a thin ice crust over a mantle similar to that of Callisto.

And, last but not least, Jupiter joins Saturn and Uranus in having rings. But these rings appear to be composed predominantly of particles only a few micrometers in diameter. The rings are only a few kilometers thick but are about 6,500 km (4,000 mi) wide at a distance of approximately 57,000 km (35,000 mi) above Jupiter's clouds.

Pioneer 11 passed by Saturn at a distance of 3,500 km (2,100 mi) on Sept. 1, 1979. In the process it discovered another ring lying just outside the already known rings of Saturn. In addition, it measured Saturn's magnetic field. The strength of the planet's magnetism is much weaker than that of Jupiter, three to five times less than anticipated. But the most surprising revelation was the fact that Saturn's magnetic axis is almost coincident with its rotational axis. This is contrary to the so-called dynamo theory, invoked to explain the magnetic fields of Jupiter, the Earth, and Mercury, which requires a significant inclination between the magnetic and rotational axes. Possibly the most important result of Pioneer's Saturn measurements is an improved knowledge of the planet's gravitational field. This will permit much better control of the Voyager trajectories when those craft arrive and will surely enhance the possibility of good data return.

Barnard's star. The next closest star to the Sun, after the Alpha Centauri system, is Barnard's star, six light-years away. It is named after the U.S. astronomer E. E. Barnard, who showed it to have the largest apparent motion across the sky, 10.3 seconds of arc per year. It has been extensively observed since the early 1900s, when Barnard did his work. One long series of photographs exists at Sproul Observatory, Swarthmore (Pa.) College, extending from 1916 through the present.

In 1963 Peter van de Kamp announced that an analysis of 2,400 plates taken from 1916 to 1962 indicated a small 24-year oscillation in the motion of Barnard's star which could best be explained as caused by an unseen companion of planetary size. But a later study utilizing measurements from the Allegheny and Van Vleck observatories cast doubt on these results.

Van de Kamp and Sarah Lee Lippincott, director of Sproul Observatory, recently completed another study of 2,700 plates taken from 1950 to 1978. A more refined measurement technique was used than in the earlier study. They announced that they had confirmed the oscillations and were now able to resolve them into two components, one with a period of 11.7 years and one with a period of 20 years. The two astronomers concluded that the observations are best explained by a model that requires two planetary objects, with masses of 0.4 and 0.8 the mass of Jupiter, orbiting Barnard's star. So, once more, the discovery of a planetary system other than our own is a possibility.

Motions in globular clusters. Kyle Cudworth of Yerkes Observatory at Williams Bay, Wis., succeeded in measuring proper motions in M3, a globular cluster in the constellation of Canes Venatici. These motions are the angular changes in positions of member stars in the clusters due to their motions across the line of sight to the cluster. Because of the great distances to most globular clusters, huge movements are required before any proper motion becomes apparent.

In the case of M3 Cudworth found proper motions amounting to only a few ten-thousandths of a second of arc per year. In all, using eight photographs of the cluster taken from 1901 to 1976, he was able to measure movement in 266 cluster stars. By combining his proper motion measurements with radial velocity values determined elsewhere, Cudworth was able to make the first astrometric distance determination for a globular cluster. He found M3 to lie at a distance of 31,000 light-years from the Sun.

Supernova of 1408. One of the most interesting objects known to astronomers is the X-ray source Cygnus X-1, thought by many to be the leading candidate for the presence of a black hole. Li Qi-bin (Li Ch'i-pin) of the Beijing (Peking) Observatory identified what appears to have been a supernova recorded by Chinese observers in 1408 in the constellation of Cygnus. In all, there were nine separate sources in which the "new" star was recorded. The positions given agree well with the position of Cygnus X-1 in the sky. Thus, it appears that another extreme object can be assigned to the growing list of supernova remnants.

The mystery of SS433. In the early 1960s a rather obscure 14th-magnitude star in Aquila was listed by Charles Stephenson and Nicholas Sanduleak as num-

Donald Lynden-Bell, University of Cambridge, Institute of Astronomy

M87, a giant galaxy more than 70 million light-years distant, was found to emit a pulse each second that contains 10^4 times the amount of energy that the Sun emits each second.

ber 433 in their list of stars showing hydrogen emission lines, thus giving it the designation SS433. It was essentially forgotten until the summer of 1978, when it was identified as the optical counterpart of a highly variable radio source, which had also been identified as an X-ray source. These three separate observations are characteristic of supernova remnants, but SS433 is not a pulsar, presumably the common form of a remnant. The two observers postulated that it may be a new form of the remains of a supernova.

Bruce Margon at the University of California at Los Angeles (UCLA) began an intensive program of observing SS433 by measuring its spectrum and brightness with telescopes ranging from the 200-in (5-m) Hale telescope at Palomar Observatory to a 60-cm instrument at Lick Observatory. The results were astounding. The Doppler shifts in the spectrum implied that there were two sources moving at speeds of up to 25,000 kps (15,500 mps) in opposite directions at the same time. Quasars show such large shifts, but never a speed of approach, only of recession. Furthermore, interstellar lines in the spectrum of SS433 imply that it is only 11,000 light-years away, well within our Galaxy. The red color of this object is due to intervening interstellar dust grains. When corrections for the absorption by this dust are made, SS433 turns out to be quite luminous, about 2,500 times as energetic as the Sun.

Most astronomers are convinced that SS433 is a binary system but not of the usual variety. There are two major competing models to explain this bizarre object. Margon and George Abell, also of UCLA, proposed a normal F-star paired with a dense neutron star.

257

Material is lost by the F-star and streams toward the neutron star, forming a disk of accreting material about the latter object. The disk becomes overloaded and material is blown off perpendicular to the face of the disk, essentially in two beams of matter. These hot beams are trapped by the intense magnetic field of the rapidly spinning neutron star. The disk precesses due to the attraction of the F-star, and the beam sweeps out a huge double cone in space, giving rise to the apparent rapid motions toward and away from the viewer on Earth. (Precession is the gyration of the rotation axis of a spinning body about another line intersecting it so as to describe a cone.)

The other model was advanced by George Collins, Gerald Newsom, and Richard Boyd of Ohio State University, who proposed a compact object, possibly a neutron star, orbiting a more massive star with a strong magnetic field. The massive star loses matter in the form of a strong stellar wind, but the ionized matter in the wind is restricted by the strong magnetic field of the star. The matter streams out in two beams, which follow the rapidly precessing magnetic axis of the star. This material is guided by the magnetic field as it bends over at large distances from the star, causing the matter to impinge violently upon a disk of cool gas surrounding the double star system. Tremendous energy is released in the two regions where the matter strikes the disk, but these two regions continually race around the disk following the precessing magnetic field of the massive star.

As of 1980 the final decision concerning the structure of SS433 had not yet been made. Some astronomers were proposing a third body, and some thought that the general theory of relativity holds the clue to the observations. This strange object has already caused considerable excitement in the astronomical community and seems certain to cause more before its ultimate nature is known.

Seyfert galaxy. A galaxy known as NGC 1275 was identified as a Seyfert galaxy in 1943. These galaxies are systems with sharp, starlike nuclei. Many Seyfert galaxies are prolific radio emitters, and NGC 1275 is one of these.

Recently this galaxy was observed with an intercontinental radio interferometer using large radio antennae in the Crimea, Massachusetts, Sweden, and West Germany. The base line of this interferometer is so large that a resolution of details as small as $\frac{2}{10,000}$ of a second of arc (well below optical resolution) is possible. On the basis of the observations Iosif S. Shklovsky of the Institute of Space Research in Moscow concluded that there is a double nucleus in the galaxy. Previous optical spectra show asymmetrical emission lines that probably arise from the combination of two Doppler-shifted emission lines. Shklovsky proposed that the two sources identified in the radio measurements are associated with the two differently shifted emission lines. By treating the two sources as two bodies orbiting each other, he was able to estimate the mass of the nucleus dynamically. His estimate of the combined mass was 300 million solar masses. But, according to the radio data, the dimensions of the objects must be extremely small. Shklovsky thus determined that they may be a pair of orbiting supermassive black holes.

Double quasar. One of the first radio sources discovered in the constellation of Ursa Major, designated as 0957 + 561 by astronomers at Jodrell Bank in the U.K., was identified with a pair of faint, blue starlike objects several years ago. Both of these objects were subsequently shown to be quasars. During the past year observers at Kitt Peak Observatory in Arizona measured the red shifts of these objects and found nearly the same values for both. This was confirmed by measurements made with the MMT. Dennis Walsh, Robert F. Carswell, and Ray Weymann, the observers at Kitt Peak argued that it was unlikely that two independent quasars so closely spaced would have identical red shifts. Instead, they proposed that what is seen is actually one object, made to appear double by a gravitational lens effect due to a massive intervening object. This effect (the bending of light by a gravitational field) is predicted by relativity theory and has been observed in starlight grazing the surface of the Sun.

But also during the year David H. Roberts, Perry E. Greenfield, and Bernard F. Burke of the Massachusetts Institute of Technology used the Very Large Array Radio Telescope of the National Radio Astronomy Observatory at Socorro, N.M., to obtain a high-resolution radio map of 0957 + 561. This map shows a complex structure with five rather than two marked concentrations. Two of the concentrations coincide with the optical images of the quasars. These results are difficult to reconcile with the gravitational lens hypothesis, and, instead, this group proposed that 0957 + 561 probably is a true double quasar. The two quasars must have formed at the same time under similar conditions.

A new sky. In 1980 two orbiting observatories were changing astronomers' view of the heavens. One was HEAO 2 (High-Energy Astronomy Observatory), called the Einstein Observatory in honor of Albert Einstein's centennial. The other was the IUE (International Ultraviolet Explorer).

The Einstein Observatory functions in the X-ray region of the spectrum. Its usefulness results from its 58-cm imaging X-ray telescope. The instrument works best for soft X-rays (0.25 to 400 keV) and is capable of resolution of three seconds of arc near the center of its 1° field of view. It has five hundred times the sensitivity of any previous X-ray satellite. In roughly the first six months of its operation it doubled the number of known X-ray sources.

The Einstein Observatory by 1980 had uncovered 70 discrete X-ray sources in the Andromeda galaxy, the first system outside our own for which this has been

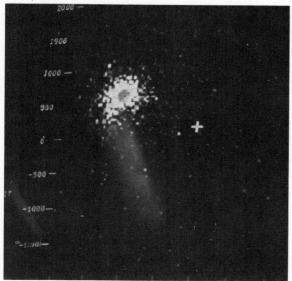

Courtesy, NASA

The star Eta Ursa Majoris was photographed by the
International Ultraviolet Explorer, which has an
ultraviolet telescope 100 times more sensitive than
those in previous satellites.

accomplished. Most of these sources are thought to be
similar to the bright X-ray sources in our Galaxy, which
means that they are supernova remnants. However,
about a dozen of the brightest sources in Andromeda,
which are seen in the central bulge of the galaxy, may
not be supernova remnants. An understanding of the
distribution of these sources in Andromeda will help
considerably in determining the way in which X-ray
sources are formed.

In our Galaxy the observatory revealed that many of
the X-ray sources previously observed with low resolution are actually multiple sources. The X-ray spectra of
supernova remnants were analyzed, and X-ray emission features corresponding to such elements were
identified. This proves that newly synthesized heavy
nuclei are products of the supernova process.

The Einstein Observatory also found X-ray sources
in extragalactic systems. For example, more than 20
quasars were determined to be X-ray sources. The
most distant quasar detected by the Einstein and positively identified with an optical counterpart is some
12×10^9 light-years away. It must be radiating, or at
least 12×10^9 years ago it was radiating, more energy
in the X-ray spectrum alone than 10 million million
Suns would radiate over the whole spectrum. The
variations, or flickering, in the X-ray flux imply that the
size of the source must be extremely compact, measured in light-hours or days. Possibly the X-ray data
will provide the first breakthrough in explaining the
quasars.

The IUE, operated by NASA in cooperation with the
U.K. Science Research Council and the European
Space Agency, provides astronomers with an ultravio-

let telescope capable of real-time control from the
ground. The instrument is a hundred times more sensitive than prior ultraviolet satellites, and for the first
time astronomers have a system with sufficient sensitivity and resolution that they can choose the objects
they wish to study on the basis of scientific considerations rather than merely brightness.

The first major efforts were aimed at the observation
of cool stars to detect stellar coronas, double stars to
search for mass exchange in the systems, novas to
better understand the nova process, globular clusters,
interstellar matter, and planets in the solar system.

See also Feature Articles: THE NEW OPTICAL TELE-
SCOPES, THE SEARCH FOR GRAVITATIONAL WAVES;
Year in Review: SPACE EXPLORATION: *Space probes.*

—W. M. Protheroe

Chemistry

Understanding the structures and properties of molecules of biological origin or with biological activity continued as a dominant concern in chemistry during the
past year. Investigators probed the anticancer activity
of an inorganic platinum compound, the chemistry of
the visual pigments responsible for color vision, and
details of the reactions that produce firefly light. Physical chemistry remained a dynamic field, spurred by
new applications for the laser and the need for improved isotope separation techniques. Chemists involved with applications of scientific discovery continued the search for alternate sources of energy.

Inorganic chemistry

Research in inorganic chemistry during the past year
remained largely focused on understanding the chemical bonding and structure of various compounds and
on syntheses and other reactions. Research was most
active in bioinorganic chemistry, energy-related photochemistry and homogeneous catalysis, and solid-state
inorganic chemistry.

Platinum anticancer drug. In the late 1960s, Bar-
nett Rosenberg and co-workers at Michigan State University discovered that certain platinum(II) complexes
have antitumor activity. [Platinum(II) is the platinum
atom with two electrons removed.] After more than a
decade of intensive study, the drug *cis*-dichlorodiam-
mineplatinum(II) (see 1a) became available for the

a   Cl—   —NH₃   Cl—   —NH₃

            Pt   Pt   b

Cl—   —NH₃   H₃N—   —Cl

cis–[Pt(NH₃)₂Cl₂]   *trans*–[Pt(NH₃)₂Cl₂]

1

(a) M + NH$_3$ (liquid) $\rightleftarrows$ [M(NH$_3$)$_x$]$^+$ (liquid) + [e(NH$_3$)$_y$]$^-$ (liquid)

(b) M + cryp + NH$_3$ (liquid) $\rightleftarrows$ [M(cryp)]$^+$ [M(NH$_3$)$_z$]$^-$ (solid)

(c) M + cryp + NH$_3$ (liquid) $\rightleftarrows$ [M(cryp)]$^+$ [e(NH$_3$)$_y$]$^-$ (solid)

treatment of certain types of cancer in humans. The initial problem of metal toxicity was largely overcome by the use of reagents that form complexes with platinum and thus assist in its removal from the body. It is also well known that, although cis-[Pt(NH$_3$)$_2$Cl$_2$] is an effective drug, its trans isomer (1b) is not an anticancer drug.

In an attempt to understand why these cis and trans isomers differ in antitumor activity and to learn why the cis isomer is so effective, the biological behavior of the isomers has been subjected to continuous detailed investigation. By the late 1970s it became generally agreed that the platinum complex acts on DNA, but the exact nature of this interaction was much less certain. During the past year Stephen J. Lippard of Columbia University, New York City, examined the reaction of both cis- and trans-[Pt(NH$_3$)$_2$Cl$_2$] with DNA that was still attached to the nucleosome core particle. In other words, this DNA was still wrapped around an assembly of histone proteins as it is in the nucleus of a cell. In this in vitro system, which models the actual cellular conditions of DNA, Lippard found that the two isomers react differently.

The cis isomer binds mainly to the DNA strands of the particle, causing the double helix structure of the DNA to unwind. This is also the way cis-platinum interacts with DNA strands that are not attached to a core structure. Thus it can be inferred that the presence of the histone proteins has little effect on the reaction of the cis isomer with DNA. The trans isomer, however, primarily forms cross-links either between the DNA chains and the protein support or between proteins in the core particle. These experiments provide a clear distinction in the kind, rather than the degree, of binding between cis and trans isomers.

Further studies by Lippard, in collaboration with William R. Bauer at the State University of New York, Stony Brook, began to focus on that portion of the DNA strand with which the cis isomer first reacts. These experiments used a small bacterial plasmid (a circular DNA molecule that exists independently of the bacterial chromosome) from *Escherichia coli* in which the sequence of its constituent building blocks, called nucleotides, is known. With this system and a special enzyme, it was possible to study the effect of the cis isomer on DNA at very low levels, approaching those at which the isomer has biological activity. Ordinarily this enzyme cleaves the plasmid at four specific sites into four fragments. When the plasmid was exposed to the cis isomer, however, the enzyme was less able to cut the DNA and the resulting fragments became fewer and larger. Furthermore, as increasing amounts of the isomer bound to the plasmid, cleavage at one site was inhibited much sooner than at the other three. After examining the nucleotide sequence at this site, the investigators tentatively concluded that the cis isomer is able to bind somewhere in a region made up of four consecutive guanine nucleotides on one DNA strand that are linked in complementary fashion to four cytosine nucleotides on the other strand. What remained to be determined was the exact binding site for cis-[Pt(NH$_3$)$_2$Cl$_2$].

Alkaline electrides. In 1974 James L. Dye and his research group at Michigan State University produced solid salts in which the anion, *i.e.*, the negatively charged ionic component, was an alkali metal (group IA of the periodic table; *e.g.*, sodium, or Na). This was a remarkable discovery because even beginning students of chemistry are taught that the alkali metals are notorious for their great tendency to give up an electron (e) and to form cations (positively charged ions) such as Na$^+$. This tendency is so large that these elements readily dissolve in liquid ammonia to give blue solutions containing the solvated electron [e(NH$_3$)$_y$]$^-$ (see 2a). With the addition of a cryptand (3), a type of compound similar to the crown ethers (which also form extremely stable complexes with alkali metal cations; see *1980 Yearbook of Science and the Future* Year in Review: CHEMISTRY: *Inorganic chemistry*), a reaction was obtained (2b) by means of which it was possible to stabilize the solid salt [M(cryp)]$^+$[M]$^-$; in this reaction M represents an alkali metal atom. X-ray analysis clearly established the structure of sodium sodide salt, which is formally analogous to common salt, sodium chloride (Na$^+$ and Na$^-$ correspond to Na$^+$ and Cl$^-$).

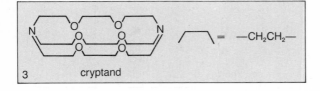

3   cryptand

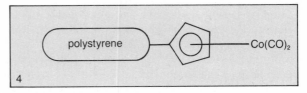

4

$$Fe_4 \!>\! C = O \xrightarrow[-H_2O]{+H^+} Fe_4 \!>\! C \xrightarrow{+H^+} CH_4 + Fe^{2+} + \text{iron carbonyls}$$

5

Recently Dye took these chemically unusual alkali alkalide salts a major step forward. This was done by replacing the alkalide anion, or the more traditional halide anion, with an electron (2c). Removal of ammonia yields an "electride" salt; *e.g.*, Na^+ and e^- correspond to Na^+ and Cl^-. In 1980 this research was in its embryonic stages, and little was known about the structures and characteristics of electride compounds. However, preliminary studies suggested that these new materials will prove to have interesting properties. For example, lithium electride was found to exist in two forms. One of the forms has extensively delocalized electrons, giving the material high electrical conductivity. This form exists above $-45°$ C ($-49°$ F), but below $-48°$ C a second form is present that appears to have locally trapped electrons, resulting in reduced conductivity.

Coal gasification and liquefaction. In recent years inorganic chemists around the world have concentrated on reactions that reduce carbon monoxide (CO) to yield hydrocarbons. Because coal can be made to yield CO, a CO reduction process allows the conversion of coal into gaseous or liquid hydrocarbons for use as fuel. In the late 1970s such a process was being done on a commercial scale, using a heterogeneous catalyst and Fischer-Tropsch chemistry (see *1978 Yearbook of Science and the Future* Year in Review: CHEMISTRY: *Inorganic chemistry*). This method, however, requires high temperature and pressure and is not too efficient. For such reasons investigators were searching for a more efficient and less costly homogeneous process.

An interesting heterogeneous-homogeneous catalyst for this reaction was recently reported by Peter C. Vollhardt and co-workers at the University of California, Berkeley. The catalyst is a cobalt carbonyl chemically attached to polystyrene (4) in such a way that the polystyrene remains insoluble and the cobalt carbonyl groups are in solution. Under rather mild conditions this system will catalyze the reaction of CO with hydrogen to yield a mixture of hydrocarbons. Preliminary results showed that hydrocarbons with numbers of carbon atoms varying from 3 through 20 are produced. The reactions involved in this process are believed to be similar to Fischer-Tropsch reactions.

A new type of reaction for the reduction of carbon monoxide to methane (CH_4) was reported recently by Duward F. Shriver and his students at Northwestern University, Evanston, Ill. This reaction depends on the protonation of (addition of positive hydrogen ions to) a polynuclear metal carbonyl anion. The most successful results to date were obtained with the metal cluster

$[Fe_4(CO)_{13}]^{2-}$. A possible mechanism for reaction is attack on the oxygen atom of CO by protons (H^+) to form water; the remaining carbide then interacts with more protons to form methane (5). This schematic does not show the complicated structure of $[Fe_4(CO)_{13}]^{2-}$ but focuses on one CO group, which is attached to two adjacent iron atoms. Protons attack the group's oxygen atom and remove it as water, thus leaving a very reactive carbide. The iron atoms in low oxidation states can provide the needed electrons to form the intermediate carbide and in effect to provide the six electrons required by the overall reaction $CO + 6H^+ + 6e \rightarrow CH_4 + H_2O$. As of 1980 it was much too early to estimate the effect that this new approach might have on the conversion of coal into hydrocarbons, but it was welcomed as a new type of reaction to be thoroughly examined.

—Fred Basolo

Organic chemistry

A truly great chemist, Robert Burns Woodward, died on July 8, 1979, at the age of 62 (*see* SCIENTISTS OF THE YEAR). His contributions to organic chemistry were monumental, and to many scientists he became a legend in his time. In addition to landmark achievements in total synthesis of complex, naturally occurring molecules, for which he received the Nobel Prize for Chemistry in 1965, he added to an understanding of the structure of many natural products, to the devel-

1 penems
2 penicillins
3 cephalosporins
4 carbapenems

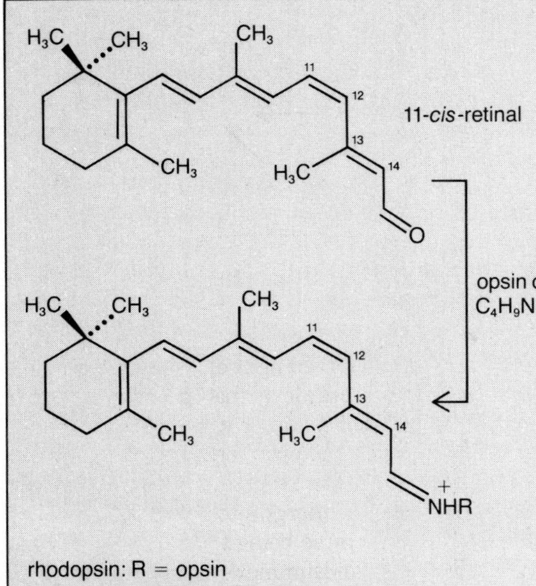

11-cis-retinal

opsin or
C4H9NH2

rhodopsin: R = opsin
retinal-butylamine combination: R = C4H9

a   luciferin

luciferase, O2

b   peroxy lactone

internal electron
transfer

c

−CO2

d   excited state

e   + light

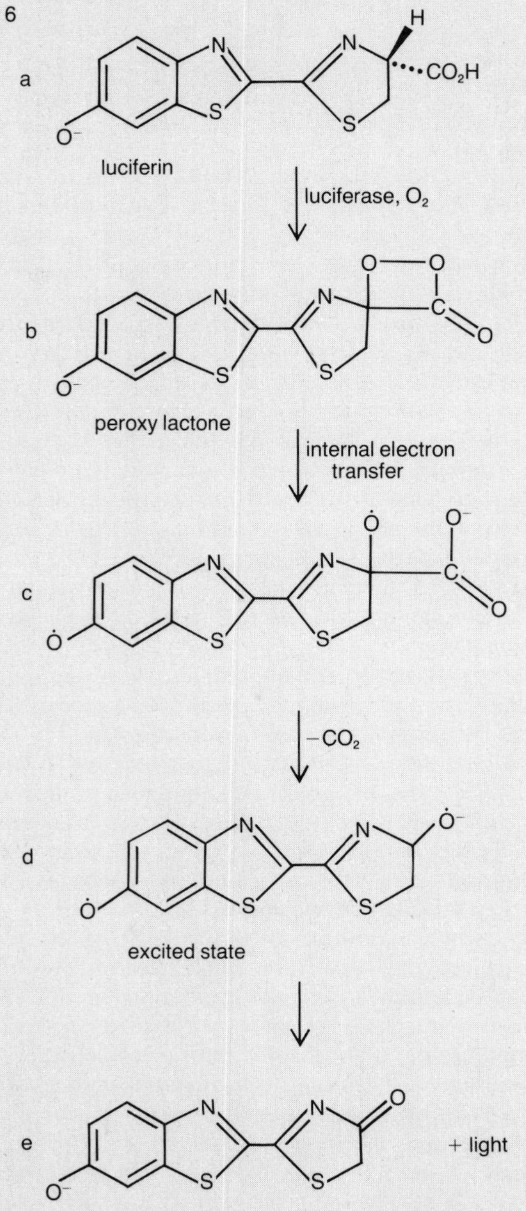

opment of relationships between structure and spectroscopic properties and of methodology in peptide synthesis, and to an understanding of the ways in which nature synthesizes molecules (biogenetic theory). Possibly his most significant contribution overall was the demonstration of strategy in synthesis. He showed that a combination of insight and an understanding of how chemical reactions occur and how they are influenced by structural constraints makes it possible to manipulate a multistep synthesis in a prescribed manner. Even so, the unexpected sometimes happens. It is a matter of record that his inquiry into an apparent anomaly encountered in the synthesis of vitamin B_{12} led to the development of a major theoretical concept—the conservation of orbital symmetry.

Even in the last year of his life, his contribution to chemistry was noteworthy. Until his death he divided his time between Harvard University in the U.S. and the Woodward Research Institute in Switzerland. Under his leadership Swiss chemists succeeded in synthesizing a new class of β-lactam antibiotic called penems. The penems (1) were designed to combine the structural elements associated with biological activity in more familiar antibiotics; i.e., the fused five-membered ring of the penicillins (2) and the double bond conjugated with the amide nitrogen of the cephalosporins (3). They are also similar to another class of promising new synthetic antibiotics, the carbapenems (4), which were reported only recently by Burton G. Christensen and his co-workers at Merck, Sharp & Dohme in New Jersey.

As anticipated, the penems are active antibiotics and, surprisingly, are active even without the acylamino side chain (R = NHCOR′) at carbon 6. The Swiss group further showed that only penems having the configuration at carbon 5 that is shown in (1)—called the R configuration—are biologically active. The implication of this work is that the sole essential stereochemical requirement for activity in penems, and presumably in other β-lactams, is the 5R configuration.

The chemistry of vision has been studied by chemists and biologists for years, yet many mysteries remain. One of these is how the combination of 11-cis-retinal with the protein opsin, in the form of the visual pigment rhodopsin, can present the brain with a rainbow of images rather than colorless forms. It is known

7

a   b   c   d   e

that in rhodopsin the retinal part is combined with the opsin part by means of an immonium group, commonly called a protonated Schiff base and abbreviated as SBH$^+$. In this respect rhodopsin is no different from the combination of retinal with a simple amine (*e.g.*, n-butylamine, n-C$_4$H$_9$NH$_2$) as in (5).

Because both rhodopsin and the retinal-amine example have the same chromophore (light-absorbing group), the SBH$^+$ grouping, they might be anticipated to absorb light of similar wavelengths. But they do not. Bovine rhodopsin absorbs at 500 nm (nanometers; 10^{-9} meters), whereas the retinal-amine structure absorbs at 440 nm. In fact, in the human eye there are three kinds of rhodopsins, absorbing at 440, 535, and 575 nm, that constitute the basis of color recognition, yet all three have the same 11-*cis*-retinal SBH$^+$ chromophore. Clearly the protein part of these visual pigments must exercise some special control on the light-absorbing properties of the SBH$^+$ chromophore.

During the past year the nature of this control was described by two groups working in collaboration, led by Koji Nakanishi of Columbia University in New York City and Barry Honig of the University of Illinois. These workers obtained evidence that electrostatic interactions between the SBH$^+$ chromophore and a point charge located on the opsin are responsible for wavelength regulation in visual pigments. Using synthetic combinations of various retinals with hydrogen, they determined that the most sensitive part of the SBH$^+$ chromophore to wavelength regulation lies between carbon 12 and the nitrogen (see 5). Based on calculations that quantify the effect of an external charge on the wavelength of absorption of model SBH$^+$ groups, Nakanishi and Honig concluded that changes in the placement of this charge at sites about 0.3 nm distant from carbon 12 to carbon 14 in rhodopsin produce the observed shifts in the wavelength maxima. This electrostatic point-charge model requires that the proteins in rhodopsins have a negative charge near the retinal, and it accounts for the fact that the same chromophore can possess different light-absorption characteristics depending on the placement of this negative charge with respect to the retinal. In model studies on simpler systems, the Nakanishi group verified that light absorption by an SBH$^+$ chromophore is indeed sensitive to the placement of external ionic groups in the manner indicated in the calculations. Possibly, tuning of wavelength absorption by a point charge is comparable

with tuning the vibration frequency of a guitar string by positioning the fret.

Vision involves photochemistry, and in any photochemical reaction absorbed light excites a molecule to a higher electronic energy level that leads ultimately to some chemical change. In other words radiant energy is transformed into chemical energy by means of molecular excitation. The reverse of this process, the conversion of chemical energy into light, is also known, a most delightful example being the emission of light by the firefly on a midsummer's night (bioluminescence). The mystery of how visible light can result from a biological or chemical reaction is of great interest, and recent research by G. B. Schuster of the University of Illinois presented some cogent answers. It has been known for some time that luminescence in the firefly depends on the conversion of luciferin (6a) to a high-energy peroxy lactone (6b), which then decomposes to the ketone (6c–6e). This decomposition occurs with sufficient evolution of energy to form the ketone in an excited state, which returns to normal by emitting light. It is the mechanism of the chemiexcitation step that has not been previously understood. From the results of chemiluminescence studies in nonbiological systems, Schuster showed that the key step is electron transfer. Thus, the decomposition of a simple peroxy lactone (7a) is accelerated by easily oxidizable hydrocarbons (Ar), which, in the process, emit light themselves. Because the intensity of the light and the rate of decomposition correlate with the ease with which the hydrocarbon gives up an electron (oxidation potential), a key step involving electron transfer from the hydrocarbon to the peroxide seems very likely. As a result the O—O bond breaks (7b), and carbon dioxide (CO$_2$) is eliminated (7c). The remaining radical ion pair "annihilates" its charges by reversing the direction of electron transfer (7d). In so doing, the chemical energy released in the peroxide decomposition is transferred to the hydrocarbon as electronic energy and

8

(Z)-propanethial-S-oxide

leads to an excited electronic state of the hydrocarbon (Ar*). This energy is released as light (7e).

A similar process is indicated for firefly luminescence. In this case, however, the luciferin molecule is ideally constituted to produce the excited state of the ketone by internal electron transfer. Electron transfer from the easily oxidized aromatic portion of the molecule to the high-energy peroxidic portion (6b–6c) results in rapid decomposition of the peroxide to give CO_2 and a charge-transfer excited state of the ketone (6d), which then emits light (6e). The mechanism has been called the CIEEL mechanism, which stands for chemically initiated electron exchange luminescence. The explanation of firefly luminescence is also applicable to other bioluminescent organisms and represents a major breakthrough in understanding how chemical energy can lead to electronic excitation.

Some of the most remarkable achievements of the year concerned the detection and elucidation of structure of compounds either that are so reactive that normally they have only a fleeting existence or that occur naturally in such small quantities that isolating enough sample for study is a major problem. The latter category includes the noxious component of onions that produces tears (the onion lachrymatory factor), which Eric Block, Robert E. Penn, and Larry K. Revelle of the University of Missouri showed to be a sulfine (8).

Proof of structure and synthesis of the female American cockroach sex excitant periplanone B was achieved as a result of the coordinated efforts of four research groups. The quest for periplanone dates back 30 years and had been repeatedly thwarted by the difficulties in obtaining enough pure material. Nevertheless, in 1976 C. J. Persoons and co-workers of the Centraal Laboratorium TNO, Delft, The Netherlands, undertook a massive cockroach-rearing project and succeeded in isolating enough active material—200 micrograms (about seven millionths of an ounce) from 75,000 females—to make a tentative assignment of structure from spectral evidence. They assigned periplanone B a germacramoid structure for which at some locations the stereochemistry was unknown. In 1979 W. Clark Still of Columbia University synthesized three of the four possible diastereoisomers of the Persoons structure by brilliantly conceived stereocontrolled routes. Bioassays by E. Arnold and J. Clardy of Cornell University, Ithaca, N.Y., showed that one diastereoisomer, which consisted of two mirror-image forms, was very active. Bioassay of the separated mirror image forms by K. Nakanishi and M. A. Adams of Columbia University showed potent activity for one form only. The absolute configuration of this form was determined; it was identical in all respects with natural periplanone B.

Finally, exciting developments continued to make news in the field of interferon chemistry. Interferons are proteins produced by the body in response to viral infection and are associated with the body's immune system. Potentially they are powerful substances in the treatment of cancer and viral diseases, but effective clinical and structural studies have been hampered by lack of sufficient material. However, using refined purification techniques and amino-acid sequencing techniques, biochemists at du Pont, Yale University, and the California Institute of Technology determined the identity and sequence of the first 20 amino acids on one end of the interferon molecule found in humans and mice. Another approach has been to manufacture interferon using recombinant DNA technology, and some pharmaceutical companies, including Biogen in Switzerland, claimed success. Although scientists were a long way from knowing the complete story about interferon, progress during the year was extraordinary and was, it was hoped, a foretaste of major developments in the years ahead.

—Marjorie C. Caserio

Physical chemistry

The use of lasers to initiate chemical reactions and to guide them into pathways leading to specific products —so-called laser chemistry—has been a focus of interest in physical chemistry in recent years. Nevertheless, as of early 1980 there were no commercial chemical processes that could be called laser chemistry. In 1979 two studies sponsored by the U.S. government offered evaluations of the benefits that could realistically be expected from laser chemistry.

A critical assessment of laser chemistry came from a report ordered by the U.S. Department of Defense and compiled by a group of physicists and chemists known as the Jason Committee. According to committee chairman William Happer of Columbia University, New York City, "[The committee] was unable to find any process under development at the national laboratories, in academia, or in industry that has the potential to be profitable during the next several years." The problem seemed to be that lasers are still too expensive for use in the large-scale processes found in industrial chemical plants.

A more hopeful outlook emerged from a joint U.S. National Science Foundation-Department of Energy (NSF-DOE) workshop on laser chemistry, which agreed that near-term use of the technique to produce chemicals in large volumes was unlikely but added that applications would come with further research. One application that could soon arrive is the use of lasers to monitor and control the progress of chemical production lines by analyzing the products.

One expectation for laser chemistry is that infrared lasers could be used to drive reactions, in part because infrared lasers are much less expensive than visible or ultraviolet lasers when their prices per unit light intensity (cost per photon) are compared. The use of infra-

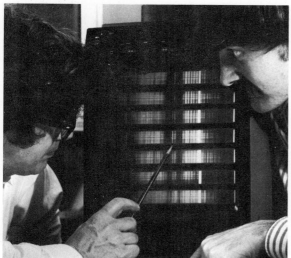

IBM scientists study novel spectral "snapshots" detailing the progress of an explosive chemical reaction. Absorption spectra were first made in infrared light and then converted to visible light for photographic recording.

red light, however, poses a problem that has been the subject of intense debate among physical chemists.

When a molecule absorbs infrared photons, it becomes excited in a specific way, vibrating with a frequency that matches the frequency of the laser. By contrast, when molecules are excited by heating them in a thermal reactor, all allowed vibrations are represented, and a mixture of reaction products results; the different products correspond to different bonds being broken when the appropriate vibration becomes too violent. One promise of laser chemistry has been that a specific reaction product could be chosen by initiat-

ing only one vibration; that is, laser chemistry could be selective. Once a molecule starts to vibrate, however, the energy of the vibration can be redistributed throughout the molecule by exciting other vibrations. Unfortunately, some experiments suggested that energy deposited by the laser is redistributed faster than the reaction can occur, and thus infrared laser chemistry is no more selective than ordinary thermal reactions are.

But a recent experiment by R. B. Hall and Andrew Kaldor of the Exxon Research and Engineering Co. in Linden, N.J., seemed to demonstrate just the opposite effect. When the Exxon chemists irradiated cyclopropane with lasers of two different frequencies, the reaction products were also different, suggesting that the reactions which formed those products took place before the laser energy became completely redistributed. Although certain details of the experiment made its interpretation controversial, late in 1979 theorists Everett Thiele, Myron Goodman, and James Stone of the University of Southern California reported on a molecular model that supported the Exxon workers. They assumed that molecular vibrations are grouped into two kinds and that redistribution of energy between vibrations in the same group is fast but that redistribution between vibrations in different groups is slow. From these assumptions the theorists could explain the Exxon results as well as the outcomes of some experiments that had been thought to show that infrared laser chemistry was not selective. The main conclusion seemed to be that experimentalists had yet to devise an experiment that could truly test whether infrared laser chemistry is or is not selective.

One very important use of lasers that was singled out by the NSF-DOE report is in the study of chemical reactions in order to control them more effectively. A prime

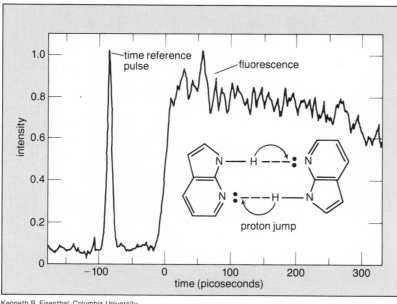

Columbia University chemists used ultraviolet laser pulses to induce a structural change in the dimer of 7-azaindole. By timing the appearance of characteristic fluorescence (seen in the plot as a sharp rise in intensity near zero picoseconds) from the excited, restructured molecule, they found that the structural change—a bonding shift of the two hydrogen atoms (proton jump) involved in holding the dimer together—takes place in less than five picoseconds (trillionths of a second).

example is combustion, the set of very rapid and complex high-temperature reactions occurring in flames. A very practical outcome of a better understanding of combustion would be the ability to design automobile engines with higher fuel economy and lower emission of pollutants.

At the Joint Institute for Laboratory Astrophysics in Boulder, Colo., chemists David Nesbitt and Steven Leone devised a laser technique that should help researchers reduce some of the complexity. Rather than burning a gas continuously, Nesbitt and Leone used very short pulses of ultraviolet laser light to ignite specific combustion reactions in a flowing gas mixture. The advantage of this approach is that reactions are initiated in a controlled, reproducible way, in part because the laser pulses are faster than the reactions themselves and in part because the laser can excite specific molecular vibrations. Moreover, as the reactions proceed, the products emit infrared radiation that can be detected by sensitive photodetectors. By following changes in the intensities and frequencies of the infrared emissions, investigators can follow the evolution with time of the reactions. Nesbitt and Leone applied their technique to several chain-reaction systems including short (millionths of a second) laser-initiated explosions of a hydrogen sulfide-chlorine (H_2S-Cl) mixture, to photodissociation reactions of such molecules as diiodomethane (CH_2I_2) and iodomethane (CH_3I), and to such ion-molecule reactions as chloride ion (Cl^-) with hydrogen bromide (HBr) or with hydrogen iodide (HI).

Another way to study combustion reactions is by infrared absorption, but the reactions proceed far too fast to record an entire spectrum from a single laser flash. Researchers Donald Bethune, John Lankard, Michael Loy, and Peter Sorokin of IBM's Thomas J. Watson Research Center in New York found a way to overcome this limitation with the use of two dye lasers. Dyes are organic materials that can be made to emit coherent radiation at many wavelengths simultaneously. Mirrors and gratings are used to separate the desired wavelength from the rest. In their investigations the IBM scientists removed the mirrors from one dye laser; consequently they were able to irradiate a sample with a wide range of wavelengths at the same time rather than one wavelength at a time. A major problem was to record the intensities of all the transmitted wavelengths simultaneously. Sensitive photographic film is suitable for visible and infrared light with wavelengths shorter than one micrometer (a millionth of a meter) but not for longer wavelengths. The investigators' solution was to convert the transmitted infrared light into visible light. To accomplish this, they tuned a second dye laser to a particular visible wave-

Workers at Columbia University employed laser light over a range of visible frequencies as an ionization source in a mass spectrometer (above). Using benzene (C_6H_6) as a sample, they found that its fragmentation pattern varied with laser frequency (right), reflecting the excitation and breaking of specific bonds.

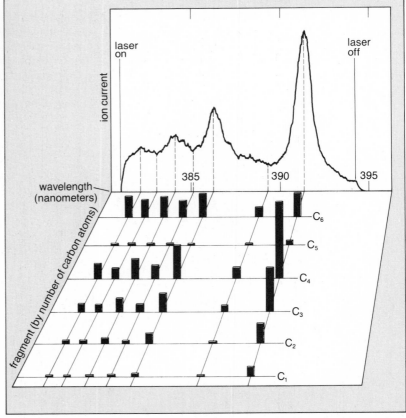

Photo and graph, Richard B. Bernstein, Columbia University

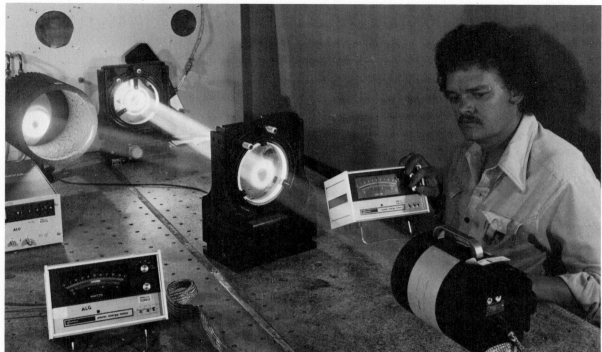

Technician at the Lawrence Livermore Laboratory in California studies characteristics of the visible light beam emerging from a copper vapor laser. The energy efficiency of lasers of this type and several other factors made them candidates for use in laser isotope separation efforts.

length and focused this light into a potassium vapor cell along with the transmitted infrared light. In the cell the transmitted infrared radiation, the focused laser light, and the potassium atoms interacted in such a way that the cell emitted visible light containing a spectrum whose details corresponded to the absorption spectrum in the infrared. In this way a broad infrared absorption spectrum could be recorded from one laser pulse of about five billionths of a second in duration, as demonstrated in a study of the explosive rearrangement of the molecular structure of methyl isocyanide. The IBM researchers believed that, with the use of other metal vapors such as cesium or rubidium, the technique could be used to record spectra in the wavelength range of 2–20 micrometers.

Among other work with lasers was a study by Kenneth Eisenthal of Columbia University and his coworkers on ultrafast laser spectroscopy of a bound pair of molecules (*i.e.*, a dimer) of 7-azaindole. The dimer is of interest because its structure is similar to that of the hydrogen-bonded base pairs in DNA. Changes in structure of the dimer under laser excitation thus could serve as a model for possible mutagenic behavior of DNA. For example, by exciting the dimer with a picosecond pulse of ultraviolet laser light and monitoring the fluorescence from the excited molecule as a function of time, the Columbia chemists found that the structural change occurs in less than five picoseconds (a picosecond is one trillionth of a second).

A second group at Columbia, headed by Richard Bernstein, used a laser in quite a different way. Bernstein's group elaborated on the growing use of lasers as the ionization source in a mass spectrometer. (The mass spectrometer is an analytical device that separates atoms, molecules, and molecular fragments according to their masses by ionizing them and passing them through electric and magnetic fields.) The group achieved two capabilities. The first was to obtain multiphoton absorption of photons from a visible-light laser. In the past multiphoton absorption had been largely the province of lasers that radiate infrared light, the photons of which are less energetic than those of visible light. In benzene, for example, as many as nine photons of visible light were absorbed, thus permitting ionization or fragmentation thresholds as energetic as 10–20 electron volts to be reached with visible photons possessing two to three electron volts of energy. The second achievement was to record sets of mass spectra with the laser tuned to different molecular absorption frequencies. In this way the fragmentation patterns could be studied and correlated with the excitation of specific bonds within the molecule. In addition to providing more specific information than could be obtained with conventional ionization by an electron beam, the Columbia chemists believed that their photoionization technique would preserve the sensitivity of mass spectroscopy to small amounts of sample that it has with electron-beam ionization.

267

Photo and diagram, Henry I. Smith, M. W. Geis, D. C. Flanders,
Massachusetts Institute of Technology

As ubiquitous as the laser seemed to be in recent months, some physical chemistry did manage to get done without it. One good example is in the preparation of isotopically pure chemicals. In recent years the most discussed and publicized application of isotope separation has been the enrichment of fissionable uranium-235 from the much more naturally abundant uranium-238 for nuclear reactors. But there are numerous applications for radioisotopes in nuclear medicine and for radioactive tracers for basic biological and chemical studies. A new method of isotope separation was devised by Nicholas Turro and Bernhard Kraeutler at Columbia University that takes advantage of the difference in the magnetic properties of light-excited molecules containing different isotopes. No laser was required; the Columbia chemists used sunlight and soap solution.

In one experiment, molecules of dibenzyl ketone were broken into two fragments by the absorption of sunlight. As an organic molecule, dibenzyl ketone contains a number of carbon atoms, some being carbon-12 (^{12}C) and some carbon-13 (^{13}C) in the ratio of about 99 to one. Unlike a laser sunlight contains many frequencies, and molecules containing either isotope are photoexcited. The difference is that the ^{13}C nucleus, or the nucleus of any isotope with an odd atomic weight, has a slight magnetic moment, whereas the ^{12}C nucleus, an isotope of even atomic weight, has none. Normally the two dibenzyl ketone fragments drift apart and undergo reactions that result in the production of a new product, diphenylethane. If the dibenzyl ketone is photoexcited in a detergent solution, however, the fragments are trapped and drift apart much more slowly. Concurrently the existence of the magnetic moment in the ^{13}C nucleus permits an electronic transition to a different quantum state, which in turn allows molecular fragments containing ^{13}C to reform dibenzyl ketone. By contrast, molecules containing ^{12}C eventually drift apart, as they do when no detergent is present. The net result is that dibenzyl ketone molecules containing ^{13}C can be separated from those containing only ^{12}C on the basis of the different reaction products. The process is not 100% efficient. In early experiments the Columbia researchers produced dibenzyl ketone in which 10% of the molecules contained ^{13}C, a tenfold enrichment. To apply the technique to other isotopes with odd atomic weights, including oxygen-17 and presumably uranium-235, all that appears to be needed is discovery of the appropriate chemical reaction.

—Arthur L. Robinson

Applied chemistry

One of the most urgent of world problems, the search for alternative sources of energy to replace the rapidly decreasing supply of fossil fuels, occupied many scien-

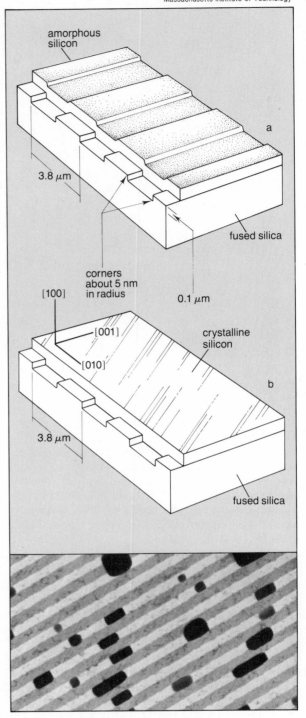

Oriented crystallization of a thin silicon film was induced in studies at MIT using a noncrystalline base of fused silica that had been grooved to microscopically precise dimensions (top). The silicon was first deposited as an amorphous film on the surface of the base (a) and then crystallized with a scanning laser beam (b). Oriented crystal growth of potassium chloride in water on a similarly grooved amorphous base had been achieved in previous work (above).

tists during the past year. Most of this review is devoted to developments attempting to alleviate the current energy shortage, including energy from biomass, solar energy, and photovoltaics (solar cells). Several recent developments in cosmochemistry related to the origin of life are also reviewed.

Biomass energy. In view of the increasing shortage of oil and natural gas worldwide attempts were being made to use nonfossilized biological energy resources containing cellulose, starches, and sugars; these included trees, agricultural crops, and waste products, known collectively as "biomass." Many biomass conversion experts believe that supplies of gasoline can be extended by the use of gasohol, usually a 9:1 mixture of gasoline and ethyl alcohol. Brazil began using alcohol produced from sugarcane for this purpose in 1975, and by 1980 it hoped to increase the alcohol content of gasohol to 20%. Eventually Brazil intended to phase out automobile engines burning gasoline or gasohol in favor of pure alcohol-burning engines. In the U.S. gasohol was being sold in several states, and a number of federal agencies were promoting its increased use on a nationwide scale. Gasohol has an octane rating some two to four points above unleaded gasoline, and it produces less air pollution.

U.S. biomass efforts in 1980 were focused largely on 14 conversion projects managed by Gary Schielbein of the Department of Energy's Northwest Laboratory in Richland, Wash. These projects involved direct combustion, direct liquefaction, and gasification of biomass feedstocks and indirect liquefaction from synthesis gas (a mixture of hydrogen and carbon monoxide). The last three processes are not expected to have an impact on U.S. energy supplies for 10–20 years.

Direct combustion was already widely practiced, especially by the forest products industry, but new developments were expected to increase utilization of forest residues and other biomass feedstocks. In 1980 the DOE had two such projects: development of a wood-fueled combustor that can be retrofitted directly to existing oil- or gas-fired boilers (Aerospace Research Corp.), and demonstration of large-scale cogeneration of industrial steam and electricity from wood (Wheelabrator Cleanfuel Corp.).

The DOE's direct liquefaction efforts centered on a project in Albany, Ore., managed by the Lawrence Berkeley Laboratory. In the fall of 1978 researchers from the laboratory developed a new process using a sodium carbonate catalyst that converts a slurry of hydrolyzed wood chips directly to an oil. In May 1979 the process was tested at the Albany pilot plant, where it produced an oil with a heating value of about 15,500 BTU (British thermal units) per lb. (Petroleum-based heating oil has values ranging from 18,300–19,000 BTU per lb.) Paul Weiss, Werner Hang, and Paul Rodewald of Mobil Research and Development Corp., Princeton, N.J., converted biomass products such as corn, castor, and jojoba oils in high yields to gasoline by passage over zeolite catalysts at 450°–500° C (842–932° F).

An indirect liquefaction process that uses garbage to make gasoline-type hydrocarbons was being developed at the U.S. Naval Weapons Center in China Lake, Calif. According to chemical engineer James Diebold very finely divided cellulose-containing municipal waste is rapidly heated to 700° C (1,292° F), at which time it is thermally decomposed (pyrolyzed) into molecules of various size. If the system is dilute and the heating time is kept short, olefins (unsaturated hydrocarbons) rather than aromatic tars or oxygen-containing organic compounds predominate in the gasification product. The gases are purified in a two-step process; carbon dioxide, hydrogen sulfide, and by-product gases are first removed, and then the low-molecular-weight olefins are absorbed into a light oil. The primary olefin produced is ethylene, which can be polymerized into high-octane gasoline hydrocarbons by a noncatalytic thermal process developed in the early 1930s. The char and gaseous by-products (carbon monoxide, methane, and hydrogen) can be burned to fuel the garbage conversion plant. Diebold estimated that half of the municipal wastes in the U.S. can be used to meet 3–4% of the nation's gasoline needs (the Iranian crisis reduced the U.S. supply by 5%) at a cost of 40–50 cents per gallon. If the process proves applicable to biomass as well as to garbage, it could meet 40–50% of the country's needs.

In 1979 two relatively large-scale attempts to produce alcohol from biomass began in the U.S.; Gulf Science and Technology Co. at Shawnee Mission, Kan., increased its cellulose-to-alcohol conversion plant from a capacity of one ton per day to 50 tons per day. By 1983, Gulf, which uses agricultural, industrial, and municipal wastes for its starting materials, expects to produce 2,000 tons of alcohol per day. The two-step process, carried out simultaneously in one vessel, uses the enzymes beta-1,4-endoglucanase and beta-glucosidase, which are obtained from the yeast *Trichoderma reesei*, to convert plant cellulose to the sugar glucose, and then uses other yeasts (*Saccharomyces cerevisiae*, *Saccharomyces carlsbergensi*, and *Candida brassicae*) to convert the glucose to ethyl alcohol.

By means of another yeast-catalyzed conversion process Donald Marata, staff engineer for the Hawaii State Energy Office, estimated that an old reconverted rum plant using molasses from Hawaii's large sugarcane crop as feedstock and *Saccharomyces cerevisiae* (the yeast used to produce beer) as the enzyme source can produce about 73 gallons of 95% ethyl alcohol every three days at a cost of $1.25 per gallon—slightly more than Gulf's prediction of $1.16 per gallon. Agri-Energies Inc. of San Diego, Calif., planned to use enzymes to convert crops and agricultural waste from California's fertile Imperial Valley to alcohol. The plant was to be run by electricity produced from geo-

Photos, Naval Research Laboratory—Authenticated News International

At the solar furnace at White Sands, New Mexico, (left) a thermochemical gas receiver (above) in 1979 became the first such device to convert sunlight into chemical energy.

thermal steam found beneath the valley floor, and its heating and air conditioning systems would operate on solar power.

Melvin Calvin, the 1961 Nobel laureate in chemistry and professor at the University of California at Berkeley, found that *Euphorbia lathyris*, a distant relative of the *Hevea brasiliensis* rubber plant, can be used to produce a mixture of hydrocarbons that can be used in a manner similar to the hydrocarbon mixture occurring in crude oil. He said that if the plants are grown in semiarid, agriculturally useless areas of the southwestern U.S., where they thrive, they could produce about ten barrels of oil per acre at a cost of about $30 per barrel, a yield that could be doubled by selective breeding. If approximately 60 million acres would be devoted to growing the plants, they could produce about 10% of the oil needs of the U.S. in five years. By 1980 Brazilian and Japanese companies had begun to grow the plants.

Because *Euphorbia*-produced oil must first be separated from solid plant materials in a process that adds to its cost, Calvin suggested that the copaiba tree (*Copaifera Langsdorffii*), which grows wild in most of Brazil, simply be tapped like a maple tree and the resulting "sap"—diesel-quality mixture of hydrocarbons (oil)—be collected. A single hole 3.75 cm (1.5 in) in diameter yields 10–20 l of oil in three hours, and if the hole is plugged it can be reopened six months later to yield an additional 10–20 l. The Brazilians began a copaiba plantation of 2,000 seedlings, and Calvin and others started work to develop better strains.

Solar energy. In June U.S. Pres. Jimmy Carter announced that federal support for solar research and development would rise to more than $1 billion in 1980 and that one-fifth of the nation's energy needs should come from the Sun by the year 2000. A number of developments took place during recent months as scientists and engineers attempted to reach that goal.

One difficulty in the use of solar energy is the problem of maintaining energy flow while the Sun is not shining. In an effort to overcome this problem a new battery system dubbed REDOX (for reduction-oxidation, the two types of chemical reactions used in this and most batteries) was developed at the Lewis Research Center of the U.S. National Aeronautics and Space Administration in Cleveland, Ohio. This system comprises a stack of flow cells, chambers in which two fluids, chromium chloride and iron chloride, are separated by a semipermeable membrane that permits passage of electrons but not of the chromium or iron. When the fluids are pumped through the cells, chemical energy is converted into electrical energy. The battery, which is as efficient as present-day lead storage batteries, is recharged by repumping the fluids through the stacks. Unlike lead batteries, which deteriorate during recharging by loss of solid lead compounds from the electrodes, no solid compounds are present in this battery, and so it lasts as long as 20–30 years. The only battery component limiting its life span is the membrane, which has been demonstrated to last up to 30 years.

Polycrystalline solar cells are much less expensive than the conventional single-crystal silicon cells used to convert sunlight to electricity, but they are also much less efficient for that purpose. Recently, however, David Ginley and Carl Seager of Sandia Laboratories in Albuquerque, N.M., increased the electrical efficiency of polycrystalline solar cells 20–100 times, into the 1–2% range, and improvements in fabrication may permit them to reach the 10% efficiency goal set by the

DOE. The combination of low cost and improved efficiency may permit home owners eventually to be able to obtain most of their electricity from rooftop polycrystalline solar panels, and utilities may produce enough electricity for entire cities from polycrystalline cells. The efficiency is increased by treating the cells with hot hydrogen gas or plasma at a relatively low, nondestructive temperature (325° C or 619° F), a process known as passivation. This treatment helps overcome the loss of electric current normally occurring at the boundary of two crystals in the polycrystalline matrix by modifying the chemical nature of the boundaries to remove "boundary traps."

One high-priority goal of materials research is the development of large, cheap, well-oriented silicon crystals, which would lower the cost of semiconducting electronic devices and make possible the inexpensive direct conversion of solar energy into electricity. Henry Smith, Dale Flanders, and Michael Geis of the Massachusetts Institute of Technology's Lincoln Laboratory in Lexington, Mass., developed a technique to grow oriented silicon crystals on the surface of an amorphous (noncrystalline) base. The new process, named graphoepitaxy, uses photolithography to etch a grating of parallel grooves two micrometers (one micrometer = about 0.00004 in) wide and two micrometers apart on the surface of an amorphous silicon dioxide (silica) glass plate. A thin film of noncrystalline silicon is then deposited on the plate and heated nearly to its melting point by a scanning laser beam. When the silicon film cools, it crystallizes and essentially becomes a single crystal that is uniformly oriented along the direction of the grating grooves. This use of an artificially created structure to control crystal growth provides an entirely new level of engineering control to crystal formation.

One possible use for the new silicon crystals is as replacements for commercially marketed silicon-on-sapphire crystals, a semiconductor material used in electronic devices. The new graphoepitaxy technique might also enable microelectronic devices to use three dimensions (instead of the current two) by sandwiching two or more layers of crystalline silicon between thin insulating layers of glass so as to increase the speed and performance of integrated electronic devices. Also, solar cells do not need silicon crystals as perfect as those in electronic devices, and so they may be the first devices in which the new crystals are used.

Angel Sanjurjo and Leonard Nanis of Stanford Research Institute International at Menlo Park, Calif., developed a new one-step process for producing high-purity silicon that is pure enough for use in solar cells at one-tenth of the cost of present methods ($5 per kilogram as compared with the current price of $60 per kilogram and a DOE 1986 goal of $10 per kilogram). When sodium fluorosilicate (a readily available waste product of the phosphate fertilizer industry) mixes and reacts with sodium, enough heat is generated to

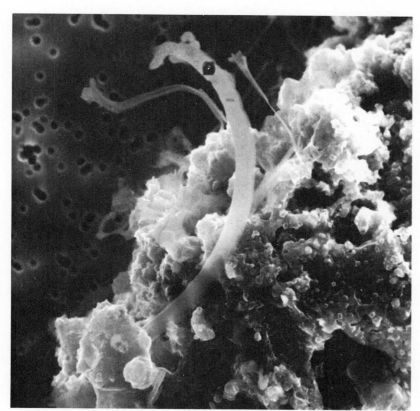

Microscopic particle collected by a U-2 aircraft flying high in the Earth's atmosphere was positively identified by highly sensitive analytical techniques as a micrometeorite, probably one of cometary origin. The achievement involved the first reported use of neutron activation analysis to determine trace element abundances in individual particles believed to be part of the dust that falls continually upon the Earth from interplanetary space. The antlerlike fibers on the particle were thought to have grown during a two-year storage period in the laboratory.

R. Ganapathy, J. T. Baker Chemical Company and D. E. Brownlee, University of Washington

produce silicon tetrafluoride. This then reacts with the sodium to produce high-purity silicon and sodium fluoride; (the latter can be sold to aluminum producers to make cryolite used in the electrolytic Hall process). Since heat is generated in the process, the reaction is self-sustaining and requires no consumption of external fuel.

Arlon Hunt of the University of California's Lawrence Berkeley Laboratory devised a new technique that he called SPHER (small particle heat exchange receiver). This process concentrates sunlight with mirrors and then focuses it on a transparent chamber filled with a mixture of air and microscopic carbon particles. Solar energy is absorbed by the particles, which then heat the air, increasing its pressure and enabling it to drive a conventional turbine to generate electricity. When the temperature reaches 649° C (1,-200° F), the carbon particles are oxidized to carbon dioxide. Carbon was chosen because of its large surface area (one gram or $1/28$ oz can be ground finely enough to yield a surface area of 70 sq m or 754 sq ft), its ability to absorb sunlight, and the small amount needed (a ten-million-watt power plant would require consumption of only 30 lb per hour). The amount of carbon dioxide emitted would be only one-thousandth of that produced by a conventional fossil-fuel-powered generating plant.

In July another system, part of a project developed by Talbot Chubb at the U.S. Naval Research Laboratory, was successfully tested by James McCrary of the Physical Sciences Laboratory of New Mexico State University at Las Cruces. Solar energy was used to heat a mixture of methane and carbon dioxide over a nickel catalyst to 925° C (1,697° F), at which temperature the gases combined in an endothermic (energy-consuming) reaction to produce synthesis gas. The heat that is evolved when the synthesis gas is burned was used to convert water to steam, which can be used to heat a building or run a power plant steam turbine. The researchers were designing a heat storage tank of molten salts (chlorides of sodium, potassium, and magnesium), which would permit the system to run continuously for up to three days without sunshine.

Origin of life. In 1979 research on cosmochemistry, the study of the chemical composition of the universe, continued with a number of new developments. Cyril Ponnamperuma of the Laboratory of Chemical Evolution at the University of Maryland in College Park reported that rocks from Greenland shown to be 3,830,000,000 years old by Stephen Moorbath of Oxford University contain small amounts of hydrocarbons (compounds of carbon and hydrogen that are found in most living organisms as well as in nonliving matter). Manfred Schidlowski of the Max Planck Institute in Mainz, West Germany, demonstrated that the ratio of the isotopes (forms of the same chemical element with different atomic weights) of carbon in the

rocks is similar to that usually found in organic substances. Inasmuch as the Greenland rocks are the oldest discovered to date and life on Earth is as old as the oldest earthly rocks, and since the Earth is considered to be 4.6 billion years old, only 800 million years elapsed between the formation of the Earth and the origin of life.

Ponnamperuma also produced additional evidence that many of the molecules required for life were being synthesized almost from the time that the Earth, planets, satellites, and meteorites first congealed from the solar nebula. From a few several-milligram samples of two meteorites (carbonaceous chondrites or carbon-containing rocks) found in Antarctica, he identified several amino acids, the building blocks for proteins found in all living matter. The deep-freeze conditions had kept the rocks unchanged from the time of their fall to Earth. The amino acids were found to be both dextrorotatory (right-handed) and levorotatory (left-handed) in their effect on polarized light, whereas all amino acids found in terrestrial plants and animals are only levorotatory. However, Ponnamperuma, in earlier successful attempts to create amino acids in the laboratory under "prebiotic" conditions, produced the same mixture of dextrorotatory and levorotatory acids as were found in the meteorites. He concluded that when amino acids were first formed on the Earth they were of both forms, but as the first living things emerged they could not metabolize the dextrorotatory acids, which thus played no role in the origin and evolution of life.

For more than three decades researchers beginning with Stanley Miller and Harold Urey, have subjected modern "primordial soups" (mixtures of water, ammonia, methane, and other materials) to electric discharges (to take the place of lightning) in attempts to duplicate the origin of organic matter (amino acids) on the primitive Earth. In 1979 Allen Bard and his postdoctoral associate, Herald Reiche, of the University of Texas at Austin likewise obtained small amounts of the amino acids glycine, alanine, serine, aspartic acid, and glutamic acid by irradiating with ordinary sunlight a mixture of water, methane, and ammonia or ammonium chloride that was catalyzed with a suspension of a semiconductor, platinized titanium dioxide. Although this catalyst is an unlikely substance for such terrestrial photosynthetic processes, other inorganic semiconductor systems, such as ferric oxide or tungsten oxide, may be capable of similar reactions. Bard considered it more likely that the prebiological synthesis of amino acids from components of the Precambrian terrestrial atmosphere was caused by sunlight rather than by sporadic bursts of lightning simulated by the electric discharge or ultraviolet light used in previous "modern" syntheses.

Steve Willner and colleagues at the University of California at San Diego reported in August that large amounts of hydrocarbons, in concentrations 1,000 times greater than astronomers had expected, are contained in huge "molecular clouds" in the area of the universe containing the constellation Sagittarius. The findings demonstrated that in space hydrocarbons are formed more easily than was previously believed, suggesting that they were much easier to form on the primitive Earth.

Hiroshi Yanagawa and colleagues at the Mitsubishi-Kasei Institute of Life Sciences in Tokyo performed experiments suggesting that many essential amino acids could have been formed from simpler substances in the primordial sea and that these acids could then have formed primitive cell-like structures. They heated a mixture of metallic elements as catalysts in water along with two simple inorganic substances, formaldehyde and hydroxylamine, all substances believed to be present in the primeval oceans, and produced 20 different amino acids in a month. Heating various combinations of these amino acids in their "modified sea medium" produced grainy aggregates, which the researchers called "marigranules" and tiny saclike structures, which they called "marisomes." Yanagawa proposed that these marigranules and marisomes could have been the evolutionary precursors for more complex cells and organisms.

—George B. Kauffman

See also Feature Article: The Chemistry of Good Cooking.

Earth sciences

Considerable activity took place during the past year in the Earth sciences. Earthquakes and floods were investigated intensively, and scientists hoped they might soon be able to provide useful forecasts of these disasters. Other subjects under study included acid rain, groundwater pollution, atmospheric carbon dioxide, and mass extinctions of species.

Atmospheric sciences

During the past year there were major developments in the following areas of atmospheric research: the general circulation of the atmosphere; the influence on global climate of increased carbon dioxide concentrations in the Earth's atmosphere; the effects of human activities on stratospheric ozone; the acidification of rain and snow; and the physical and dynamical properties of the ionosphere.

Global weather experiment. The massive global meteorological experiment that was set in motion in 1966 through the efforts of the National Academy of Sciences came to fruition during 1979. Over a one-year period ending on Nov. 30, 1979, 147 nations deployed scientists and a wide array of instruments all over the

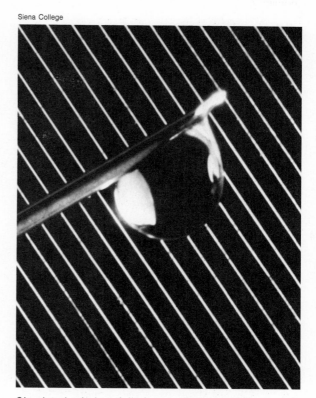

Simulated raindrop falls from syringe through a disdrometer, a device that computerizes the diameter and frequency of raindrops and may prove to be an effective means of analyzing rainstorm data.

Earth. This program has produced unique, detailed observations of the entire atmosphere up to an altitude of 30 km and of the upper layers of the ocean. Such complete information is needed to develop and test procedures by which theoretical models of the global atmosphere are used to make weather forecasts one to two weeks in advance.

The heart of the observational system was a system of five geostationary satellites in orbit around the world to keep it under constant surveillance. Three were controlled by the United States, one by Japan, and the other by the European Space Agency. For the first time simultaneous detailed observations were made of the entire tropics, and complete histories of hurricanes, typhoons, and other tropical cyclones were recorded. Such histories were also obtained for the more frequent cyclones of middle and higher latitudes.

In addition to the three geostationary satellites the National Oceanic and Atmospheric Administration (NOAA) operated two polar orbiting satellites giving radiometric data from which vertical temperature and humidity profiles could be calculated. Such information is of particular value over the vast oceans in the Southern Hemisphere, where there are virtually no other measurements.

As part of the global experiment special research activities were devoted to the study of the West African

273

and Asian monsoons. These experiments should shed some light on the factors governing the onset of the vitally important summer monsoons and their accompanying rains.

The quantity of data collected during the global experiment was enormous and will serve atmospheric scientists for a long time. The observations should appreciably enlarge knowledge about the evolution of cyclonic storms. It should lead to a better understanding of the nature of the general circulation of the Earth's atmosphere and the factors that control it. As a consequence better estimates can be made of the limitations of atmospheric predictability, and improved forecasts should become possible for longer time periods. It is hoped that research employing global data also will assist in the development of techniques for predicting climatic abnormalities.

Ozone. In 1979 the U.S. National Academy of Sciences published a report by its Panel on Stratospheric Chemistry and Transport chaired by Harold I. Schiff of York University, Ont. The panel reaffirmed the concerns expressed in academy studies issued in 1976 and 1977 by stating "that continued release of halocarbons into the atmosphere will result in a decrease in stratospheric ozone." The report went on to say that recent analyses show that chlorofluoromethane emissions at the rates prevailing in 1977 would almost certainly lead to greater ozone depletions than were earlier estimated.

Although there were no appreciable increases over the past four years in the production of fluorocarbons for aerosol spray cans, there was substantial growth in the use of Freon F-22 ($CHClF_2$) for use in refrigeration and of methyl chloroform (CH_3CCl_3) for use as a solvent. These are significant contributors to stratospheric chlorine, the substance that serves to reduce ozone amounts.

Unfortunately, it is difficult to obtain precise measurements of total stratospheric ozone because it is highly variable in time and space. The academy report concluded that it is unlikely that direct measurements would make it possible to detect a decrease of ozone of less than 5% attributable to human activity. Even if the release of halocarbons were totally stopped at the time of detection of a man-made reduction of ozone, the decrease would be expected to continue for another 15 years or so.

Carbon dioxide and climate. Although there still is uncertainty about whether or not total stratospheric ozone has been decreasing, no doubts exist about the trend of carbon dioxide concentrations in the Earth's atmosphere. The measurements made for many years, mostly at the Mauna Loa Observatory in Hawaii and at the South Pole, show distinct annual cycles of carbon dioxide (CO_2), reflecting interactions with vegetation. But on the average over recent years CO_2 has been increasing at a rate of about one part per million (ppm)

per year and now stands at about 335 ppm. It was about 290 ppm in the year 1900.

Most experts believe that the major source of atmospheric CO_2 is the combustion of fossil fuels. Nevertheless, some have argued that the biosphere has been a net contributor rather than a sink of CO_2. In a 1979 publication Wallace S. Broecker and his associates at Columbia University concluded that over the last two decades changes in the biomass of the world's forests have made contributions to atmospheric CO_2, though they are small in comparison with the contributions from the burning of fossil fuels.

The oceans are the major sinks of CO_2 and are mostly responsible for the fact that about half of the CO_2 coming from fossil fuels remains in the atmosphere. Unlike certain substances such as water vapor, which remains in the atmosphere only about 11 days on the average, the residence time of carbon dioxide is measured in years.

Future concentrations of atmospheric CO_2 will depend on the types and quantities of fuels used. It appears to many authorities that the major sources of electrical power in the early part of the next century will be coal and nuclear systems. It has been predicted that atmospheric CO_2 will reach 600 ppm by about the year 2030 if the use of fossil fuels continues to increase at a rate of 4% per year, the rate that was prevailing until a few years ago. If fuel consumption increases at only 2% per year, CO_2 should reach 600 ppm by perhaps 2050.

During the past year Gordon J. F. MacDonald, chief scientist at Mitre Corp., suggested that if the United States and the Soviet Union began producing synthetic fuels at a combined rate of two to three million barrels a day the CO_2 concentration of 600 ppm might be reached as early as 2010. A panel of experts assembled by the National Academy of Sciences disagreed with MacDonald's analysis and concluded that the date of CO_2 doubling is most likely to be between 2030 and 2050, as noted above.

There is a growing conviction that such development will have profound effects in the Earth's climate. Carbon dioxide absorbs some outgoing terrestrial radiation while being transparent to incoming solar radiation. Syukuro Manabe and Richard T. Wetherald at the Geophysical Fluid Dynamics Laboratory at Princeton University updated their analyses by which mathematical models of the general circulation of the global atmosphere are used to evaluate the consequences of an average CO_2 concentration double that at the beginning of this century. Their latest results indicated that it is likely to lead to an average global surface warming amounting to 2° to 3.5° C (3.6° to 6.3° F).

There still are uncertainties about heat exchanges with the oceans, but a panel of scientists concluded that if the rate of transfer of heat into the deep waters is greater than now anticipated there would be slower

John W. Goerg—New York State Dept. of
Environmental Conservation

Environmental Protection Agency

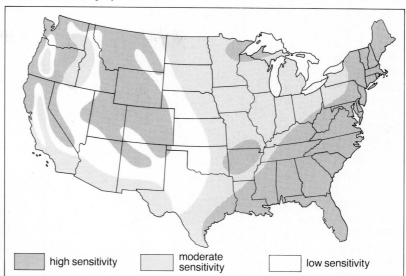

high sensitivity   moderate sensitivity   low sensitivity

Lime diluted with water is spread on the surface of a lake in the Adirondack Mountains in an effort to counteract harmful effects of acid rain. The map at the right indicates the varying sensitivity to acid rain in areas of the continental United States.

atmospheric warming than predicted by the existing models. The net effect would be to delay the time of the approximate 3° C (5° F) warming somewhat.

The polar regions would be expected to experience more warming than the lower latitudes, and the consequences for weather patterns would be very important. For example, storm tracks would be changed, and the timing of monsoons would be altered. Sea levels would rise because of the melting of land-locked ice in polar regions. At this time little can be said in detail about changes of temperature, precipitation, evaporation, and soil moisture at particular places.

Acid rain. The increasing acidity of rain and snow and its effects on lakes and streams was called to world attention in the early 1970s by Scandinavian investigators. Over recent years it has been getting increasing notice in the U.S. and elsewhere.

The combustion of fossil fuels and various smelting operations release large quantities of sulfur dioxide into the atmosphere. Chemical processes that involve water vapor convert the sulfur compounds into sulfuric acid, either in the form of droplets or as coatings on the surface of tiny smoke or soil grains. These acidic particles serve as condensation nuclei for the formation of cloud droplets. When rain or snow forms in an atmosphere rich in sulfates, the precipitation reaching the ground is acidic.

Nitrogen oxides emitted into the air from motor vehicles or other sources can be converted to nitric acid. It serves functions similar to its sulfuric acid counterparts and also contributes to the acidity of precipitation.

According to reports by the Environmental Protection Agency, since the 1930s the average acidity of some lakes in the Adirondack Mountains of New York state has increased so much that no fish have survived. The average pH dropped from 6.5 to 4.8 (that is, the acidity increased by a factor of about 50) over the last four decades. Until fairly recently it was assumed that the acid-rain problem was mostly restricted to heavily industrialized areas. It now is known that even areas such as the Rocky Mountains, once thought to be relatively clean of atmospheric pollutants, experience acidic precipitation. A directive from U.S. Pres. Jimmy Carter in 1979 set in motion a major research program to determine the mechanisms of production and transport, in the atmosphere, of sulfuric and nitric acids and their effects on fish and vegetation.

Snow augmentation. It is known that when ice-nucleating substances such as finely divided silver-iodide particles are introduced into a supercooled cloud, ice crystals are created. In a matter of minutes the crystals grow large enough to fall toward the ground in the form of snow. There is considerable debate among cloud physicists as to whether or not this kind of cloud seeding can cause increases of snowfall by amounts large enough to have economic significance in such activities as farming or hydroelectric power generation. Snowfall increases of more than about 10% of the amounts normally experienced on the mountainous watersheds in the western U.S. would be economically significant.

The strongest evidence that this can be done came from a series of experiments conducted from 1960–70 near Climax, Colo., by scientists at Colorado State University. Over the so-called target areas 10–30% more snow was observed on seeded days when the air temperature at the 500-mb (millibar) atmospheric pres-

Microwave radiometer in a space satellite senses microwave emissions from various levels of the Earth's atmosphere and thus can gather data about developing patterns of weather and track existing weather systems.

sure level was $-11°$ to $-20°$ C ($12°$ to $-4°$ F).

During the past year this experiment received a great deal of attention. In particular, Peter Hobbs at the University of Washington and his associates examined the physical basis for partitioning the data and its interpretation in the light of snowfall occurrences outside the target areas. Doubts were raised about the degree to which the overall experimental results support the hypothesis that ice-nuclei seeding can increase snowfall from winter clouds over mountainous regions.

A new investigation over the Sierra Nevada that will serve to test this hypothesis was in the advanced planning stage in 1980 under the sponsorship of the U.S. Water and Power Resources Services (formerly the Bureau of Reclamation). It was designed to take into account the lessons learned in earlier experiments, such as the ones carried out by Colorado State University and one conducted by the Bureau of Reclamation over the San Juan Mountains of Colorado between 1970 and 1975.

Severe storms. The growing recognition of the costs in deaths and injury and in property damage caused by violent thunderstorms led to several ambitious programs of basic and applied research that are relying on new observational and data analysis techniques. During the period April to June 1979 a large

data-gathering project was mounted in Oklahoma as part of the Severe Environmental Storms and Mesoscale Experiment. The principal goal of this project was to improve the understanding and prediction of organized thunderstorms. This requires better information about processes near the ground that are favorable for storm development and about the interactions of thunderstorms and their environments.

In and around Denver, Colo., NOAA began to design, construct, and test a system for supplying "radically new local scale weather services." The system would use new radar and other remote sensing techniques to obtain a "continuous detailed, high resolution, three-dimensional picture of all relevant meteorological parameters over an urban area." Continually updated forecasts for periods of up to a few hours would seek to pinpoint the time and place of occurrence of severe weather events. The forecasts would be disseminated by means of readily accessible and easy to understand video displays, presumably via television.

Lightning. Although a great deal is known about thunderstorm electricity, some important mysteries remain. A large research project known as Thunderstorm Research International Program (TRIP) has been engaged in the investigation of the dynamical, microphysical, and electrical nature of thunderstorms. Interest in such a program was stimulated by a dramatic episode on Nov. 14, 1969, when Apollo 12, on its way to the Moon, was struck twice by lightning as it was leaving the launch pad at the John F. Kennedy Space Center in Florida. TRIP began in 1976 with a series of field programs in Florida. In 1979 the field observations were carried out near Socorro, N.M.

There still is considerable debate over the process by which electric charge is generated and separated in clouds. The preponderance of opinion is that charging involves the interaction of ice and water, mostly in regions of the cloud where temperatures are between about $-10°$ and $-20°$ C ($14°$ and $-4°$ F).

During TRIP simultaneous measurements were made of cloud electrification and of the vertical air motions in thunderstorms. The latter were obtained by Roger Lhermitte at the University of Miami, Fla., who used three Doppler radars. He speculated that the nature of vertical velocities in the subfreezing parts of clouds is more important in explaining cloud electrification than is the quantity of rain that is produced by the clouds.

By means of rapidly responding electronic systems, new observations were made of the sequences of events associated with cloud-to-ground lightning. According to the work of E. Philip Krider at the University of Arizona and his associates, the current rise in a lightning stroke is much faster than was thought earlier. The currents in an average Florida lightning stroke reach peaks of 10,000 to 20,000 amps in periods of the order of 0.2 microseconds or less.

Authenticated News International

Scientists release research balloon carrying instruments to measure wind speed, temperature, and humidity in an effort to determine how air pollution travels through hilly regions.

Radar measurements of the upper atmosphere.
In 1958 William E. Gordon at Cornell University proposed that existing radar technology could be used to measure the properties of the ionosphere at heights above 100 km (60 mi). This led to the development of equipment that employs large antennas and operates at frequencies (50 to 1,300 MHz) that suffer little ionospheric refraction. The radar signals are reflected because of small, random fluctuations in atmospheric refractive index that result from random thermal motions of the individual gaseous species. The equipment, known as incoherent radars, measures the densities, temperatures, and motions of ions and electrons. Recent research by means of similar radar techniques made it possible to measure wind speeds and turbulence at altitudes below about 100 km.

James C. G. Walker, at the National Astronomy and Ionosphere Center in Arecibo, Puerto Rico, recently summarized the development of incoherent scatter radars. He concluded that more are needed throughout the world in order to obtain a better understanding of the dynamics of the entire upper atmosphere.

—Louis J. Battan

Geological sciences

The past year was one of intense activity in virtually every field of geological science. It is no exaggeration to say that never before in history have so many people been engaged in the study of the Earth. The twin spurs of a renewed theoretical enthusiasm engendered by the geological "revolution" of the 1960s and by current energy and environmental concerns are largely responsible for this geological renaissance, but it has occurred in many areas of study not obviously related to these factors.

Geology and geochemistry. No scientific breakthroughs or even major changes in emphasis occurred during the past year. The fact that 1979 marked the one-hundredth anniversary of the founding of the United States Geological Survey provided an occasion for U.S. geologists to take a long view of their discipline. (*See* Feature Article: SURVEYORS OF A NATION.) At the convention of the Geological Society of America in San Diego a session was devoted to the geological work of Grove Karl Gilbert, a geologist who worked for the Survey during its early years.

Exploration for energy sources. The search for new sources of energy continued to receive a high priority throughout the U.S. geological community. In September the Society of Exploration Geophysicists reported that, although exploration for oil and gas declined somewhat worldwide, seismic exploration in the U.S. and adjacent waters was at a higher level than at any time since 1959.

Despite the accident at the Three Mile Island nuclear-fueled electric-generating plant in Pennsylvania (*see* ENERGY) and increasing opposition to the building of new nuclear-fueled generating plants in the U.S., the price of uranium held steady in 1979 and exploration and production activity continued at a high level. Two plants constructed in Florida during 1978 to recover uranium oxide from phosphorites, for example, were expected to supply an appreciable percentage of total U.S. production in 1980.

As the demand for domestic sources of energy increased, so did the demand for men and women trained to locate and develop these sources. Undergraduate and graduate student enrollments in college and university geology departments, which had been high during the past several years, showed no sign of decline. Academic departments were apparently operating at or near their capacities. There were, however, signs that trustees and administrators might resist attempts to increase the instructional capacity of geology departments as a result of the overall austerity and contraction in higher education.

Geologists inevitably have become involved in the discussion which has arisen out of the seeming conflict between two national goals, that of developing domestic sources of energy and raw materials on the one

277

Largest operating centrifuge in the U.S. is being used to study such geological phenomena as Earth subsidence over coal mines. By subjecting scale models of Earth structures to various loads, the centrifuge enables scientists to predict how full-sized Earth structures will be affected by loads.

hand and that of preserving and enhancing the quality of the environment on the other. The American Institute of Professional Geologists published a Mineral Resource Position Statement containing recommendations aimed at encouraging mineral exploration and production. Several of these recommendations involved changes in government policy to encourage the development of domestic resources, including tax incentives, stockpiling, and changes in policy to encourage private exploration and production on federal land including areas designated as wilderness. The authors of the statement claimed that the high price of energy resulting from failure to develop domestic resources has, in fact, led to environmental deterioration as, for example, in forest depletion.

The search for energy not only resulted in increased exploration activity but also in many studies aimed at achieving fundamental understanding of the origin of petroleum. E. C. Copelin of the Union Oil Co. of California delivered a paper at the convention of the American Association of Petroleum Geologists held in Houston, Texas, in April. He suggested that the generation of oil begins early in the depositional cycle, the source of hydrocarbons being overlying waters rich in phytoplankton.

Environmental geology. Strong interest in environmental geology continued in 1979. Environmental and engineering geologists increasingly were turning their attention to sophisticated and complex interdisciplinary studies, many of which involved assessing the

consequences of natural and man-made events over long periods of time. Two reports issued by the U.S. Geological Survey on the potential hazards of explosive volcanic eruptions in the northwestern U.S. were indicative of this trend. It was reported that an eruption of Mt. St. Helens in southwestern Washington, identified as the most active explosive volcano in the contiguous U.S. during the past 4,500 years, would cause a failure or overtopping of the Swift Dam unless 100,-000 ac-ft of storage capacity were maintained behind the dam. Mt. St. Helens did erupt in March 1980, the first volcanic eruption in the contiguous 48 states since 1917, but did not immediately threaten the dam.

The Geological Society of London devoted part of its May issue to a series of articles on the prediction of volcanic eruptions. In one of these articles it was pointed out that the prediction of eruptions cannot help avert disasters because volcanic catastrophes do not occur at the beginning of eruptions. From the standpoint of human welfare the crucial problem is the ability to predict whether an eruption will end in a dangerous climax. Most eruptions do not.

It became clear during the year that the advice of geologists and geophysicists was becoming more significant as engineers and architects sought to make decisions on the location of new structures. For example, construction of the Auburn Dam in northern California was delayed until further studies could be made on earthquake risks. Recent seismic activity in surrounding areas led to a reassessment of the view that the dam was located in an area of low seismic activity.

Plate tectonics. The hypothesis of plate tectonics by 1980 was firmly established as the ruling paradigm of contemporary geology, having recently made significant inroads in Eastern Europe and the Soviet Union, where until recently resistance to it was rather intense. The present state of the hypothesis was revealed by K. Burke and A. M. C. Sengor in their "Review of Plate Tectonics," which appeared in the September issue of *Reviews of Geophysics and Space Physics.* They concluded that "Revision of the basic principles of plate tectonics has not proved necessary, but intensive studies have revealed subtleties that may not have been clearly appreciated in the earliest research. For example, although continental lithosphere is a product of plate tectonic processes, various studies have shown that plate kinematics cannot be usefully employed for detailed description of continental tectonics." It appeared that geology was in a period that Thomas Kuhn called "normal science" in his *Structure of Scientific Revolutions.* In such a period an attempt is made to accommodate anomalous phenomena to the ruling paradigm rather than to regard them as evidence against the paradigm.

The study of tectonics continued to be one of the most active in geology. There was some indication that the preoccupation with plate convergence at continental margins, which had dominated discussions in recent years, might be abating. In April an international conference at the Imperial College of Science and Technology, London, dealt with the features of classical orogenic belts (regions where mountains have formed, especially by folding of the Earth's crust). The more than 300 scientists who attended the conference heard papers dealing with subduction of continental lithosphere, gravity sliding, and high pore pressure.

Plate tectonics was invoked not only in explanations of orogenies and continental drift but also in the explanation of geological phenomena having a relationship to plate motion that seemed less obvious. Raymond Siever discussed plate-tectonic controls on diagenesis, the process by which sediments are transformed into rocks. He said, "Tectonics plays a prime role in determining the mineralogy and texture of a sediment, not only in the primary assemblages and stratigraphic patterns, but in their diagenetic histories as well."

Robert D. Regan, James G. Marsh, and Samir Vincent writing in the September issue of *Geoexploration* claimed that gravity and magnetic data derived from satellite measurements can play a significant role in mineral exploration. The regional rather than local views of the Earth provided by satellite data were in-

Mt. St. Helens in the state of Washington sends a plume of smoke, ashes, and debris up to 20,000 feet above its summit. The eruption, which began late in March 1980, was the first for the volcano since 1857 and the first in the contiguous 48 United States since Mt. Lassen erupted in 1917.

Wide World

creasingly important not only because of the economic potential of mineral deposits so found but also because such observations help reveal the relationships between plate tectonics and ore deposits.

The Deep Sea Drilling Project continued its program of ocean-floor exploration with the "Glomar Challenger." Oceanic crust was penetrated on the East Pacific Rise, the Middle American Trench, and at the mouth of the Gulf of California. Plans were made to extend the international program of ocean drilling using the "Glomar Challenger" into the Atlantic during the period from late 1979 until late 1981. Subjects of projected study include paleoenvironments of the southeastern Atlantic Mesozoic and Cenozoic, subsidence history of the oceanic crust, and mechanisms of crustal thinning during continental rifting.

Paleontology. Vertebrate paleontology, a subject largely unrelated to the economic needs of society and only slightly influenced by recent developments in tectonics, remained an active field of study, presumably because of the widespread intrinsic interest in the history of life. Dinosaurs, which have long been a subject of popular as well as scientific interest, were receiving renewed attention from paleontologists. The hypothesis that, contrary to earlier opinion, these reptiles might have been warm-blooded was a subject of intense debate. Attention was by no means confined to dinosaurs, however. Papers were published concerning the phylogeny, classification, and ecology of virtually every major group of vertebrates. Several significant fossil discoveries were made during 1979. Wann Lang-

ston, Jr., of the Texas Memorial Museum reported that recent discoveries of the fossil remains of the giant Texas pterosaur would contribute substantially to an understanding of the structure and function of this spectacular flying reptile.

Activity in the field of invertebrate paleontology was also intense. J. William Schopf of the University of California at Los Angeles brought together a group to be called the "Precambrian Paleobiology Research Group" to study the origin and earliest history of life. In support of this group Schopf contributed the $150,000 Alan T. Waterman Award that he received from the National Science Foundation in 1977 for his work in the study of Precambrian life. His contribution was matched by a grant from the U.S. National Aeronautics and Space Administration.

Interdisciplinary efforts to solve complex geological problems were evident in attempts to provide physical explanations for widespread episodes of extinction in the history of life. Walter Alvarez in a paper delivered at the annual meeting of the American Geophysical Union in Washington, D.C., suggested a means of testing the hypothesis that the occurrence of supernovas might lead to the extinction of organisms. Supernovas, according to Alvarez, result in increased levels in the atmosphere of certain elements, including iridium, and this in turn may lead to higher concentrations of those elements in accumulating sediments. He reported a 25-fold increase in concentrations of iridium in certain sediments in northern Italy deposited about 65 million years ago, a time that roughly corresponds with wide-

Nine-foot-long scapula (shoulder blade) is prepared for plaster mold at the site where it was discovered in western Colorado. James Jensen (center), who found the bone, believes that it was a part of the largest dinosaur that ever lived, a brachiosaurus that stood between 50 and 60 feet tall and weighed 80 tons.

Reuben J. Ross, Jr., U.S. Geological Survey

Chinese and visiting paleontologists crack rock in an attempt to find fossil trilobites in Wufeng Shale. The two signs mark the boundary between the top of the Ordovician Wufeng Shale and the bottom of the Silurian Longmaxi Formation. The site is on a tributary valley north of the Yangtze Gorge and downstream from Chongqing (Chungking).

spread extinctions between the Cretaceous and Tertiary periods.

Other developments. Geologic mapping, important as a means of compiling geological information and as a foundation for further investigations, continued to occupy the attention of many geologists. Perhaps the most ambitious mapping project in recent years was the attempt of more than 100 geologists from academic institutions, U.S. government agencies, and private industry to begin together an integrated series of maps reflecting the latest geological, mineralogical, and energy resources information available for the Pacific region. Paul Richards, chief of the U.S. Geological Survey Circum-Pacific Map Compilation Project, reported that the geographical and base maps at a scale of one to ten million had been published and that the compilation of other maps was progressing well.

International cooperation in geological studies was strikingly evident in 1979 as it has been for several decades. A number of U.S. and European geologists took advantage of the improved accessibility of China to visit important geological localities there. A group of Ordovician stratigraphers, led by Reuben Ross, Jr., visited China in October 1978 as guests of the Geological Society of China. They attended and gave lectures and visited significant Ordovician localities. In June a seven-member delegation from the Subcommission on the Devonian System of the International Stratigraphic Commission went to China for discussions with their Chinese colleagues and examination of critical Devonian sections. Another indication of China's scientific contacts with the U.S. was the presence of a Chinese delegation at the annual convention of the American Association of Petroleum Geologists in Houston. Wang Ping, a Chinese petroleum geologist, delivered a paper on the Gudao oil field in the Shengli (Sheng-li) district of China.

—David B. Kitts

Geophysics. Several major developments took place in geophysics during the past year. In the U.S. deep crustal reflection profiling in the southern Appalachian Mountains suggested that they were formed by shallow overthrusting during episodes of continental collision and are underlain by relatively undeformed Paleozoic sedimentary rocks. Groundwork for the prediction of three major earthquakes began in the U.S. and Japan in areas where the possibility of a major earthquake had been identified using plate-tectonic concepts. The feasibility of a direct test of the plate tectonics hypothesis was demonstrated using space-age geodetic technology. Preliminary results indicated that motion between the North American and Pacific plates is essentially restricted to the vicinity of the plate boundary and that the North American plate behaves as a rigid body.

Studies of crustal structure. A major discovery about the origin of the southern Appalachian Mountains was announced by the Consortium for Continental Reflection Profiling (Cocorp) in 1979. Deep crustal reflection profiles in Georgia, North Carolina, and Tennessee revealed that crystalline rocks exposed in the southern Appalachians form a sheet underlain by relatively flat-lying layered rocks.

The crystalline rocks are inferred to have been thrust at least 250 km (155 mi) to the west during episodes of plate collision and suturing of continental fragments to the North American continent. The underlying layered rocks visible in the reflection cross sections at depths varying from 6–10 km (3.7–6.2 mi) are probably Paleozoic sedimentary rocks, which, by inference, cover an extensive area of the central and southern Appalachians. Cocorp researchers pointed out that these sediments are a potential—and unexplored—source of hydrocarbon deposits.

Seismic gaps. Three of the more than one dozen seismic gaps located along plate boundaries through-

281

Laser interferometer is used deep in an abandoned gold mine shaft near Boulder, Colorado, to measure stresses that affect the size and shape of the Earth. It can detect vibrations minute in size.

out the world came under increased scrutiny in 1979. According to the theory of plate tectonics many of the world's large earthquakes result from the sudden release of elastic strain energy stored in the boundaries, which separate the mobile, rigid plates that form the Earth's outer shell. A seismic gap delineates a region along a plate boundary where large earthquakes are known to occur but that has remained unbroken for at least the past 30 years. The three seismic gaps under observation are located in central Japan in the Tokai district between Tokyo and Nagoya, in south-central Alaska near Cape Yakataga, and in southern California along the big bend of the San Andreas Fault north of Los Angeles.

Many Japanese Earth scientists, earthquake engineers, and government officials responsible for disaster prevention expect that a great earthquake will strike the Tokai area in the near future. In that region the mean return period of great earthquakes is estimated to be 120 years. Earthquakes of magnitude 8.4 hit this area in 1707 and 1854. Many critical facilities, includ-

ing the route of the Tokyo–Osaka high-speed express trains and several nuclear reactors, are located in the affected area. Official concern was heightened by the recent recognition of significant strain accumulation in the region and the identification of a marked seismic gap off Japan's Pacific Coast. In response to growing concern the Great Earthquake Countermeasure Law was enacted in Japan in December 1978 to coordinate earthquake prediction activities, to evaluate possible earthquake precursors, and to issue an earthquake-warning statement based upon imminent prediction information whenever possible.

Interest and concern about the 240-km-long (150-mi-long) Yakataga, Alaska, seismic gap increased following the magnitude 7.7 St. Elias earthquake of Feb. 28, 1979. This was the first major earthquake in the U.S. since a 7.2 earthquake shook Hawaii on Nov. 29, 1975. Although the St. Elias earthquake caused only minor damage in the sparsely settled region, the event alarmed seismologists because it filled the eastern quarter of the seismic gap that lies between the rupture zones of the 1958 earthquake to the east and the great Alaskan earthquake of 1964 to the west. In the 80 years since the gap was last ruptured in 1899–1900, elastic strain equivalent to as much as 4.8 m (16 ft) of fault displacement is believed to have accumulated. Ongoing studies in the Yakataga gap region, including seismograph, strain meter, and tiltmeter networks, strong-motion monitoring stations, and detailed geologic investigations of faults and coastal landforms, were intensified and expanded as a consequence of the St. Elias earthquake.

Concern over the possibility of an earthquake on the 320-km-long (200-mi-long) segment of the San Andreas Fault located north and east of Los Angeles intensified as a result of changes in geodetic strain that occurred in 1979. This segment of the San Andreas Fault, which last broke in the 8.3 earthquake of 1906, is also centered on the southern California uplift.

Annual surveys of geodetic networks in southern California revealed that between 1974 and 1978 the region underwent nearly uniform contraction in a north-south direction and also a decrease in land area. Over the past year, however, this trend began to reverse, with most networks showing east-west extension and an increase in land area with little north-south contraction. The geodetic network at Palmdale, Calif., near the middle of the seismic gap, also showed an accelerated shear strain rate parallel to the San Andreas Fault. Coupled with an observed reduction in stress normal to the fault plane, these conditions suggest that the tendency for an earthquake to occur has increased. Theoretical and laboratory studies of faulting show that the point of frictional instability is reached when the shear stress on the fault equals 80% of the effective normal stress. Until baseline values for the actual stresses are known, strain changes observed during 1979 cannot by themselves provide an accurate assessment of the imminence of an earthquake.

An analysis of the southern California uplift re-leveling project begun in 1978 revealed that the bulge underwent a partial collapse between 1974 and 1978. The 84,000-sq km (32,433-sq mi) region extending from near Point Arguello eastward to the Arizona border with its center near Palmdale, Calif., bulged upward by up to 45 cm (17.7 in) between 1961 and 1974. The relationship between deflation of the uplift, changes in crustal strain, and the potential for a large earthquake was poorly understood, however, and continued to be the focus of ongoing research.

Another factor adding to the geologic puzzle was the increase in radon emission in some water wells in the region. Large changes in radon flux were reported to have preceded large earthquakes in the Soviet Union and China. Radon, a short-lived radioactive gas, is commonly monitored because it is easier to measure than other nonradioactive gases present in ground water. Two wells located northeast of Los Angeles showed a twofold increase in radon concentration beginning in June 1979 relative to a two-year baseline. The short history of the radon measurements made their correlation with phases of the uplift and strain changes difficult. The increase, however, may have been a precursor of the Imperial Valley earthquake on Oct. 15, 1979.

Imperial Valley earthquake. Southern California and northern Baja California in Mexico were shaken by a strong earthquake on Oct. 15, 1979. The magnitude 6.4 event ruptured the Imperial and Brawley faults, which form a part of the San Andreas system. The scientific importance of this earthquake is twofold. First, it represents the best documented case of repeated seismic slip on a fault during the historic period. Second, the wealth of strong ground motion data and near-field geodetic data made it the best recorded earthquake to date.

Surface faulting reoccupied fault traces broken in the 7.1 earthquake of 1940. However, the two events were far from identical, with significant differences in the amount and pattern of surface rupture observed. Surface faulting in the 1940 event locally exceeded 6 m (19 ft), while the maximum offset in the 1979 event was 75 cm (30 in). Curiously, no surface offset of the fault was observed above the 1979 epicenter, near the location of maximum movement in 1940.

Following the October earthquake sympathetic fault slip was reported on several other faults in the region. A 32-km-long (20-mi-long) segment of the San Andreas Fault located 48 km (30 mi) N of the northernmost extent of surface faulting slipped by up to ⅛ inch. Movement on the Superstition Hills fault, 32 km NW of the Imperial fault exceeded ½ inch. Sympa-

Steel-reinforced concrete pillars on the east side of the Service Building of Imperial County, California, were virtually sheared at ground level as a result of the 6.4-magnitude earthquake that struck the region in October 1979. The building had been engineered to withstand a quake with magnitude as great as 8.

thetic displacement on these faults also accompanied the 1968 Borrego Mountain earthquake.

Instrumental records of the strong ground motion caused by the earthquake promised to yield a better understanding of the faulting process than had previously been possible. More than 20 instruments were sited within 16 km (10 mi) of the fault. Peak horizontal acceleration and velocity exceeded 1.7 times gravity and 100 cm per second, respectively. Structural damage in the largely agricultural region was relatively minor, although the Imperial County Service Building failed and had to be demolished. Built in 1974 according to earthquake safety codes of the time, the structure was heavily instrumented. Accelerograms recorded during its failure provided important data for structural engineers.

Geodynamics. A direct test of the plate tectonics hypothesis on a global scale using space technology for long-range geodesy began to supply some preliminary answers. The plate tectonics hypothesis presupposes that the stable plates that form the outer shell of the Earth behave as rigid bodies with relative motions being accommodated at the boundary between adjoining plates. The most precise determination of plate motion currently available relies upon the record of reversals of the Earth's magnetic field as indicated by the cooling oceanic crust at spreading centers. Consequently, average motions over periods shorter than about a million years are unknown.

Direct measurement of the distance between points separated by continental distances became possible by using very-long-baseline interferometry (VLBI). Cross-correlation of simultaneous observations of extragalactic radio sources by two or more radio telescopes allows the distances between the telescopes to be determined. Another system, employing optical telescopic observations of the laser geodynamic satellite (LAGEOS), provides similar information. VLBI and LAGEOS experiments being conducted in California across the San Andreas Fault showed a high rate of crustal strain across the North American-Pacific plate boundary. Results obtained were in rough agreement with plate-displacement rates determined by conventional geodetic methods and by observations of seafloor spreading.

Repeated observations of a 3,850-km-long (2,400-mi-long) baseline between Owens Valley, Calif., on the western edge of the North American plate, and Haystack, Mass., limited the rate of separation between the two observatories to less than ½ inch per year. The North American thus appears to behave as a nearly rigid plate, as predicted by theory. A more exhaustive test of the hypothesis, involving dozens of observatories and several other space techniques for geodesy was in the planning stage in 1980. A rigorous test of the theory will require about ten years.

—William L. Ellsworth

Hydrological sciences

Efforts to improve the effectiveness of flood forecasting, analyses of groundwater contamination, monitoring of ocean surface layers, and investigations of unusual assemblages of deep-ocean fauna were among the major developments in the hydrological sciences during the past year.

Hydrology. Flood-related damages in the United States in 1979 were estimated at $4 billion, with more than 100 lives lost. The damage total was second only to that of 1972 ($4.4 billion), when Tropical Storm Agnes was responsible for approximately 75% of the destruction.

Flood-related disasters outside the U.S. were also substantial in 1979. In Brazil heavy rainfall flooding caused 204 deaths in the southeastern regions. In the Dominican Republic floods in northern areas killed 32 people and caused extensive damages to farmland during the spring, and Hurricane David added to the destruction later in the year. The 1979 monsoon flooding in India was the worst in more than 50 years, with over 2,500 deaths and 30 million people displaced. More than one-third of West Bengal was inundated, and extensive evacuations of major cities were required. Flooding in some areas of Calcutta exceeded three meters (ten feet) in depth.

In the U.S. a troubling aspect of 1979 was the number of events that caused significant damage. Of the year's total loss $2 billion occurred in Texas alone, mostly in the southeastern region. These events followed upon the disastrous flash floods that resulted in 33 fatalities in the Big Hill and Big Country area of Texas Aug. 1–4, 1978, from Tropical Storm Amelia. Texas exemplified a disturbing trend in which flood damages were shifting from large rivers to smaller tributaries and headwater catchments. A headwater catchment is the mountainous or upper portion of a river system, and it receives its water from precipitation as opposed to tributary streams.

Flood forecasting. To reduce damages and fatalities in these areas it is important to develop effective flood forecasting systems. Flood forecasting systems consist of three major components: input data collection, forecast of river flows, and dissemination of flood warnings. Collection of input data consists of radar readings of storm systems from which precipitation is estimated, precipitation measurements by rain gauges, and precipitation forecasting through interpretation of storm structures (by U.S. National Weather Service personnel). The transformation of precipitation estimates into river flows is accomplished through the use of a hydrological model. Based on precipitation and river flow forecasts, warnings are issued that can be broadcast over radio and television. In all three areas there were significant developments.

Precipitation inputs, which are important for flood

Residents of Festus, Missouri, tour the town by boat in April 1979 as a result of flooding by the Mississippi River. Flood damages in the U.S. in 1979 were estimated at more than $4 billion, second only to 1972.

forecasting, vary statistically in time and space. To estimate precipitation in a particular area a network of rain gauges is installed. A number of studies during the year addressed the problem of finding statistically accurate estimates for areal precipitation. It is clear that while precipitation networks have been in operation for many years, continued work is being conducted by both universities and government agencies to improve their operation. In the United Kingdom this effort was being led by the Institute of Hydrology, which developed procedures for evaluating its rain gauge network and applied the results to the Wessex Water Authority and Southwest Water Authority regions. In evaluations of major flood events recommendations for improved rainfall data collections and for additional automated rain gauges that send radio signals to forecast centers are often made. Radar data are also important for predicting precipitation rates and in devising effective warning systems.

In runoff and river forecasting recent developments include improved methods for utilizing data transmitted during the flood. This capability is required if the data from automated precipitation networks are to be fully utilized. Since about 1970 the U.S. National Weather Service has been shifting from empirical curves for estimating basin runoff to an extensive mathematical computer model that simulates the hydrologic cycle (and response) of the river basin. While this model may be effective for long-term water-balance analyses, because of its data requirements it may not be as useful for forecasting flash floods on headwater catchments. Recent research indicated that considerably simpler models that can effectively utilize data collected during the storm may be preferable.

Some of these results were scheduled to be present-ed at an international symposium on the Application of Recent Developments in Hydrological Forecasting to the Operation of Water Resource Systems, called by the International Association of Hydrological Sciences (IAHS) and to be held April 15–19, 1980, in Oxford, England. The aims were to review developments in hydrological forecasting data systems, to discuss advances in forecasting, and to present applications of these techniques. The symposium may have a significant impact on flood forecasting in many smaller countries because their weather services often look to the IAHS for scientific guidance.

The development of the public warning system led to a significant decrease in flood-related fatalities, especially in the U.S. In flood situations in which sufficient warning time exists, loss of life is low compared with property damage. Flood warnings can also lead to reduced property damage by allowing the use of emergency procedures such as removal of mobile property and sandbagging. In the spring 1979 flood on the Red River of the North, an estimated $90 million of damages were saved by means of these procedures. The U.S. National Weather Service estimated that its warning system saved $1 billion in 1979 alone. Unfortunately, forecast warnings are most difficult to make in flash flood situations due to both the localized nature of the precipitation and the short time interval between the onset of precipitation and the occurrence of the flood. In recognition of the problem of flash floods the American Meteorological Society held a conference on that subject March 18–20, 1980, in Atlanta, Ga.

Applied research. In 1979 the World Meteorological Organization (WMO) received approval to coordinate the transfer of operational hydrologic models among various countries. To be known as the Hydro-

285

logical Operational Multipurpose Subprogram (HOMS), this effort was to be implemented within the Operational Hydrology Program (OHP) of WMO. A significant problem for the hydrological and meteorological services of many countries is the lack of resources and expertise to utilize and develop hydrological models based on the most current techniques. Often these services do not know whether models exist or how to obtain them. HOMS hoped to meet that need.

The central core of the program was to be the HOMS reference manual, which would offer information concerned with setting up and operating a hydrology project, and would also include a brief description of all the available hydrological modeling components. The manual would guide users in the selection and use of appropriate models. Often a variety of alternative models would be available, each at a different level of technological complexity and designed for application under different conditions. The use of the models will involve training of personnel, particularly in the less developed countries. This training was to be handled through already established programs within WMO.

The model components of HOMS were to be developed in response to needs identified by WMO member countries and would be derived from those models available to national hydrological and meteorological services and provided by those services to HOMS. The model components that would initially have priority are those concerned with data collection and processing from observational stations. They would be used for purposes of hydrological forecasting, in particular for the operation of reservoirs and regional planning of water resource development.

Basic research. The problems concerned with groundwater contamination continued to attract the attention of hydrologists. As an outgrowth of groundwater-contamination research a special session was held at each semiannual meeting of the American Geophysical Union (AGU).

The session held during the spring meeting focused upon using the unsaturated zone as a barrier in waste disposal. The unsaturated zone, which has a moisture level below saturation, is that part of the soil column between the land surface and the water table. The chemical and biological reactions that take place in this zone are extremely complex yet vitally important in evaluating the impact of waste-disposal sites on groundwater systems. An important research aim is the development of mathematical models that correctly mimic the transport physics and chemical behavior of these waste products. No model has yet been developed that incorporates all of the physical, chemical, and biological processes that are operative in the unsaturated zone beneath a typical waste-disposal site. Nevertheless, such an all-encompassing model may not be required for specific applications as long as the crucial characteristics for the particular problem are

included. Current research is developing these models for specific situations and testing the results with information from the field.

A special session on synthetic organic contaminants in groundwater was held during the fall meeting of the AGU. These compounds are present in organic pesticides, in by-products of industrial processes, and in many industrial and household products (for example, cleaning agents). These products are also cancer-causing agents at low concentrations. The U.S. Environmental Protection Agency has not, as yet, set maximum contaminant levels in drinking water for all organic compounds, but for those that do exist the standards are between one and ten parts per billion (ppb). For Endrin, it is 0.2 ppb; Toxaphene, 6 ppb; and for 2,4,5-TP Silvex, 10 ppb.

Current research focuses on measuring and monitoring the contaminants, the mathematical modeling of their transport in groundwater systems, and their chemical reactions in the unsaturated and saturated groundwater zones. It is important to note that efforts to decrease air and surface water pollution have tended to increase the potential for organic chemicals to enter the groundwater because of the increased use of ground-disposal systems as receptors of organic wastes.

—Eric F. Wood

Oceanography. Studies of the world's oceans during the past year ranged from large-scale monitoring of the surface layers to investigations of animals found clustered around vents of warm water welling up from the seafloor.

Ocean monitoring. One of the important differences between studies of the ocean and those of the atmosphere is that the latter benefit from a well established network of routine weather observations. This monitoring network developed because such observations are needed for forecasting weather conditions. No such requirement applied to the oceans, where the task is in any case much more difficult because of the oceans' enormous unpopulated areas, as well as the frequency and extent of their storms and the physical problems of obtaining subsurface measurements.

By 1980, however, the need for ocean monitoring was becoming more apparent, and new techniques were becoming available for doing the job. The need arose because of the influence of the ocean surface layers on weather and climate and the possibility that improved forecasts of the former and understanding of the latter would be possible if a running account could be kept of the storage and transfer of heat in the ocean. The main uses of such information would be on land, where agriculture and other human activities are concentrated. Yet some ocean activities, such as the harvest of living resources, would also benefit if it should become possible to make good predictions of the location and abundance of fish populations.

Courtesy, U.S. Geological Survey, Woods Hole, Massachusetts

Foraminifer from the Miocene Epoch (26 million to 7 million years ago) was found off the coast of South Carolina by AMCOR (Atlantic Margin Coring Project) in a drill hole that penetrated 307.9 meters. The project, sponsored by the U.S. Geological Survey, revealed that relatively fresh to brackish water occurs beneath much of the Atlantic continental shelf.

Until recently ocean monitoring has been superficial and scattered, carried out for the most part by merchant ships that routinely report to the weather network such data as sea-surface temperatures and near-surface wind velocities; some measurements of ocean surface circulation can also be obtained from navigational data. In the last few years some merchant and naval ships have been using expendable bathythermographs (XBT's), instruments that report temperature profiles to depths of 500 m (1,640 ft) or more. Important storage of heat occurs in the layer between the sea surface and the top of the thermocline, and the XBT measures the thickness and heat content of this layer. (The thermocline is the stratum in which water temperature decreases rapidly from surface values to those of the deep ocean.) Coastal and island stations also contribute to ocean monitoring, by, for example, measuring sea levels that are affected by the heating and circulation of near-surface waters.

The possibilities of ocean monitoring by remote sensing expanded greatly in the last few years with the development of Earth-oriented satellites. These are now well-established elements in the meteorological network, and some oceanic data are already routinely available. One example is sea-surface temperatures in cloud-free areas. While meteorological satellites can measure vertical profiles of atmospheric properties, they cannot penetrate the sea surface because the ocean is so opaque to electromagnetic radiation. But experiments in 1978–79 showed promise of overcoming to some extent even that limitation.

A satellite devoted to demonstrating the possibility of monitoring the ocean, Seasat 1, operated for about 100 days in late 1978, and the first results of its measurements appeared early the next year. Most of the instruments being tested operated at microwave wavelengths capable of penetrating clouds, and the characteristics they measured included ocean surface elevation, surface temperature, winds, waves, and sea ice distribution. The measurement by an altimeter of the elevation of the sea surface can lead directly to an indication of surface and subsurface ocean currents because the currents are usually geostrophic; that is, pressure gradients are balanced by the Coriolis force resulting from rotation of the Earth, and the pressure gradients are indicated by the sea-surface slope. The slopes are

287

R. E. Cheney, J. G. Marsh, "SEASAT altimetry observations of dynamic ocean currents in the Gulf Stream region." Geodynamics Branch, NASA, Goddard Space Flight Center

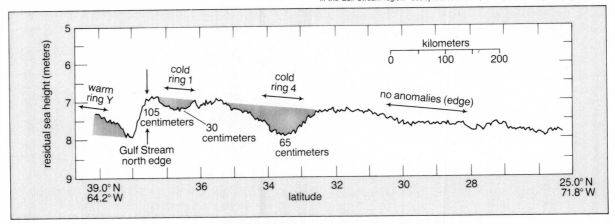

Seasat 1 satellite used an altimeter to measure differences in the levels of the ocean surface. By so doing the satellite revealed the position of the Gulf Stream and also the locations of several cold and warm current rings with differences in elevation of as little as 20 centimeters.

small—for example, across the Gulf Stream, one of the most energetic currents, the slope is only one meter in 100 km (3.3 ft in 62 mi)—and so the altimeter must have a precision of the order of centimeters. Furthermore, the orbit of the satellite and the shape of the geoid (the surface around the Earth that coincides with mean sea level in the oceans) must be known with comparable precision. Yet despite these difficulties, passes of the satellite registered the position of the Gulf Stream and also revealed the location of a series of cold and warm rings with elevational differences of as little as 20 cm. With further refinements it seems likely that satellite altimetry will permit the monitoring of near-surface currents and, coupled with other

measurements, will track their transport of heat.

Information on the near-surface ocean can also be obtained from drifting buoys that report positions and measurements via satellites to ground stations. During the 1979 Global Weather Experiment this method was extensively exploited to obtain data from the Southern Hemisphere. For this experiment the principal interest was in measuring atmospheric pressure (for calculating winds) and sea-surface temperature, but information on ocean currents was also obtained from the trajectories of the buoys. Several hundred buoys were deployed south of 20° S in early 1979, and maps of buoy tracks, temperature anomalies, sea-surface temperature, and surface atmospheric pressure were

Swiss oceanographer Jacques Piccard tests a new research submersible in Switzerland's Lake Geneva.

produced. Early results, while confirming the generally accepted picture of Antarctic circumpolar circulation, showed intriguing details and variations that were not previously recognized.

Seawater is relatively transparent to acoustic energy, especially at low frequencies, but the transmission of that energy is affected by water characteristics between the transmitter and the receiver. Though this is an inconvenience when one is hunting submarines or fish, it may provide a powerful method for monitoring these characteristics. A recent proposal was to use acoustic travel time changes along a variety of paths to determine the intervening field of sound speed. From this, one can estimate the water circulation. This will be particularly useful for examining motion in eddies about 100 km (60 mi) in diameter, where much of the ocean's "weather" seems to be concentrated. The method is analogous to a medical X-ray procedure for looking at two-dimensional displays of structure and therefore has been called acoustic tomography. It promises to make possible monitoring of the interior of the ocean on a scale as large as, for example, the entire North Atlantic.

Ocean eddies. The features of ocean weather mentioned earlier that contain much of the ocean's kinetic energy are eddies with diameters from less than 100 km to more than 1,000 km and with rotation in either clockwise or counterclockwise direction. North Atlantic eddies have been studied in a large U.S.-Soviet experiment known as POLYMODE, the field program of which continued through much of 1979.

Part of the effort, the Local Dynamics Experiment 400 km (250 mi) west of Bermuda, was designed to obtain specific information on temperature, salinity, pressure, and current velocity with sufficient accuracy for testing theoretical models. Many of the velocity measurements were made by moored instruments; subsurface floats located acoustically were used to track some of the eddies. Another experiment, largely the work of Soviet participants, traced eddies as they moved through a large region extending from 26° N to 34° N and produced regular "weather" maps of their distribution.

Flow in the ocean was found to be disorderly, and eddies of different sizes and behavior abound. Eddies can travel over considerable distances, carrying anomalous water properties and heat to other regions. The strongest eddies are near the Gulf Stream, and, although they commonly extend through the water column, they tend to be weaker near the bottom. The field data were used to improve numerical models, which are generating eddies with realistic duration, size, and energy. The models allow one to run long-term experiments; they suggest that even the extensive POLYMODE experiment has been too short-lived to be truly representative of oceanic conditions. But if measurements are to be made over three to four years,

Tube worms, some as long as three meters, are found clustered on the ocean floor around vents emitting clouds of warm, sulfur-laden water. The vents are in areas of seafloor spreading.

the remote sensing monitoring methods discussed earlier will be critical to their success.

Hydrothermal vent fauna. The occurrence of seafloor spreading and the associated features of plate tectonic theory are now accepted by most Earth scientists. Until now the investigations have been conducted primarily by geologists and geophysicists, but recent discoveries have dramatic biological and chemical implications.

Visual observations have had an important role in exploration of the seabed near spreading centers. Studies of the Galápagos Rift were made with a towed device capable of photographing half an acre of seafloor at a time (the so-called Angus, acoustically navigated underwater system) and a research submersible (in this case, the U.S. craft "Alvin"). In 1977 the first observations showed completely unexpected assemblages of marine life at depths of 2,500–2,700 m (8,-200–8,900 ft); in 1979 biologists joined the investigation to assess the meaning of this discovery.

Vents on the seafloor were seen emitting clouds of bluish-white (indicating the presence of colloidal sulfur) and warm (up to 17° C, 63° F) water in a region where the ambient water temperature is about 2° C (36° F). Clustered around the vent areas was a remark-

289

Photos, courtesy, Carl I. Sisskind, Scripps Institution of Oceanography

Sample recovered by a new piston corer (far right) developed by the Scripps Institution of Oceanography reveals the distinctly laminated sediments that are lost in the chewed-up core (right) recovered by a conventional rotary drill.

able grouping of giant clams, mussels, limpets, and extraordinary tube worms (reaching lengths of three meters [ten feet] and possibly members of a new phylum). Even near the surface such an assemblage would have been noteworthy, but at those depths far from known sources of food it was most unusual.

The densest colonies were of filter-feeding animals, suggesting a source of particulate food. Yet at such depths, where no light penetrates, the food could not be produced by photosynthesis. Collections in the emergent vent waters revealed large concentrations (estimates run as high as 10^8 or 10^9 cells per milliliter) of sulfur-oxidizing bacteria, indicating a chemosynthetic base for the food chain. The bacteria are believed to oxidize hydrogen sulfide in the vent water to sulfur and sulfate, using this energy to fix carbon dioxide into the organic matter that is consumed by the waiting multitudes. The likelihood of this proposed system was supported by the finding that the relative abundance of carbon-13 in the flesh of vent mussels was much too low for the food source to be photosynthetic. The food is produced below the seafloor, where large bacterial populations line the walls of the fissures through which the waters laden with hydrogen sulfide ascend.

Life around the hot springs is ephemeral, as observations of dead clam shells have indicated. The vents may be active for 10–20 years, the activity then shifting elsewhere along the axis of the spreading seafloor. Vent animals developed several strategies to cope with such changes. Growth is very rapid—analysis of radionuclide ratios in a giant clam have shown growth

rates about 500 times those of Atlantic Ocean deep-sea clams—and some species have long-lived planktonic larvae that are borne by the abyssal currents on lengthy recolonization expeditions.

Demonstrations of the existence of hydrothermal vents caused a reappraisal of the origin of seawater composition. It was previously believed that elements were brought to the sea by rivers and runoff from the continents; the seafloor was considered to be a sink and not an important source of minerals. Estimates of hydrothermal injections now suggest that large volumes of seawater percolate through cracks in the seafloor, providing a continuous exchange of elements. The fixation of insoluble metallic sulfides near the vents is evidence of an important and continuing mineral-forming process.

It is not known how widespread the occurrence of deep-sea thermal vents may be. Vent area communities may extend for hundreds of miles along the axial ridge of the Galápagos Rift and very likely will be found in other regions in which the seafloor is spreading. During 1978 further discoveries were made, by a French-American-Mexican expedition on the East Pacific Rise (south of Baja California), with columnar edifices up to 10 m (33 ft) high and colonies of dead giant clams indicating recent hydrothermal activity. And farther north, 70 km (45 mi) southwest of San Diego, accumulations of mineral deposits and dense colonies of tube worms similar to those near Galápagos were recently observed at depths of 1,800 m (5,900 ft). The concentrations of animals and the milky appearance of the near-bottom water suggest that a similar chemosynthetic food chain has been operating along this active fault zone.

Production in oceanic waters. It has long been known that photosynthetic production is high in coastal regions where nutrient levels in the water are high. In the open ocean, on the other hand, concentrations of inorganic nitrogen and phosphorus are low, sometimes immeasurable, and the standing stock of phytoplankton is low. Yet it now appears that in these apparently infertile regions growth rates of plant cells remain close to the maximum.

An indication of this is the fact that the ratios (by atoms) of the major elemental constituents of marine phytoplankton—carbon, nitrogen, and phosphorus—are usually about 106:16:1, whether the cells are from coastal or oceanic waters. Recent experiments demonstrated that these ratios are achieved in the laboratory only at high growth rates when nutrients are not a limiting factor. This paradox can be explained if nutrients are provided not only by physical processes, such as upwelling, but also by regeneration of nutrients that are organically bound. This can be accomplished by bacterial degradation of detrital material and by the excretion of soluble nutrients by zooplankton and fish. To the extent that such recycling is effective, nutrient availability is not the primary limiting factor in oceanic waters.

The euphotic zone of the open ocean (the upper layers into which sufficient light penetrates to permit the growth of green plants) in this respect resembles a continuous laboratory culture operating at steady state. The phytoplankton biomass is kept at a low level by zooplankton grazing. Despite the impoverished appearance of conditions in the open ocean the systems there are capable of accomplishing about 80% of the total photosynthetic carbon fixation in the entire body of water. Much of this is apparently accomplished by small (less than 10 μm in diameter) naked flagellates that are extremely difficult to sample and culture, and the applicability of these concepts to such organisms remained to be tested.

—Warren S. Wooster

Crewman aboard a research vessel checks one of the air guns that is part of a system also comprising a 240-channel recording device and ten minicomputers for gathering seismic data on the seafloor.

UPI

Electronics and information sciences

Progress continued to be made during the past year in improving the capacity and speed of information and communications systems. Major developments included the invention of a new computer language, an efficient means of varying the speed of an induction motor and thereby saving a considerable amount of energy, and a new frequency allocation of the electromagnetic spectrum.

Communications systems

Communications systems continued to be a dynamic area of technology. The past year was marked by technical advances; tremendous growth in communications requirements, driven in part by the energy shortage; and many experiments and products specifically oriented to the transfer of information. This was also the year of WARC, the World Administrative Radio Conference, as well as a period of significant regulatory and legislative action.

Throughout 1979 relatively deserted shopping centers and malls could be seen in large metropolitan areas as consumers were forced to curtail unnecessary outings to conserve gasoline. Plans were made by some employers to shorten workweeks in order to lessen fuel consumption by commuters. Airline schedules were overhauled, and at times scheduled flights had to be canceled for lack of aviation fuel. These events firmly established the potential benefits of communications systems for home and business applications.

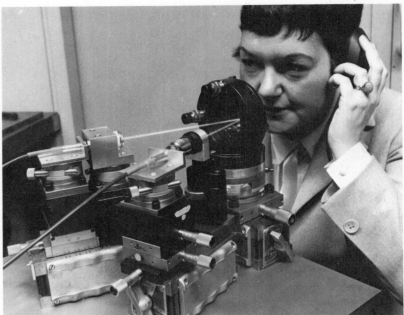

West German engineer demonstrates light-powered telephone by speaking into a vibrating membrane that is part of an array of components which will convert speech into modulated light and vice versa. A laser supplies the total energy for the system, which is attempting to employ nothing but optically powered elements between the exchange and the subscriber.

Home communications. The two most common home communications instruments are the telephone and the television set. Telephone-based systems are usually simpler to implement and have varying degrees of automation. As an example, more than 200 pay-by-phone systems already exist.

An electronic system based on the use of an ordinary television set as a computer terminal is referred to as a videotex, a term provisionally adopted by the International Telecommunication Union. First introduced in 1978 in the United Kingdom, by 1980 more than two dozen videotex systems existed or were planned in eight countries. They represented a great variation in function, ranging from simple captioning of television programs to aid deaf persons to highly interactive systems that include a keyboard for data input by the person using the system. Interactive systems have great potential for applications involving information retrieval and consumer transactions. For example, subscribers would be able to browse through newspapers and reports on television as the screen becomes a window on a full reference library. Also department store offerings could be perused by using television as an electronic catalog.

Continued advances in electronics, such as more sophisticated microprocessors, will allow subscribers to have a small but powerful computer and storage facilities attached to their videotex sets. This will provide added flexibility as information received through the videotex can be processed locally by the subscriber to meet individual requirements.

During the past year several companies announced nationwide personal-computing and home-information services, providing functions such as text editing, airline ticketing, newswire access, electronic mail, and interaction between subscribers. Videotex-based directory assistance and Yellow Pages services were also tested by American Telephone and Telegraph Co. (AT&T).

Business systems. The communications needs of businesses were spurred by the energy situation. One example was renewed interest in teleconferencing, a facility that enables organizations to conduct meetings by using television technology. Although the capability for and indeed a limited number of such systems have existed for some time, the cost of teleconferencing has been high. But as the cost of travel increases and the cost of the communications facilities decreases, the economics of teleconferencing become more attractive. The integration of teleconferencing with videotex systems may eventually lead to the "home office," enabling many workers to perhaps reduce the number of days they must travel to a central office.

Businesses continued to extend the use of communications systems both in regard to the automation of a single office and to the interconnection of multiple locations. Communications can provide greater accessibility to computational facilities and centralized data banks, as well as furnishing a network for the distribution of electronic documents. These applications require new systems with greater reliability and capacity than most existing voice networks. A number of organizations including Xerox, Satellite Business Systems, and General Telephone and Electronics continued to develop such systems.

Advances were also made in the design of new public data networks. EURONET, developed by the European Economic Community (EEC), became operational in mid-1979. Initially it was to be used only as a research tool by the academic community for purposes of testing, but eventually it was intended to provide a common data network that would interconnect all the members of the EEC.

Major changes in voice communications also took place during the year. Radical improvements were made to the private branch exchange, the heart of most business voice communications systems. Incorporating computers in the private branch exchange not only provided for increased voice functions, such as speech filing systems, but also opened the way for integration of voice and data networks. Speech filing systems such as that announced by AT&T in 1979 provide for the creation and distribution of voice messages. They also provide for delayed delivery to take advantage of lower rates for off-peak transmission. Integrated voice and data networks have the potential for both cost reduction and improved function by minimizing the equipment and facilities required. The merger of voice and data could also lead to new applications such as voice annotation of coded documents.

Transmission technologies. Most of the applications and systems discussed above are critically dependent on improvements in basic communications transmission technology. The two major areas in which these improvements have been realized are satellites and fiber optics. The reliability and performance of satellite transmission are ideal for applications requiring the transfer of large quantities of data. One example was an experiment set up by Teleglobe Canada that relayed European newspapers to Montreal for the large Italian and French communities there. Use of satellites for telephone communications, however, has been hampered by the voice-garbling echoes resulting from transmission delay due to the 45,000-mi-long satellite path. In the summer of 1979 AT&T announced a new integrated circuit designed to eliminate echoes in satellite voice transmissions. It was estimated that satellite usage for voice transmission increased by more than 300% in the fourth quarter of 1979 as a result of this echo-cancellation device.

The cost of satellite usage, measured in investment per circuit per year, continued to drop. The cost for a single circuit declined from $32,500 in 1965 to $800 in 1979. These costs were expected to fall even further, based on increased usage combined with availability of the space shuttle for satellite reuse.

Fiber optics transmission technology continued to generate great interest. Fiber optics systems transmit messages as light waves through long glass fibers. This technology has a reliability as much as 100,000 times higher than typical voice lines, with an average of one error in each 1,000,000,000 binary units of information. Fiber optics also was demonstrated to have a potential for extremely high capacity. An experiment performed by Bell Laboratories demonstrated digital information transmission at a rate of 2×10^{11} binary units of information per second. However, the cost of laser signal sources and amplifiers along the path of the fiber resulted in high costs for fiber optics systems in comparison with copper wire except when their unique properties, such as freedom from electromagnetic interference or high capacity, are needed. This situation seemed sure to change as technological advances continue.

The reliability and performance of such systems depend on the silicon purity of the glass fibers. As fibers become more pure, fewer amplifiers will be required. In March 1979 the Nippon Telegraph and Telephone Co. announced an improvement in the transmission efficiency of optical fiber by a factor of three over re-

Courtesy, AT&T Co

Bell Laboratory scientist (right) holds a silicon wafer containing more than four dozen chips designed to eliminate echoes in voice transmissions of 1,800 miles and beyond. A fellow worker at the left holds a single chip mounted in an integrated circuit.

RCA scientist holds a solid-state laser he developed at company laboratories. Light from the laser can be coupled into optical fibers for transmission of data at efficiencies as high as 70%.

sults obtained a year earlier. In fact, improvements of approximately a factor of 100 have been achieved in the past 12 years. Also in 1979 the RCA Corp. described an experimental laser technology that could eventually provide a much less expensive signal source for fiber optics systems that would also be more reliable.

The applications in the home described above require an inexpensive means of transmitting large quantities of data. Both satellite technology and fiber optics systems show great promise in this area. In 1979 plans were announced to develop receive-only satellite Earth stations. As the licensing requirement for these facilities was dropped, the stage was set for providing a service where a person could receive large quantities of data via satellite and use low-speed terrestrial facilities such as the telephone for transmission of data.

Regulation. The regulatory environment for communications systems varies widely from country to country. In many nations the communications facilities and services are provided by a government-owned monopoly. In others services are furnished by private corporations operating under the sanction of a central control or licensing agency. In the U.S. in 1980 there were more than 1,500 companies engaged in offering communications services. In addition to public utility commissions in each state the Federal Communications Commission (FCC) was created by the U.S. Con-

gress in 1934 to oversee common carriers on national interstate issues.

In 1971 the FCC concluded an inquiry begun in 1966 into the relationship between the providers of data-processing services and equipment and the common carriers (such as telephone companies). The FCC determined then that there was no need to regulate the data-processing industry, as the high level of competition there was the most effective form of regulation. The FCC also determined that communications services should be offered only by regulated carriers. A hybrid service was described that allowed the providers of communications services to engage in data processing when it was incidental to the basic communication service. Conversely, it also allowed providers of data-processing services to engage in communications when such communication was only incidental to the primary data-processing service.

As communications and computer technologies evolved, these distinctions became less and less clear. Consequently, in 1976 a second computer communications inquiry was instigated by the FCC to establish more clearly the relationship between the providers of data-processing and communications services. Some of the issues to be addressed by this inquiry were whether a regulated common carrier could provide a data-processing service, and, if so, whether that service should or should not be regulated; the relationship between communication and computational equipment and the appropriate regulation of such equipment; and the regulation of integrated data-processing and communications services. In July 1979 the commission released its tentative decisions. In this action it classified service offerings as voice, basic nonvoice, and enhanced nonvoice.

Voice service is simple telephone transmission as it now exists. Basic nonvoice service is the transmission of subscriber data where the carrier routes the data through the network to its appropriate destination providing error detection or correction as appropriate. Enhanced nonvoice services are defined as any service more than basic nonvoice, especially where computer processing applications are used to alter the data entered by the subscriber. The commission stated that carriers should be able to use any computer processing capability necessary in providing voice and basic nonvoice services. If, however, a carrier wishes to provide computer processing as part of an enhanced nonvoice service, the carrier must provide a separate organizational structure to offer this service. Significant clarification will be required to achieve a final decision that can be simply and straightforwardly implemented.

WARC. The International Telecommunication Union (ITU) is the body of the United Nations that allocates use of the entire radiowave spectrum for everything from amateur radio to microwave ovens and radar systems. Every 20 years the ITU convenes a

World Administrative Radio Conference (WARC) to decide how the electromagnetic spectrum should be divided and what services should be provided on what frequencies. In 1979 the WARC was attended by representatives of 142 nations and ended after 74 days. The 1,900 representatives generated a final document containing 2,000 pages of frequency allocations.

Allocations were increased for mobile services such as communications to ships, cars, and airplanes, and a 7% increase was agreed on for the portion of the shortwave spectrum set aside for amateur services. Other action substantially increased the available positions for satellites and allowed more flexibility for countries placing satellites in orbital positions that are most efficient both technically and economically for particular areas. The conference left unresolved, however, two of the most sensitive issues—allocations for shortwave broadcasting and reservation of frequencies in orbital positions for geostationary satellites. These issues were scheduled to be addressed by a series of ITU conferences in the early- and mid-1980s.

—James D. Atkins

Computers and computer science

Developments of interest in the computer field in the past year included an important new computer language, a new algorithm for linear programming, and new laws designed to protect privacy with respect to personal information stored in computer data banks.

A new computer language. The most significant event in the area of computer software in 1979 was the introduction of a major new computer language, Ada,

a language that will probably take its place alongside FORTRAN, COBOL, PL-1, BASIC, and Pascal as one of the most important and most widely used computer languages in the world. By 1978 a major project to develop a high-order language sponsored by the U.S. Department of Defense had produced a document called "Steelman." It specified the requirements of the language to be developed, and contracts had been awarded to four companies for the development of detailed specifications of a language that satisfied these requirements. This was not meant to be a cooperative effort on the part of those companies but was rather a competition. The languages produced by the companies carried code names: Blue, Green, Yellow, and Red. After a period of intensive evaluation two of the companies, Softech Inc. and SRI International were eliminated from the competition. The surviving firms were Intermetrics Inc. of Cambridge, Mass., and CII Honeywell Bull, a French affiliate of Honeywell, Inc.

New contracts were awarded for the final competition, which called for delivery of formal language specifications, a reference manual, and an experimental translator, by April 1979. The winner was CII Honeywell Bull. Its "Green" language was selected to become the standard language for program development in the U.S. Department of Defense. The code name Green was dropped, and the language is now known as Ada, named after Augusta Ada, the Countess of Lovelace, who was the daughter of the poet Lord Byron. She worked with the British mathematician and inventor Charles Babbage, whose computer design in 1834 contained many of the basic concepts of modern computers. Her published examples of how that computer

HP-85 computer developed by Hewlett-Packard Co. packs into an 18-pound unit a powerful central processor, a keyboard with a 20-key numeric pad, a high-resolution display tube, and a thermal printer. The computer uses an enhanced version of the BASIC language with editing capabilities.

Courtesy, IBM Corp.

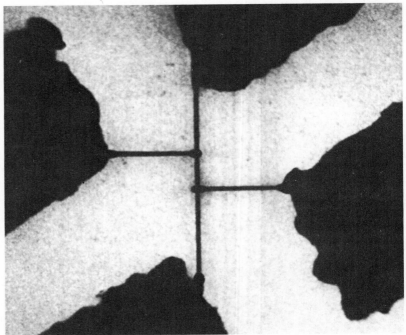

Smallest electronic circuit elements ever fabricated and tested were produced by IBM scientists. The three fine lines connecting the four terminals at the right are each only 50 nanometers (billionths of a meter) wide and 30 nanometers thick. The longest measures 1,000 nanometers, and the shortest 600 nanometers. They are used for investigations of superconductivity and other physical phenomena at small dimensions.

might be used are considered to be the first computer programs ever written.

The project leader of the group that designed Ada was Jean Ichbiah, a French computer scientist. In the early 1970s he joined a French computer software company, Compagnie Internationale pour l'Informatique, one of the firms that eventually merged to form CII Honeywell Bull. A research project at CII in 1972–76 produced a language, LIS, which contained many features that were later incorporated into the design of Ada.

Although the kernel of the group that produced Ada was French, the effort was an international one, participated in by experts in computer languages from other parts of Europe and from the United States. The international nature of the effort, especially the fact that the language was designed in Europe for the U.S. Department of Defense, may lead to acceptance and use of the language far beyond the U.S. defense community. A proposal was made to the International Organization for Standardization that Ada become one of its standard languages.

The fact that so many different computer languages already exist raises questions about the need for a major new one. In answer to such questions Ichbiah pointed out that the current standard languages, such as FORTRAN, COBOL, and PL-1 represent the thinking of the 1950s and early 1960s. Since that time a number of languages, including SIMULA, Pascal, and ALGOL 68, have introduced important new ideas, such as data types, modularization, and task synchronization. Ada combines many important features that were only available separately in widely different languages.

A long and detailed preliminary reference manual was produced for Ada. Suggestions for corrections and improvements were solicited for inclusion in a final version of the language definition document to be released in 1980. It was expected that only relatively small changes would be made. Work on the production of compilers for the Department of Defense that will translate Ada into the machine language of a number of different computers was expected to start in 1980.

A polynomial-time algorithm. "A Soviet Discovery Rocks World of Mathematics" was the title of an article in the *New York Times* on Nov. 7, 1979. The discovery occurred in a mathematical area of computer science known as complexity theory. A Soviet mathematician, L. G. Khachian, published a new algorithm for the solution of linear programming problems. He appeared to prove that the algorithm could solve all such programs in "polynomial time." This came as a surprise to most theoreticians, who had thought that such a solution could not be found.

The following discussion is an attempt to explain in nontechnical language the meaning and significance of this development. An algorithm may be defined informally as a method or a set of rules for solving a problem. Algorithms can be expressed as computer programs, and the study of algorithms is thus of fundamental interest to computer scientists.

Even though an algorithm exists that is guaranteed to solve a problem, the corresponding computer program may take so long to execute as to make that method of solution impractical. As an example, one can consider an almost trivial problem, a list of all possible arrangements of the first n integers. This can be im-

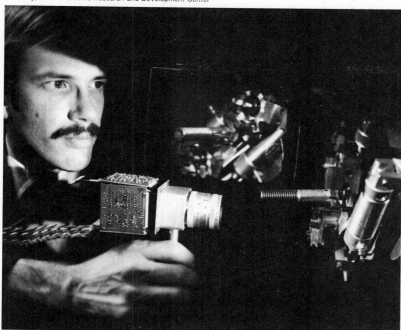

Automated inspection system developed by General Electric Co. consists of a solid-state television camera, here being focused on the threads of a bolt, and a minicomputer that is programmed to determine whether or not a part is satisfactory.

plemented in a simple computer program, and for $n = 3$ it will quickly produce the listing 123, 132, 213, 231, 312, 321. The number of such arrangements is $n!$, the product of the integers. It is a characteristic of $n!$ that it grows extremely rapidly with n. For $n = 25$ the program would have to list 25! or about 1.55×10^{25} different arrangements, and for $n = 50$ the number would be about 3.04×10^{64}. There are 3.1536×10^{8} seconds in a year, and so even if a computer could list one arrangement per nanosecond (a billionth of a second) it would still take it about 50 million years to finish listing the arrangements for $n = 25$. It would have run out of paper long before that.

There are practical problems for which the only known algorithms require a number of operations of the order of $n!$ One is the "traveling sales representative" problem—to find the shortest route that would take a sales representative through each one of n different cities and then back home. It is easy to write a computer program that considers every possible route and finds the shortest, but even for moderate values of n the calculation on the fastest imaginable computer would take essentially forever.

Another trivial problem is to list all of the subsets of the set $\{1,2,3 \ldots n\}$ integers. For $n = 3$ there are eight such subsets $\{\ \}$, $\{1\}$, $\{2\}$, $\{3\}$, $\{1,2\}$, $\{1,3\}$, $\{2,3\}$, $\{1,2,3\}$. The first, $[\ ]$, is the null set that has no elements. For any n there are 2^n subsets. The value of 2^n also grows rapidly with n, though not nearly as fast as does $n!$. Thus 2^{100} is approximately 1.27×10^{30}, and the listing of this many sets would take billions of years on the fastest computer.

It is known that for any positive constants a and k,

a^n grows much faster with n than n^k. For example, as n gets very large 2^n grows very much faster than n^2. If the number of operations needed to carry out the computer program that represents an algorithm is of the order of a^n or $n!$, it is not practical to use that algorithm for a large n. But if a positive integer k exists such that the number of operations required to carry out the program is less than n^k, the algorithm is called a polynomial-time algorithm. Such algorithms are considered to be relatively efficient. If k is small, it may be practical to use them for calculations involving fairly large values of n.

There exists a large class of problems for which no polynomial-time algorithm is known but for which it has not been proved that it is impossible to find such an algorithm. The traveling sales representative problem is in this class. Another is the problem of finding all of the prime factors of an integer. Experts in the field do not think that polynomial-time algorithms will ever be found for these problems, but they cannot eliminate that possibility.

Until 1979 the general linear programming problem was in that class. Linear programming problems are important in many areas of business and industry. Firms confront them as they seek to minimize cost or maximize profits subject to the constraints of labor, capital, and various resources.

The simplex algorithm developed by George Dantzig in 1947 is used in a large number of computer programs that have been developed to solve general linear programming problems. It works well in practical situations and solves quite large problems in a reasonable length of time. However, it is not a polynomial-time algorithm. Mathematicians have been able to construct examples that would take essentially forever to solve by the simplex algorithm. This is a worrisome situation, and it would be much more comfortable to have a practical algorithm that can be proved to work in polynomial time.

The new linear programming algorithm published by Khachian is a polynomial-time algorithm, but this does not guarantee that it will be of any practical significance. It is hoped, but is by no means certain, that the new ideas introduced by Khachian will lead to new and more efficient computer programs than now exist for solving such problems. For a further discussion of Khachian's discovery, *see* MATHEMATICS.

Computers and privacy. In recent years there has been increasing public awareness of the use of computers to store and access large files of data. The names of almost everyone who participates in the economy along with considerable amounts of personal data appear in a large number of data banks. For example, nearly everyone who works in the U.S. has an entry in the huge data bank maintained by the Social Security Administration and another in the bank maintained by the Internal Revenue Service. Anyone who uses credit appears in large data banks maintained by credit bureaus. Anyone who has life insurance appears in a data bank maintained by the insurance industry. Aside from these huge banks with tens of millions of entries in each, there are many smaller ones that list and cross-list large segments of the population.

The use and possible abuse of computer technology to maintain and manipulate large amounts of personal information about individuals pose a serious threat to

"It seems that their databank has all the information that's in our databank, plus information that's not in our databank, plus information about our databank."

s. harris

Sidney Harris

privacy. In most free nations of the world the right to privacy is recognized as a fundamental right without which most other rights can be threatened.

In the U.S. the federal Privacy Act of 1974 affirmed the right of every person to know which federal government records are collected and maintained about him. The act provides for access to such records and the right to have such records changed and corrected under appropriate circumstances. It also provides that the information collected by the government for specific purposes cannot be disclosed for other purposes.

The 1974 act applies only to data collected by the U.S. government. That act set up a Privacy Protection Study Commission, whose major charge was to recommend the extent to which the privacy protection with respect to government data should be extended to data collected by individuals or by private companies. The study commission report in 1977 set up a number of principles to be followed in connection with all data banks. Persons about whom records are kept should have the right to see, copy, and correct these records. They should also have an assurance of confidentiality. Information should be used only for the purposes for which it was collected, and should be released only to those who have a valid need to know the information contained in such records.

Following the recommendations of the Privacy Protection Study Commission and also as a result of a "privacy initiative" by President Carter, a number of bills were introduced in the U.S. Congress in 1979 addressing two areas in which privacy is considered to be especially important: financial information and medical records. A law passed in late 1978, the Right to Financial Privacy Act, limits access to a person's financial records by government agencies. The Fair Financial Information Practices Act would extend these limits to anyone seeking such access. Another bill introduced in 1979 was designed to safeguard personal medical records and personal information collected through federally funded research projects.

There are some serious problems associated with the implementation of the protection of privacy promised by these laws. It is difficult to guarantee the confidentiality of data. Serious attempts to abide by the guidelines suggested by the privacy study commission and to comply with the provisions of existing and proposed privacy laws can be expensive. In July 1979 the American Bankers Association estimated that it would cost the banks between $50–100 million per year to comply with the provisions of the proposed Fair Financial Information Practices Act.

A number of European countries moved ahead of the U.S. in the privacy protection area. For example, a strong privacy protection law has been in effect in West Germany since the beginning of 1978. During 1979 there was serious concern expressed by international corporations about the effect on international

Domains in magnetic bubble film of gallium-substituted garnet are reduced in size (center portion) by bathing the material in laser light and then rapidly cooling it. This annealed film can support memory-system bubbles that are stabler than those in the original film.

communications of the various laws that have been enacted in different countries concerning privacy of data about persons in that country. International standardization in this area is clearly desirable but may be difficult to achieve.

—Saul Rosen

Electronics

To understand the direction electronics is taking, one must become aware of the types of signals managed by electronic equipment. Electronic circuits are designed to process two kinds of electrical signals, analog and digital. An analog signal is one having a magnitude that varies continuously. These signals abound in our environment. For example, the loudness of music tends to vary in a continuous manner. An automobile accelerates or decelerates continuously. Temperature is another example; it rises or falls continuously. Digital signals, on the other hand, have discrete values only. These are the kind of signals represented by strings of zeros and ones that a computer processes.

Owing to the remarkable progress achieved in recent years in placing tens of thousands of digital circuits on a silicon chip having an area less than two square centimeters (referred to as large-scale integra-

tion, or LSI), the microcomputer has become the dominant device in electronic equipment. It is economical, versatile, and reliable. Although most physical quantities are analog in nature, because of the availability of the microcomputer it pays to convert them to digital quantities.

There are compelling reasons for doing this. A microcomputer is programmed to perform specific tasks. If these tasks are changed, the microcomputer is simply reprogrammed. This is generally less costly than changing the electronic circuit elements (hardware) to perform the new task. Another advantage of digital signals is that, because digital electronic circuits are repetitive, large-scale integration and its attendant low cost and high reliability are easily obtained.

The microcomputer. The heart of a microcomputer is the microprocessor. It performs basic arithmetic operations (addition and subtraction), is capable of making simple logic decisions, and controls the sequence of operations when a program is executed. The memory stores the program and the partial results obtained during a calculation. Information to be processed is entered through an input device, such as a teletypewriter or a video unit. The results are transferred to an output device, which typically is a printer or a video display.

The number of binary ones and zeros, called bits, that a microprocessor can handle in one step is an important consideration. Prior to 1978 most units processed eight bits. In 1978 a number of manufacturers made available 16-bit microprocessors. A 16-bit device can address larger memory spaces, provide greater precision, and is faster than its 8-bit cousin.

The memory used in the microcomputer is characteristically composed of transistors and is referred to as a semiconductor memory. There are two types of semiconductor memories, the read-only memory (ROM) and the read-write, or random-access, memory (RAM). Data can be only read from a ROM; it is therefore used for storing programs and routines that are frequently used. Data can be written into and read out of a RAM; it is therefore used for storing numerical results in a calculation.

Currently available ROM and RAM memory chips store up to 64 K bits, where K = 1,024 bits of memory space. Memories of this size are adequate for a large variety of applications and satisfy the needs of many computer hobbyists. When a system is used in business applications, for example, additional memory, called bulk memory, is required. In 1979 megabit (one million bit) magnetic bubble memories became commercially available.

The bubble memory. Bubble memories provide medium-speed data storage at a cost that is competitive with an earlier form of bulk memory, the "floppy disk." Like the disk the bubble memory is nonvolatile; if power is removed from it, the information is not lost and is again available when the power is restored. One important advantage over bulk storage devices that are mechanically dependent, such as the disk, is that no moving parts exist in a bubble memory. This ensures good operating reliability.

In a bubble memory magnetic domains, under the influence of a suitable magnetic field, travel in a material such as garnet. These domains, or bubbles, move in well-defined magnetic patterns. The presence of a bubble at a place in the pattern corresponds to a one and its absence to a zero. A rotating magnetic field moves the bubbles along their paths. Appropriate circuits are connected to the memory for the writing in and reading out of data.

Other microcomputer developments. A special-purpose microcomputer on a single chip that consumes only 200 mw of power made its bow in 1979. Called the MAC-4, it was developed by Bell Laboratories for telecommunications applications and can handle 4-, 8-, 12-, and 16-bit data. With a special instruction most of the chip's circuitry can be turned off and the power drain reduced to microwatts.

Another interesting microcomputer on a single chip introduced in 1979 was the analog microcomputer. In addition to the typical elements found in a digital mi-

MAC-4 single-chip microcomputer is compared in size with a standard small paper clip. Consuming only 200 milliwatts of power, the MAC-4 can handle 4-, 8-, 12-, and 16-bit data.

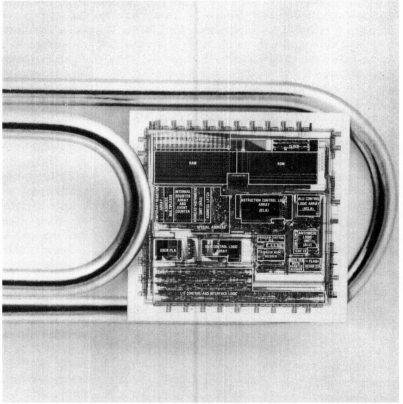

Courtesy, Bell Laboratories

crocomputer, analog-to-digital (A/D) and digital-to-analog (D/A) converters were fabricated on the same chip. The A/D converter takes an analog signal, such as temperature, and converts it to an equivalent digital signal to be processed by the microcomputer. Upon completion of the program the digital result is then converted to an analog signal by the D/A converter. Because most physical quantities in our environment are analog in nature, the analog microcomputer provides a direct interface with the physical world.

Electronics and energy conservation. In 1976 Arthur D. Little, Inc., funded by the U.S. Federal Energy Administration, released a report analyzing the power consumption of electric motors in the United States. It found that electric motors account for 64% of the total electricity consumed in the nation and that 40% of that amount was used to drive industrial motors. It was estimated that in 1979 some 20 million motors having a rating of one horsepower or more were in use. These motors find wide application in the processing industries for driving blowers, compressors, and pumps. Invariably in these applications there is a need to control the speed of the driving motor.

Controlling the speed of a direct-current motor is straightforward and economical. Such a motor, however, is expensive, bulky, and not very fit for operation in an industrial environment. On the other hand the alternating-current induction motor is ideal for such an environment, being rugged, reliable, and economical. It suffers, however, from a serious shortcoming: its speed cannot be changed easily.

A typical solution to this problem has been to operate the induction motor at its nominal speed (perhaps 3,-600 or 1,800 rpm) and use a mechanical method to vary the rate of a process. For example, in a motor-driven pump the motor runs at full speed and a valve is used to vary the rate of flow of a liquid. This is inefficient and wasteful of electrical energy. What is required is a reduction of the speed of the motor itself, thereby conserving energy.

An efficient means of varying the speed of an induction motor was announced by Exxon Corp. in 1979. Using microprocessor control it is possible to change the voltage and frequency simultaneously in order to vary the speed of an induction motor efficiently. Based on field tests Exxon estimated an average energy savings of at least 30%, and, translated in terms of oil, a savings of 600,000 bbl a day. Although speed controllers for AC motors exist, they are costly, bulky, and inefficient because of their use of transformers, inductors, and capacitors. These components have been eliminated in the system announced by Exxon wherein a microprocessor plus appropriate transistor circuits are used to vary the speed.

During the past year a number of utilities, including Detroit Edison and Arkansas Power and Light, conducted experiments with residential load management.

In this method of energy conservation a coded radio signal is transmitted by the utility to its customers during times of peak loads. The signal selectively turns off and on a home electrical appliance, such as an air conditioner or a water heater. This approach avoids the necessity for switching on another power-generating unit during peak power demands, thereby conserving fuel.

In a typical system for the control of residential power usage a digitally coded FM signal is transmitted by the utility. Installed in the customer's residence, an FM receiver picks up the signal and decodes it. The decoded signal actuates the appliance's thermostat circuit, turning it off for a fixed period of time. If no further signal is received after this time has elapsed, the appliance turns on and operates normally. If the peak demand remains high, another signal is transmitted to turn off the unit and the cycle is repeated.

Consumer applications. There was much activity in 1979 in regard to the improvement and development of new electronic products for the consumer. The microcomputer was the key element in nearly all of them. To highlight a few of these applications, National Semiconductor Corp. delivered its one millionth integrated circuit chip to Mattel Inc. for use in the firm's line of electronic games. The RCA Corp. introduced a microcomputer-controlled television set. The computer is programmed to turn on and off different channels of a television receiver at selected times over a seven-day period.

Using an 8-bit microprocessor and a number of ROM's to yield a 64-kilobyte (65,536 eight-bit word capacity) read-only memory, foreign language translators appeared in 1979. Some 1,500 words of English and a foreign language were stored in their memories. In another version the translator speaks and displays words, phrases, and sentences in English and in a foreign language. In addition, plug-in modules were available that provide more than 1,000 phrases in French, German, and Spanish.

The microcomputer also made inroads on the automotive industry. Ford Motor Co. made available a digital speedometer and fuel gauge. In the company's most expensive Lincoln model an alphanumeric display that indicates the condition of the automotive system was offered. Not to be outdone, General Motors Corp. offered a unit for its Cadillac Seville which, using a two-digit code, displayed as many as 25 failure modes.

In October 1979 Federal District Judge Warren Ferguson in Los Angeles ruled that it was lawful to record commercial television programs on a home video recorder. A suit had been filed by MCA, Inc., and Walt Disney Productions against a number of defendants, including the Sony Corp. of America. The plaintiffs charged that the sale of home recorders violated copyright protections. Judge Ferguson's ruling in favor of

Computer-operated FD500 AutoProgrammer can automatically turn on a preselected television show in advance, switch from one channel to another, and turn itself off. It can be programmed to do this for up to seven days.

the defendants cleared the way for the expansion of this fast-growing segment of consumer electronics.

Electronic blackboard. Bell Laboratories unveiled an electronic blackboard in 1979. Looking like any other blackboard (it measures 1.3 m high × 1.6 m wide), it can be mounted on a wall or on a portable stand. Writing is done with ordinary chalk and mistakes can be corrected using an ordinary eraser. About three centimeters thick, the blackboard consists of two plastic sheets in front of an aluminum-honeycomb/aluminum-sheet sandwich. Writing causes the front plastic sheet to touch the rear plastic sheet. Contact between these sheets generates a voltage that represents the position of the chalk on the board.

The voltage is converted to digital pulses, which are transmitted at 1,300 bits per second over telephone lines to video monitors. The writing is retained as electrical charges on a special surface in a storage tube. These charges are scanned continuously by an electron beam that is synchronized with the monitor's beam, producing an image of the handwriting. If there should be a power failure, the information is retained.

Talking typewriter. Considerable progress was made in the synthesis of speech during the past year. One interesting example is a talking typewriter, which can be a useful aid for the blind. An adapter that senses the keyboard and transfers the data to a microprocessor is installed in a magnetic media typewriter. Basic speech sounds (phonemes) and pronunciation rules are stored in a memory.

The microprocessor is programmed to synthesize sounds in order to make them intelligible. Depending on the keyboard data, appropriate phoneme commands at the rate of 15 per second are obtained by the microprocessor from the memory. Each command contains eight bits; six bits define the phoneme, and two bits define inflection levels. The phonemes are modified and blended by the microprocessor to ensure good speech quality.

—Arthur H. Seidman

Information systems and services

As industrialized nations move into a "dossier society," one in which a great deal of personal information is collected and filed for computerized search, the security of these files and the protection of privacy become matters of concern to individuals, to industry, and to government. The General Accounting Office (GAO) reports that the potential for misusing personal data increases as data files are centralized, as the number of users increases, and as greater volumes of data are shared. While absolute security of data stored in a computer system is an impossibility, a balance can be achieved between the economics that may result with multiuser data-processing systems and the added cost of providing an appropriate level of protection for personal information as required by the federal Privacy Act of 1974.

U.S. Pres. Jimmy Carter enunciated two basic principles necessary to protect personal privacy. First, standards must be enacted for handling sensitive personal records, and individuals should be told what kind of information is being collected about them, how it will be used, and to whom it will be disclosed. Second, limits must be set on the government's right to gain access to and use personal information so as not to threaten individual liberties. To implement these principles Carter proposed minimum privacy standards for federally funded public assistance and social service programs. He called upon the states to develop privacy protection for state record-keeping systems, particularly for their social service and criminal justice information systems. He also urged private employers to secure their employment and personnel records, and commercial credit grantors to provide adequate privacy protection in accordance with the principles outlined above.

U.S. information systems and services. In the United States the National Crime Information Center maintains a computerized criminal history file with records of individual offenses provided by the federal

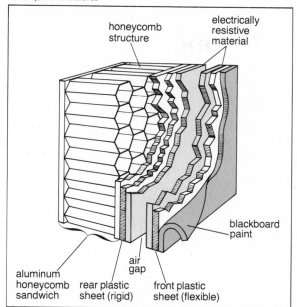

Writing on an electronic blackboard (right) is displayed on a nearby terminal and also on a remote monitor not shown in the photograph. The blackboard consists of two plastic sheets in front of an aluminum honeycomb/aluminum sheet sandwich. Writing causes the front plastic sheet to touch the rear one and generate a voltage that represents the position of the chalk on the board.

government and a number of states. The purpose of this clearinghouse, which is part of the Federal Bureau of Investigation, is to enhance the administration of justice by providing nationwide access to criminal history information.

The Securities and Exchange Commission implemented a program with the Securities Information Center, Inc., to maintain computerized data on lost, stolen, and counterfeit securities. Brokers and banks dealing with the public must report missing securities to the data bank, and when these organizations receive securities they query the data bank to determine whether these items have been reported lost or stolen. If, as anticipated, the records contribute to the recovery of missing securities and provide accurate information about the extent of the problem, the service will be continued.

Computer-related crime was becoming increasingly common and serious. These are crimes such as theft, extortion, sabotage, and vandalism that are perpetuated through the use of computers or that caused intentional damage to computers. The U.S. Senate Committee on the Judiciary (Criminal Justice Subcommittee) prepared an updated computer-crime bill that would make fraud by computers a federal crime. Meanwhile, a National Computer Crime Data Center was established in Los Angeles to aid in the investigation and prosecution of computer-related crimes. The Center collected and disseminated computer-crime information including case summaries describing the types of crimes committed, the procedures used, and material

dealing with computer crime from judicial, business, and computer industry points of view.

Another problem that has become more serious in recent times in the U.S. concerns control of illegal aliens. Aliens residing in the U.S. hold identification cards, but many of these "green cards" have been counterfeited. To control this problem the Immigration and Naturalization Service embarked on a program known as ADIT, Alien Documentation, Identification, and Telecommunications. An automated information system will create and issue fraud-proof identification cards and will process and display authenticating data to identify aliens during inspection at ports of entry into the country. By 1980 the card production facility had been implemented, but the second component of the system, consisting of card readers and video display terminals connected to centrally located U.S. Department of Justice files, was not yet operational. When fully implemented and placed at primary points of entry, the ADIT system was expected to provide a fast, accurate check to confirm card authenticity and would thus eliminate one aspect of the illegal alien problem.

In the field of health information the National Library of Medicine (NLM), which already provided such clinical information services as MEDLINE (MEDLARS On-line) and TOXLINE (Toxicology Information On-line), added new data bases on medical history and hospital administration. HISTLINE (History of Medicine On-line) contains about 40,000 citations to recent literature (from about 1970) on the history of medicine, including references to individuals, institutions, drugs, and diseases. The Health Planning and Administrative data base contains citations to the literature that are concerned with health care planning, management, human resources, financing, and related subjects. It was produced in cooperation with the Asa S. Bacon Memorial Library of the American Hospital Association and the NLM.

International information systems and services. Information services develop in response to the needs of the times. A case in point is a new terrorism data base offered by Risks International with headquarters in Alexandria, Va. The files contain detailed information on 5,000 significant terrorist incidents which have taken place since 1970. Recorded for computer searching are the date and time of each incident; country, city, street address, nationality and name of targeted person or company; weapons used; damage in U.S. dollars; and number of people killed or wounded. If the terrorist activity is a kidnapping or a hijacking, specialized information about these events is recorded. By examining the patterns of terrorism, this data bank enables an organization or individual to assess the risks involved in certain international assignments so that additional precautions may be taken.

The Fawcett Library, established by the London Society for Woman's Services in 1926 (now the Fawcett Society), contains what is acknowledged to be one of the finest collections in the world of information and literature about women. It consists of more than 20,-000 books and several thousand pamphlets, periodicals, press clippings, archives, photographs, and letters, mostly related to women's suffrage and the social conditions of women from 1860 to 1930. This collection was supplemented with more current material provided by the Equal Opportunities Commission of the U.K. government, including a collection of nonsexist career literature, teaching materials, and children's books. In order to improve access to this collection, the library card catalogs were being converted into machine-readable formats and would be made available on computer-output microfiche. Called BiblioFem, this bibliographic service was available from the City of London Polytechnic college.

The development of a Direct Information Access Network for Europe (DIANE) was given high priority by the European Council of Ministers. Effort was to be expended to publicize DIANE, to develop a market for scientific and technical information within the European Community, and to improve and expand the information services provided through Euronet, the European communications network. To promote DIANE a special help desk was established to answer user queries about the network, and a launch team was to assist information services in marketing their products in new areas.

The Saudi Arabian National Center for Science and Technology (SANCST), located in Riyadh, coordinated and supported technological developments in that country. Cooperative U.S.-Saudi Arabian projects were sponsored by a Joint Commission of Economic Cooperation and monitored by the National Science Founda-

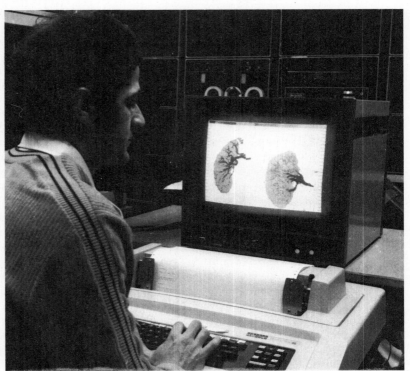

Full-color television picture reveals a healthy human kidney (left) and a diseased one (right). Made by combining 128 X-ray pictures, this composite view is part of a computerized angiography technique developed by West Germany's electron-synchrotron center in Hamburg. The colors are a function of the rate of blood flow in organs.

tion/SANCST Program Office. A Saudi Arabian Scientific and Technological Data Base and Information System was being designed by Informatics, Inc. By means of computer terminal and satellite communication, Saudi professionals would be able to access information from throughout the world concerning agriculture, medicine, petroleum, water, and mineral resources. Another U.S. company, Warner-Eddison Associates, Inc., was organizing a Financial Information Center at the request of the Saudi Arabian Ministry of Finance and Economy. This automated on-line system was being designed to handle all internal library functions of the Ministry, including acquisition, cataloging, circulation, and administrative operations. It was also to be capable of carrying out both manual and on-line reference searches and would monitor and provide current awareness services of international economic literature.

White House Conference. The convening of the White House Conference on Library and Information Services in November 1979 was the culmination of many years of local and state meetings and an important milestone in the evolution of information sciences and services in the U.S. Approximately 1,000 delegates and alternates attended the conference along with a large number of observers and interested individuals and organizations; these included President Carter, who addressed the opening session. It was the largest such conference ever held, but size alone did not make it important; its significance lay in the content, the provocative ideas, and the resolutions passed by the

convention for submission to Carter for endorsement and legislative action.

The conference organizing committee, the National Commission on Libraries and Information Science (NCLIS), in its report, *Toward a National Program for Library and Information Services: Goals for Action—An Overview,* stated that "the total library and information resource in the United States is a national resource which should be developed, strengthened, organized, and made available to the maximum degree possible in the public interest." In assessing the present state of libraries and information services NCLIS concluded that existing programs had developed in an uncoordinated way and that a national framework for planned, systematic growth of library and information services in both the public and private sectors was needed. To develop such a framework preliminary conferences were held in every state and territory, resolutions were passed, and delegates and alternates were elected to attend the national conference. There, again, the delegates met in working groups to hammer out resolutions for presentation at the plenary session.

The basic issues developed by NCLIS for formulating and implementing a national program for library and information services were: (1) to ensure that basic minimums of library and information services adequate to meet the needs of all local communities are satisfied; (2) to provide adequate special services to special constituencies; (3) to strengthen existing statewide resources and systems; (4) to ensure basic and continuing education of personnel essential to the im-

Designer applies a light pen to a computer terminal to specify the part of a vehicle structure that he wishes to have analyzed. The system is being used to help designers create safer vehicles by the most efficient use of materials.

Courtesy, General Motors Corp.

plementation of a national program; (5) to coordinate existing federal programs of library and information service; (6) to encourage the private sector (comprising organizations that are not directly tax-supported) to become an active partner in the development of the national program; (7) to establish a locus of federal responsibility charged with implementing the national network and coordinating the national program under the policy guidance of the National Commission; and (8) to plan, develop, and implement a nationwide network of library and information service.

—Harold Borko

Satellite systems

Applications satellites are Earth-orbiting satellites that utilize their vantage points in space for economic benefit and military purposes rather than scientific research. There are three basic classes of applications satellite systems: communications, Earth observation, and navigation. Users are individual and groups of nations, and private industrial concerns.

The U.S. and the Soviet Union still dominated such activities because of their large booster rockets, which they also used to launch satellites for other nations. Yet France, Japan, and China, as well as the European

Commercial communications satellite system that would cover the 48 contiguous states of the U.S. was proposed by Hughes Communications, Inc. The satellite channels would be leased to industry and government.

Courtesy, Hughes Aircraft Company, Space and Communications Group

Space Agency (ESA), continued development of their own space launch capabilities. ESA is a consortium comprising Belgium, Denmark, France, West Germany, Ireland, Italy, The Netherlands, Spain, Sweden, Switzerland, the U.K., and others with observer status. ESA members planned future use of the French-developed booster (Ariane) in competition with the U.S. McDonnell Douglas Delta launch vehicle, or the space shuttle, still under development. In December 1979 the first of four test flights of Ariane was completed successfully from the French launch facility at Kourou, French Guiana. ESA hoped to capture eventually 20–25% of the satellite launch market.

Communications satellites. Of all types of applications satellites, the one that has exhibited the greatest activity in growth and economic value is the communications satellite. The rapid growth of national and international communications during the 1970s resulted primarily from the use of satellites. The International Telecommunications Satellite Organization (Intelsat), a consortium of 102 nations of which the Communications Satellite Corp. (Comsat) is the U.S. member, continued to grow in size and capability. Global transmissions of telephone, television, facsimile, and digital data are provided by Intelsat 4 and 4A spacecraft in geostationary orbit. (A geostationary, or geosynchronous, orbit is at an altitude of 35,900 km (22,300 mi) above the Equator. At that height a satellite travels at the same angular velocity as the surface of the rotating Earth, and thus remains at a constant point above the Earth. Three such satellites can provide global coverage except at the highest latitudes.) At the beginning of 1980 Intelsat had five satellites in operation stationed over the Atlantic, Pacific, and Indian oceans plus one standby at each location.

Three domestic satellite systems were operational in the U.S. Western Union Corp. owned and operated Westar satellites to transmit telegrams, mailgrams, telex, and high-speed facsimile data. On Aug. 9, 1979, NASA launched a third Westar satellite on a cost-reimbursable basis. Placed in geosynchronous orbit due south of New Orleans above the Galápagos Islands, Westar 3 was capable of transmitting color television, 600 two-way telephone calls, or high-speed data. Through the satellite Western Union Telegraph Co. and Video Communications, Inc., joined to provide entertainment programming to remote areas. The service was to include news, sports, and movies. Geographical areas which could be reached included North and Central America, the Caribbean, and parts of the Gulf of Mexico and the Atlantic and Pacific oceans.

RCA Corp. operated a Satcom satellite system for commercial leased lines, as well as cable and pay-television distribution services. A third Satcom was launched for RCA by NASA on Dec. 6, 1979. During transfer to geosynchronous orbit four days later, all contact was inexplicably lost. Insurance coverage amounted to $50 million to cover spacecraft and launch service costs, and up to $27 million for lost services. As a consequence aerospace insurance underwriters were expected to become more cautious of satellite investments.

Comsat General Corp., a subsidiary of Comsat, leased the capacity of Comstar satellites to the Bell divisions of American Telephone & Telegraph Co. (AT&T) to form the third U.S. domestic system. Comsat announced that consideration was being given to development of a satellite television service to homes in the U.S. by direct transmission to small rooftop antennae. This would be a joint venture with Sears, Roebuck and Co.

In December 1979 Hughes Communications, Inc., a subsidiary of Hughes Aircraft Co., applied to the Federal Communications Commission (FCC) for authorization to develop a new domestic U.S. satellite system. Hughes Aircraft is a major producer of communications satellites.

In 1979 Intelpost, International Electronic Post via satellite, underwent trial tests between London, New York City, and Washington, D.C. Argentina, Belgium, Canada, West Germany, France, The Netherlands, Switzerland, the U.K., and the U.S. agreed to participate in Intelpost field trials.

Marisat, the maritime satellite communications service developed by Comsat General, entered its fourth successful year of operation in 1980. It provided high-fidelity voice, data, telex, and facsimile service to the U.S. Navy and commercial vessels.

As a result of the success of Marisat the International Maritime Satellite Organization came into being in July 1979 to provide the next generation of commercial maritime satellite communications services. Of the 29 countries in the new organization the U.S. had the largest ownership share, 22.5%. The Soviet Union had 15.7%, and lesser amounts were taken by the U.K., Norway, Japan, Spain, Australia, India, New Zealand, and Egypt. Decisions were to be made in 1980 concerning future requirements. Competitive offers to provide satellite capacity were received from Marisat, Intelsat, and the ESA.

Elsewhere, Canada was conducting experimental color television broadcasts to small user terminals using its Anik communications satellite system. Early in 1980 the Soviet Union launched a communications satellite to provide television and telephone links to extreme northern Siberia and remote regions of Soviet Central Asia.

China expressed interest in technology associated with domestic broadcast satellites similar to the U.S.-built Japanese BSE satellite built by the General Electric Co. Australia, assisted by Canada, was planning a

SAGE (Stratospheric Aerosol and Gas Experiment) satellite awaits launching on top of Scout booster rocket (left). The spacecraft will track and measure volcanic emission flows in the stratosphere caused by such eruptions as that of La Soufrière (right) on the West Indian island of St. Vincent.

Photos, courtesy, NASA

Landsat 3 is checked prior to its launch by the U.S. National Aeronautics and Space Administration. From its polar orbit the satellite gathers and transmits data concerning the Earth's resources.

domestic satellite system. An application for one transponder was placed with Intelsat. Fifty-one receive-only stations would be used throughout the country. In Indonesia availability and success of the Palapa communications satellite system were largely responsible for the increase in the number of telephone sets from 200,000 to 600,000 in the past ten years.

On the military side a U.S. Navy FleetSatCom 2 was launched into geosynchronous orbit over the Atlantic Ocean in May 1979. Weighing more than one metric ton in orbit, the spacecraft was designed to provide high-priority secure communications between U.S. aircraft, ships, submarines, ground stations, the Strategic Air Command, and the National Command Authority network for Atlantic, European, and African areas. A similar FleetSatCom 1 was launched in 1978 covering the Pacific areas.

Earth observation satellites. This category of applications satellites consists of three major types: meteorological, Earth resources, and military reconnaissance.

Weather satellites. In June 1979 NASA launched a polar-orbiting weather satellite for the U.S. National Oceanic and Atmospheric Administration (NOAA). Designated NOAA 6, it provided global weather data along with TIROS-N, launched in 1978. NOAA 5 was

placed in standby service. Two geostationary weather satellites, together with two ESA and Japanese craft, provided continuous global weather photos and such data as cloud heights, except for the polar regions.

NASA launched the Stratospheric Aerosol and Gas Experiment (SAGE) satellite in February 1979 to measure effects of aerosol concentrations in the atmosphere. Understanding was gained about how pollutants might be transported globally and their possible effects upon climate.

Earth resources satellites. The two U.S. remote sensing satellites, Landsat 2 and Landsat 3, continued global observation and transmission of multispectral data from their polar orbits despite some operational problems. A major portion of NASA's efforts in 1979 was devoted to maintaining a flow of data to an increasing number of operational users.

Failures of one of the two tape recorders aboard Landsat 2 and two of the three aboard Landsat 3 resulted in plans to deploy transportable receiving stations to several foreign countries. The next Landsat was scheduled to be launched in September 1981. However, delay in development and escalating costs of a thematic mapper that would achieve improved environmental data were causing concern. Landsat 2 and Landsat 3 were not designed to last beyond 1981.

Information obtained from the Landsats was in use in more than 100 countries. Major interests in data ranged widely from crop inventories to flood assessment and mineral exploration.

In a related area of Earth observation the U.S. Geological Survey awarded a contract to Comsat General to provide near real-time hydrological information services via satellite beginning in the latter half of 1980. Water-level sensors and small, self-powered data collection platforms were to be installed at 75 sites in remote areas of New England, Pennsylvania, Colorado, and Arizona. Periodically, data were to be transmitted via a commercial communications satellite to an Earth station in New Jersey, processed in Massachusetts, and relayed to survey headquarters in Virginia.

Military reconnaissance satellites. The U.S. in 1958 launched its first recoverable satellite designed to return photographs to the Earth. The Soviet Union followed in 1962. Since then both nations have developed sophisticated systems to observe selected targets from orbit and to return photographic, radar, and other data to military commanders. These systems are considered to have a stabilizing effect in maintaining world peace. The political turmoil in the Middle East in late 1979 caused such surveillance to be increased greatly.

In December 1979 United Nations Secretary-General Kurt Waldheim formed an international panel to study a French proposal for an international reconnaissance satellite agency to be operated by the UN. Findings and recommendations of the panel were due in June 1981.

Navstar, the U.S. Air Force Global Positioning System, is in its second year of development. Twenty-four such satellites are expected to be operational by 1985.

Navigation satellites. The U.S. Navy has had a navigational satellite system, Transit, in operation since 1960. Established primarily to update inertial guidance systems of Polaris submarines, it became used increasingly by commercial surface ships. Accuracy of position is provided to within 550 ft. Despite increased demand for Transit, production economies have lowered the purchase price of its onboard receiv-

er/computer from $25,000 to less than $10,000 in the past five years.

An improved U.S. Air Force Global Positioning System, Navstar, was in the second year of development. Problems occurred, such as the onboard rubidium standard atomic clocks sometimes failing to operate. An eventual system of 24 satellites was expected to be fully operational in 1985, with civilian access anticipated five years later.

—F. C. Durant III

Energy

The last year of the 1970s could be considered a watershed for energy in the United States and in the world. Three events set in motion processes that seemed certain to have continuing and major impacts on the development of the energy industries and on energy consumption for decades to come. These events were the nuclear accident at the Three Mile Island reactor near Harrisburg, Pa.; the decision by U.S. Pres. Jimmy Carter that energy prices would rise in the U.S. to at least world levels, phased in over a 28-month period; and the loss by the moderate forces of their control of pricing in the Organization of Petroleum Exporting Countries (OPEC), which led to unrestricted and unchallenged price increases throughout the year.

Three Mile Island. The worst crisis yet experienced for commercial nuclear power in the U.S. began on March 28, 1979, at Unit 2 of the nuclear power facility on Three Mile Island, ten miles southeast of Harrisburg, Pa. The events that unfolded in the following minutes, hours, and days brought into sharp focus the issues surrounding the development of nuclear power as a major energy source.

Unit 2 on Three Mile Island was powered by a nuclear reactor. The reactor, using uranium, generated

U.S. Pres. Jimmy Carter wears protective boots as he is escorted through the control room of the Three Mile Island nuclear power plant in April 1979, soon after the reactor accident.

Key component of an advanced superconducting generator, a 13-ft, 1½-ton rotor, is spun at 3,600 rpm at −452° F. Such a generator should produce as much electricity as a conventional one twice as large.

heat as a result of nuclear fission, and the heat in turn produced steam to drive a turbine in order to generate electricity. In a pressurized water reactor such as Unit 2 the core, consisting of fuel rods, is cooled by water. If the core is left uncovered because of a loss of coolant, the temperature will first rise to roughly 1,200° C (2,200° F), damaging the fuel rods and producing hydrogen. If the core remains uncovered, the temperature will continue to rise to the melting point of the uranium fuel, about 2,900° C (5,200° F). At this level a meltdown occurs and very large quantities of radioactive materials could be released, the worst accident that can occur at a commercial nuclear plant.

On March 28 at Three Mile Island a feedwater system pump failed. The flow of water to the steam generators stopped, and the plant's safety system automatically shut down the steam turbine and the electric generator. The temperature of the reactor coolant began to increase. As the pressure within the reactor built up, a pressure valve opened to relieve the strain. Within eight seconds the reactor automatically scrammed; that is, its control rods automatically dropped into the reactor core to halt its nuclear fission. Fourteen seconds after the initial pump failure, emergency feedwater pumps automatically started. Everything was proceeding as planned in the reactor design.

However, the operator did not notice that valves were closed on the emergency feedwater lines and that the pressure release valve was stuck open. At this time if the control room operators had realized that the pressure valve was stuck and had acted to close a backup valve, or if they had left the plant's high-pressure injection pumps on, nothing would have happened at Three Mile Island except the relatively minor inconvenience of a reactor shutdown.

Instead, however, the operators shut down the high-pressure injection pumps because they did not realize that there was more water leaving the system than was being added and that the core was being uncovered. About two and half hours after the initial failure the blocked valve backup to the pressure release valve was closed and the loss of coolant stopped. However, the water level in the reactor was then below the top of the core and the damage continued.

From the beginning public knowledge of what was going on at Three Mile Island was greatly confused. Two days after the accident Gov. Richard Thornburgh of Pennsylvania advised pregnant women and preschool children to leave the region within a five-mile radius of Three Mile Island. Schools were closed, evacuation plans were developed, and public apprehension began to build. On Saturday, March 31, a new concern became evident concerning a potential hydrogen explosion inside the reactor. This proved groundless, but it greatly intensified the fear surrounding the accident. The chairman of the Nuclear Regulatory Commission stated at a news conference that day that a precautionary evacuation within a 20 mi-radius from the reactor might be necessary. The emergency preparedness offices in the affected counties were deluged with citizens asking for information. On April 1 Presi-

Table I. Installed Nuclear Power in Major Non-Communist Countries

Country	Numbers of reactors		Capacity (000 of gross electrical kilowatts)	
	12/78	11/79	12/78	11/79
Canada	8	9	4,790	5,590
France	14	16	6,840	8,760
Germany, West	10	11	6,410	8,350
India	3	3	620	620
Italy	4	4	1,490	1,490
Japan	18	22	11,500	15,120
Spain	3	3	1,120	1,120
Sweden	6	6	3,850	3,850
Switzerland	3	4	1,060	2,030
United Kingdom	32	33	8,790	9,010
United States	71	71	54,120	54,180
Total	172	182	100,590	110,120

Source: U.S. Department of Energy.

Dozens of cars lined up at a gas station in Los Angeles on May 9, 1979, the first day of the odd-even gasoline rationing plan in the state of California.

dent Carter visited the facility, and by Sunday afternoon it was finally concluded that the hydrogen bubble was no problem; there was, however, no immediate public announcement of this. On April 2 the acute phase of the accident was over, but it was not until April 7 that the evacuation shelter at Hershey, Pa., was closed, and the governor's advisory was not withdrawn until April 9.

In 1980 the accident at Three Mile Island was still under investigation. Carter had appointed a commission headed by John G. Kemeny, president of Dartmouth College, to conduct a comprehensive study of the accident. The commission reported to Carter on Oct. 30, 1979. Its major conclusion was:

To prevent nuclear accidents as serious as Three Mile Island, fundamental changes will be necessary in the organization, procedures, and practices—and above all—in the attitudes of the Nuclear Regulatory Commission and, to the extent that the institutions we investigated are typical, of the nuclear industry.

This conclusion speaks of *necessary* fundamental changes. We do not claim that our proposed recommendations are sufficient to assure the safety of nuclear power.

The commission's report contained a large number of findings and an equally large number of recommendations. Among the latter were the following: the Nuclear Regulatory Commission should be restructured as an independent agency with a single administrator at its head; the utility industry and its suppliers should establish a program setting appropriate safety standards and conduct independent evaluations of the achievement of those standards; an agency-accredited training institution for operators should be established; and the design of the instrumentation at reactors should be improved.

Additional work in health-related radiation effects research and in the education of health professionals and emergency-response personnel in the vicinity of nuclear power plants was also urged. *See* Feature Article: Hazards of Low-Level Radiation. The commission believed that there should be an emergency response plan, reviewed and approved by the Federal Emergency Management Agency, prior to the granting of any operating license. Finally, one of the major problems identified by the commission was the incorrect, uncoordinated, and confusing information released during the accident. The commission recommended that the utility provide information to the public and that the responsibility for state actions be centralized within a single agency. By early 1980 no formal action on the recommendations had been taken other than a minor restructuring of the Nuclear Regulatory Commission.

The aftereffects of the Three Mile Island accident will be felt for many years. By early 1980 all but two of the nuclear reactors ordered since 1974 had been canceled. Opening of new nuclear plants slowed, and construction of plants already approved was delayed or

The first insulated 550-kilovolt reactor capacitor switch is tested by the Bonneville Power Administration near Seattle, Washington. The device is expected to reduce the cost of switching large capacitor and reactor banks.

suspended. The question of whether nuclear power could be expanded was the subject of intense debate by the public, the U.S. Congress, and the administration. The issue promised to be an important one in the 1980 presidential election.

The financial effects of the accident were also large. Public utilities with nuclear plants under construction or ready to go onstream were encountering major financial problems because of the delays in completing those plants. The utility that owned the Three Mile Island reactor was under intense financial pressure. Thus, the future of commercial nuclear power in the U.S. was uncertain. That fact, in turn, raised serious problems with respect to the future energy situation of the U.S. and the world.

Energy prices. During the spring and summer of 1979 gasoline shortages such as those that followed the OPEC embargo of 1973–74 returned to many parts of the U.S. Long lines formed at gasoline stations in many areas, and rationing plans were instituted in many states. Reacting to the oil shortage triggered by the shutdown of petroleum production in Iran, President Carter held a long domestic summit conference at Camp David, Md. He emerged from that conference with a series of proposals to Congress. The thrust of his proposals was that the U.S. must reduce its reliance on oil flowing from the Middle East. He imposed a quota on imports as an immediate step, and called for a massive development of domestic energy resources as the long-term solution to reducing imports. The keystone underlying these recommendations was the removal of the subsidy to domestic energy consumption that had been achieved by holding domestic energy prices below world levels.

On May 31, 1979, price controls on domestic crude oil began to be phased out. The impact on domestic crude oil prices was dramatic. The average price rose from $9.46 per bbl in January 1979 to more than $14 by August and continued to rise throughout the year. The average price of regular gasoline rose from 68.95 cents per gal in January 1979 to 108.91 cents at the end of January 1980, an increase of 58% over a 12-month period. Heating oil sold to residential customers rose from 50.2 cents per gal at the beginning of the heating season in October 1978 to 82.2 cents in October 1979, a rise of 64%. The price of natural gas, which had been decontrolled on a phased basis in 1978, rose 26% over the same period. Thus by 1979 consumers of oil and gas in the U.S. were facing the realities of the higher costs of these fuels.

The price developments within the U.S. for other forms and sources of energy were not so dramatic, since in the case of electricity, prices were still con-

Table II. U.S. Energy Production, Consumption, Imports, and Exports, 1973–1979
In 10^{15} BTU's

Year	Production	Consumption	Imports	Exports
1973	62.4	74.6	14.7	2.1
1974	61.2	72.7	14.4	2.2
1975	60.0	70.7	14.1	2.4
1976	60.1	74.5	16.8	2.2
1977	60.4	76.5	20.0	2.1
1978	61.3	78.4	19.2	2.0
1979	63.2	78.2	19.1	2.8

Source: U.S. Department of Energy.

Table III. U.S. Energy Production by Source, 1973–1979
In 10^15 BTU's

Year	Coal	Crude oil and natural gas liquids	Natural gas	Hydroelectric power	Nuclear electric power	Other	Total
1973	14.4	22.1	22.2	2.9	0.9	0.1	62.4*
1974	14.5	21.0	21.2	3.2	1.3	0.1	61.2*
1975	15.2	20.1	19.6	3.2	1.9	0.1	60.1
1976	15.9	19.6	19.5	3.0	2.1	0.1	60.1*
1977	15.9	19.8	19.6	2.3	2.7	0.1	60.4
1978	15.1	20.7	19.5	3.0	3.0	0.1	61.3*
1979	17.8	20.4	19.2	3.0	2.8	0.1	63.2*

*Totals may not equal yearly sum due to independent rounding.

Source: U.S. Department of Energy.

trolled by the state public utility commissions and in the case of coal there were no price controls in effect. The price of coal delivered to utilities under contract increased through September 1979 by only 8% from the level in January, while spot prices were actually lower than they had been in September 1978. The average retail electricity price to residential customers rose 21% from January to October 1979, reflecting the fact that more than 70% of the electricity was generated from coal, hydropower, or nuclear energy, the costs of which did not rise nearly as much as those of petroleum and natural gas. However, the price of delivered electricity does not include the costs involved in nuclear plant construction delays, and thus it can be expected to increase sharply once those costs are passed to the consumers.

The major change in energy policy in the U.S. in 1979 thus resulted from the executive actions to allow the price of energy to consumers to rise. The portion of the energy program proposed by President Carter that requires congressional action had not been implemented by the beginning of the congressional session in January 1980. The major elements of this proposed program were a substantial commitment to the building of synthetic energy plants through a governmental agency, the enactment of a windfall profits tax on oil companies, and the establishment of an Energy Mobilization Board to hasten the approval process for new energy facilities.

OPEC developments. The Organization of Petroleum Exporting Countries reacted to the shutdown of production in Iran by raising prices for its products throughout the year. For example, the FOB cost of crude oil from Nigeria increased from $14.84 per bbl in January 1979 to $26.37 in October 1979. More and

Chemist checks equipment for laboratory-scale coal liquefaction. By adding pyrite to coal before liquefaction, Sandia Laboratories hopes to increase by 10 to 15% the liquid fuel recovered from the coal.

Courtesy, Sandia Laboratories

Table IV. Crude Oil Consumption for Selected Major Non-Communist Countries, 1973–1979
In 000,000 bbl per day

Year	Japan	West Germany	France	United Kingdom	Canada	Italy
1973	5.0	2.7	2.2	2.0	1.6	1.5
1974	4.9	2.4	2.1	1.8	1.6	1.5
1975	4.6	2.3	1.9	1.6	1.6	1.5
1976	4.8	2.5	2.1	1.6	1.7	1.5
1977	5.0	2.5	2.0	1.6	1.7	1.5
1978	5.1	2.6	2.0	1.7	1.7	1.5
1979*	5.2	2.7	2.1	1.7	1.8	1.5

*1979 estimated on eight-month basis.

Source: U.S. Central Intelligence Agency.

Mirror elements are placed in a heliostat on Weissfluh mountain in eastern Switzerland. The Swiss Center for Atomic Research developed the device as part of a two-year study of solar power.

more oil was sold on the spot markets rather than under long-term contracts, and prices of that oil continued to leapfrog. At the OPEC summit meeting in December 1979 the cartel was unable to agree on a pricing policy for 1980. Effective control of prices was shifting from the core Persian Gulf countries led by Saudi Arabia to other OPEC members.

Table V. OPEC Production by Country, 1979
In 000 bbl per day

Country	Year average	% change from 1978
Saudi Arabia	9,740	+20.9
Kuwait	2,227	+19.4
Iran	2,895	−44.4
Iraq	3,568	+35.7
Qatar	518	+ 6.8
United Arab Emirates	1,796	− 2.0
Algeria	1,260	+ 2.9
Libya	2,092	+ 5.0
Nigeria	2,317	+21.3
Gabon	212	− 5.7
Indonesia	1,590	− 2.9
Venezuela	2,336	+ 8.0
Ecuador	223	+10.5
Total OPEC	30,774	+ 5.0

Source: Adapted from Croll, Donald O., "Growth in a Year of Crisis," *Petroleum Economist,* January 1980.

The long-term implications of these developments remained uncertain. Because the OPEC price had been maintained at levels below those which a profit-maximizing cartel would impose, the breakdown of cartel discipline led to price increases rather than price decreases. However, the long-term impact of the failure to agree on pricing policy was expected to depend upon the policies pursued by Saudi Arabia, which accounts for almost one-half of Arab OPEC production. The Saudis were major forces for price moderation during 1979, and early in 1980 were resisting the continued rapid escalation of OPEC prices.

What did become clear was that the unity within OPEC with respect to pricing and production policies had been broken. This was reflected in a leapfrogging of prices by OPEC members to take advantage of short-term market situations. Whether or not it will be reflected in a competitive search for additional markets should there be a decline in petroleum demand remains to be seen.

Production and consumption. Total energy consumption in the U.S. declined in 1979 by about 1%. This small decline in total consumption, however, hid a significant shift in the consumption of primary energy types. For example, the consumption of coal in the U.S. rose 7%, while that of natural gas, petroleum, and nuclear energy declined. The biggest percentage decline occurred in nuclear electric power, down by 7% in 1979 compared with 1978. Petroleum consumption declined 3% as did consumption of natural gas. Imports to the U.S. continued their drop from the 1977 high, while exports from the nation showed a significant increase.

U.S. energy production rose 3%, the entire increase being represented by a gain in coal production of 18%. It should be recognized, however, that this percentage increase in coal was not as significant as it appeared because 1978 production had been reduced by the coal strike during the first quarter of that year.

The major non-Communist countries did not mirror the U.S. decline in crude oil consumption. Consumption rose in Japan, West Germany, France, and Canada. On the production side OPEC output showed a substantial increase of 5%, even though production in Iran declined 44% from 1978 levels. Total world production rose 5% for the year.

The behavior of the OPEC countries during the year deserves some explanation. As indicated above, 1979 was a year of rapidly rising OPEC prices. These increases were matched by substantial increases in output, especially by Saudi Arabia, Kuwait, Iraq, and Nigeria. These production rises, in the face of the price increases mentioned above, provided evidence that OPEC prices were still below the profit maximization level for the cartel as a whole.

From the point of view of world supplies it was clear that 1979 as a whole was not a year of supply stringency in crude petroleum. The shortages of gasoline in the U.S. during the spring and summer of 1979 resulted from regulatory and allocation activities and controlled prices rather than shortfalls in world supplies. The import quotas announced by President Carter in July were actually at levels above current levels of imports and therefore did not constrain supply to the U.S.

Future outlook. World energy markets were experiencing great uncertainty as of early 1980. The decline in cohesion in the OPEC cartel was resulting in immediate substantial increases in the world price of oil, especially on spot markets. However, the continued increase in world production and the decline in petroleum consumption already registered in the U.S. and likely to spread because of economic conditions to the rest of the industrialized world pointed toward an oil glut in the short run. The reaction of the OPEC countries to this glut, if it should occur, will test the cohesiveness of the organization.

The rate of growth in installed nuclear capacity in the world declined sharply in 1979. That decline was expected to persist as questions about the ultimate safety of nuclear technology are assessed. Clearly, within the U.S. and also in the other major industrial non-Communist countries, the future of nuclear power is open to question. For coal, continued price decline in real terms is expected to lead to its rapidly expanding use in the U.S. and in western Europe.

—William A. Vogely

Environment

During 1979 there was more hard thinking than ever before about the precise nature of the linkage between energy use and economic growth; much new data became available about the health effects on humans of chemicals, nuclear fallout, and nuclear accidents; and a far-reaching discussion of endangered species was published. More meaningful results on the effect of environmental stress on humans became available.

Up to 1979 much of the thinking and writing about the future either was based on simple extrapolation of past trends or else argued about the inevitability of major future departures from those trends. In 1979 there became evident the fruits of much thinking about the precise form the future would take, based on careful analyses of many different types of phenomena, ranging from fossil fuel supplies to shifts in the character of the popular belief system.

Energy and economic growth. Sidney Sonenblum pointed out that there are two sets of beliefs about the way in which energy use and economic growth are linked. In the first view energy is unique as an input to modern economies, and nothing else can be substituted for it. Under this view energy is a prerequisite for economic growth because it makes investment and labor productive and because it is the essential ingredient to technological progress. Given this belief, any decrease in the availability of energy is interpreted as leading inexorably to a lowered rate of economic growth. Two groups of people employ this notion in different ways: technologists, as an argument for developing new energy technologies, and those fearful of the consequences of continued economic growth, as the rationale for reduced energy use.

The second belief concerning the linkage between energy and economic growth holds that energy is only one of several inputs to economic growth, with the others having relatively greater influence. While conceding that energy is obviously necessary for growth, they maintain that energy conservation or expansion would have only modest impacts on the economic growth rate. Clearly, one's choice of policies for managing the economy will be critically affected by which of these two contrasting views one holds.

Some of the most revealing writing on this matter in recent months came from Bruce Hannon, the winner in 1975 of the Mitchell First Prize, an international award for work on limits to growth. Hannon proposed a comprehensive theory that encompasses both natural communities of plants and animals and economies dealing with the role of energy in system performance and growth. He argued that energy can indeed function as a limit to growth, with the rate of growth decreasing as an energy limit is reached. Though this sounds like Sonenblum's first belief, Hannon then went on to argue that the energy limit may be raised, by the introduction of new energy-generating technology, or may be lowered, by depletion of energy stocks. He supported these ideas with examples from England and Wales in the period from 1700 to 1815. From 1710 to 1740 society there was in a steady state, dependent on agriculture and woodburning. From 1740 to 1770 growth occurred but at a constantly decreasing rate as a limit in coal production was approached. This limit was set by the difficulty in pumping water out of coal mines. After 1770 rapid development of the steam engine eliminated several kinds of limits to growth: water could be pumped out of the coal mines, and so coal production increased, thus allowing expanded iron production; this, in turn, resulted in vast improvements in both agriculture and industry. Thus Hannon's theory includes both of the beliefs described by Sonenblum.

In another part of his theoretical system Hannon argued that, while the components of an ecosystem strive to maximize their total energy storage, the overall system strives to minimize the energy of metabolism per unit of stored energy in the plants and animals. The result, in the steady state (equilibrium), is a system with the largest possible amount of living material stored, given the constraints of available water, air, soil, and sunlight. In short, living systems, such as the assemblage of plants and animals in a forest or a lake, tend to maximize the ratio of their mass to the energy input into the system.

The reason that environmentalists are so fascinated with this view is that modern technological societies strive to do just the opposite: to maximize the energy use per unit of biomass (the people living in the society). Hannon has an interesting way of viewing this situation. He says that in the heavy use by the United States of fossil fuels stored over very long periods of time the territory of the nation is being expanded in time rather than in space. However, when those stocks

of fossil energy are depleted, this new type of limit will contract sharply.

Given this perspective by Hannon, a new study by David Root and Lawrence Drew takes on particular significance. They asked why the amount of petroleum discovered per unit of exploratory drilling drops off so sharply after the initial phases of exploration. Examining this issue in terms of the relative numbers of oil fields of various sizes, they discovered that U.S. oil fields consist of 275 expected to yield more than 100 million barrels of crude oil each and a very large number (about 20,000) of much smaller fields. The very large fields tend to be discovered early and the small ones late: it is easier to find an elephant than a shrew. It should be no surprise, therefore, that the number of barrels of new oil discovered per foot of exploratory drilling in the U.S. dropped from 52 to 18 just from 1973 to 1976.

Health effects. For years some scientists, such as Ernest Sternglass, have been proposing the controversial hypothesis that radiation released into the environment from bomb tests or nuclear reactors has a statistically demonstrable impact on infant mortality rates. During 1979 an elaborate new analysis by Joseph Lyon, Melville Klauber, John H. Gardner, and King Udall of the relationship between childhood leukemias and fallout from nuclear testing in Nevada suggested that Sternglass had correctly identified a hazard. The new study was extraordinarily comprehensive, and it is difficult to see how it would be vulnerable to criticism on methodological grounds.

The study was based on death certificates for all childhood neoplasms (cancer) in Utah residents between 1944 and 1975. These were split into groups by type of cancer, the amount of fallout from Nevada bomb tests experienced in the Utah county of residency, the age of the child, and the time of death. Leukemia death rates were clearly higher for children who

U.S. Coast Guard cutter in August 1979 tows a long snakelike barrier across the entrance to the Brownsville (Texas) ship channel in an effort to block an oil slick moving northward in the Gulf of Mexico from a huge spill off the Mexican coast.

had lived in Utah counties where there had been high fallout, relative both to low-fallout Utah counties and to other parts of the United States. After making various necessary statistical adjustments, the researchers found that the leukemia death rate in children exposed to high concentrations of fallout was about 50% higher than it otherwise would have been.

While the attention of the public was focused on the accident at the Three Mile Island reactor in Pennsylvania (*see* ENERGY), a scientific controversy developed about another incident on which far more information was available, near Kyshtym, southeast of Moscow, in late 1957. During 1979 a dissident Soviet refugee and distinguished biologist, Zhores Medvedev, published a book summarizing all known information about the incident; this work subsequently was reexamined by several scientists in the United States. The latter document did not question that nuclear contamination occurred over a large area (50 by 100 km). However, it argued that the cause was fallout from a nuclear bomb test rather than Medvedev's explanation: explosion of a waste disposal site.

The portions of documents about the incident which were released by the U.S. Central Intelligence Agency (CIA) leave little doubt that there were one or more very large explosions at the Kyshtym plant. The precise wording used is explicit that the explosion lit up the night sky for a great distance and that subsequently there were a "tremendous" number of casualties in hospitals in the region. A CIA report of May 23, 1958, stated that Soviet visitors to the world's fair in Brussels "stated independently but consistently that the occurrence of an accidental atomic explosion during the spring of 1958 was widely known throughout the U.S.S.R." Medvedev also provided transcripts of two interviews by the British television company Granada with former residents of the Kyshtym area. It is clear from these reports that hospitals in the entire area were "crammed with victims of the Kyshtym catastrophe," and that a large region was so contaminated with radioactivity that all food from the area had to be measured with radiometers as late as 1967. Perhaps most convincing of all, Medvedev found that from 1939 to 1958 virtually all the cities of the Urals had a population growth factor of at least two; however, from 1936 to 1970 the population of Kyshtym declined from 38,000 to 36,000.

Another environmental hazard that received considerable attention in 1979 was the herbicide 2,4,5-trichlorophenoxy acetic acid, and other phenoxy herbicides. These substances are sprayed over large tracts of coniferous forest in order to kill broadleaved plants that would compete with the commercial tree crop. In Oregon and northern California evidence accumulated suggesting that these substances are associated with an unusually high incidence of miscarriages and of babies born dead or deformed. The variety of malfor-

UPI

Geiger counter is used to detect radioactivity near the Three Mile Island nuclear power plant on March 31, 1979, three days after the accident at one of the plant's reactors.

mations was surprising; they included cleft palates, eye deformities, displaced hips, and anencephaly (poorly developed or absent cerebrum and lack of a skull vault). The frequency with which these usually rare conditions occurred in the sprayed area was startling: anencephaly, for example, appeared with 13 times the national average incidence. The Environmental Protection Agency reported that in one group of sprayed counties hospital records showed a miscarriage rate significantly higher than in areas where herbicides had not been used.

Endangered species. Norman Myers during the year published one of the most comprehensive analyses of the endangered species problem. He explained some ways in which exotic organisms can be useful to man; for example, manatees eat up water weeds that clog canals, and tropical forest trees provide firewood or exotic organic chemicals. Myers concluded that a significant cause of the loss of animal species is man's destruction of their habitats, particularly tropical moist forest, which he claimed is being destroyed at the rate of 245,000 sq km (94,600 sq mi) per year. He also pointed out that destruction of the forest that supports endangered species leads to flash flooding downstream after the forests are no longer present to absorb a high proportion of the rainfall. This flooding, in turn, causes the water level in the rice paddies to become too high

Czechoslovak News Agency/Keystone

Park bordering the town of Most in Czechoslovakia is a reclaimed mining waste dump.

to grow the new high-yielding rice varieties that have short stems.

Deforestation implies that firewood runs out, to be replaced by dung that should have been used as fertilizer. Also, reservoirs and hydropower installations lose efficiency through siltation from erosion. In short, species extinction is merely one of many symptoms of an underlying problem, excessive resource exploitation.

Environment and stress. While developing large-scale, mathematical models of nations for exploring future impacts of various policies, systems teams discovered country-to-country differences in production that could not be accounted for by any "hard variables"; the residual factor had something to do with international differences in human behavior. Further research showed that these national characteristics follow people when they emigrate; for example, the incidence of suicide among various national groups of U.S. immigrants is correlated to the incidence in their countries of origin.

This type of observation led Austrian researcher J. Millendorfer into an investigation of the relationship between various measures of national average cultural values and mental health. He found that an index of national average incidence of suicides plus accidents strongly correlated to another index for divorces plus psychoses. Countries high in the suicides plus accidents measure were the same countries that were high in the divorces plus psychoses measure. The theory is that all of these phenomena are produced by stress.

The interpretation Millendorfer puts on these results is that the underlying phenomenon being measured is "close human relationships." This, in turn, is related to the degree of disintegration of the global system. In short, as the relationships between mankind and the environment become less balanced, this will be reflected in the way people relate to one another.

The future. Two interesting studies on the future became widely available during the past year, one from Willis Harman and the other from a group at the University of Wisconsin headed by John Steinhart. Both of them suggested that life in about 2050 will of necessity be quite different from what it is now. Harman argues that humanity has arrived at its present state by following a paradigm, or belief system, that first brought us the industrial revolution. He believes that this paradigm is showing clear signs of a breakdown. To illustrate, there are not enough meaningful jobs, technology is being misapplied, and the habitability of the planet is not being preserved.

Harman's work makes a convincing case that a new paradigm is necessary; the Steinhart study shows where that paradigm might lead. It describes an imaginary United States in 2050, in which the total amount of energy used is 47% of that used in 1975 and energy use per capita is 34% of the 1975 figure. In fact, what is described is a 2050 United States very much like a big 1970 Switzerland. In the Steinhart model only 7% of the 2050 U.S. population lives in cities of more than 100,000 population, down from 28% in 1970. Cities of 25,000 to 100,000 would hold 29% of the total population, up from 17% in 1970. Thus, the Steinhart model has as one of its central features a move away from large urban centers. Associated with this decentralization is a major change in agriculture and transportation, with, for example, a much higher proportion of food being produced and consumed locally. An enormous decline in the use of oil and gas, no nuclear power, and a great increase in solar heating and in generating electricity by harnessing the power of the

318

Sun and wind are also implied. Walking, cycling, and mass transit would be the principal means of passenger transportation.

The driving force behind this scenario is necessity. Only by conserving energy can the U.S. make a sufficiently rapid conversion to a viable life-style after oil and gas are depleted, given available capital.

In short, a main theme in environmental sciences during the year was consideration of the relative costs and benefits of further growth versus stability. Further growth of the type recently experienced comes at too high a price. The inescapable conclusion is that the future must be qualitatively different.

—Kenneth E. F. Watt

Food and agriculture

World food production declined slightly during the year. The ever increasing price of petroleum used for fertilizers, herbicides and pesticides, and fuels caused the entire food system to become more expensive. There were, however, some significant breakthroughs on the horizon that gave promise of helping to hold down food costs.

Agriculture

World agricultural production dropped in 1979 for the first time in seven years. Virtually all of the decline occurred in the developed countries, where output fell almost 3%, while production in the less developed countries held nearly steady. All major industrialized countries except the U.S. experienced declines; Soviet output fell 12%, largely because of a sharply reduced grain harvest.

The U.S. embargo on grain and other products as retribution against the U.S.S.R. for its invasion of Afghanistan sparked interest among both producers and consumers as to the possible effect on grain prices. U.S. grain stocks (wheat, feed grains, rice, rye) approximated 74 million metric tons by the end of 1979, equivalent to 5.2% of annual world use. It had been expected that the Soviet Union would substantially increase its purchases of wheat and corn and thus significantly decrease stocks in the U.S., but the embargo changed that picture markedly.

U.S. agricultural exports in 1979 were expected to reach approximately $32 billion. Crop receipts were estimated to be approximately $60 billion and livestock receipts about $69 billion. Cash receipts would total $129 billion, compared with $111 billion for 1978, but production expenses, led by fuel and equipment costs, would account for approximately $112 billion. In general, farmers were spending more to produce food. They had survived rising prices by becoming more efficient and productive, but in the process they had become increasingly dependent on purchased inputs such as fertilizer, fuel, equipment, and chemicals to control weeds and insects.

Research priorities. Close cooperation between the scientist and the farmer in the U.S. has resulted in a food production system that is the envy of the world. Some wondered whether this working relationship had already been maximized or whether there would be new breakthroughs that would allow production costs per unit of food to continue at the current, relatively low value.

Greater photosynthetic efficiency is one high-priority area of current research. At present, crops are able to convert into food energy only 2 to 3% of the solar energy that reaches a given area of land, so there is considerable room for improvement. Another important research goal is improved biological nitrogen fixation. Corn requires relatively large quantities of nitrogen fertilizer, whereas legumes fix nitrogen through symbiosis with a microorganism called *Rhizobium*, which carries specific genes for nitrogen fixation. Scientists at the University of Illinois reported that

Taro, growing in a marsh in Hawaii, has many uses. Its roots and leaves provide a staple food in Polynesian diets, while European processors are beginning to use the roots in manufacturing plastics.

there is hope of incorporating these genes into cells of the corn plant, although several technical problems have yet to be solved. In pursuing this goal, the plant geneticists must also consider such factors as yield and resistance to pests.

A significant increase in livestock resources could be realized through improved use of feeds, disease control, and genetic improvement. All three research areas must be pursued simultaneously. Each year more than 50 million cattle and buffalo and 100 million sheep and goats throughout the world are lost to diseases and parasites. The U.S. alone loses $20 billion annually as a result of animal diseases. Reducing this loss by as much as 50% is a realistic goal.

Work carried out by scientists at Colorado State University (CSU) and supported by the National Science Foundation was focusing on improving range beef production systems. There are 1,200,000,000 ac of range in the U.S., most of it in the mountainous West and the Great Plains. Data developed by agronomists and range scientists suggest that beef can continue to meet a major portion of the U.S. protein needs without draining grain supplies, but the key to the strategy is obtaining greater productivity from the range.

The Economics, Statistics, and Cooperatives Service of the U.S. Department of Agriculture (USDA) estimated that the U.S. produces some 40,000,000,000 lb of marketable beef each year, some 80 to 90% of which is brought to slaughtering weight with grain, principally corn. The investigators at CSU believed that, if proper adjustments could be made in the beef system, grass-fed beef could be produced for about 40% of the cost of grain-fed beef. Their figures show that feeding or dryland pasture is about 2.7 times more energy-efficient than corn and 5.7 times more efficient than alfalfa (at least in Colorado where marginal acreage and pumped irrigation make alfalfa costly). By comparing energy input to actual pounds of beef produced, they determined that range-grass feeding of yearlings was about 3.5 to 7.4 times as efficient as total confinement feeding on various types of corn rations.

There were several barriers to increased use of range, however. Paramount was consumer preference —and hence higher prices—for marbled beef, obtained by feeding grain. Other impediments were rapid increases in land values and federal policies restricting the use of public lands.

An important area of research involved agricultural productivity. In terms of grain equivalents, it was estimated that the Earth could produce 40 times as much food as at present. Biological limits to productivity had not been reached for any major food crop or animal product. The world record for corn production in 1979 was 22,139 kg per ha (353 bu per ac), but the theoretical maximum yield was almost three times greater. Future advances would focus on managing the entire complex of systems involved in food production, including land, water, energy, pest control, tillage, fertilizers, and even climate.

Energy self-sufficiency in agriculture. Agricultural production in the developed countries is energy-intensive. Hence, energy availability problems in important producing areas, including North America and Europe, have made it critical for agriculture to set a goal of energy self-sufficiency. For the immediate future major emphasis would be placed on methane production from animal wastes and other biomass substrates, wind energy, solar energy, and production of alcohol to be mixed with gasoline (gasohol) or diesel fuel (dieselhol) or used as a fuel source by itself.

Animal fecal wastes, cornstalks and related cellulosic materials, and wood, bark, lignin, and related materials can be converted to methane in the presence of microorganisms of the genus *Clostridium* under anaerobic conditions. The Solar Energy Research Institute of the U.S. Department of Energy reported that some animal fecal-waste digesters can produce a steady supply of fuel gas with 60 to 65% of the heating value of natural gas. The methane thus derived can be used to power most activities that would otherwise re-

Gasohol, a mixture of 10% alcohol and 90% gasoline, is pumped into a car in Indiana. Researchers continued their efforts to find substitutes for pure gasoline.

Mary Ann Carter

Komondor dog seems to have a natural protective instinct for sheep and may be used increasingly on range lands in the West to ward off such predators as coyotes and foxes.

quire natural gas. Fecal matter from a mature cow can produce 40–50 cu ft (1.1–1.4 cu m) of gas each day, which, conservatively, is equivalent to 20,000 BTU's of heat. About 50 cows would be needed to heat an average home on a very cold day.

Wind has been used as an energy source in agriculture for many decades. Its principal disadvantages are lack of reliability and consistency, but a new generation of wind-driven electrical generating equipment gave promise of overcoming these deficiencies. One type, developed by the U.S. National Aeronautics and Space Administration and the Department of Energy (DOE), has two airfoil vanes that rotate regardless of wind direction; it looks rather like a 22-ft eggbeater. It can provide power with winds as low as 13 mph, develops maximum power with 27- to 40-mph winds, and automatically shuts down at higher wind velocities. It can produce 11 kw of electricity, enough to cool roughly 1,400 lb of milk per day. By means of heat recovery equipment the waste heat from cooling the milk can be used to heat water to wash down the facility and to wash the cows' udders before milking. On a larger scale propeller-type windmills 300 ft in length were being used by DOE near Medicine Bow, Wyo., to test the concept of a "wind energy" farm.

Solar energy, which was becoming popular as an alternate energy source for heating and cooling buildings, has many on-farm applications, including heating not only the farmhouse but also sheds, barns, farrowing pens, and brooders. Solar-powered hot-air drying is a low-energy, cost-effective means of partially drying grain crops.

Sugar- and starch-based agricultural products and the cellulosic materials associated with them (*e.g.,* cornstalks) are potentially excellent sources of alcohol. In terms of energy input sugar crops are the most efficient. A major thrust in the U.S. was to encourage the development of on-farm systems for the production of alcohol. A key factor in this program was the need for a ready source of inexpensive energy for the digestion, fermentation, and distillation processes. A second factor, related to the selling price of the undistilled residue, is called (for grain crops) distillers' dried grains and solubles. This residue can be used as a high-protein supplement for livestock and in the production of pet food, and, when properly processed, is suitable for human consumption. Increased use and, hence, value of the residue would lower the cost of producing alcohol considerably.

The alcohol can be blended with gasoline at a level of either 10 or 20% and the resultant fuel burned in internal combustion engines. Typically, a mixture of 90% gasoline and 10% ethanol (two-carbon alcohol) is referred to as gasohol. The addition of alcohol to diesel fuel yields dieselhol, which can be burned in semitrailers, tractors, and other farm machinery. A blend of butanol (four-carbon alcohol) and diesel fuel produces the best mixture. Machinery can also be adapted to use alcohol alone.

Achieving on-farm energy self-sufficiency would require a combination of these methods, together with a standby system of normally available commercial fuel. Research scientists were also investigating more exotic alternatives. There are several members of the genus *Euphorbia* which produce significant quantities of a milklike emulsion of hydrocarbons in water. Melvin

321

Calvin of the University of California at Berkeley reported that he had observed a tree in the tropical jungles that produces virtually pure diesel fuel. Every six months or so this tree, of the species *Copaifera Langsdorffii*, yields 15 to 20 liters of hydrocarbon that apparently can be placed directly into the fuel tank of a diesel-powered engine. Significantly for agriculture, it is possible that hydrocarbons could be used not only for fuel but, after further treatment, would yield some of the chemicals needed in modern farming. Along related lines the USDA launched a substantial program involving a desert shrub called guayule, which might become a source of natural rubber.

—John Patrick Jordan

Nutrition

The ninth edition of the Recommended Dietary Allowances (RDA's) was released by the Food and Nutrition Board of the U.S. National Academy of Sciences late in 1979. These allowances, first published in 1943 and revised periodically, are used as goals in planning food supplies and as guides in interpreting food consumption records. The statistical data, together with the complete commentary and discussion, are supplied on request by the Food and Nutrition Board.

The RDA's are released in three tables, each divided into values for various age groups and for pregnancy/lactation as follows: (1) energy allowances as mean values and as the range of customary energy output, together with mean heights and weights; (2) the Recommended Dietary Allowances for protein, fat-soluble vitamins, water-soluble vitamins, and minerals; and (3) estimates of adequate and safe intakes of se-

lected vitamins, trace minerals, and electrolytes. The energy allowances for young adults assume light work, and they include mean kilogram-calorie (kcal) and range values.

For women aged 11–14, 15–18, 19–22, and 23–50 years, the mean energy needs range from 2,000 to 2,200 kcal, and for men in the age ranges 11–14, 15–18, 19–22, and 23–50, from 2,700 to 2,900 kcal. For the older age groups (51–75 and 76 and over) the energy allowances assume a 2% decrease in basal metabolic rate per decade and reductions in activity of 200 kcal per day for men and women aged 51–75, 500 kcal for men over 75, and 400 kcal for women over 75. The maximum range for adults allows for differences in energy needs of plus or minus 400 kcal at any particular age, emphasizing the wide variation in energy needs within any group of people. The data are based on research studies of persons living under a wide variety of conditions.

The allowances are only estimates of the amounts of essential nutrients that each healthy person must consume in order to have reasonable assurance that his physiological needs will be met. The recommendations are high enough to meet the needs of those with the highest requirements, thus assuring an adequate intake for most of the population.

The ninth edition had few changes from the previous edition released in 1973. What changes there were reflected data from studies that interpreted the influences of climate, economic status, and distribution of population in the U.S. The RDA's can be met by food, and the recommended amounts of nutrients should be present in the daily diet of people in the U.S. However, the RDA's do not allow for nutrients lost in wasted food

Poster displayed at 80 major U.S. airports was sponsored by the National Heart, Lung, and Blood Institute.

or destroyed when food is prepared, cooked, and served. Such losses must be considered in evaluating the actual intake of individuals.

It was probable that the revised RDA's would trigger a revision of the food-labeling regulations, especially since recommended intakes of protein had been reduced for most age groups. Also, the table on safe and adequate vitamin and mineral intakes should initiate a requirement that quantities of certain potential health hazards such as sodium be included on labels. Although efforts to control sodium intake have focused on table salt (sodium chloride), many "safe" additives provide an even greater dietary supply of sodium.

Nutrition and patient care. The RDA's are designed to cover average healthy people. The nutritional needs of persons suffering from trauma, such as burns or wounds, may be much greater than the RDA, and this is also true for persons with fever or infection and those who are being treated for wasting disease. Nonetheless, the RDA's suggest a base from which increases can be judged by professionally qualified persons responsible for giving aid to individuals with greater needs. Unfortunately, studies have shown that many patients have not benefited from the contribution that good nutrition could make to their recovery or rehabilitation therapy. Resistance to eating or even anorexia (refusal of food), combined with negligence by professional staff, can result in disaster for the patient involved. Commercial organizations have made great advances in formulating concentrated, nutritionally balanced products to supply the nutrient needs of the ill or injured person. Intravenous hyperalimentation or gastro-nasal tube feeding can be resorted to in severe cases with good results and minimum tissue atrophy during recovery.

Cortez F. Enloe, editor of *Nutrition Today*, a strong supporter of closer cooperation between medical staff, dietitians, nutritionists, and nurses in patient care, reported the "exhilarating news that the New York Academy of Medicine has not only set up a subcommittee on nutrition and established a section on the subject in the academy, it has taken a policy stand on nutrition that provides strong and unequivocal guidance for its members in daily practice." He believed that this move would serve to improve the nutritional care of patients and enhance the prestige of the dietitian, slowly but surely influencing thinking on the subject throughout the U.S. and Canada.

Nutrition for the very young. Observance of the International Year of the Child in 1979 focused special attention on the dietary needs of the very young. Adequate maternal nutrition, especially in regard to the role of protein and calories, was being reemphasized, partly because of a realization of its importance for brain and lung development during prenatal life. Furthermore, infants with birth weights of under two pounds have a relatively poor chance of survival.

Roy M. Pitkin, chairman of the Committee on Nutrition of the Mother and Preschool Child, Food and Nutrition Board, National Academy of Sciences, stressed the positive correlation between total maternal weight gain and birth weight. Optimal protein utilization in pregnancy seems to require a minimum of 30 kcal per kilogram of body weight per day. The average weight gain in normal pregnancy is 10 to 12 kg (22 to 27 lb). The rate of weight gain is more important than the total, with only 1 to 2 kg (2 to 4.5 lb) to be gained during the first trimester, followed by a linear gain of 395 g (14 oz) per week until term. Limiting weight gain in the last months of pregnancy could result in serious deprivation of the fetus. Even placing an obese pregnant woman on a low-calorie diet is questionable, since calorie restriction may limit essential nutrients. Research at Syracuse (N.Y.) University indicated that the use of energy- and/or sodium-restricted diets during pregnancy, common among young, low-income women, is associated with lower nutrient intake.

Pitkin emphasized the need to supply the pregnant woman with all nutrients in the amounts specified by the RDA. Since the brain and lungs are among the first

Children in Upper Volta line up to receive milk provided by the government. Modern farming methods have increased production, but not all have benefited.

A. Holbrooke—United Nations

organs to reach the maximum cell count, adequacy of nutrients early in pregnancy is especially urgent. The fetus is an "iron parasite," and if maternal supplies of iron are minimal, anemia often develops. Thus iron supplementation is necessary and must allow for the poor absorption characteristic of iron compounds. However, except for iron and possibly folacin, nutrients required in pregnancy can be met through diet. Multivitamin and mineral supplements should not be a substitute for a balanced diet. The problem remains one of reaching the client early and motivating her to consume a diet supplying the specified amounts of nutrients. According to Margaret K. Snowman and Marjorie V. Dibble of Syracuse University, the young, low-income woman responds best when contacted in her home by a person who serves as an intermediary between her and the professionals.

The UN has estimated that 400 million children in the world are hungry. That any of these should be in the U.S., despite the various government-subsidized feeding and nutritional education programs, is something of a dilemma. Evaluation of these programs by researchers supports the hypothesis that changes in dietary behavior are slow and often transitory. Fashion also plays a role, however. The shift back and forth in emphasis on breast feeding is an example, and has had an especially negative effect on infant feeding practices in less developed countries. Also, at times, accelerated growth rates have been confused with infant obesity and attributed to one food or method of feeding.

Reviews of the data indicate that infants can be well fed by various procedures, although none is more efficient, less expensive, or more convenient than breast-feeding. For example, breast milk appears not to decrease the absorption of a trace dose of iron, and this, together with the high bioavailability of iron in breast milk, suggests that exclusive breast feeding is an effective means of preventing iron deficiency in early infancy. Solid vegetable foods, on the other hand, appear to have an inhibitory effect on iron absorption.

Ascorbic acid. An assessment of the revised RDA's is incomplete without some discussion of the controversy over the value of megadoses of certain chemical compounds, identified rightly or wrongly as nutrients. Among these, ascorbic acid (vitamin C) has received the most publicity, largely because of the theories of Albert Szent-Gyorgyi and Linus Pauling, who suggest doses several hundred times the RDA quantity of 60 mg for adults. Ironically, ascorbic acid is probably the nutrient most often deficient in the average diet. It is unstable and may be destroyed or lost during storage, processing, and cooking. Thus, although the cole vegetables (cabbage, broccoli, etc.) are initially rich in the vitamin, the food as eaten may have only negligible amounts. This leaves the citrus fruits as the staple supply of ascorbic acid, but in recent years orange juice has to some degree been replaced by "orange drinks"

with varying and often unreliably labeled ascorbic acid content.

The nature of ascorbic acid is something of a mystery. To be sure, it functions as a vitamin in that a dietary deficiency results in characteristic symptoms which are relieved by ascorbic acid therapy. However, Szent-Gyorgyi, who was awarded a Nobel Prize in 1937 for his research on vitamin C, believes that ascorbic acid is the center of the life of the cell, promoting cell division and preventing pathological or uncontrolled cell growth. In his view ascorbate, the salt form, is life's most important chemical.

Laymen frequently ask not only how much but how often and with what foods nutrients should be consumed. Generally, nutrients seem to be utilized better if they are consumed in regular patterns of three to five meals daily. Diet supplements such as vitamin pills and iron compounds are absorbed into the blood more readily when taken with meals. Time-release products now on the market are said to supply nutrients such as ascorbic acid throughout the day, but this claim awaits more thorough investigation.

—Mina W. Lamb

Life sciences

Investigations in the life sciences during the past year were highlighted by efforts to slow the progress of Dutch elm disease, to understand the complex interactions between plants and pollution, and to exploit microbial fermentation in the synthesis of alcohol and other basic chemicals. Molecular biologists continued their probing of the many fundamental differences in gene structure and function between bacteria and higher organisms and offered evidence to support a model of the way in which proteins are secreted from cells. Zoologists studied a special "sixth sense" of chemical perception in animals and the blood chemistry of high-flying ducks.

Botany

During the year investigators working with plants recorded findings of importance in the fields of pathology, ecology, physiology, and genetics.

Fungal diseases. In 1909 a specimen of the European elm bark beetle was discovered in Massachusetts, signaling the beginning of the battle for survival of the American elm (*Ulmus americana*). This beetle and an American relative carry spores of a fungus, *Ceratocystis ulmi*, that devastates the elm with Dutch elm disease. Beetles breed under the bark of dead or dying branches, and in about eight weeks a new generation flies off to healthy trees to feed and spread the fungus. When the fungus reaches vascular tissue, the tree produces a substance to block the vascular flow and thus

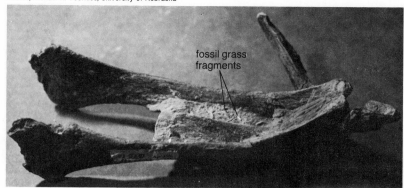

fossil grass
fragments

Fossil skeletons (bottom) of an extinct rhinoceros, Teleoceras major, *that lived in Nebraska about seven million to ten million years ago were discovered to contain plant fragments indicative of their diet. Mineralized parts of three species of grass were taken from the rib cage or oral cavity, including the tongue bones (left), of several* Teleoceras *specimens. The find shed light on the animals' feeding habits and on late Miocene environment.*

block the internal spread of the fungus. Consequently sap flow is diminished and wilting results, but the fungus keeps spreading nonetheless, and the tree dies in one to three years. The fungus also may be transmitted through natural root grafts between neighboring trees.

Initially Dutch elm disease in the U.S. was fought largely through sanitation—pruning diseased branches, removing affected trees, and burning or burying the wood. By the 1950s DDT sprays were being used to kill the beetles with some success in retarding the progress of the disease, but a ban on DDT use in 1969 removed it from the battle, leaving the task to some less effective sprays. By 1976 estimates indicated that the U.S. had lost 54% of its American elms, while the northeast part of the country alone had lost 75%. The disease continued to spread westward.

By the late 1970s a variety of new techniques held promise at least for preserving greater numbers of elms for longer than might have been expected. Several new fungicides could be administered directly to the vascular tissue of elms through holes bored into the lower trunk or even into the roots. Chemical sex attractants were being used to lure beetles to traps for collection and destruction. Resistant trees were being identified in the belief that their propagation would lead to resistant strains. Most experts remained cautious because all techniques are limited: fungicide treatments last but one or two years, beetle entrapment captures only a small percentage of these insects, development of resistant strains of trees takes a long time, and sanitation was not being carried out in many areas that could act as brood sources for beetles. Perhaps the American elm will be saved as a species, but it will never again be the dominant shade tree once found in many northeastern and midwestern U.S. communities.

Two Washington State University researchers suggested a new approach to the control of fungal infections, which are a major problem in agriculture and other efforts requiring plant culture. I. B. Maiti and P. E. Kolattukudy observed that some fungi attack plants by penetrating the otherwise protective cover called cutin and reasoned that, if one or more enzymes were involved in the destruction of cutin, inhibition of such enzymes could result in plant resistance to infection. Eventually, they succeeded in isolating an enzyme, called cutinase I, from *Fusarium solani pisi,* a fungal pathogen of the common pea. This enzyme was shown

325

to be inhibited both by antibodies developed in rabbits immunized by cutinase and by the chemical diisopropylfluorophosphate. Because cutinase is not found in the normal metabolism of plants, it might be feasible to develop antipenetrants—chemicals that attack fungal cutinase when sprayed on plants—that would effectively repel fungus attack without harm to the host plant.

Infrared thermometry. A group of researchers in Arizona, P. J. Pinter, Jr., and associates, showed that infrared thermometry can be used to detect diseased plants. Their technique is a development of recent interest in remote-sensing technology as a tool to detect crop stresses for agricultural purposes. Infrared thermometry uses an infrared-sensitive thermometer that is passed over plants to measure radiant leaf temperatures. Since higher leaf temperatures are exhibited during water deprivation than when water supply is ample, this type of thermometry can detect water stress. In the event that elevated temperatures are detected even when water supply is ample, stress may be due to decreased ability of the plant to take up water, which in turn may be caused by disease.

These researchers used infrared thermometry on sugar beet and cotton plants in Arizona, choosing fields in which certain fungi were known to cause root-rot in the crops: *Pythium aphanidermatum* in sugar beet and *Phymatotrichum omnivorum* in cotton. Plants were classified into three categories based on the appearance of the root system: healthy, slightly diseased, and moderately diseased. When temperature measurements taken of plants in the three categories were compared, it became apparent that slightly diseased plants showed no significant deviation from normal in leaf temperatures, probably because a significant portion of their root systems had not been destroyed. The leaves of moderately diseased sugar beets, however, averaged 2.6°–3.6° C (4.7°–6.5° F) warmer than healthy plants; in cotton this difference averaged 3.3°–5.3° C (5.9°–9.5° F). The investigators felt that infrared thermography would not be limited to detecting these two soil-borne fungal diseases but would be useful in detecting biological and physical plant stress due to a range of causes.

Plants and pollution. Studies continued on the effects of atmospheric pollutants on plants. In one, Danish researcher Jens C. Tjell and co-workers demonstrated that 90–99% of the total lead content in grass comes from deposition of atmospheric lead on the plant surface. Most of the atmospheric lead in the Northern Hemisphere originates from automobile exhausts, and previous research had reported the greatest effect on plants to be within 50–100 m (165–330 ft) of roadways, where an estimated 10% of the lead is deposited. Plants raised increasingly farther from roadways would be expected to gain from the air a diminishing proportion of their total lead uptake. How-

ever, the experiments of these researchers, carried out on Italian rye grass (*Lolium multiflorum*) grown one kilometer (0.6 mi) from the nearest highway, showed that no more than 10% of plant lead comes from the soil. Thus, accumulation of lead in crop plants from atmospheric sources may be of greater consequence than previously thought.

As a result of another study, J. C. Noggle of the Tennessee Valley Authority concluded that atmospheric sulfur compounds are absorbed by plants in amounts that increase as sulfur compounds in the soil decrease. This report added a new dimension to recent concern about the rising acidity of rain in some parts of the world. It has been known for some time that atmospheric sulfur dioxide is harmful to plants when exposure is as low as 0.5 ppm for three hours. Noggle pointed out, however, that modern agricultural practice has not provided for adequate sulfates in the soil for optimum crop production. In the past both sulfur-rich manure and inorganic sulfates were added to provide the major nutrients of nitrogen, potassium, and phosphorus, but no longer is manure an important fertilizer and commercial fertilizers contain little sulfur. In greenhouse experiments Noggle showed that some crop plants apparently compensate by increasing their uptake of sulfur dioxide and hydrogen sulfide from the air. Hence, if the concentration of sulfur compounds in air remains below toxic levels, it can be beneficial. This investigator did not offer this finding in

Root tips of sala (Gaultheria shallon) *penetrate two seeds of the parasite* Boschniakia hookeri. *Contact of the seed embryo by the growing host root tip allows the host-parasite relationship to develop.*

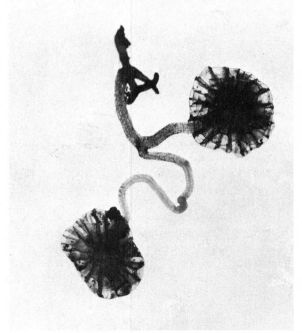

From "Growth of host root establishes contact with parasitic angiosperm Boschniakia hookeri," S. Olsen & I. D. Olsen, NATURE, vol. 279, pp. 635–636, fig. 2, June 14, 1979

support of industrial pollution but suggested that the cost of applying additional fertilizers to make up for atmospheric sulfur compounds removed in antipollution efforts should be considered in the cost of cleanup.

Underground activities. Interesting relationships exist between many plants and their parasites. As an example, the broom-rape family Orobanchaceae contains plant-root parasites that somehow attach to their hosts underground. The genus *Orobanche* is characterized by parasitic plants whose seeds germinate when stimulated by some chemical released from the host plant. The parasitic relationship subsequently is established when contact is made between the growing parasite embryo and a root of the host plant. This process ensures a relatively high probability of establishment of the host-parasite relationship. Sigurd and Ingrith Olsen of the University of Washington discovered a different technique by which the host-parasite relationship involving the parasite genus *Boschniakia* is initiated. They observed that seeds of *Boschniakia hookeri* fail to germinate unless their seed coats are penetrated by an advancing root tip of certain members of the family Ericaceae, such as *Arctostaphylos uva-ursi*, the bearberry. After a bearberry root tip penetrates a *Boschniakia* seed and establishes contact with the embryo, tissues of both grow together and a tuber forms. In early 1980 the cause of attraction was still unknown.

A much different relationship exists between a fairly large group of fungi and their prey, which happen to be small nematodes, commonly called roundworms. Nematode-trapping fungi develop looplike traps with some of their hyphae (filaments), which are capable of holding the nematode as they attempt to pass through. A mechanism for binding the nematodes was demonstrated recently by Birgit Nordbring-Hertz and Bo Mattiasson of the University of Lund in Sweden. They reported that a very common nematode-trapping fungus, *Arthrobotrys oligospora*, actually produces a protein called a lectin that binds to certain carbohydrates on the surface of the nematode, thereby holding it fast even against its struggles. Within one hour the fungus grows a short hypha into the nematode for nutritional purposes.

"Big bang" flowering. The family Dipterocarpaceae contains impressive trees, many of which exceed 60 m (200 ft) in height. These trees are characteristic of lowland forests of Southeast Asia, where they are known for their failure to flower on an annual basis. At intervals of three to ten years most of these trees flower in profusion (as many as four million flowers per tree). Although different species of trees bloom the same year, the time of flowering is staggered. According to H. T. Chan and others who carried out studies at the Pasoh Forest Reserve, southeast of Kuala Lampur, Malaysia, the flowering pattern is correlated with dependence on insects called thrips (order Thys-

From "Action of a nematode-trapping fungus shows lectin-mediated host-microorganism interaction," Birgit Nordbring-Hertz and Bo Mattiasson, NATURE, vol. 281, pp. 477–479, fig. 1, October 11, 1979

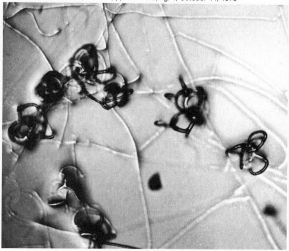

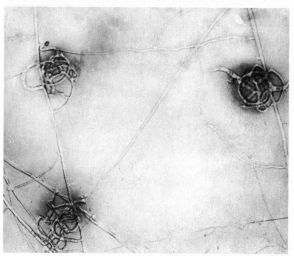

Experimenters probing the microscopic capture organs of nematode-trapping fungi (top) simulated natural prey with red blood cells, which adhere to the traps. Within an hour of capture the cells disintegrate, and the capture organs lose their turgidity (above).

anoptera) for pollination. When the first dipterocarps come into bloom, populations of thrips increase explosively and effectively pollinate successively blooming species. The first dipterocarp to flower might seem to lose out on this mechanism, even though it is essential to the initiation of it, because the thrip populations would be building during its time in bloom. It was shown that one such plant, *Shorea macroptera*, could produce seeds asexually if its flowers were not pollinated. This overall situation seems to be a good illustration of how a group of related plants maintain a mutualistic relationship by blooming the same year and utilizing the same pollinators. They avoid competition by blooming sequentially.

A similar relationship was reported for two Rocky Mountain wildflowers by U.S. investigators Nicholas Waser and Leslie Real. *Delphinium nelsonii* and *Ipo-*

mopsis aggregata flower sequentially and are pollinated by hummingbirds. During two favorable years, 1975 and 1976, both species were observed to flower abundantly and to produce seed well. A 1977 winter drought led to a drastic reduction in flowering for *D. nelsonii* during 1977 and 1978 but not so for *I. aggregata*. Yet seed production for the latter was lowered greatly, and the investigators noted a corresponding decline in frequency of appearance of the broad-tailed hummingbird (*Selasphorus platycercus*) during the latter two years. They concluded that the two wildflowers share use of the hummingbird for pollination and that the failure of *D. nelsonii* to attract the bird led to failure of *I. aggregata* to be pollinated as well.

Genes and hormones. In a paper published in 1979 in the *American Journal of Botany*, Soviet botanist M. K. Chailakhyan attempted to relate genetic and hormonal factors in certain developmental processes in plants. With respect to hormonal regulation of growth, Chailakhyan was able to show that genetic control of dwarfism is mediated by amounts of gibberellic acid (GA_3), a growth promoter, and such growth inhibitors as quercetin-glycosyl-coumarate, found in pea dwarfs. Experiments with peas, corn, wheat, and other plants showed that the retarding effect in dwarfs is directly proportional to the number of their genes known to be associated with dwarfing and may be due to the production of greater amounts of growth inhibitors, which inactivate the effect of growth promoters.

In investigating hormonal regulation of sex determination, Chailakhyan used species of dioecious plants for study. Individual plants of dioecious species are either male or female, and differences in chromosomal makeup in the plants are reflected in the physiological differences between sexes. Female plants have two X chromosomes, on which it is assumed the genes for production of female flowers reside. Male plants have one X and one Y, on which (probably on the Y) the genes for production of male flowers reside. Studies showed that leaves produce certain hormones classed as gibberellins, which travel to apical buds and induce them to produce male flowers. Roots produce other hormones called cytokinins, which may travel to apical buds and induce the formation of female flowers. Thus a specific hormonal balance is needed to produce one kind of flower or another, and in an environment common to both sexes of plant, genetic differences must determine the different hormonal balances. The exact mechanism of interaction remains to be discovered.

—Albert J. Smith

Microbiology

At one time the U.S. obtained its industrial alcohol, organic acids, and neutral solvents from the microbial fermentation of glucose derived from starch in grain, chiefly corn. It then became more economical to synthesize these substances chemically from petroleum products. In recent years, owing to the high cost of petroleum as well as to supply shortages, microbiologists have been directing renewed attention toward the use of microorganisms to produce industrial organic substances and also to produce alcohol and methane for fuel.

Some authorities believe that ultimately a large proportion of energy in the U.S. will be obtained from renewable biomass produced by photosynthesis. Microorganisms will be used to convert the biomass into usable products. It seems unlikely, however, that corn and other cereals will be used for the microbial fermentation of alcohol for use as fuel because of two overriding factors. First, the combination of American energy-intensive farming methods and the energy input required to ferment and distill the alcohol would likely exceed the alcohol's usable energy content. Second, owing to widespread hunger, world opinion would not permit extensive amounts of grain to be diverted to alcohol for fuel. However, the use of agricultural products for the microbial fermentation of chemical feed stocks is considered to be both economically feasible and socially acceptable. Chemical feed stocks are those relatively simple chemical compounds that are used as starting materials in the synthesis of such complex products as plastics.

Much interest has been shown in the microbial fermentation of cellulosic materials to produce alcohol and methane as fuels. Cellulose is the largest biomass component of the Earth's renewable resources. The U.S. is estimated to produce more than 900 million metric tons of cellulosic waste alone. Most of cellulose occurs as a lignocellulose complex containing large fractions of crystalline cellulose. Because cellulose-utilizing microorganisms have little ability to break down lignocellulose, a chemical or mechanical pretreatment of the complex is necessary to disrupt the lignin-cellulose bonds and to decrystallize the cellulose fibers. The cost of pretreatment is a major expense in the overall process.

Recent research has also centered on the use of thermophilic (heat-loving) microorganisms to ferment cellulosic materials. The potential advantages of thermophiles, compared with microorganisms that grow at ambient temperatures, are more rapid growth, increased enzyme activity, and greater enzyme stability.

Microbial fermentation of cellulosics produces not only methane and alcohol but also single-cell protein, which can be isolated from the resulting microbial biomass. Indeed, many researchers believe that the production of both fuels and protein will be necessary if alcohol and methane are to be made and sold on a competitive basis.

The synthesis of chemical fertilizers containing fixed nitrogen—*i.e.*, combined with other elements in a form that living organisms can use—requires the input

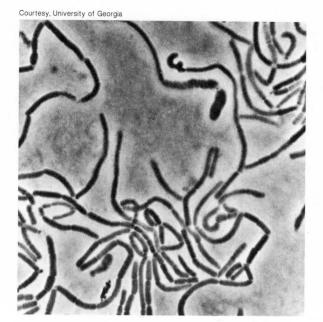

Courtesy, University of Georgia

Bacterium collected in 1978 from hot springs was found to ferment a wide range of sugars to ethanol at temperatures as high as 78° C (172° F). It may have applications in industrial alcohol production.

of considerable energy. Thus, research on biological nitrogen fixation owes much of its impetus to the energy shortage and the high cost of petroleum. Nitrogen is the nutrient that most commonly limits crop productivity. The most studied biological nitrogen fixation system is the symbiosis between species of the bacterial genus *Rhizobium* and such legumes as clover, soybeans, alfalfa, peas, and beans. In *Rhizobium*-legume symbiosis the bacteria first adhere to the root hairs of the plant and then infect them. Next, bacteria-filled root nodules are formed, and finally the bacteria in the nodules differentiate into enlarged forms, called bacteroids, that fix nitrogen.

Species of *Rhizobium* exhibit a high degree of host specificity; for example, the species that infects clover will not infect other legumes. Several years ago expression of host specificity in the *Rhizobium*-legume symbiosis was shown to be due to the interaction of certain legume proteins, called lectins, that attach to specific sugars on the surface of the bacterium. Subsequently it was found that clover lectin binds both to sugars on the bacterial surface and to related sugars on the surface of the clover root hair itself. Thus, the selective adherence of the bacterial symbiont to its specific plant host is accomplished via a specific cross-bridging between plant and bacterium by the plant lectin.

In the microbial nitrogen-fixing process the enzyme complex nitrogenase converts molecular nitrogen to fixed nitrogen, but it also may evolve significant amounts of hydrogen at the same time. Hydrogen evolution is dependent on the input of a large amount of microbial energy, and can consume as much as 40% of the energy involved in the nitrogen-fixing process. Yet, some bacteroids in the *Rhizobium*-legume symbiotic system do not evolve hydrogen. It was shown that these bacteroids possess hydrogenase, an enzyme complex that oxidizes hydrogen, and that the evolved hydrogen is recycled. Evolution of hydrogen by nitrogenase and its oxidation by hydrogenase in the hydrogen-recycling process serves the physiological role of protecting the oxygen-sensitive nitrogenase complex from excessive oxygen, because oxygen is used in the hydrogenase reaction. Energy is also produced by the hydrogenase reaction, and consequently some of the energy expended in hydrogen evolution by nitrogenase is gained back. Hydrogen-recycling systems also were identified both in blue-green algae (cyanobacteria) and in other bacterial nitrogen-fixing systems.

Certain nonleguminous plants form nitrogen-fixing root nodules in symbiosis with actinomycetes, a form of "higher" bacteria. Such nodulated plants are often pioneers in nutrient-poor soils, and they participate in soil enrichment early in some ecological successions. Such is the case for the alder tree. Formerly there had been little study of nodules from such systems because of the difficulties of working with woody tissue containing phenolic substances; these chemicals inactivate enzymes upon rupture of the cells for enzyme isolation and study. Recently scientists at the University of Wisconsin overcame these difficulties. They found that the actinomycete-alder nitrogen-fixing system was similar to other microbial nitrogen-fixing systems with respect to the energy-dependent, hydrogen-evolving nitrogenase system. This was further evidence for the homology preserved in the evolutionary development of biological nitrogen-fixing systems. (For a detailed account of nitrogen-fixation research, see *1979 Yearbook of Science and the Future* Feature Article: FOOD, FAMINE, AND NITROGEN FIXATION.)

Indian scientists from New Delhi reported that the use of chemical fertilizers can be reduced by one-third if blue-green algae are applied to rice paddies. Blue-green algae not only fix nitrogen but also are thought to aid in the adjustment of oxygen and sulfide concentrations optimal for growth of the rice plant. It was further reported that blue-green algae can establish themselves almost permanently if inoculation of the rice paddies is done repeatedly for three or four cropping seasons. This kind of technology is cheap and, thus, relevant for poor rice farmers for whom the high cost of chemical fertilizers poses a serious constraint in adopting high-yielding varieties of rice.

The Japanese are considered to be world leaders in industrial microbial-fermentation research. A recent novel approach was the use of immobilized, living microbial cells to produce end products of commercial importance. In one instance Japanese scientists found that carrageenan, a polysaccharide (complex sugar)

329

Courtesy, Andrew A. Benson; photo, W. W. Wight

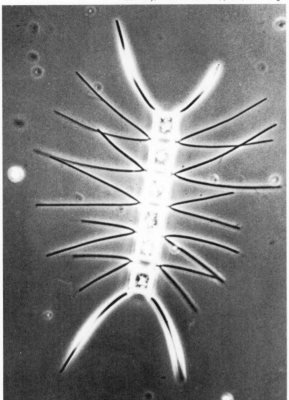

Work with Chaetoceros decipiens *showed that such marine diatoms cope with potentially toxic arsenic compounds that they absorb from seawater by safely incorporating the arsenic into their membranes.*

isolated from seaweed that becomes a gel under mild conditions, was a highly suitable substance in which to immobilize microbial cells. When a hollow tube was packed with living yeast cells immobilized in a carrageenan matrix and suitable nutrient was passed through the matrix, the number of living yeast cells remained constant while they continously produced alcohol for longer than a month. Similar results were obtained for the production of an amino acid by immobilized, living bacterial cells. The advantage of using immobilized microorganisms is that more of the nutrient is converted to end product because the nutrient is not being utilized to supply energy for microbial multiplication.

Another novel Japanese approach was the use of "coupled fermentation by energy transfer." In one experimental system the amino acid glutamine was produced by a combination of dried bakers' yeast and the enzyme glutamine synthetase, which had been isolated from a bacterium. When sugar was added to a reaction mixture containing this combination and a source of glutamate, the yeast fermented the sugar and formed the molecule ATP. This energy-rich compound, which serves as the "dollar" in the energy economics of all organisms, in turn supplied energy for the conversion of glutamate to glutamine by glutamine synthetase.

A final noteworthy experiment by Japanese workers was the culturing of microorganisms under conditions in which a particular desired enzyme was caused to accumulate in high amounts in the microbial cells. The cells were then added directly to a reaction mixture to take advantage of the catalytic activity of the accumulated enzyme. This procedure was used experimentally in the formation of certain amino acids from chemical precursors.

U.S., West German, and Scottish scientists working jointly recently reported that they had succeeded in introducing genes from hepatitis B virus into the bacterium *Escherichia coli.* This bacterium thus acquired the ability to synthesize hepatitis B viral proteins, which possibly could be used as a vaccine to stimulate antibody formation against the virus. This experiment established the feasibility of commercial vaccine production from viral protein antigens synthesized in microbial cells.

Microbiologists from Nagoya University, Japan, isolated bacteria that have the ability to accumulate phosphate in high concentration within their cells. This finding suggests that sewage could be inoculated with these bacteria during the biological sewage-treatment process to remove phosphate. So treated, the sewage effluent then could be discharged to a stream or lake without the consequences of phosphate pollution, a condition that leads to undesirable growth of algae and aquatic plants.

Kerogen is the generic name for high-molecular-weight organic matter, insoluble in organic solvents, that occurs naturally in geological sediments. It is a major component of oil shales and, moreover, is said to be the most abundant type of organic matter on the Earth, but little is known of its origin and of its detailed molecular structure. Workers in West Germany and France demonstrated that kerogen contains distinctive long-chain hydrocarbons of the type found to occur in cells of evolutionarily primitive bacteria called archaebacteria (*e.g.,* the methane-producing bacteria) and also in petroleum. This observation suggests that kerogen is a "molecular fossil" of archaebacteria and also raises the interesting possibility that petroleum may have been formed at least in part by archaebacteria that dominated the environment soon after life on the Earth began.

In 1977, when geologists first photographed volcanic hot-water vents in the Galápagos Rift in the eastern Pacific, the scientific community was astonished to find the vents teeming with life. The vents are at a depth of 2.5 km (about 1.5 mi), where no light penetrates and the water temperature is normally only a few degrees above freezing. Only scant nutrients reach the deep ocean floor, those which drift down from the surface. To observe an abundance of life here, including huge clams, gigantic tube worms, and other new species of organisms, was quite unexpected.

In 1979 scientists descended to the bottom to collect living specimens and samples of sediment and water. A basic question concerned the nature of the primary food source. Experimental evidence indicated that chemoautotrophic bacteria were the primary producers. These bacteria gain their energy by the oxidation of hydrogen sulfide given off by the volcanic vents, and they convert carbon dioxide to organic matter. In this way the bacteria multiply and thus become the source of food for other organisms. This situation is most unusual because the general rule is that primary producers are photosynthetic forms of life.

—Robert G. Eagon

Molecular biology

Much of the literature of molecular biology describes studies of gene structure and function carried out using bacteria. The cells of higher organisms (eucaryotes) differ from bacteria (procaryotes) in some obvious ways: they are much larger, and they contain nuclei and other membrane-surrounded intracellular bodies such as mitochondria and chloroplasts. Never-

theless, the attention paid to bacteria and bacterial viruses has been justified because the basic facts of molecular biology are nearly the same in procaryotes and eucaryotes. All living cells contain chromosomes, which consist of lengthy DNA molecules. The genetic information in the chromosomes is embodied in the sequence of the four nucleotides—adenine (A), thymine (T), guanine (G), and cytosine (C)—that make up the DNA structure. That information is transcribed from the gene into a corresponding sequence of nucleotides in the RNA molecule. The RNA nucleotide sequence serves as a message and is in turn translated by the protein-synthesis machinery, the ribosome, into the amino-acid sequence of a protein. The amino-acid sequence determines the structure and, ultimately, the function of the protein molecule.

This scheme for the storage, transmission, and use of genetic information must be vastly superior to alternatives because it has been conserved in all currently evolved cells. But past research had uncovered some differences between procaryotes and eucaryotes with respect to RNA and protein synthesis, and newer information reopened the question of the evolutionary relationship of procaryotes and eucaryotes.

It has been known for some time that there are

In the eucaryotic chromosome, DNA strands are wrapped at intervals around cores of basic proteins called histones (below left, a) to form a series of structures called nucleosomes (b). Under the electron microscope unfolded fragments of DNA from eucaryotic chromosomes resemble beads on a string (right).

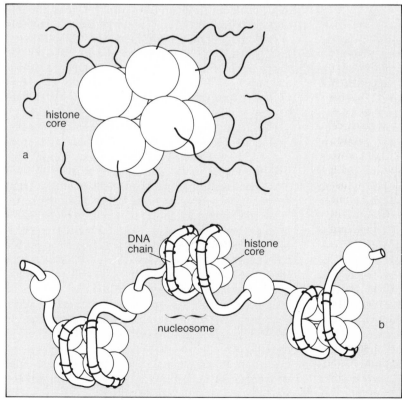

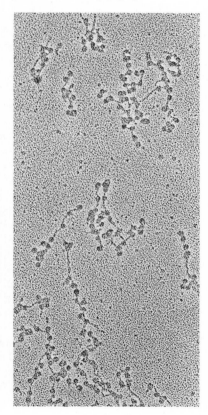

(Left and right) John Finch, MRC Laboratory of Molecular Biology

fundamental differences in the packing of bacterial and eucaryotic chromosomes. The bacterial chromosome is thought to be simply a naked DNA molecule, whereas a eucaryotic chromosome consists of DNA wrapped around a core of basic proteins called histones and condensed further by interaction with other proteins. Moreover, nearly all of the nucleotide sequences in bacterial DNA are unique and are transcribed into RNA. Eucaryotic DNA, on the other hand, contains many repeated sequences of unknown function, and much DNA characterized by unique sequence is not represented in the RNA transcripts found in the cell cytoplasm.

Recombinant DNA studies have provided a partial explanation for the absence in the cytoplasm of RNA sequences that represent all of the DNA in the chromosome. Recombinant chromosomal DNA fragments have been shown to contain a number of intervening sequences; i.e., sequences that lie between those that code for amino-acid sequences in proteins. Put another way, many eucaryotic genes are fragmented. They are completely transcribed in the nucleus, but the RNA transcript is not transported to the cytoplasm intact. Instead, the intervening stretches of RNA nucleotides (corresponding to the intervening sequences of chromosomal DNA) are cut out, and the remaining coding portions are spliced together to produce the final cytoplasmic messenger RNA. The discarded intervening sequences, in several of the cases that have been studied, are actually longer than the preserved coding portions.

The mechanism by which the intervening sequences are removed is of considerable interest. During the past year a number of eucaryotic genes were sequenced; that is, the precise order of nucleotides in the genes was determined. When the sequence of each gene was compared with the sequence of its corresponding cytoplasmic messenger RNA, it became possible to determine the nucleotide sequence in the vicinity of the sites that are cut and spliced during the removal of intervening sequences from the initial, nuclear RNA transcript. Comparison of a number of such splicing sites revealed certain similarities—in fact, enough similarity to suggest that the sequence at the splicing site is recognized by the splicing mechanism.

Some years ago it was discovered that animal-cell nuclei contain a number of stable RNA molecules of low molecular weight. Several of these were sequenced, but because the function of these molecules was unknown the sequences were uninterpretable. What a surprise it was, then, to discover that one of these stable nuclear RNA's contains a sequence that is exactly complementary to the sequences common to the splicing sites described above. Thus it appears that complementary base pairing, such as that found in the double strands of DNA (A pairs with T, G pairs with C), joins the two splicing sites at either end of an intervening sequence. The two sites are held together by a base-pairing interaction with a second RNA molecule, allowing a splicing enzyme to cut and reseal the originally oversized RNA transcript.

Why bother with extra material inside genes when it has to be cut out of the transcript en route to the cytoplasm? In early 1980 no one yet knew, but it was suggested that the coding portions of genes correspond to "domains" of the finished protein; i.e., subregions having distinct functions. Separating these domains by noncoding bits of DNA would facilitate evolution by allowing the coding regions to be genetically reshuffled intact, with the breaks and splices all located somewhere within the intervening sequences. Such recombination would not have to be precise because any coding errors made at the splicing sites would be cut out along with the intervening sequences.

Further differences between procaryotic and eucaryotic gene expression have turned up in details of transcription of RNA itself. The enzyme RNA polymerase, which effects transcription, has been purified from a large number of bacteria. In every case the enzyme contains five protein subunits: a core of four subunits (two identical) needed to extend growing RNA molecules and a fifth (called sigma) needed for initiation of RNA chains. In every bacterium studied, a single class of RNA polymerase is responsible for the synthesis of three different kinds of RNA: messenger RNA, ribosomal RNA, and transfer RNA. In eucaryotes, by contrast, there are three classes of RNA polymerase, each with many distinctive protein components. One of the different RNA polymerases is required for the synthesis of each major kind of RNA. Moreover, while bacterial RNA polymerase will transcribe DNA in vitro (outside the living cell and in an artificial environment) without additional factors, each of the eucaryotic RNA polymerases requires different protein factors to initiate RNA synthesis.

The biggest surprise to date in this connection came from a comparison of procaryotic and eucaryotic promoters. The promoter is a region of DNA, found originally in bacteria, to which RNA polymerase binds; such binding is necessary for proper initiation of RNA transcription. So many bacterial genes have been sequenced that it is possible to determine which nucleotides are common to all, or most, bacterial promoters. It is also possible to determine which nucleotides are covered when RNA polymerase simply binds to a DNA fragment containing a promoter. When these possibilities were explored, it was found that two regions of DNA are important: one is about 10 nucleotides before the actual start point of transcription and the other is about 35 nucleotides before the start point. Thus, in bacteria, RNA polymerase binds to a nucleotide sequence spanning at least 25 nucleotides and then slides or reaches 10 nucleotides "downstream" toward the start point to start synthesis of RNA.

Very little comparable information was available from eucaryotic systems until last year. Then, workers in the laboratory of Donald Brown at the Carnegie Institution of Washington (D.C.) established an in vitro system for the transcription of a cloned gene of the toad *Xenopus laevis*. The gene in question coded for "5S" RNA, a ribosomal RNA transcribed by RNA polymerase III. A DNA fragment containing the gene and some additional DNA at each end was cloned by inserting it into a bacterial plasmid, a small, circular molecule of DNA that replicates in the bacterium independently of the bacterial chromosome. This process was accomplished in such a way that the ring of plasmid DNA could be cut open and digested piecemeal, creating a series of deletions that reached from the plasmid DNA into the cloned *Xenopus* DNA fragment, terminating at various points prior to or inside the 5S RNA gene.

This manipulation yielded several surprises. First, removal of DNA "upstream" (in front) of the start site, including the 10–35 nucleotide region that would correspond to a bacterial promoter, had no effect on 5S RNA transcription. Second, removal of the middle third of the cloned gene abolished transcription entirely. Finally, removal of the beginning part of the gene in such a way that DNA from the bacterial plasmid was connected to the middle third of the cloned gene resulted in a product whose transcription was begun in the bacterial DNA at roughly the proper number of nucleotides upstream from the middle third of the gene. These results mean that the "promoter" for the Xenopus 5S RNA gene, *i.e.*, the nucleotide sequence that directs RNA polymerase to initiate transcription, is located inside the gene. This is clearly different from every known bacterial case. It remains to be determined whether other eucaryotic RNA polymerases will recognize promoters of either type or follow an entirely new plan.

In addition to the requirement for splicing, eucaryotic RNA containing coding sequences differs from bacterial messenger RNA in other ways. To describe these differences it is convenient to recall that all DNA and RNA have a polarity, or direction, that is determined by the chemical linkages between successive nucleotide units. One end of a DNA or RNA molecule is called the 5′ end, and the other the 3′ end. RNA synthesis always occurs from the 5′ end toward the 3′ end. In bacteria the messenger RNA that directs the synthesis of proteins on the surface of ribosomes is identical to the RNA molecule that is first transcribed from DNA. In eucaryotes messenger RNA is always modified at the 5′ end and usually modified at the 3′ end. Both modifications occur in the nucleus prior to export of the RNA to the cytoplasm. Modification at the 3′ end consists of the addition of 50–200 units of adenine. The function of this "polyA" tail is not known. At the 5′ end, modification consists of adding a single guanine unit, in an unusual chemical orientation, to the first nucleotide of the primary transcript. The guanine and the first nucleotide of the transcript are also subsequently decorated with several methyl groups. The new structure thus formed is called a cap, and the process is termed capping. Caps were first discovered on viral messenger RNA but subsequently were found to be required for translation of all eucaryotic messenger RNA. Work during the past year determined why caps are required and how viral RNA molecules get their caps.

Caps are required to initiate protein synthesis efficiently in eucaryotes but not in bacteria. Nearly all bacterial messenger RNA's contain, several nucleotides upstream from the AUG triplet (U refers to the nucleotide uracil) that will initiate the protein, a sequence that is complementary to a sequence near the 3′ end of the structural RNA of the ribosome. The resulting complementary base pairing places the AUG at the correct site to initiate the mechanism that will build the protein. Eucaryotic messenger RNA's do not have such a recognition sequence. Instead, eucaryotic ribosomes recognize the capped 5′ end of the messenger RNA and then slide down to the first AUG triplet to begin protein synthesis. These results have important consequences for attempts to synthesize eucaryotic proteins in bacteria and the reverse. For efficient synthesis of a eucaryotic protein in bacteria, the eucaryotic gene must be fused to bacterial RNA in such a way that the ribosome recognition sequence is positioned optimally with respect to the first AUG. Conversely, bacterial messages must be capped before they can be translated by eucaryotic ribosomes. Moreover, capping the first message in a bacterial RNA that codes for several proteins will allow synthesis of only the first protein. Because every eucaryotic message needs a cap, it follows that each will code for only one protein, and the method bacteria use to coordinate the regulation of neighboring genes—namely, their transcription into a single large RNA molecule—cannot be used by eucaryotes.

Viruses carry few capabilities of their own for synthesis and must depend on many of those of the bacterial and eucaryotic cells that they infect. If caps are required for protein synthesis in eucaryotes and if the machinery for producing caps is in the eucaryotic nucleus, how can viruses confined to the cytoplasm acquire caps for their own messages? Quite simply, they steal them. Studies of the transcription of influenza virus RNA in vitro showed that the viral messenger RNA, transcribed in this case from the RNA carried in the virus, contains a cap transferred from cellular messenger RNA. The experiments of Michele Bouloy and Robert Krug of the Sloan-Kettering Institute for Cancer Research in New York City used eucaryotic β-globin messenger RNA molecules whose caps were radioactively labeled. Their work revealed that 10–15 nucleotides in addition to the cap were cut from the β-globin RNA and used to initiate the viral messages.

333

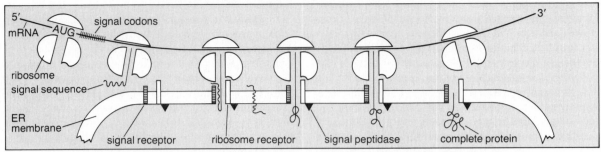

Adapted from "Newly Made Proteins Zip Through the Cell," Jean L. Marx, SCIENCE, vol. 207, no. 4427, pp. 164–167, January 11, 1980

According to the signal hypothesis, proteins destined for secretion by cells carry special amino-acid signal sequences that allow them to pass into an intracellular membrane system, the endoplasmic reticulum (ER), that functions in transporting proteins out of the cell. The messenger RNA (mRNA) coding for such a protein contains a string of codons for the signal sequence after its start codon (AUG). A ribosome synthesizing a protein from the mRNA first synthesizes this sequence, which attaches to a receptor site on the ER membrane. In addition, a second receptor on the membrane binds to the ribosome itself. The binding interactions are thought somehow to open a channel in the membrane for the protein to pass through to the interior space of the ER. During this passage the protein's signal sequence is cut off by the signal peptidase enzyme. Ultimately the entire protein passes into the ER.

Because the virus provides the enzyme that steals cellular caps, it may be reasonable to seek specific inhibitors of that enzyme activity as a basis for treatment of influenza infection.

Following description of some ways in which detailed comparison of RNA transcription and translation reveals striking differences between bacteria and eucaryotes, it seems appropriate to conclude with exciting new results on the synthesis of membrane and secreted proteins that emphasize instead the unity of cellular biochemistry. Over the past decade experiments in a number of laboratories, particularly that of Günter Blobel at the Rockefeller University in New York City, have indicated that proteins destined for secretion by cells contain special amino-acid sequences called signal sequences that are crucial for transport of the protein across the cellular membranes. For several proteins the signal was shown to be a peptide of 15–30 amino acids at the beginning of the protein chain. This "leader" peptide, believed to bind to specific receptor sites on cellular membranes while the protein was being made, functioned in the membrane transport necessary for secretion but was then unneeded. Indeed, an enzyme in the membrane cleaved the leader peptide from the rest of the protein during transport.

This model for protein secretion, called the signal hypothesis, was strongly supported last year by experiments on bacteria from the laboratory of Jonathan Beckwith at Harvard University Medical School. There, genetic engineering was used to fuse the gene that codes for the easily measured enzyme β-galactosidase to the beginning parts of genes that code for transported proteins. The enzyme indeed was found to be made with a leader sequence that was cleaved as a consequence of transport, but of greater significance was the observation that genes which failed to be transported possessed mutations lying exactly in the leader sequence. Thus the details of this model, which had been worked out in mammalian cells, were confirmed in bacteria.

—Robert Haselkorn

See also Feature Article: THE REMARKABLE CELL MEMBRANE.

Zoology

During the past year advances in developmental biology brought science closer to achieving a clone of a mammalian species. Neurobiologists investigated the capacity of nerves in the central nervous system to regenerate and found new mechanisms involved in animal navigation. Chemical perception in snakes, feeding behavior in whales, and adaptations of birds to high altitudes were studied, and analysis of meteorites uncovered the existence of amino acids of extraterrestrial origin.

Developmental zoology. During development cell communication may occur via interaction of the surface membranes of adjacent cells. For example, the membrane specialization found at the point where nerve cells and muscle cells meet is characterized by clusters of receptors for the neurotransmitter acetylcholine. Although these receptors are scattered over the muscle cell membrane, at nerve-muscle junction points ovoid clusters five to ten micrometers (a few ten-thousandths of an inch) across are found that increase the cell's sensitivity to acetylcholine a thousand-fold at a site adjacent to the nerve cell that releases the transmitter. If embryonic muscle cells are cultured in the absence of nerves, these clusters still develop and thus might be considered preformed sites on muscle cells for the formation of neuromuscular junctions. Recent evidence from the laboratories of Melvin Cohen at Yale University and Gerald D. Fischbach at Beth

Israel Hospital in Boston, however, indicate otherwise. When cultured embryonic muscle cells were exposed to pieces of living nervous tissue, neuromuscular junctions developed but not necessarily at the sites of the preformed clusters. In fact, these clusters subsequently disappeared, with their components apparently migrating to the site of nerve-muscle contact. Similar results were obtained when dead nerves were laid across developing muscle cells. Apparently, there is some factor in the nerve cell membrane that induces synthesis or migration of receptor sites in the muscle cell membrane.

The understanding of embryonic differentiation may be increased as the result of a line of investigation being pursued at the Max Planck Institute for Experimental Medicine, Göttingen, West Germany. Using the small free-living nematode *Caenorhabditis elegans*, Günter von Ehrenstein and Einhard Schierenberg worked out the complete developmental cell lineage from egg to hatching at the 550-cell stage—the first case of a completely documented developmental pattern. Additional aspects make this organism a useful model system: genetic crosses can be done, the life cycle is completed in only 3.5 days, and the gene content is small (an estimated 2,000 –4,000 genes). The

Göttingen group went on to characterize seven temperature-sensitive nematode mutants that alter embryonic development at elevated temperatures by inducing abnormalities of the timing of cell division and embryonic cell migration. Analysis of the nature of these mutants promises to yield new insights into the fundamental controls of development.

Apart from these basic discoveries in developmental biology, the most exciting reports described applied research directed ultimately toward cloning a mammalian species. Karl Illmensee of the University of Geneva announced that he was able first to transfer the nucleus from a mouse embryo cell into a recently fertilized egg of a second mouse and then to remove the nucleus of the recipient egg together with the nucleus of the sperm cell that fertilized it. This manipulated egg was transplanted into the uterus of a pseudopregnant surrogate mother, and a normal mouse was born with genetic traits that were solely the characteristics of the mouse strain from which the embryo-cell nucleus was taken. If and when experiments are done to determine if nuclei taken from adult mouse cells will also function similarly, the attempts can be called cloning in the full sense of the word.

Two other techniques for manipulating normal

More than 40 unusual footprints found in fossilized mud of an ancient lake bottom in Connecticut were interpreted as the first evidence of swimming by large carnivorous dinosaurs. Photos show central toe impressions and flanking claw streaks apparently made by the left and right feet of one dinosaur species (left and center) and by the left foot of a second, smaller species (right). Sketch at left reconstructs a hypothetical swimming posture for Megalosaurus, a dinosaur known to have lived in the region about 180 million years ago, when the tracks were made.

1 meter

(Top) Walter P. Coombs; (bottom) adapted from "Swimming Ability of Carnivorous Dinosaurs," W. P. Coombs, SCIENCE, vol. 207, no. 4436, pp. 1198–1199, March 14, 1980; art by Matthew Hyman

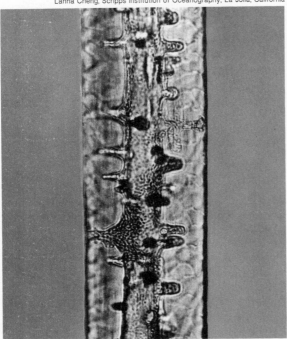

Lanna Cheng, Scripps Institution of Oceanography, La Jolla, California

Mystery of San Diego Zoo's green-tinted polar bears was solved when examination of their fur showed that green algae were living in the hollow cores of many of the coarse guard hairs of the bears' outer coat.

mammalian reproductive processes were also reported during the year. Peter Hoppe of Jackson Laboratory, Bar Harbor, Maine, developed a procedure for obtaining mice with genetic traits derived solely from one parent. Immediately after fertilization of a mouse egg, Hoppe removed the sperm nucleus from the egg and stimulated the remaining egg nucleus to duplicate its genetic material. The egg was then transplanted into a surrogate mother for development, and healthy mice were born. Because both sex chromosomes were derived from the maternal nucleus in this procedure, all offspring were female. Pierre Soupart of Vanderbilt University, Nashville, Tenn., reported yet another technique that yields a similar result. He was able to make two unfertilized mouse eggs fuse together using a special virus preparation. The resulting cell had the same chromosome count as an egg-sperm combination and underwent development to the 64-cell stage. Implantation in a surrogate mother was not attempted. These experiments indicate that there is nothing special that the sperm contributes to embryonic development other than chromosomes and a perturbation of the egg-cell membrane. All of these techniques have implications for animal husbandry as well as for the possibility of human cloning.

Neurobiology. In 1976 Soviet scientists L. A. Matinian and A. S. Andreasian reported that, if enzymes known to prevent scar formation were injected into the spinal cords of rats paralyzed by surgical sev-

ering of the spinal cord, nerve regeneration occurred, allowing the rats to walk again. Confirmation of these findings and clinical application would be a start toward helping millions of people who have suffered damage to the central nervous system. Recently, a group from the University of Maryland School of Medicine at Baltimore, led by Lloyd Guth, reported that these results seemed to be in error. When the Baltimore group cut the cords with a fine blade as had the Soviets, six out of eight rats healed and started to walk without enzyme treatment. Microscopic observation of these lesions indicated that some small nerves had not been cut. When the operating procedure was changed by first passing a surgical probe under the cord, cutting, and then lifting the probe through the cut to ensure that all fibers were severed, all 92 rats so handled remained paralyzed despite postoperative enzyme treatment. Guth and his team concluded that the recoveries seen by the Soviets were the result of incomplete surgical procedure and not enzyme therapy.

Other findings were reported, however, indicating that a clinical procedure for nerve regeneration may someday be possible. Katherine Kalil and Thomas Reh of the University of Wisconsin observed in baby hamsters that severed nerves in the pyramidal tract, which passes from the sensory-motor cortex of the brain to the brain stem, can regenerate in a functionally useful way. Similar encouragement may be drawn from the successful work of Richard J. Wyatt at the National Institute of Mental Health, Bethesda, Md., who grafted a functioning section of the brain of one rat onto the damaged brain of another. The idea of partial brain transplants is revolutionary, but apparently possible.

The sensitivity of animals to the Earth's magnetic field and its significance for orientation were being studied by Charles Walcott of the State University of New York, Stony Brook, and several other investigators. Several years ago, using small battery-powered wire coils attached to pigeons, Walcott varied the strength and direction of the magnetic field surrounding the bird's head during flight. When field polarity was reversed by switching battery connections, pigeons would fly in a direction 180° from the home roost, but only under cloudy conditions. Apparently, at least some species of birds can make use of both solar and magnetic compasses, depending on conditions. More recently similar observations of a magnetic sense were observed in honeybees by James Gould of Princeton University. Using a superconducting magnetometer, Gould found that the heads of honeybees contain magnetic particles of two types: single domain crystals of magnetite large enough to maintain their magnetic moments (memory) and crystals small enough to line up with an external magnetic field surrounding them (sensor). Though these are the necessary prerequisites of a magnetic homing system, it is not clear how the generated information is read by the bee. Walcott and

X-ray of female brown kiwi taken 15 hours before egg laying reveals the enormous disproportion between egg size and body size. Recent studies by U.S. and New Zealand scientists explored some of the evolutionary factors influencing egg size and the reproductive advantages of an oversized egg.

Gould collaborated to locate the magnetic sensor in pigeons. In preliminary studies a one-millimeter (0.04-in) piece of tissue on one side of the bird's head behind the eye was identified as containing magnetite crystals. In 1980 research was being conducted to determine how this tissue functions to provide information for navigation, if indeed it does. (*See also* PHYSICS: *General developments.*)

Organismal zoology. Bruce Means of the Tall Timbers Research Station in Tallahassee, Fla., developed a tracking technique involving radiotelemetry to follow movements of the eastern diamondback rattlesnake. A paraffin-coated radiotransmitter, which is force-fed to the snakes, is retained as long as one year in the digestive tract. Means found that rattlesnakes have a keen sense of navigation, ranging as far as a mile away from a home tree stump to which they return year after year. They do not feed often and in the wild can live as long as 12 months on fat reserves.

A rodent bitten by a rattlesnake often scurries off to die at a distance from the encounter. Several minutes after striking, the snake follows the precise path of the envenomed prey and will cross fresher paths of other rodents to get its particular meal. Kent M. Scudder and David Chiszar of the University of Colorado reported that subsequent tracking of prey involves tongue-flicking behavior with the tongue picking up chemical clues and transferring them to a vomeronasal organ in the roof of the mouth. (The vomer is a skull bone between the nose and the mouth.) Gordon Burghardt of the University of Tennessee noted that if the opening to this organ in the snake's mouth is sutured closed or if the nerves leading from it are cut, tracking behavior stops. Interestingly, blockage of the vomeronasal sys-

tem also abolishes courtship behavior in snakes. This discovery correlates with knowledge of vomeronasal organ function in rodents, where it is involved in the receipt of sexual information by means of chemical attractants.

An ingenious feeding behavior was observed among humpback whales by Chuck Juarasz of Glacier Bay, Alaska. The krill and small fish that are staples of these whales' diets are usually dispersed in the ocean as in a very thin soup. If a volume of water—say, 30 m (100 ft) across in its horizontal dimension—is surrounded by bubbles rising from the ocean floor, krill have a tendency to move away from the bubbles toward the center. Taking advantage of this behavioral phenomenon, a feeding humpback whale will swim upward in a slow spiral from about 15 m (50 ft) below the surface, emitting air through its blowhole. The angle of the spiral is such that the bubbles and the whale reach the surface simultaneously. Surfacing in the center with its mouth open, the whale reaps the benefits of this krill-concentrating mechanism.

Zoologists are constantly being amazed by adaptations that organisms have made to their environments. One long-standing question is how birds can survive and function at altitudes that are harmful to other species. Barbara R. Grubb in Knut Schmidt-Nielsen's laboratory at Duke University, Durham, N.C., made some observations pertinent to this question. At high altitudes birds and mammals breathe more rapidly than normal (hyperventilate), which results in two things: more oxygen is brought into the lungs, and carbon dioxide is expelled in large quantities from the blood. The loss of carbon dioxide affects blood chemistry by making it more alkaline, which in turn leads to

Adapted from "A unique form of locomotion in a stomatopod—backward somersaulting," Roy L. Caldwell, NATURE, vol. 282, pp. 71–73, November 1, 1979

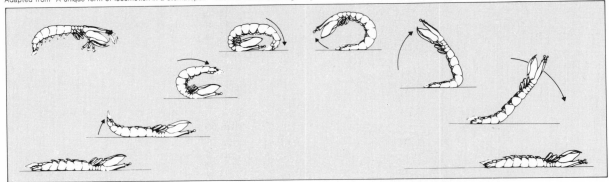

A unique form of locomotion — backward somersaulting — was discovered to be a life-saving tactic of the marine stomatopod Nannosquilla decemspinosa *when it finds itself exposed on the beach at low tide. The two-centimeter-long crustacean rolls onto its back, flexes its tail over its body and onto the sand in front of its head, and rolls forward to complete the flip, often repeating the process 20–40 times.*

blood vessel constriction. This latter condition reduces blood supply to the brain, and brain cells can become oxygen deficient and die.

Grubb found in ducks under hyperventilation conditions that blood flow to the brain remained close to the rate observed during normal breathing. In mammals, under similar conditions, blood flow to the brain would have been reduced 50–75% of normal, with impairment of brain function. Clearly, birds have some mechanism that prevents blood vessel constriction in response to low carbon dioxide levels, and it is this mechanism that allows high-altitude survival. More recently Grubb was trying to determine if the proportionately larger hearts of birds may be an adaptation to the lower oxygen concentration at high altitudes in that it allows more oxygen to be transported to the tissues.

Hookworm, trachoma, schistosomiasis, malaria, and filariasis are parasitic diseases estimated to infect at least 500 million people in the world, primarily in less developed tropical countries, according to Barry R. Bloom of the Albert Einstein College of Medicine in New York City. Development of livestock programs in these countries is also retarded by other parasitic dis-

eases. There has been a resurgence of interest in controlling these diseases ecologically, chemotherapeutically, or immunologically. The World Bank urged that health programs be coupled to economic programs that it funds in less developed countries. Science, however, must provide more information before the problem can be solved.

At a recent conference in West Germany sponsored by the World Health Organization, membrane biology was identified as a major common denominator for all parasitic diseases. Studies of parasitic membranes are relevant to the modes of action of antiparasitic drugs, and membrane-bound antigens (molecules that stimulate the body's immune defenses) may be of particular importance in the development of new diagnostic techniques and immunization measures. Such intracellular parasites as those which cause malaria also interact with the host-cell membrane during movement into and out of the cell, and African trypanosomes, which cause sleeping sickness, are known to have the capacity for extensive variation of chemical structure and antigenic characteristics of their surface membranes. Schistosomes, a kind of flatworm, are most remarkable,

Male scorpionfly Hylobittacus apicalis (on left) copulates with female after engaging in a mating ritual that includes providing her with captured prey (in this case, a blowfly). Biologists recently noted that some males mimic female behavior in the presence of other males in order to steal nuptial prey for their own use. Such transvestite males copulate more frequently and avoid some of the risks involved in catching their own nuptial prey.

having the ability to incorporate into their own surface membranes a variety of host membrane components, including blood-group components and histocompatibility antigens, and thus mask their own antigens by mimicry. Control of parasitic diseases may well depend on understanding these membrane phenomena.

Environmental zoology. For 45 years it was thought that there were two species of North Atlantic eels distinguished only by two characteristics: one is found in North American streams and has 107 vertebrae, and the other lives in European streams and has 115 vertebrae. Both are migratory and are thought to spawn in the Sargasso Sea, where the eggs develop into larvae, which drift for about two years prior to their metamorphosis into elvers. The elvers then swim up rivers into freshwater, where they grow to adults before returning to the sea to spawn and die. About 20 years ago the two-species concept was challenged by the British biologist Denys Tucker, who contended that there was only one species and that drift patterns of larvae resulted in growth differences and different times for metamorphosis, which would explain the differences in numbers of vertebrae. Depending on where the larvae drifted, they were attracted to freshwater rivers either in Europe or America. To date, genetic and biochemical studies of proteins have found no conclusive evidence that there are two species; thus the Tucker hypothesis could be correct. Determining whether there are two distinct breeding populations or one mixed population is important to managing this fishery, which amounts to $20–30 million annually worldwide. West Germany made two research ships available in 1979 to work on this problem. Larvae were collected at various locations and growth analyzed, larval drift patterns were studied, and attempts were made to track adult eels and elvers during migration. In the near future these efforts should provide sufficient data to solve the "old eel problem."

The British Antarctic Survey was undertaking studies of the adaptation strategies that polar organisms use in combating the challenge of wide temperature ranges with long periods of subfreezing temperatures. The mite *Alaskozetes antarcticus* is an important component of a sparse collection of Antarctic terrestrial invertebrates. Freezing is lethal to all life stages of this mite, yet obviously it survives. Investigators found that this mite can withstand a body temperature of −26° C (−15° F) by synthesizing and retaining glycerol in its body fluids, especially in the juvenile stages. In the range 0°–10° C (32°–50° F) *Alaskozetes* can also maintain a metabolic rate two to three times greater than that of mites from temperate zones. The life cycle takes two to three years, and the ability to avoid freezing along with the elevated metabolic rate allows mixed populations of instars (stages between molts) to survive the polar winter and to use the short summer period for growth and reproduction.

For many endangered species, loss of habitat by conversion from a natural ecosystem into a man-made environment is the primary force threatening survival. One prime example was thought to be found in the case of the snail darter and the Tellico Dam in the U.S. Under provisions of the 1973 Endangered Species Act, completion of this Tennessee dam had been delayed for several years on the grounds that it would destroy the sole river habitat of an endangered fish. In 1979 political pressure finally succeeded in restarting dam construction, but it seemed that the snail darter may still have a chance as a species. Some 2,000 transplanted snail darters appeared to be thriving in a new location in another Tennessee river.

Large mammals, though subject to the hardships of habitat loss, are in the most danger from humans because of direct killing. The World Wildlife Fund (WWF) indicated that rhinoceros numbers are dwindling fast primarily because of poaching. Of five species only 20,000–30,000 individuals are thought to exist in the world. In some African reserves poaching has reached one animal per day. This devastating slaughter caused the WWF to postpone its project to save the elephant and to devote immediate attention to rhino conservation. The rhino is sought by poachers for its horn, which is sold in the Middle East as dagger handles and in the Far East as a medicine.

Chance mating of a male gibbon and a female siamang produced a hybrid offspring termed a siabon. Studies of its chromosomes provided clues as to how species of lesser apes diversified.

Sister Moore, Atlanta, Georgia

Whales continue to be hunted and numbers are shrinking, but two important protective measures were adopted at the most recent meeting of the International Whaling Commission: the number of operating factory ships, which process whale carcasses at sea, was limited, and a whale sanctuary was established in the Indian Ocean in an area of 40 million square miles. Perhaps these developments and reduced quotas will result in increased whale populations and lessen the grave danger of their extinction.

Evolutionary zoology. Usually evolutionary zoologists study mineralized remains of animals that lived in the past. In 1977, however, an unusual find was made in Siberia; an intact 90-kg (200-lb) juvenile woolly mammoth was discovered encased in ice by a gold miner. The specimen was kept frozen by Soviet scientists and anatomical observations were made. Recently, tissue samples were given to Allan Wilson at the University of California at Berkeley and Morris Goodman at Wayne State University, Detroit, Mich., for biochemical and electron microscopic analyses. Rarely do scientists get a chance to work with protein samples from tissue believed to be 27,000–44,000 years old. Although they were able to study the amino-acid sequences of collagen and albumen isolated from the tissue, neither investigator succeeded in isolating from the tissue the molecule about which paleo-biochemists dream, DNA. If intact DNA or genes could be obtained, the molecules could be cloned with modern laboratory techniques and proteins synthesized, thus allowing a comparison of modern gene function with genes that were active long ago.

Understanding of chemical evolution was increased, however, by a discovery of Cyril Ponnamperuma of the University of Maryland. He examined a meteorite recovered from Antarctica for possible signs of organic material. His analyses showed that both the interior and exterior of the meteorite contained amino acids. Furthermore, the amino acids were a mixture of both left-handed and righ-handed isomers; "handedness" in this sense relates to the ability of solutions of these molecules to bend polarized light to either the left or right. Their extraterrestrial, nonbiological origin is confirmed by this observation because biological systems on Earth contain only left-handed forms of the amino acids.

Ponnamperuma's discovery indicates that prebiotic reactions which produce some compounds necessary for life occur elsewhere than on the Earth and also offers evidence for chemical evolution in the universe. It consequently bears on studies concerning the origin of life on Earth and on estimates of the chances of extraterrestrial life being found.

—Warren D. Dolphin

See also Feature Articles: PRIMATE INTELLIGENCE; LIFE IN THE JUNGLE CANOPY; BIOLOGICAL PEST CONTROL.

Materials sciences

During the year materials engineers demonstrated that ceramics could survive the heat and rotational stresses of an operating engine and could also safely contain high-temperature radioactive wastes. Metallurgists sought to prevent the problems caused by particles of alumina incorporated into steel during deoxidation.

Ceramics

The use of ceramics for the fabrication of blades and other turbine components has been a goal of the materials engineering community since the introduction of the aircraft turbine engine in the early 1940s. Ceramic components can withstand much higher temperatures than the metallic superalloys currently used for such purposes, and ceramic parts can operate without the cooling air requirements that significantly reduce the efficiency of all-metal engines. Several attempts to use oxide ceramics or mixtures of ceramics and metals, called cermets, have failed. However, the

Stress test is performed on fiberglass mesh impregnated with polyester resin. The material is soft and sticky at first but becomes tough and rigid from the Sun's rays. It may be used in the space program.

Hughes Aircraft Co.

first phase of the most recent assault on this problem, the use of non-oxide ceramics such as silicon nitride or silicon carbide, reached a major milestone during the past year.

The program of the U.S. Defense Advanced Research Projects Agency, conducted by the Garrett Corp., showed that a ceramic-bladed rotor, consisting of hot pressed silicon nitride blades attached to a central metal disk, could survive the full temperatures and rotational speeds of a real operating engine. This feat represented a significant advance for the ceramic industry. The failure of other ceramic components in these engine tests, however, showed that many engineering difficulties remain in the design and construction of complex, multistage engines. In view of the progress already made and the 25% to 55% increase in efficiency that could be achieved by increasing turbine temperatures with the use of uncooled ceramics, the U.S. Department of Energy initiated two new industrial programs for the development and demonstration of advanced gas turbine engines for automotive use.

While silicon nitride was the principal ceramic considered for most turbine and diesel engine applications, several developments during the past year could provide other important future options. The Carborundum Co. opened a major new facility for the production of sintered silicon carbide components. Advances in silicon carbide hardware included valve lifters that operated successfully in a racing-car engine during 3,000 mi of competition. Sintered silicon carbide was also under evaluation for turbocharger rotors, pushrods, precombustion chambers, pistons, piston caps, cylinder liners, and exhaust components.

The General Electric Co. reported progress in its effort, supported by the U.S. Air Force, to design a ceramic turbine rotor with blades that would be loaded principally in compression rather than tension. This would be accomplished by containing the ceramic blades within a cooled, circumferentially wrapped composite hoop. If such a design could be refined enough to compete in level of efficiency with a conventionally bladed rotor, the likelihood of silicon nitride and perhaps other ceramic materials succeeding in the turbine environment might be substantially improved.

In an outgrowth of the impressive performance of carbon-carbon composites in reentry vehicle nosetip and rocket nozzle applications, several engine companies experimented with them as major new materials of construction for turbine engine components. These graphite-fiber reinforced composites are extremely light and temperature-resistant. Furthermore, they do not appear to suffer from extreme sensitivity to flaws and the brittleness characteristic of conventional ceramics. They do, however, have oxidation problems. But if satisfactory protective coatings, reinforcement designs, and fabrication techniques can be developed, these composites could have a bright future as ul-

Courtesy, Corning Glass Works

Cross sections of ceramic supports for catalysts reveal varying cell densities. Such ceramic "honeycombs" are used to improve the efficiency of catalytic converters in automobile engines.

trahigh-temperature turbine engine components.

Although U.S. construction of new nuclear power plants may well be slowed by the accident at the Three Mile Island reactor in 1979, many other countries were expanding their nuclear facilities. France expected to generate half its electricity in nuclear plants within the next six years, and the U.K. was planning five new nuclear plants within the next decade. However, the safe disposal of nuclear wastes from such plants remained an important concern. These wastes cannot be released into the atmosphere and, depending on their radioactive half-lives, must be stored for periods up to 10,000 years. Ceramic glasses and ceramic canisters received increased attention as favored means of immobilizing these potentially dangerous materials.

The incorporation of radioactive waste elements into specially formulated, stable glasses effectively minimizes the risk of their accidental release. France, the U.K., and Canada have already stored such glasses under real underground burial conditions for almost 20 years to test their stability, and France built the world's first production-scale facility for the conversion of nuclear wastes into these storable glasses. Despite the relative inertness of the glasses most storage schemes

341

call for them to be securely sealed within specially designed containers. Radioactive waste masses that produce low heat can be stored simply in cement or concrete canisters. More intense, higher-temperature waste would have to be stored in impervious, much more heat-resistant canister materials. Dense alumina (Al_2O_3) capsules for this purpose were recently developed by a Swedish firm.

Many portable or mobile systems, including the electric car, depend for an energy source on the availability of high-energy density batteries (those that can store large amounts of energy in a small, lightweight unit). Although lithium-sulfur dioxide and lithium-thionyl chloride batteries have great potential for these applications, their development has been slowed by the possibility of explosive reactions when they are damaged or contaminated. The Altus Corp. in Palo Alto, Calif., recently announced its development of ceramic seals that reliably withstand erosion from the lithium battery's reactants and that also protect it from external damage and contamination. The cells with such seals have apparently demonstrated excellent shelf life, resistance to severe impact, and the ability to withstand internal and external short circuits and intensive heating.

The conversion of solar energy to electrical or chemical energy is an important potential solution to the world's shrinking supply of oil. The possibility of forming fuels photochemically from plentiful supplies of water, nitrogen, oxygen, and carbon dioxide is attractive. In this regard the conversion of solar energy to electricity or fuel by reduction-oxidation events at the junction between a semiconductor and a liquid electrolyte solution was receiving increased attention. The semiconductor/liquid cell has inherent advantages: the junction is easy to form, and the cell appears to work almost as efficiently with inexpensive polycrystalline semiconductors as it does with single crystals. An exciting potential use for these cells would be the direct photoelectrolysis of water to form hydrogen for use as a fuel. The most efficient such cell under investigation in 1980 utilized ceramic strontium titanate, $SrTiO_3$, as the photoelectrode. An active search for still more efficient ceramic photoelectrodes and for other photoelectrochemical reactions that could yield useful fuels was under way.

The U.S. space shuttle, scheduled for its first launch in 1980, suffered several delays during the past year. One of these resulted from difficulties with ceramic thermal protection tile. Consequently, the Lockheed Missiles and Space Co. was speeding development of a second-generation ceramic thermal protection material called fibrous refractory composite insulation (FRCI). The new material incorporates 20% of 3M Company's "Nextel," a high-strength, large-diameter aluminoborosilicate fiber in a matrix of the pure silica (SiO_2) fibers previously used. In addition to its direct strengthening of the fibrous insulation, the Nextel apparently contributes a minute amount of boron that helps to fuse together the high-purity silica fibers. The resultant insulation is stronger, tougher, and somewhat more temperature-resistant than the current tile material. If current qualification tests are successful, FRCI tiles may be used on the second flight orbiter. The Nextel fiber itself can withstand prolonged exposure to 1,400° C (2,600° F), and promises to be an attractive substitute for asbestos because it is also strong, abrasion-resistant, flexible, and capable of being woven into cloth or tape.

Several other new materials appeared recently. One

Ceramic thermal protection tiles are applied to the body flap of the U.S. spacecraft shuttle Orbiter 2. They will protect the craft from the intense heat it will encounter when reentering the Earth's atmosphere from space.

Courtesy, NASA

of the most interesting involved the formation of cubic boron nitride on a metallic substrate by the reactive evaporation of an alloy, containing principally boron, in the presence of ammonia gas. Cubic boron nitride is one of the hardest materials known and is an excellent cutting tool, but until now it has been prepared only by extremely high-pressure processing techniques and has been very expensive.

The new process, developed by the Battelle Columbus Laboratories, utilizes alloying additions that may serve as nucleating agents for the cubic boron nitride phase and as barriers to the transformation from the cubic form to the hexagonal form, which is normally more stable at typical use temperatures. The Battelle process also uses relatively low-temperature deposition to build in growth stresses that may help stabilize the cubic structure and avoid elevated temperatures that might favor reversion to the hexagonal form. In 1980 the process was still at an early stage of development, and much remained to be done before useful cubic boron nitride products could be expected from it. For example, initial deposits contained only about 20% of the desired cubic boron nitride phase, the remainder being iron boride and hexagonal boron nitride. It would be desirable for the material to be at least 90% cubic boron nitride.

The United Technologies Research Center (UTRC) had developed graphite fiber-reinforced glass matrix composites that can be used up to approximately 600° C (1,100° F), but are subject to degradation by fiber oxidation at elevated temperatures. UTRC recently demonstrated that the use of silicon carbide fibers to reinforce the glass matrix could achieve for these composites both good mechanical properties and good high-temperature stability. At the year's end UTRC was studying new glass and glass-ceramic matrices that might allow use of the composites at temperatures of 1,000° C (1,800° F) or more.

—Norman M. Tallan

Metallurgy

Steelmaking processes involve the selective oxidation of impurity elements from liquid iron, with the major impurity, carbon, being oxidized to form gaseous carbon monoxide. The other impurities, upon oxidation, are transferred from the liquid iron to the steelmaking slag. Consequently, when the desired composition for the steel has been reached by means of these selective oxidation processes, the steel contains a higher-than-desirable concentration of dissolved oxygen. The removal of this oxygen, after separation of the steelmaking slag and before solidification of the steel, is achieved by deoxidation.

The most commonly used deoxidizing agent is aluminum, which has a greater chemical affinity for oxygen than does iron and therefore reacts with the dissolved oxygen to form solid alumina (Al_2O_3). Particles of alumina subsequently incorporated in the solid steel are known as inclusions. With the increased production of continuously cast steel and because of the particular problems caused by the formation of alumina as the product of deoxidation, it has become increasingly important that steelmakers obtain an understanding of deoxidation. Toward this end an experimental study of the formation of alumina inclusions in steel was conducted.

The experiments were designed to examine the influence on alumina inclusions of such variables as the time and rate of stirring of the metal after addition of the aluminum, and the initial concentration of oxygen in the metal. The metal used was an iron-nickel alloy containing 10% by weight of nickel and between 100 and 500 parts per million (ppm) of dissolved oxygen, to which was added 0.1% by weight of aluminum.

After deoxidation under controlled conditions the metal was frozen to form cylindrical ingots, which were then sectioned both horizontally and vertically. The distributions of the inclusions and clusters of inclusions were determined by light microscopy of metallographically polished sections. After "excavating" individual inclusions and clusters by chemical dissolution of the surrounding metal, the configurations of the inclusions were determined by scanning electron microscopy (which provides a three-dimensional view of small objects).

The observed distribution of the inclusions required the classification of two types of regions: those containing clusters of inclusions and those, which made up most of the volume of the ingots, that did not contain clusters. The clusters were normally observed at the top surface of the ingot and at the outer edges of the ingot where the liquid steel had been in contact with the alumina crucible. Of particular interest was the wide variation in the morphologies of the inclusions. Five types were identified: dendritic (treelike), faceted (three-dimensional with well-formed flat faces corresponding to crystallographic planes), thin plates, spheres, and clusters (large agglomerates of individual faceted or dendritic inclusions).

It was found that the holding time, *i.e.*, the time elapsing between the addition of the aluminum to the liquid metal and the freezing of the melt, had a pronounced effect on the morphology and composition of the inclusions and also on the formation of the clusters of inclusions. In essentially stagnant melts with an initial oxygen content of 200 ppm no clusters were formed with holding times of less than two seconds, and small clusters, few in number and located exclusively at the top surface of the ingot, were formed in five to ten seconds. At longer holding times these clusters increased in size and began to appear adjacent to the crucible wall. The number of inclusions on the top surface increased from 0.015 per sq mm after a hold-

343

An amorphous metal ribbon is produced by ejecting a molten iron-nickel-boron alloy onto a spinning cold copper wheel. For use in electrical equipment amorphous metals promise efficiency and low cost.

ing time of five seconds to 0.51 per sq mm after 16 minutes, and the corresponding coverage of the top surface by clusters increased from 0.033% to 6.78%. The mean size of the clusters followed a similar trend, increasing from 0.01 sq mm after ten seconds to greater than 0.1 sq mm after two minutes of holding time. All three of these parameters began to decrease with longer holding times, and massive clusters (those greater in area than one square millimeter) were only found after intermediate holding times. The number of inclusions per square millimeter in the clusters increased rapidly to 18,300 after 30 seconds and then slowly decreased to 8,400 after 60 minutes.

It was found that the behavior of the inclusions in the "nonclustered" regions was quite different. The mean volume percentage of inclusions remained constant until ten seconds of holding time, after which it rapidly decreased to zero, and the predominant morphology was found to vary with holding time. Faceted inclusions were only found with holding times of 60 seconds or less; dendritic inclusions were only found with holding times of 30 seconds or less; platelike inclusions with holding times of 2 seconds or less; and spherical inclusions only with holding times of less

than one second. Although silica and iron aluminosilicate inclusions were found with holding times of less than one second, all the inclusions occurring at greater holding times were alumina.

The influence of stirring was observed by varying the power input to the inductively heated melt (which varied the extent of induction stirring of the melt) and by mechanical stirring of the melt by means of an alumina rod. Both induction and mechanical stirring were found to influence the formation of clusters; induction stirring influenced the extent to which the clustering process progressed, and mechanical stirring influenced the size and location of the clusters. Variation in the time of stirring influenced the extent of removal of the clusters. An increase in the stirring rate caused rapid increases in both the percentage of the area at the top of the ingot covered by clusters and the number of clusters per unit area. At intermediate rates of mechanical stirring a number of massive clusters were found, although no such clusters were found at either low or high rates of mechanical stirring. In induction-stirred melts the percentage by volume of inclusions and the number of inclusions per square millimeter in the nonclustered regions decreased from 0.11% and 1,400, respectively, with no stirring to values too small to be measured at high rates of induction stirring. In contrast, variation in the rate of mechanical stirring had little effect on the volume percentage of inclusions in the nonclustered regions.

Variation in the intial concentration of dissolved oxygen had a pronounced effect on the morphology of the inclusions. It was found that the inclusions in the clusters were dendritic and platelike in melts of low initial oxygen content and were spherical in melts of high initial oxygen content. Faceted inclusions occurred in the nonclustered regions of all ingots, with the number of these inclusions decreasing with increasing initial oxygen content. Although the number of clusters per unit area at the upper surface of the ingot was relatively independent of the initial oxygen content, the percentage of the top surface occupied by clusters increased with increasing initial oxygen content to a maximum of 7.9 at 300 ppm oxygen; however, the percentage decreased with further increases in the initial oxygen content.

The results of this study showed that stirring of the melt is the major factor influencing the formation of alumina clusters. The number of clusters formed increases with increased stirring rate, and the very large number of small clusters located near the crucible walls in rapidly stirred melts indicates that high stirring rates can cause the mechanical breakup of clusters. Within ten seconds of holding time in stagnant melts the inclusions are randomly distributed throughout the melt; if the melt has an initial oxygen content of less than 200 ppm, these inclusions are predominantly dendritic with the dendrite branches radiating

344

from a central origin. Because a dendritic inclusion has a much larger collision cross-sectional area than has a single spherical inclusion of the same mass, the number of collisions between dendritic inclusions per unit time in stirred melts is much greater than that between spherical particles. Alumina is not wetted by liquid iron, and so a collision between two inclusions will cause them to stick to one another. Sintering of the compact then begins. (Sintering is a diffusion-controlled process in which the system attempts to minimize its energy by minimizing the ratio of its surface area to volume.)

With a holding time of less than one minute the number of inclusions per unit area in the clusters increases with time because the rate at which inclusions are added to the clusters by collision with them is greater than the rate of growth of the individual inclusions. A further factor in the evolution of the inclusions is the influence of the radius of curvature on the surface energy of the inclusion and, thus, on the solubility of alumina in the metal. This effect is such that, within a cluster, inclusions of smaller radius of curvature will redissolve while those of larger radius of curvature will grow. Calculations indicated that an inclusion with an initial radius of curvature of 0.15×10^{-4} cm which is completely surrounded by inclusions of radius of curvature 0.3×10^{-4} cm can completely dissolve in less than ten seconds.

Once formed, the clusters either rise to the surface of the melt under the influence of the buoyancy force caused by the difference between the densities of alumina and liquid iron, or they collide with and adhere to the walls of the alumina crucible. This characteristic of sticking and sintering is the cause of the major problem encountered in the continuous casting of deoxidized steel. Unless the liquid steel being poured into the tundish (the reservoir that feeds metal to the nozzles of the casting strands) has been thoroughly stirred, the melt will contain a large number of alumina particles. As the melt flows through the nozzle, the predominantly dendritic inclusions will collide with and stick to the nozzle, thus providing sites for the entrapment of particles passing into the nozzle. The addition of more particles to the clusters eventually causes the formation of a bridge across the entire nozzle and blocks the flow of metal to the casting strands.

—David R. Gaskell

Mathematics

Without question the most noteworthy accomplishment in the mathematical sciences during the past year was the announcement that a previously unknown Soviet mathematician had discovered a revolutionary way to solve one of science and industry's most common and vexing problems, linear programming.

News of the accomplishment spread quietly among European and U.S. scientists during the summer, and reached a crescendo of public notice with announcements in October and November on the pages of *Science News*, *Science*, and, shortly thereafter, the *New York Times*. It is rare indeed for the *Times* to take notice of a mathematical discovery, but the importance of this new procedure seems to warrant unprecedented attention.

The story began a decade earlier when the Soviet mathematician N. Z. Shor published in the journal *Kibernetika* a new algorithm (step-by-step procedure) for determining the minimum value of a function in a certain type of problem. Shor's novel method used multidimensional ellipses (called ellipsoids) to control the path of descent to the minimum value. Yet his idea lay fallow for nearly a decade.

Shor's algorithm was noticed about two years ago by Leonid Genrikhovich Khachian, a 25-year-old theoretical mathematician working for the computer center of the Soviet Academy of Sciences in Moscow. Khachian recognized that Shor's strategy could be applied to an important class of mathematical problems, the so-called linear programming problems, in a way that improved on established methods of solution. He adapted Shor's algorithm to this purpose and discovered that it worked remarkably well; not only did it provide a computational alternative to existing methods, but also in certain important cases it reached a solution much faster than any other method. His paper on this topic was submitted for publication in October 1978, and it appeared in outline form in the May 1979 issue of *Doklady*, the proceedings of the Soviet Academy of Sciences.

News of the Khachian paper reached Stanford (Calif.) University during the summer, where it attracted the interest of visiting Hungarian mathematicians Laslo Lovasz of the University of Szeged in Hungary and Peter Gacs of the University of Rochester (N.Y.). Gacs and Lovasz reconstructed the theory behind Khachian's proofs from the outline that appeared in *Doklady* and circulated it among colleagues in a simple typed form. It was this version that enabled the news to spread quickly among the U.S. research community; indeed, for nearly six months the informal Gacs and Lovasz treatment was the only available English-language version of the algorithm.

Linear programming is perhaps the most important mathematical technique in use today, at least if importance is judged by any economic or utilitarian measure. By some estimates nearly one-fourth of the scientific computation time of all the computers in the world is devoted to solving linear programming problems. Efficient solutions to these problems can save industry millions of dollars each month and can make enormous differences in the functioning of the national economy. Modern economics and management science

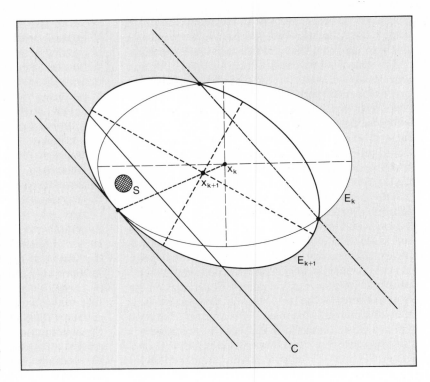

Converging ellipsoids illustrate Shor-Khachian's algorithm for linear programming. A sequence of ellipsoids E_k centered at x_k eventually converge to a solution in the set S. If x_k lies on the wrong side of linear constraint line C, a new ellipsoid E_{k+1} is constructed so that its center X_{k+1} is closer to C than was X_k and so that it encloses half of E_k as well as S.

depend almost totally on everyday solutions to linear programming problems.

As its name implies, linear programming deals with "linear" problems—those in which changes in scale of the data are reflected by corresponding changes in scale of the solution. Such models describe many economic situations, such as one in which the production of twice as much of a product requires twice as much raw material. The general linear programming problem is to optimize—that is, to maximize or to minimize—some desired outcome subject to a variety of linear constraints. Thus, managers need to maximize profits or to minimize costs, and economists wish to minimize unemployment or to maximize productivity; these goals and others can be achieved with greatest efficiency by following the dictates of the solution to an appropriate linear programming problem.

But solving these problems is no easy matter. Often the constraints number in the hundreds or even thousands, with as many or more variables. The first reasonable method of solving these problems—indeed, the only known way until Shor and Khachian did their work—was devised during World War II in an attempt to resolve the logistical problems of maintaining steady supplies to distant troops subject to the constraints of wartime scarcities. This solution was devised by George Dantzig, now of Stanford University, and published for public use shortly after the end of the war.

Dantzig's algorithm is conceptually simple. One begins by visualizing the constraints as outlining a complicated polyhedron. (That the faces of the polyhedron

are flat rather than curved is due to the linearity of the constraint equations.) All points on this enormous polyhedron, called a simplex by geometers, are candidates for the solution; they comprise the feasible options. To find the best of these feasible points, Dantzig's method relies on two key ideas: that the optimal point —the solution—must be one of the vertices of the simplex, and that the sure way to find it is to climb steadily uphill (or downhill) along the edges. At each vertex Dantzig's algorithm picks the route of steepest slope that leads in the direction of the solution: uphill for a maximum, or downhill for a minimum. Eventually it will find the answer.

But eventually is often not soon enough. It is not at all uncommon for applications of this "simplex algorithm" to take several days, even on today's high-speed computers. Indeed, in 1972 it was shown that some linear programming problems are so complex that as the number of constraints gradually increases the time required for the simplex algorithm to solve the problem grows exponentially. This discovery made linear programming appear to be what computer scientists now call a "hard" problem, because computers cannot realistically cope with problems that have solution times that increase exponentially.

Fortunately, the typical linear programming problem does not present such difficulties, and the simplex algorithm usually produces a solution to it in a reasonable amount of time. But that it sometimes fails is a significant flaw that many researchers hoped to overcome. Moreover, the recent realization that some problems are inherently beyond the reach of any computer solution motivated much research into the distinction between "hard" and "easy" problems. The latter, while not actually easy, are those with solution times that grow slowly (that is, polynomially) rather than exponentially. Dantzig's simplex algorithm made linear programming appear to be a "hard" problem and in that sense was described as a "hard" algorithm, but no one knew if there were any other algorithms for linear programming that might be "easy."

Khachian's genius was that he recognized that Shor's algorithm could provide an "easy" solution to linear programming problems. This perception was all the more remarkable given the enormous resources that had been expended in linear programming for more than one-third of a century. Even though numerous variations on the simplex algorithm were devised, they all shared the fundamental property of following the edges of the simplex and moving uphill or downhill to the solution. Many who worked on the "hard" vs. "easy" problems became convinced that the simplex strategy of inexorable progress toward the goal was unnecessarily stupid and that no algorithm could hope to provide an "easy" solution if it were not sufficiently smart to occasionally sacrifice by moving away from its goal in return for greater benefits in future steps.

The problem is in many ways like that facing a mountain climber. Without any maps the climber might spend many days climbing uphill only to discover that he really was scaling just a minor peak. Far better would be the vision provided by a map (or an aerial view) that would permit the climber to find a path down into a valley from which the major ascent can begin. Foresight, intelligence, or good luck are needed to find the most efficient route to the top; blind perseverance in walking consistently uphill will frequently prove fruitless.

Shor's algorithm does not have this handicap. It uses a series of multidimensional ellipsoids to encircle the solution and gradually converge to it. The approximations to the solution, provided by the centers of the ellipses, sometimes move away from and sometimes move toward the solution. But Khachian was able to show that the approximations provided by Shor's algorithm always will converge to the solution and that the time required for this convergence grows polynomially rather than exponentially as the number of constraints or variables increases. Thus in one step Khachian proved that linear programming is not really a "hard" problem as the simplex algorithm sometimes made it appear, and he provided an alternative computation that can be used in those cases when the simplex algorithm proves too slow.

The Shor-Khachian algorithm is remarkably simple. When the ellipsoids are expressed in matrix notation, the entire algorithm can be expressed in just two formulas that can be understood and calculated by any college sophomore science or engineering student. Indeed, the algorithm has even been programmed into a hand-held calculator. However, the task of providing a computer program that will work efficiently on the large linear programming problems typical of industrial and government applications is far from solved. The need to calculate matrix inverses in the Shor-Khachian algorithm introduces roundoff error at an alarming rate, and it is entirely possible that the intrinsic computer error will grow more rapidly than the algorithm will converge, yielding nothing but nonsense in the end. It will take finesse and patience to overcome these difficulties, and by early 1980 hundreds of research groups were working on this aspect of the problem.

According to William F. Lucas of Cornell University, Ithaca, N.Y., the Shor-Khachian algorithm will probably in a short time provide significant computational improvement for a certain class of linear programming problems, but will not replace the simplex method for the ordinary problems that it handles well. But perhaps more important is the possibility that the ideas behind this algorithm will provide breakthroughs in other related problems. Integer programming, for instance, is a common variety in which the data and solutions must be in whole numbers (because they represent, for example, assignment of people to jobs). Integer programming problems are now solved by a fairly ineffective method derived from the simplex algorithm. The key idea behind the Shor-Khachian algorithm—to encircle the solution with easily computed geometric shapes of rapidly decreasing size—is sufficiently powerful that some variation on its details may well lead to major improvements in other types of mathematical programming problems as well.

—Lynn Arthur Steen

Medical sciences

The use of bacteria to produce two important and rare medical compounds, human growth hormone and interferon, was an important breakthrough in the medical sciences during the past year. Also, new light was shed on three leading causes of death and disability: atherosclerosis, diabetes, and influenza. A dental scientist reported that fluoridation may help retard the development of gum disease.

General medicine

Among the many developments in medicine during 1979 was an increased understanding of diabetes as a disease with a complex collection of causes. Human interferon and human growth hormone were produced by genetically engineered bacteria in the laboratory, an accomplishment that was expected to allow researchers to establish new clinical uses for those

Portable insulin pump maintains tight control over the diabetes of a young patient while allowing him considerable freedom of action.

rare materials. Applications of the techniques of molecular biology to study of the influenza virus allowed scientists to track that ever-changing disease agent. And two new drugs held promise for troublesome conditions, severe acne and genital herpes.

Diabetes. A young teenager showing off his skateboarding skill while wearing a small insulin pump strapped to his waist illustrates one of the most practical developments in diabetes therapy in 1979. Research into that disease produced an impressive assortment of results, but most will influence patient treatment only in the future. The information accumulated indicates that diabetes, which affects almost 5% of the U.S. population, is not a single disease or even just two forms but is a complex collection of conditions, each preventing normal control of the body's carbohydrate metabolism.

Even the names for the diseases changed during 1979 to better reflect physicians' understanding of the underlying causes of diabetes. A task force of diabetologists christened as "insulin-dependent diabetes mellitus" the form of the disease formerly known as juvenile diabetes. Patients with that condition produce little or no functional insulin naturally and are dependent on insulin injections. The disease formerly called maturity-onset diabetes, in which patients make insulin but do not respond adequately to it, was renamed "non-insulin-dependent diabetes mellitus."

The most striking finding from researchers studying insulin-dependent diabetes was a virus clearly linked to a case of the disease. A ten-year-old boy developed symptoms of diabetes in the spring of 1978 and died after a week's hospitalization. Abner Notkins and Ji-Won Yoon of the U.S. National Institute of Dental Research at Bethesda, Md., isolated a virus from the boy's pancreas. When that virus was grown in laboratory cells and injected into susceptible mice, it destroyed insulin-producing cells in the mice. Those animals also developed symptoms of diabetes.

Notkins pointed out that the virus was not the sole cause of most cases of diabetes. He identified the virus as Coxsackie B4, a common infective agent. Almost half the population of the U.S. has been exposed to that virus, while less than 0.1% suffer from insulin-dependent diabetes. While implicating a virus helped to explain the seasonal fluctuations of diabetes onset and offered hope for a future vaccine, other factors such as the patient's genetic makeup and immune system still seemed to be intricately involved in the disease. Notkins and colleagues stressed that they could not yet say whether viral infection seldom, frequently, or generally plays a role.

Further evidence for participation of the immune system in insulin-dependent diabetes and for a potential treatment strategy was presented by Arthur Like of the University of Massachusetts at Amherst. Like suppressed the immune systems of rats that had characteristics resembling human insulin-dependent diabetes. He found that the treatment cured 36% of the diabetic animals, bringing the glucose concentration in

348

their blood to normal levels, and it prevented the later occurrence of diabetes in other susceptible rats.

Another cause of insulin-dependent diabetes—one that is probably rare—was first identified by Arthur Rubenstein of the University of Chicago. A patient with high levels of circulating insulin, but showing diabetic symptoms, responded to insulin injections. The patient's own insulin was produced in abundance, but Rubenstein showed that it was abnormal in the region that binds to the insulin receptors on the surface of cells. Thus, the circulating insulin was not effective in regulating carbohydrate metabolism. Rubenstein suspected that the abnormality was inherited.

Though preventing or curing any of the forms of insulin-dependent diabetes remained a task for the future, medical researchers in 1979 made significant advances toward providing insulin more conveniently and more effectively to those whose bodies could not make adequate amounts for themselves. Patients in Ontario, Canada, and also in Connecticut began wearing experimental portable insulin pumps at home, school, work, and play. The battery-driven device, worn on a belt, injects insulin under the patient's skin on a preset schedule—small doses at regular intervals around the clock and larger doses before scheduled meals and snacks. Philip Felig of Yale University, New Haven, Conn., reported that the pump lowered blood glucose levels of those patients to normal and kept the urine free of sugar.

Still better treatment for patients would be a device that works more like a normal pancreas—continuously sensing blood glucose levels and delivering appropriate doses of insulin. The problem has been to develop a small but reliable sensor. In 1979 researchers made progress on two alternative approaches. In a chemical maneuver scientists Michael Brownlee and Anthony Cerami of Rockefeller University in New York City attached a sugar group to an insulin molecule, which remained effective as a hormone. That sugar handle could be grasped by a plant protein called a lectin and would be released when other sugars became available. The scientists proposed that such a system of lectin-bound insulin-sugar implanted into the bloodstream in a permeable tube would release insulin appropriately in response to high levels of blood glucose.

Nature's own insulin providers, certain pancreatic cells, were the basis for other insulin-replacement research. Insulin-producing cells growing on the outer surface of a permeable tube controlled blood glucose levels in dogs and rats, Clark Colton of the Massachusetts Institute of Technology reported. In other laboratory research Paul Lacy of Washington University at St. Louis, Mo., transplanted insulin-producing cells directly into rats, using two procedures to evade the rats' immune systems. The cells functioned successfully for more than 100 days, encouraging scientists to believe that transplantation of human pancreatic cells eventually may be feasible.

Arrows indicate arrays of reoviruses (below) in a single mouse beta cell. Such viruses, being studied by Abner Notkins (right), destroy beta cells in the pancreas of mice, producing a diabeteslike syndrome.

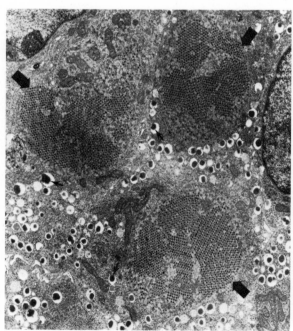

Capuchin monkey operates light switch for William Powell, paralyzed from the neck down by an accident. Such monkeys have been trained to aid handicapped people and have learned to open doors, pick up articles from the floor, ring doorbells, and turn on television sets.

Until that time, however, insulin must be provided from outside the body. Scientists at Eli Lilly and Co. continued to pursue the use of genetically engineered bacteria as an abundant source of the human material. Human insulin was first produced by bacteria in 1978, but it was more than a year before its biological activity was demonstrated. In September 1979 Lilly received permission from the National Institutes of Health at Bethesda, Md., to work with those bacteria in batches of more than 10 l (10.6 qt), and the pharmaceutical company announced that clinical trials of the human insulin were planned for the near future.

The other major type of diabetes, the non-insulin-dependent disease, was also explored in 1979. Again the major development was increasing awareness of the variety of conditions that could lead to the disease symptoms. The disease is characterized by normal, or even high, levels of insulin to which the receptors on cell surfaces do not adequately respond. In some cases the patient has a shortage of receptors; in others the receptors are insensitive.

Michele Muggeo and C. Ronald Kahn of the National Institutes of Health reported in March a new treatment for diabetes patients who are so insensitive to insulin that they would respond inadequately to even 1,000 times the usual dose. In these cases the problem was that the patients produce antibodies to their own receptors, and the antibodies prevent normal binding of insulin. Muggeo and Kahn successfully treated those patients with plasma exchange to remove the antibodies from the blood and make the receptors more sensitive.

Scientists also uncovered a new explanation for a regimen long known to help patients with non-insulin-dependent diabetes. Exercise was demonstrated in 1979 to increase the number of receptors on the cells of healthy subjects, thereby increasing a person's sensitivity to insulin.

Human growth hormone and interferon. Drugs for the future manufactured by means of genetic engineering became more of a certainty as a result of laboratory developments in 1979 and early 1980. Bacteria were developed that produce medically important compounds currently in seriously short supply. While none of the bacterially produced materials reached clinical trials, scientists expected several to be available for tests on humans within a year.

In July 1979 two California laboratories announced almost simultaneously bacterial production of human growth hormone. The limited amounts of that material available from human cadavers had been successfully used to treat children with pituitary dwarfism, a rare congenital defect. Preliminary experiments indicated that growth hormone can control gastrointestinal bleeding and promote healing of burns. But only with a greater supply of the hormone can those possibilities be investigated in clinical trials.

Abundant growth hormone seemed close at hand when a special laboratory strain of the bacterium *Escherichia coli* was manipulated to manufacture the hu-

350

man form of growth hormone by means of gene splicing, or recombinant DNA (deoxyribonucleic acid), techniques. Each research team joined genetic material of bacteria with genetic material containing the information for human growth hormone. The teams used different methods to persuade the altered bacteria to make foreign protein. At Genentech, Inc., the South San Francisco research firm that in 1979 produced human insulin with recombinant DNA, scientists chemically constructed a segment of DNA including a "start" signal that the bacteria recognize. That synthetic piece was linked to DNA copied from the natural human gene for growth hormone. The other research group, at the University of California at San Francisco, attached the human growth hormone gene to a natural bacterial gene for another protein so that the product includes part of the bacterial protein and human growth hormone.

While growth hormone has promise as a drug for several conditions, more excitement centered on bacterial production of human interferon. That protein, which was discovered more than 20 years ago, is manufactured by cells in the body when they are infected with a virus. Interferon has promise as a potent fighter against a wide variety of viruses and also as a cancer drug. However, experiments with interferon have been severely limited by the scarcity of material. As with growth hormone only the human type of interferon is active in people, so animals cannot supply material for clinical trials. Despite the cost of up to $15,000 to treat a single patient, the American Cancer Society in 1980 had a 150-patient test under way, and in 1979 the National Cancer Institute (NCI) in Bethesda, Md., announced that it would soon begin large-scale clinical experiments.

In January 1980 a small international research firm, Biogen S.A., of Geneva, announced that its scientists had succeeded in using bacteria to make interferon. Charles Weissmann of the University of Zurich in Switzerland led the team that modified laboratory bacteria so that they would produce human interferon, and demonstrated that the product was active; it killed viruses in laboratory-grown human cells. The Biogen scientists believed that moderate amounts of bacterially produced interferon would be available for clinical trials within a year and that its cost would be only a small fraction of the current price, perhaps about $10 per patient.

Bacterial production of interferon was expected to spur further applications of gene-splicing techniques. Interferon had been thought to be one of the most difficult goals for the method. In their experiments the Biogen scientists had to sort through 20,000 lines of bacteria to find the one carrying the gene for human interferon. But the work went more quickly than expected, requiring less than two years. Thus, bacterial interferon production was hailed as both an impressive

demonstration of the power of recombinant DNA technology and as a major step toward investigating whether interferon has potential as a new wonder drug.

Tracking influenza. While human influenza was relatively dormant in 1979, research on the viruses responsible for the disease flourished. New techniques for analyzing viral genes allowed scientists to examine how influenza viruses evolve from one epidemic to the next. Surprising results highlighted the studies of both the major shift in viral surface characteristics that defines each pandemic era, when a new form of the virus sweeps around the world, and the series of smaller changes within a pandemic era.

Recombinant DNA methods allowed scientists in several laboratories to explore the major viral changes that allow a new form of the influenza virus to evade the immune response people had developed to the previous strains. In 1979 genetically engineered bacteria produced for study large amounts of the gene for the major surface protein from each of three influenza viruses, one that infects birds and two that caused human pandemics ten years apart. The amount of variation among the genes was surprising. The surface proteins of the two influenza strains infecting people

Using an automatic pipette, a technician transfers material containing organisms generated by recombinant DNA techniques. Such gene-splicing has produced human insulin that will soon be tested.

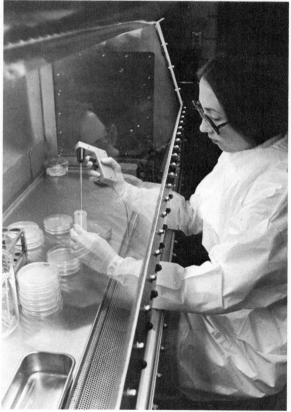

Courtesy, Eli Lilly and Co.

were no more similar to each other than to the protein of the strain that was infecting birds. Therefore, it was impossible to tell whether new human strains arise from adopting genes from animal viruses or whether they represent reemergence of human viruses that had circulated years earlier.

The components packed within the virus, as well as the surface proteins, vary gradually as the virus evolves, as Peter Palese of Mount Sinai School of Medicine in New York City demonstrated in 1979. He compared the genetic material from ten viruses causing influenza in eastern Asia in 1977 and found variations in seven of the viruses' eight genes. He speculated that changes in those internal proteins might make a virus reproduce in human cells more rapidly or spread more efficiently, giving the virus a selective advantage especially early in an epidemic.

Palese also demonstrated that human influenza viruses can swap genes. In 1977 and 1978 two different strains of influenza A caused epidemics, and some people were infected simultaneously with both. Palese analyzed an influenza A virus isolated in California in 1978 and discovered that the virus contained four genes, including those for the two surface proteins, from one of the circulating influenzas and four genes from the other. That new "recombinant" virus seemed to have an advantage over its parent with the same surface proteins, because only the recombinant was collected in the U.S. later in 1978 and 1979. However, the parent types still circulated in other areas of the world. Only from future epidemics will virologists learn whether the recombinant virus will prevail.

In vitro fertilization. Health authorities in Virginia approved in January 1980 the first clinic in the U.S. for the conception of human embryos outside the mother's body. Prompted by the successful birth in 1978 in the U.K. of a child conceived from an egg and sperm combined in a laboratory procedure, nearly 2,500 childless couples contacted the Eastern Virginia Medical School in Norfolk in hopes of using in vitro fertilization to reproduce. However, Mason Andrews, chairman of obstetrics at the school, expected the clinic to be able to treat only 50 couples the first year.

Earlier, in March 1979, an advisory board to the U.S. Department of Health, Education, and Welfare reported that research involving fertilization of human eggs in the laboratory is "ethically acceptable." That report was the first step toward restoring federal support, which had been prohibited in 1974, for such research projects. The board stated that experiments involving in vitro fertilization without implanting the embryo can only be done to obtain scientific information otherwise unavailable. The experiments would require the consent of participants fully informed of the procedures and must not allow embryos to be kept in the laboratory more than 14 days. For experiments in which an embryo is to be transferred into a woman's womb, the board stipulated that the egg and sperm used must come from that woman and her husband.

Male and female contraceptives. Clinical trials were announced in January 1980 for a new category of chemical contraceptives. These potential birth control drugs were styled after the natural brain compound that regulates both male and female sexual function. Scientists predicted that a new female contraceptive of this type could be ready for general use by the mid-1980s and a similar male contraceptive available a few years later.

The chemical under consideration is a peptide hormone, a chain of ten amino acids. That simple but potent substance, called LHRH (luteinizing hormone-releasing hormone), is the master signal in the brain that controls development of secondary sex characteristics, the menstrual cycle, spermatogenesis, and aspects of sexual behavior such as libido. Experiments with modified copies, called analogs, of the natural LHRH led scientists to believe that such substances would interfere with sperm production or conception but would sustain other essential sexual functions. LHRH and its analogs had already been used successfully to aid infertile men and women. However, higher doses were found to interfere with sperm production, egg release from the ovaries, and production of progesterone, a hormone required for pregnancy.

One potent and long-lasting LHRH analog, called a "superagonist," was scheduled for two-year clinical trials in both men and women to begin in 1980. That analog is at least 140 times more potent than the natural LHRH. Preliminary studies by Samuel S. C. Yen at the University of California at San Diego showed that daily injections of the analog into women can inhibit egg release while allowing the subject to maintain adequate amounts of estrogen. In a 16-week study Yen showed that the ovaries were still functioning while the contraceptive was effective. In another approach to female contraception Yen gave the analog to women on two successive days in the middle of their menstrual cycles and found that it shortened the cycle, so that a pregnancy probably would not be possible.

In men administration of the superagonist was shown to affect two hormone pathways differentially. When it was infused into subjects, testosterone levels stayed normal but the levels of follicle-stimulating hormone, which triggers sperm production, fell. In the study to begin in 1980 the superagonist will be injected daily, and sperm and hormone levels will be monitored. The study, to be carried out by David Rabin at Vanderbilt University School of Medicine in Nashville, Tenn., will use volunteers recruited from patients who have asked for a vasectomy.

Chemists at several laboratories continued to look for additional useful analogs of LHRH. Wylie Vale of the Salk Institute for Biological Studies in La Jolla, Calif., and Andrew V. Schally of Tulane University

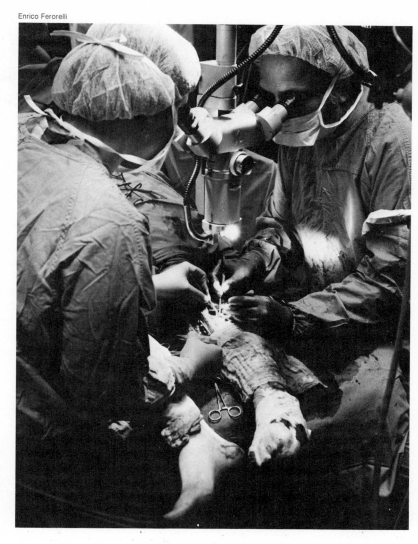

Enrico Ferorelli

With the aid of high-powered microscopes two surgeons can perform delicate operations simultaneously. In this process special miniature tools are used to make barely visible sutures in severed arteries and veins.

School of Medicine in New Orleans, La., developed potent chemicals that effectively block the action of LHRH and thus are called antagonists. The most potent antagonists are copies of LHRH modified at several positions, and they bind to LHRH receptor sites on cells more than 25 times as tightly as does LHRH. Vale found that the antagonists prevent normal menstrual cycles in female rats and can dramatically reduce sperm production in male rats.

The scientists said that they expected LHRH analogs to have fewer side effects than the steroids now used as female contraceptives. The LHRH analogs act more specifically and are more rapidly degraded by the body.

One other, quite different candidate for a male contraceptive entered the birth control arena in 1979. Scientists in China reported that a chemical derived from cottonseed oil inhibits sperm formation. That substance, call gossypol, was tested on approximately 4,000 men in China, and it was more than 99% effective as a contraceptive. It did not seem to alter hormone levels in the blood.

Experimental brain grafts. A piece of brain from one rat grafted onto the damaged brain of another survived to benefit the recipient animal, an international team of scientists reported in May 1979. The investigators said that the finding opens up a new area of research that in the long run could aid patients with Parkinson's disease and other motor disorders.

Parkinson's disease, which is characterized by uncontrollable, jerky movements, is thought to be caused by loss of brain cells that manufacture a key brain chemical called dopamine. Patients can be helped by L-dopa, a drug that stimulates dopamine production in the brain, but that drug is not completely effective and has some undesirable side effects. In their experiments with rats Richard Wyatt of the National Institute of Mental Health at Rockville, Md., and colleagues at the University of Colorado in Boulder and at the Karolinska Institute in Stockholm destroyed dopamine-producing cells in the brains of rats. Those rats then exhibited behavior that the scientists believe is the equivalent of tremors in human Parkinson patients.

353

Nine of the rats next received tissue containing healthy dopamine-producing cells from the brains of rat fetuses. The tissue was injected into a cavity of the brain just above the region that had received connections from the original dopamine-producing cells. The Parkinsonlike behavior of most of the rats was reduced within four weeks after the brain cell transfer. The transplanted cells thrived in the host, growing fibers into the brain. There was little evidence of scarring or other abnormal growth even nine months after the transplant. The scientists did not know why the rats did not biologically reject the transplanted tissue but suspected that the immune system's activity is limited in the brain.

The scientists cautioned that the results are just the first step in exploring grafts as treatment for brain disorders. They pointed out that behavioral implications of the grafts and their safety and long-term stability remained to be explored. A major issue in the clinical application of this technique to human brains would be the source of the graft. The use of human fetal brains would not be medically or ethically feasible. But other parts of a patient's own body might be a suitable source. To address that possibility scientists began studies in which they transplanted dopamine-producing cells into the brains of rats from other areas of the nervous system.

Motor problems associated with normal aging may share a cause with Parkinson's disease, according to a different research effort reported in October 1979. John F. Marshall and Norberto Berrios noticed that the impaired swimming ability of elderly rats resembles the swimming difficulties of young adult rats whose dopamine-producing cells had been damaged. Administration of drugs that stimulate dopamine activity, such as L-dopa, allowed the older rats to swim even more vigorously and successfully than the young adult rats, Marshall and Berrios reported. The results indicate that such drugs might improve the mobility of normal senior citizens.

Microsurgery. One after the other, four fingers were surgically reattached to the torn left hand of 28-year-old Eddie Safford. The fingers had been severed in an accident at a Boston bookbindery. The 23-hour replantation operation at Massachusetts General Hospital in Boston in June set a record for the length of time a finger can be preserved before reattachment. Reattachment of the last digit, the little finger, was completed 28 hours after the accident occurred.

That same month in New York City eight surgeons at Bellevue Hospital Center performed another replantation feat. The first known successful reattachment of both legs followed an accident in which a man's legs had been cut off by a subway train. Several other accidents followed by replants in New York City during the summer focused attention on the dramatic technique. Replants were performed on a police officer, a motor-cyclist, and a 17-year-old music student, all injured in traffic or subway accidents.

Improvements in equipment and increased numbers of surgeons trained in replantation were responsible for the growing success of the specialized surgery. Replant surgeons view their work through microscopes that magnify up to 40 times, and they use suture material so fine that it is almost invisible to the naked eye. Estimates of the number of replantations done in the U.S. ranged as high as 1,000 in 1979, and survival rates of 70% to 90% of the replanted limbs and digits were reported by most teams of surgeons.

Surgery in China has gone beyond the reattachment of severed and preserved parts, visitors to China reported. Chinese surgeons have reconstructed hands lost in accidents. The first patient had a new hand constructed in a 12-hour operation in October 1978; two of the patient's own toes were surgically attached to a prosthetic device implanted in his wrist. In September 1979 a hand for another patient was built of three toes attached to a metal palm. The reconstructed hands, although inferior to the natural ones, did allow movement of digits and normal sensations. The first patient just a year after the operation was able to do calligraphy with his reconstructed hand.

Microsurgery allowed physicians to intervene delicately to correct abnormalities within the body as well as to restore severed parts. For example, to treat spina bifida, a condition in which a sac of fluid protruding from the spinal column causes paralysis, surgeons were able to remove the sac without damaging adjacent nerves. Brain surgery especially benefited from the increased ability to make fine connections. The use of microscopes increased the success rate from 50% to 90% in one type of brain operation, according to a report from Johns Hopkins University in Baltimore, Md. Aneurysms, weak points of an artery that bubble out and leak blood, were corrected in that surgery.

Microsurgery even allowed physicians to prevent strokes by implanting a stretch of artery to bypass a blocked blood vessel in the brain. A 1979 study reported that such surgery was significantly more successful than drug treatment in preventing strokes. These techniques were added to the growing list of more common microsurgical procedures, which included reversal of tubal sterilizations, placement of muscle-skin flaps over large wounds, and transplantation of bone and blood vessels when a tumor is removed.

Drugs for acne and herpes. Drugs announced in 1979 offered hope to victims of two troublesome, long-lasting medical conditions, acne and herpes infection. NCI dermatologists announced the new acne treatment. A drug being considered in cancer prevention, an analog of vitamin A, cleared the skins of patients with severe and extensive acne that had resisted treatment with antibiotics, hormones, and X-rays. Among 14 patients with scarring, cystic acne, 12 were completely

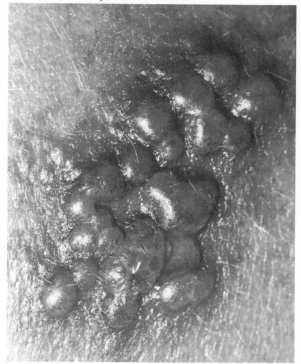

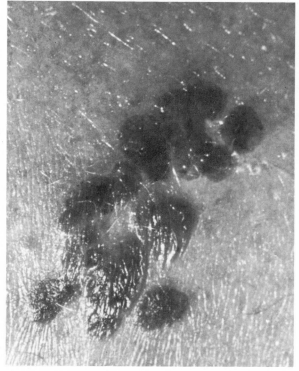

Genital herpesvirus sores (top) become significantly smaller (bottom) after four days of treatment with an experimental drug called 2-deoxy-D-glucose. A venereal disease that has no cure, genital herpes can cause fetal deaths in pregnant women and may also cause cancer of the cervix.

cleared of acne by the experimental drug and the others showed a 75% improvement. Even 20 months after the 4-month treatment the acne in those patients had not recurred. The treatment seemed to work by inhibiting secretions of the sebaceous glands associated with hair follicles. Long-term trials of the drug, called 13-cis-retinoic acid, were expected to take approximately three years.

The new possibility for treatment of genital herpes was a chemical that interferes with herpes virus multiplication in laboratory experiments. Herbert Blough and Robert Giuntoli of the University of Pennsylvania School of Medicine at Philadelphia were the first to explore its clinical action. Genital herpes is the second most common venereal disease in the U.S., and it presents a serious risk to babies as they contact herpes lesions during birth. In initial tests Blough and Giuntoli treated 18 women with the chemical 2-deoxy-D-glucose and treated a control group with a placebo. The experimental drug rapidly relieved pain in the patients and reduced the duration of symptoms from 15 days to 3 days. Among patients with recurrent infections 90% showed improvement when taking the drug. Blough said that 2-deoxy-D-glucose might be approved for commercial distribution as early as 1981.

Mastectomy. Radical mastectomies were performed on approximately 25,000 breast cancer patients in the U.S. in 1979, or on about one out of six women with early breast cancer. A less disabling and less disfiguring surgical procedure was recommended in June by a panel of cancer authorities at the NCI. The modified procedure is removal of the breast and some underarm lymph nodes, leaving intact chest muscles that had been removed in radical mastectomies.

The recommendation was based largely on a study of almost 1,700 women at 35 medical centers. Over an average of 70 months there was little difference in cancer recurrence between those who had undergone a radical mastectomy and those who had had a simple breast removal followed with radiation treatment. An Italian study presented to the NCI panel offered hope that even less drastic surgery may be possible for some breast cancer in the future. Among 150 women with small cancers diagnosed before they spread beyond the breast, half had the entire cancerous breast removed and the others had only the cancerous part of the breast removed. After five years the survival rate was 90% in both groups. Thus partial removal of a breast appeared to be a promising procedure.

—Julie Ann Miller

Vascular diseases

In 1980 the leading cause of death and disability in the industrialized nations was atherosclerosis, which is characterized by thickening and obstruction of arteries by cholesterol and other fibrous and fatty material.

Major risk factors for the development of atherosclerosis are hyperlipoproteinemia (including elevated plasma cholesterol), hypertension, cigarette smoking, and diabetes mellitus. Data from the Honolulu Heart Study, confirmed by other reports, show that low levels of high-density lipoproteins (HDL) are an important risk factor; the ratio of HDL to low-density lipoproteins may be more important in determining relative risk than is the total plasma cholesterol.

Damage to the arterial lining (endothelium) is probably always necessary as a precursor to atherosclerosis. This may be caused by the stresses to the artery from hypertension and also by excessive lipoproteins. Recent attention to the role played by the tiny blood cells, platelets, in the production of these lesions has been intense.

Platelet-endothelial interactions. After platelets adhere and aggregate at tiny breaks in the arterial endothelium, there is release of a number of biochemical agents leading to further aggregation. Arachidonic acid is released by enzyme action from the platelet membrane phospholipids. It is then rapidly metabolized through a series of complex interactions, producing thromboxane A_2 (TXA_2), which has profound effects on the interaction between platelets and the blood vessel wall.

Platelets do not adhere to healthy vascular endothelium; when the wall is damaged, however, the cells stick to the exposed subendothelial substance, collagen. They then form an aggregate and secrete the contents of their granules. One such released factor is a mitogen, which stimulates smooth muscle growth and may lead to the gradual development of the endothelial thickening characteristic of atherosclerosis. Another substance released is TXA_2, which induces further platelet aggregation and intense arterial constriction.

The arterial wall protects itself from the effects of TXA_2 by synthesizing prostacyclin (PGI_2) from precursors in the wall itself. This substance, in contrast to TXA_2, causes marked dilatation of arteries; it also is a potent factor in preventing aggregation of platelets. It is assumed that in normal individuals a balance between the production of TXA_2 and PGI_2 prevents marked arterial obstruction.

Accumulated clinical data show that abnormal platelets are present in patients with atherosclerosis and its complications, such as heart attack (myocardial infarction) and stroke. Whether such platelets are inherently defective or are responding secondarily to a plasma factor or to the atherosclerosis itself is unknown.

Vascular spasm and hypertension. Investigators speculate about the cause of sudden heart attack and stroke in patients with relatively stable and fixed atherosclerotic obstruction. Autopsy examinations often show no signs of new occlusion overlying the fixed, old atherosclerosis. Recently, Attilio Maseri and coworkers from Italy demonstrated that coronary artery spasm frequently accompanies angina pectoris at rest (inadequate arterial blood supply, producing oxygen lack and chest pain) and even myocardial infarction. The cause of the spasm may be related to temporary platelet aggregation superimposed on the old arterial occlusion, with consequent increased obstruction and secondary spasm caused by the release of TXA_2. Small platelet plugs found in the peripheral arteries of animals with experimentally induced infarction support this speculation. Thus, the final common pathway of arterial obstruction leading to heart attack and stroke may be a combination of temporary platelet aggregation and coronary spasm induced by TXA_2 released from the platelets.

Fundamental knowledge about the causes of hypertension is still lacking, but epidemiologic studies show that obesity is a definite major risk factor and high dietary salt intake is a likely one. Increased sympathetic nervous system activity in experimental rats plays a role in the genesis of animal high blood pressure; whether this is related to hypertension in the human is unknown.

Diagram reveals how single-transducer echocardiography is used to detect valvular and chamber abnormalities of the heart. T is the transducer; CW the chest wall; RV the right ventricle of the heart; LV the left ventricle; AO the aorta; MV the mitral valve; PPM the posterior papillary muscle; and LA the left atrium. A, B, C, and D are paths that single beams of sound may take through chambers of the heart.

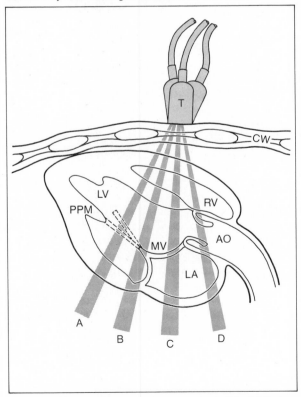

Adapted from "Research Related to Noninvasive Instrumentation," Donald C. Harrison, CIRCULATION, vol. 60, no. 7, December 1979, pp. 1569–1574

Diagnostics. The cornerstone of vascular disease diagnosis remains the X-ray filming of contrast media injected directly into the artery (angiography). Anatomic obstruction of blood vessels in virtually every part of the body may now be demonstrated by these techniques. Because angiography requires puncture of an artery and injection of foreign material, it presents minor risks to life and limb. Consequently, intensive efforts at developing noninvasive methods of vascular diagnosis continue. Such measures would be extremely useful in mass screening for latent vascular disease and in determining the effect of treatment.

Electrocardiography (EKG). This long-established noninvasive method records electrical signals from the heart, disclosing the heart rhythm and rate and reflecting changes in heart size and from damage. EKG performed during exercise (the EKG stress test) measures heart rate and waveform response to predetermined amounts of physical work; the presence of myocardial ischemia (tissue anemia) as a result of coronary obstruction causes changes in the EKG waveform and sometimes in blood pressure and heart rate. These tests, usually done on a treadmill or bicycle, may indicate significant coronary disease in patients with specific chest pain complaints, but they are less useful in screening those without symptoms. They are also helpful in determining how much cardiac work can be performed safely and as a baseline for future comparative measurements.

Portable tape recorders were developed to monitor cardiac rate and rhythm for 12 to 24 hours and are used in patients who faint because of inadequate cardiac output. Additionally, such recordings are able to document the extra heart beats (PVC's) coming from the ventricles of infarction patients; the frequency and types of these PVC's correlate with subsequent risk of sudden death.

Ultrasound. Sound waves reflected from cardiac tissues (echocardiography) disclose heart chamber size, the status of myocardial contraction, and heart valve and tissue configuration. Although echocardiography does not provide direct information about vascular disease, it is a useful indirect assessment of major heart muscle damage caused by coronary obstruction. A new variation is two-dimensional echocardiography, which provides real-time video displays of the silhouette, size, and motion of the heart.

Radioisotopes. The image of blood flowing through arteries provides a noninvasive picture of vascular anatomy. When red blood cells or macroaggregates of albumin are labeled with radioisotopes, sensitive radiation cameras may detect the transmitted gamma radiation as these substances circulate through the vascular system. High-speed filming and computer processes permit accurate video displays of both vascular flow and cardiac wall motion. Similarly, the concentration by the myocardium (middle muscular layer of the heart wall) of radioactive thallium-201 is related to blood flow through arteries into heart muscle. Thallium-201 is taken up by normal myocardium; the relative concentrations of radioactivity in areas of heart muscle thus will reflect blood-flow abnormalities or infarcted tissue. The combination of an EKG stress test and thallium injections at peak exercise loads provides highly sensitive and specific information about the presence or absence of significant coronary obstructive disease. Another isotope, technetium pyrophosphate, binds to calcium inside damaged myocardial cells and is used to confirm myocardial infarction.

Treatment. *Atherosclerosis prevention.* Attempts to modify the major risk factors of atherosclerosis have had mixed success. Changing one's dietary fat intake causes a significant reduction in plasma cholesterol; research results are inconclusive, however, as to whether such alterations affect morbidity and mortality from atherosclerosis. The cholesterol-lowering drug Clofibrate was used in large-scale controlled European and U.S. studies but failed to decrease coronary events significantly.

Pediatrician helps first grader use an exercise bicycle. The girl is taking part in a project aimed at preventing young children from becoming early high-risk candidates for coronary heart disease.

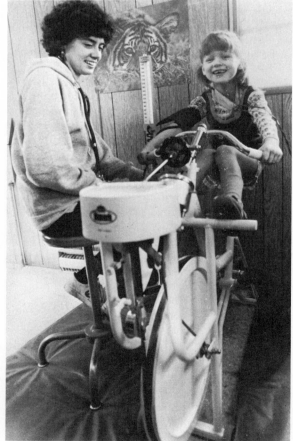

More hopeful was evidence derived from a U.S. Veterans Administration study on antihypertensive drugs; stroke incidence was significantly reduced by such treatment. U.S. government-sponsored MRFIT (Multiple Risk Factor Intervention Trial) studies are aimed at reducing multiple-risk factors. By 1980 conclusive data were not yet available.

In the U.S. there was a substantial decrease in cardiovascular mortality from 1968 through 1977. Why this happened is unclear. Possibly a general decrease in cigarette smoking, decline in beef and saturated-fat consumption, more public exercise programs, and better blood-pressure control have been responsible. Hard evidence supporting this hypothesis was unavailable.

Arterial operations. Use of the saphenous vein from the leg to bypass coronary arteries and obstructed femoral arteries had by 1980 become commonplace. This procedure had a mortality risk of only 1–2% in many major medical centers. Nevertheless, controversy continued regarding the level of illness at which such surgery is necessary. Most investigators agreed that patients with significant (greater than 70%) occlusion of the left main coronary artery or with similar degrees of obstruction of all three main arteries should have a bypass in order to prolong life. Controlled data suggest that in such patients this operation does improve chances of survival. Those with disabling angina pectoris who cannot be treated effectively with medication also should have a bypass operation. Marked disagreement existed, however, about the value of these techniques in prolonging life expectancy in those with less severe coronary obstructive disease. Unequivocal data show that the operation relieves the symptoms of angina in most patients, but medical treatment often is equally successful. When there is substantial impairment of cardiac muscle function, a bypass operation is not likely to improve longevity or cardiac output.

Similar operations performed on the cerebral circulation may reduce the risk of stroke in certain groups of patients. Clear-cut indications for such surgery were not yet available.

Medical therapy. Because of the interest in platelet-arterial wall interactions a vigorous search began for compounds inhibiting platelet activity. Clinical trials of aspirin and other antiplatelet drugs were for the most part inconclusive. However, a large-scale study from Canada demonstrated that the risk of stroke in hypertensive men over 60 was markedly reduced by aspirin when compared with other antiplatelet drugs. Sulfinpyrazone, another anti-inflammatory agent, was given to a large group of myocardial infarction survivors and its action was compared with that of a placebo. The group treated with sulfinpyrazone had a markedly reduced incidence of sudden death for at least six months compared with the patients given placebos. The action of sulfinpyrazone most likely was not related to antiplatelet activity but perhaps to a membrane-stabilizing action on the myocardium.

Recent experimental evidence indicated that prostacycline given intravenously to animals inhibits the formation of blood clots. Researchers showed that prostacycline protects the oxygen-starved myocardium in animals both by reducing the amount of cardiac work and by inhibiting platelet aggregation and preserving myocardial cell integrity. Further intensive studies of the potential usefulness of prostacycline and the suppression of TXA_2 are under way.

Nitroglycerine given either under the tongue or intravenously clearly inhibits blood vessel spasm. Some patients, however, do not always respond sufficiently to such agents. Newer calcium blocking ("slow-channel") drugs such as Nifedipine and Verapamil were demonstrated to be useful in preventing coronary spasm in patients with angina when they are at rest.

—Irwin J. Schatz

Dentistry

The dental profession in the U.S. during 1979 intensified efforts to increase access to dental services for all segments of the public. The American Dental Association (ADA) at its annual session in Dallas, Texas, in

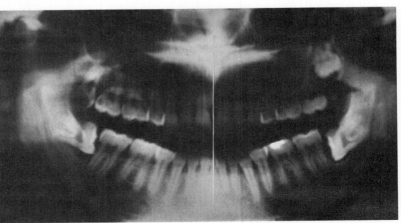

Horizontally impacted lower wisdom tooth (lower left) reveals bone destruction near second molars. The wisdom tooth at the upper left is afflicted with caries (cavities), while that at the upper right is impacted. Dentists concluded that wisdom teeth should be removed when there is evidence of follicular enlargement and also when these teeth develop soft-tissue inflammatory conditions and nonrestorable carious lesions.

October overwhelmingly approved a blueprint for a massive access program. The purpose of the program would be to focus existing resources of the ADA toward improving access to comprehensive dental care for six underserved population groups: the poor and working poor; the elderly; residents of remote areas; the handicapped; the institutionalized and homebound; and employees without dental insurance. ADA officials explained that fundamental to the program is the concept that improving access is a "shared responsibility" to be shouldered by the dental profession, government, the private sector, and the individual.

Prevention of dental disease is closely linked to an access program. Thus, the U.S. government's fresh infusion of $10 million for the expansion of community water fluoridation was an important step in reducing tooth decay rates. New statistics released by the U.S. Department of Health, Education, and Welfare (HEW) disclosed that 20% of teenagers who drank fluoridated water from birth have teeth that are totally free of cavities.

The federal government over the past several decades has been involved in fluoridation research, endorsement, and promotion, but until 1979 no federal funds had been provided to communities so that they could implement fluoridation. "We now have about 108 million people drinking water that has adjusted natural fluorides," according to Robert Faine, deputy chief of the dental disease prevention activity at the Center for Disease Control in Atlanta, Ga. "We have about 70 million more people to go to include all who have access to community water systems. That's about 8,670 additional systems to be fluoridated by the year 1990," he said.

Fluoridation and gum disease. Fluoridation's value in decreasing dental decay has been documented for more than three decades, but in recent months a dentist suggested that fluorides may also significantly retard the development of periodontal or gum disease. Leonard Zeldow of Binghamton, N.Y., reported at the annual session of the ADA in Dallas that topical fluoride solutions seem to improve gum problems and help rebuild supporting bone tissue. Topical fluoride therapy treatments focusing on the destruction of the bacterial causes of periodontal disease in many cases made surgical corrective treatment either unnecessary or secondary, he said.

Zeldow described intensive fluoride therapy by self-administration at home using a traylike device called a toplicator. The toplicator is custom-fabricated to fit tightly over the teeth, and the patient receives instructions for its use from the dentist. The fluoride is dropped in gel form in the tray, and the patient is instructed to self-administer the treatment once daily until his next visit to the dentist's office. Several applications a week are expected to be sufficient for effective treatment.

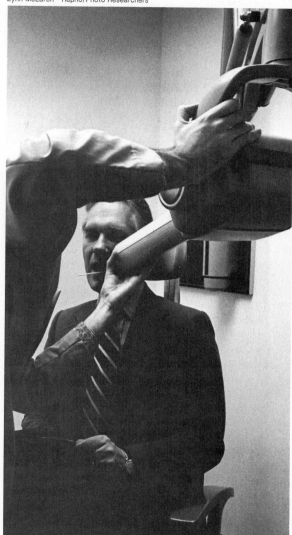

Patient has teeth X-rayed by a dentist. According to a U.S. government radiation research scientist the amount of radiation received from dental X-rays is minimal and poses a negligible threat to health.

New denture techniques. A University of Tennessee denture expert and a behavioral scientist offered suggestions aimed at increasing the comfort of denture wearers. By observing some simple preventive measures at home, denture wearers can help prevent "embarrassing denture slippage," said T. H. Shipmon of Memphis, Tenn. One of the primary reasons dentures become loose and lose their stability is because of a natural loss of the supporting jawbone structure. Denture patients lose approximately 2 mm (0.08 in) of jawbone every year. Because of the loss of supporting bone and soft tissues and because of the resultant facial changes, the average denture needs to be replaced or remade every five or six years.

Regular checkups play an important role in a preventive program for the denture patient, Shipmon explained. Many people mistakenly think that dentures mean an end to regular dental visits. On the contrary denture patients need to have an oral evaluation at least once a year so that major problems, such as abnormal bone loss, can be spotted early. "Denture wearers also should make it a point to eat a well-balanced diet. This will help minimize bone loss and will increase tolerance of the soft tissue to the denture," Shipmon said. He also suggested that denture wearers should take special care to chew straight up and down, placing equal weight on both sides of the jaw. Food should be divided equally between the right and left side, and the patient should chew with both sides simultaneously.

From another point of view successful denture treatment is frequently influenced by how well the patient copes with emotional, social, and cultural needs. Of all these factors, perceived need is one of the most important affecting an individual's desire for dental treatment, said Helen Gift of Chicago, director of the ADA Bureau of Economic and Behavioral Research. Total patient commitment is a leading emotional factor vital for successful denture treatment.

X-rays and safety. New research strongly confirmed the fact that the amount of radiation received from dental X-ray examinations is minimal and virtually harmless, according to a radiation research scientist in the U.S. government. "The use of radiation in the healing arts is recognized as the largest man-made component of radiation dose to the United States' population. Approximately 145,000 X-ray units in dental offices throughout the country are used to make 300 million dental radiographs each year," said James W. Miller of Silver Spring, Md., special assistant for dentistry in the Bureau of Radiological Health of the Food and Drug Administration. But in spite of this, dental radiographic examinations were estimated in 1970 to contribute only about 3% of the total adult per capita mean active bone marrow dose of radiation. Recent research data indicated that dentistry's contribution to the mean active bone marrow dose decreased significantly after 1970.

Miller urged dentists to continue following the ADA recommendations on X-ray examinations. As a result the "amount of radiation received will be so small as to be virtually harmless." For another view, *see* Feature Article: HAZARDS OF LOW-LEVEL RADIATION.

Dental restorations. By using fine-quality silver amalgam dentists can provide patients with dental restorations that look and function like natural teeth except for the color. To assist in the long-term retention of large amalgam restorations dentists use various types of pin techniques, including one called the "threaded pin system" in which a pin is inserted into a hole cut into the dentin or pulp chamber of the tooth. The number and placement of pins can vary with the size of the cavity. Generally, the safest place to insert pins is at the four corners of the tooth.

Because of the large increases in the prices of gold and silver dentists began turning to nonprecious metals as possible substitute materials in restorative treatment. Five of ten high-copper amalgams received good marks in a two-year study by the National Institute of Dental Research. Scientists found that substituting copper for most of the tin in silver fillings improves physical and mechanical abilities.

—Lou Joseph

Veterinary medicine

The nuclear accident at Three Mile Island near Harrisburg, Pa., in March 1979 affected not only the adjacent human population but animals as well. In 1965 the procedures to be followed with regard to livestock and the food supply in such an emergency had been detailed in a symposium on disaster medicine. On the basis of these recommendations state agencies advised dairy farmers in the Three Mile Island area to keep their cows confined under cover, thus removing the potential for contamination of the milk supply by the radioactive iodine released into the atmosphere.

By contrast, pet owners were ill-prepared to cope with the problems of fallout or evacuation as these related to their animals. Although precise figures were not available, the approximately 200,000 persons evacuated from the area would be expected to own about 40,000 dogs and 50,000 cats. Many evacuees took their pets with them or had them boarded at kennels or veterinary hospitals, but others did not have this option because public evacuation centers were not equipped to admit pet animals. Some persons confined their pets before leaving, but the majority took the worst possible course—that of abandoning them in the street.

To help pet owners who might face such situations in the future, a University of Pennsylvania veterinarian, David Kronfeld, formulated recommendations to be considered whenever evacuation of the human population becomes desirable or mandatory. The four options he suggested for handling pets were:

1. Confinement. Because the alternatives may be impractical for the great majority of pets, first consideration in most cases should be given to confinement at home. At best, boarding facilities would be overcrowded and may require evacuation later; the family garage is probably the best place. If water is available, a healthy dog can go without food for two or three weeks; if food is supplied, it should be dry (moist food will spoil) and relatively unpalatable to prevent overeating. Even if usually friendly toward each other, dogs must be confined separately from cats.

2. Evacuation. Since pets are often considered members of the family, taking them along may be mutually beneficial but only if their size and temperament per-

Photos, Paul Felix—Camera Press/Photo Trends

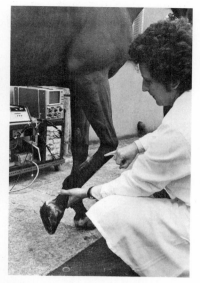

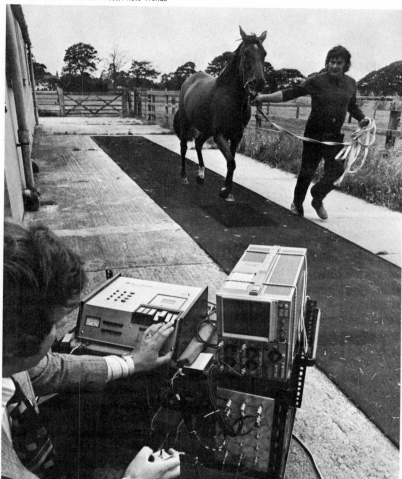

Horse is trotted over a force-plate (left), which determines with the aid of a computer how well it has recovered from lameness. Horizontal stripes on a horse's leg (above) were caused by "firing," a method of curing lameness by applying red-hot irons to increase blood circulation. Such treatment has been criticized as inhumane and ineffective and is being replaced by the use of carbon-fiber implants in the leg.

mit and provisions for their care are made beforehand. Veterinarians near Three Mile Island were besieged with requests for medication (also available at drug stores) to prevent motion sickness in dogs. Crating may be desirable or necessary, but unmanageable animals should be left home. Relatively few persons have the facilities or patience required to transport animals any great distance.

3. Euthanasia. Although not generally recommended, euthanasia may be the best or only solution in an emergency, especially if a pet is likely to endanger persons or other animals. The procedure is best left to an expert, but veterinary hospitals near Three Mile Island were unable to supply all the services requested. A gun should be used only by someone accustomed to handling it.

4. Abandonment. Many persons believe freedom is preferable to confinement for their pets (even under normal conditions) and think the animals can fend for themselves. However, scavenging and fighting resulting from a sudden increase in the stray dog population would be injurious to the animals and create problems for the people who remain behind. Exposure to radia-

tion also is less likely if animals are confined.

The quadrennial World Veterinary Congress sponsored by the World Veterinary Association convened July 1–7, 1979, in Moscow. Approximately 1,300 Soviet veterinarians and 3,000 from outside the U.S.S.R. were in attendance. Emphasis at the scientific sessions was on health of farm livestock, regulatory (governmental) veterinary medicine, and public health. V. L. Tharp, president of the American Veterinary Medical Association (AVMA), was elected to be a vice-president of the Congress.

Despite objections raised by AVMA and other interested groups, the U.S. Department of Defense proposed to reduce the size of the U.S. Army Veterinary Corps and Air Force Veterinary Service. Earlier, Congress had recommended their elimination altogether. The current proposal called for an immediate reduction in Veterinary Corps personnel by 10% and eventual replacement of another 30% by nonveterinary specialists. The intention to substitute civilians for military veterinarians doing research was especially criticized by AVMA officials, who pointed out that the specialty training afforded by military service attracted

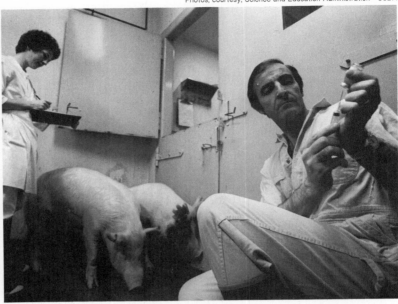

Cell cultures from female swine infected with porcine parvovirus are examined (above left). The disease causes fetal deaths and small litters. A veterinary scientist (above right) prepares to test a vaccine developed to combat the virus; it proved to be both effective and safe.

many young veterinarians and that qualified civilian specialists would consider the pay scale inadequate.

The U.S. Postal Service issued an embossed envelope honoring veterinary medicine, the First-Day-of-Issue ceremony for which was held July 24, 1979, at the annual meeting of the AVMA in Seattle, Wash. At the presentation Regional Postmaster Joseph Morris expressed hope that "this envelope will encourage greater recognition and understanding of the services you—our nation's veterinarians—provide day in and day out in so many ways throughout the country....While it commemorates past accomplishments of the veterinarians of America, it also calls attention to the varied aspects of your work today."

An Arthur D. Little Manpower Study in 1978 had predicted that the supply of veterinarians in the U.S. would exceed demand by as many as 8,300 within a decade, but this was refuted by incoming AVMA president William Jackson. He contended that the increase in numbers "can be absorbed into private practice by a top-notch public relations program, making the public more aware of what [the veterinary profession] can do." In addition to increasing personal contact of individual veterinarians with the public, Jackson said that the AVMA will have to advertise as a professional organization.

A study by the Bureau of Health Manpower projected a larger supply (54,900) of veterinarians by 1990 than that forecast by the A. D. Little study (51,000) but also a larger demand (52,300 vs. 41,600). The difference in supply was accounted for by the expectation of there being 26 instead of 24 schools (currently 23) in operation during the 1980s. Although the bureau did not explain how it arrived at the demand figure, it determined that the area of greatest shortage is for farm animal practitioners in rural areas and suggested that "non-financial incentives may be more successful in attracting veterinarians to this area of practice." This contradicted the widely held belief that income was the main reason for recent graduates to prefer small-animal practice.

The projections in the A. D. Little study were based largely on existing patterns of veterinary services. Rather than concede the report to be a blueprint for unemployment, however, a number of prominent veterinarians believed the reverse would be true if certain changes were made in the system. Richard Talbot, dean of the College of Veterinary Medicine at Virginia Polytechnic Institute in Blacksburg, said: "Expanded and better services should be our challenge for the future. We should find improved ways to deliver our services, find new outlets for our services—such as government and industry, particularly agribusiness—and we must market our services more aggressively and more competitively." He recommended sharing of facilities to provide better service at less expense; less emphasis on appearance of buildings and dispensing of medications; and more training in preventive medicine, nutrition, and specialized diagnostic services to increase competence as consultants to large livestock operations. "What we need to do and can do," he concluded, "is ethically market our abilities and our services in ways that will make the general public aware that our services are valuable to them."

A recently completed AVMA survey of veterinary practitioner incomes in 1977 indicated an average net of $33,977 for those treating large animals only and $37,141 for those dealing exclusively with small animals. Lower incomes for those in mixed practice reduced the overall average to $33,437. This was up from $16,770 in 1965, but when adjusted for the Consumer Price Index it represented an increase of only 3.8%. For owners of veterinary practices (excluding veterinarians employed by them) the income adjusted for return on capital investment was $20,588, a decrease of 17.4% since 1965 after adjustment for the price index.

Female veterinarians, who accounted for about 6.8% of the 23,237 private practitioners surveyed, had incomes averaging $18,331. Women veterinarians were, on the average, about nine years younger than men and thus had less experience (5.4 vs. 12.9 years); they also worked an average of nearly four hours less per week. The income for all practitioners averaged $11.79 per hour, and most worked more than 55 hours per week. A large increase in the number of women veterinarians was expected in the near future due to the fact that 37.5% of the 2,353 students in the 1978–79 class were women (34.7% of total enrollment).

—J. F. Smithcors

Optical engineering

One event likely to have a tremendous effect in the "information age" of the 1980s is the maturing of optical information processing into a field of practical technology and engineering and above all into a powerful new form of computing, a field perhaps best called "opto-digital computing." No person probably has greater claim to fame in this development than Dennis Gabor, who died in London in February 1979 (*see* SCIENTISTS OF THE YEAR). When the Nobel Prize for Physics was awarded to Gabor in 1971 for his invention of holography, this field of three-dimensional lensless photography had already attained world fame, not only in the scientific and engineering community but in a wide popular sense as well.

Born in Budapest, Hung., in 1900 Gabor studied in Berlin where he obtained a doctoral degree at what later became the Technische Universität Berlin with a thesis on "Oscillography of Traveling Waves with Cathode-Ray Oscillography." It was natural for him to go on to work for the world-famous German electrical firm Siemens & Halske in Berlin, where he stayed on as an engineer from 1927 to 1933. He then emigrated to Great Britain and eventually became a British citizen. The work that would eventually earn him the Nobel Prize and that has so fundamentally influenced the field of optical engineering was published while Gabor was employed at the Thomson-Houston Compa-

Photos, G. W. Stroke, "Optical Computing," IEEE SPECTRUM, vol. 19, December 1972, pp. 24–41

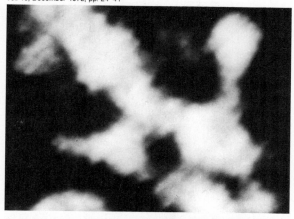

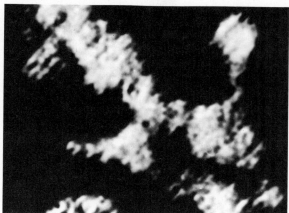

Holography and optical computing have been combined into a technique for sharpening electron micrographs, which are often taken out of focus to enhance contrast. Blurred image of a virus (top) resolves detail to five angstroms. Sharpened image (bottom) has twice the resolution.

ny, Ltd., in Rugby. It was entitled "A New Microscopic Principle" and appeared in the British scientific periodical *Nature* in 1948. Rarely has a single piece of published research exemplified better just how short a paper may be in order to qualify for a Nobel Prize, provided the paper contains not only the basic suggestion but an experimental proof as well! It and two subsequent papers contain concepts that more than 30 years later still remained to be fully understood. These papers may be found reprinted in their entirety in G. W. Stroke, *An Introduction to Coherent Optics and Holography,* 2d ed., Academic Press, 1969.

Gabor held the chair of Electrical Engineering at the Imperial College of Science and Technology, University of London, from 1949 until his retirement in 1967, but he continued an active career until his death, spending about half of each year as a staff scientist at Columbia Broadcasting System (CBS) Laboratories in Stamford, Conn. During this last period he also co-authored several papers on fundamental aspects of

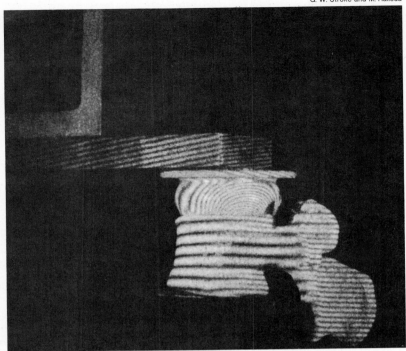

Holographic interferogram of a human vertebra under stress consists of a single photographic plate on which two holograms of the object—before compression and after compression—have been superimposed. Illumination of the interferogram with laser light yields an image covered with interference fringes that highlight regions of deformation on the surface of the vertebra.

holography with G. W. Stroke, then a scientific consultant to CBS Laboratories. Gabor's Nobel Prize address, entitled "Holography, 1948–1971," may be found reprinted in the June 1972 *Proceedings of the IEEE,* and a still useful popular introduction to the field coauthored by Gabor, Stroke, and Winston E. Kock appears in the U.S. journal *Science* of July 2, 1971.

In addition to his scientific work, Gabor also published a number of books dealing with the general theme of societal aspects of science and technology, partly in connection with his activities in the Club of Rome. Among these, *The Mature Society* and *Inventing the Future* are most widely known. Gabor received many honors for his work even before being awarded the Nobel Prize, including fellowship in the Royal Society, 1956; the Cristoforo Colombo Prize of the Genoa (Italy) International Institute of Communications, 1967; The Thomas Young Medal and Prize of the Royal Photographic Society, 1967; the Holweck Medal and Prize of the Société Française de Physique, 1971; and the Medal of Honor of the Institute of Electrical and Electronics Engineers (IEEE) in the U.S., 1970.

Holography may well be called the basis of modern optical engineering. In scope and influence it rivals the fields of communications and information sciences and, in fact, has come increasingly to include developments in these fields, based on the original contributions of U.S. mathematicians Norbert Wiener and Claude Shannon, among others. Through recent developments in technology, including the laser, as well as in the underlying mathematics, all three fields of endeavor are attaining new levels of importance and in-

terest in many areas of science and engineering, including physics, astronomy, medicine, and biology. In fact, many of the most impressive applications of holography, beyond its three-dimensional imaging capabilities, appear to be of a computational nature. In combination with digital computers, for example, holography is gaining increasing importance as a new field of engineering in the form of opto-digital computing. Even as early as the late 1950s holographic principles were used to reconstruct images of the Earth with coherent light. The images originally had been recorded with radar waves and stored on photographic film in a form later recognized as truly holographic.

Fundamentally a hologram consists of a diffraction grating generally produced through interference, using laser light, on photographic plates (although it can also be produced artificially with the aid of digital computation). Upon illumination of the developed plate with a beam of laser light, a process called reconstruction takes place in which multidimensional images emerge from the information stored in coded form on the plate. This process is quite similar to the reconstruction of music encoded in the grooves of a phonograph record, in which a pickup is made to vibrate as it follows the mechanical deformations of the grooves. In fact, the similarity between holographic storage and reconstruction of images and phonograph recording and reconstruction of music and sound recently resulted in the production of phonograph records and playback machines using the principles of holography.

In applying holography to both pictorial and sound recording and reproduction, one makes use of the associative storage of two light waves A and B such that wave A may be extracted from the hologram (*i.e.*, reconstructed) by illumination of the hologram with wave B under a wide variety of exploitable conditions. Perhaps most remarkable in this associative principle is the fact that wave B, which may originate from a single point, is by itself sufficient to produce wave A, which in turn may consist of millions of different picture points (*i.e.*, of tens of millions of data "bits"). This situation is somewhat similar to the recall of an entire book of thousands of pages, each with hundreds of words, with the aid of a simple "title" that perhaps consists of only a single word; say, "Bible."

The ramifications of this associative property, with its enormous storage capabilities, are only becoming slowly appreciated by nonspecialists and some specialists alike in the fields of data storage and communications. Completely new, opto-digital computers, which operate in parallel rather than serially with enormous speed and capacity, are currently within the domain of realization, and some of their aspects already have been demonstrated in the laboratory. The reconstruction of sharp images from blurred photographs (*e.g.*, caused by vibrations or out-of-focus conditions) represent one of the earliest examples of this type of optical computing. Recently these principles have been extended to reconstruction of X-ray images by means of the new technique of computer tomography, itself the subject of the 1979 Nobel Prize for Physiology or Medicine (*see* SCIENTISTS OF THE YEAR.)

Perhaps the most dramatic and, at the same time, most representative example of the newly emerging field of opto-digital computing is the reconstruction of images of atoms and of molecules in crystals tomographically, *i.e.*, section by section, as if they could have been observed in an optical microscope capable of resolving objects on the atomic level. This achievement was recently described, as a culmination of Gabor's original hopes, by Stroke, M. Halioua, R. Sarma, and V. Srinivasan, in "Imaging of Atoms: Three-Dimensional Molecular Structure Reconstructions Using Opto-Digital Computing" in the *Proceedings of the IEEE* for April 1977.

With respect to the engineering aspect of holography, as so often happens in the history of science and technology, one of the first and most surprising applications turned out to be the accidental discovery of "holographic interferometry." In this technique a hologram record is made of the same object in two successive states; for example, before and after it has been slightly displaced or deformed, as in the case of an airplane wing, automobile tire, or even part of the human body. Rather than being recorded separately, however, these images are superimposed on a single photographic plate. Subsequent illumination of the plate with laser light produces a three-dimensional picture of the object crossed by "zebra-stripe" bands

Scientist checks laser beams in device developed at IBM for measuring laser wavelengths. Its convenience and accuracy should broaden horizons for research that makes use of tunable dye lasers.

called interference fringes. As on a geographic map, these interference fringes represent the topographic height differences between the two states (positions) of the object's surface; they may be used for establishing mechanical structural properties, diagnostic determination of defects in construction, and other purposes. Applications to the study of the living human eardrum were recently demonstrated, and other promising applications of holographic optical engineering in medicine and biology exist, including ultrasonic diagnostics.

—George W. Stroke

Physics

Attempts to produce a coherent picture of the fundamental forces of nature and of the underlying structure of the atomic nucleus and its constituent particles continued to preoccupy and perplex physicists in recent months. The possibility for low-cost solar cells seemed closer at hand as investigators gained a better understanding of the effects of structural defects in semiconductors. New findings underscored the significance of extremely weak magnetic fields for certain forms of life.

General developments

Research in physics during the past year was highlighted by studies of superfluid helium, the behavior of elements under extremely high pressure, and the significance of magnetic fields for living organisms. Prospects for nuclear fusion reactors brightened as new laser fusion designs were tested successfully.

Magnetic fields and life. The nerves of the human body carry electrical signals with ease. All body sensations are, in fact, waves of electric polarization that ripple along nerve fiber. When these waves reach the brain, they induce nearby currents which can be detected outside the skull. The electroencephalogram (EEG) traces which, for example, reveal the alpha waves of the brain are recordings of these currents. In recent years scientists have found that the magnetic fields that accompany these nerve signals can also be detected near the brain, and with greater resolution. The key is a superconducting quantum interference device called a SQUID, which can measure very small magnetic fields (less than one billionth of the Earth's field). Oscillating electric fields are smeared out by the resistivity of the skull; magnetic fields are not.

Using SQUID detectors, investigators in 1979 pursued exploration of the correspondence between what a person feels and which part of the brain responds. For example, Samuel Williamson and co-workers at New York University found that when a particular finger is stimulated by an electrode, the neuromagnetic response appears in a very small region of the cerebral cortex. Shifting the stimulus from the little finger to the thumb moves the brain activity a distance of two centimeters (a little less than an inch) on the cortical surface. Although human "circuits" produce very weak fields—the weakest ever detected—they may help explain the complex interworkings of human perception of and reaction to the world.

Ability to sense such small fields also has led to diagnosing effects deep within the body. David Cohen and colleagues at the Massachusetts Institute of Technology's National Magnet Laboratory studied traces of magnetic dust deposited in the walls of human lungs, not by direct probing, but by measuring with a SQUID magnetometer the minute fields that the dust produced. Volunteers inhaled magnetite dust (a form of iron oxide) and then were placed in a strong magnetic field. The dust aligned with the external field, so that when it was turned off, the dust itself produced a small field that could be detected outside the body. Cohen's group remeasured this field at intervals for several months, relating its declining strength to the amount of dust still remaining in the lungs at a particular time. It was known that there is a short-term clearance of dust from the lungs by a carpet of mucus, which moves steadily up toward the throat. This mechanism eliminates most of the dust, but to do better requires that a kind of white blood cell ingest the dust. Striking in Cohen's results is the fact that the cigarette smokers in the volunteer group had only a weak long-term clearance; the cells simply were not doing their work. After 11 months only 10% of the magnetic dust remained in the nonsmokers' lungs, but about 50% was left in the smokers' lungs. Further progress may show how smokers lose this long-term capability.

Research continued to suggest that birds, bees, and even bacteria had been using magnetism long before humans discovered even the simplest properties of the

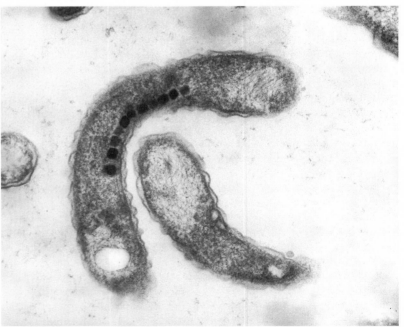

Internal chain of magnetite crystals stands out in electron micrograph of a magnetic bacterium that has been sliced through its long axis. Magnification is about 53,000 times.

Courtesy, Richard Blakemore and Richard Frankel; photo by D. L. Balkwill lodestone. Since 1975 Richard P. Blakemore of the University of New Hampshire and others have accumulated evidence to show that bacteria in many different kinds of watery environments in the Northern Hemisphere contain iron-rich crystals. They also swim consistently to the north. The bacteria make their own internal magnets by synthesizing and stringing together chains of tiny magnetite crystals that fall within the narrow range of sizes for single magnetic domains. If the crystals were larger, there would be several domains per crystal, each oriented differently, so that the tendency for the chain to align with the Earth's magnetic field would be partially self-canceling. Smaller crystals would have less than a domain and consequently a weaker response. The bacterial "choice" of size appears just right for optimum strength of alignment. Changing the magnetic field artificially showed that the bacteria adjust their course within a second, a response that fits a simple calculation based on the relaxation time of the magnetite chains.

It seems that bacteria find it useful to swim north because in general the Earth's north magnetic pole draws magnetic objects downward as well as northward. For magnetic bacteria downward is toward the sediment, where they live most of the time. Other creatures have also been found to carry magnetic material—honeybees in front of their abdomens and pigeons near or in their skulls—although the link between these deposits and the animals' exceptional navigational abilities remains to be demonstrated.

Because the Earth's field is not particularly strong, it was long thought that magnetic effects have been unimportant in the evolution of life forms. These recent developments demonstrate, however, that minute specks of iron compounds can provide a valuable mechanism for guidance, and even the extremely weak fields associated with normal nervous system functions may somehow be important to the organisms that generate them.

Visible quantum effects. When cooled to temperatures approaching absolute zero (−273° C, or −460° F), helium first liquefies and then begins to exhibit superfluidity, a state characterized by an assortment of unusual phenomena including frictionless flow and the ability to creep up and over the walls of containers. The theory that attempts to explain such behavior begins by assuming that the superfluid state is ruled by large-scale quantization; *i.e.*, that the laws that parcel properties like mass, energy, and momentum into discrete values on helium's atomic and subatomic levels also hold true for superfluid helium in bulk. A consequence of this theory is the expectation that superfluid helium cannot move with any arbitrary momentum or energy; instead it must move in quantum steps.

Recently Richard E. Packard, Edward J. Yarmchuk, and Michael J. V. Gordon at the University of California at Berkeley created an experimental situation that made it possible to photograph this effect. In a cylindrical container 2 mm in diameter by 25 mm long (1 mm = 0.039 in) they spun superfluid helium, which in accordance with theory formed a stationary array of whirlpools, or vortices, that increased stepwise in number only when the container's rotation reached certain critical velocities. To make the vortices visible, electrons were allowed to be sucked into each one; an electric field was then applied to pull the electrons out of the vortices and onto a phosphor screen. Now that these vortices can be seen directly, the Berkeley group can study how they form and disperse, probing the underlying quantum mechanical laws more deeply.

Pushing toward laser fusion. The race to prove the scientific feasibility of controlled thermonuclear fusion for energy production is directed down two main avenues. The traditional approach traps hot ionized gas, or plasma, in a "magnetic bottle," where the nuclei

Standing patterns of whirlpools in a rotating container of superfluid helium stepwise increase in number according to quantum laws as rotational speed is increased. Whirlpools were made visible by filling them with electrons, which were then projected onto a phosphor screen.

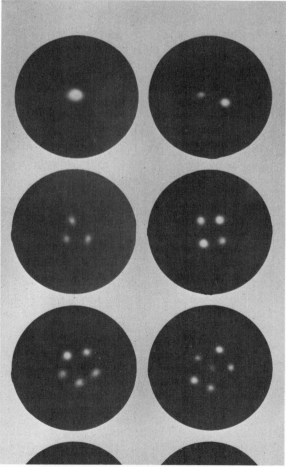

can collide, fuse together, and produce energy. A newer approach relies on imploding a small target of fuel. This compression rapidly increases temperature, forcing nuclei together under conditions that allow them to fuse. The all-important question for this second technique is what form of energy can compress pellets to the necessary extent. In the late 1970s electron and ion beams were being tried, but most effort was going into sharply focused, energetic lasers. During the past year the Shiva laser system at the Lawrence Livermore Laboratory of the University of California reached a significant milestone on the road to fusion.

In Shiva, 20 laser beams strike the target in pulses shorter than a nanosecond (one billionth of a second). In early 1980 it was the most energetic of all laser systems but still delivered only a tenth of the energy that would be needed to attain break-even (that is, a condition in which energy produced equals laser energy delivered to the target). In the past, laser bombardment reached high target temperatures using a target pellet design called the exploding pusher, which allows a rapid, supersonic shock-wave form of delivery of the laser pulse energy to the target. But these experiments fell far short of the plasma densities needed. Although Shiva was too weak to give both high temperature and high density, recent work showed that new designs in pellets and laser pulses can reach high densities, thus proving that at least in principle much of the fundamental physics of the compression is understood.

The targets are glass "microballoons" about 0.3 mm in diameter that are filled with deuterium-tritium gas, which is the reaction fuel. In the new design the glass is coated with thin layers of metal and plastic. When the laser pulses strike simultaneously from many directions (to keep spherical symmetry on the target), the plastic layer vaporizes and drives the metal layer inward, squeezing the fuel comparatively slowly and smoothly. This "spaced" compression requires somewhat longer laser pulse times, but it avoids the supersonic shock waves that form from a fast implosion and thus the sudden premature heating that had prevented achievement of high fuel densities in the past. In tests during 1979 the gas reached an ion temperature of only a few thousand electron volts (keV, or about 10,-000° C), compared with nearly ten keV in earlier experiments. The earlier work, however, had given peak densities only a fraction of the liquid density of the deuterium-tritium fuel, whereas recent experiments yielded densities 50–100 times the liquid density. Overall, demonstration that high density is realizable raised expectations that in the near future a more energetic set of lasers will give simultaneously the high temperatures and high densities needed to achieve and eventually exceed break-even.

Squeezing the elements. High-pressure physics advanced on a broad front in recent months, as scientists came closer to a possible final goal: superconducting hydrogen. Squeezing a substance hard enough, thus reducing its volume and raising its electron density, must eventually force it to become a metal. If this process is carried further to higher pressures and the temperature of the material is kept sufficiently low, theorists widely believe that any substance probably can be made into a superconductor, capable of carrying currents without energy losses from resistance.

At Cornell University, Ithaca, N.Y., Arthur L. Ruoff and David A. Nelson, Jr., added experimental support to this general view by making xenon become metallic. Xenon is the first element from the noble-gas column of the periodic table to show metallic behavior. The experiment was performed at 32° above absolute zero (32 K, or about −241° C), and the metal formed at about 320,000 times atmospheric pressure.

At still lower temperatures sulfur displays interesting new properties. Earlier work had shown that sulfur becomes metallic at room temperature under high pressures. Recently several groups of investigators in the U.S. and the U.S.S.R. pursued sulfur's metallic state down to liquid helium temperatures and apparently found the predicted transition to the superconducting state. Somewhere below about 10 K (−263° C), the metal superconducts, under a pressure of 200,-000–500,000 atmospheres.

Such high pressures seem to make practical use of these properties out of the question, but it is the very uncertainty of the field that makes this judgment itself questionable. Physicists dream of a superconducting hydrogen or oxygen that, once produced at high pressure, will remain condensed and superconducting when the pressure is removed. Theoretical predictions for hydrogen's superconducting transition temperature have ranged from nearly absolute zero to room temperature, depending on the applied pressure. Thus some excitement occurred when Peter M. Bell and Ho-Kwang Mao at the Carnegie Institution of Washington, D.C., made solid hydrogen at room temperature. They began by squeezing a tiny sample of liquid hydrogen in a pressure vessel at very low temperatures. They then sealed the vessel, allowed it to warm up to room temperature, and squeezed the sample still further, using a small tabletop press. At 57,000 times atmospheric pressure, the sample first formed geometric plates and then a single transparent solid mass. This behavior agreed quite well with theory. At about 360,000 atmospheres, its density was estimated at about two-thirds that of water, which is a density slightly lower than that found in the high-pressure, metallic phase of hydrogen that was reported by investigators at the Lawrence Livermore Laboratory in 1978 (see *1980 Yearbook of Science and the Future* Year in Review: PHYSICS: *General developments*).

Theoretical links between this newly found solid state, the metallic state discovered earlier, and the possible superconducting state are not well understood.

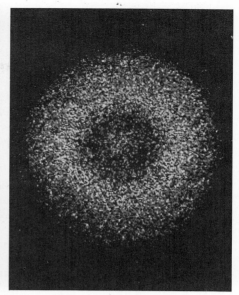

Development of the 24-beam Omega laser system (left) and of techniques to visualize imploding nuclear fuel pellets (right) form part of the efforts at the University of Rochester to harness fusion energy.

The problems of detecting electrical properties and even of making an accurate measurement of the pressure are primary stumbling blocks to rapid progress. The implications are broad, however, and go beyond Earthly laboratories. Deep in the interiors of Jupiter and other giant gaseous planets, hydrogen may form solid and metallic phases. This possibility has significance for the evolution of these worlds and the way in which their magnetic fields are generated.

—Gregory Benford

High-energy physics

The past year in high-energy physics was marked by major developments on both theoretical and experimental fronts.

Unification of weak and electromagnetic forces. The forces in nature seem to be of four types: the familiar gravitational force; the weak interaction, which is responsible for beta decay in radioactive nuclei; the electromagnetic force between electric charges, which keeps electrons bound to the atomic nucleus; and the strong interactions, which act between nucleons (protons and neutrons) in the nucleus and between their presumed constituents, the quarks. For many years these forces appeared to have little in common, though many physicists suspected they must somehow be closely connected. A major advance in understanding this connection occurred during the past several years with the development and gradual experimental verification of a unified theory of the weak and electromagnetic interactions.

Much of this "electroweak" theory is due to the work of Sheldon Glashow, Abdus Salam, and Steven Wein-

berg, who shared the 1979 Nobel Prize for Physics for their contributions (*see* SCIENTISTS OF THE YEAR). In it the quarks and leptons (the latter include the electron, muon, and recently discovered tau particle, together with their respective neutrinos) are treated as pointlike objects and are grouped together in multiplets. Members of a multiplet interact with each other in a well-defined way. One multiplet, for example, contains the lightest particles: the u quark, d quark, electron, and electron neutrino. Electromagnetic forces are due to the exchange of photons (packets of electromagnetic radiation) between the quarks and leptons; the weak force is due to the exchange of particles called intermediate bosons. Both the photon and intermediate bosons have intrinsic spin of one unit, while the quarks and leptons have spin $\frac{1}{2}$. Unlike the photon, however, which has zero rest mass, the intermediate bosons are predicted to have rest masses about 100 times that of the proton. These particles cannot be produced with existing accelerators but should be accessible with the next generation of accelerators, currently under construction at Fermi National Accelerator Laboratory (Fermilab) and Brookhaven National Laboratory in the U.S. and at the European Organization for Nuclear Research (CERN) in Geneva.

Experimental discovery of the intermediate bosons is eagerly awaited. The electroweak theory, however, already has an impressive body of experimental evidence to support it. As of early 1980 all the data were in good agreement with the simplest version of the theory as it was formulated independently by Weinberg and Salam. A particularly important experiment was the discovery at CERN of a type of weak interaction that does not change the electric charge of the participating particles. Experiments at the Stanford Linear Accelerator Center (SLAC), which studied parity violation in inelastic electron scattering by nucleons, were crucial tests (for a description of these terms and the SLAC experiments, see *1980 Yearbook of Science and the Future* Year in Review: PHYSICS: *High-energy physics*). Important as well were experiments at various accelerators to study neutrino scattering.

The electroweak theory also predicts the existence of another yet undiscovered type of particle, the so-called Higgs bosons, which must exist for the theory to be internally consistent. These particles may be difficult to find because there is no firm prediction of their mass, even as far as order of magnitude, and they are expected to be very short-lived and to have complicated decay modes.

Grand unified theories. The great success of the electroweak theory has led many theorists to attempt a more encompassing unified theory, which would include the strong interaction and possibly gravity. These attempts, all still unproven, go under the name of grand unified theories.

Scientists fine tune world's first frameless cylindrical drift chamber before its installation at the Los Alamos Meson Physics Facility. The device will be used in attempts to detect a very rare type of muon decay.

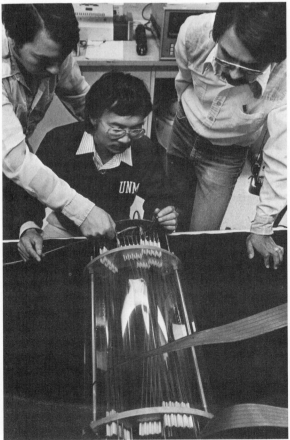

Courtesy, Los Alamos Scientific Laboratory; photo by LeRoy N. Sanchez

In widening the electroweak theory to incorporate the strong interaction, quarks and leptons become intimately tied together so that decays of quarks into leptons become possible. Thus certain conservation laws that prevent baryons (such particles as protons and neutrons, which consist of three quarks) and leptons from transforming into each other—laws previously thought to be inviolable—would be only approximately true. A striking prediction of these theories is that a proton or neutron can decay into leptons through the simultaneous decay of two of the three constituent quarks. Because the quarks decay into leptons by a weak interaction, however, this process would be extremely rare. In these theories proton lifetime is estimated to be about 10^{31} years. This means, for example, that one proton in a person's body might decay every 1,000 years or so. Hence, although confirmation of this possibility is obviously of great importance, it requires an experimental tour de force. In the early 1980s detectors with active volumes of thousands of tons of matter were being built deep underground to obtain the required sensitivity.

Just as the weak interactions come about through the exchange of an intermediate boson, the interaction that transforms quarks into leptons occurs through the interchange of a massive particle. Theoretical estimates place the mass of this particle at about 10^{15} times the mass of the proton. (A water droplet of this mass would be just visible to the naked eye!) Because it seems unlikely that the enormous energies required to create these particles experimentally will ever be attainable, detecting the decay of the proton with the predicted lifetime appears to be the crucial experimental test of the theory.

At energies comparable to the mass of this particle (about 10^{15} GeV, or billion electron volts), the interaction that transforms quarks into leptons and vice versa is expected to be comparable in strength to the strong interactions. Such energies are thought to have occurred in the very early universe, at times on the order of 10^{-35} seconds after the "big bang." Thus the grand unified theories have important implications in cosmology. In particular, they may help explain two long-standing cosmological puzzles: the large imbalance between the observed quantities of matter and antimatter in the universe and the much greater abundance of photons compared with baryons (about a billion to one). Within a unified theory of this type it is possible to construct plausible scenarios that would give rise to these asymmetries.

Quantum chromodynamics. A possible theoretical framework for describing the strong interactions has been evolving over the past several years. The general framework of this theory seems correct, but many details remain to be worked out. In it the strong interactions are due to the exchange of spin-one particles (those with one quantum unit of angular momentum)

Massive CHARM particle detector, which uses marble slabs for targets, dwarfs experimenters at CERN's proton synchrotron. Located in the synchrotron's neutrino beam, the detector will be used alone and in combination with other detectors to study the quark structure of nucleons, neutrino-electron scattering, and muon polarization.

called gluons between the quarks that make up the strongly interacting particles. In analogy with electric charge, the quarks and gluons possess a different attribute called color charge. There are six kinds of color charge, figuratively labeled red, blue, green, and their "complementary" colors. Unlike electric charge, however, free or solitary color charges are thought not to occur. All hadrons (collectively the baryons and mesons) are expected to be color-canceling combinations of a red, a blue, and a green quark or of a quark and an antiquark with complementary color charge. Color charge and therefore quarks and gluons are said to be confined; they cannot be observed directly. By analogy with quantum electrodynamics, which deals with the interactions of electric charges, the theory of color charge is called quantum chromodynamics.

It should be emphasized that quark confinement is only a postulate. No theoretical proof of quark confinement has been presented. Experimentally only one group (headed by William Fairbank at Stanford University) of the many that were searching for the fractional electric charges that free quarks should exhibit ($\frac{1}{3}$ or $\frac{2}{3}$ that of the electron) reported positive results. As of early 1980 no other group had duplicated Fairbank's results.

Although it may turn out that color confinement is not quite absolute, quantum chromodynamics shows great promise. Calculations in the theory are difficult; because of the strong coupling of the quarks and gluons to each other, generally only approximate predictions are possible. This hurdle, together with the presumed impossibility of observing quarks and gluons directly, makes it difficult to devise a critical test of the theory. The experimental evidence does seem to be consistent with the theory, and in the spring and sum-

mer of 1979 experiments at the new accelerator in Hamburg, West Germany, gave indirect evidence for the existence of gluons (*see below*).

New accelerators. In the past year data from two new accelerators began to make their mark on the field. Both of these are electron-positron colliding beam machines. The PETRA storage ring at the DESY laboratory near Hamburg is capable of storing counterrotating electron and positron beams, with total energies exceeding 35 GeV. This makes PETRA by far the most powerful electron-positron collider until a comparable machine in the U.S. comes into operation in 1980. Both of these machines were built to exploit the very rich new fields of physics opened up by lower energy storage rings.

According to quantum chromodynamics, when an electron and its antimatter counterpart collide, their annihilation can form a quark and antiquark. Because of color confinement these can never show themselves directly. Instead they produce two oppositely directed jets of particles containing hadrons. Thus the bulk of the events at high energy are expected to show two collinear, oppositely directed groups of tracks. A small fraction of the time, it is predicted that one of the quarks will radiate a gluon, just as an electrically charged particle can radiate a photon. The gluon gives rise to a third jet of particles. Such three-jet events indeed were found at PETRA with about the expected frequency, an observation that added strong support to the basic ideas of quantum chromodynamics.

The second electron-positron storage ring to start experiments during the past year was CESR at Cornell University. This accelerator can store beams as energetic as 8 GeV; it was constructed especially to study new particle states formed from *b* quarks, which carry

371

(Top, left and right) CERN COURIER, November, 1979, p. 359;
(bottom) courtesy, Fermilab

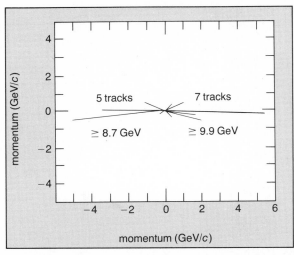

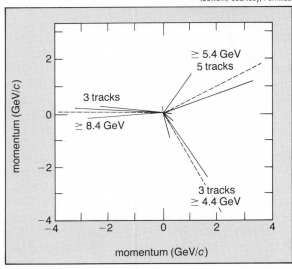

Computer reconstructions of two electron-positron collision events in the TASSO detector at PETRA are compared (top). Each event produces about a dozen charged particles; the length of each particle track is proportional to the particle's momentum. On the left is an example of the most common type of event, with two oppositely directed jets. The reconstruction on the right shows a rarer three-jet event. (Bottom) Günter Wolf of DESY interprets the third jet as evidence of gluon production.

the quantum property known variously as beauty or bottom and which were discovered at the proton accelerator at Fermilab. To produce particles containing *b* quarks, each electron beam must have an energy greater than about 5.5 GeV. Previous experiments at Fermilab and DESY had indicated the existence of three upsilon states, which are bound states of a *b* quark and its antiquark. Only the two lower energy upsilons, however, were detected with certainty. Soon after experiments started at CESR, the third upsilon was found. It is expected that a rich spectrum of new states will be seen in the energy range accessible to CESR.

A fascinating connection between high-energy physics and international diplomacy developed in early 1979 with the signing of a formal agreement for cooperation in science between the U.S. and the People's Republic of China. In conjunction, the U.S. agreed to assist China in the construction of a 50 GeV proton synchroton to be built near Beijing (Peking) not far from the Ming Tombs. Prototype magnets for the machine will be built at Fermilab with the participation of Chinese physicists. During the year Chinese scientists were also involved in experimental programs at CERN, DESY, and SLAC.

—Michael J. Longo

Nuclear physics

Research in nuclear physics in recent months was productive as experimenters continued to push their studies to ever higher energies and thus to more microscopic probing of nuclear structure and behavior. A major advance in unifying the description of physical phenomena continued to take shape as experimental and theoretical studies lent support to a new model of nuclear structure developed by Franco Iachello of Yale University (see *1980 Yearbook of Science and the Future* Year in Review: PHYSICS: *Nuclear physics*).

Structure of helium nuclei. Recent results obtained at the Stanford Linear Accelerator Center (SLAC) by R. Arnold and his collaborators raised new and as yet unexplained questions about the structure of some of the very lightest nuclei. It has long been recognized that the scattering of electrons represents one of the cleanest ways in which to examine the structure of nuclei. In a very real sense SLAC's linear accelerator is simply a two-mile-long electron microscope lying on its side. Its energetic electrons interact with nuclei under study only through the electromagnetic force—the most thoroughly understood force in nature—without the ambiguities that arise when the strong nuclear force, which holds nuclei together, is directly involved.

The new electron scattering results appeared to show that the two protons and the one neutron in the helium-3 nucleus repel one another, leaving essentially a hole in the middle that is vastly more pronounced than any current model of nuclear structure would permit. This finding is particularly disturbing because it has long been felt that an understanding of this extremely simple nucleus with only three component parts is a prerequisite to obtaining a microscopic understanding of more complex situations.

This new result poses some fascinating possibilities, among them that three nucleons can interact in ways not previously suspected or that the scattering of electrons is being influenced in unexpected fashion by the presence of the cloud of virtual pi mesons (pions) that are involved in binding the helium nucleus together. Resolution of this puzzle will occupy a significant fraction of research in nuclear physics in coming months.

Deep inelastic scattering. When it first became possible to examine the interaction of heavy nuclei, among the most important discoveries was the fact that an entirely new process, termed deep inelastic scattering, was present. In this process, in contrast to any that had previously been known and through mechanisms not as yet understood, a substantial fraction of the total energy initially appearing as relative motion of the interacting nuclei is transferred into internal excitation energy. The hot excited fragments formed during the collision then move apart from one another, essentially under the influence of their mutual electrostatic repulsion. Following the discovery of deep inelastic scattering by John Huizenga of the University of Rochester in New York several years ago, the mechanisms by which this energy transfer is accomplished pose important problems and have been the subject of intensive activity worldwide.

Ricardo Broglia of the State University of New York at Stony Brook and Aage Winther of the Niels Bohr Institute in Copenhagen suggested that the energy of relative motion might first be converted into excitation of the so-called giant resonances, in which the entire nucleus is forced to vibrate very much in the nature of a liquid drop, and that subsequently the energy as-

K. T. R. Davies, K. R. Sandhya Devi, M. R. Strayer, "Physical Review C," vol. 20, no. 4, fig. 8, October, 1979

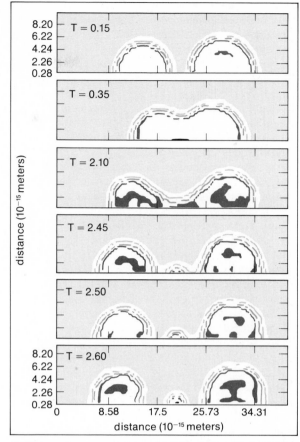

Collision of two nuclei, krypton-86 and lanthanum-139, at an energy of 710 MeV is simulated in a series of computer plots developed from mathematical calculations by British and U.S. physicists. Contoured areas relate regions of equal nuclear density. Times (T) are in units of 10^{-21} seconds. After coalescing, the model nuclei separate, forming a neck that breaks in two places to leave behind a small fragment similar to an alpha particle.

sociated with this vibration could be coupled into more complex motions and excitations of the nuclear system. During the past year Russell Betts and his collaborators at Yale University obtained the first experimental information that confirms this suggestion. By studying the interaction of carbon and aluminum nuclei they were able to freeze the energy transfer process—in effect, before it was completed—and found characteristic signatures of the process in which the original giant resonance vibrational energy was being converted into the much more complex underlying excitations. Current interest centers on searching for similar phenomena in much heavier nuclear systems and on understanding the relative importance of the different characteristic giant resonance vibrations that are permitted to a nuclear system by quantum laws.

Obviously this transfer of energy takes a certain

amount of time, albeit very small. Huizenga and his collaborators at the University of Rochester and at the Lawrence Berkeley Laboratory in California suggested that there is a unique one-to-one relationship between the amount of energy transferred and the time taken to accomplish that transfer, but as of early 1980 there was no direct experimental confirmation of this simple assumption. Recently, Walter Greiner and his associates at the University of Frankfurt in West Germany proposed a very interesting experiment that might resolve the question. They noted that when colliding nuclei are near one another there is a substantial probability that electrons from the original clouds about those nuclei can be ejected as so-called delta electrons. This process can happen when the nuclei are either coming together or receding from one another following the collision and, according to quantum mechanics, the contributions—both before and after the collision —must be added coherently. Consequently, should a deep inelastic interaction occur, a time delay will be introduced between ejection of the delta electrons in the initial and final parts of the interaction. This delay will result in a phase shift between the two contributions and a predictable oscillation in the number of delta electrons emitted as a function of their energy. Should experimental studies currently under way both at the GSI facility in Darmstadt, West Germany, and at Yale University confirm this suggestion, it would represent the first direct measurement of the time scale involved in these very rapid nuclear processes, on the order of 10^{-20} seconds.

Meson production in heavy-ion collisions. With the availability of extremely high-energy heavy ions from the Bevalac at the Lawrence Berkeley Laboratory and the Synchrophasotron at Dubna in the Soviet Union, great interest has been attached to searches for phenomena, first predicted by T. D. Lee and G. C. Wick of Columbia University, New York City, that would be possible under these high-energy conditions. In particular, Lee and Wick suggested that under the conditions of very high compression that might occur in an ultrahigh-energy collision it might be possible to obtain entirely new kinds of nuclear matter in which much of the mass of the neutrons and protons involved would disappear and then reappear in the form of pion clouds—a sort of pion soup in which the diminished nucleons would be suspended. As a first step toward investigating this fascinating idea searches have focused on the possibility of so-called pion condensates, which would form as "droplets" of pions during the collisions. Recently a team led by Walter Benenson and involving scientists from Michigan State University, the Lawrence Berkeley Radiation Laboratory, the Institute of Nuclear Studies in Tokyo, Indiana University, Osaka University in Japan, and the University of Paris used the Lawrence Berkeley Bevalac to examine heavy-ion collisions. They found a very sharp

peak in the energy spectrum of negatively charged pions at a production angle directly in line with the incident heavy-ion beam. The fact that there is a corresponding minimum in the positively charged pion spectrum leads to the conclusion that the effect is caused by the electric field of the heavy ions during the collision. These studies are still in their infancy but will be pursued because they may provide one of the possible signatures for phenomena that might be expected on the way to obtaining this new kind of nuclear matter, if indeed it exists.

Similarly, attention is being focused on the possible existence of shock waves induced in the nuclear matter during these very high energy collisions. Under such conditions the actual nuclear velocities are greater than the velocity of sound in nuclear matter, and shock waves analogous to those produced by supersonic aircraft would be expected. From measurement of the characteristic angles in such shock waves, if they can be identified, it is possible to measure the degree of compression that occurs and thus the extent to which the experimental situation approaches that predicted by Lee and Wick. In the early 1980s only the Berkeley and the Dubna facilities provided adequate energy to permit the study of such phenomena.

Hyper nuclei. The lambda particle, the lightest one possessing the quantum property called strangeness, is only 20% heavier than a neutron or proton and differs from the neutron, for example, only in having this strangeness. Because it does differ from the neutron, however, it is not prevented by the Pauli exclusion principle from occupying a quantum state that is already full of neutrons or protons, as would be the case for another nucleon. It has long been recognized that for this reason it would make a most interesting probe for the deeply lying structure of nuclei. It would provide a method of examining the character of the nucleon orbits not near the nuclear surface but rather deep in its interior and the extent to which the behavior of nucleons is different under such conditions.

Many years ago Herman Feshbach and Arthur Kerman of the Massachusetts Institute of Technology recognized that the interaction in which an incoming kaon (K meson) brings one unit of strangeness into the collision and a pion emerges to conserve energy and momentum would be one particularly simple way of converting one of the neutrons in a target nucleus into a lambda particle. This transformation would result in a so-called hyper nucleus (because the lambda particle belongs to a class called hyperons) and thus permit study of just the desired interaction. Recently a French-West German collaboration led by Bogdan Povh carried out such a reaction using kaon beams from the CERN accelerator in Geneva and targets of oxygen and carbon to produce just the type of reaction envisaged by Feshbach and Kerman. In early 1980 results were still somewhat preliminary, but already a fascinating puzzle was emerging. Characteristic of the behavior of neutrons in nuclei is the fact that it makes a very considerable difference whether the intrinsic spin of the neutron is aligned parallel or antiparallel to its orbital angular momentum. This is the so-called spin-orbit coupling that is of central importance in determining the spectroscopy of the nuclear quantum system. Because the lambda particle is so similar to the neutron, it had been fully assumed that it would display very similar spin-orbit characteristics. It was thus extremely surprising to find that the lambda particle apparently displays a spin-orbit reaction that is no more than one-tenth that of a neutron. No explanation is currently available for this puzzle, which may well be the first of many as this new field of hyper nuclear physics is opened up with the availability of kaon beams from high-energy particle accelerators.

One of the most interesting aspects of hypernuclear physics is the prospect that it could shed important new light on the quasi-particle picture of physical systems. The idea of a quasi-particle—*i.e.*, a disturbance in a medium that behaves as a particle and that can carry size, shape, energy, momentum, and other properties characteristic of objects—has been extremely useful in some pursuits of solid-state and plasma physics, as well as in particle and nuclear physics. The low excited states of strongly interacting systems can be reproduced easily by simple excitations of properly chosen quasi-particles and by collective excitations of the system. Only in the nucleus, however, do scientists now have a suitable probe, the lambda particle, with properties that simulate a nucleon in the nucleus yet make the particle quite distinct.

—D. Allan Bromley

Solid-state physics

Solid-state physics occupies a special place within the subfields of physics because of the strong interaction between fundamental research in the discipline and practical applications. The question being asked more frequently is not whether fundamental research will have practical implications but rather how soon these implications will have an important effect. There is also influence in the opposite direction. Practical advances often open questions or provide certain clues that lead to important new fundamental advances. These aspects of solid-state physics will be stressed below in a review of a pair of recent advances.

Another characteristic of solid-state physics is the interrelation between advancements in fields that superficially may appear quite different. The examples to be discussed, although part of independent lines of research, are both associated with structural defect levels (*e.g.*, crystal-lattice vacancies) in covalently bonded semiconductors (materials whose atomic bonds are formed of shared electron pairs). Realization

Column 26 meters (85 feet) high forms part of the new 25 MV electrostatic accelerator at Oak Ridge National Laboratory. In combination with other equipment the device will accelerate ions with masses as high as 150.

of the central importance of structural defects has completely changed theoretical ideas of amorphous semiconductors and has raised the possibility, inconceivable a decade ago, that these materials may be of practical importance for the direct conversion of solar energy to electricity. In a parallel development it has become apparent that such defects play the dominant role in the formation of Schottky barrier rectifiers in certain key materials. Whereas these rectifiers have been a vital element in solid-state electronics for half a century, until recently they have defied fundamental understanding of their key electrical property, the barrier height (*i.e.*, the electrical "turn-on" voltage).

Amorphous semiconductors and solar energy. Attention was first focused on amorphous, or noncrystalline, semiconductors a decade ago when U.S. physicist Stanford R. Ovshinsky reported that an increase in voltage above a certain minimum value could create a drastic change in the electrical properties of certain covalent amorphous materials. While hopes that these materials might produce a new family of electronic devices to challenge the transistor proved to be too optimistic, amorphous devices have found application as specialized memory elements in computers.

375

There has been a large advance in the basic understanding of amorphous semiconductors since 1970. At that time the dominant theory of their fundamental electrical properties centered on the idea of a very basic difference in the nature of the band gaps in crystalline and amorphous semiconductors. To properly explain what this means, the nature of band gaps in crystalline materials should be considered.

In crystalline materials there is a very well-defined range of discrete energy levels, or quantum states, that electrons cannot possess (*see* figure 1). This range forms the band gap that gives crystalline semiconductors their very special properties. In the atoms of a pure crystal at sufficiently low temperature, the quantum states lying below the band gap (the valence band) are completely filled with electrons, whereas those lying above the band gap (the conduction band) will be completely empty. Thus, there are no electrons in quantum states that allow them to carry electric current when an external electric field is applied. As a result the material is an insulator. However, by raising the temperature or introducing the correct atomic impurities (dopants) into the semiconductor crystal lattice, or both, electrons can be placed in the conduction band or removed from the valence band (creating positively charged "holes"). Thus, electrons are placed in quantum states in which they can move freely through the crystal in response to an external field. This ease of movement is one consequence of the sharp band edge that characterizes crystalline semiconductors. By a sharp band gap, one means that there is a sharp transition in the relative number of available quantum states that electrons can occupy.

A decade ago the situation was thought to be quite different for amorphous semiconductors. For them,

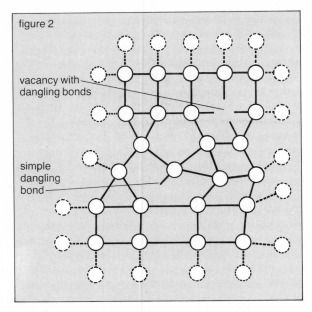

Schematic model of amorphous silicon atoms shows examples of a simple dangling bond and a vacancy with dangling bonds.

due to the lack of crystalline order, there was believed to be no well-defined band edge and, thus, no abrupt transition in the quantum states that could conduct electricity at the forbidden gap. Rather, the allowed quantum states were believed to "tail" into the forbidden gap. The "tail" states would be localized in space so that they could not conduct electricity. Thus, in contrast to crystalline materials, it was predicted that the electrons in the lowest conduction-band quantum states inherent in the amorphous semiconductor could not efficiently conduct. However, new work on carefully prepared amorphous samples and new theoretical results (based on different starting approximations) indicated that amorphous materials could have sharp band edges similar to those of single crystals.

These conflicting results led naturally to the question of whether the earlier evidence of band tailing demonstrated a property fundamental to amorphous materials or was due to defects produced in the material during its preparation. Even if the material was perfectly pure, structural defects could produce the observed states. Basically, such defects are due to unsatisfied, or "dangling," covalent bonds (*e.g.*, a silicon atom in amorphous silicon bonded only to three silicon neighbors and not the four necessary to chemically saturate the four valence electrons of the silicon atom). This, in turn, would lead to an isolated dangling bond that would produce states in the forbidden gap (*see* figure 2). Such other defects as vacancies (an atom missing from a lattice site) or vacancy complexes (a complex involving more than one missing or "out-of-position" atom) could also be present.

The question of whether the tail states are funda-

Graph compares quantum state density in the band gap region for single-crystal silicon (dashed line) and for amorphous silicon with sharp band edges (light solid line) and without them (heavy solid line).

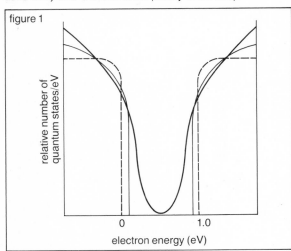

mental was very important not only theoretically but practically. If these states are fundamental, then electrons that are excited (*e.g.*, by light) from the valence to the conduction band cannot move significant distances before becoming trapped in the tail states. Thus, one could not make solar cells from amorphous materials. However, if these states were due to defects and if the defects could be removed or neutralized, then amorphous materials could be so used.

If one assumes that the basic level of structural defect is the unsatisfied covalent bond, one can start to see how such defects can be eliminated. It is well known that a simple way of satisfying such a dangling bond is by making it a covalent bond with an atom that can form only a single covalent bond. Hydrogen, fluorine, or chlorine are examples of such atoms. In fact, this approach has been found to be very important in integrated circuit technology where it is critical to reduce the number of dangling bonds at the silicon-silicon dioxide interface.

As often happens in solid-state physics, practical developments did not wait for complete resolution of theoretical questions. Thus, the empirical attempt to neutralize defects went forward parallel with fundamental work. Groups at Harvard University and RCA Laboratories and in Scotland during the 1970s found that adding hydrogen to amorphous silicon as it was grown transformed the material to one that had the same sort of sharp band edges as crystalline silicon and whose conductivity could likewise be changed by doping. These results gave additional evidence that "tailing of states" into the gap observed in the 1960s is not a fundamental property.

A group at RCA Laboratories appeared to be the first to appreciate the practical implications for solar cells and to act on that appreciation. One problem with practical solar energy conversion is that the intensity of sunlight arriving on the surface of the Earth is relatively low per unit area. Crystalline silicon devices, which have been quite suitable for uses in space (where cost of the devices is insignificant compared with other costs), are much too expensive to manufacture for use on the Earth where the cost of providing energy is a critical factor. Amorphous silicon solar cells, however, can be prepared economically because they can be formed by relatively inexpensive techniques; manufacture of silicon cells by ion-sputtering, evaporation, or chemical deposition methods is much less costly than growing single crystals, cutting wafers, and forming junctions and contacts, all of which are necessary for creating single-crystal solar cells. Using amorphous silicon in combination with hydrogen, RCA investigators achieved efficiencies for transformation of solar to electrical energy in excess of 5%, compared with about 15% for the more expensive single-crystal silicon cells. More recently, Ovshinsky announced improved amorphous silicon solar cells made by using

fluorine rather than hydrogen to satisfy the dangling bonds. In 1980 his company, Energy Conversion Devices, signed a $25 million contract with a large oil company to hasten development of these solar cells.

In 1980 it was not yet clear if amorphous materials would play a key role in practical solar energy efforts. Nevertheless, disproving a theory that was once widely accepted has opened the way for such possibilities.

Lattice defects and Schottky barrier rectifiers. Strangely enough, one of the oldest and most important solid-state devices has been the subject of intense fundamental research in the last few years. This is the Schottky barrier rectifier, named for the German scientist who in the 1930s helped explain its behavior but not the underlying reasons. To form a Schottky barrier, a metallic layer is placed on a semiconductor. For a large number of metals it is found that current flows in one direction but not in the other. These devices first came into prominence before World War II as simple devices for radio signal reception. During the war they were the subject of intensive research because of their importance in radar and other systems. Because a favored semiconductor material in their fabrication was germanium, considerable effort was placed in producing purer and more perfect germanium crystals and in understanding the properties of those crystals. It was this work that helped lay the foundations necessary for development of the transistor, integrated circuits, and other solid-state devices.

Fundamental understanding of the Schottky barrier, however, remained elusive for many decades. In recent years a new generation of experimental tools has made it possible to obtain, on an atomic level, rather complete knowledge of the clean surfaces of semiconductors. Simultaneously, theoretical methods have progressed to the point where detailed calculations can be made of

Graph illustrates the relationship between current and voltage for a Schottky barrier rectifier.

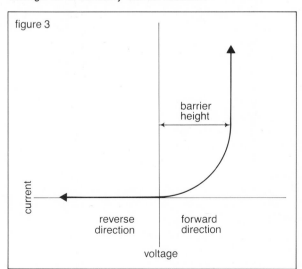

the electronic structure of the surface layer of atoms. However, since these calculations depend on knowing the exact position of all atoms, they have been made more difficult by the necessity of determining these positions experimentally. In some cases a combination of experiment and theory has been used to determine atomic surface positions. This problem is quite acute: for covalent semiconductors positions of atoms at the surface have been found to differ by 15–25% from positions inside the crystal.

In the last few decades several theories have been derived to explain the fundamental properties of the Schottky barrier. The most important of these properties is the barrier "height." This is the applied voltage necessary to start current flow in the "forward" direction. (In the "reverse" direction of an ideal Schottky barrier, no current will flow no matter how large the applied voltage.) This concept is illustrated in figure 3.

Much recent work has concentrated on 3-5 semiconductor compounds, so called because they are made from elements in the third and fifth columns of the periodic table. In the past year work at Stanford University and the Xerox Corp. made it clear that none of the existing theories for the Schottky barrier was correct. All of them were based on the assumption of an ideal planar boundary between the metal and semiconductor, an assumption that the recent experiments proved false. It was found, furthermore, that semiconductor material moved out into the metal, raising the possibility that structural defects were being produced in the semiconductor. In addition, not only was behavior of the Schottky barrier confirmed to be essentially independent of the metal atom, but also its barrier height was found to be the same even if oxygen rather than a metal was used. Together these experiments suggested that Schottky barrier formation did not involve a direct interaction between the added atom and the semiconductor but rather a process in which the added atoms perturbed the semiconductor surface and formed vacancies or other structural defects that were responsible for establishing the barrier height. This new model is currently being explored in depth.

Schottky barriers are becoming of increasing importance in the manufacture of high-speed solid-state devices based on the use of 3-5 compounds. In silicon technology the control elements of such devices are normally formed by a metal oxide-silicon structure. However, as mentioned above, to make silicon-silicon dioxide structure work, the density of dangling-bond states between the semiconductor and the oxide must be kept at a very low value. Such a solution has not been achieved for interfaces between 3-5 compounds and their oxides. As a result, Schottky barrier control elements are used instead. For some very promising 3-5 compounds, however, the Schottky barrier height is not sufficient to allow even the use of Schottky barrier control elements. Understanding the role of defects in Schottky barrier formation has stimulated work aimed at fabricating Schottky barriers such that their heights can be increased—and possibly even tailored—for various applications. Such an accomplishment would have widespread importance in the semiconductor industry.

—William E. Spicer

Psychology

The year was marked by the appearance of critical reactions to the chimpanzee language demonstrations that had captured the imagination of professional psychologists and public alike during the 1970s. This criticism was spearheaded by Herbert Terrace of Columbia University, who published five major pieces on the topic during 1979: (1) a highly critical review of David Premack's book on intelligence in apes; (2) a lead article in *Science* (November 23) on his own language research with a young chimpanzee; (3) an article in the November issue of *Psychology Today* summarizing the major critical points; (4) an experimental report of operant research with pigeons that demonstrates behavioral capacity essentially equivalent to that which Terrace believes to have been unambiguously shown by the higher primates; and (5) a book entitled *Nim*, the nickname of the chimpanzee that Terrace had studied.

The heart of the disagreement involved the interpretation of the learning demonstrated by Beatrice and R. Allen Gardner's Washoe (and her numerous successors), using a modified form of American Sign Language (ASL); Premack's Sarah, communicating by placement of plastic chips of varying color and shape; and Duane Rumbaugh's Lana, trained to communicate by operating a computer. Terrace does not question the ability of these primates, or of his own Nim, to learn an impressively large number of signs, which they can use to express their wants to trainers. What he does question is the evidence that any of them has really used even a rudimentary form of grammar in putting the signs together in meaningful strings, which is the generally accepted criterion for language.

Careful review of the filmed records of these animals' behavior, again including Nim, persuaded Terrace that the preponderance of what at first seemed to be meaningful strings of signs could also be explained on the basis of the animals' rapid response to inadvertent cuing by their trainers or subtle imitations of the trainers' signs. Terrace therefore concludes that these demonstrations all attest to the excellent ability of the primates to solve problems on the basis of the rewards they are typically given but do not provide an adequate empirical basis for the proposition that they have actually used any form of grammar.

This criticism is all the more trenchant coming as it

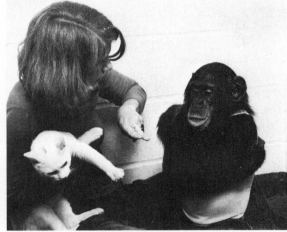

Chimpanzee Nim signals "me" (upper left), "hug" (upper right), and "cat" (lower left) to trainer. In spite of such achievements Nim was the subject of a report by Herbert Terrace in which the author questioned whether any nonhuman primate has been able to put learned signs together in meaningful sequences. Whenever primates seem to have done this, Terrace argued, they are only responding rapidly to inadvertent cuing by their trainers or are imitating the trainers' signs.

does from a highly respected and behaviorally oriented experimentalist. Terrace somewhat ruefully admits that he named his chimpanzee Neam Chimpsky (an obvious reference to behaviorist B. F. Skinner's long-time critic, linguist Noam Chomsky) on the assumption that his results would in fact demonstrate linguistic capacity.

An even more embarrassing attack on alleged chimpanzee language was published (in the November issue of *Psychology Today*) by Thomas Sebeok and Jean Umiker-Sebeok, two Indiana University linguists who have studied the use of signs by animals, especially in animal-training situations. They are most critical of the ASL research featuring Washoe, pointing to many recorded instances which indicate that insufficient attention was paid to the possibility that the trainers were unintentionally providing subtle but crucial cues. More detailed accounts of their work are available in *Speaking of Apes: A Critical Anthology of Two-way*

Communication with Man and also in *What the Speechless Creatures Say* (both 1980).

The proponents of primate linguistic communication will undoubtedly respond to the criticisms, and it is to be hoped that their responses will include new and more carefully controlled research. Meanwhile, it can safely be said that neither of the two extreme positions should be held seriously today: to wit, that the higher primates other than man use only signs in their communication, or that they have been shown without question to use a grammar approximating that utilized by young human organisms. Which of these two positions or, more realistically, which kind of compromise position will ultimately come to be accepted will depend on the outcome of future research. (*See* Feature Article: PRIMATE INTELLIGENCE.)

Chinese psychology. The revival of psychological enterprise in China was one of the most significant events of the year. In 1979 a delegation of California psychologists visited Beijing (Peking) University, where plans for new and resumed publications of scientific journals (*e.g.,* the first issue of *Acta Psychologica Sinica* since 1967) were described. The new attitude toward psychology generally and Western psychology in particular dates from the fall of the radical "gang of four" in 1976. Psychologists had been among the more suspect elements in the academic and professional community during the Cultural Revolution.

By and large, the research interests of contemporary Chinese psychologists appeared to parallel those of their Western colleagues. For example, the Psychology Institute of the Chinese Academy of Sciences in Beijing has sections on developmental psychology, sensory and perceptual processes, physiological psychology, and theoretical studies. The physiological section recently studied animal reactions to drugs and human reactions to acupuncture anesthesia. In the latter research it was found that success was markedly facilitated by the patient's confidence in the technique.

In addition to the institutes, which were being organized in major cities, psychology was being actively developed within the universities. At Beijing University the department of psychology was only two years old, psychology formerly having been a specialty within philosophy. It was now one of 21 departments and, like most of the others, was in need of new facilities. No foreign publications had been received for about two decades.

The California psychologists were interested in the theoretical climate of the new Chinese psychology, which tends to stress applied and industrial problems. Asked about Chinese reactions to the views of Freud and Skinner, Jing Jizheng (Ching Chi-cheng), deputy director of the Beijing University psychology department, replied: "We can answer the question in a clearcut way, with a negative answer to Freud. . . . and there are certain limitations if we want to apply behaviorism to the higher cognitive processes."

The centennial. The centennial of the formal initiation of scientific psychology by Wilhelm Wundt at the University of Leipzig in 1879 was celebrated by a number of events. Because the International Congress of Psychology (the major international organization of psychologists) meets only every three years, its observance was scheduled for 1980. A weeklong program was held in Leipzig, East Germany, with a number of sessions devoted to commemoration of Wundt's work.

In the U.S., in addition to various commemorative programs at meetings, the centennial was observed by publication of a book, *The First Century of Experimental Psychology,* edited by Eliot Hearst of Indiana University and written by a group of prominent experimentalists. Although it was estimated that only about 10% of contemporary U.S. psychologists consider themselves "experimental" psychologists, they nevertheless play a significant role within the discipline.

Sidney Harris

Schematic memory. Research and theorizing in the field of memory continued to develop rapidly. Long ignored by most psychologists, memory and forgetting were becoming recognized as pervasive and crucial problems. Under the influence of behaviorism interference theory (the view that most, if not all, forgetting is due to active blocking out of old associations by new ones) had displaced the orthodox decay theory (the commonsensical notion that old memories tend to fade away, as from some weakening of their neurophysiological basis, much as muscles weaken from lack of use). Although the interference theory is by no means dead, it was in turn replaced as the dominant theory by a new emphasis on organization (the more or less hierarchical ordering of the meaningful encoding—neurophysiological recording—of memories) as a part of the strong current focus on information processing and related cognitive processes.

The latest and, in some respects, the most promising new approach is the concept of schematic memory. As psychologist Jean Mandler of the University of California at San Diego explains in a review article, this form of organization theory holds that a schema "is formed on the basis of past experience with objects, scenes, or events and consists of a set of (usually unconscious) expectations about what things look like and/or the manner in which they occur." She points out that schemas provide "a more powerful set of retrieval cues than does a taxonomic organization... [and] are automatically activated by familiar situations regardless of age, culture, or schooling."

The schema concept appears to offer an unusually high potential for future theory and research. It also appears to bring memory research closer to everyday life than is the case with the typical laboratory study.

Unconscious reading: short-term memory. An especially significant and potentially important development in the area of information processing was the recent discovery by Anthony Marcel of the Applied Psychology Unit at Cambridge University of what he labeled "unconscious reading." Marcel found that when a very brief presentation of a common word is followed immediately by a mask consisting of a jumble of letters and digits, there is an interruption in the encoding of the stimulus. The subject is rarely able to identify the word itself but often shows signs that it has indeed been processed up to a point (for example, by giving common associates of the word, such as "king" when the presented word was "queen"). Apparently the conscious recognition of the stimulus and the verbal report on it are blocked by the disruption of processing by the mask. Nevertheless, the early stages of processing, preceding conscious identification, are permitted to occur. These results are consistent with the view that processing of different features of verbal materials occurs in simultaneous parallel channels. Some aspects of a word's meaning can therefore be processed at an unconscious level.

The richness of automatic encoding in human perception that this phenomenon suggests is reminiscent of the earlier demonstration, by Delos Wickens at Ohio State University, of the so-called "release of proactive inhibition." Wickens's procedure consists of a series of trials in the short-term memory paradigm (three words presented briefly, to be remembered; followed by about 20 seconds of some mental task, such as arithmetic operations, sufficiently demanding to prevent active rehearsal; then a recall test of the three words). The unique part of this experimental design is the use of related words (*e.g.*, birds' names) for the first three or four trials, followed by a shift to some other type of word on the crucial test trial (*e.g.*, names of trees). The typical result is that memory for the word triads becomes progressively poorer, presumably because of the buildup of interference among the highly similar terms, with a dramatic improvement in recall of the test words on the changed dimension.

The greatest release of this kind has been shown for shifts such as that illustrated above (birds to trees) and from words to numbers. Very little release has been found between word parts; *e.g.*, from verbs to adjectives. Wickens's procedure not only provides a sensitive means of assessing the degree of encoding relationship between various stimulus conditions but also is, conceptually, a neat combination of interference and organization theory. Moreover, as Wickens emphasized, it is a powerful demonstration of both the complexity and the automaticity of the encoding process.

Return of the maze. Another development of more than usual interest was the return to favor of the maze as an instrument to measure animal learning. The first maze was developed about 1900 for use with rats. It was long and complex, having been modeled after the famous maze at Hampton Court in England.

Over the first half of the 20th century the length and complexity of rat mazes were progressively reduced, until finally a single choice point (the so-called T-maze) became the preferred instrument for many experimentalists. This occurred primarily because it was felt that elimination of the interaction among successive choices (mostly right and left turns) would permit a clearer delineation of the determinants of the choice. Subsequently, the T-maze was itself reduced by removal of the T (or choice point); all that was left was a straightaway with start and goal boxes, permitting study of even simpler questions about activating and inhibiting factors. As the operant-conditioning movement initiated by Skinner attracted an increasing number of adherents, even the runway was largely abandoned in favor of a single testing chamber, often with only one manipulandum (a bar for the rat to press, an illuminated disk for the pigeon to peck).

The return of the maze was a side effect of the "cognitive revolution," specifically, the application of cognitive questions to the problems of animal learning and memory. In the main, the various pieces of apparatus described above are singularly unfitted to the task of providing inferences about cognitive structures. The maze, on the other hand, readily permits such inferences. This is especially true of the so-called radial maze, typically consisting of a central starting area with several arms leading from it.

The problems being addressed in this maze research involve the structure of memory and the development of cognitive maps. Other, somewhat more unusual, problems are those of foraging strategies used by various forms of predatory animals and experimental analyses of exploratory behavior, useful to the behavioral biologist as well as to the comparative and experimental psychologist in developing more ecologically satisfactory theoretical accounts of adaptive behavior in animals.

—Melvin H. Marx

Space exploration

Probes to Jupiter and Saturn revealed much new information about those planets and their moons during the past year. Among the most striking discoveries were that Jupiter has a ring and a fourteenth moon and that Saturn has two additional rings. Also during the year Soviet cosmonauts set a new space duration record.

Manned flight

Technical problems coupled with underestimates in systems testing and costs continued to delay the first flight of the U.S. space shuttle orbiter "Columbia." Na-

Engineers inspect the aluminum slosh baffles that line the interior of the one-half million-gallon external fuel tank of the space shuttle. The baffles are designed to diffuse the movement of the fuel during launch.

tional Aeronautics and Space Administration (NASA) officials held out some hope for a first flight during 1980. In other developments two Soviet cosmonauts spent 175 days aboard the Salyut 6 space station, breaking the old space duration record set by a Soviet crew in 1978. The U.S. space station Skylab, lived in by three trios of U.S. astronauts in 1973–74, met a spectacular demise in July 1979 as it entered the atmosphere and broke up over Western Australia.

Space shuttle. Space shuttle program managers were encouraged in late December 1979 when three test shuttle orbiter main engines were fired together for 520 seconds, the normal launch-to-orbit duration, at the National Space Technology Laboratories in Mississippi. Previous attempts had been hampered by component failures, although test engines had been fired singly for the full duration during the preceding months.

The orbiter's glass tile heat shield system, a departure from earlier heat shields, was also presenting technical problems. Orbiter "Columbia" was ferried partially completed in March from Palmdale, Calif., to NASA's John F. Kennedy Space Center in Florida. Revi-

sions had to be made in the techniques and adhesives used to bond the fragile silica-glass heat shield tiles to the craft's aluminum skin, and while some technicians were bonding tiles to one part of the spacecraft others were removing them somewhere else. The orbiter heat protection system totals more than 30,000 tiles.

Aside from the difficulties with the tiles and main engines on the "Columbia," other elements of the shuttle system, such as the strap-on solid rocket boosters, the main engine fuel tank, and the launch complex at Kennedy Space Center seemed in early 1980 to be on schedule for a first orbital flight test. NASA was restructuring the shuttle funding plans because of cost overruns amounting to some 20% more than cost estimates at the outset of the program. Much of the research and development work on new technology for the shuttle was bypassed or delayed because of budget limitations.

In August 1979 the 35 shuttle astronaut candidates, who had been in training during the previous year, were declared ready for flight assignments. NASA received 3,278 applications for astronaut candidates in a two-month recruiting campaign late in 1979.

Skylab. Space station Skylab reentered the Earth's atmosphere on July 11, 1979, after six years in orbit. As its orbit rapidly decayed in the final weeks, flight controllers influenced the space station to enter the atmosphere while it was over low-density population areas on the Earth.

The space station proved to be remarkably sturdy, for on its final orbit telemetry received by a mid-Atlantic tracking station showed that it was still intact at an altitude when it should have been breaking up. Half an orbit later Skylab entered the atmosphere and broke up over Western Australia with no injuries or property damage. Several large fragments survived reentry and were recovered.

Soviet manned flight. Soviet cosmonauts Lieut. Col. Vladimir Lyakhov and flight engineer Valery Ryumin broke the manned flight duration record by staying aboard space station Salyut 6 for 175 days. Fellow cosmonauts Vladimir V. Kovalenok and Aleksandr S. Ivanchenkov had set the previous record of 139.6 days in the same station during 1978.

Lyakhov and Ryumin were launched from the Tyuratam Cosmodrome near Leninsk, Kazakhstan, on Feb. 25, 1979, aboard Soyuz 32 and docked with the space station 26 hours later. Using the Soyuz orbital maneuvering engine as a tug, the crew boosted Salyut from an orbit ranging from 302 to 330 km (187 to 205 mi) to one 308 to 338 km (191 to 210 mi).

The cosmonauts spent the first several days activating the space station and replacing several modular components in a preventive maintenance program aimed at lengthening the space station's operational lifetime. Scientific equipment used aboard Salyut 6 by Lyakhov and Ryumin included the Yelena telescope for measuring gamma radiation and electrons in near-Earth space and the Kristall electric furnace for processing materials in zero-gravity conditions. Among materials investigated in the furnace experiments were rare earth metals provided by France, semiconductor crystals for electronic applications, and optical-quality glass and glass fibers for investigating possible commercial space manufacturing techniques.

The Kristall furnace was among 2.5 tons of supplies and fuel brought up to Salyut 6 by the unmanned Progress 5 resupply spacecraft on March 14. In addition to fuel and replacement modules for maintenance work, Progress 5 hauled up mail, clothing, a clothes drier, and a television receiver. With the television receiver the crew could see entertainment programs from Soviet broadcasting stations as well as text and drawings from spacecraft and experiment handbooks telecast from the Soviet control center. The first use of Earth-to-spacecraft television was on March 24.

Additional supplies and equipment were later flown up aboard Progress 6 and 7 spacecraft. The maneuvering engine of Progress 6 was used late in May to boost the Salyut-Soyuz-Progress cluster to an orbit ranging from 333 to 352 km (206 to 219 mi). Each Progress spacecraft was used as a trash can for discarded equipment and waste before being jettisoned to reenter and vaporize over the Pacific. A Progress 7 engine burn early in July boosted the cluster to an orbit ranging from 399 to 411 km (247 to 255.4 mi).

An attempt to visit Salyut 6 with a second crew failed April 11 when the Soyuz 33 maneuvering engine malfunctioned during the approach for docking. Nikolai Rukavishnikov and Georgy Ivanov, a Bulgarian, returned to Earth after 48 hours in space.

Soyuz 34, flown unmanned, was launched June 6 to take supplies to the Salyut crew and to check out changes in the Soyuz maneuvering engine system. Lyakhov and Ryumin loaded exposed film and completed experiment equipment aboard their Soyuz 32 spacecraft for its unmanned return to Earth, keeping Soyuz 34 for their return home.

During their stay in space Lyakhov and Ryumin maintained muscle tone and general physical conditioning through the use of a treadmill exerciser, a bicycle ergometer, and the *Pengvin* (Penguin) suits in which arm and leg muscles work against elastic spring

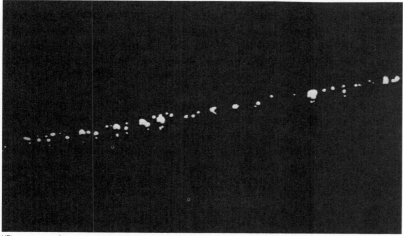

Fragments of Skylab light up the night as the U.S. space station reenters the Earth's atmosphere and breaks up over Western Australia.

UPI

Soviet cosmonauts Vladimir Lyakhov (left) and Valery Ryumin guide Soyuz 32 toward a rendezvous with the space station Salyut 6. The two remained aboard Salyut 6 for 175 days in 1979, setting a new record for length of time spent in space.

devices in the suit. Ryumin was the first space crew member to experience no weight loss during a flight.

As a part of deactivating Salyut prior to return to Earth, Lyakhov and Ryumin donned spacesuits and went outside through the airlock to remove and jettison an entangled radio telescope antenna and to retrieve scientific experiment equipment and materials samples exposed to space. The two cosmonauts returned to Earth on August 19 after 175 days aboard the space station. Soviet flight surgeons reported that they were in excellent physical condition and had readapted quickly to Earth life. In a post-flight press conference Ryumin said, "Our expedition confirms once again the effectiveness of work in space aboard a long-term orbital station."

Soviet space planners were evaluating Salyut 6 for further manned expeditions and as a test bed for an improved version of the Soyuz spacecraft. An unmanned Soyuz T (Transport) was launched December 16 to dock with the space station.

The Soyuz T was described by Salyut design engineer and former cosmonaut Konstantin Feoktistov as having significant improvements over the standard Soyuz, including an onboard digital computer for controlling spacecraft maneuvers and improvements in the life support, flight control, and descent systems. When operational, the Soyuz T version was expected to be manned by three cosmonauts. Soyuz crews had been reduced from three to two after the accident involving depressurization during reentry of Soyuz 11 in 1971 and the death of three cosmonauts. A life-support package replaced the third crew couch in subsequent Soyuz entry modules.

Soyuz T was also fitted with solar panels for electrical power generation. Dependence upon storage batteries in earlier versions of Soyuz forced docking with the space station at the first opportunity or the alternative of entry and landing under dangerous conditions.

Plans by China. In recent months China began training a cadre of candidate astronauts for future manned space missions. A seven-year space research program started in March 1978 by the Chinese National Science Congress included plans for a manned orbiting laboratory.

Armed Forces deputy chief of general staff Wu Xiuquan (Wu Hsiu-ch'üan) told journalists accompanying U.S. Secretary of Defense Harold Brown in January 1980 that "we are doing research and a man in space is possible. But it is not our top priority."

—Terry White

Space probes

As 1979 ended, Pioneer 10 was exploring the outer reaches of the solar system. At a distance of approximately 2,400,000,000 km (1,500,000,000 mi) from the Sun the probe reported that cosmic radiation becomes erratic, indicating that the probe probably was approaching the heliospheric boundary where the influence of the Sun gives way to that of intergalactic space. Launched on March 3, 1972, the probe crossed the orbit of Uranus on July 11, 1979, and continued on its way toward Pluto's orbit. It was expected to cross the orbit in 1987, at which time radio communications with it will no longer be possible. After leaving the solar system the probe will be headed generally to the center of the constellation Taurus.

News from Mars. As 1980 began, scientists participating in Project Viking were in general agreement that no form of life known on Earth was present at either landing site on the Martian surface. Experimental results that could have indicated the presence of such life forms were caused by nonbiological reactions. For example, the labeled-release experiment produced data that could have been caused by microbiological metabolic activity. However, the consensus was that the data were produced by a strong oxidant in the Martian soil, perhaps hydrogen peroxide.

The possibility of microorganisms living in Martian rocks rather than soil remained. E. I. Friedmann of Florida State University pointed out that such organisms found in the rocks of the dry valleys of southern Victoria Land in Antarctica exist in an environment similar to that of Mars. Friedmann suggested that microorganisms could be present in Martian rocks, but that it would be impossible to know they were there because the scientific instruments aboard the Viking landers were not designed to detect them. The scientists decided that the question of life on Mars could not be answered conclusively without a further probe to the planet.

Probing Jupiter. At the beginning of 1979 Voyager 1 was approaching Jupiter and taking photographs of it. Late in January and early in February the probe began sending to Earth telemetric data from ten scientific experiments as well as some 15,000 photographs. During this period the probe's narrow-angle camera took a picture every 96 seconds for 100 hours. Jupiter during that time made ten revolutions. The resulting film became a record of the planet's complex atmospheric activity.

Voyager 1 made its closest approach to Jupiter on March 5. It had survived the trip through interplanetary space with only a few minor problems. The probe approached within some 275,960 km (172,475 mi) of the surface of the planet. Pictures made of its turbulent atmosphere showed storms as large as 14,000 km × 40,000 km (8,700 mi × 24,800 mi) and wind velocities as high as 400 kph (250 mph). Particularly detailed pictures were obtained of the Great Red Spot.

Sensors reported that there is a torus (ring) composed of large numbers of doubly ionized sulfur atoms around the planet at a distance of some 144,000 km (90,000 mi). The temperature of the plasma in places reached 300,000,000° C. Project scientists pointed out that the energy required to produce such ionization would amount to some 500,000,000,000 w, equal to the total electrical power generating capacity of the U.S. Other sensors reported a "flux tube" connecting Jupiter with its satellite Io, containing currents measuring 5,000,000 amp.

Pictures made by Voyager 1 as it crossed the planet's equatorial plane at a distance of some 1,200,000 km (745,200 mi) from the giant planet on March 4 showed that Jupiter has a ring around it as do its sister planets Saturn and Uranus. The ring is believed to be only 29 km (18 mi) thick, which accounts for its having gone

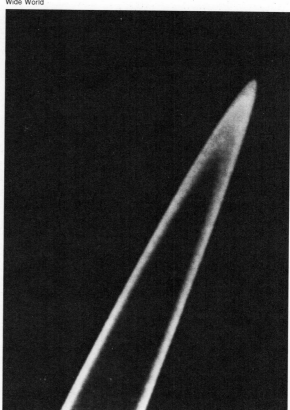

Ring around Jupiter was first detected by Voyager 1. Believed to be only 29 kilometers (18 miles) thick, it was discovered accidentally during a search by Voyager for additional Jovian satellites.

undetected in observations from the Earth. However, it is about 6,500 km (4,000 mi) wide. Its outer edge is some 57,000 km (34,000 mi) above Jupiter's visible cloud tops. The discovery was made accidentally. As the probe crossed the planet's equatorial plane, the shutter of the narrow-angle camera was opened for 11.2 minutes. The purpose was to record any Jovian satellites that had not previously been detected. While the shutter was open, the camera platform moved slightly, causing the image to appear as six wavy lines instead of one very faint image. If the platform had not moved slightly, the single image could have been so faint as not to have been detected.

"We targeted the camera off the planet for no reason other than to get off to the side of the planet, and, incredibly, the edge of the ring fell in our field of view," said Bradford A. Smith of the University of Arizona and team leader for the Voyager imaging experiments. He went on to add, "My best guess would be that it is dark material, and may be due to the break-up of a satellite moon that wandered too close." The tremendous gravitational pull of the planet would have shattered and pulverized a smaller body.

If pictures of Jupiter's turbulent atmosphere and

385

Courtesy, Jet Propulsion Laboratory/NASA

Volcanic eruption on Io, photographed by Voyager 1, rises some 260 kilometers (160 miles) above the surface of the satellite. Io and the Earth are the only two bodies in the solar system known to be volcanically active.

ring delighted mission scientists, they were even more pleased with images returned of the Jovian moons. During the encounter pictures were made of Amalthea, Io, Europa, Ganymede, and Callisto.

After being printed in color, Io was dubbed the "pizza" satellite because of its orange-red hue and pitted surface. The pictures also revealed that Io was volcanically active, the only body in the solar system other than Earth known to be so. While depressions or sinkholes are obvious on its surface, there appear to be no impact craters. This topography indicates either that the surface is being renewed by some process or that it has been eroded away. One picture of Io showed two erupting volcanoes, one of which was throwing material in an arc some 260 km (160 mi) above its surface.

Equally as fascinating were pictures of Ganymede, the largest of Jupiter's moons. Its surface resembles a desert floor on the Earth, criss-crossed by the tracks of a giant dune buggy. In reality they are probably cracks in the floor of the moon similar to structures along the San Andreas Fault in California.

Callisto, next outward of the Jovian satellites from Ganymede, presented scientists with even a more intriguing sight. On its surface is a large, white circular depression approximately 320 km (200 mi) in diameter. This crater has several concentric interior rings. Apparently it is the result of an impact by a large meteor that melted the icy crust of Callisto, which then refroze, fixing the rings as they now appear. The moon also has a number of smaller craters, more than those detected on neighboring Ganymede. This difference in-

dicated that Callisto is probably the older of the two Jovian satellites.

Voyager 1 also took pictures of Europa from some 1,920,000 km (1,200,000 mi), and they showed large linear features that probably are surface fractures. The probe also took long-distance pictures of Amalthea, innermost of Jupiter's moons. It appears to be an irregular, reddish body measuring 130 km (80 mi) by 220 km (136 mi).

Among other things Voyager 1 determined about Jupiter was that lightning is frequent in its atmosphere and that there are also gigantic auroras that appear on the dark side of the planet. New data were gathered concerning the Jovian bow shock wave, the point where the planet's magnetic field interacts with the solar wind. The probe passed in and out of the bow wave several times on its approach to Jupiter. Having finished its mission to Jupiter on April 13, Voyager 1 swung past it and set course for Saturn, with which it was scheduled to rendezvous in November 1980.

Voyager 2 began its studies of Jupiter on April 26. Its science sequences of the planet were modified as a result of the findings made by Voyager 1. Among these were different views of the planet's ring from various angles, time-lapse sequences of Io, and more observations made on the dark side of Jupiter. The probe made its closest approach on July 9 at a distance of 646,560 km (404,100 mi).

The probe's cameras sent back more pictures of Io, Callisto, Ganymede, and Europa. The images of Europa showed that moon to be extremely flat and apparently unable to support large, topographic features. Since there are few craters visible, it is assumed the surface of Europa is younger than Ganymede or Callisto. In describing its surface, Laurence Soderblom of the U.S. Geological Survey said "It is as if the crust was cracked and then just sat there—just like an eggshell."

Additional pictures were obtained of Jupiter's ring. They were made both from above and below it and showed up also in pictures made as Voyager 2 receded from the planet.

More than 150 pictures were made of Io during a ten-hour volcano watch. They showed changes in the appearance of volcanic deposits on the surface and a lack of activity by the most active volcano photographed by Voyager 1. However, six of the volcanoes photographed by Voyager 1 were present in pictures from Voyager 2.

Pictures made by Voyager 2 of the upper atmosphere of Jupiter, when compared with those from Voyager 1, showed changes in atmospheric flow patterns near the Great Red Spot. Other photographs provided more data for scientists seeking to explain the dynamics of the planet's complex atmospheric activity.

The high point of the Voyager 2 mission occurred on July 8. Pictures made of Jupiter's ring definitely revealed the presence of a new moon of the planet, its fourteenth known satellite. It was estimated to be only 30 to 40 km (18 to 25 mi) in diameter. With a period of seven hours and eight minutes, it moves at an orbital velocity of 30 kps (67,000 mph), making it the fastest moving satellite in the solar system. Following its encounter with Jupiter, Voyager 2 was targeted for a meeting with Saturn in August 1981 and a rendezvous with Uranus in January 1986.

Exploring Venus. As 1979 began, U.S. scientists were analyzing the wealth of data returned to Earth by Pioneer Venus 1 and 2, the latter of which consisted of five subprobes that entered the Venusian atmosphere on Dec. 9, 1978. Pioneer Venus 1 had gone into orbit about the planet five days earlier.

Early analysis of data from both probes proved that the searing heat of the atmosphere and surface of Venus are due to a "runaway greenhouse effect," in which the Sun's radiation is trapped near the planet's surface. The clouds surrounding the planet are arranged in three well-defined and distinct layers and consist largely of oxygen, water vapor, and sulfur dioxide. The Venusian surface, as depicted by radar maps

Photograph from Voyager 2 shows atmospheric features of Jupiter in region extending from the planet's equator to its southern polar latitudes in the vicinity of the Great Red Spot (upper right).

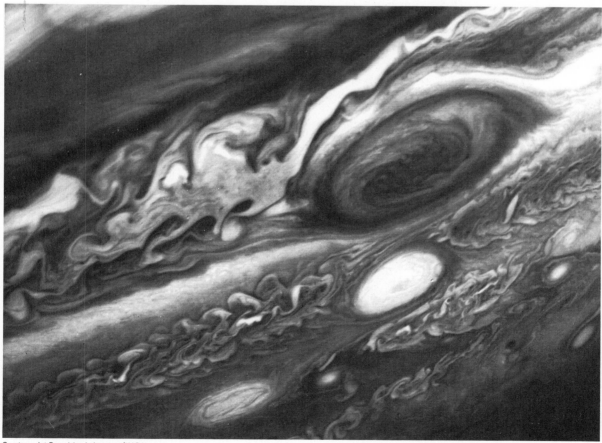

Courtesy, Jet Propulsion Laboratory/NASA

from Pioneer Venus 1, is similar to that of the Earth, with both relatively flat areas and high mountains. The surface in the region where the Pioneer Venus 2 day probe landed was covered with a layer of fine dust. Night probes detected at an altitude of 13 km (8 mi) what may be fires on the surface of the planet.

Other discoveries include the fact that the solar wind interacts with the Venusian atmosphere several times more strongly than previously supposed. Also, the two probes identified ten chemical constituents of the Venusian atmosphere and ten ions in its ionosphere. The composition of the atmosphere is approximately 97% carbon dioxide, 1–3% nitrogen, 250 parts per million (ppm) helium, 6–250 ppm neon, and 20–200 ppm argon. Beneath the cloud layer water vapor, sulfur dioxide, and oxygen exist in minute amounts.

One significant finding by the two probes was the presence of several hundred times more primordial argon and neon on Venus than on the Earth. Data returned from the Soviet probes Venera 11 and Venera 12, which also landed on Venus in December 1978, confirmed the findings. One Soviet scientist said, "the ratio of argon 36 to argon 40 on Venus was 200 to 300 times higher than on Earth."

Probing Saturn. On Aug. 20, 1979, Pioneer 11 began taking pictures of Saturn while still 10,080,000 km (6,300,000 mi) from the planet. It made its closest approach on September 1, when it passed within 20,800 km (13,000 mi) of Saturn's cloud tops. As had the Voyagers and Pioneer Venus probes, Pioneer 11 (designated Pioneer Saturn upon its arrival at the planet) provided scientists with much new data.

The probe's voyage from Jupiter had not been without danger. It was struck by at least five micrometeoroids measuring between ten micrometers and one centimeter in diameter. It also came dangerously close to a collision with what may be a small natural satellite of Saturn. Nearing its closest point to Saturn and only 23 minutes after crossing the ring plane, Pioneer Saturn passed about 1,500 km (930 mi) beneath and within 2,500 km (1,500 mi) slant range of an unknown and uncharted body some 100 to 300 km (62 to 186 mi) in diameter.

Among Pioneer Saturn's major findings were the discoveries of the eleventh and twelfth natural satellites of the planet and what may well be a thirteenth moon as well. The eleventh satellite has a diameter of about 400 km (250 mi), while that of the twelfth appears to be about 170 km (105 mi). The probe also discovered two new rings of the planet, designated the F and G rings. The former is separated from the A ring by a 3,600-km (2,240-mi) gap. The latter lies between the orbits of Saturn's satellites Rhea and Titan, about 500,000 km (312,500 mi) above the planet's cloud tops.

Another discovery was that Saturn has a magnetic field, thus joining the Earth and Jupiter. However, the size of the field appears to be 20% weaker than that of Jupiter, extending only 100 planetary radii outward from Saturn. The field is some 1,000 times stronger than that of the Earth.

Measurements of Saturn's gravitational field indicate that the planet is flattened by some 10% at its poles by its rapid rotation and that it is not an oval body. Analyses of the field along with temperature profile measurements suggest that the core of Saturn is about twice the size of the Earth but is so compressed that it contains about 11 Earth masses of matter, probably iron and rock.

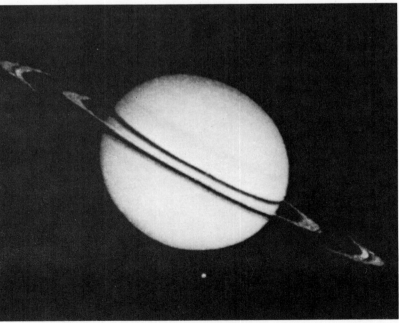

Computer-enhanced photograph of Saturn and its rings was taken by Pioneer 11 from a distance of 2.4 million kilometers (1.5 million miles). The small bright spot below the planet is its moon, Rhea.

Saturn seems to radiate two and a half times more heat into space than it receives from the Sun, with the temperature of its upper atmosphere being some 5° C (9° F) warmer than previously believed. Additionally, Pioneer Saturn reported that the planet has radiation belts of high-energy protons and electrons comparable in intensity to the Van Allen belts of the Earth; however, the region they occupy is some ten times larger. These belts are interrupted by Saturn's rings, which act as mirrors to bounce the charged particles back and forth between the planet's poles.

Pictures of the cloud tops of the planet do not reveal the extreme turbulence in that region associated with Jupiter and, to a lesser degree, Venus. Studies made of the satellite Titan show that it has a cloud-top temperature of −198° C (−324° F). This coldness eliminates an internal heat source as a means of warming the satellite's surface. However, there may be some atmospheric heating by the greenhouse effect.

As did the Voyagers at Jupiter, Pioneer Saturn studied the various natural satellites of its target planet. These included Phoebe, Iapetus, Hyperion, Dione, and Mimas on the approach to Saturn, and Tethys, Enceladus, Rhea, and Titan, after the planetary encounter. They were photographed in visible and ultraviolet light. Titan, however, being larger than the planet Mercury and known to have an atmosphere, received special attention, being scanned in the infrared spectrum as well. Iapetus appeared to be an icy globe some 1,450 km (900 mi) in diameter; however, it could as well be a rocky body with only one hemisphere covered with snow or ice.

Future prospects. In 1979 Japan announced plans to become the third country, after the United States and the Soviet Union, to launch space probes. That country's space agency proposed a probe that would be launched in January 1985 to investigate plasmas in interplanetary space and the atmosphere of Jupiter and Halley's Comet.

NASA's hopes for a probe that would be sent toward comet Tempel 2 and Halley's Comet were dashed in 1979 when the U.S. Office of Management and Budget struck such a probe from the agency's fiscal 1981 budget. To answer the problems not solved by the Viking probes of Mars, NASA scientists urged a Mars soil-sampler probe that would return soil to Earth, a roving vehicle to be landed on the planet, or a small airplane that could be released from a Mars probe.

NASA and the European Space Agency (ESA) signed an agreement on March 29 for a joint International Solar Polar Mission (ISPM) to be launched in early 1983. Under the agreement NASA and ESA each would provide a probe that would be launched into orbits that circle over the Sun's poles. Launched by the space shuttle and, it was hoped, by the Inertial Upper Stage, the two probes would travel initially toward Jupiter rather than the Sun. Once within Jupiter's tremendous gravitational field, they would be swung out of the ecliptic plane that contains the orbits of the Sun's planets and into trajectories so that one probe would fly over the north pole while the other would fly over the south pole. In the summer of 1987 the two probes would circle over their respective poles and gather information in those regions, never before explored, on the solar wind, heliospheric magnetic fields, solar and cosmic radiation and interplanetary dust, and the solar corona. The mission would end on Sept. 30, 1987.

Scientists in France were developing special floating probes to be ejected into the atmosphere of Venus by balloons in a vehicle to be sent to that planet by the U.S.S.R. in 1984. The instrumented balloons were to float at an altitude of 56 km (34 mi) above the surface of Venus and telemeter scientific data to a Soviet probe orbiting the planet.

—Mitchell R. Sharpe

Transportation

The technological thrust of developments in transportation in 1979 continued, as in recent years, to be devoted to fuel conservation. This was to be achieved by means of more efficient engines, the use of lighter materials, and changes in vehicle design. While such efforts also included many projects designed to make transportation safer and more environmentally acceptable, the strong move toward stiffer regulations in those areas—which was characteristic of the 1970s—appeared to be easing somewhat.

Air transport. Advanced-technology, fuel-efficient jet aircraft engines were being developed during the year by General Electric Co. and the Pratt & Whitney Aircraft Group of United Technologies Corp. for the U.S. National Aeronautics and Space Administration (NASA) Energy Efficient Engine (E3) project. Project goals included a 12% reduction in fuel consumption, a 50% decrease in the performance deterioration rate of engine fuel consumption, and a 5% improvement in direct operating costs. The engines also would be required to meet Federal Aviation Administration (FAA) noise regulations and Environmental Protection Agency (EPA) emissions limits.

Both manufacturers completed design work and were developing components and related technologies. Among advances incorporated in both engines were active clearance controls (automatic sensing and adjustment of clearances between compressor and turbine components for greatest efficiency), new lightweight metal alloys and composites, and digital electronic control systems.

The General Electric E3 was designed to have a takeoff thrust of 36,500 lb and a 14% improvement in fuel consumption over comparable conventional engines. Its turbofan blades were made of titanium, with

Courtesy, Wright-Patterson Air Force Base

Pilotless research aircraft developed by the U.S. Air Force and U.S. National Aeronautics and Space Administration awaits its first test flight at Edwards Air Force Base in California. In July 1979 it was carried aloft under the wing of a B-52 and then released for a 22-minute flight that was controlled from the ground.

a housing of steel and Kevlar, a high-strength synthetic fiber. Kevlar and graphite epoxies were to be used in the engine nacelles. Active control of component clearances would be accomplished by regulating the flow of cooling air through assemblies to control thermal expansion and contraction. The engine's digital electronic control was to monitor engine temperatures and relay commands to the clearance control systems. The digital control would also monitor inputs from aircraft controls and other engine sensors for use in optimizing engine performance and efficiency. There was to be a backup system in the event of failure.

Pratt & Whitney's E3 engine was designed to produce 41,000 lb of takeoff thrust. Fuel savings were estimated at 15%. The turbofan would be made of titanium, the fan containment ring of Kevlar and aluminum, and the nacelle largely of graphite epoxy. This engine would also have integrated active and passive clearance controls.

United Technologies also announced its decision to build a new engine for mid-size air transports, those carrying from 150 to 200 passengers. To be called the JT10D and featuring major fuel savings, it was to be built as a joint project with two partners, Motoren- und Turbinen-Union of West Germany, with a 13% interest, and Fiat S.p.A. of Italy, with a 4% interest. In all probability it would be built as a family of engines, with thrusts ranging from 25,000 lb to 35,000 lb. First engine test runs were scheduled for early 1982. Total development costs were estimated at about $1 billion, of which $300 million had already been spent for preliminary research and development.

Advanced transport aircraft technology studies were accelerated by McDonnell Douglas Corp. after it was awarded two contracts under NASA's Aircraft Energy Efficiency program. One contract, for $15.8 million, allowed the Douglas Aircraft Co. to continue into 1982 the work it had begun in 1977 on improving aircraft operating efficiency by the use of winglets (vertical wing-tip extensions), active (automated) controls, supercritical wings (which permit subsonic aircraft to maintain efficient cruise speeds close to the speed of sound), and engine nacelle design changes. The other contract, for $168,000, was to examine substitution of advanced turboprop engines for the two tail-mounted turbofan engines on the McDonnell Douglas DC-9. The turboprop engines would feature a new eight-to-ten-blade prop-fan propeller being developed by NASA and a division of United Technologies. The new propeller was only half the diameter of those on conventional turboprops but, according to United Technologies, was 20–35% more fuel-efficient.

Development of a new low-level, wind shear alert system neared completion at the FAA's National Aviation Facilities Experimental Center in New Jersey. Scheduled for installation at 60 U.S. airports over the next three years, the new detection and warning system was designed to detect significant changes in the horizontal speed or direction of air by means of sensors 30 ft off the ground about a mile from the ends of runways. Data from the sensors would be relayed by radio to the control tower, where a computer would determine whether the wind velocity at any of the sensors differs by 15 knots or more from the velocity at a centrally located sensor. Controllers would be warned by audible alarms and flashing lights on their displays if the 15-knot threshold is exceeded. They then would notify pilots so that they could take appropriate action.

An automated electronic flight progress system to replace the flight progress strip now used by air traffic controllers was being developed by Sanders Associates, Inc., under a $2.6 million FAA contract. Under the current system, as a plane leaves one controller's area and enters another's, data on the flight—identity, route, and assigned altitude—are automatically typed out on strips of paper that are mounted in order on a rack for the controller taking over. Any changes in altitude or route must be updated by hand and manually typed into a central computer. The new Electronic Tabular Display Subsystem would present the flight data on an electronic display next to a controller's radarscope, and the controller could enter changes in flight plan with a touch of the finger on the display face. The system should reduce the clerical workload of controllers, enabling them to concentrate on other traffic control functions. Sanders was scheduled to deliver the engineering model in February 1980, and the FAA, if satisfied, planned to install the system in air traffic control centers in 1984 and 1985.

Predicting an expanding air cargo market in the 1980s, Airbus Industrie, a European consortium, rolled out the first A300C4 retrofitted convertible passenger/cargo version of its popular twin-engine, wide-body A300 transport. The manufacturer foresaw possible sales for such convertible air transports of as many as 120 units by 1993. The first C4, which would cost about 10% more than the A300, was ordered by Hapag-Lloyd AG of Hamburg, West Germany, an air charter carrier, and was scheduled for 1980 delivery. It was designed for 24-hour conversion from a passenger aircraft handling up to 315 persons to an all-cargo aircraft capable of transporting 42 tons of payload. Rapid loading and unloading, with a claimed turnaround time of 45 minutes, were to be accomplished by use of ball mats, roller tracks, and electrical drive units; these could be fitted to or released from the passenger floor by quick-release fasteners.

Lockheed Corp. began test flights with the first production model of its three-engine, wide-body L-1011-500, which was slated to go to Pan American World Airways. The transport was to contain a number of technological advances, including a 4.5-ft tip extension on each wing, active (automatic) aileron controls, high-thrust turbofan engines, a catalytic ozone converter, automatic brakes, and a new digital autopilot. The combination of the wing-tip extensions and the improved Rolls-Royce engines was expected to boost fuel efficiency by approximately 6% as compared with previous L-1011s.

Lockheed was also researching a new "flatbed" air

McDonnell Douglas DC-9 Super 80 is repositioned for final assembly. Its fuselage length is 147 feet 10 inches, an increase of more than 14 feet from the DC-9 Series 50.

cargo transport, which it claimed could "revolutionize the aviation field the way semitrailer combinations changed the ground transportation industry." The new design would feature a basic airframe with an open flatbed area between the flight station and the tail section. Cargo would be carried in individual container units that fill the flatbed area, which would be built low to the ground purposely to permit easy loading and unloading. Individual containers would be carried as is, with their sides and top becoming part of the aircraft's fuselage. If needed, the containers could be covered with a lightweight fiberglass cocoon. The aircraft could also carry passengers in a pressurized module, which likewise could be rolled onto the flatbed. Lockheed-Georgia Co. was working under a NASA contract to determine the technical and economic feasibility of developing such an aircraft in the 1990s.

A hybrid blimp-helicopter capable of lifting more than 75 tons of cargo was proposed by Goodyear Aerospace Corp. as a means of combining the heavy-lift capability of airships with the vertical-lift capability of helicopters. The helium-filled airship, about half the size of the rigid-frame, hydrogen-filled "Hindenburg," would have helicopterlike rotors for lift and propellers for horizontal motion. Helium capacity would be 2.5 million cu ft. Goodyear Aerospace maintained that construction of such an airship would require no technological breakthroughs, and it estimated that development of the first prototype would cost $85 million and take 5½ years. Possible transport advantages of such a craft include a reduction in port congestion because ships could be loaded away from docks, the delivering of supplies to places where conventional airfields do not exist, and the transporting of materials for such construction projects as offshore drilling rigs. Goodyear Aerospace estimated the price of such airships at $7 million apiece if built in lots of 20. (*See* Feature Article: THE AIRSHIP RETURNS.)

Highway transport. General Motors Corp. introduced the Chevrolet Citation, the first of its X-body series of automobiles that it hoped would enable it to meet the U.S. government's requirement for a 27.5-mpg (miles per gallon) fleet average by 1985. The 2,500-lb Citation is 800 lb lighter and 20 in shorter than the Chevrolet Nova, which it replaced. But, according to GM, the new car, with EPA ratings of 38 mpg on the highway and 29 mpg in the city, is about 60% more fuel-efficient than the Nova. Innovations include front-wheel drive, a transverse-mounted engine (to save space and weight and increase traction), and a compact six-cylinder engine able to fit in the same space as the standard four-cylinder engine. Serviceability of the car was enhanced by use of a unique miniframe, or cradle, that enables modular replacement of the engine and powertrain.

General Motors also announced development of a new zinc-nickel oxide battery for electric automobiles that is lighter, more efficient, and longer-lived than conventional lead-acid batteries. The firm claimed that the new batteries can power a test vehicle, built on a Chevette body, at 50 mph for 100 mi between charges and that they will last 20,000–30,000 mi. The breakthrough, according to GM, was made possible because of components that allow repeated rechargings without deterioration or power loss. Replacement of the new batteries would cost more than $1,000, making the electric auto more expensive to operate than a gasoline-powered car. But GM expected the electric to be competitive in price in about five years.

The U.S. Department of Energy unveiled its ETV-1 electric test vehicle, which it said could provide a realistic alternative to the internal-combustion auto within six years. The car, for which the General Electric Co. was prime contractor, was designed to accelerate from 0–30 mph in nine seconds, maintain 55 mph on a 5% grade, pass another vehicle at 60 mph, and have a

While still moving at 30 miles per hour, a truck is weighed electronically in 0.05 seconds on a scale only 27 inches long. The device can weigh as many as 9,000 trucks per day.

Courtesy, StreeterAmet Division, Mangood Corp., photo by Joseph J. Lucas, Jr.

Adapted from information obtained from General Electric Research and Development Center

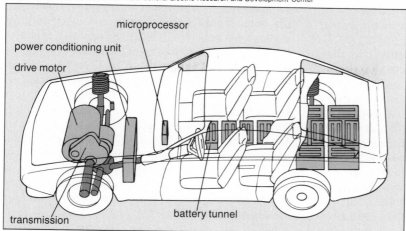

power conditioning unit
microprocessor
drive motor
transmission
battery tunnel

ETV-1 electric test vehicle, developed by the U.S. Department of Energy, is designed to accelerate from 0 to 30 mph in nine seconds, maintain a speed of 55 mph on a 5% grade, and have a range of 100 miles at a steady 45 mph. The batteries could be recharged for about $1.

range of 100 mi at a steady 45 mph. The department claimed that the batteries could be recharged for about $1. Technological advances contributing to ETV-1 design goals included more efficient, longer-lived lead-acid batteries, transistors to control motor speed, regenerative braking to recharge batteries, aerodynamic design, and lightweight materials. The batteries were expected to last three years, at which time they would be replaced for about $700. The ETV-1 was designed to be mass-produced for about $6,400.

For making electric motors more efficient, Exxon Corp. reported development of a new technology that it called an alternating-current synthesizer (ACS). Exxon predicted that by 1990 the ACS, which grew out of research into electric cars, could save the U.S. one million barrels of crude oil per day. According to the company the ACS employs a microprocessor that produces alternating current of desired frequency and voltage from fixed-voltage electricity. Thus, a motor can be made to operate at optimum speed. Exxon said that it has built an automobile with an ACS-equipped motor for power in acceleration and on grades and a gasoline engine for use on level ground and for recharging the batteries.

Baltimore, Md., was selected as the initial proving ground for a joint U.S. Department of Transportation-U.S. Department of Energy program to test petroleum-independent automotive technology. Under a $170,620 federal grant as many as five transit buses powered by gas-turbine engines would be placed in service during a year. The chief advantage of the gas turbine is that it does not require petroleum-based fuels but can burn virtually any fuel, including alcohols, liquefied natural gas, liquid hydrogen, vegetable oil, and mineral oil. The Baltimore test was to be the first part of a three-phase program that would place up to ten preproduction gas-turbine buses in two other cities, followed by ten production models in two more cities. The turbine engines would be tested for fuel economy, safety, reliability, emissions, noise, and vibration.

The U.S. Department of Transportation's Transbus design, an advanced city bus able to kneel for easy loading and unloading and equipped with ramps and wide doors for the handicapped, was dealt a serious blow when no manufacturer, domestic or foreign, submitted a bid to build it. The manufacturers said that such a vehicle, which they estimated would cost about $230,000, would be far too expensive to build since advanced-design buses already in production meet virtually all Transbus design standards yet cost less than half as much. The builders also claimed that certain Transbus standards contradict each other and would be physically impossible to meet.

New electronic truck-weighing scales that allow large vehicles to be weighed while in motion were installed by the Indiana State Highway Commission at twin weighing stations on an interstate highway. The scales, designed by a unit of Mangood Corp. of Chicago, were the first of their kind to be installed in the U.S. They made the weighing operation quicker and more efficient by allowing vehicles to continue rolling at 30 mph while being weighed.

A dump trailer constructed of fiberglass-reinforced plywood was being manufactured by Williamsen Truck Equipment Corp. of Salt Lake City, Utah. The 33.8-cu yd trailers were designed primarily for coal hauling. Their fiberglass-reinforced side panels are coated inside with a slick gel that prevents loads from sticking. In fact, the original purpose in designing the trailers was to solve the problem of coal sticking to metal trailers. Among other benefits claimed by the manufacturer are corrosion resistance, abrasion resistance, better insulation, and lighter weight.

Pipelines. Backers of five large, long-distance coal-slurry pipelines that would move low-sulfur coal located in the west-central U.S. to utilities throughout the nation again failed to win federal eminent-domain rights to cross state and private properties, especially the tracks of railroads. There were, however, reports of further eminent-domain gains through state courts.

Backing of pipelines by the Carter administration was evidenced by its support of such eminent-domain legislation, as well as legislation to give an Energy Mobilization Board the power to expedite clearances for such projects. The U.S. Department of Energy also indicated its belief that coal-slurry pipelines are a necessity for the future by its construction of a $10-million coal-slurry pilot test plant near Pittsburgh, Pa. Designed primarily to generate data on slurry transport of coal in underground mines, the plant was being built aboveground to avoid the problems and delays of working underground. The government also expected the facility to be useful for testing equipment and pipeline materials and for training operators.

The facility consists basically of three closed loops of 6-in-, 12-in-, and 18-in-diameter pipe with horizontal, vertical, and sloped segments. Sensors placed at intervals along the lines were to measure pressure, flow, density, and accumulation of solids and provide the operator with a printout of the data. Responses to emergency situations were designed to be automatic should the operator fail to act.

A consulting firm, Arthur D. Little, Inc., reported completion of laboratory work and engineering studies conducted over the last two and a half years on the possible use of liquid carbon dioxide as a coal-slurry carrier. While still in the design stage, the proposal envisioned recovery of the carbon dioxide from the commercial burning of coal at either end of the pipeline. Flowing freer than water, the liquid carbon dioxide could be recycled for reuse in the pipeline or used for enhanced recovery in depleted oil fields. Future plans included a test system at the company's Cambridge, Mass., facility, followed by construction of a pipeline system 50–150 mi long.

To help speed the flow of crude oil through a pipeline, the Continental Oil Co. (which was renamed Conoco, Inc.) reported development of a chemical additive that temporarily changes the oil's physical properties to allow it to flow faster without increasing pipeline pressure. Tests were scheduled for its use on crude oil flowing through the huge 48-in-diameter Trans-Alaska Pipeline System. Earlier tests on small-diameter lines were conducted by both Continental Oil and Atlantic Richfield Co.

Railway. Railroad innovations to reduce the weight of rolling stock and thus conserve fuel continued to be tested successfully in piggyback operations for the movement of both trailers and containers. The Southern Pacific Transportation Co. reported that its prototype "double-stack" container car passed all testing procedures in regular operations. The new car, about 45% lighter than conventional trailer-container flatcars, carries 40-ft containers stacked two high in a recessed well so that there are no roadway clearance problems. The lightweight cars thus allow both greater payload and reduced fuel consumption. In 1980 the company was scheduled to build a triple-unit articulated version of the car that will carry six 40-ft containers stacked two deep over a length of only 141 ft.

The Atchison Topeka and Santa Fe Railway Co. reported similar success with its "Ten-Pack" cars, which consist of ten single-trailer cars combined into one articulated unit. The railroad operated ten-car unit trains, with a capacity for 100 trailers, between Chicago and Los Angeles and reported fuel savings of nearly 6,000 gal per 4,000-mi round trip as compared with a conventional freight train. The cars, which consist of little more than a frame and a platform for trailer wheels, weigh 35% less than conventional piggyback equipment and require only three rather than four diesel locomotive units.

While still limited in scope, U.S. railroads were experimenting with the use of solar power at remote points where conventional power was not readily available. For example, the Santa Fe, Southern, and Seaboard Coast Line railways were using photovoltaic cells (which convert sunlight directly into electricity) to provide electric power for line and grade-crossing signals isolated from power lines. Other roads such as the Southern Pacific and Burlington Northern were using solar energy for powering track circuits and communications. The Southern Railway was mounting solar cells on a fleet of 80 cabooses to provide electricity for rear-of-train warning flashers. These 4 ft × 4 ft arrays require no maintenance other than washing, and, at $2,000 for an entire system, their cost is less than that of a generator-driven system.

A solar-powered railway communications system was scheduled to be constructed by the Solar Power Corp., a U.S. firm, for the Australian National Railways. The solar cells were to be used to recharge batteries powering a 72-channel integrated microwave-VHF (very high frequency) radio system for the new Tarcoola–Alice Springs Railway. A railway spokesman said that the system should also facilitate diesel fueling and maintenance procedures.

A new tank car that promises to reduce empty backhauls was developed and tested by the Union Tank Car Co. with the help of Goodyear Aerospace and Amoco Oil Co. The new car, called the 2-4-1, eliminates the need to clean the interior between loads of incompatible bulk commodities or to deadhead (i.e., to move empty, usually on return trips) between compatible loads. A flexible, chemically coated rubber/nylon diaphragm divides the car into two chambers so that no surface is ever touched by both commodities. Each chamber has its own separate fillers and outlets. Filling one chamber pushes the diaphragm snugly against the opposite wall of the other chamber. Amoco used the car to carry clean base oil from an Indiana refinery to a plant in Illinois and return with motor oil additives. The car thus eliminated a 400-mi empty backhaul or the need to take the car out of service for cleaning.

Subway in Atlanta, Georgia, began operations in mid-1979 with an 11-minute ride over a 6.7-mile (10.8-kilometer) route. Eventually the system will comprise 53 miles (85 kilometers) of rail linking the central city to its suburbs.

The Association of American Railroads' technical center in Chicago began tests of a minicomputer to relay train data to engineers. To be conducted in a locomotive cab simulator, the tests, as part of the association's Track/Train Dynamics Program, were designed to produce a simple computer system that will improve train handling. Noting that virtually the only information feedback on train conditions that the engineer now receives comes from the first locomotive unit, the association researchers surveyed engineers on the types of data and displays they need. Using the responses, they began working to design a system that would use simple, durable, off-the-shelf components to provide the desired information to the engineer at the time he or she needs it. Such information includes performance of trailing power units, location and diagnosis of engine problems, acceleration and deceleration of train components, track profile, brake pressure, drawbar force at the rear of the train, and disposition of loads and empties.

Test runs of RoadRailer equipment were conducted over the Seaboard Coast Line tracks at speeds up to 79 mph, with sustained running at nearly 65 mph, according to Bi-Modal Corp., the developer of RoadRailer. This innovative train consists of a locomotive pulling self-contained but interconnected RoadRailers, which are trailers with interchangeable rail and truck wheels. It required a special waiver from compliance with normal Federal Railroad Administration (FRA) railroad safety regulations. Conditions included a 15-car limit on train length and no commingling with other types of rail rolling stock. Seaboard Coast Line expressed enthusiasm about the potential of the new train, and Bi-Modal predicted passage of the brake test well before the FRA's two-year deadline.

Water transport. The major deep-sea ports of the U.S. were rapidly becoming radar controlled in a manner similar to that of air traffic control centers. With funds provided by a special act of Congress the U.S. Coast Guard began awarding contracts for installation and maintenance of Vessel Traffic Service (VTS) radars to provide real-time surveillance of marine traffic approaching and departing from major U.S. ports. These include Valdez, Alaska; Houston/Galveston, Texas; San Francisco, Calif.; New York, N.Y.; and, soon, New Orleans, La., and Seattle, Wash.

The VTS-radar system was designed to detect even small vessels at long range and in high seas, and is sophisticated enough to allow detection of marine traffic and fixed objects that are separated by short distances. It also is able to minimize the effects of rain and fog. Utilizing advanced communications, the Coast Guard Vessel Traffic Center at each port collects radar data from throughout the port area for transmission to ships' masters and pilots.

Further advances were reported on the integrated tug-barge concept, in which an oceangoing tug locks into a large slot in the rear of a huge barge. Halter Marine Inc. received a $37-million contract to build two 133-ft, 18,200-BHP (brake horse power) catamaran tugs. They were to be used to propel huge tanker barges to form units 691 ft long and 95 ft wide, with a cargo capacity of 47,000 deadweight tons and a loaded draft of 40½ ft. The integrated units form a rigid ship for "unrestricted ocean service" and would incorporate the latest safety and pollution-control features, including inert gas systems, segregated ballast, double bottoms, and a patented bulbous bow for better seakeeping qualities. Deliveries were for September 1980 and January 1981.

The U.S. Maritime Administration was giving wind-powered ships another look as a result of the sharply rising fuel costs for oceangoing vessels. It awarded a $138,840 contract to a seven-member research team of maritime experts headed by the president of the Wind Ship Development Corp. of Norwell, Mass., to make a 12-month study of wind propulsion. This was a continuation of a similar study by the University of Michigan, completed in 1975, which concluded that a commercial sailing vessel was not then an economically feasible alternative but might soon become so as petroleum costs rise.

In all probability any wind-powered merchant ships would use hybrid propulsion systems, with fuel-powered engines for use in calm seas, for maneuvering in harbors and restricted waterways, and for improved open-sea navigation. Advancements in ship technology should enable any modern sailing cargo vessel to utilize wind far better than could the ships of the 19th century. For example, modern sails are not only aerodynamically designed for better performance but also are made of more durable synthetic materials. Special hull coatings provide better protection and reduce friction, and modern communications equipment should help wind-powered ships both utilize and avoid weather as appropriate.

—Frank A. Smith

U.S. science policy

One of the most curious aspects of the scientific endeavor is that, although it is almost entirely occupied with the search for knowledge, it knows so little about itself. How else could one explain the fact that, after a decade of warnings from the leadership of the scientific community about the "mindless dismantling" of the scientific enterprise by an unappreciative federal government, the beginning of the 1980s found U.S. science in better shape than ever?

In a testimonial address to the 1979 winners of the National Medal of Science, Philip Handler, president of the National Academy of Sciences, declared: "Our national research endeavor has been spectacularly successful in all disciplines—witness the glorious accomplishments of those whom we honor this evening. Moreover, our science was never more productive than it is today."

A similar appraisal from the president of the Carnegie Institution of Washington—a noted basic research organization—contained an element of disbelief: ". . . I find the nation's basic research enterprise as a whole surprisingly healthy despite increasing concerns about reductions in support, increasing federal regulation, and misplaced priorities."

To find the nation's research enterprise in such vigorous bloom as it entered the decade of the '80s was indeed a surprise to many—and not only because of the pessimism that had prevailed within the scientific community during the 1970s. In an address to the National Academy of Sciences celebrating the centenary of the birth of Albert Einstein in March 1979, Pres. Jimmy Carter acknowledged the difficult years:

"American science found itself beleaguered by two very different kinds of anti-intellectualism: on the one hand, by the romantic anti-rationalism of the counterculture and, on the other, by the veiled hostility of a national Administration that distrusted the academic and scientific community.

"The latter represented the most serious threat. Federal policy toward science became infected with a simplistic search for the quick fix. Research that seemed to promise a quick payoff was more amply funded, while support of basic research was allowed to decline.

"The future of our scientific and technological primacy was put at risk."

U.S. Pres. Jimmy Carter stresses the need for new energy sources as he stands on the roof of the west wing of the White House to dedicate a newly installed solar heating system (background).

UPI

As it turned out, according to most knowledgeable observers, the country did not actually lose its "primacy" in scientific research, but there was good evidence to suggest that it might have lost its scientific supremacy among the nations of the world. A few decades earlier, about three-quarters of the contributions to the world's scientific literature originated in the U.S.; at the end of the 1970s, the fraction was closer to one-third. Another third came from Western Europe and Japan, and an equivalent amount from the Soviet Union and other nations of Eastern Europe.

With respect to technology the situation was markedly worse. Except for a few areas of very high technology—such as computers and microprocessors—the U.S. was slipping badly. There was painful evidence of this in international surveys of productivity and, collaterally, in the increasing deficits in the U.S. balance of trade with other advanced nations.

The year 1979 was marked by extraordinary efforts on the part of the national leadership to diagnose the disease and to propose remedies. The symptoms were easy enough to describe: across the broad range of U.S. technology, from steelmaking to the manufacture of electronic components, there was a decline in the introduction of truly innovative procedures and a leveling off in the growth of productivity per unit of labor. Both adversely affected the competitive position of U.S. industry in world markets and, ultimately, the value of the dollar.

The quest for productivity. Productivity was very much a factor in U.S. science policy in 1980. In February the director of the Office of Management and Budget, the secretary of the treasury, and the chairman of the Council of Economic Advisers joined in this statement:

"The disappointing performance of productivity has been an important factor behind the inflation of the last few years. In the early 1960's, productivity gains averaged more than 3 percent per year. In recent years, productivity increases have dwindled to about 1 percent, and a sizable decline occurred in 1979.

"Improvement in productivity growth would obviously have highly beneficial effects. Besides reducing the rise of costs and prices, increased productivity would mean higher real output and improved living standards for Americans. However, bettering our productivity performance cannot be achieved quickly or at low cost.

"Indeed, since we do not fully understand the causes of the slowdown in productivity, we are hampered in our efforts to deal with it. We do know, however, that basic research and development and a stronger pace of business investment in new plant and equipment are indispensable ingredients for increased economic efficiency.

"The budget for 1981...contains additional funds for basic research and development, continuing the strong federal backing for basic research begun in fiscal 1978. The budget does not contain new tax incentives for investment. . . ."

Therein lay a key policy decision of the Carter administration. Many of the industries suffering from slowdowns in productivity had several characteristics in common: they had enjoyed their most rapid growth as a result of important technological breakthroughs in decades past and were now spending a relatively small percentage of their income on R and D (research and development).

Typically, these industries saw their salvation in terms of fiscal incentives (such as lower taxes on capi-

Saturn V rocket, once scheduled to boost an Apollo manned spacecraft to the Moon, lies rusting on the ground at the Kennedy Space Center in Florida, replaced by the space shuttle. Many such craft and their support structures at the space center are being taken apart for scrap metal.

Syndication International/Photo Trends

tal gains) that would encourage investment and in accelerated depreciation allowances that would increase tax write-offs. The decision of the White House to go the route of increased R and D rather than tax reductions represented not only a policy of fiscal restraint but also a declaration of faith in the promise of technological research.

Budgetary bonanza for R and D. The commitment to scientific research was spelled out by President Carter in his introduction to the federal budget for fiscal year 1981:

"In the long run, economic growth depends critically on technological development. For many years, this country has led the world in producing new technology. We are in danger of losing this leadership. The 1981 budget continues my long-standing commitment to reverse the trends of the past two decades and provide for major and sustained increases—above the rate of inflation—for research and development programs. Obligations for research and development will increase by 13%; for basic research by 12%. . . . I believe these are among the most important expenditures we can make. The payoff, particularly for basic research, is long-term, but immense. We benefit today—in new industries, in millions of jobs, in lives saved, and in lives protected—from the investments in science made decades ago. We must continue such investments today to reap similar returns tomorrow."

In dollar terms, the administration was recommending to Congress that federal obligations for the support of basic research be increased by $543 million (to $5.1 billion in fiscal 1981) and for all R and D by $4.2 billion (to $36.1 billion). The largest increases were proposed for the Department of Defense, whose obligations for total conduct of R and D were larger than those of any other federal agency and accounted for approximately 45% of all federal support for R and D. Obligations were estimated to increase by $2.8 billion, or 20%, over fiscal 1980.

The department planned to raise its support for basic research by 21%, with an unusually large fraction going to university campuses. Most of the funds, however, would be devoted to the development of major strategic and tactical weapons, including a new cargo transport aircraft to increase the U.S. forces' rapid deployment capabilities and continued development of the M-X mobile intercontinental ballistic missile.

An increase of 13% in basic-research funds was proposed for the Department of Energy, as well as greater overall support for longer-term R and D on solar, fossil, and fusion energy sources. A decrease was proposed, however, for work on the controversial breeder reactor.

Budgetary allocations to the National Aeronautics and Space Administration provided for continued development of the much-plagued space shuttle. New initiatives for which funds were committed included the development of a gamma-ray observatory "to obtain fundamental knowledge of the nature and origin of our universe," advanced space communications technology, and improvements in aircraft design and performance.

The only federal agency primarily concerned with the support of basic research is the National Science Foundation (NSF), and an increase of 16.9% was proposed for that segment of its activities. Within this category the largest gain was for mathematical and physical sciences, which had suffered particular neglect since 1967. But even larger increases were proposed for engineering and the applied sciences within the NSF. These would increase 22.5% and reflected the administration's ambition to raise the productivity of U.S. technology through R and D. The budget provided for cooperative relationships between government and industry in quest of the goal.

The specific activities listed in the fiscal 1981 budget to carry out the Carter administration's "new emphasis" on technological innovation included: "increased support by the NSF of joint-industry research teams leading to the advancement of industrial technology; NSF and Department of Commerce support for research and development on technologies that are basic to the improvement of several industrial sectors; increased support for the small business innovation program of the NSF to stimulate development of new processes and products to encourage private investments; and initiation of a basic automotive research program in cooperation with industry."

Government-industry collaboration. Taken at face value the proposed program for collaborative programs of research supported by the government and jointly carried out by industry and academia raised a number of questions. Antitrust legislation currently in effect served to discourage collaborative research in industry. Many argued that the problems of lagging U.S. technology were also rooted in such factors as inflation, high interest rates, and shifting regulatory policies.

These questions were posed to Philip Smith, one of the principal members of the staff of the White House Office of Science and Technology Policy.

"There is no question," Smith said, "that inflation and regulatory policies have presented particularly difficult obstacles to the increase of productivity through technology, but nevertheless we feel that underlying everything is a need for new knowledge. We believe we need to stimulate more long-range research, sponsored by government, but undertaken by industry or in cooperation with industry.

"The strategy we're using in the development of the automotive research program is essentially that the time is now ripe for exploring new relationships between government, industry, and universities. We're using a variety of techniques to arrange different combinations of people working on basic research in a cooperative mode.

"But each time you approach one of these large industrial complexes in order to work out some kind of collaborative arrangement between government and industry, you run into all kinds of problems. We've been working with the Justice Department in clarifying some of the anti-trust legislation. Right now we're working on some guidelines that may remove some of the ambiguity about where cooperation is feasible and where it is not."

A well-regarded forecast by the Columbus (Ohio) Laboratories of the Battelle Memorial Institute on the probable levels of R and D expenditures in 1980 suggested that private industry was following the lead of the federal government in pouring more money into the search for new materials, processes, and ideas. According to Battelle industrial funding in 1980 was expected to grow 21% over 1979—representing an unprecedented increase of more than $5 billion to a total of more than $29 billion. Industry funding of R and D would thereby constitute 47% of the national expenditure for R and D, a total of $61.8 billion.

The forecast noted that trends in real R and D effort "are continuing the upward movement established over much of the past decade. Since 1973, real R&D effort has increased at a six-year average rate of 2.67 percent, and the projections for 1980 suggest that the seven-year average rate will increase to about 3.3 percent. Battelle estimates that during the decade of the 1980's real R&D activity will increase at an average annual rate of approximately 3 percent."

Other efforts toward innovation. The national concern about the decline in productivity and innovation was reflected in the extraordinary number of con-ferences, symposia, and studies that were held in 1979 to deal with the problem. One of the longest and most ambitious studies was carried out under the direction of Jordan Baruch, assistant secretary of commerce for science and technology. Finally issued toward the end of the year, it offered major "Industrial Innovation Initiatives." These included not only efforts to increase the store of technical knowledge and clarification of the antitrust policy but also improvements in the regulatory system, enhancement of the transfer of information from government laboratories to industrial firms, strengthening the patent system, fostering the development of small innovative firms, and facilitating labor/management adjustment to technical change.

One of the strongest signals received by the federal government with respect to the decline in technological innovation was a study performed for the National Science Foundation indicating an almost precipitous falloff in the formation of small high-technology firms. These are enterprises formed to exploit an exciting new idea and then funded by venture capital. Some fail, but a number suddenly take off and create powerful new industries almost overnight. In the late '60s such small firms were being formed by the hundreds; by the mid-1970s, according to data published by the NSF, new starts had decreased to almost zero.

The fiscal 1981 budget for the NSF provided for a quadrupling of its support "to provide an opportunity and an incentive for small science and technology-based firms to help solve technical problems that could have significant benefit to the public"—from $3 million to $13 million.

The new approach to regulation. Regulatory reform, considered by many industrial leaders to be a sine qua non in any national effort to stimulate innova-

George Wald, a Nobel Prize-winning biologist, addresses an antinuclear rally on the Boston Common.

tion and productivity, also received major attention. A White House document issued in December by Richard Neustadt, assistant director of the domestic policy staff, acknowledged that the regulatory structure of the government was cumbersome. It reported that some 58 regulatory agencies, including 18 independent commissions, issue about 7,000 rules and policy statements per year. Of these roughly 2,000 are legally binding rules with a significant effect on state and local government or the private sector, and 100 have a major economic impact.

Although there was general agreement that the structure of legislation establishing regulatory procedures would require major surgery at some time in the future, a White House executive order issued in 1979 provided something more in the nature of a Band-Aid. It established a regulatory analysis review procedure that required policymakers in regulatory agencies to give greater attention to the cost of regulations—*e.g.*, the cost of vehicle emission controls to the ultimate purchaser of an automobile. A regulatory council was established in order to coordinate significant regulations and to develop a calendar that would provide a broad overview of the potential effect of such regulations on the economy.

Competition in the international market. Another impediment to the competitiveness of U.S. industry was spelled out by Handler in his talk to the winners of the National Medal of Science:

"On one side we confront a potential military adversary whose government controls all aspects of their national life and deliberately invests in military preparation, including R&D, a far larger fraction of its Gross National Product than will our country, in the absence of a military emergency. The challenge to the relevant American scientific community is to assure that we compensate in quality what we are unwilling to pay for in quantity.

"That, in fact, we do so reasonably well is made possible by the fact that a disproportionate fraction of our most talented physical scientists and engineers is drawn into defense research because of its great intellectual challenges, its exciting technical opportunities, and its relatively generous support. At the same time, those nations which are our most successful competitors in the international marketplace for technology invest and engage in very little military R&D. Their competitive success may rest, at least in some part, on the circumstance that German and Japanese counterparts of our brightest scientists and engineers, shielded by the American military umbrella, are designing superior consumer products for the American market; no easy solution to that dilemma is evident."

A report from the Worldwatch Institute provided supporting data. In the U.S. and Great Britain more tax money is spent on military R and D than on all civilian programs combined. But France allocates only 30% of the government R and D budget to the military, West Germany 11%, and Japan 2%.

Whether the new programs proposed by the White House would help to solve the dilemma of international competition for U.S. industry remained to be seen. But there was some early evidence that the academic community was prepared—indeed eager—to cooperate. At the spring 1979 meeting of the American Physical Society, its president, Lewis Branscomb, chief scientist for the IBM Corp., declared, "In the immediate future, there will be some increase in industry support, but in the long range, there will be a great deal more support. The industry connection is the wave of the future."

Industry and academic scientists joined in discussing several models of such partnerships. An agreement between Harvard University and the Monsanto Co. provided long-term support (up to 12 years) for Harvard's medical faculty. Monsanto scientists worked side by side with their Harvard counterparts; an intricate patent agreement dealt with the often complex question of how to dispose of marketable research results. Several other preeminent research institutions—including the Massachusetts Institute of Technology and the California Institute of Technology—offered similar arrangements to industrial partners in campus research.

The tilt toward China. Two of the most significant developments in U.S. science policy occurred around the end of 1979. The increased government harassment of several Soviet scientists, including the world-famous physicist Andrei Sakharov, produced a ground swell of resentment among U.S. scientists so powerful that it threatened to end a 21-year-old program of formal scientific exchanges between the United States and the Soviet Union. A number of U.S. scientists notified their Soviet counterparts that they would no longer participate in such exchanges, either as visitors or as hosts. The most serious blow was delivered in February 1980 when the U.S. Academy notified the Soviet Academy of Sciences that it was suspending participation in a program of bilateral symposia and conferences for a period of six months, citing the harsh treatment of its foreign associate Sakharov as a principal reason for this action.

At the same time, the U.S. and China announced the first meeting of a Joint Commission on Scientific and Technological Cooperation in January 1980. During the meeting the two nations signed protocols for cooperation in Earth sciences—earthquake studies in particular. In addition, the two nations agreed to explore possibilities for cooperation in several other research areas, including environment, transportation, basic sciences, aviation, statistics, nuclear energy, electronics, telecommunications, and construction and urban planning.

—Howard J. Lewis

Scientists of the Year

Honors and awards

The following is a selective list of recent awards and prizes in the areas of science and technology.

Architecture and civil engineering

Ewing Medal. The 1979 James Alfred Ewing Medal was presented by the Institution of Civil Engineers in Great Britain to Sir Alfred Pugsley for "his outstanding contributions in the major engineering disciplines of aeronautics, civil engineering and marine technology, particularly in the field of structural safety, which have won him international recognition and renown."

Honor Awards. The American Institute of Architects extended its 1979 Design Honor Awards to nine new structures and to six others classified as renovations. The list of new buildings included: in New York City, Citicorp Center (Hugh Stubbins & Associates), a 900-ft-high aluminum office tower, which rises over an open plaza and encloses business establishments; an 18-ft-sq cedar vacation cabin in Washington (Arne Bystrom), "every inch [of which] was designed with function and esthetics in mind"; the Undergraduate Science Center at Harvard University (Sert, Jackson & Associates); the Joan Miró Foundation building in Barcelona, Spain (Sert, Jackson & Associates); the Johns-Manville World Headquarters near Denver, Colo. (The Architects Collaborative); the Angela Athletic Facility of St. Mary's College in Notre Dame, Ind. (C. F. Murphy Associates); the 22-block-long Portland (Ore.) Transit Mall (Skidmore, Owings & Merrill and CHNMB Associates); the Pembroke Dormitories at Brown University in Rhode Island (Lyndon Associates); and a private home on Bainbridge Island, Wash. (Morgan and Lindstrom). The six renovated structures that were honored included: the St. Louis Art Museum (Hardy Holzman Pfeiffer Associates); the Chicago Public Library and Cultural Center (Holabird & Root); Gunwyn Ventures, a four-story office building in Princeton, N.J. (Michael Graves); the Center for American Arts at Yale University (Herbert S. Newman Associates); the Louisville Museum of Natural History and Science (Louis & Henry); and the Mechanics Hall in Worcester, Mass. (Anderson Notter Finegold).

Pritzker Prize. Philip Johnson was named recipient of the first annual $100,000 Pritzker Architecture Prize, which the Hyatt Foundation sponsors to honor "outstanding endeavors" by an architect or group of architects. Johnson was selected for "doing more than anyone in the world to keep Modern Architecture lively and unpredictable."

Astronomy

Bruce Medal. The Astronomical Society of the Pacific named William A. Fowler of the California Institute of Technology recipient of the 1979 Catherine Wolfe Bruce Gold Medal. Fowler undertook research on the origins of the elements, including the production of deuterium and helium during the "big bang." He has also studied the release of gravitational and nuclear energy from massive objects.

Chapman Medal. The Royal Astronomical Society of Great Britain presented its Chapman Medal to Eugene N. Parker of the University of Chicago for his work on the theory of solar wind.

Cleveland Prize. Three scientists were jointly awarded the American Association for the Advancement of Science-Newcomb Cleveland Prize for their work in astronomy. Patrick M. Cassen and Ray T. Reynolds, both of whom are associated with NASA/Ames Research Center in California, and Stanton J. Peale of the University of California at Santa Barbara, were selected for "Melting of Io by Tidal Dissipation," which was published in the March 2, 1979, issue of *Science.* The report accurately predicted the existence of volcanism on Io, one of Jupiter's satellites.

Franklin Medal. Sir Bernard Lovell of the University of Manchester and director of the Nuffield Radio Astronomy Laboratories was given the 1980 Benjamin Franklin Medal by the Royal Society of Arts in Great Britain.

Gould Prize. The $5,000 Benjamin Apthorp Gould Prize was presented to Irwin I. Shapiro of the Massachusetts Institute of Technology for his "scientific accomplishments in the astronomy of precision."

Imperial Prize and *Japan Academy Prize.* Yoshihide Kozai of the Smithsonian Astrophysical Observatory was awarded both the Imperial Gift Prize and the Japan Academy Prize for his research in celestial mechanics. Kozai has undertaken extensive studies on minor planets, artificial satellites, the motion of Saturn's moons, and zonal harmonics.

Pierce Prize. D. A. Harper, Jr., of the University of Chicago received the Newton Lacy Pierce Prize for "his outstanding contributions in infrared observations of stars, planets, interstellar gas and dust, and distant galaxies, based on innovation in the development of instruments and on careful calibration of the signals." In presenting the award the American Astronomical Society also called attention to Harper's observations of faint astronomical objects from airborne telescopes and his contribution toward the development of the Winston radiation detector.

Smith Medal. Ralph B. Baldwin, president of the Oliver Machinery Co., received the J. Lawrence Smith

Arthur Davidsen

Medal from the National Academy of Sciences for "original investigations of meteoric bodies." Baldwin has also done considerable research that concerns the Moon, novas, eclipsing binary stars, stellar atmospheres, and spectral classification of stars.

Trumpler Award. The 1979 Robert J. Trumpler Award was presented to Gary D. Schmidt of Lick Observatory who was honored for developing a photoelectric technique for mapping polarized radiation emitted by galaxies and galactic nebulas.

Warner Prize. The 1979 Helen B. Warner Prize for astronomy was given to Arthur Davidsen of the Johns Hopkins University. He was honored for developing and launching a rocket-borne ultraviolet radiotelescope used to measure the Lyman-alpha emission line of hydrogen in quasar 3C 273.

Watson Medal. The National Academy of Sciences named Charles T. Kowal of Hale Observatories recipient of its James Craig Watson Medal. Kowal, who was given a $5,000 honorarium, discovered Jupiter's thirteenth and fourteenth moons, scores of supernovae, and the miniplanet Chiron, which is located between the Saturn and Uranus orbits.

Chemistry

AIC Medal. Melvin Calvin of the University of California at Berkeley, recipient of the 1961 Nobel Prize for Chemistry for tracing the carbon cycle of photosynthesis and discovering its intermediate products, was awarded the 1979 Gold Medal of the American Institute of Chemists.

Bingham Medal. The Society of Rheology awarded its 1979 Bingham Medal to William W. Graessley of Northwestern University. His studies have included the structural aspects of polymer rheology, polymerization reactor engineering, and statistical mechanics of cross-linked systems. He has also contributed to an understanding of how molecular structure and inter-molecular interactions influence the properties of polymer liquids and networks.

Broida Prize. The American Physical Society presented its first Herbert P. Broida Prize in Atomic and Molecular Spectroscopy or Chemical Physics to Robert W. Field of the Massachusetts Institute of Technology. He was cited "for his design and execution of elegant and original laser spectroscopic studies of isolated small molecules, for providing new techniques such as optical-optical double resonances and for the development of stimulated emission pumping of molecules leading to a whole class of new molecular laser systems." The $5,000 honorarium also recognized Field's "exploitation of intramolecular perturbations, which act as 'windows' on missing electronic states."

Chemical Sciences Award. The $5,000 National Academy of Sciences Award in Chemical Sciences was presented to Linus Pauling "for his studies which elucidated in structural terms the properties of stable molecules of progressively higher significance to the chemical, geological, and biological sciences."

Cope Award. Gilbert Stork of Columbia University received the Arthur C. Cope Award of the American Chemical Society for developing new methods of constructing molecules in which rings of atoms are present and then applying these methods to the synthesis of several natural substances belonging to that category. These include the alkaloids yohimbine (a tranquilizer), aspidospermine (a respiratory stimulant), and camptothecin (an antitumor agent), and other compounds of complex molecular structure.

Davy Medal. The Davy Medal of the Royal Society of Great Britain was given to Joseph Chatt for "his distinguished contributions to transition metal chemistry and the understanding of catalysis."

Garvan Medal. Helen M. Free of Miles Laboratories received the Garvan Medal of the American Chemical Society for developing diagnostic test systems involving chemical reagents. Her work led to the introduction and expansion of dip-and-read tests for urinary constituents now accepted as standard procedures.

Langmuir Award. For "significant impact on the scientific understanding of the subtle forces in molecules," William Klemperer was given the 1980 Irving Langmuir Award in Chemical Physics by the American Chemical Society. A longtime member of the Harvard University faculty, Klemperer was honored among other reasons for determining the structural details of many important molecules and how electrical properties determine molecular behavior.

Lippincott Medal. The 1979 Ellis R. Lippincott Medal, jointly sponsored by the Coblentz Society, Optical Society of America, and Society for Applied Spectroscopy, was awarded to E. Bright Wilson of Harvard University. His development of matrix methods for the calculation of normal coordinates of molecular vibrations has had wide influence on other scientists—a prerequisite for receiving the award.

Nobel Prize. The 1979 Nobel Prize for Chemistry was awarded jointly to Herbert Brown and to Georg Wittig, both of whom have profoundly influenced the course of modern chemistry. Brown, who received his doctorate from the University of Chicago in 1938 and joined the faculty of Purdue University in 1947, followed two principal themes in his research. The first concerned the preparation and reactions of inorganic compounds of hydrogen and boron and related compounds of hydrogen and aluminum. This research led to the introduction of a new class of reducing agents that have become standard tools of the organic chemist. In later years Brown explored a group of organic compounds in which boron atoms are present. The second theme of Brown's research was the study of chemical reactions that take place in stages involving the appearance and disappearance of organic species that bear a positive electrical charge. The molecular structures and chemical behavior of these so-called carbonium ions or carbocations were the subject of sometimes heated controversy during the 1950s and 1960s. Brown's active participation in that debate contributed to substantial advances toward one of the perennial goals of chemistry, the correlation of the

Georg Wittig (left) and Herbert Brown

(Left) UPI; (right) Wide World

molecular structure of compounds with the courses and rates of their reactions.

Wittig received his doctorate in 1926 from the University of Marburg in Germany and became professor emeritus at the University of Heidelberg in 1965. His research interests complemented those of Brown. Instead of studying compounds of boron, Wittig concentrated on compounds of phosphorus; instead of reactions involving positively charged intermediates, Wittig concentrated on those with negatively charged species, called carbanions. The Nobel committee noted Wittig's achievement in employing phosphorus compounds in the synthesis of substances in which the molecules contain pairs of carbon atoms linked by the sharing of two pairs of electrons.

Nuclear Chemistry Award. Arthur Poskanzer of the Lawrence Berkeley Laboratory was named recipient of the American Chemical Society's 1979 Award for Nuclear Chemistry. Poskanzer, who received a $3,000 honorarium, was cited for "exceptional work in the use of high energy nuclear reactions." He discovered 29 isotopes, mostly of light elements. Some scientists had predicted that lithium-11 and beryllium-14, two of Poskanzer's discoveries, could not exist because they would lie beyond the boundaries of nuclear stability.

Perkin Medal. Herman F. Mark, long associated with the Polytechnic Institute of New York, received the 1980 Perkin Medal from the Society of Chemical Industry, which made the selection in consultation with five other societies. Mark is credited with contributing many of the materials, methods, and principles basic to modern polymer science.

Pfizer Award. Frederick C. Hartman of the Oak Ridge National Laboratory was given a $2,000 honorarium as recipient of the 1979 Pfizer Award in Enzyme Chemistry. He was cited for contributing to the design and use of the so-called "affinity labeling" technique, which is employed to identify the essential amino acids found in the enzymes that metabolize carbohydrates.

Plyler Prize. The Earle K. Plyler Prize for notable contributions to molecular spectroscopy was given to George Pimentel, deputy director of the National Science Foundation, "for his development of and contributions to chemical lasers, matrix isolation spectroscopy and rapid-scanning infrared spectrometers."

Priestley Medal. The American Chemical Society awarded its prestigious 1980 Priestley Medal to Milton Harris, who retired as vice-president and research director of Gillette Co. in 1966 and later served as chairman of ACS's board of directors. Unlike most past recipients of the Priestley Medal, Harris was not honored for basic research. His preoccupation has been to use "basic knowledge to solve some practical problem." Under his direction, Gillette developed such products as the polymer-coated razor blade and devised a new chemical process used during the styling of hair. Harris explained: "The trick is to break disulfide bonds in the hair fibers temporarily, shaping the hair while the bonds are broken and then allowing them to reform to lock the fibers into place as curls or waves."

TIF Founders' Prize. The 1978 Texas Instruments Foundation Founders' Prize was awarded to Chandra K. N. Patel of the Bell Telephone Laboratories in New Jersey. Patel, who received a $35,000 honorarium, was lauded for his broad range of scientific achievements. Among other things, he designed and developed the powerful carbon-dioxide laser. In addition, his research on tunable spin-flip-Raman lasers has produced high-resolution measurements in molecular-gas spectroscopy.

Wolf Prize. The Wolf Foundation in Israel presented its 1979 prize in chemistry to Herman F. Mark, professor emeritus of the Polytechnic Institute of New York. Mark received a $100,000 honorarium, one of five such prizes given each year to outstanding scientists in various fields.

Earth sciences

Abbe award. The 1980 Cleveland Abbe Award for Distinguished Service to Atmospheric Sciences was given to Jule G. Charney and Joseph Smagorinsky by the American Meteorological Society. The two were cited "for their scientific leadership of the Global Atmospheric Research Program which after a decade has culminated in the remarkably successful Global Weather Experiment." Charney was associated with the Massachusetts Institute of Technology, while Smagorinsky was with the National Oceanic and Atmospheric Administration.

Agassiz Medal. The triennial Alexander Agassiz Medal was awarded in 1979 to Henry M. Stommel, senior scientist at the Woods Hole Oceanographic Institution, for "major advances in the understanding of ocean circulation and the distribution of water masses."

Bowie Medal. The American Geophysical Union named Frank Press, director of the administration's Office of Science and Technology Policy, recipient of the William Bowie Medal "for outstanding contributions to fundamental geophysics and for unselfish cooperation in research."

Bucher Medal. The American Geophysical Union honored Edward E. Irving of Canada's Department of Energy, Mines and Resources with its Walter H. Bucher Medal. Irving was selected for his work in paleomagnetism and paleoclimatology, which provided early evidence for the theory of continental drift.

Day Medal. The 1979 Arthur L. Day Medal was given to Walter M. Elsasser by the Geological Society of America. Since his retirement in 1974, Elsasser has been adjunct professor at the Johns Hopkins University. He is credited with developing the dynamo theory of the Earth's magnetic field and contributing to a growing understanding of magnetic reversals in rocks.

Ewing Medal. Wallace S. Broecker of the Lamont-Doherty Geological Observatory received the Maurice Ewing Medal from the American Geophysical Union for his studies on the physical, geological, and geophysical processes in the ocean. Broecker, whose use of radioisotopes in the study of oceanic processes is well known, is given credit for important contributions to an understanding of the carbon cycle and for studies of the possible effects of climatic change.

Fleming Medal. Syun-Ichi Akasofu of the University of Alaska was given the John Adam Fleming Medal by the American Geophysical Union "for original research and technical leadership in geomagnetism, atmospheric electricity, aeronomy and related sciences."

Meisinger Award. Richard A. Anthes of Pennsylvania State University was named recipient of the 1980 Clarence Leroy Meisinger Award by the American Meteorological Society "for research and modeling in tropical cyclones and mesoscale meteorology."

Penrose Medal. The Geological Society of America named J Harlen Bretz recipient of its 1979 Penrose Medal. Before retiring in 1947, Bretz taught for 33 years at the University of Chicago and won wide recognition for his studies of limestone caverns.

Rossby Medal. The American Meteorological Society named Sean A. Twomey of the University of Arizona recipient of its 1980 Carl-Gustaf Rossby Research Medal. He was cited "for extensive contributions to the development of many areas of atmospheric science, including aerosol and cloud physics, radiative transfer and remote sensing from satellites."

Second Half Century Award. André J. Robert, director of the Canadian Meteorological Centre in Montreal, and Frederick G. Shuman, director of the National Meteorological Center in Camp Springs, Md., were named co-recipients of the 1980 Second Half Century Award by the American Meteorological Society. The two were cited "for scientific leadership in the construction of different and original operational primitive equations models that produced significant benefits to Canadian and U.S. weather services."

Sverdrup Medal. "For his studies of bottom water formation in the Arctic and Antarctic seas and of the earth's water balance, and for his inspiring leadership in international cooperation among oceanographers," Haakon Mosby, former rector of the University of Bergen in Norway, was awarded the 1980 Sverdrup Gold Medal by the American Meteorological Society.

Electronics and information sciences

ACM Distinguished Service Award. The Association for Computing Machinery presented its 1979 Distinguished Service Award to Carl Hammer, director of computer sciences for Sperry Univac. Hammer was selected by the association for his "professional, managerial and technical contributions, both nationally and internationally."

Eckert-Mauchly Award. The Institute of Electrical and Electronics Engineers (IEEE) Computer Society and the Association for Computing Machinery named Robert S. Barton of the Burroughs Corp. first recipient of the ACM/IEEE Eckert-Mauchly Computer Architecture Award. Barton, who is known primarily for his work on the design and engineering of a series of Burroughs computer systems, was cited for a 25-year record of accomplishment, leadership, and innovation.

Edison Medal. Albert Rose, a longtime fellow of the technical staff of RCA Laboratories in Princeton, N.J., was the recipient of the 1979 Edison Medal presented by the Institute of Electrical and Electronics Engineers. Rose, whose award included a $10,000 honorarium, was cited "for basic inventions in television camera tubes and fundamental contributions to the understanding of photoconductivity, insulators and human and electronic vision."

Ericsson Prize. Robert D. Maurer of the Corning Glass Works and Charles K. Kao of the International Telephone and Telegraph Corp. were named joint recipients of the 1979 Ericsson International Prize. The triennial award, which included gold medals and an honorarium worth about $25,000, recognized their contributions to long-distance optical fiber transmission. Maurer was specifically cited for research that led to the development of practical, workable methods of producing high-purity glass waveguides for telecommunications. Kao was commended for early recognition of the feasibility of using glass fibers as a telecommunications medium.

Goode Award. The American Federation of Information Processing Societies presented its 1979 Harry Goode Memorial Award to Herman H. Goldstine of the Institute for Advanced Study (IAS) in Princeton, N.J. Goldstine received the honor "for his support and major contributions to the development of the ENIAC [an early all-electronic digital computer]; for his pioneering work on the logic, design and coding of electronic computers; for his leadership role in the design, construction and use of the IAS machine at the Princeton Institute for Advanced Study; for his significant contributions to the theory and practice of matrix computations; for his encouragement of young scientists and mathematicians to explore the use of electronic computers; and for his pioneering analysis of the history of computing."

Hopper Award. Stephen Wozniak of Apple Computer, Inc., of California received the 1979 Grace Murray Hopper Award from the Association of Computing Machinery. He was cited "for his many contributions to the rapidly growing field of personal computing and, in particular, to the hardware and software for the Apple Computer."

Lamme Medal. The Institute of Electrical and Electronics Engineers named James M. Lafferty recipient of its 1979 Lamme Medal for contributions "to thermionic emitters and to high-vacuum technology as applied to high-power vacuum switches." Lafferty is associated with the General Electric Research and Development Center in Schenectady, N.Y.

Marconi Fellowship. Yash Pal, director of the Space Applications Centre of the Indian Space Research Organization, was selected by the Marconi Fellowship Council to receive the sixth Marconi International Fellowship. The $25,000 annual grant honors achievements in communications science and technology that are especially beneficial to mankind. Pal was chosen for his work on the Satellite Instructional Television Experiment (SITE), the purpose of which is to bring instructional television to the rural villages of India. Pal has not only helped design the hardware used by SITE but has also been involved in developing television programs to meet the needs of SITE's special audience.

NAE Founders Award. The National Academy of Engineering gave its Founders Award to David Packard of the Hewlett-Packard Co. "for his pioneering role in engineering, manufacturing, and entrepreneurship of advanced electronic technology and for enlightened public service leadership in many fields."

Turing Award. The Association for Computing Machinery presented its 1979 A. M. Turing Award to Kenneth E. Iverson of the IBM Thomas J. Watson Research Center in New York. Iverson was honored for "his pioneering effort in programming languages and mathematical notation resulting in what the computing field now knows as APL, for his contributions to the implementation of interactive systems, to educational uses of APL, and to programming language theory and practice."

Energy

Fermi Award. The U.S. Department of Energy named Harold M. Agnew and Wolfgang K. H. Panofsky joint recipients of the 1978 Enrico Fermi Award. This award, which includes a gold medal and a $25,000 honorarium, acknowledges "exceptional and altogether outstanding scientific and technical achievement in the development, use, or control of atomic energy." Agnew, who is president of General Atomic Co. in San Diego, Calif., was lauded for "his many innovative contributions to nuclear physics and nuclear weaponry, his dynamic leadership of the Los Alamos Scientific Laboratory," and for his contributions to U.S. national security. Panofsky, director of the Stanford Linear Accelerator Center, was cited for "his very important contributions to elementary particle physics; his leading role in advancing accelerator technology; his positive influence on younger scientists; and the scientific advice he has generously given to the U.S. government."

Environment

Aeroacoustics Award. The American Institute of Aeronautics and Astronautics presented its 1979 Aeroacoustics Award to Harvey H. Hubbard of the NASA Langley Research Center in Virginia. He was cited "for outstanding scientific contributions to understanding and reducing the generation, propagation, and effects of aircraft noise."

Browning Award. F. Raymond Fosberg, an internationally recognized authority on the ecology of tropical islands and botanist emeritus of the United States National Museum of Natural History, received the 1979 Edward W. Browning Achievement Award for Conserving the Environment.

Environmental Quality Award. The National Academy of Sciences presented its 1979 Award for Environmental Quality to Alexander Hollaender, senior research advisor with Associated Universities, Inc., which operates the Brookhaven National Laboratory in New York. Hollaender was honored with a $5,000 honorarium for his "study of the effects of ultraviolet and ionizing radiation and organisms, and possible protection of human cells against radiation hazards."

INMM Award. William A. Higinbotham of the Brookhaven National Laboratory was first recipient of the Distinguished Service Award of the Institute of Nuclear Materials Management. His concern about nuclear safeguards began in 1944, when he worked on the Manhattan Project at Los Alamos, N.M.

Szilard Award. The American Physical Society Forum on Physics and Society named F. Sherwood Rowland recipient of the 1979 Leo Szilard Award for Physics in the Public Interest. Rowland, who is associated with the University of California at Irvine, was selected for "his identification and warnings of the hazards of the release of chlorofluorocarbons to the Earth's protective ozone layer."

Food and agriculture

Appert Award. F. John Francis, a member of the faculty of the University of Massachusetts and chairman of the Institute of Food Technologists' Expert Panel on Food Safety and Nutrition, was given the 1979 Nicholas Appert Award. His main research interests include the chemistry and physiology of fruits and vegetables after harvest, colorimetric techniques for assessing the quality of food products, and, most recently, special emphasis on pigments, especially on their degradation, and on color and quality of foods.

Babcock-Hart Award. The 1979 Babcock-Hart Award, which is sponsored by the Nutrition Foundation and administered by the Institute of Food Technologists, was given to Robert H. Cotton, chief food scientist at the ITT Corp. While employed at the National Research Corp. he helped develop a process for vacuum evaporation of orange juice for concentrate, and while serving as a member of the White House Conference on Food, Nutrition and Health, he helped develop Astrofood, a fortified cakelike snack that provides substantial nutrition when eaten with milk. He also helped commercialize the retort pouch for ITT Continental Baking and served as first director general of the Chile Foundation, a center for applied research and technology transfer.

Borden Award. Boyd L. O'Dell of the University of Missouri at Columbia was named recipient of the 1979 Borden Award in Nutrition for his studies on the nutritional requirements for zinc and its role in intermediary metabolism.

Elvehjem Award. The 1980 Conrad A. Elvehjem Award for Public Service in Nutrition was given to Bernice K. Watt, who, before her retirement, directed the compilation of tables of food composition for the U.S. Department of Agriculture. She was largely responsible for the production of *Agriculture Handbook No. 8,* which includes data for 17 nutrients in nearly 2,500 foods.

International Award. The 1979 International Award of the Institute of Food Technologists was presented to John Hawthorn, head of the Department of Food Science and Nutrition at the University of Strathclyde, Glasgow. The award recognizes outstanding efforts to promote the international exchange of ideas and understanding in the field of food technology. Hawthorn, who was appointed to the first chair of food science established in the United Kingdom, studied the movement of radioactive materials through the food chain during the late 1950s and helped found both the British Institute of Food Science and Technology and the International Union of Food Science and Technology.

Johnson Award. The 1980 Mead Johnson Award for Research in Nutrition was given to John D. Fernstrom of the Massachusetts Institute of Technology at Cambridge. He was cited for fundamental contributions to the understanding of the role of dietary constituents in the functioning of neurotransmitters in the central nervous system.

Osborne and Mendel Award. John W. Suttie of the University of Wisconsin at Madison received the 1979 Osborne and Mendel Award of the Nutrition Foundation for his extensive work on the vitamin K system.

Technology Award. The Institute of Food Technologists presented its 1979 Food Technology Industrial Achievement Award to the Armour Research Center of Armour & Co. and to Grumman Allied Industries for their development and manufacture of a hypobaric system for the transportation and warehousing of fresh fruit, vegetables, and meat. The system, which combines low pressures with high humidity and low temperature and calls for the continuous release of such undesirable gases as ethylene and carbon dioxide, is designed to extend the life of perishable commodities as much as six times greater than normal.

Wolf Prize. The Wolf Foundation in Israel presented its 1979 prize in agriculture to Jay L. Lush of Iowa State University and to Sir Kenneth Blaxter of the Rowett Research Institute in Scotland. The two shared the $100,000 honorarium, one of five such prizes given each year to outstanding scientists in various fields.

Life sciences

AIBS Award. The American Institute of Biological Sciences named H. C. Chiang of the University of Minnesota recipient of its 1979 Distinguished Service Award. He has long been involved in international programs for biological pest control.

Albert Lasker Award. Walter Gilbert of Harvard University and Frederick Sanger of the Laboratory of Molecular Biology in England shared a $15,000 Albert Lasker Basic Medical Research Award in 1979 for their independent development of new methods of rapid sequencing of DNA. Gilbert's method uses chemical reagents to break the DNA molecules into fragments, while Sanger's method relies on enzymatic reaction in its sequencing procedure.

BSA Awards. The Botanical Society of America selected four scientists in 1979 to receive its annual Merit Awards. David W. Bierhorst of the University of Massachusetts was cited "for his incisive and significant investigations of vascular cryptograms, especially *Psilotum* and *Tmesipteris*, for the painstaking studies of lesser-known ferns, and for his comprehensive book on the morphology of vascular plants." Margaret H. Fulford of the University of Cincinnati was honored "for her excellent studies of the morphology and taxonomy of the leafy liverworts, for her syntheses regarding the phylogeny of liverworts, and for her distinguished career as a teacher and investigator in bryology." Anton Lang of Michigan State University was singled out "for his extensive and diverse contributions to developmental botany—especially the physiology of plant hormones, flowering, plant response to environment, cell differentiation, and organ formation, for numerous efforts in behalf of international botany, including many editorial tasks, and for coordinating the research of others as director of several laboratories." Samuel N. Postlethwait of Purdue University was commended for "his contributions to the art of botanical teaching, specifically for his longstanding love of students and his development of the audio-tutorial system of laboratory instruction, and for research on the morphology of corn."

Cole Award. Michael Edidin and Richard Cone, both members of the Johns Hopkins University faculty, were selected by the American Biophysical Society to receive the 1979 Kenneth S. Cole Award. Working independently, the two found that cell membranes are highly fluid. Proteins and other molecules are thus able to act as pathways for messages as they pass through the membranes. The fluid nature of cell membranes was previously unknown to scientists.

Gairdner Award. Walter Gilbert of Harvard University and Frederick Sanger of the Medical Research Council Laboratory of Molecular Biology in England were given $10,000 each as recipients of 1979 Gairdner Foundation Awards. Gilbert was cited for "his contributions to our understanding of gene replication and regulation, and of the development of methods for sequencing of DNA and their application to studies of gene organization." Sanger was honored for "his development of methods for the sequencing of DNA" and for contributions "to new concepts of gene structure."

Leidy Medal. The Academy of Natural Sciences presented its Leidy Medal to E. O. Wilson, curator of entomology at Harvard University. Wilson's scientific contributions include the first evolutionary analysis of caste systems among ants, the identification of certain pheromones, and the outlining of a pheromone "vocabulary" used in ant communications.

Louisa Horwitz Prize. Two biochemists shared the $25,000 Louisa Gross Horwitz Prize for 1979: Frederick Sanger of the Medical Research Council Laboratory of Molecular Biology in England and Walter Gilbert of Harvard University. Sanger was cited for his recent studies on the DNA and RNA molecules, which "in a sense eclipse his earlier work by their bold originality and outstanding impact on future research in the study of biology and medicine." Gilbert was honored because he "has single-handedly provided more information concerning the molecular aspect of gene regulation in bacteria than any other investigator. In the course of these investigations, he has developed fundamentally new techniques, wherever necessary, and these have served not only to enhance his own scientific work but that of a great many investigators throughout the world."

Lounsbery Award. Michael Brown and Joseph Goldstein of the University of Texas were named joint recipients of the Richard Lounsbery Award for Biology and Medicine. The award carries with it a $50,000 honorarium and a $20,000 travel and research grant. Brown and Goldstein were selected for discovering the cell receptor that accepts low-density lipoproteins and thereby signals cells to decrease cholesterol synthesis.

Luck Award. The James Murray Luck Award for Excellence in Scientific Reviewing was presented to Alan Robison of the University of Texas "for his insightful and perseverant contributions to the recognition of the pervasive biological importance of cyclic adenosine monophosphate." The award carries with it a $5,000 honorarium.

Moore Award. The Society of American Foresters presented its 1979 Barrington Moore Memorial Award to Alex L. Shigo, a principal plant pathologist with the U.S. Department of Agriculture's Forest Service.

407

Shigo, one of the few persons designated a Pioneering Scientist by the forestry agency, has undertaken research on methods of preventing and arresting decay and discoloration of living trees.

Ricketts Award. The 1979 Howard Taylor Ricketts Award was presented to James E. Darnell, Jr., of Rockefeller University for demonstrating that adenovirus DNA, which is produced in virally infected cells, is transmitted into very long nuclear precursor molecules, and that subsequently these molecules are cleaved, and selected portions are further modified to form the functional messenger RNA. Darnell's work has provided a model for messenger RNA synthesis in all living cells.

Rosenstiel Award. Brandeis University named César Milstein recipient of its eighth annual Lewis Rosenstiel Award for Distinguished Work in Basic Medical Research. Milstein, a biochemist at the Medical Research Council Laboratory of Molecular Biology in England, received a $5,000 honorarium for his research in antibodies, which is said to be revolutionizing the field of immunology.

Schmitt Award. Stephen W. Kuffler of Harvard University was selected to receive the 1979 F. O. Schmitt Lectureship Medal and Award. The neuroscientist was cited for his work concerning the chemical mediation of nerve-muscle synaptic transmission and for establishing one of the world's major centers of neurobiology at Harvard.

Smith Medal. William R. Taylor, emeritus professor at the University of Michigan, was given a $5,000 honorarium as recipient of the Gilbert Morgan Smith Medal in Phycology. He was honored "for his outstanding contributions to the knowledge of the marine algae of Florida, the Caribbean Sea, the northwest Atlantic and tropical Pacific oceans."

Stone Award. Marc S. Collett of the University of Colorado Health Sciences Center and Peter T. Lomedico of Harvard University were named recipients of the ninth annual Wilson S. Stone Memorial Award by the University of Texas M. D. Anderson Hospital and Tumor Institute. Collett was cited for his work on the structure and function of the avian sarcoma virus transforming gene. He helped identify, purify, and characterize the Rous sarcoma virus transforming gene product pp60^{src} and determine its mode of action. Lomedico was honored for his research on the structure and expression of insulin genes. Among other things he was the first to show a 23 amino acid sequence on the NH_2-terminal end of the proinsulin translation product.

Materials sciences

Acta Metallurgica Medal. David Turnbull of Harvard University was given the 1979 *Acta Metallurgica* Gold Medal for a lifetime of contributions to metallurgy and solid-state science. He was honored especially for providing "a substantial part of our present understanding of nucleation and growth in crystals, diffusion in solids and liquids, of solid-state reactions and the nature of the glassy state."

New Materials Prize. Three persons shared the American Physical Society's International Prize for New Materials "for their discovery of intermetallic compounds and alloys exhibiting unusually high superconducting transition temperatures, and for their demonstration that these materials retain their superconductivity under conditions of high currents and fields." The honored trio included John K. Hulm of the Westinghouse Research Laboratories in Pittsburgh, Pa., J. Eugene Kunzler of Bell Telephone Laboratories in Murray Hill, N.J., and Bernd T. Matthias of Bell Telephone Laboratories and the University of California at San Diego.

Mathematics

Steacie Prize. David W. Boyd of the University of British Columbia was awarded a 1978 Steacie Prize for his work in functional and numerical analysis.

Waterman Award. The fourth annual Alan T. Waterman Award of the U.S. National Science Foundation was presented in 1979 to William P. Thurston, a

William P. Thurston

topologist at Princeton University. The award, established by the U.S. Congress in 1975, includes a $50,000 grant for research or advanced studies during each of three successive years. Thurston was selected for "achievements in introducing revolutionary new geometrical methods in the theory of foliation, function theory, and topology."

Wolf Prize. Two French mathematicians, Jean Leray and André Weil, were named co-recipients of the $100,000 Wolf Prize in Mathematics for 1979. Leray, who applied algebraic topology to specific problems "taken from amongst the most challenging of the science of our times," developed theories that not only opened up solutions to whole classes of differential equations but also altered the direction of research in algebraic topology. Weil is given credit for the development of algebraic geometry and its applications in analysis, number theory, and algebra.

Mechanical engineering

Propulsion Award. The American Institute of Aeronautics and Astronautics named Arthur J. Wennerstrom recipient of its 1979 Air Breathing Propulsion Award. Wennerstrom, who has been Aerospace Engineer/Research Group Leader at the U.S. Air Force Aero Propulsion Laboratory in Ohio, was cited "for noteworthy engineering excellence in innovative compressor design which significantly advanced the state of the art for compressor system technology."

Medical sciences

Berson-Yalow Award. Helena Wachslicht-Rodbard and Jesse Roth of the U.S. National Institute of Arthritis, Metabolism, and Digestive Diseases received the 1979 Berson-Yalow Award from the Society of Nuclear Medicine. The two received the prize for developing a method that enabled them to study whole body insulin receptors in humans. Their technique was expected to be useful in the study of diabetes and other disorders of glucose metabolism.

Coolidge Award. Herbert M. Parker, president of H.M.P. Associates, Inc., of Richland, Wash., was the recipient in 1979 of the William D. Coolidge Award of the American Association of Physicists in Medicine. Long concerned with environmental science and the development of radiation exposure standards, Parker developed radiation protection programs associated with the U.S. atomic bomb project.

Gairdner Award. The Gairdner Foundation in Canada presented 1979 International Awards to James W. Black of the Wellcome Research Laboratories, to Elwood V. Jensen of the University of Chicago, and to Charles R. Scriver of McGill University/Montreal Children's Hospital Research Centre. Black was honored for "his role in the identification of amine receptors

and in the development of the receptor-blocking drugs, Propanolol and Cimetidine." Jensen was cited for "his discovery of steroid receptors which has led to the elucidation of the action of steroid hormones and to the development of tests guiding endocrine treatment for cancer of the breast." Scriver was selected for "his contributions to understanding of genetic disease and, in particular, the detection of genetically-determined disease in large population groups, and the development of treatment programs for these disorders." Each received a $10,000 honorarium.

General Motors Prizes. Henry S. Kaplan of Stanford University, Sir Richard Doll of Oxford University, and George Klein at Sweden's Karolinska Institute each received $100,000 from the General Motors Cancer Research Foundation as winners in 1979 of the first General Motors Cancer Research Prizes. Kaplan led in the development of treatment that changed Hodgkin's disease from an illness that was usually fatal to one that was highly curable. Doll was one of the first to reveal the connection between cigarette smoking and lung cancer, while Klein demonstrated that the body's immune system and cancer are interrelated.

Hazen Award. The first annual Lita Annenberg Hazen Award for outstanding achievements in clinical research was presented in 1979 by the Mount Sinai School of Medicine, New York City, to Jesse Roth of the National Institute of Arthritis, Metabolism, and Digestive Diseases. Roth made important contributions to the understanding of diabetes, explaining how the disease can exist in a person with a large excess of insulin. The $100,000 prize is to be split each year between a scientist whose work is honored and young physicians selected by the winner to work with him or her in biomedical research.

Lasker Award. Roger W. Sperry of the California Institute of Technology was awarded a 1979 Albert Lasker Basic Medical Research Award, and with it a $15,000 honorarium, for developing the technique of "split brain" research, during which he severed the bundle of nerve fibers that connects the two halves of the brain. He discovered that the two hemispheres then function independently and the right brain does not know what the left brain is learning. Sperry also found that the two halves of the brain govern two sets of activities and that there is no one dominant hemisphere for all mental processes.

Nobel Prize. Allan Cormack of the U.S. and Godfrey Hounsfield of the U.K. shared the 1979 Nobel Prize for Physiology or Medicine, awarded by Sweden's Royal Caroline Medico-Chirurgical Institute. They won the award for their development of the computerized axial tomography (CAT) scanner, an instrument that can produce a detailed X-ray picture of a selected section of the human body. A conventional X-ray plate, a two-dimensional representation of a three-dimensional object that is made by directing a beam of X-radiation

Allan Cormack

Godfrey Hounsfield

through the object, is not adequate for such problems as finding a tumor or a blood clot in the brain. In the CAT scanner electronic detectors replace the photographic plate of the conventional X-ray system, and the X-ray source delivers many short pulses of radiation as it and the detectors are rotated about an imaginary axis through, for example, a patient's head. This process produces a sharp image of that particular cross section, one that allows physicians to detect tumors and clots.

Born in Johannesburg, South Africa, in 1924, Cormack studied physics and engineering at the University of Cape Town. After receiving bachelor's and master's degrees there, he studied for two more years at the University of Cambridge in England. In 1956 he went to Harvard University as a research fellow and in 1957 joined the physics faculty of Tufts University in Medford, Mass. At Tufts he published a mathematical analysis of the process of absorption of X-rays as they pass through layers of tissues that differ in density. He demonstrated that details of a flat layer could be calculated from measurements of the attenuation of X-ray beams passing through it from many angles. Cormack became a naturalized U.S. citizen in 1966.

Hounsfield was born in 1919 and grew up tinkering with machinery on his father's farm in Nottinghamshire, England. During service with the Royal Air Force in World War II he became skilled at working with radar, and after the war he attended and was graduated from the Faraday House Electrical Engineering College in London. He then went to work for EMI, Ltd., where he extended the capability of a computer so that it could interpret X-ray signals so as to form a two-dimensional image of a complex object such as the human head. He built a prototype head scanner and body scanner at EMI.

Passano Award. Donald Steiner of the University of Chicago received the 1979 Passano Award, given by the Passano Foundation, for his research "elucidating the mechanism by which insulin is synthesized in the human body." Steiner in 1966 discovered and characterized proinsulin, the precursor molecule from which insulin is formed, and in 1976 did the same for preproinsulin, the precursor of proinsulin.

Radiological Society Award. F. Mason Sones, Jr., of the Cleveland (Ohio) Clinic Foundation was presented in 1979 with the gold medal of the Radiological Society of North America. Sones received the award for his pioneering work in the field of coronary arteriography.

Roentgen Medal. Russell Morgan, dean emeritus of the Johns Hopkins University School of Medicine, was the recipient in 1979 of the Roentgen Medal, given for outstanding advances in radiology by West Germany's Roentgen Museum Society. Morgan perfected image intensification in radiology, which improved X-ray pictures for diagnostic purposes.

VA Award. The Veterans Administration Medical Research Service presented its highest award to Roger H. Unger of the University of Texas Southwestern Medical School in Dallas. Unger was named Senior Medical Investigator for his work with the pancreatic hormone glucagon.

Wightman Award. Claude Fortier, chairman of the department of physiology at Laval University in Quebec City, received from the Gairdner Foundation in 1979 the $25,000 Wightman Award for "outstanding leadership in medicine and medical science." Fortier's research concerned the relationships between the central nervous system and glands such as the thyroid, pituitary, and adrenal.

Wolf Prize. Roger W. Sperry of the California Institute of Technology, Arvid Carlsson of Gothenburg University in Sweden, and Oleh Hornykiewicz of the University of Vienna shared the 1979 Wolf Prize for Medicine and the $100,000 honorarium. The Wolf Foundation in Israel each year gives five such prizes to scientists in various fields.

Optical engineering

Abbe Award. The New York Microscopical Society in 1979 presented the Ernst Abbe Award to Albert Crewe of the University of Chicago. The prize is given to a person whose contributions to the science of microscopy are "deemed to be as remarkable as Ernst Abbe's"; the innovations of Abbe in the 19th century led to great improvements in microscope design. Crewe pioneered in the development of the scanning electron microscope.

Ives Medal. The Optical Society of America presented its 1979 Frederic Ives Medal to Nicolaas Bloembergen of Harvard University for his "achievement in establishing the theoretical framework of nonlinear optics, his sustained innovative contributions to the explorations of all aspects in the field of nonlinear optical phenomena and his successes in the role of teacher and interpreter of science."

Kingslake Award. Norm Brown, an optical engineer at the Lawrence Livermore Laboratory of the University of California at Berkeley, received in 1979 the Rudolph Kingslake Award of the Society of Photo-Optical Instrumentation Engineers. Brown developed a new method for calculating the shapes of aspheric lenses and mirrors.

Mees Medal. Koichi Shimoda of the University of Tokyo was awarded the 1979 C. E. K. Mees Medal by the Optical Society of America. He was honored for his contributions to quantum optics and double resonance spectroscopy and for "his generous contributions to international cooperation in physics through conference organization and publication guidance."

Michelson Medal. The Franklin Institute awarded the Albert A. Michelson Medal in 1979 to Richard Brewer of IBM Corp. Brewer received the honor "for his many discoveries and contributions to laser physics in the area of nonlinear interaction of intense laser light with molecules."

Richardson Medal. The 1979 David Richardson Medal of the Optical Society of America was awarded to William P. Ewald of the Eastman Kodak Co., who was cited for his numerous contributions to applied optics, particularly in the fields of projection and stereoscopy, as well as for "inspired service as a teacher and consultant both within the Eastman Kodak

Company and to the optics community in general."

Royal Medal. For "outstanding contributions to the design and development of the X-ray microscope and the scanning electron microprobe analyser (scanning electron microscope)," Vernon E. Cosslett was given a 1979 Royal Medal by the Council of the Royal Society in Great Britain. He is emeritus reader of electron physics at the University of Cambridge.

Wood Prize. Peter Franken of the University of Arizona received the 1979 R. W. Wood Prize "for his pioneering discoveries of optical second harmonic generation, optical mixing, and optical rectification." The Optical Society of America, which presented the award, commented: "These studies revolutionized modern optics by stimulating the development of what is now the subject of nonlinear optics with all its vast ramifications."

Physics

Achievement in Physics Medal. Jules Carbotte of McMaster University received the 1979 Medal for Achievement in Physics from the Canadian Association of Physicists. Carbotte's research centered on positron annihilation and thermalization and on the theory of superconductivity in relation to microscopic parameters.

Acoustical Society Medal. Richard Bolt, a former professor at Massachusetts Institute of Technology and Stanford University, was named winner of the 1979 Gold Medal of the Acoustical Society of America. Bolt received the prize "for outstanding contributions to acoustics through research, teaching and professional leadership."

Ballantine Medal. Benjamin Abeles and George Cody of the Exxon Research and Engineering Co. shared the 1979 Stuart Ballantine Medal, awarded by the Franklin Institute. They won the prize for their research on thermal conduction in semiconductors and for their development of germanium-silicon alloys used in thermoelectric power generators.

Bohr Medal. Charles Townes of the University of California at Berkeley in 1979 received from Prince Henrik of Denmark the Niels Bohr International Gold Medal. The Dansk Ingenirforening chose Townes because of his central role in the inventions of the maser and the laser.

Born Medal. The 1979 Max Born Medal and Prize was awarded by the British Institute of Physics and the (West) Germany Physical Society to John Bryan Taylor of the U.K. Atomic Energy Administration's Culham Laboratory. Taylor was selected "for his work on the theory of plasmas, particularly in relation to controlled nuclear physics."

Boys Prize. The British Institute of Physics presented the 1979 Charles Vernon Boys Medal and Prize to Derek Robinson of the U.K. Atomic Energy Administration's Culham Laboratory for his studies of the magnetic properties of pinched discharges.

Cresson Medal. Steven Weinberg of Harvard University was the recipient of the 1979 Elliott Cresson Medal, awarded by the Franklin Institute. Weinberg was honored for his research on developing a unified theory of weak and electromagnetic interactions.

Davisson-Germer Prize. Joel Appelbaum and Donald Hamann, both of Bell Laboratories, shared the 1979 Davisson-Germer Prize of the American Physical Society for their "pioneering analysis of the electronic structure of semiconductor surfaces."

Einstein Award. Tullio Regge of the Institute for Advanced Study in Princeton, N.J., and the University of Turin, Italy, received in 1979 the Albert Einstein Award from the Lewis and Rosa Strauss Memorial Fund. Regge won for his research on particle scattering, stability of collapsed objects in general relativity, and symmetries in field and particle dynamics.

Europhysics Prize. The 1979 Hewlett-Packard Europhysics Prize was shared by five physicists: Eric A. Ash of University College in London, Jeffrey H. Collins of the University of Edinburgh, Yuri V. Gulaev of the Institute of Radio Engineering and Electronics in Moscow, Kjell A. Ingebrigtsen of the Norwegian Institute of Technology at Trondheim, and Edward G. S. Paige of the University of Oxford.

German Physical Society Prize. Helmuth Möhwald of Dornier Systems Ltd. and Hans Reithler of the 3rd Physics Institute of the Rhenish-Westphalian Technical University shared the 1979 Physics Prize of the (West) German Physical Society. Möhwald received the award for his research on the transfer properties, phase transitions, and molecular dynamics of organic charge-transfer crystals. Reithler was honored for his experimental confirmation of the scattering of neutrinos by electrons.

Glazebrook Medal. Thomas Pickavance, former chairman of the European Committee on Future Accelerators, was awarded the Glazebrook Medal and Prize in 1979 by the British Institute of Physics. The Institute honored Pickavance "for his many contributions to the construction and utilization of large particle accelerators both in the U.K. and the rest of Europe."

Herzberg Medal. Gordon Drake of the University of Windsor in Canada was named winner of the 1979 Herzberg Medal by the Canadian Association of Physicists. Drake devoted his research efforts to atomic processes, including radiative transitions, electron-atom scattering, and atom-atom scattering.

Holweck Prize. André Blandin of the University of Paris in Orsay, France, was named winner of the 1979 Holweck Medal and Prize by the British Institute of Physics and the French Physical Society. Cited for "his outstanding contributions to the theory of metals," Blandin was a pioneer in determing the differences between surface and bulk structure of a solid.

Max-Planck Medal. Markus Fierz, emeritus professor at the Swiss Federal Institute of Technology in Zürich, was awarded the 1979 Max-Planck Medal by the (West) German Physical Society. Fierz provided the basis for the elucidation of a general law of nature according to which the statistical behavior of a particle is determined by its internal spin.

Michelson-Morley Award. Hans Wolfgang Liepmann of the California Institute of Technology was named winner in 1979 of the Michelson-Morley

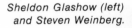

Sheldon Glashow (left) and Steven Weinberg.

UPI

Award, presented by the Case Institute of Technology. Liepmann was honored especially for his work on the dynamics of liquid helium, which increased the understanding of fluid motion at low temperatures.

Nobel Prize. The 1979 Nobel prize for Physics, presented by the Royal Swedish Academy of Sciences, was shared by Sheldon Glashow and Steven Weinberg of Harvard University and Abdus Salam of the Imperial College of Science and Technology in London. They achieved the honor for their complementary efforts in formulating a theory that encompasses both the electromagnetic interaction and the weak interaction of elementary particles. Electromagnetism explains the properties of light and the chemical behavior of atoms, while the weak interaction accounts for certain forms of radioactive decay and for reactions among the lightest particles—electrons, neutrinos, and muons.

The central achievement of the prizewinners was the selection, from among many possible theories, of one that not only explains the known facts about the electromagnetic and weak interactions but also makes it possible to predict the outcome of new experiments in which elementary particles are made to impinge on one another. The results of several experimental tests agreed with the predictions of the theory.

Glashow and Weinberg were each born in New York City, and both were graduated from Cornell University in 1954. After achieving a Ph.D. at Harvard, Glashow taught at the University of California and then returned to Harvard. Weinberg obtained his doctorate from Princeton University and also taught at the University of California before going to Harvard.

Salam was born in Jhang Maghiana, now in Pakistan. After attending the Government College at Lahore, he received a Ph.D. from the University of Cambridge, England. In 1957 he became professor of theoretical physics at Imperial College of Science and Technology and in 1964 took the additional position of director of the International Centre for Theoretical Physics at Trieste, Italy.

Oberth Medal. Friedwardt Winterberg of the University of Nevada Desert Research Institute was awarded the 1979 Hermann Oberth Gold Medal by the Herman Oberth-Wernher von Braun International Foundation for Space Flight. Winterberg was the first to propose what is known as "impact fusion," nuclear fusion achieved by means of acceleration of macroparticles at fuel targets.

Royal Medal. The Council of the Royal Society of Great Britain presented a 1979 Royal Medal to Sir Charles Frank, emeritus professor of physics at the University of Bristol, for "his outstanding original contributions to the theory of crystal growth, dislocations, phase transformations and polymers."

Schottky Prize. The 1979 Walter Schottky Prize for Solid-State Research was awarded by the (West) German Physical Society to Heiner Müller-Krumbhaar of the University of Hannover, West Germany. Müller-Krumbhaar received the honor for developing a theory that makes possible detailed predictions about the surface structure and growth rates of crystals.

Steacie Prize. Walter N. Hardy of the University of British Columbia was awarded a 1978 Steacie Prize for "recent observations of the microwave spectrum of isolated pairs of ortho-H_2 molecules in solid matrix of para-H_2 molecules."

Warren Award. Farrel Lytle of EXAFS Co. and Edward Stern and Dale Sayers, both of the University of Washington, were named winners of the Bertram Eugene Warren Diffraction Physics Award by the American Crystallographic Association. The three were honored for their development of extended X-ray absorption fine structure (EXAFS) spectroscopy, a technique useful for investigating atomic structures.

Welch Award. Gert Ehrlich of the University of Illinois received the 1979 Medard W. Welch Award from the American Vacuum Society. Ehrlich was cited "for contributions to our understanding of the microscopic force laws by which atoms residing on solid surfaces interact with the substrate and each other."

Wetherill Medal. The Franklin Institute in 1979 awarded the John Price Wetherill Medal to Elias Burstein of the University of Pennsylvania for his research on the optical properties of solids and their applications in photoconductive technology.

Wolf Prize. Giuseppe Occhialini, one of the founders of the National Institute for Nuclear Physics in Italy, was named by the Wolf Foundation of Israel as the winner of the 1979 Wolf Prize for Physics. Occhialini was honored for two major discoveries: electron-positron pair combination and detection of the pion.

Psychology

AAAS Socio-Psychological Prize. The American Association for the Advancement of Science awarded its 1979 Socio-Psychological Prize to Ronald Wilson of the University of Louisville for his studies of the early mental development of identical versus fraternal twins. Wilson's research showed that identical twins become more alike with age while fraternal twins become less so.

Applications in Psychology Award. Joseph Wolpe of Temple University received from the American Psychological Association its 1979 Distinguished Contribution Award for Applications in Psychology. Wolpe was cited "for his outstanding contribution to the understanding and modification of abnormal behavior, and in particular for his pioneering work that led to the establishment of behavior therapy."

Scientific Contribution Award. Three psychologists were chosen by the American Psychological Association as recipients of its 1979 Distinguished Scientific Contribution Award. John Atkinson of the University

413

of Michigan was cited "for his powerful analysis of human motivation conceptualized as the interplay of the personal and situational forces that influence changes in activity over time." Gordon Bower of Stanford University was selected "for his powerful analytic and conceptual insights into the acquisition, representation, and use of knowledge." John Garcia of the University of California at Los Angeles achieved the honor "for his highly original, pioneering research in conditioning and learning."

Space exploration

Contribution to Society Award. The American Institute of Aeronautics and Astronautics (AIAA) presented its 1979 Aerospace Contribution to Society Award to Richard Johnston of the Lyndon B. Johnson Space Center of the National Aeronautics and Space Administration (NASA). Johnston received the honor "for exceptional leadership in the application of space flight technology to ground-based health care systems."

Goddard Astronautics Award. Maxime Faget of NASA's Johnson Space Center received from the AIAA its 1979 Goddard Astronautics Award for outstanding contributions to the design and development of manned space flight systems and also for his leadership abilities.

Space Systems Award. The AIAA gave John Casani of the Jet Propulsion Laboratory its 1979 Space Systems Award "for his personal contributions as the principal architect and system designer of the Galileo Project, a pioneering attempt at planetary explorations."

Transportation

Guggenheim Medal. Edward Heinemann, president of Heinemann Associates, was presented with the 1979 Daniel Guggenheim Medal by the American Institute of Aeronautics and Astronautics (AIAA). Heinemann received the honor "for outstanding achievement in the innovative design of military airplanes."

Kremer Trophy. Paul MacCready, an aeronautical engineer and glider expert from California, received the Kremer Trophy for designing the "Gossamer Albatross," which became the first man-powered aircraft to cross the English Channel. Bryan Allen, the pilot and "engine," was awarded a gold medal. Other members of the team were given bronze medals that bore the inscription: "The Kremer cross channel man-powered flight challenge won 12 June 1979."

Potts Medal. Richard Whitcomb of the Langley (Va.) Research Center received the 1979 Howard N. Potts Medal from the Franklin Institute "for his outstanding and innovative contributions to transonic flight." Whitcomb discovered and verified the "area rule," a method of designing aircraft to reduce drag and increase speed.

Science journalism

AAAS-Westinghouse Science Writing Award. The Westinghouse Electric Corp. in conjunction with the American Association for the Advancement of Science presented three awards in recognition of outstanding writing in 1979 on the natural sciences and their engineering and technological applications, excluding medicine, in newspapers and general circulation magazines. For newspapers with a daily circulation of more than 100,000 the winners were Karen Freiberg and Martha Mangelsdorf for "We're Running Out," a series of articles in the *Wichita Eagle and Beacon* about the water supply in Kansas. For newspapers with a daily circulation of less than 100,000 the prize was given to Joseph Donohue for his article "Low-level Radiation . . . How Safe?" in the *Press* and *Sunday Press* of Atlantic City, N.J. For general circulation magazines Thomas Canby won the award for his article "The Search for the First Americans" in the *National Geographic.*

AIP-U.S. Steel Award. Dennis Overbye, an editor for *Sky and Telescope* magazine, received the 1980 American Institute of Physics-U.S. Steel Foundation Science Writing Award in Physics and Astronomy. Overbye gained the honor for his article "The Wizard of Space and Time" in *Omni* magazine.

Bernard Award. The National Society for Medical Research presented its 1978 Claude Bernard Science Journalism Award to Bruce DeSilva of the Providence, R.I., *Journal-Bulletin* and Joan Arehart-Treichel of *Science News* magazine. DeSilva won his prize for a series of articles on cancer that appeared in the Providence *Sunday Journal*, while Arehart-Treichel was honored for her article "Brain Proteins: Matter over Mind" in *New York* magazine.

Grady Award. The James T. Grady Award for Interpreting Chemistry for the Public was presented by the American Chemical Society in 1979 to Edward Edelson, science editor of the *New York Daily News.* Edelson's articles for the newspaper were lauded for their accuracy, clarity, and timeliness.

Washburn Award. Mary D. Leakey, director of Olduvai Gorge Excavations in East Africa, where she has worked for more than 40 years, received a gold medal and a $5,000 honorarium from the Museum of Science in Boston when she was presented with the 1980 Bradford Washburn Award for contributing to public understanding of science. Leakey was specifically honored for an article that appeared in the April 1979 issue of *National Geographic* magazine. Entitled "Footprints in the Ashes of Time," it reported "a startling discovery in East Africa—tracks left in hardened volcanic ash by hominids that walked upright at least 3.6 million years ago." The footprints were found in the Laetolil area of Tanzania and pushed back the known history of man by half a million years.

Lisa Randall

John Andersland

Miscellaneous

National Medal of Science. U.S. Pres. Jimmy Carter awarded the 1979 National Medal of Science, the highest honor accorded U.S. scientists and engineers by the federal government, to 20 recipients. They are: Robert Burris of the University of Wisconsin for his research on the biochemistry of nitrogen fixing; Elizabeth Crosby of the University of Michigan for her research into comparative human neuroanatomy; Joseph Doob of the University of Illinois for his work on probability and mathematical statistics; Richard Feynman, of the California Institute of Technology for his explanation of the behavior of subnuclear particles; Donald Knuth of Stanford University for his design of efficient algorithms that have formed the basis of computer programs; Arthur Kornberg of Stanford University for research into the reproduction of DNA; Emmett Leith of the University of Michigan for his pioneering work in holography; Herman Mark of the Polytechnic Institute of New York for advancing the study of polymers; Raymond Mindlin of Columbia University for his work in mechanical engineering and theoretical mathematics; Robert Noyce of the Intel Corp. for his research on semiconductor devices for integrated circuits; Severo Ochoa of the Roche Institute of Molecular Biology for his discoveries concerning the cell's citric acid cycle, through which it manufactures energy; Earl Parker of the University of California at Berkeley for advancing the understanding of the way materials act when under stress and pressure; Edward Purcell of Harvard University for his research on the structure of atoms and on interstellar magnetic fields; Simon Ramo of TRW Inc., for his efforts in developing microwave electronics; John Sinfelt of Exxon Corporate Research Laboratories for his work on catalytic systems that remove pollutants from automobile exhaust; Lyman Spitzer, Jr., of Princeton University for his theory of star formation and his research on nuclear fusion; Earl Stadtman of the National Institutes of Health for explaining the metabolic process of bacteria that survive without oxygen; George Stebbins, Jr., of the University of California at Davis for developing a theory of plant evolution; Paul Weiss of Rockefeller University for his contributions to understanding the nervous system; and Victor Weisskopf of Massachusetts Institute of Technology for his research in particle physics and on nuclear reactors.

Science Talent Awards. The Science Talent Search, sponsored by the Westinghouse Educational Foundation and administered by Science Service, resulted in 1980 in a tie for first place for the first time in its 39-year history. Co-winners were Lisa Randall from Stuyvesant High School in New York City and John Andersland of East Lansing High School, East Lansing, Mich. Randall's research concerned Gaussian integers, numbers of the form $a + bi$, where a and b are integers and i is the square root of -1. Her paper developed conditions about the form a Gaussian integer must possess in order to be a perfect number, that is, to be a positive integer equal to the sum of its positive integral divisors other than itself. Andersland studied the characteristics of mutant cells in African violets, concentrating on those that cause white leaves.

415

Obituaries

The following persons, all of whom died in recent months, were widely recognized for their scientific accomplishments.

Blodgett, Katharine Burr (Jan. 10, 1898—Oct. 12, 1979) U.S. research scientist, developed (1938) a non-reflecting "invisible" glass that is used in automobile windshields, store windows, telescopes, cameras, and submarine periscopes. Blodgett applied 44 layers of one-molecule-thick transparent liquid soap—totaling about four-millionths of an inch thick—to a sheet of glass, thereby causing the reflection of the soap film to neutralize the reflection from the glass itself. Blodgett, who was the first woman to become a research scientist at General Electric Co. (1918), conducted studies in both chemistry and physics with Nobel laureate Irving Langmuir. Together they published papers in technical journals on the quantitative measurement of flow of electric current under prescribed conditions, and, after her graduate study, the improvement of tungsten filaments in electric lamps. In 1926 she received the first Ph.D. in physics ever awarded to a woman by the University of Cambridge. After returning to General Electric, Blodgett invented a color gauge that could measure the thickness of film within one-millionth of an inch. This gauge proved indispensable to metallurgists, physicists, and chemists, who were able to measure transparent or semitransparent films without the aid of costly optical instruments. She also devised a smoke screen that saved thousands of lives of Allied troops during the North African and Italian invasions in World War II.

Blokhintsev, Dmitry Ivanovich (Jan. 11, 1908 [Dec. 29, 1907, old style]—Jan. 27, 1979), Soviet physicist, was instrumental in the development of nuclear energy in the U.S.S.R. and was in charge of directing construction of the country's first nuclear power plant at Obninsk in 1954. As director (1956–65) of the Joint Institute for Nuclear Research at Dubna, near Moscow, Blokhintsev announced the discovery of synthetic element No. 104 in 1964. This breakthrough represented the twelfth radioactive element heavier than uranium to be created by mankind. Blokhintsev was graduated from Moscow University (1930), where he later served as professor of physics (1936–56). In 1960 he chaired the Organizational Committee of the ninth International Conference on Physics and High Energies in Kiev. His major scientific contributions were in the fields of solid-state quantum theory, the physics of semiconductors, the theory of chain reactions, and particle physics. At the time of his death he was head of the Laboratory of Theoretical Physics at the research institute in Dubna.

Chain, Sir Ernst Boris (June 19, 1906—Aug. 12, 1979), German-born biochemist, was a joint winner of the Nobel Prize for Physiology or Medicine in 1945 for

Sir Ernst Chain

isolating and purifying penicillin. Chain studied chemistry and physiology at the Friedrich-Wilhelm University in Berlin but left Germany in 1933 because of racial persecution. After a short time in London and at Cambridge he went to the University of Oxford, where he worked in the field of chemical pathology with Howard Florey. Starting from Sir Alexander Fleming's discovery of the antibacterial properties of *Penicillium notatum* mold, he managed to isolate pure penicillin and by 1941 the new drug had been tested on patients dying of staphylococcal infections. Although the first two tests failed, the third was successful, and by 1945, when Chain, Florey, and Fleming were awarded the Nobel Prize, penicillin had been recognized as a dramatic advance in medical science. In 1948 Chain went to Rome as scientific director of the International Research Centre for Chemical Microbiology. There he discovered a new penicillinlike substance in penicillin fermentations that was later characterized as the nucleus of the penicillin molecule, 6-aminopenicillanic acid. The subsequent isolation and characterization of this nucleus led to a long series of penicillins effective against bacteria that had been resistant to penicillins obtainable by fermentation. Chain returned (1961) to England to become professor of biochemistry at the Imperial College of Science and Technology, London. He was knighted in 1969.

Chapple, Charles C(ulloden) (April 27, 1903—March 23, 1979), U.S. pediatrician, developed in the mid-1930s the Isolette incubator, which was instrumental in the care of premature and feeble infants. Chapple's invention was superior to earlier incubators and minimized such life-threatening conditions as the

416

infants' lack of breathing capacity, their susceptibility to infection, and their vulnerability to atmospheric changes. After receiving his M.D. from the University of Michigan, Ann Arbor, Chapple interned there at University Hospital. Although the greater part of his career was spent in Philadelphia as a senior physician at the Children's Hospital of Philadelphia and as a professor at the University of Pennsylvania, Chapple later served as chief of clinical studies for the Veterans Administration in Washington, D.C., and professor (1966–72) of pediatrics at the University of Nebraska College of Medicine. His other accomplishments included the early diagnosis and treatment of congenital dislocation of the hip in infants. Chapple also disproved a tenet in medical textbooks that congenital hip dislocation in infants could only be discovered once an infant could stand. After detecting the condition in his daughter, he discovered a method that enabled early diagnosis and treatment of the malady.

Cousteau, Philippe Pierre (Dec. 30, 1940 – June 28, 1979), French oceanographer and cinematographer, was the son of Jacques-Yves Cousteau, the world-renowned oceanographer and coinventor of the aqualung. A highly respected and dedicated oceanographer in his own right, Cousteau worked with his father as a diver and photographer on the research ship "Calypso." Together they made expeditions to Turkey, Greece, the North Sea, Italy, Africa, and Tunisia. On a trip to the Red Sea in 1963 they filmed *World Without Sun*, which won an Academy Award as best documentary feature in 1964. He also filmed the television series "The Undersea World of Jacques Cousteau," which won ten Emmy awards. In 1965 he participated in an experiment of the Conshelf Saturation Dive Program by living 328 ft (100 m) underwater with five other aquanauts for 30 days. Cousteau filmed that experiment for a National Geographic Society television special. Upon the creation of the Cousteau Society in 1974, Cousteau and his father became the society's executive producers for "The Cousteau Odyssey," a series of television specials. He was coauthor with his father of *Les Requins* (1970; *The Shark*) and wrote articles for such magazines as *Sea, Skin Diver,* and *Oceans.* Cousteau was killed when the seaplane he was piloting crashed into a sandbank in the Tagus River in Portugal.

Focke, Henrich Karl Johann (Oct. 8, 1890 – Feb. 25, 1979), German aircraft designer, designed the first helicopter certified as airworthy, the Fw 61; in 1936 it made the first free flight of a rotary-wing aircraft. Unlike the fixed-wing airplane, Focke's helicopter did not depend on forward speed to remain airborne. Focke removed the risk and difficulty of landing at high speeds by devising a vertical takeoff and landing, and solved the problem of torque by mounting two rotors on lateral outriggers. The controllability of his "mechanical housefly" was demonstrated by Hanna

Henrich Focke

Reitsch, who manuevered the copter to rise, hover, and fly in the confined space of Berlin's Deutschland Hall. His firm, Focke-Wulf Flugzeugbau AG, founded with Georg Wulf in 1924, was taken from him by the Nazis in the 1930s. He therefore had no part in the design of its World War II aircraft, the famed Fw 190 fighter and the Fw 200 Condor. In 1937 he founded Focke-Achgelis & Co. to construct helicopters, and in 1942 his Fw 61 set an altitude record of 23,290 ft (7,100 m) that stood for 12 years. After the war Focke worked in several countries, including France, the U.K., The Netherlands, and Brazil. In 1958 Focke-Achgelis, later incorporated into the aircraft company VFW-Fokker, built West Germany's first helicopter.

Forssmann, Werner (Aug. 29, 1904 – June 1, 1979), German surgeon, shared the Nobel Prize for Physiology or Medicine in 1956 with André F. Cournand and Dickinson W. Richards. As an intern Forssmann demonstrated on himself that a catheter inserted into a vein at the elbow could safely be maneuvered all the way to the heart. In 1929 Forssmann published a paper describing "probing of the heart." He suggested that drugs could be administered directly to the heart without penetrating the chest wall, pericardium, and heart muscle. This contribution to medical technology was largely ignored for nearly 12 years before Cournand and Richards perfected the procedure. Cardiac catheterization, as it is now called, enables physicians both to study the conditions under which the diseased human heart functions and to make more accurate diagnoses of underlying anatomic defects. The three physi-

417

Werner Forssmann

cians were awarded the Nobel Prize for discoveries concerning heart catheterization and circulatory changes. For much of his life Forssmann was director of surgery at the Evangelical Hospital of Düsseldorf in West Germany.

Frisch, Otto Robert (Oct. 1, 1904 — Sept. 22, 1979), Austrian-born physicist, together with his aunt Lise Meitner in 1938 conceptualized and described the splitting of a neutron-bombarded uranium nucleus into two or more fragments that must fly apart at high speed. The two physicists named this process nuclear fission. Frisch subsequently demonstrated the high energy of fission fragments and realized that an explosive chain reaction could be achieved. He helped persuade U.S. scientists to take his discovery seriously and during World War II worked on the development of the first atomic bomb at the U.S. Army's laboratory at Los Alamos, N.M. Earlier in his career Frisch had been associated with Otto Stern at the University of Hamburg, where he demonstrated that atoms of helium behave as waves when reflected from the surfaces of crystals. Leaving Germany in 1933 because of Hitler's racial policies, he spent five years at Niels Bohr's Institute for Theoretical Physics in Copenhagen. There Frisch measured the radioactivity produced by neutrons in rare earths. After World War II he became a professor at the University of Cambridge. Among his achievements at Cambridge was the invention of Sweepnik, a device that semiautomatically measures particle tracks in bubble chambers.

Gabor, Dennis (June 5, 1900 — Feb. 8, 1979), Hungarian-born physicist, was awarded the Nobel Prize for Physics in 1971 for his invention of holography, a lens-less method of three-dimensional photography that allows the viewer to study an object as if he or she were seeing it through a window rather than on the surface of a photographic plate. Initially Gabor used a conventional filtered light source to develop the basic technique, but holography was not widely used until the invention of the laser, which amplifies the intensity of light waves. Gabor worked in Berlin until 1933 and then went to Great Britain, where in 1947 his work on improving the flat images seen through an electron microscope led to the discovery of holography. Besides photography, holography has been used in such fields as medicine, topographical mapmaking, communications, and computer technology. Gabor was reader in electronics (1949–58) and professor of applied electron physics (1958–67) at the Imperial College of Science and Technology, London. In 1967 he joined the Columbia Broadcasting System Laboratories at Stamford, Conn., as a staff scientist. His publications include several books on the social implications of technological change, among which are *Electronic Inventions and Their Impact on Civilization* (1959), and *The Mature Society* (1972). His most celebrated book, *Inventing the Future* (1963), warns of the problems that are associated with war, overpopulation, and increased leisure.

Hagihara, Yusuke (March 28, 1897 — Jan. 29, 1979), Japanese astronomer, devoted his life to the study of celestial mechanics and was internationally recognized as an authority in the field. His scholarship was evidenced by a massive five-volume work, *Celestial Mechanics,* a reference known to every student of astronomy, published between 1970 and 1976. Other works include *Beyond Nebulae* (1949), *General Astronomy* (1955), *Stability in Celestial Mechanics* (1957), and *Theories of Equilibrium Figures of a Rotating Homogeneous Fluid Mass* (1970). After graduating from Tokyo University in 1921, Hagihara was sent by the Japanese government to study in the U.K. under Sir Arthur Eddington and Henry F. Baker at the University of Cambridge. He visited observatories in France, Germany, and the U.S. before returning to Japan to earn his Ph.D. He then became a professor at Tokyo University and served as director (1946–57) of the Tokyo Astronomical Observatory.

Harding, Gerald William Lankester (Dec. 8, 1901 — Feb. 11, 1979), British archaeologist, played a crucial role in preserving the Dead Sea Scrolls as director (1936–56) of the Jordanian Department of Antiquities. With virtually no formal schooling, he worked in various jobs until his interest in Egyptian hieroglyphics induced Sir Flinders Petrie to accept his services during the 1926–32 excavations near Gaza, Palestine. From 1932 to 1936 he assisted J. L. Starkey at Lachish, Palestine, and deciphered inscriptions recording the destruction of the town in biblical times. In 1947 the first manuscripts of the Dead Sea Scrolls were accidentally discovered by shepherd boys in a cave at Khirbat Qumran on the northwest shore of the Dead Sea. Harding immediately recognized the importance of this find and directed the first official excavations at the site. The recovery of these documents enabled scholars to reconstruct the history of Palestine from the 4th century BC to AD 135 and to clarify the relationship between early Christianity and Jewish religious traditions. Harding later undertook important archaeological work in Lebanon and Jordan.

Harrison, George Russell (July 14, 1898—July 27, 1979), U.S. physicist, was a longtime (1930–64) professor of physics at the Massachusetts Institute of Technology (MIT) and the compiler in 1938 of the MIT Wavelength Tables, a widely used basic spectrographic reference. Harrison was an expert in using optical spectroscopy to study the complexities of the atom, and after his retirement (1964) he continued to refine and improve "ruling engines," or machines that etch the grooves on diffraction gratings. A graduate of Stanford University, he taught at his alma mater and was a National Research Council fellow at Harvard University before joining the faculty of MIT. During World War II Harrison was chief of the optics division of the National Defense Research Committee, and, while chief of research (1944) at Gen. Douglas MacArthur's headquarters, he developed an infrared sniperscope so that soldiers could engage in night warfare. His writings include *Atoms in Action* (1938), *Practical Spectroscopy* (1948), and *Lasers* (1971).

Haworth, Leland J(ohn) (July 11, 1904—March 5, 1979), U.S. physicist, established Brookhaven National Laboratory as one of the world's foremost scientific research centers as its director from 1948 to 1961. Under Haworth's guidance Brookhaven expanded its facilities by designing and operating such "big machines" as a graphite research reactor, the first reactor designed for peacetime research; the Cosmotron, the first particle accelerator to achieve proton energies greater than one million volts; and the alternating gradient synchrotron, which was the most powerful accelerator in the world for many years. Haworth earned (1931) a Ph.D. at the University of Wisconsin, where he taught from 1930 to 1937. After brief periods at the Massachusetts Institute of Technology, where he helped develop microwave radar, and at the University of Illinois, where he assisted in the development of one of the first time-of-flight systems for the direct determination of slow neutron velocities, he joined (1947) Brookhaven as assistant director in charge of special projects. During his directorship Haworth also was vice-president (1951–60) and president (1960–61) of Associated Universities Inc. (AUI), a nonprofit organization that operates Brookhaven under a government contract. In 1961 he was appointed a member of the U.S. Atomic Energy Commission and helped construct a major governmental planning document, the 1962 Report to the President on civilian nuclear power. After serving (1963–69) as director of the National Science Foundation, Haworth returned as special consultant to AUI until his retirement in 1975.

Heizer, Robert Fleming (July 13, 1915—July 18, 1979), U.S. archaeologist and anthropologist, participated in archaeological expeditions to Mexico and Central America that increased the understanding of ancient civilization on the North American continent. Together with John A. Graham, Heizer unearthed the earliest example of Mayan monumental architecture and writing in the Pacific Coast highlands of Guatemala. This find suggests that the ancient Mayan civilization probably began in the highlands rather than the hot, tropical lowlands where most of the Mayan ruins were found. On an expedition to Mexico Heizer discovered (1968) in La Venta a 100-ft-high (30.5-m-high) pyramid that is thought to be the oldest in the New World. He was also a recognized authority on California archaeology and spent numerous hours studying Sir Francis Drake's landing on the coast and the history of aboriginal Indians in the state. These interests resulted in a wealth of papers and books numbering over 400. Heizer wrote *Man's Discovery of his Past* (1962), and was co-author of *The Four Ages of Tsurai* (1952), *Prehistoric Rock Art of Nevada and Eastern California* (1962), and *The Other Californians* (1971). A graduate of the University of California, Heizer served as professor of anthropology at the Berkeley campus and director (1948–60) of the University of California Archaeology Survey.

Kowarski, Lew (Feb. 10, 1907—July 27, 1979), physicist, was a pioneer in pre-World War II research on atomic energy and during the postwar period helped found the European Organization for Nuclear Research (CERN). Born in Russia, he left his native land following the Bolshevik Revolution and studied in Belgium and France before joining the research team of Frédéric Joliot-Curie and Hans von Halban. Together they realized the possibility of a chain reaction resulting from nuclear fission, and when World War II broke out Kowarski continued this work in Britain and Canada. He had become a French citizen in 1939 and returned to France after the war to help build the country's first two atomic stockpiles. In 1952 he founded CERN and in 1954 became director of the scientific and technical services division. From 1963 he held visiting professorships at several universities in the U.S. and after his retirement in 1972 remained a consulting physicist to CERN.

Lowell, Francis Cabot (Aug. 6, 1909—Dec. 30, 1979), U.S. physician, developed the first well-controlled therapy for allergies by employing immunotherapy, a treatment consisting of antigens or antigenic preparations. Immunotherapy remains the general treatment for hay fever, asthma, and other related diseases. Shortly before his death Lowell was also granted a patent for a treatment that substantially alleviated the asthmatic reaction from which many people suffer when exposed to cats. An injection of a cat-dandruff extract made from cat pelts was proved widely effective. Lowell was graduated in 1936 from Harvard Medical School, where he taught from 1958 to 1976. He joined Massachusetts General Hospital in 1958 as chief of the allergy unit and physician in the medical services division. He was appointed by the U.S. Food and Drug Administration in the early 1970s to head a panel of seven experts from the private sector who evaluated the effectiveness of nonprescription cold remedies. Their findings, made public in 1976, indicated that few of the active ingredients in nonprescription cough and cold remedies could be judged safe and effective. Lowell also served as chief of the allergy clinic at Massachusetts Memorial Hospitals (now University Hospital), and as allergy consultant to the department of medicine of the New England Medical Center Hospital and to the Veterans Administration Hospital, both in Boston.

Merritt, H(iram) Houston (Jan. 12, 1902—Jan. 9, 1979), U.S. neurologist, co-developed (1936) with Tracy J. Putnam the antiseizure drug Dilantin (diphenylhydantoin), used to combat epileptic seizures and to treat abnormal heartbeats. Merritt's discovery was a significant breakthrough because phenobarbital was the only other drug available to treat epilepsy and its use was limited because of its sedative effect. Shortly after graduating (1926) from Johns Hopkins University, Merritt joined the faculty of Harvard University and conducted research at Boston City Hospital. In 1944 he moved to New York City to become chief of neuropsychiatry at Montefiore Hospital and a member of the faculty at Columbia University. At Columbia he became (1948) chairman of the neurology department, and from 1958 to 1970 he was dean of the College of Physicians and Surgeons and vice-president in charge of medical affairs at the university. Merritt's writings include some 215 scientific papers, as well as a standard textbook on neurology and a book on the effects of syphilis on the brain.

Natta, Giulio (Feb. 26, 1903—May 2, 1979), Italian chemist, won the Nobel Prize for Chemistry in 1963 together with Karl Ziegler of West Germany for their work on the development of high-polymer plastics and their industrial applications. In 1952 Ziegler polymerized ethylene (*i.e.*, he changed the gaseous state to a plastic one by uniting hydrocarbons) and produced the plastic resin, super polyethylene. Two years later Natta, who was working on the polymerization of propylene, an abundant gas that was relatively inexpensive, introduced isotactic polypropylene by following Ziegler's catalytic principle. The plastic was found to be a strong homogeneous crystal structure that could be molded into solid objects, spun into fiber as strong as nylon, and spread into film as clear as cellophane. This

development proved useful in the manufacture of detergents, auto parts, fabrics, and film. Earlier Natta had developed catalytic syntheses for methanol, formaldehyde, and bityraldehyde. Other plastics that he produced included a new polystyrene and a polybutadiene. Natta studied chemical engineering in Milan and subsequently taught in Pavia, Rome, and Turin. In 1938 he was appointed professor at Milan Polytechnic and director of its industrial chemistry research institute, where he succeeded in polymerizing propylene gas into highly ordered chains of molecules.

Nervi, Pier Luigi (June 21, 1891—Jan. 9, 1979), Italian engineer, revolutionized architecture with stunning and daring designs characterized by tilted arches, curved ceilings, and a feeling of space. Nervi, who considered concrete the finest construction material available, invented ferrocemento, a reinforced material of steel mesh and cement mortar. After graduating (1913) in civil engineering from the University of Bologna, he began (1923) his career as an engineer and contractor in Rome. Some of his most notable designs in Italy included the cinema Augusteo in Naples; a municipal stadium in Florence; a prefabricated 309-ft (94-m) span arch for the Turin exhibition hall; the Pirelli Building (1955–59) in Milan, the country's first skyscraper; and two sports palaces for the 1960 Olympic Games held in Rome. Nervi also designed, with Marcel Breuer and Bernard Zehrfuss, the UNESCO headquarters in Paris. His last work was a massive audience hall for the Vatican. Nervi taught (1947–61) at the University of Rome and was Charles E. Norton professor (1961–62) at Harvard University. Among numerous honors he received the gold medals of the Royal Institute of British Architects (1960) and the American Institute of Architects (1964).

Payne-Gaposchkin, Cecilia (Helena) (May 10, 1900—Dec. 6, 1979), U.S. astronomer, achieved a position of eminence in her chosen field as an authority on variable stars, as the first woman to earn a tenured professorship at Harvard University, and as head of the university's department of astronomy from 1956 to 1960. After graduating from Newnham College at the University of Cambridge, she pursued graduate studies in the U.S. In 1923 she became associated with the Harvard College Observatory and simultaneously studied for her Ph.D. at Radcliffe College. When she was awarded a Ph.D. in 1925, she became the first in the history of the college to earn a doctorate in astronomy. After her marriage in 1934 to Sergey Gaposchkin the couple collaborated on an extensive study of variable stars, especially novas. These stars, which also include supernovas, Cepheid variables, long-period variables, eclipsing variables, and irregular variables, exhibit changes in brightness, color, size, and atmosphere. Together they examined 1,500 specimens and in 1935 reported their observations in three treatises. The next year Payne-Gaposchkin suggested that supernovas "differ only in scale from that of a normal galactic novae," and in 1938 she and her husband published evidence for this conclusion. Payne-Gaposchkin also conducted studies on the Sun and on pulsating and exploding stars, and performed analytical research on astronomical photographs.

Ponti, Gio(vanni) (Nov. 18, 1891—Sept. 15, 1979), Italian architect, was a spectacularly brilliant innovator whose best known work (in collaboration with Pier

Pictorial Parade

Gio Ponti

Luigi Nervi and others) is the delicate 34-story Pirelli Building in Milan. The skyscraper, completed in 1959, was the first great success of its kind in Europe. Ponti turned away from neoclassical Fascist architecture between World Wars I and II and championed modernism. Demonstrating his versatility, he founded the Italian architectural review *Domus* in 1928, designed the interiors of Italian liners such as the "Andrea Doria," designed scenery and costumes for La Scala theater in Milan, and designed furniture and fixtures for the home. He was also an architectural historian and critic. Ponti's factories, hospitals, offices, and other buildings went up in cities worldwide, including Buenos Aires, Stockholm, New York City, and Islamabad, Pak.

Rolf, Ida P(auline) (May 19, 1896—March 19, 1979), U.S. biochemist, developed a deep-massage technique known as "Rolfing," which involves the manipulation of soft tissues of the body so that the ear, shoulder, hip, knee, and ankle are in perfect alignment. Rolf first practiced her method in 1940, when she re-

stored the use of a hand and an arm to a piano teacher by using yoga exercises. Rolf, however, advocated her method for promoting physical efficiency and emotional well-being rather than for chiropractic or osteopathic use. When she began teaching her technique in the U.S. and Europe, she referred to it as "Structural Integration." After graduating from Barnard College in New York City, Rolf became an assistant in biochemistry at the Rockefeller Institute (now Rockefeller University). While employed there, she earned a Ph.D. in biological chemistry from the College of Physicians and Surgeons of Columbia University, and became an associate at the institute. During the last 40 years of her career Rolf worked in applied physiology, and in 1975 she founded the Rolf Institute in Boulder, Colo.

Tomonaga, Shinichiro (March 31, 1906—July 8, 1979), Japanese physicist, was joint recipient with Julian S. Schwinger and Richard P. Feynman of the Nobel Prize for Physics in 1965 for developing basic principles of quantum electrodynamics. Although the three scientists worked independently, it was learned after World War II that each had reached essentially the same conclusions, though using three separate approaches. Their efforts made the theory of quantum electrodynamics (the electric and magnetic effects on subatomic particles) fully consistent with the special theory of relativity. After graduating (1929) from Kyoto Imperial University, Tomonaga joined the Institute of Physical and Chemical Research and worked with Yoshio Nishina, a pioneer in nuclear physics. In 1941 he became professor of physics at Bunrika University (later Tokyo University of Education), and from 1956 to 1962 he was president of the university. Tomonaga also played a leading role in the Pugwash

Shinichiro Tomonaga

Wide World

Conference, which campaigned against the spread of nuclear weapons. His most important work in English is *Quantum Mechanics* (1962).

Velikovsky, Immanuel (June 10, 1895—Nov. 17, 1979), Russian-born scientific writer, was a controversial author whose unorthodox theories of human history and the way in which the solar system evolved created a furor among scientists but won him an immense following. Velikovsky received an M.D. from the University of Moscow in 1921 and later practiced medicine in Palestine. His psychiatric training under Wilhelm Stekel, a student of Sigmund Freud, led to a practice in psychoanalysis and a deep interest in Freud's analysis of the subconscious of Moses. After extensive studies in ancient mythology and in legends of the Jews and other Mediterranean peoples, Velikovsky concluded that some tales were not myths but actual occurrences. In his book *Worlds in Collision* (1950) he proposed that about 1500 BC a large fiery fragment of the planet Jupiter broke off and went into orbit around the Sun, eventually becoming the planet Venus. He further theorized that during its travels this fragment came close to the Earth about 1450 BC and was responsible for such events described in the Old Testament as the descent of manna, the parting of the Red Sea, and the plagues of Egypt. He attributed the founding of Rome and the destruction of Sennacherit to later approaches by the fragment to Earth. Velikovsky's other books include *Ages in Chaos* (1952), *Earth in Upheaval* (1955), *Oedipus and Akhnaton* (1960), and *Velikovsky Reconsidered* (1976), a collection of articles by Velikovsky and others refuting the criticism leveled against him. Interestingly, his works contain astronomical predictions—including the existence of magnetism in Moon rocks, radio waves that emanate naturally from Jupiter, and high atmospheric temperatures on Venus—that were proved true in the course of later scientific investigations.

Wallis, Sir Barnes Neville (Sept. 26, 1887—Oct. 30, 1979), British inventor, became known for his invention of the rotating bouncing bomb, which, when dropped from an aircraft, skipped over the water and exploded after it had sunk to the base of the retaining wall of a dam. This bomb, used during World War II by the Royal Air Force (RAF) on the Möhne and Eder dams in Germany's industrial Ruhr area, produced a devastating effect. Wallis trained as a marine engineer before joining the airship department of Vickers in 1913 as a designer. In 1930 his R100 airship flew to Canada and back but was not developed after its companion ship, the R101, was lost. Turning to aircraft, he employed his geodetic system in the RAF's Wellington bomber in World War II. His researches into detonation effects produced not only the "dambuster" bombs but also the 12,000-lb "Tallboy" and the 22,000-lb "Grand Slam." He was also responsible for the bombs that destroyed the German warship "Tirpitz," the V-

Sir Barnes Wallis

rocket sites, and Germany's railway system. As chief of aeronautical research and development (1945–71) at the British Aircraft Corp. Wallis produced for supersonic aircraft the Swallow variable sweep wing and in 1966 a new form of hollow airfoil or wing; in 1971 he designed an aircraft that could fly five times the speed of sound and needed a runway only 300 yd long. Wallis became a fellow of the Royal Society in 1945 and an honorary fellow of Churchill College, Cambridge, in 1965, and was knighted in 1968.

Woodward, Robert Burns (April 10, 1917—July 8, 1979), U.S. chemist, was awarded the Nobel Prize for Chemistry in 1965 for the syntheses of sterols, chlorophyll, and other substances once thought to be produced only by living things. A giant in the field of synthetic organic chemistry, Woodward was also responsible for the syntheses of strychnine, lysergic acid, reserpine, and in 1972 vitamin B-12 (then the most intricate molecule ever constructed in a laboratory). He was instrumental in determining the structure of such complicated organic compounds as penicillin and terramycin. At an early age Woodward displayed an enthusiasm for chemistry and constructed a laboratory in his parents' basement. After earning a Ph.D. from the Massachusetts Institute of Technology at the age of 20, he joined (1941) the faculty of Harvard University. In 1944, together with William E. Doering, Woodward synthesized quinine and in 1947 protein analogues. At Harvard he was successively named professor of chemistry (1950), Morris Loeb professor (1953), and Donner professor of science (1960). At the time of his death Woodward was working on the synthesis of the antibiotic erythromycin.

Contributors to the Science Year in Review

C. Melvin Aikens *Archaeology.* Chairman, Department of Anthropology, University of Oregon, Eugene.

James D. Atkins *Electronics and information sciences: Communications systems.* Staff member, Corporate Technical Committee, IBM Corp., Armonk, N.Y.

Fred Basolo *Chemistry: Inorganic chemistry.* Professor of Chemistry, Northwestern University, Evanston, Ill.

Louis J. Battan *Earth sciences: Atmospheric sciences.* Director, Institute of Atmospheric Physics, University of Arizona, Tucson.

Gregory Benford *Physics: General developments.* Professor of Physics, University of California, Irvine.

Harold Borko *Electronics and information sciences: Information systems and services.* Professor, Graduate School of Library and Information Science, University of California, Los Angeles.

D. Allan Bromley *Physics: Nuclear physics.* Henry Ford II Professor and Director, Wright Nuclear Structure Laboratory, Yale University, New Haven, Conn.

Marjorie C. Caserio *Chemistry: Organic chemistry.* Professor of Chemistry, University of California, Irvine.

Warren D. Dolphin *Life sciences: Zoology.* Professor of Zoology and Executive Officer of Biology, Iowa State University, Ames.

F. C. Durant III *Electronics and information sciences: Satellite systems.* Assistant Director, National Air and Space Museum, Smithsonian Institution, Washington, D.C.

Robert G. Eagon *Life sciences: Microbiology.* Professor of Microbiology, University of Georgia, Athens.

William L. Ellsworth *Earth sciences: Geophysics.* Geophysicist, U.S. Geological Survey, Menlo Park, Calif.

Lawrence E. Fisher *Anthropology.* Assistant Professor of Anthropology, University of Illinois at Chicago Circle.

David R. Gaskell *Materials sciences: Metallurgy.* Professor of Metallurgy, University of Pennsylvania, Philadelphia.

Robert Geddes *Architecture and civil engineering.* Dean, School of Architecture and Urban Planning, Princeton University, Princeton, N.J.

Robert Haselkorn *Life sciences: Molecular biology.* F. L. Pritzker Professor and Chairman of the Department of Biophysics and Theoretical Biology, University of Chicago.

John Patrick Jordan *Food and agriculture: Agriculture.* Director, Colorado State University Experiment Station, Fort Collins.

Lou Joseph *Medical sciences: Dentistry.* Manager of Media Relations, Bureau of Communications, American Dental Association, Chicago, Ill.

George B. Kauffman *Chemistry: Applied chemistry.* Professor of Chemistry, California State University, Fresno.

David B. Kitts *Earth sciences: Geology and geochemistry.* Professor of Geology and Geophysics and of the History of Science, University of Oklahoma, Norman.

Mina W. Lamb *Food and agriculture: Nutrition.* Professor emeritus, Department of Food and Nutrition, Texas Tech University, Lubbock.

Howard J. Lewis *U.S. science policy.* Director, Office of Information, National Academy of Sciences, Washington, D.C.

Michael J. Longo *Physics: High-energy physics.* Professor of Physics, University of Michigan, Ann Arbor.

Melvin H. Marx *Psychology.* Research Professor of Psychology, University of Missouri, Columbia.

Julie Ann Miller *Medical sciences: General medicine.* Life Sciences Editor, *Science News* magazine, Washington, D.C.

W. M. Protheroe *Astronomy.* Professor of Astronomy, Ohio State University, Columbus.

Arthur L. Robinson *Chemistry: Physical chemistry.* Research News Writer, *Science* magazine, Washington, D.C.

Saul Rosen *Electronics and information sciences: Computers.* Director, Computing Center, and Professor of Computer Science, Purdue University, West Lafayette, Ind.

Irwin J. Schatz *Medical science: Vascular diseases.* Professor and Chairman of the Department of Medicine, John A. Burns School of Medicine, University of Hawaii, Honolulu.

Arthur H. Seidman *Electronics and information sciences: Electronics.* Professor of Electrical Engineering, Pratt Institute, Brooklyn, N.Y.

Mitchell R. Sharpe *Space exploration: Space probes.* Historian, Alabama Space and Rocket Center, Huntsville.

Albert J. Smith *Life sciences: Botany.* Professor and Chairman of the Department of Biology, Wheaton College, Wheaton, Ill.

Frank A. Smith *Transportation.* Senior Vice-President, Transportation Association of America, Washington, D.C.

J. F. Smithcors *Medical sciences: Veterinary medicine.* Editor, American Veterinary Publications, Santa Barbara, Calif.

W. E. Spicer *Physics: Solid-state physics.* Stanley W. Ascherman Professor of Engineering, Stanford University, Stanford, Calif.

Lynn Arthur Steen *Mathematics.* Professor of Mathematics, St. Olaf College, Northfield, Minn.

George W. Stroke *Optical engineering.* Professor of Electrical Sciences and Director of the Electro-Optical Sciences Laboratory, State University of New York, Stony Brook.

Norman M. Tallan *Materials sciences: Ceramics.* Chief Scientist, Air Force Materials Laboratory, Wright-Patterson Air Force Base, Ohio.

William A. Vogely *Energy.* Professor and Chairman of the Department of Mineral Economics, Pennsylvania State University, University Park.

Kenneth E. F. Watt *Environment.* Professor of Zoology and Environmental Studies, University of California, Davis.

Terry White *Space exploration: Manned flight.* Public Information Specialist, NASA Johnson Space Center, Houston, Texas.

Eric F. Wood *Earth sciences: Hydrology.* Assistant Professor of Civil Engineering, Princeton University, Princeton, N.J.

Warren S. Wooster *Earth sciences: Oceanography.* Professor, Institute for Marine Studies, University of Washington, Seattle.

Index

This is a three-year cumulative index. Index entries to feature and review articles in this and previous editions of the *Yearbook of Science and the Future* are set in boldface type, *e.g.*, **Astronomy.** Entries to other subjects are set in lightface type, *e.g.*, Radiation. Additional information on any of these subjects is identified with a subheading and indented under the entry heading. The numbers following headings and subheadings indicate the year (boldface) of the edition and the page number (lightface) on which the information appears.

> **Astronomy 81**–254; **80**–255; **79**–262
> black hole physics **80**–370
> climatology **79**–148
> computer simulated galaxies il. **80**–297
> cosmology **80**–88
> Einstein's theories **80**–79
> honors **81**–401; **80**–406; **79**–410
> laser use in simulation **80**–367
> Native American influence **79**–214
> optical telescope **81**–198

All entry headings, whether consisting of a single word or more, are treated for the purpose of alphabetization as single complete headings and are alphabetized letter by letter up to the punctuation. The abbreviation "il." indicates an illustration.

425

Acknowledgments

6   Photographs and illustrations by (left to right, top to bottom) Zig Leszczynski —ANIMALS ANIMALS; John Youssi; John Youssi; Ron Villani; courtesy, U.S. Department of Energy; courtesy, General Electric Research and Development Center

1768

To extend the tradition of excellence of your Encyclopaedia Britannica educational program, you may also avail yourself of other aids for your home reference center.

Described on the next page is a companion product—the Britannica 3 bookcase—that is designed to help you and your family. It will add attractiveness and value to your home library, as it keeps it well organized.

Should you wish to order it, or to obtain further information, please write to us at

Britannica Home Library Service
Attn: Year Book Department
P. O. Box 4928
Chicago, Illinois 60680